The Vietnam

WAR

ITS OWNSELF

By

James E. Parker, Jr.

This is a Second Edition
August 2016

Copyright 2014 by James E. Parker, Jr
Printed and bound in the United States

Cover Design: Erika Gizelle Santiago

ISBN-13: 978-1503361393

ISBN-10: 150336139X

Dedication

South Vietnamese Army Generals
Tran Van Hai and Le Van Hung

Table of Contents

Acknowledgement

John J. "Jack" Lyons Jr.; Gilbert P. Spencer; Sgt. Maj. Cecil Bratcher, USA (Ret.); Robert M. Dunn, Linda Dunn; Lt. Col. Larry D. Peterson, USA (Ret.); Col. John Woolley, USA (Ret.); and Lt. Gen. Robert Haldane, USA (Ret.), helped tremendously with the early U.S. Army chronology.

Col. Leonard L. Lewane, USA (Ret.), the former commander of the Quarterhorse; Col. Edward J. Burke, USA (Ret.), the secretary of the 28thInfantry Association; and Andrew Woods at the McCormick Research Center, 1st Division Museum, provided detailed background information on 1st Division operations in Vietnam.

Merle Prebbinow helped enormously in getting at the North Vietnamese side of the story on the battle for Skyline. A Vietnamese linguist and friend of the highest order, he translated more than 700 pages of North Vietnamese Army (NVA) histories and accounts of the Skyline battle. With each translation he added comments that put the report in context.

Would also like to especially recognize Mac Thompson, a former United State Agency for International Development (USAID) employee who worked upcountry Laos during the war and still travels there often from his home in Bangkok. He answered every question on mapping and terrain feature. Mac knows the area around the Plaine des Jarres (PDJ) like few other people on the face of this good earth and was often able to make sense of conflicting reporting on locations and movements.

Mike Ingham, aka "Hardnose," made significant contributions to the research of the Skyline Battle, giving his personal account of events. He has constantly insisted on sharing just equal responsibility for the successful defense of the ridgeline, despite the gathered evidence that he was one of the battle's principle heroes. Certainly at its darkest hour, he and Hog were the only Americans in the valley.

Hugh Tovar was also very supportive during this process of getting the Lao program facts together.

I also thank author Ken Conboy who has been very gracious with his time. He has a unique understanding of the Secret War and how it fits into the overall picture of Southeast Asia fighting.

Central Intelligence Agency (CIA) compatriots from Laos who helped with interviews and comments include Jimmy Assuras, Jerry F., Dave Campbell, Eli C., Gordon Dibble, Norm Gardner, Jim Glerum, Dunc Jewell, Dick Johnson, Shep Johnson, Dick Kustra, Vint Lawrence, Stu Methven, Hugh Murray, Tom Norton, Dave Nutley, George O'Dell, Lena Uckele and Joe Glasgow.

Air America pilots who have contributed include Dick Casterlin who was in Laos for a very long time doing a variety of jobs; he has great recall of the whole program from its inception to its conclusion. Also Jerry Connors, Izzy Freedman, Brian Johnson, Allen Cates, Wayne Knight, Bob Noble, George Taylor and Steve Stevens. Les Strouse from Continental Air Services Incorporated (CASI) also helped with details.

All the Ravens have been helpful, especially Karl Polifka, who has a very sharp eye for detail and a talent for writing. Other Ravens who have contributed are Ed Gunter, H. Ownby, Bryon Hukee, Spike Milam, Fred "Magnet Ass" Platt, Hal Smith, Steve Wilson, John Wisneiwski, Darrell Whitcome, "Growth" and Chuck Heines.

Retired USAF officers who have helped include Gerry Frazier, Ray Roddy and Jessie Scott.

FAGs and ops assistants who have contributed include Spotlight (Precha Nithisupa), Wild Bill (Wiboon Suwanawong), Smallman (Somchai Tankulsawat), Judy (Nhia Vang), Lucky (Lew Yang) and Va Xiong.

Royal Thai Army retired Generals Chewthai

Sangtaweep (aka Saen) and Chinnasotta Picha, in addition to retired Colonel Chat Phon, were very forthcoming with insights on the battle and other details.

Glenn R., Don K., Tom F. and Jim D. provided invaluable help in reporting on the last days in South Vietnam. Terry Barker helped with accounts of our experiences together in Vi Thanh. George Taylor corroborated details of the actual evacuation of the CIA contingent from Can Tho. Bonnie Myers, daughter of the captain of the *Pioneer Contender*, the late Edward C. Flink, located the ship's log and other official reports that expanded my recollections. Ron Ross of Alaskan Barge and Transport helped me to complete the story of Tugboat Control and the hectic scene at Vung Tau on 1 May 1975.

Matt Phair provided information on the Marines unit that boarded the *Pioneer Contender* at the mouth of the Bassic River and was on it through the evacuation of refugees from Vung Tau.

I extend special thanks to Doan Huu Dinh and Nguyen Ky Phong, proud former citizens and soldiers of South Vietnam, who provided information on the deaths of General Hung and General Hai.

I also thank Terry Barker, Fred Brugger, Morris Hitson, Paul Prester, Sedgwick Tourison, Ron Brown, Dr. Lewis M. Stern, Dr. William M. Leary, Dr. Matt Oyas, Linda Dunn and Henry W. Turner for their contributions to the overall manuscript. Special thanks to Aaron Aylsworth for his considerable time in shaping the manuscript, especially the introduction. Paul Carter and Thomas Briggs also provided enormous help in the final construction of the introduction.

Most of the photos are from the private collection of Mike Ingham, Dave Campbell, Hugh Tovar, Mac Thompson, Dick Johnson, Digger O'Dell, Dave Kouba, Lena Uckele, Joe Glasgow, Jim Glerum, the author's and others. Some of the photos and maps used are in the public domain, easily accessible from open-source sites on the

Internet including Wikipedia, Wikimedia Commons and the CIA World Factbook.

Thanks go to Terry Belanger, a demanding, marvelously talented copy editor. After her death, her daughter Barbara Johnson stepped in as my syntaxer and grammatologist. She has been just as marvelous.

Most of all, I thank my wife, Brenda, who always supported and encouraged this work.

Introduction

I served five years on Southeast Asia (SEA) battlefields. Went over as 22-year-old 2nd Lt platoon leader in the 1st Division in 1965 and saw a year's combat northwest of Saigon, in the Tay Ninh, Minh Thanh and Cu Chi areas.

Jim Parker, enroute Vietnam 1965

In 1971 I returned to Southeast Asia as a Central Intelligence Agency (CIA) paramilitary case officer working with the Hmong guerrillas upcountry Laos. In one significant battle our rag-tag 4,000 man CIA army under command of Hmong war lord Vang Pao – with U.S. combat air support - beat 27,000 NVA in the Battle for Skyline Ridge.

Skyline Ridge

After the Lao cease fire and the U.S. military pullout from Vietnam I was transferred to the Delta of SouthVietnam where I liaised with the ranking SouthVietnamese Army (ARVN) commanders south of Saigon. This included General Tran Van Hai, the ARVN 7th Division commander, whose headquarters was located on the Cambodian border below the Parrot's beak.

General Tran Van Hai

Across from Hai's forces inside Cambodia was a North Vietnamese military staging area. Soon after South Vietnam's Ban Me Thuot province fell in early 1975, it began to swell with North Vietnamese soldiers certainly intent on moving

to the under belly of Saigon for the final assault
by the North Vietnamese to take the country.

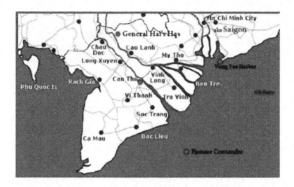

Hai's forces were the only opposition between
this large, powerful communist assault unit and
Saigon.

I would meet Hai two and sometimes three times
a week for discussions on the fighting in his area
and other information he had on the fighting
throughout South Vietnam.

Although helpful, he hated me and the U.S.
government I represented to have put him and
his men in this untenable position. We had
blundered our mission to SouthVietnam from
start to the soon-to-be-finished, he said. He
wondered how we could go from the best military
in the world in 1945, when we beat the Germans
and the Japanese, to getting our asses whipped
by little North Vietnam... and in going about
that getting so many of his countrymen killed.

"How did this happen, Mr. CIA man?" He
asked again and again.   His look always fierce

and unwavering. His haunting question loudly resonating in the quiet tent he used for an office.

I had no answer then ... nothing in my on-the-ground experience in SEA helped explain how we had done so badly ... we had won every battle I was in.

Over the years, I have searched for answers to Hai's question. What I have found is laid out in the prelude. As one who was there, it's what makes sense to me. Refer to my bibliography for sources – nothing is invented -- but understand that I am a story teller and this is my story, my understanding, on how the United States came to be in a fight it lost in Southeast Asia. You want someone else's understanding of how Vietnam happened, buy their book.

What follows the prelude are the details of my five years on Southeast Asia (SEA) battlefields. Some of these accounts are taken from my previous books, LAST MAN OUT, CODENAME MULE and THE BATTLE FOR SKYLINE RIDGE. The book ends with my escape from Vietnam on May 1, 1975, two days after the American Embassy was evacuated.

It is my personal accounting of the Vietnam War, the only start-to-finish memoir from among all personal accounts of the three million Americans who served.

James E. Parker, Jr
August 2016

Prelude

Part I

The Beginning of the First Anglo-Vietnam War

European missionaries began arriving in Vietnam in the 17th century and by 1850 there were 300,000 Roman Catholic converts in Annam (central Vietnam) and Tonkin (in the north).

Most of the priests and bishops were French and Spanish nationals, implying a certain inherent responsibility on the French and Spanish governments in Europe for their safety and, by extension, their Vietnamese Christian converts.

There were concerns because generally speaking the Catholics were looked upon with suspicion by the rural Vietnamese who held strongly to traditional Asian values and beliefs. Also the Catholics were not well received by national leaders.

Soon after Tu Duc ascended the throne as the fourth emperor of the Nguyen Dynasty of Vietnam in 1847 all Vietnamese Catholics were ordered to either renounce their religion or be branded on the face with the mark of a heretic.

This rallied most of the European powers against Vietnam, putting Tu Duc in the ranks of crazy third world despots, denying him any understanding or sympathy from the West.

In 1857, on orders from Tu Duc, Spanish Catholic bishop José María Díaz Sanjurjo, and another missionary, were beheaded. This was neither the first nor the last such incident; however, on previous occasions the French government had overlooked the provocations.

Sanjurjo's execution happened when the British Empire was absorbing Burma (present-day Myanmar) as it expanded its colonial holdings east from India.

The French government, also in the business of colonizing third world countries, was aware of the British expansion and sent a punitive expedition to Vietnam. Ostensibly it was because of the persecution of Catholic clergy but probably it was to compete with the British Empire for land in Southeast Asia unclaimed by other European countries.

Consequently, in September 1858, a joint French and Spanish force landed and took control of the city of Da Nang in central Vietnam, a short distance from Tu Duc's royal court in Hue.

This was followed by a 3,500 soldier French assault on Saigon in the south.

Tu Duc's national militia initially put up resistance but their antiquated weapons and tactics were no match for the French, who suffered more from the climate and disease than from enemy resistance.

As result of the successful French campaigns against Da Nang and Saigon, Tu Duc was forced to sign the Treaty of Saigon on June 5, 1862. The treaty required Vietnam to:

- Permit the Catholic faith to be preached and practiced freely;
- To cede the southern provinces of Bien Hoa, Gia Dinh and Dinh Tuong (and the small island of Poulo Condore) to France;
- To allow the French to trade and travel freely along the Mekong River;
- To open Da Nang, Quang Yen and Ba Lac (at the mouth of the Red River that runs through Hanoi) as trading ports;
- And to pay an indemnity of a million dollars to France and Spain over a 10-year period.

Emperor Tu Duc

The French placed the three southern Vietnamese provinces under the control of its Ministry of Navy and thus – with minimal resistance - was born the French colony of Cochinchina, with its capital at Saigon.

Adding to Emperor Tu Duc's troubles at the time – to France's advantage - were continuing internal rebellions... literally hundreds of small uprisings took place throughout the country during the middle of the century.

With the Vietnamese government preoccupied with maintaining civil order, France consolidated its military's hold on the region and at every turn asserted its influence in the Vietnamese culture.

Cambodia

Cambodia, at the time, had been reduced to a vassal state of the Siam kingdom (now known as Thailand), which had annexed and occupied Cambodia's western provinces, including Angkok. The Khmer empire was also at odds with Vietnamese groups in the eastern portion of the country.

French colonel soldiers in Tonkin

After the French colony of Cochinchina was firmly

established with the treaty of Saigon, King Norodom of Cambodia requested French protectorate status for his kingdom. On August 11, 1863, Norodom signed a treaty in Phnom Penh that allowed the Cambodian monarchy to remain, but power was largely vested in a resident French general to be assigned. According to the treaty France was also specifically in charge of Cambodia's foreign and trade relations.

So, unlike in Vietnam, the French were looked on as protectors of the Khmer culture and were welcomed into Cambodia.

Laos

With the French in Cambodia on Siam's east, and with Burma, on the west annexed by the British Empire, the peaceful, mostly agrarian monarchy was now caught between two aggressive colonial powers.

Obvious problem faced by the government in Bangkok was how to defend its distant, often hard to identify borders. For example, in middle of the 19th century there was no clearly understood north-south border between Cambodia and the Kingdom of Luang Prabang. No survey had ever been taken where Siam ended and Vietnam began.

Plus there was some question on the specific domain of the Kingdom of Luang Prabang, which lay across the Mekong River to the north of Siam. Contiguous to most other Southeast Asia countries, the king of Luang Prabang maintained independence in the region by paying tribute to China and Vietnam as well as Siam.

But the King had little control of the countryside out from the capital.

With France and England now on the scene in Southeast Asia, and having just lost influence in Cambodia, Siam sought to emphasize their influence in the Luang Prabang kingdom by deploying Siamese troops there in a show of force.

There were scattered unsuccessful efforts by local militia to oppose these Siam soldiers, but by the 1860s it seemed as though the land north and northeast of the Mekong would soon disappear as a distinct national entity, becoming a regional sub-nationality of the Siamese kingdom, separate from French, British, Chinese and Vietnamese land.

French explorers went on several expeditions up the Mekong River to investigate the situation north of the Mekong and find possible trade opportunities for French Cambodia and Cochinchina. This led to the 1885 establishment of a French consulate in Luang Prabang.

Siam, aware of this new diplomatic French mission and fearful of French intention, asked the French to sign an acknowledgment that recognized Siam's suzerainty over the separate kingdom north and east of the Mekong.

France complied.

For similar reasons of identifying primacy in the different regions of shifting regional control, the French drew up a Second Treaty of Saigon, signed by Tu Duc on March 15, 1874. It reiterated the stipulations of the 1862 agreement in which Vietnam recognized the full sovereignty of France over the three southernmost provinces. Further, to clarify trade agreements in northern Vietnam, this second treaty opened the Red River as well as the ports of Hanoi, Haiphong and Qui Nhon to French commerce.

In 1888, roaming Chinese irregular militia known as the Black Flags, attacked and sacked Luang Prabang.

The Siamese contingent fled, but Auguste Jean-Marie Pavie, the vice-counsel of the French consulate, organized the defense of the town and evacuated the family of the elderly King Oun Kham to safety.

French foreign legion troops from Hanoi soon arrived to expel the Black Flags from the region. Following his return to the city, King Oun Kham requested a formal, continuing protective relationship with France.

On March 27, 1889, the king signed a treaty turning his region into a protectorate of France.

Siam protested, to no avail.

Auguste Jean-Marie Pavie

The border to the Luang Prabang kingdom was clearly drawn to the north with China and to the east with Vietnam. Pavie negotiated with the English and in early 1896 signed an accord recognizing the border with British Burma.

There was no established southern border so Pavie argued for all he thought he could get and demanded French protectorate status over all lands east of the Mekong from Laung Prabang down to Cambodia.

Hearing this, Siam rushed troops and administrators into its eastern extremes but was not able to assert governance so distant from Bangkok.

After several border disputes, an armada of French warship gathered in the Gulf of Siam. Pavie sent an ultimatum to Bangkok, the Siam capital, compelling the kingdom to recognize French control over the entire eastern side of the Mekong River, or the French would attack the capital city.

This new country proposed by Pavie was composed of the traditional Laung Prabang mountain kingdom of King Oun Kham and the "panhandle," the previous Siam land down to Cambodia between the Mekong River and Vietnam. In negotiations with Bangkok, Pavie called this country "Laos" for the first time.

Siam, expecting British help that did not materialize, in time accepted the new Lao borders as structured by the French. The administrative capital of this new country was established in Vientiane. Luang Prabang remained the seat of the royal family, whose power was reduced to figureheads while the actual power was transferred initially to the French vice consulate and resident-general.

A French colonial governor was later installed in Vientiane and the country was organized into ten provinces. To finance the colonial government, France imposed taxes on the population; however, Laos was never able to pay the cost of running its own country and France had to go to Hanoi and Saigon every year to get money to help Laos pay its bill.

Like the Cambodians, the French were very well received by the Lao in the countryside, especially in Vientiane.

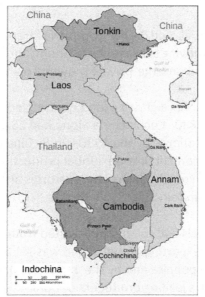

French Indochina

France Tightens Control

While the French developed the notion of bringing Western civilization to Indochina, its military and commercial leadership was driven primarily by profit in the way it exploited its new colonial holdings, especially in Vietnam. Each region had a separate governor who wielded enormous power, a situation that encouraged self-interest, corruption, venality and heavy-handedness.

Emperor Tu Duc remained as a figurehead in Hue, but from the late 19th century he exercised less and less political power as the French played local mandarins, communities and religious groups against each other to maintain order.

Colonial officials and French companies transformed Vietnam's thriving subsistence economy into a colonial system, based on large privately owned plantations.

The amount of rice-growing land quadrupled in the 20 years after 1880. Cochinchina alone had 25 gigantic rubber plantations. By the 1930s, Indochina was supplying 5 percent of total global production of raw rubber. The French constructed factories and minded for coal, tin and zinc.

French officials and colonists benefited from growing, selling and exporting opium. Land was set aside to grow opium poppies and by the 1930s Vietnam was one of the world's leading producers of opium.

The French also imposed an extensive taxation system

on the Vietnamese, which included an income tax, a poll tax on all adult males and stamp duties on a wide range of publications and documents. They also imposed what was called the "corvee," which required males to complete 30 days of unpaid work on government roads and buildings.

Harnessing and transforming Vietnam's economy required local support. There were only 11,000 French troops in Vietnam in 1900 so the French relied on locals trained to support colonial rule. Vietnamese held positions of authority in local government, businesses or economic institutions, such as the French Bank of Indochina.

French colonialism did provide conspicuous benefits for Vietnamese society, one of the more noticeable of which was education. French missionaries, officials and their families opened primary schools, conducting lessons in both the French and Vietnamese languages. The University of Hanoi was created by French colonists and became an important national center of learning. A small number of Vietnamese students were given scholarships to study in France. These changes were particularly significant in the cities; there was little or no attempt to educate the children of peasant farmers. The syllabuses at these schools reinforced colonial control by stressing the supremacy of French values and culture.

Colonialism produced a physical transformation of Vietnamese cities. Traditional buildings, some of which had stood for a millennium, were torn down and replaced with buildings of French architecture and style.

Significant business tended to be conducted in French, rather than local languages. French restaurants, bars and brothels abounded. If not for the climate and people, some parts of Hanoi and Saigon could have been mistaken for parts of Paris.

But this French paradise was not to last. Other world events would, in time, affect its tranquility and legality.

Larger World Events and the Shaping of Ho

In 1904 Japan annexed Korea and began to expand its influence throughout the Pacific Rim of the Far East. This went almost unnoticed in the United States.

In the summer of 1914 the Hungarian/Austrian archduke was assassinated in Sarajevo, Serbia and within months, for a variety of associated reasons, England declared war on Germany. In August 1914 Germany attacked and defeated the Russian army in Poland. The next month the German army attacked France.

With the world preoccupied with the war in Europe, on October 31, 1914, Japan attacked and captured Tsingtao, China, just across the Yellow Sea from Korea.

The United States was finally drawn into the war in Europe and declared war on Germany on April 6, 1917.

In May 1917, German Gotha airplanes attacked Folkestone, England leading to 95 civilian deaths with 195 injured. The concept of strategic bombing of purely civilian targets introduced the term of **"Total War"** into the lexicon of 20thcentury war.

In June 1917 the first American troops landed in France and by 1918, 10,000 U.S. soldiers a day were arriving to fight the Germans.

By November 1918 Germany was overwhelmed on the battlefield and signed an armistice.

World War I was over.

Joseph Stalin

In 1924 Stalin took power in Russia after Vladimir Ilyich Lenin's death.

Japanese on the march

The Japanese army invaded Manchuria in 1931 and, to make their expansionist policies official, declared war on China in 1937.

Adolph Hitler

Adolph Hitler took power in German in 1933 and in 1939 his armies invaded Poland.

Ho Chi Minh

In 1941, Ho Chi Minh returned to Vietnam.

Ho Chi Minh was born on May 19, 1890, the second son to a family of farmers living in Kim Lien, Central Vietnam. His birth name was Nguyen Sinh Cung, but when he was 10 years old his father gave him a new name: Nguyen

Tat Thanh ("Nguyen the Accomplished"). Later in Paris he identified himself as Nguyen Ai Quoc ("Nguyen the patriot"). Finally he took the name by which he is best known, Ho Chi Minh ("He who enlightens").

As a young man Ho traveled to Saigon where he obtained a job as a cook aboard a French steamship bound for France. He spent the next two years traveling around the world, visiting cities in Europe, Asia, North America, and perhaps Africa and South America as well. He settled in London during the height of World War I and became involved in leftist and anti-colonial activities.

Following World War I, Ho helped found the Association for Annamite Patriots, an organization composed of Vietnamese nationals living in France who opposed the French colonial occupation of Vietnam.

He authored a petition demanding the end of the French colonial exploitation of Vietnam, which he attempted to present to the world powers at the Versailles Peace Conference, held in the aftermath of World War I. His petition was never officially recognized, but his effort became well known. Later he founded the journal Le Paria, which spoke for opponents to the French colonial regime in Southeast Asia.

Identified for his value to the international communist movement, Ho traveled to Russia for the first time in 1923 where he was introduced to influential Soviet leaders including Leon Trotsky, Vladimir Ilyich Lenin and Joseph Stalin.

While in Russia, Ho was embraced by Comintern (shortened title for the Communist International, aka the Third International) and trained as one of its many foreign operative.

Founded by Lenin in 1919 the Comintern was dedicated to organizing the international pro-Soviet movement. Comintern agents were deployed from Russia throughout the world to fight "by all available means, including armed force, for the overthrow of the international bourgeoisie and for the creation of an international Soviet republic as a transition stage to the complete abolition of the State."

In 1925 Ho went to China (a trip certainly coordinated by Comintern) where he formed the Thanh Nien, an organization composed of Vietnamese exiles dedicated to revolution in their home country.

Ho was forced to leave China after a couple of years when Chiang Kai-shek, the leader of the Nationalist Party (Kuomingtang), instituted a vicious crackdown on left-wing radicals, imprisoning and executing hundreds of communists and labor activists.

Ho returned to the Soviet Union where he attended the Moscow Sun Yat-sen University – again certainly under the auspices of Comintern - and spent the next few years making trips to China to recruit members for Thanh Nien.

In 1928 he returned to Asia by way of Europe as a senior Comintern agent. He founded the Vietnamese Communist Party (VCP) in Hong Kong, was arrested by

British authorities for his involvement in revolutionary activities and was imprisoned for two years.

Upon his release, Ho returned to Moscow where various Indochinese communist movements were pulled together under his name.

In 1941 the Soviet Comintern directorate in Moscow sent the 51 year-old Ho Chi Minh back to Vietnam. On his return he became the prominent figurehead in the foundation of the Viet Nam Doc Lap Dong Minh ("League for the Independence of Vietnam"), known simply as the Viet Minh.

****

In September 1940, as part of its Far East expansionist policies, the Japanese moved into Vietnam. Vichy French colonial authorities agreed to allow this Japanese occupation under the condition that the pro-Axis French colonial administration not be dismantled. Japan agreed.

More "Total War"

Pearl Harbor

The Japanese Imperial Navy, the aggressor in the Pacific, attacked Pearl Harbor December 7, 1941.

Four days later Germany declared war on the United States.

During World War II, the battles between Germany and Russia constituted the largest military confrontation in the history of mankind. It was characterized by a **"Total War"** of unprecedented ferocity, wholesale destruction, and immense loss of life due to combat, starvation, exposure, disease, and massacres.

Operation Barbarossa

The majority of all Germans soldier casualties in World War II were lost to the Russian on its eastern front in Operation Barbarossa.

Poland which was invaded and occupied by Germany (from which the Germans launched Barbarossa), suffered six million killed, mostly civilian.

The Soviet Union lost 10 million soldiers defending Russia from the Germans and altogether suffered 25 million casualties.

China lost 14 million civilians and soldiers, mostly to the Japanese.

With Germany spent in its unsuccessful attack on Russia, and with the power of Japan slowly eroded by its army's efforts to control all of China, the defeat of the Axis forces was assured. Certainly the United States was successful in the war because of the U.S. industrial base's rapid conversion to the production of war material, Roosevelt's political/civilian war managers and the gallant efforts of the common American doughboys. But not to be overlooked in understanding the history of WW II was Germany's and Japan's enormous losses to Russia and China, which contributed significantly to the ultimate win by allied forces.

The Office of Strategic Services (OSS) Deer Team visited the Viet Minh jungle camp in North Vietnam near the end of World War II. Ho Chi Minh was sick much of the time. General Vo Nguyen Giap, known as Mr. Van, seemed to be the one in charge, the alpha animal. Center left to right, are Rene Defourneaux, Ho Chi Minh, team leader Allison Thomas, Vo Nguyen Giap.

Yalta and Potsdam:
Deciding what the New World will look like

Churchill, FDR and Stalin

On June 6, 1944 Allied forces landed at Normandy and drove directly into the heart of the German homeland. By early 1945 German defeat seemed assured. Franklin D. Roosevelt, Winston Churchill and Joseph Stalin meet at Yalta in February 1945 to decide on the war's end game.

Preparatory to Yalta, Stalin's conditions on joining the American fight against Japan was discussed with the US

Ambassador to Russia, Averell Harriman, in 1944. On December 14 of that year, Stalin delivered to Harriman his demands.

- He would move 30 of his divisions from the western front to join 30 of his division positioned in eastern Russia to attack Japanese forces occupying Manchuria, and would control that part of China until Chinese forces could assume reasonable governance.
- That Russia would assume a lease on the Port Arthur/Darien seaports and regain management of the Manchurian railroad.
- Russia would also re-take control of several islands near Japan that it had also claimed in years past.

In Yalta, Roosevelt, tired from his travels (he would die within weeks of his return home), met privately with Stalin and Stalin's Foreign Minister, advised on by Harriman. He would not agree to Russia's re-acquisition of the Manchurian railroad, saying it should be run as a joint Soviet/Chinese endeavor. Roosevelt also said all condition were subject to coordination with Chiang Kai-shek. Stalin conceded on those two points but got Roosevelt to agree not to announce the particulars of the agreement – even within his government - so as not to give the Japanese advance word… and he wanted the agreement written up and held in tight security. Roosevelt, with Harriman at his side, complied only showing the draft to his military advisers at Yalta, but not to the US Secretary of State. The written agreement was hand carried back to Washington and place in a White House safe. Chiang was not notified until after Roosevelt's death in April.

In April 1945 on FDR's death, Harry S Truman assumed the office of US President.

In Europe Allied armies raced for Berlin: Americans from the west, Soviets from the east. Soviets entered the shattered capital first on April 23. Two weeks later, on May 7, 1945, Germany surrendered.

Churchill, Truman and Stalin

At the end of July 1945, in Potsdam, Germany, Stalin confirmed his intentions to join the fight against Japan per the agreements arranged with Roosevelt and Harriman at Yalta. During the conference, French representatives requested the return of all French pre-war colonies in Southeast Asia. Their request was granted.

Then Came August 1945

Little Boy

On the 6th of August 1945, the United States dropped an atomic bomb—named Little Boy—on Hiroshima, killing 75,000 people instantly and injuring more than 100,000.

Soviet Invasion of Manchuria

On the 8th the Soviet Union invaded Manchuria spearheaded by "penal" battalions to clear the country of Japanese military. These forces eventually gave way to Soviet engineer units which dismantled all equipment in former Japanese factories which had been built in Manchuria over the previous ten years, packaged the equipment up and shipped it to Russia. This included turbines in Manchuria's hydro-electric plants. Soviet administrators also looted the Manchurian banks, sending massive amounts of gold bullion to Moscow banks, replacing them with worthless Soviet "occupation yuan." Soviet forces themselves moved to ports of entry from lower China – including Port Arthur and Darien - to frustrate Chuang Kai-shek's American trained anti-communist armies from moving north and to allow time for Mao Zedung's forces to establish a significant presence in the previous communist-free area. Manchuria in time became critical terrain in the China civil war.

Fat Man

On the 9th, a second, and more powerful, atomic bomb – named Fat Man - was dropped on Nagasaki; to this point in time the ultimate **"Total War"** weapon.

On the 10th, the 38th parallel was set as the delineation between the Soviet and United States occupation zones in Korea.

On the evening of the 14th, Emperor Hirohito announced his country's surrender by public radio.

Japan signed the surrender agreement in Tokyo Bay formally ending World War II in the Pacific on September 2, 1945. On this same day, Ho Chi Minh proclaimed the independence of Vietnam with this statement: "We hold the truth that all men are created equal, that they are endowed by their Creator with certain unalienable rights, among them life, liberty and the pursuit of happiness."

The French Return to Vietnam

Ignoring Ho Chi Minh's American-cloned proclamations in the north, on September 13, 1945 the British landed in Saigon to disarm the Japanese and to prepare for the arrival of French troops.

In North Vietnam, 150,000 Chinese Nationalist soldiers, consisting mainly of poor peasants, arrived in Hanoi after razing Vietnamese villages during their march down from China.

In South Vietnam on September 22, 1945, fourteen hundred French soldiers released by the British from former Japanese internment camps, entered Saigon and went on a deadly rampage attacking Viet Minh. They were aided by some of the 20,000 French civilians who lived in Saigon at the end of the war.

In October 1945, thirty-five thousand French soldiers arrived in South Vietnam to restore French rule. They were immediately taken on by the Viet Minh, launching the first Anglo-Vietnamese war.

The Chinese under Chiang Kai-shek agreed in February 1946 to withdraw from North Vietnam and allow the French to return in exchange for French concessions in Shanghai and other Chinese ports.

The population of all Vietnam in 1945 was approximately 46.5 million, almost three times what it was when the French first arrived in 1858. The majority of the people lived in the north.

In Laos, French-educated King Sisavang Vong refused to cooperate with home-grown Lao nationalists at the war's end and was deposed when the Lao Issara declared the country independent. In April 1946 at the request of Sisavang Vong, the French asserted its pre-World War II role as the country's administrator and reinstated Sisavang Vong as king.

The United States Retrenches from "Total War" of World War II

After the Japanese surrendered in the fall of 1945 the public outcry in the United States was: "Bring the boys home."

In Washington, D.C., the thought also was to bring the troops home, so as to reduce the size and expense of the military. Not considered so much was how many U.S. troops were needed to enforce new policy, police the end-war agreements established in Yalta and Potsdam and protect U.S. in the new alignment of world power.

Washington was also thinking, "What's our post Atomic Bomb/World War II foreign policy?"

The Marshall Plan was part of the U.S. answer to a way ahead in Europe, an area used to putting itself back together after war. Various castles and fortress there are testament to the many previous fights/wins/losses. Fighting wars and making peace and new boundaries afterwards is the history of Europe.

As for the Far East, U.S. planners first thought was to support the Soviet-approved, U.S. State Department-suggested division of Korea at the 38[th]parallel. Soviet forces, which had moved through Korea in the attacks on Manchuria early August 1945, moved down to the vicinity of the 38th and stopped. U.S. Army forces came up to the southern part of this demilitarized zone (DMZ) in early 1946.

China after WW II was involved in a great civil war, between the Soviet supported armies of Mao Zedung and the US supported armies of Chiang Kai-chek. General George Marshall visited China in an effort to bring the conflict to a close. He ordered a cease fire as he sought ways to engineer a coalition government. Chiang complied, Mao did not. Plus the Soviets continued their occupation of Manchuria to facilitate the infiltration of Mao's armies into Manchuria, while at the same time continuing to frustrate Chiang's Army from moving in great numbers up into the region to establish control.

Adding to this was the general disdain General "Vinegar Joe" Stilwell held for Chiang Kai-chek. Stilwell was the chief American adviser to the China Nationalist Army. Any failings of the multi-million men in the National Army he blamed on Chiang, who never sought Stilwell's favor. He pointedly did not learn how to speak English and never kowtowed to the westerners.

Also the "Ol' China" hands in the State Department were mostly born and raised in China, sons of US Missionaries. While they spoke fluent Mandurian and/or Cantonese, they did not see Mao as a devout communist who had sold his soul to the Russian for providing his army with war support, but as someone who represented the Chinese people. All things considered the State Department lent its influence to Mao Zedung.

General Marshall picked up on the general US Army and US State Department thinking and openly criticized Chiang. Marshall seemed to regard Chiang pretty much as the union leader of buck-tooth Asian laundry men, not at all comparable to say, European leaders. Tragically for pro-American Asian forces in the east Asia, after leaving China, Marshall went back to be the U.S. Secretary of State and then Secretary of Defense.

Chiang was toast.

George Kennan – Princeton (1925)

In 1946, the Washington, D.C. search for a post-atomic Bomb era of foreign policy found some solutions with arrival of George Kennan's famous "long telegram" from the U.S. Embassy in Moscow. It addressed the need for a policy of **"Containment"** of the Soviets to avert another **"Total War."**

On September 18, 1947 the Central Intelligence Agency (CIA) was created as a follow on to the Office of Strategic Services (OSS) of World War II. Despite Douglas MacArthur and J. Edgar Hoover objections it was set up as an independent organization responsible to the President.

Cominform (Communist Information Bureau) was founded in the Soviet Union later the same month the CIA was created. It took up where Comintern had left off (when this organization was suspended in World War II) to promote worldwide communist movement. It clearly had different mission from the USA's CIA. It was more like the Soviet Union's Cold War Department. Almost all future Soviet international mischief and rebel-rousing could be traced back to Cominform or to Stalin's office.

French Struggle to Re-Assert Control of Vietnam: First Indochina War

In November 1946, after a series of violent clashes with the Viet Minh, French forces bombarded Haiphong harbor and occupied Hanoi, forcing the Viet Minh forces to retreat into the jungle and mountains of North Vietnam.

Vo Nguyen Giap

The following month 30,000 Viet Minh launched a counter-attack and with that began an eight-year struggle known as the First Indochina War. "The resistance will be long and arduous, but our cause is just and we will surely triumph," declared Viet Minh military commander Vo Nguyen Giap.

Throughout Vietnam the state of war with the French actually simplified Ho's political problems. The Vietnamese did not have to be Communist to join the fight against the French, and the ranks of the Viet Minh swelled with patriotic volunteers.

From October 7 through December 22, 1947, the French conducted a series of attacks on Viet Minh guerrilla positions in North Vietnam near the Chinese border. Although the Viet Minh suffered over 9,000 causalities, most of the 40,000 soldier Viet Minh force slipped away through gaps in the French lines.

Korea: 'Containment' Triumphs as U.S. Policy

In Korea, with the DMZ established, U.S. troops began to withdraw from the peninsula leaving South Korea under the leadership of United States-aligned Syngman Rhee, who worked closely with the U.S. State Department through its embassy in Seoul.

Shtykov   Kim Il Sung

In North Korea, first supreme commander was Russian General Terentii Shtykov 1946-1947, who instigated land reform that took all land ownership from the public and transferred it to the government. Then in 1947 Kim Il Sung was selected as president by the Soviet embassy. Most historians suggest Kim was a combined product of Cominform, Shtykov and Stalin. Korean was not his first language, because in his first taped speech he had difficulty speaking Korean. (He was most probably Russian of Korean extraction). The name Kim Il Sung was taken from a Korean resistant leader killed near the end of World War II.

One Soviet official said they made President Kim Il Sung from "nothing."

Whatever Kim's background, Kim was closely controlled by Shtykov, who remained as the Soviet Ambassador to North Korea.

U. S 'Containment Policy' Players

Harry S. Truman - No college
President of the United States 1945 to 1953

A professional politician, Truman was selected as FDR's vice president in 1945 and assumed office as the 33rd president of the United States on Roosevelt's death. Truman won election outright as president over Thomas E. Dewey in 1948. He was followed in office in 1952 by Dwight D. Eisenhower.   His advisers included Dean Acheson, Robert Lovett, John McCoy and Averell Harriman.

Dean Acheson -   Yale (1915) Skull and Bones
Secretary of State 1949-1953

Dean Acheson, Truman's secretary of state, helped define foreign policy through the Marshall Plan, Truman Doctrine, and formation of the North Atlantic Treaty Organization (NATO). Close to Averell Harriman.

Robert Lovett – Harvard (1921) and Yale (1918) Skull and Bones
Under Secretary of State 1945 -1949
Assistant Secretary of Defense 1949-1951
Secretary of Defense 1951 to 1953

Out of Harvard, Lovett worked for Brown Brothers Harriman on Wall Street and was spotted by Averell Harriman. Lovett became Truman's secretary of defense after General George Marshall. Helped create CIA, NATO. He became known as one of the U.S. architect of the "Cold War."

John McCloy - Harvard (1921)

Assistant Secretary of War 1941-1945
Military Governor and High Commissioner for West
Germany 1946-1949

A War Department official and later U.S. official to Germany, John McCoy was spotted by Averell Harriman in the private sector and invited into top level of U.S. government. He advised FDR on Japanese internment and on Truman's decision to drop atomic bombs on Japan.

Averell Harriman – Yale (1913) Skull and Bones
Ambassador at Large and confidant of
Presidents Franklin D. Roosevelt and Harry
Truman 1934-1953
Governor of New York 1954-1958
Ambassador at Large and confidant to President
John F. Kennedy and Lyndon Johnson. 1961 to
1968

1891 Averell Harriman was born into the family of railroad baron E.H. Harriman. After graduating Yale, he inherited the largest personal fortune in America. A few years later, at 24 years old, this tall, distinguished young man with a slight stutter, was vice president of the

Union Pacific Railroad Co. and director of the Illinois Central Railroad. A few years later he expanded his transportation holdings into sea transports, which led to his partnership with the Soviet government in the Georgian Manganese Concessions.

In the 1920s he consolidated his financial holdings into the industry-leading Wall Street firm of Brown Brothers Harriman & Company along lines of an old-fashion investment house, in which partners would sit at their large roll-top desks in a large room and discuss international business and finance that, when the company became involved, always seemed to turn a profit. Except maybe the Soviet Manganese Concessions.

Though mostly involved in solid no-risk U.S. investments, Harriman's company invested in a forerunner of Pan American Airways. In publishing, Harriman's firm developed a national magazine called Today, "an independent journal of public affairs" whose first subscriber was FDR; Today eventually merged with NewsWeek.

Harriman coached crew at Yale, was a champion croquet player, owned some of the best racehorses and bird dogs in the world and was a top level polo player. He personally developed the Sun Valley Ski Resort.

He was an elitist with a very persuasive personality who clearly held himself above most anyone he encountered. As maybe was his right. There was no American businessman more successful than young Averell Harriman in the Roaring 20s.

In 1934, encouraged by his older sister (also an extreme elitist) Mary Ramsey, Harriman left his financial empire at Brown Brothers Harriman & Company in New York City to their younger brother and moved to Washington, DC, to take up politics.

He was first appointed - due in some measure to Mary's influence - to head the National Recovery Administration, part of FDR's New Deal. This was a significant appointment and by all accounts Harriman applied his considerable organizational skills to good advantage.

In 1941, as World War II loomed, he was selected by President Franklin D. Roosevelt as a special envoy to Europe to help coordinate the Lend-Lease program, and to work with Winston Churchill in refining the Atlantic Charter. He and Churchill subsequently went to Moscow to negotiate the terms of the Lend-Lease agreement with Stalin. There, he promised $1 billion in aid to Russia, technically exceeding his brief, but ensuring Stalin's friendship and gratitude. Exceeding his brief with the Soviets was to characterize much of his high level US diplomacy thereafter.

Harriman was appointed ambassador to the Soviet Union in 1943 and served there until January 1946 where he enjoyed a relatively close relationship with Stalin.

Harriman counseled FDR at the Tehran Conference in late 1943 and, near World War II's end, at the Yalta Conference. At the conference he and Roosevelt had private consultations with Stalin and his Minister of Foreign Affairs, in which the only other American in the room, "Chip" Bohlen, a State Department Ambassador and FDR's Russian interpreter, thought Stalin caught Roosevelt and Harriman "napping."

After Roosevelt's death, Harriman attended the final "Big Three" conference at Potsdam at the elbow of the new U.S. president, Harry Truman, and insured that concessions to Stalin ostensibly to help in the end fight with Japan were given the authority of "approved treaty."

While he remained guarded about overall Soviet intentions in official dispatches as U.S. Ambassador, he became good friends with Walter Duranty, the New York Time's Moscow bureau chief. Harriman is quoted as saying he "...learned more from this journalist... than from any diplomat." However, columnist Joe Alsop, among many others, said Duranty was a KGB agent. At the very least he was a Soviet apologist and sympathizer who had a reputation among other journalist as an "out and out liar."

In the 1960s Anatoliy Golitsyn, a defector to the United States from the KGB, suggested that W. Averell Harriman had been "recruited" as a Soviet spy while he was the U.S. ambassador to the Soviet Union. That is not true. Harriman had no exploitable weaknesses and was probably unrecruitable. What could the Soviets offer? But he did have an enormous ego with ambitions to move among world leaders who would decide the future of the world. It would be typical of the Soviet KGB to say that was probably a vulnerability that could be manipulated. And because he was manipulable, they may have considered him recruited. Certainly Stalin's friendship was very meaningful to Harriman.

Shortly before he left Moscow Harriman was given a carved Seal of the United States which he hung over the desk in his study. It was a KGB bug, however, discovered years later. In one of his last meeting with Stalin, his daughter commented on how handsome the lead horse was in a parade of Soviet cavalrymen. Stalin gave her the horse and had it shipped back to one of Harriman's breeding farms on a Soviet aircraft.

When Harriman returned to the United States, he worked hard to get George Kennan's Long Telegram into wide distribution before his posting in April 1946 as the U.S. ambassador to England. He didn't say long in England, returning to Washington to take the appointment as secretary of commerce.

He was subsequently in charge of the Marshall Plan from 1948 to 1950. When the Korean War broke out in June 1950 he became a special assistant to President Harry S. Truman and was near the Oval Office through the end of Truman's administration.

He helped appoint the men around Truman and was a conspicuous ally of his good friend, Secretary of State Dean Acheson. Harrison was reported to have convinced Truman to fire the unpopular Secretary of Defense Johnson to make way for Harriman's friend Lovett. Harriman also played a significant role in the way President Truman handled the Korea war and the impertinent MacArthur.

Truman's Five-Star Army Generals

United States has had only five 5-Star U.S. Army Generals, all promoted during World War II to ensure they ranked higher than allied commanders.

5-Star General Hap Arnold held the joint positions of 5-Star General of the Army and 5-Star General of the Air Force.   He was taught how to fly planes by the Wright Brothers and was the first of three pilots in the U.S. military. He went on to build the aviation division in the U.S. military and in World War II led the 2.5 million men in the U.S. military air corps with75,000 planes. He retired from the military in 1946 for health reasons and died four years later.

The remaining four 5-Star Army generals greatly impacted U.S. military strategy and U.S. foreign policy after World War II:

5-Star General George Marshall
US Army Chief of Staff 1939-1945
Secretary of State 1947-1948
Secretary of Defense 1950-1951

During World War II, General Marshall provided significant leadership to allied campaigns in Europe and the Pacific. Created the Marshall Plan for Europe at the war's end. He opposed U.S. involvement in China. Did not like Chiang Kai-chek.

5-Star General Omar Bradley
Chairman of Joint Chief of Staff 1949-1953

"Set your course by the stars, not by the lights of every passing ship"   Soft spoken and polite, General Omar Bradley, chairman of the Joint Chiefs of Staff, objected to dismantling of the U.S. military after World War II. Though he did not personally like MacArthur was the only dissenting vote among Truman advisers to dismiss him from Command in Korea.

5-Star General MacArthur
Supreme Commander for the Allied Powers in Japan
1945-1951
Commander-in-Chief of the United Nations Command in
Korea 1950-1951

Operating under **"Total War"** ideals, 5-Star General Douglas MacArthur refused to obey Truman's **"Containment"** and **"Limited War"** objectives. His position was unwavering, frequently stating that there is **"no substitute for victory**." He tried to negotiate with Mao Zedung to end the Korean War without consultation with Truman and sent a letter to Congress pointing out Truman's lack of support to his war strategy. Relieved of duty by President Harry S. Truman on 11 April 1951 for insubordination.

5 Star General Eisenhower
Supreme Allied Commander in Europe 1943-1945
Commander of the North Atlantic Treaty Organization
(NATO) 1950-1952
President of the United State 1952-1960

While Eisenhower did not hold a U.S. government or
U.S. military office during most of Truman's
administration, he was never far from the headlines.
Popular, he represented the loyal opposition of the
Republican party to Truman's management of the
Korean War. In running for president in 1952 he
promised to "visit" Korea as President and bring the war
to an end. He took office as the 34th President of the
United States January 20, 1953.

**Eisenhower did not like Truman or Harriman or
Kennedy or Johnson or McNamara.
Especially he did not like Truman or McNamara.**

******

On August 29, 1949, the Soviet Union exploded a nuclear device, dubbed "Joe 1." This greatly affected Washington, D.C., discussions on U.S. foreign affairs way-ahead in the nuclear age. Kennan's **"Containment"** policy – greatly bolstered by Harriman's endorsement - dominated as an alternative to a future **"Total War."** With Little Boy and Joe 1 now part of the **"Total War"** weapons inventory, "**annihilation**" and "**mutual annihilation**" became part of the equation... and that was unacceptable to U.S government leaders.

Enter the Dragon

Oct 1, 1949 Mao Zedong became Chairman of the newly constituted PRC (People's Republic of China) when Chiang Kai-shek's Nationalist Army fled to the island of Taiwan. All China fell under Mao's communist control.

On December 6, 1949, two months after winning the civil war Mao took a private train to Moscow for a two month visit, ostensibly to celebrate Stalin's birthday.

Acheson spoke to the Washington, D.C. press club on January 12, 1950 about U.S. "**Containment**" thinking… and showed how U.S. defense lines had been drawn around the world. The outermost protective arch that he drew of the Pacific rim did not protect Southeast Asia (SEA), Taiwan or Korea.

End January 1950, Ho Chi Minh arrived in Moscow for talks with Mao and Stalin. Stalin, who controlled the meetings, asked China to provide North Vietnam with war supplies to use in expanding communist influence in SEA. In return Russia would re-supply China with new equipment.

Almost immediately after the Stalin/Mao/Ho conference, China began sending military advisers and modern weapons to the Viet Minh. Some that includes weapons that had been provided to the Chinese Nationals by the United States. With the influx of new equipment and Chinese advisers, General Vo Nguyen Giap transforms his guerrilla fighters into conventional army units that included five light infantry divisions and one heavy division.

After Mao and Ho had returned to their respective countries, North Korea's Kim Il Sung went to Moscow on March 7, 1950. Stalin did not coordinate with Mao but (according to Russian reports) agreed to Kim's plan for invasion of South Korea. (Some historians have suggested he ordered Kim to attack the south as a means of drawing China closer and more dependent on the USSR.)

A Top Secret National Security Council (NSC) report 68 – "United States Objectives and Programs for National Security" -- was signed by President Truman on 14 April 1950. Five years in the making, Kennan's "**Containment**" ideas now became official U.S. foreign policy.

In May 1950 Mao agreed with Kim Il Sung's plan to invade the South Korea. He understood that Chinese and Russian advisers would be involved. He did not think the United States would interfere because:

- The U.S. defensive line that Acheson had drawn outlined the countries the United States pledged to defend did not include Korea.
- The United States had only very recently been involved in the peninsula ('46-'47). Had only around 500 soldiers on the ground there.
- The United States had gone from 8,000,000 men in uniform at the end of World War II, to now five years later, to around 1,500,000 men total worldwide… an 82% percent drop in U.S. military strength. The United States did not have any apparent military means to challenge the North Koreans invasion.
- The general orientation of U.S. foreign policy was toward Europe. The United States had not interfered when the communist were taking over China.

Truman's "Containment" wins out over MacArthur's ' "Total War"

Nine North Korean divisions invaded South Korea on 25 June 1950.

On June 27, 1950, President Truman, after meeting with advisers, pledged that the United States would prevent South Korea soldiers and officials from being pushed into the sea. He turned to MacArthur to head up the United Nations Command (UNC) forces that would be deployed to save South Korea.

Three days later Truman ordered U.S. ground troops into South Korea to confront the North Koreans. Truman described the invasion of North Korean troops as a "monolithic" Soviet-backed attack.

General Walton H. Walker's 8th Army was created from available forces on active duty in the Pacific and deployed to southeast South Korea near the port city of Pusan. In the United States, military reserves were mobilized.

North Korean forces captured Seoul on June 28, 1950.

U.S. Army Major General William F. Dean and elements of his 24th Infantry Division were deployed in front of 8th Army forces as a maneuver element to engage and slow the North Korean move south. These forward-deployed US forces fought gallantly but were rolled over by the tank supported North Korean assault. General Dean was captured by the North Koreans and many of his 24th Division soldiers killed, wounded or captured.

Throughout the summer of 1950 there was fierce fighting as the North Korean forces tried to break the Pusan defensive perimeter of the U.S. 8th Army. Operating so long so far to the south however, their thin supply lines became over-extended.

On 23 August U.S. military brass met in Tokyo to decide future strategy. First up in the meeting was the question, "if an invasion of U.S. forces is called for to relieve pressure on the 8th Army, what are our options?" Several invasion locations were mentioned.

At the end of the meeting MacArthur rose and delivered one of his most persuasive speeches, arguing that Inchon was the right location.

Most of the U.S. military brass at that meeting thought it was wrong for a long list of reasons. If the best U.S. military thinkers thought it was too difficult, reasoned MacArthur, then certainly the enemy would too.

MacArthur agreed that Inchon with its narrow, maybe mined, approach channel, its shifting tides of up to 30 feet and the mud flats exposed at low tide would make the landing difficult. But those factors should not rule it out, and he gave an example of a successful invasion years before under similar circumstances.

MacArthur emphasized that with Americans boots on the ground at Inchon, Seoul could be recaptured within a couple of weeks. That would cut the only supply route the North Koreans used to supply their forces far in the south.

With the bulk of the North Korean invasion force cut off and isolated in the Pusan area, the UNC would win the war.

For 45 minutes he spoke and at the end...Inchon, it was. It may have been his finest hour.

On September 15, 1950, 1st Marine Division and 7th U.S. Army Division invaded Inchon against almost no resistance. A total of 75,000 US soldiers were off loaded from 261 ships.

Seoul was recaptured by end of the month and tens of thousands of North Koreans were cut off in the south of the Korean peninsula. Maybe 30,000 made their way back to North Korea, but thousands were captured and sent to POW camps on Koje-do Island in the South China Sea. Also sent to those camps were South Korean communists and people policed up on the battlefield whose allegiance could not be determined.

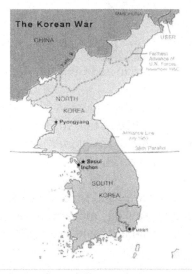

On October 7, 1950, with President Truman approval (and with General Marshall encouragement to "do what was necessary") MacArthur forces launched north across the 38th parallel to find and kill the remaining North Korea Army. Truman specifically told MacArthur to advance with Republic of South Korea (ROK) forces in the lead.

President Truman and General MacArthur

15 October 1950 President Truman and General met on Wake Island 15 Oct 1950 to talk strategy and for Truman to share some of the glory MacArthur achieved for his successful Inchon invasion.

Stalin (probably) encouraged Mao to react. Chinese leadership, in turn, said any movement of the U.S. army up to its border would not be tolerated.

Intelligence was clear that China had moved some of its huge armies from encampments across from Taiwan up north into Manchuria, next to Korea. MacArthur did not believe those Chinese were moving to attack U.S. forces in North Korea, however. There was no signal intelligence, because the Chinese had little in the way of radios. And there was no visual evidence of large number of the enemy in the hills south of the Yalu, because the Chinese only moved at night, and stayed hidden during the day. Chinse soldiers caught moving from hiding positions during the day were shot by their officers. MacArthur couldn't see them, and didn't hear them… and had always held that the Chinese were non-confrontational. And per Stilwell and Marshall, inept as soldiers.

MacArthur persists in his view despite the capture of Red Chinese soldiers south of the Yalu River. And there were reports from some allied intelligence teams on movement of the Chinese military south into North Korea. There were also reports by some U.S. Airmen of soldiers marching south of the Yalu toward UNC troops.

And as MacArthur said later at hearings in Washington, D.C., that those reports seemed to stand out in hindsight, but at the time, even the CIA figured the Red Chinese had only around 75,000 soldiers inside North Korea which tracked with MacArthur's G-2 estimates.

Final movement by UNC forces to the Yalu River border began 24 November, [On this same day a USAF, or possibly a South African, airstrike on a suspected enemy position in North Korea killed Mao Zedung oldest son,

Mao Anying, who was part of an advance Red Army advisory team. Those around Mao, afraid of his reaction, did not tell Mao for several weeks.]

MacArthur's 8th Army in the west and X Corps in the east moved closer to the Yalu, in what was described as a "reconnaissance in force."

Then on the night of 24 November, MacArthur's force, hoping to be home by Christmas, were suddenly attacked by 300,000 Red Chinese who charged in human waves, screaming, bugles and whistles blowing.

It was the greatest ambush of American forces in our country's history.

MacArthur's troops were thrown back all across the front. Some units were destroyed. In other instances, like the Chosen Reservoir, UN forces were surrounded. All allied units in MacArthur's command retreated in various stages of organization from the overwhelming onslaught.

In reaction, Truman did not allow MacArthur war planes to blow the four main bridges across the Yalu that the Chinese needed to support their assaults and he did not allow him to hit resupply depots inside China.

Starting in early 1951 MacArthur's UN forces launched Operation Thunderbolt and broke out of Chinese encirclements of the Chosen Reservoir and, along with other allied forces holding out in pockets of resistance, fought their bloody way south.

As UNC forces were pushed south, Chinese forces retook Seoul, lost it again and dug in near the old DMZ along the 38th parallel. Minor scuffles ensued. (Seoul was lost, retaken, lost and retaken within five months in 1950).

With the rout of UNC two prong advance, the Red Chinese forces were soon far south from their border. Their human wave attack had resulted in severe casualties. Like the North Koreans before them, they were now beginning to strain their re-supply lines, even with the help of Soviet rail.

Responding to the loss of momentum by the Chinese, on 1st of February 1951 the Soviet delegation to the UN suggested peace talks in Korea. The United Nations agrees that a peaceful solution should be sought and talks tentative were set for August 1951.

With the promise of a white flag there was a stand down to the fighting, which allowed time for the Red Chinese and the North Koreans to regroup and resupply their forward most troops.

MacArthur was enormously frustrated with President Truman's acquiescence to the UN orders under the pretense to discuss peaceful negotiations. Truman's apparent efforts to seek "armistice" rather than "victory" seemed to MacArthur to be short sighted. He saw no value whatsoever to **"Limited War"** verse **"Total War."**

MacArthur was especially frustrated at not be allowed to take the initiative at a time he had the Red Chinese at a disadvantage.

So without consulting Washington, on the 24th of March, MacArthur issued an ultimatum to Mao to pull his forces back north across the Yalu or face sure destruction.

Before any response was received from Mao, on April 5, 1951, MacArthur wrote Congress about the lack of support from the Truman administration.

Truman, outraged at MacArthur's insolence, met with his advisers and, based on their recommendation, fired the national hero.

MacArthur returned home with hundreds of thousands of people lining his every route.

A quarter million people filled the National Mall and along the route from the Washington Monument to the Capitol to cheer the war hero on April 19, 1951 when he addressed a joint session of Congress.

He began by saying, *"I stand on this rostrum with sense of deep humility and great pride — humility in the weight of those great American architects of our history who have stood here before me; pride in the reflection that this home of legislative debate represents human liberty in the purest form yet devised."*

Then, standing in the belly of the beast, he said:

- East Asia was as important to the U.S. as West Europe.
- China had emerged as a country to be watched because they had become a warrior nation with "increasingly dominant, aggressive tendencies."
- Appeasement does not work; begets sham peace and war.
- We rightly took on North Korea after its invasion of the south and were kicking its ass back to where it came from when Red China intervened with numerically superior ground forces.
- It takes innovations and cooperation on our side to beat an enemy like Red China. U.S. politicians did not support the U.S. military.

MacArthur said that he had asked for help. " I did not receive it."

He went on to say, "I have from the beginning believed that the Chinese communists' support of the North Koreans was the dominant one. Their interests are at present parallel with those of the Soviets, but I believe that the aggressiveness recently displayed not only in Korea but also in Indo-China... reflects predominantly the same lust for the expansion of power which has animated every would-be conqueror since the beginning of time."

"I do not believe in war," MacArthur continued. "But once war is forced upon us, there is no other alternative than to apply every available means to bring it to a swift end. ... War's very object is victory, not prolonged indecision. In war there is **"no substitute for victory."** He ended by saying, "... that old soldiers never die; they just fade away... [I am just] an old soldier who tried to do his duty as God gave him the light to see that duty. Good Bye."

However, his great oration before Congress was not persuasive --- "**Limited War**" and civilian control of the U.S. military prevailed.

In fact, MacArthur's ouster was the end – at least temporally - of "**no substitute for victory**" as a U.S. battle plan. That attitude, however noble, was part of "**Total War**" global thinking. And with Little Boy, Fat Man and Joe 1, if the US kept on in making "**Total War**" then the stakes ultimately become MAD, "**mutually assured destruction**." Which in the name of all humanity, the U.S. did not want.

China turning communist deeply affected the world balance of power. Truman with his adviser corps understood the bigger picture of the importance of establishing a civil relationship with an independent new China - and stopping this new communist country of half a billion people from tying into a Russian confederation. This was more important than MacArthur's "victory" in Korea.

If China acted in concert with Russia, world power would potentially shift to the communist.

History has proved that Truman and his advisers were right and MacArthur was wrong. MacArthur was probably a better general than Truman was a president, certainly when comparing MacArthur's World War II and Inchon successes against Truman's low approval numbers during his presidency. Truman's very limited efforts to support Chiang Kai-Shek was spun by the Republican Party as the main reason the communist won in China. Plus McCarthyism painted Dean Acheson and his lot as soft on communism.

Back to the Korea War itself, the fight intensified along 38th parallel as peace talks were set up. The first talks were July 10, 1951 in Kaesong, on the border between North and South Korea, and then at the neighboring village of Panmunjom. Chief UN Negotiator Admiral C. Turner Joy arrived the first day to take a seat across from the Chief North Korean negotiator, General Nam Il. The legs of his chair had been cut several inches lower than the North Korean's, a harbinger of things to come. The United Nations came to negotiate peace, though the North Koreans used the opportunity to publicly belittle the West's effort to impose its will on its peninsula.

The return of POWs was a big issue. The United States made mistakes after World War II by forcibly repatriating Russian soldiers captured by the Germans – even though they begged not to be returned to Russia. Because, as they feared, when they returned they were sent to special isolation camps, most never to be seen again.

Complicating peace talks was the Chinese/North Korean manipulation of communist POW inmates in the Koje-do POW camp off the southern coast of South Korea. Communist agitators had been planted in the POW population and riots ensued whenever North Korean chief negotiator General Nam Il called for them.

Then on 5 March 1953, Stalin died and, not coincidentally, Korean peace talks suddenly found traction and surged ahead. On 27 July 1953 a Korean Armistice was signed.

The Korean War for all intents and purposes was over. It was, however, according to U.S. General Mark Clark, "an armistice without victory."

Clark, like MacArthur, did not understand that the principle of "**No substitute for victory**" ran, in this instance, against Washington, D.C. "**Containment**" thinking. Clark's comments reflect U.S. military thinking pre-Little Boy and Fat Man.

A POW swap was set up in October 1953, although there were issues. A convocation was called in Geneva, Switzerland, during the spring of 1954 – away from Korea - to resolve these problems.

United States Commits to South Vietnam

Back in Southeast Asia, in the summer of 1951 CIA case officer James W. (Bill) Lair arrived in Thailand to work with the Thai Police to create what was euphemistically referred to as the police aerial resupply unit (PARU). It was a force designed to protect the country's extensive northern border. If communist Chinese forces moved into SEA in a military action similar to their invasion of South Korea, the PARU would be the Thai military's vanguard.

During May and June 195, Giap's Viet Minh army was

surrounding by French forces in the Red River delta southeast of Hanoi. French reinforcements, combined with air strikes and armed boat attacks resulted in the wholesale slaughter of the Asians, with 10,000 Viet Minh killed and wounded. Giap forces remain encircled.

French military leaders, encouraged by their successes in the delta asked Washington in September 1951 for more military assistance to maintain their momentum against the communist guerrilla insurgents. They had them surrounded.

Truman was supportive of efforts against the communist, but was preoccupied with the war in Korea. No U.S. material was provided.

The Beginning of the End of France in Southeast Asia

Left to their own devices, during the next month French forces linked up in Hoa Binh southwest of Hanoi in an effort to lure Giap out into a major battle.

However, Giap avoided the conventional warfare that he had waged before, and did not move into the baited battlefield. Instead he sent his forces to attack the French, not where they were concentrated, but against their vulnerable outposts on the Black River, especially those between Hoa Binh and Hanoi.

Giap's men followed up hit-and-run attacks with fast retreats into dense jungles. Nibbling at their edges, his goal was to cut the supply lines to the far-flung French positions throughout the Red River valley.

Giap's tactics worked. Supply routes down the Black River to Hoa Binh were cut. Although the French were in relatively large units, they were isolated, and had to fight their way out back to Hanoi. Casualties for each side surpassed 5,000.

In October 1952 Giap continued to gain the initiative by next attacking French positions along the Fan Si Pan mountain range between the Red and Black Rivers. The French forces here, like those in Hoa Binh, were forced to fight their way to alternate positions.

Viet Minh in North Vietnam

By the end of 1952, despite taking enormous casualties, the Viet Minh military organization had grown stronger and more experienced in their fight against the French colonialists. Plus they were receiving an abundance of new recruits and an almost limitless amount of military supplies from China.

Most important, the Viet Minh had the initiative on the battlefield. The French were falling back across a wide front in North Vietnam. They had been out-General-ed by Giap.

Part II

Laos' Strategic Importance

On January 20, 1953, Dwight D. Eisenhower was inaugurated as the 34th U.S. president. On a first name basis with most of the British leadership, he also had legions of friends in the French military and followed events closely in Vietnam. He was disappointed that despite U.S. government support, the Indochina war was not going well for the French. Its military did not seem to have any long-range plans since the Red and Black River campaigns. More and more they committed men just to counter moves of the Viet Minh insurgency.

In the spring of 1953 Giap began to consolidate his divisions in the west/northwest of North Vietnam where there were no French targets. This led the French to believe that he and his Chinese advisers may be planning attacks into peaceful neighboring Laos.

Note: Below Phongsali in Red, "DBP" stands for Dien Bien Phu)

In reaction to the buildup of pre-invasion Viet Minh divisions along the Lao border, a regiment of French Expeditionary soldiers was sent to Xam Nua (aka Sam Neua) in the mountains of northeast Laos to reinforce the 1,200-man joint French/Lao garrison there protecting the Royal Lao provincial government staff.

Once on the ground April 17, 1953, the commander of the reinforcements said Xam Nua was not defendable because of the high mountains - east toward the Lao/North Vietnamese border - that overlooked and dominated established Xam Nua defensive positions. The commander ordered the planes that brought his regiment into Laos to return to pick up just his soldiers.

Chaos reigned on the airfield as the planes returned.

Subsequently the French Expeditionary command in Vientiane – accepting the military analysis of the French reinforcement commander -- ordered all remaining French/Lao military forces and local Lao officials to abandon Xam Nua and head overland toward French positions on the Plaine de Jars (PDJ).

When Giap saw the French garrison riot he launched one of his divisions into Laos to create a blocking position east of the PDJ and sent three divisions charging after the fleeing French and Lao... killing almost all.

When the smoke cleared, communist Lao (Pathet Lao) leaders set up permanent headquarters in the abandoned Xam Nua, Laos.

A third Viet Minh column to the north was led by the

combat-toughened 148th regiment of the Viet Minh 316th Division, supported by 200,000 porters bringing in supplies directly from China. Attacked by French planes, road builders for the army of porters struck a new route through forest, built submerged bridges across rivers and in all ways possible hid the long columns heading to the invasion staging area in the heretofore little known Dien Bien Phu valley of Vietnam, a few miles from the Lao border.

On command, the well-outfitted 316[th]Division headed west across the border with plans to drive on Luang Prabang along river valleys deep in the Lao interior.

They ran into a problem 10 miles inside Laos when the advancing 148th Regiment soldiers came to the small Lao village of Sop Nao, which was guarded by a 30-man Chasseurs Laotiens (Lao light infantry) platoon under the command of a French lieutenant and several French noncommissioned officers.

The Chasseurs Laotiens' defensive position, surrounded by steep, jagged mountains and almost impregnable jungle, straddled the Nam Houa River valley.

The lieutenant contacted his regional commander about the sudden appearance to his front of main line Vietnamese forces and was advised that Viet Minh were invading Laos all along the border. He was ordered to hold for as long as he could.

While this probably meant death for the Sop Nao Chasseurs Laotiens, it was common for French rear commands to order forward isolated posts, like this one, to stay and fight against Viet Minh attacks.

Chasseurs Laotian

It was an accepted loss for the French Indochina Expeditionary military force in their management of approximately 800 fortifications scattered throughout Indochina, most in Vietnam.

For six days the small platoon held out against wave after wave of attackers – like the Spartans at Thermopylae -- before pulling back to join its main unit, a full company of 300 Chasseurs Laotiens positioned 20 miles to the west, at the confluence of the Nam Ou and Nam Noua rivers. A place called Muong Khoua.

Nam Ou

Captain Teullier, the commander of this garrison was told by the French commander in Laos to attempt to hold his position for 14 days to give time for defensive fortifications to be built north of Luang Prabang.

For 34 days the combined French/Lao force held at Muong Khoua. The 316th Viet Minh division finally diverted around the position to continue its way south toward Luang Prabang.

They were ambushed along the way by French forces and were finally stopped by fortifications just completed on the outskirts of town.

Behind schedule, with the beginning of the monsoon rainy season, Giap ordered the greatly extended division back to North Vietnam.

On the way back, it overran the gallant French garrison at Muong Khoua, killing all but four of the defenders.

The Xam Nua riot and later the loss of Muong Khoua was front-page news in all the French newspapers.

Only eight years since the end of World War II, the French were tired of war and there was no peaceful end in sight in SEA. Their casualties in SEA were hovering near 100,000.

The commander of the French forces in Indochina was replaced in the late summer of 1953. The new commander, almost on his first day, received intelligence that indicated the Viet Minh planned to return down the Nam Noua/Nam Ou River valleys in Laos to attack Luang Prabang again during the next dry season.

With the Chasseurs Laotiens' position at Muong Khoua erased, on November 20, 1953, the new commander established a blocking "hedgehog" defense in the Dien Bien Phu valley of Vietnam to stop any Viet Minh advance into Laos.

Almost immediately Giap started to mass his forces to surround the new French positions. Using the pathways – most hidden from view from the sky -- made by the porters from China during the previous campaign – an army of porters began to bring in an enormous amount of munitions and supplies that included at least 200 artillery pieces, enough to completely ring the Dien Bien Phu valley. Some of the artillery had been captured from UN forces in Korea.

Faced with the Viet Minh buildup around Dien Bien Phu, the French pleaded for U.S. help, but President Eisenhower, just finished with the Korean War, would not commit American troops.

The End of the First Indochina War

In the early morning of March 13, 1954, outnumbering the defending French nearly five-to-one, 50,000 Viet Minh began their assault against the fortified French Expeditionary Force positions circling the Dien Bien Phu runway.

North Vietnamese attacking at Dien Bien Phu

Viet Minh artillery prevented aircraft from landing, forcing the French to rely on erratic parachute drops for resupply.

It was as bloody a fight as ever recorded in the history of man. Certainly it was as Bernard Fall said, "Hell in a very small place."

The United States made out-of-sight contributions to the French defensive efforts. The CIA-owned Civil Air Transport (CAT) made air drops to the besieged French position. Almost all the parachutes used by the French came from U.S. depots in the Philippines. One of CAT's most storied pilots, "Earthquake McGoon," was shot down over Dien Bien Phu.

French troops soon ran out of fresh water and medical supplies and made a desperate final appeal for help to Washington. Because Eisenhower had ruled out committing American troops, the U.S. Joint Chiefs of Staff now considered two other possible military alternatives: a massive conventional air strike by B-29 bombers or the use of tactical atomic weapons.

President Eisenhower dismissed both options after getting a strong negative response from Britain,

America's chief foreign ally.

However in a mid-April 1954 speech, maybe uncoordinated with Eisenhower, Vice President Richard Nixon said that "to avoid further Communist expansion in Asia and Indochina we must take the risk now of putting our boys in, I think the Executive has to take the politically unpopular decision and do it."

Supplies parachuted into Dien Bien Phu

The international conference to help resolve lingering issues in Korea was convened in Geneva, Switzerland. With the fight for Dien Bien Phu coming to a conclusion, the conference's mission was expanded to look for peaceful options in Vietnam.

Because the U.S. did not recognize the communist government of Mao Zedong (represented by Chou En-lai), General Bedell Smith represented the United States at the conference table; the U.S. Secretary of State spent time standing in the halls. The British, who chaired the conference, and the French had complicated long-standing differences of policies that bubbled below the surface throughout the conference.

On May 6, 1954, forces under the command of Viet Minh Colonel Nguyen Huu An, detonated munitions under the French "Elaine 2" hilltop position at Dien Bien Phu, a vantage that overlooked the French command post. The building on top and most of the hill top were destroyed, leaving only a massive hole on the crest. Colonel An's men occupied the blown-apart hill top without opposition.

Cratered top to "Elaine 2" after Viet Minh explosion of tunneled in munitions

The next day all fighting just came to an end, and at 5:30 t h e evening of May 7, 1954, the French officially surrendered. By now, an estimated 8,000 Viet Minh and 1,500 French had died in this battle. Hundreds of French wounded lay scattered about the spent battlefield.

Wounded French soldier

In war-weary France -- as a direct results of the Dien Bien Phu defeat -- a new government was formed in Paris which conceded all French territorial claims in Indochina.

In response to this, the Geneva Convention now composed of - France, China, USSR, United States, England, Cambodia, Laos, the Viet Minh and the government of what would be South Vietnam - considered future options.

Peace Accords Shape Next Battlefield

The peace accords that were finally reached - heavily influenced by the unified communist representatives - were hastily negotiated and drafted. Parts were so vaguely and haphazardly written as to be almost unintelligible. Some small parts were translated into different languages to mean different things.

However there was consensus on the main items:

- That a 60-mile DMZ was to be established near the 17th parallel as a divide between a North and a South Vietnam.
- Civilians on both sides of that line were granted free movement back and forth for a 300-day period.
- Elections in 1956 were mandated to unite the two territories.
- Laos was given its unconditional independence.

The United States and South Vietnam did not sign the

accords because of one of the main provisions that called for elections in 1956. Ho Chi Minh was the undisputed leader of the movement to gain Vietnamese independence. Now that the French were vanquished - and with the bulk of Vietnam's population in the north under Ho's direct control -- elections in 1956 would surely go his way.

Though not a signee, President Eisenhower welcomed the Geneva Accords' partition of the north and south at the 17thparallel. He saw it as a similar situation to Korea divided at the 38th parallel, with the communist to the north and pro-democratic forces to the south. His initial thinking was also if Laos was denied to the North Vietnamese, the DMZ would contain the communists in the north.

Laos created a natural bottle for the North Vietnamese, Eisenhower was fond of saying, and it was up to South Vietnam to keep the cork in the bottle.

"Deny Laos to the North Vietnamese," Eisenhower's military people insisted, "falls in line with National Security Council (NSC) thinking on '**Containment**.' We don't allow a toppled domino effect on small non-communist countries, like South Vietnam. It is worth our time and money and the risk of U.S. prestige. We can 'contain' communist expansion in SEA... if the North Vietnamese are denied Laos."

Immediately after the conference, the United States promised $100 million to help start up a government in South Vietnam and in doing that, took the initiative – and seemed to take responsibility – to protect democracy in SEA. Without Eisenhower's avowed support, there was absolutely no chance for the survival of a South Vietnam.

Indochina with Vietnam divided at the 17th parallel

The government that was brought together in the south faced many economic, political and social challenges. What was needed was a strong, charismatic leader who could unite the many factions behind a coherent ideology and start-up plan.

The problem was that few pro-American leaders fit the bill. Most prominent personalities had either joined the communists or had been killed by the French in the preceding conflict.

Probably the best of the available candidates, Ngo Dinh Diem, deftly separated himself from the few contenders and became the prime minister of South Vietnam in June

1954. (Note: Although Ngo is the surname, this individual is commonly referred to as "Diem.")

Diem, a Roman Catholic in the overwhelmingly Buddhist country, encouraged Vietnamese Catholics living in communist North Vietnam to take advantage of the 300-day free pass period allowed by the Geneva Accords and move south. Nearly one million Catholics took advantage and moved.

At the same time, some 90,000 communists in the south went north, although as many as 10,000 committed Viet Minh fighters were instructed by Hanoi to quietly remain behind.

In September of 1954, the United States, France, Great Britain, New Zealand, Australia, the Philippines, Thailand and Pakistan formed the Southeast Asia Treaty Organization, or SEATO. The United States saw SEATO as essential to its global Cold War policy of "**Containment**" of communist expansion in SEA. In addition to SEATO countries, South Korea sent forces to fight North Vietnam incursions in the south.

November 1954

April 1955

Like Hitler before his rise to power in Germany, **TIME** magazine featured Ho Chi Minh on its cover on November 22, 1954. The lengthy accompanying article profiled the new North Vietnamese president in glowing rhetoric. "Ho Chi Minh, dedicated Communist," the article read, "is a matchless interplay of ruthlessness and guile."

On 4 April 1955, five months after Ho's **TIME** cover/article, the magazine featured Ngo Dinh Diem. The cover story was rich with colorful, sometimes satirical, language of how inept this leader of free South Vietnam was.

The media was picking sides. International media soon followed the **TIME** opinion, emphasizing "Good Ho, Bad Diem."

One of the first pieces of business under the new Vietnamese government in Hanoi was to create the National Liberation Front (NLF) to continue the fight for South Vietnam.

The communist auxiliary in the south eventually became known as the People's Liberation Armed Forces (PLAF), which the Americans and Diem referred to as Viet Cong (VC), an abbreviation of Viet-nam Cong-san (or Vietnamese communists).

The Ho Chi Minh Trail

Maintaining contact between the NLF and the VC became a problem when overland traffic was stopped from crossing the 17th parallel in Vietnam in late 1955.

There was some surreptitious sea traffic, although the most common route north-to-south and south-to-north was on the mountain trail that ran west of the 17th parallel through Laos and Cambodia. It has been in place since at least World War II; a rough path that in 1958 took upwards to six months to travel from top to bottom.

In 1958 the trail began to expand with use.

Then in May 1959 the North Vietnamese 559th Transport Group was created to make major improvements the entire length of the trail.

Group 559 (which stood for the 5th month of 1959) was set up entirely of southern Viet Minh soldiers from the Region 5 area (and specifically from the area from Nha Trang-Binh Dinh up to Danang) who had regrouped to North Vietnam.

The first commander of Group 559, Colonel Vo Bam, was a native of Quang Ngai Province in South Vietnam and was the individual most responsible for building the trail into an expressway.

He started with less than 1,000 workers but by 1973 Group 559 had just over 100,000 personnel working the trail, making improvements and moving material up and down from North Vietnam to communist enclaves in Laos and Cambodia.

Ho Chi Minh Trail approximately 1965

Eventually the total length of all the different side trails to the route would be approximately 12,000 miles and would include an oil pipeline, way stations, foot paths and roads that supported heavy vehicles.

With the new transport pathway in place more than 4,000 Vietnamese soldiers, originally born in the south, were sent from North Vietnam to infiltrate back into their home regions of South Vietnam.

NVA Colonel Vo Bam

VC forces began to establish safe sanctuaries in Cambodia and Laos accessible by the improved 559th's super highway... that came to be known as the Ho Chi Minh Trail. From these safe heavens resupply was made to new communist cells formed by communists inside South Vietnam... in the Mekong Delta alone, 37 armed companies were created and run from sanctuaries in Cambodia.

North Vietnam Girds for the Second Indochina War

To fuel the North Vietnamese war machine with soldiers, a wartime draft was instituted in the north that included all able-bodied citizens. Soldiers from the ranks of refugees who fled from the south in opposition to Diem's oppressive policies were also recruited.

Belying Ho's carefully constructed façade of the kindly and gentle "Uncle Ho," the new administration – to clearly establish its authority — massacred North Vietnamese farmers by the thousands in a Soviet-style "land reform" campaign.

In fact, land reform in North Vietnam was very similar in style to the way it was implemented in North Korea 1946/1947. There were other similarities between the way North Korea and North Vietnam were initially organized. Even the two local leaders: Some historians argue that Ho and Kim were responsive Comintern/Coiminform agents: nothing more, nothing less.

Diem Tried by Fire

In the United States, President Eisenhower followed events in Vietnam closely and supported Ngo Dinh Diem's vigorous anti-communist campaigns launched in late 1954. To help Diem's effort to pacify the countryside, U.S. military advisers arrived in South Vietnam in February 1955. Diem himself was advised by U.S. Air Force Col. Edward G. Lansdale, USAF, who was attached to the Central Intelligence Agency (CIA).

Diem came from the same region of Northcentral Vietnam as Ho Chi Minh but was a very different character. Educated by the French, Diem was a devout Catholic who had studied for the priesthood and had a Catholic bishop brother. His base morality, however, was impacted by his understanding of Confucianism and the way traditional Asian society worked. For example, Diem assigned most high-level government positions to close friends and family members, including his younger brother, Ngo Dinh Nhu, who was his closest adviser. This was typical Asian organizational management.

Ngo Dinh Nhu, Ngo Dinh Can and Ngo Dinh Diem

Careful not to be seen as a U.S. puppet, Diem and his brothers developed their own ideology: a benevolent inspired alternative to communism that emphasized human dignity. The government's focus on family and social groups was meant to foster an attitude of human kindness — supposedly emanating from the top levels of the new Saigon government. This, Diem thought, would be an effective middle ground for the rural Buddhist. A government based on benevolence was also helpful in maintaining good relations with its democratic mentor/protector, the U.S.

However, the realities of the new South Vietnamese government policies were almost always a heavy-handed, brutal, unsympathetic response to any dissent.

There was always a traditional, cultural gulf between the urban, Catholic, western-educated, light-skinned Diem and the dark skinned, Buddhist farmers who made up most of the South Vietnamese citizenry.

Some in the U.S. government became concerned that Diem did not have any staying power because his civilian support was primarily in the minority urban upper class of his country. He was encouraged to win the "Hearts and Minds" of the farmers in the delta and around Saigon rather than just brutally, impersonally impose his government's will.

By the end of 1955, Diem conspicuously ran Saigon and maintained strong contact with the various power brokers in the field. However, the countryside fell more and more under VC control because

- The warlords did not channel rural support up to the government in Saigon.
- Diem's minority Catholic beliefs made him vulnerable to charges of answering to western powers. He did not establish a sense of national pride.
- Diem's meager efforts to identify with the predominately common people around Saigon were not successful.

This was not initially apparent to Vietnam observers halfway around the world in Washington.

Although Ho Chi Minh remained president of the Democratic Republic of (North) Vietnam, day-to-day responsibilities of running the country was left to others, due what was said to be Ho's old age and "failing health."

It was as if the unseen hands of his communist mentors in Moscow were satisfied with the part he had played to this point in developing North Vietnam, but were moving to another stage, taking a more prominent military tact to conquer South Vietnam.

But Ho continued to be the face of small undeveloped North Vietnam and was employed to enhance the overall international efforts of the communists.

As 1960 broke, the conflict in Vietnam was gaining international attention and a worldwide protest movement began. Rallies were held in support of the VC and the rhythmic chant "Ho, Ho, Ho Chi Minh" rang out at peace marches.

In the face of all this attention Diem did not rise to the challenge. He never gave the impression to foreign observers that he was capable of winning the support of the majority of the people in South Vietnam.

Unlike North Vietnam, there was a limited sense of prosperity in the south. Instead there was doubt about the viability of a separate South Vietnam. At every turn Diem's family-run government was found to be corrupt and, as time went on, ineffective.

In April 1960, 18 distinguished nationalists in South Vietnam send a petition to President Diem advocating full government reforms. Diem ignored their advice and instead closed several opposition newspapers and arrested journalists and intellectuals.

All this did not go unnoticed by the international media.

Discouraged, but undeterred in its commitment to support Diem's regime, on May 5, 1960, the United States announced the increase in the number of military advisers to South Vietnam from 327 to 685 men.

In November 1960 a failed coup against President Diem by disgruntled South Vietnamese Army officers brought on a harsh crackdown against all perceived "enemies of the state." Over 50,000 people were arrested; many were tortured and killed.

Laos Becomes 'the Belle of the Ball'

Diem paid a state visit to Washington where President Eisenhower labeled him the "miracle man" of Asia and reaffirmed U.S. commitment. "The cost of defending freedom, of defending America, must be paid in many forms and in many places ... military as well as economic help is currently needed in Vietnam," Eisenhower stated.

As for Laos during this time, no one there had any experience running "a free and independent nation," as created by the Geneva Accords of 1954. Various political/military factions out of Hanoi, Bangkok, Paris, Washington, Luang Prabang and Savannakhet maneuvered for control in the somnolent shadows of a country that was made of the backyards of most SEA countries. Without a history of running matters of state and greatly influence by its neighbors, the situation was so confusing that in the late 1950s a foreign diplomat said, "If you think you know what's happening in Laos, you just don't know the facts."

Eisenhower sent U.S. Army Special Forces military advisers to the small land locked Laos, beefed up the CIA effort there and funneled money into Savannakhet's Royal Lao Army (FAR) General Phoumi Nosavan coffers, all with no apparent success.

Laotians did not seem impressed that so much was being made of them and that their critical geographic location – laying along the western borders of both North and South Vietnam - played such a significant role in this budding confrontation among the world powers.

It just lay there in the foothills of the Himalaya, so un-unified and un-coordinated it could not do anything.

In the north the hills tribesmen were called Meo, or roughly "savages." The people in the south panhandle had been part of Thailand up until the late 1800s and had Thai roots/language. The population epicenter around Vientiane and Luang Prabang only had a small group of leaders, who did not unite the mountain "savages" with their countrymen, the former Thais in the panhandle.

By comparison, the new government and military in Saigon, firmly under Diem's control, looked better. Corrupt, sure, but its representatives looked good in liaison meetings with US officials and its soldiers marched sharply on parade fields. Diem's administration had been trained by the French and knew how to showcase themselves.

Lao neutralist (communist-leaning) Captain Kong Le and Savannakhet's General Phoumi Nosovan fought an artillery battle for Vientiane, Laos in 1960. Kong Le finally retreated to the Plaine de Jars (PDJ), a breathtakingly beautiful 250 square-mile high-mountain plateau 100 miles northeast of Vientiane, and, with North Vietnam Army help, took control of the entire region.

Both the neutralist and communist forces received substantial air support from the Soviet Air Force based out of Hanoi. Soviet aircraft was parked and serviced at several PDJ airfields.

With continuing political instability in Vientiane and with anti-West armies controlling first Xam Nua and then the PDJ, the future of an independent Royal Lao government was in doubt.

CIA case officer Stu Methven, out of the U.S. Embassy in Vientiane, met Asian mountain war lord Vang Pao (aka VP) in the PDJ northeast. Vang Pao had been an officer in the French/Lao forces in the early 1950s and had been part of a French relief column to Dien Bien Phu, arriving in the area about the time of the French defeat in 1954. He was a FAR Army general and the leader of the White Hmong tribe.

Despite the FAR's well-deserved reputation for incompetence, Vang Pao was an effective, intelligent, respected leader with tremendous presence and an uncanny acumen for mountain guerrilla warfare. He impressed Methven with his singular potential to challenge the increasing North Vietnamese/Soviet control of the Lao northeast, centered around the PDJ.

As Eisenhower was coming to the end of his eight years as president, Diem continued to struggle as the United States' hope in Saigon, and landlocked Laos was proving to be an almost unsolvable problem in his "deny Laos" strategy in Southeast Asia.

However, in one of his last official acts, President Eisenhower signed a "Covert Action" approval for the CIA to work clandestinely with local Asian forces to fend off North Vietnamese aggression and intrusions into Laos. Air America was organized and Vang Pao irregulars were armed and trained.

There were few other bright spots on the pro-democratic front in SEA.

President Eisenhower with President-elect
President Kennedy

January 19, 1961, the day before Kennedy's inauguration as the 35th President of the United States, a meeting was convened in the White House at the president-elect's suggestion to get Eisenhower's comments and recommendations on the situation in Laos.

Eisenhower was accompanied at the meeting by Secretary of State Christian A. Herter, Secretary of Defense Thomas S. Gates Jr., Secretary of the Treasury Robert B. Anderson and General Wilton B. Persons the White House Chief of Staff.

Kennedy was accompanied by three designated secretaries - Dean Rusk (State), Robert S. McNamara (Defense) and C. Douglas Dillon (Treasury) - and Clark M. Clifford, a close Kennedy adviser.

Clifford's memo for the record on the meeting reported that while Herter and Gates spoke the most (also reported in Kennedy's notes) at the end, President Eisenhower, Clifford wrote, stated that Laos is the present key to the entire area of Southeast Asia. If Laos were lost to the Communists, it would bring an unbelievable pressure to bear on Thailand, Cambodia and South Vietnam. President Eisenhower stated that he considered Laos of such importance that if it reached the stage where we could not persuade others to act with us, then he would be willing, *"as a last desperate hope, to intervene unilaterally."*

In several subsequent interviews Secretary of State Dean Rusk said that he had read Clifford's memo and said that it captured the thrust and details of the meeting.

General Persons also drafted a memo for Eisenhower that tracks with Clarks account, but he also quoted the phrase Eisenhower often used that if North Vietnam was contained by Laos it would cause a "bottle" effect that South Vietnam could keep corked.

Robert S. McNamara's notes, as McGeorge Bundy put it in an August 24, 1965, memorandum to President Johnson, did "not correspond . . . to Dean Rusk's recollections of the meeting."

McNamara's notes read: "*President Eisenhower advised against unilateral action by the United States in connection with Laos.*" He told his biographer Deborah Shapley years later that at that meeting "*Eisenhower warned Kennedy that if the United States intervened in Laos, 'the Sino-Soviet bloc' could hit back with far greater forces.*" McNamara also told the biographer Shapley that when he left that meeting he thought, "'*My God, what a hell of a mess.' And I don't recall that in the next ninety days I had any clear solutions to the problem."*

Whatever the intent, whatever the words used, Eisenhower said clearly that Laos should be "denied" to the North Vietnamese in a military sense. Kennedy may have heard "denied" in a political sense. McNamara apparently did not understand what was being said. He left the meeting unclear of a way forward in Southeast Asia and in fact nothing he did later as secretary of defense indicates that he was aware of the advice from the former commander of all World War II allied forces in Europe. Certainly there had been no mention by Eisenhower of the United States committing any ground forces to South Vietnam as a way to counter communist aggression in SEA.

The next day -- January 20, 1961 -- John Fitzgerald Kennedy declared in his inaugural address as the 35th U.S. president, "We shall pay any price, bear any burden, meet any hardship, support any friend, oppose any foe, to insure the survival and the success of liberty."

A few days later – to counter Kennedy's inaugural promises -- Soviet premier Nikita Khrushchev pledged support to all "wars of national liberation" throughout the world, which specifically included the North Vietnam insurgency in South Vietnam.

Camelot

Despite the well-intended advice from Eisenhower and the grand inaugural rhetoric, the youthful Kennedy administration was inexperienced in matters of war, especially in Southeast Asia. As he himself said, McNamara did not have a clue.

When Eisenhower left office, most of the Republican government office-holders left with him and there was not an experienced institutional carry-over to Democrat Kennedy's Camelot court. War planning went from men experienced in war to the incoming secretary of defense, 44-year-old Robert McNamara, along with his "best and brightest Whiz Kids," civilian planners recruited from the academic community. Experienced top-level military personnel in the Pentagon either went along with their new civilian superiors, or were retired.

President John F. Kennedy's civilian advisers included Robert S. McNamara, McGeorge Bundy, Walt Rostow, his brother Robert "Bobby" Kennedy, Dean Rusk, Lyndon Johnson and Averell Harriman.

Robert Strange McNamara –   Harvard MBA 1939
Secretary of Defense 1961-1968

Born into a middle class family in California, Robert McNamara was an Eagle Scout and attended the University of California at Berkley. He was a Phi Beta Kappa and an influential member of the university president's student advisory group.

He went on to excel at the Harvard School of Business, where his gift in managing numbers and data was noted. Not only could he quickly absorb an enormous amount of information on most any subject, he had the talent to translate that information into mathematical or sequential form. He became known as a brilliant statistician who could coalesce factual data effortlessly to win arguments.

After getting his Harvard MBA he did a stint in the private sector before he was offered at job on the Harvard Business faculty to teach business management systems. When the United States entered World War II McNamara joined a group of other Harvard professors into a "system's control" task force that was deployed around the world to help in the management of strategy resources. Of note was his analysis of which aircraft the Army Air Corps should be using against specific targets. After the war his group of Harvard Whiz Kids were hired in masse by Henry Ford II to help save the Ford Manufacturing Company from insolvency. Every year General Motors increased its share of the U.S. auto market, more and more marginalizing the Ford product.

McNamara moved steadily up the management ladder, often amazing colleagues with his ability to dominate high-level conference debates with his pervasive guile, command of facts/figures and his self-confidence. He became a favorite of Henry Ford, who was known to call out McNamara to visitors to explain Ford company policy.

On November 9, 1960 he was appointed president of the Ford Motor Company and moved into the enormous office of the president on the 12th floor of Ford headquarter. Less than a month later, on December 7th President-elect John Kennedy sent his brother-in-law, Sargent Shriver, to meet with McNamara in his office. Shriver wasted no time in this meeting. He said the president-elect would like to offer McNamara the office of secretary of the treasury. McNamara said he was not remotely qualified. Shriver then said he was authorized to offer McNamara the job as secretary of defense, and again McNamara said he was not qualified.

Shriver asked if McNamara would do the president-elect the courtesy of meeting him in Washington, which he accepted. In two subsequent meetings with McNamara at his Georgetown residence, Kennedy won him over, and McNamara left his new job with Ford, which paid a yearly salary of $410,000 with stock options worth into the many millions over

the course of the next few years. As secretary
of defense his new salary was $25,000 a year,
but he took it because his life ambition was "to
make a difference"... to play in the big leagues
and to deal with world leaders, to impact
history. Plus, consorting this president of the
United States was enormously appealing.

In accepting the job he made Kennedy pledge to
give him complete authority at the Department
of Defense (DOD).

His impressive smarts, self-confidence,
statistical talents and lessons learned climbing
up in the Ford corporate ladder helped him in
his interaction with others in Kennedy's
Camelot Court.

However, he did not have a rudimentary
understanding of land, air and sea combat or
the U.S. profession of arms. Early on, his
contributions to Cabinet-level discussions on
military matters were hardly astute; some of his
statements were painfully naive. At an early
meeting with Kennedy, McNamara brought the
whole top tier of the Pentagon, but the meeting
was awkward and the Pentagon people
reported that they were embarrassed.

McNamara also remembered things sometimes
differently from others. For example, he
reported to biographers that Kennedy soon
concluded that landlocked Laos was
indefensible for practical purposes and "not

worthy of engaging the attention of great powers."

This may not have been Kennedy's early thinking at all.

Despite his inexperience in military matters, he became a close associate and friend of President John Kennedy and a confidant of Attorney General Bobby Kennedy. On Kennedy's assassination, McNamara moved his allegiance to President Lyndon Johnson.

More than any other individual, he set the United States on a course that involved U.S. troops on the ground in South Vietnam. He left the office of secretary of defense on February 29, 1968... within the month of the TET Offensive... probably he was fired.

McGeorge Bundy –   Yale (1940)   Skull and Bones
Chairman of the National Security Council 1961-1966

As chairman of the National Security Council (NSC) McGeorge Bundy reorganized the NSC to prevent easy access to the president by the military's Joint Chiefs of

Staff. He and McNamara spoke for the military. Bundy left office in January 1966 to become president of the Ford Motor Company.

Walt Rostow – Yale (1940)
Chairman of the National Security Council 1966-1969

Walt Rostow replaced Bundy as Chairman of the NCS in 1966. He was rumored to take his orders from Harriman more so than from President Johnson.

Bobby Kennedy – Harvard (1948)
Attorney General 1961-1964

When word reached Robert Kennedy about the assassination of his brother, he sought immediate solace with McNamara in McNamara's office in the Pentagon. Kennedy said the Johnson administration deviated from his brother's policies in Vietnam and said the idea that Americans were fighting to end communism in Vietnam was "immoral."

Dean Rusk – Rhodes Scholar out of University of California/Berkley 1940
Secretary of State 1961-1969

Dean Rusk was a long Time State Department official. He was part of a group in the 1940s that suggested dividing Korea at the 38th parallel. Rush believed his role as Secretary of State was to support the president, first Kennedy and then Johnson rather than make policy.

Lyndon Johnson –   Texas State (1930)

Vice President of the United States 1961-1963
President of the United States 1963-1969

A long time politician, Lyndon B. Johnson was disliked by most in the Kennedy family, but was deemed necessary for JFK to win the 1960 election. As president he was greatly influenced by public opinion, the media and McNamara.

Averell Harriman – Yale (1913) Skull and Bones
Ambassador at Large 1961-1969

[Also see information on Harriman in a listing of President Truman advisers.] Out of Washington while the Republican Dwight Eisenhower was president, Harriman was elected governor of New York in 1954. He was a candidate for the Democratic Party's presidential nomination in 1952 and again in 1956 but lost out to Adlai Stevenson both times. Although unsuccessful in his bid for the White House, Harriman remained a respected senior adviser in the Democratic Party.

In the Kennedy administration, he became a favorite adviser of the president, who called him the "crocodile."

As Kennedy's emissary Harriman went to Geneva in 1961 and, using his "influence" with Soviet leadership, negotiated the Geneva Accords of 1962, which in effect kept the United States and other non-communist armies out of Laos – disregarding Eisenhower's advice on military strategy in the area and denying the United States any chance of winning a ground war in Southeast Asia.

He followed up the good-deal-for-the-communist accords by arranging his appointment as an undersecretary of state for Southeast Asia affairs, certainly a position beneath his normal assignment. Remember he had run for President a few years before. He used his authority to keep the U.S. military out of the communist sanctuaries in Laos and off the Ho Chi Minh Trail.

Hard of hearing by this time, he famously would turn his hearing aid volume down when he was in the company of people he did not wish to talk with. William Colby, the CIA director, claimed that in meeting Harriman in his State Department office to request support and supplies to the local guerrillas under the CIA's control in Laos, Harriman would conspicuously turn his hearing aid down. Colby, not to be put off, would revert to shouting which could be heard in neighboring rooms.

Finally with the Lyndon Johnson and the Democrats out of office in 1968 (but controlling Congress), Harriman and his wife, Pamela, former daughter- in-law of Winston Churchill, became the Democrat's power couple in Georgetown, criticizing the Republicans at every turn in their efforts to leave Vietnam with some vestige of honor.

Averell Harriman was awarded the Soviet Union's Order of the Patriotic War, First Degree in 1985.   40 years after Yalta. 10 years after the U.S. defeat in Vietnam.

William Sullivan –   Harvard (1947)
Assistant to Harriman in Geneva 1961-1962
Ambassador to Laos 1964-1969
Ambassador to the Philippines 1973-1977

In one of his first State Department assignments to the U.S. Embassy in Bangkok, William Sullivan met with the Viet Cong in northern Thailand... the circumstance of which have never been explained. After other State Department assignments in Southeast Asia, he was selected by Averell Harriman to work as Harriman's deputy in meetings with the Soviets in Geneva in 1962.

From 1964 to 1969 Sullivan was the U.S. ambassador to Laos to work with Harriman back in Washington to ensure that the U.S. Army stayed out of Laos. Like Harriman, he insisted on compliance with the Geneva Accords of 1962 that he helped create.

As ambassador he would take second-hand and sometimes third-hand word from known communist sympathizers that U.S. planes had bombed civilian areas of Laos to summarily castigate the U.S. Air Force.

Sullivan worked with Secretary of State Kissinger in 1973 to close out the American military involvement in Vietnam.

As Ambassador to the Philippines in May, 1975 he objected to Washington about the large numbers of South Vietnamese seeking refuge in the Philippines after their escape from communist Vietnam when Saigon fell. Sullivan suggested in diplomatic channels that they be sent back "home."

He went on to be the last U.S. Ambassador to Iran 1977-1979. Because he pointedly did not carry out President Jimmy Carter's specific instructions in his official dealing with the Shad (he thought the will of the Iranian people was with the Iranian Muslim clerics), he was recalled shortly before the Iranians took over the U.S. Embassy late 1979.

He was quoted in retirement (See Roger Warner's *Shooting at the Moon*) that it was appropriate that we left Vietnam "with our tails between our legs," because he thought we should have lost. He felt the United States had/has an inflated opinion of its righteousness.

US Military Advisers to Kennedy

When Kennedy took office as president, his military advisers included General George H. Decker, USA, General Curtis LeMay, USAF and General David M. Shoup, USMC:

**General George H. Decker   Lafayette College
Army Chief of Staff 1960-1962**

Army Chief of Staff George H. Decker, who worked his way through college, told the President Kennedy soon after he came to the White House that the U.S. Army should go into Laos with the intention to fight and win the war there. USAF General Curtis LeMay agreed. This advice lost out to McNamara's "counterinsurgency" ideas on fighting the war in South Vietnam.

General Curtis LeMay   Ohio State
USAF Chief of Staff 1961-1965

General LeMay, who worked his way through college, was a tough, in-your-face advocate of air power. "Bomb 'um back to the stone age," he'd say. "Don't give an inch. "If our problems don't get solved in Laos, we'd do the job from the air."

General David M. Shoup   DePauw University
Commandant of the Marine Corps 1960-1963

General David Shoup was awarded the Medal of Honor in World War II. He opposed plans for combat in Vietnam, and later said that "every responsible military man to my knowledge" was against the war there as well.

GEN William C. Westmoreland   West Point Military Academy
Military Commander in Vietnam 1964-1968

A favorite of McNamara's, in January 1964 General Westmoreland became commander of Military Assistance Command, Vietnam (MACV). He was known for highly publicized, positive assessments of U.S. military prospects in Vietnam. As the war progressed, the strengthening of communist combat forces in the South led him to regular requests increases in U.S. troop strength... from 16,000 when he arrived to its peak of 535,000 in 1968 – shortly after TET - when he left. His removal was seen by some government observers – like McNamara's removal -- as the results of the enemy's TET offensive.

The stance of Kennedy's civilian and military adviser can be summarized:

- For a strong military stand in Laos: **Decker** and **LeMay**
- For counterinsurgency in South Vietnam: **McNamara, Bundy, Rostow** and **Westmoreland**
- For not deploying U.S. military in South Vietnam: **Shoup**
- For not deploying U.S. military to SEA at all: **Robert Kennedy**
- For going without serious intent on win: **Harriman and Sullivan**

Kennedy had strained relations generally with members of the Joint Chiefs of Staff due Cuba and, reluctant to take their advice, turned to McNamara, Harriman and Bundy.

Kennedy Mulls McNamara's "Counterinsurgency" in Southeast Asia

Despite Eisenhower's recommendation that Laos should be the focus of United States' involvement in Southeast Asia due to its pivotal, strategic location, McNamara made a convincing case to Kennedy that our focus should be on South Vietnam instead, primarily for the following reasons:

- Diem's government administrators had, for the most part, been trained by the French, and seemed to understand the Western principles of organization and how to take meetings. They were easy to deal with.
- The South Vietnamese president was a Catholic, like our president. Washington and Saigon operated by committee and trusted in God.
- The South Vietnamese military looked sharp on the parade field. They were marketed as competent to fight the Viet Cong "insurgency."
- The Lao government in Vientiane, by comparison, was inept. The Lao military was among the worst in the world and almost all other government departments did not work.
- Laos was landlocked. When McNamara's logistic strategists and academic Whiz Kids looked at supporting a military effort in SEA, they saw an extensive coastline in South Vietnam with deep-water ports in place. But with Laos, the only protected way to get troops or supplies in was through Thailand and then hundreds of miles inland. Coming into a Lao

battlefield through Vietnam was not
considered.
- The South Vietnam citizenry, especially Saigon
  night people, had had extensive dealings with
  the French. They knew how to make the
  Americans, those who came early, very
  comfortable. Generally speaking, the U.S.
  advisers who came once, wanted to come back
  to South Vietnam. Especially the bachelors.
- South Vietnam was bucolic and exotic… about
  as good a place to have a war as any place in
  the world.

South Vietnam in time became the land where
Kennedy's Camelot administration threw down the
gauntlet. This we will protect, it said, for organizational
and political rather than tactical military reasons. It just
made more sense to McNamara and the "best and
brightest" corps of Whiz Kids he brought from the
private sector. He was supported in the field by
General Westmoreland, who McNamara had put in
charge of field operations. Harriman offered no
comment. In many respects Harriman thought dealing
with Diem was below him. He traditionally cast his lot
with world leaders on the order of Stalin, Churchill,
Truman and MacArthur.

So NSC's report 68 ideas of countering communist with
"containment" gave way to **"counterinsurgency."** NSC
resolutions under past presidents were not often
quoted as foundations for Kennedy's foreign policies.

Also because **"counterinsurgency"** by definition allowed
as how the enemy was not contained, but was loose in

the countryside, the term "**limited war**" became the phrase to explain the change in policy. Reacting to North Vietnam military initiatives, "**flexible response**" entered the lexicon, appearing in more and more accounts of United States and South Vietnamese field activities. Our foreign policy had become something of a crossword puzzle.

Westmoreland said initially that this "**limited war**" was not a "**war of attrition**," but to appease his Washington, D.C. bosses he came around to accepting the intent of that strategy. Westmoreland's thinking was that we win if we kill more of them than they kill of us.

That was an enormously bad strategy because the North Vietnamese had an almost limitless supply of young soldiers. Also, if ever the ravages of war tipped in the allies favor, North Vietnam could conceivable call on the Chinese for a million or more replacements. The attrition war favored the North Vietnamese.

Conducting a war of attrition resonated with some in the Pentagon, however, because it came from bedrock military thinking that had won World War II, when the war machines at America's disposal were like scythes cutting the enemy down on battlefields.

In South Vietnam, however, those machines were not as adapt when the actual fighting was in among the citizenry. In the jungle, under two and three layers of foliage, artillery and mortar will not achieve much. The aircraft that had won the skies and brought the angry wrath of American military might down on our enemies in World War II could offer little help on the jungle floor and in times of bad weather.

Also, North Vietnam was not an industrialized country. There were few targets for our bombers.

To make this war acceptable to the U.S. men who would fight it, a tour of duty was set for 12 months. This meant part of the fighting forces was always just learning its way on the battlefield. There were always "new guys" to be trained. Plus, one-year tours of duty for war managers meant the United States could just go on and on with the war.

In the early stages of U.S. planning to fight a war to contain communism in Southeast Asia, questionable decisions were made in tactics, battlefield selection, equipment and length of duty. Also – more simply - U.S. war managers did not take the advice of our most experienced military leaders, who had won World War II.

Plus, there were no conspicuous Pentagon effort to use lessons learned from post-World War II/ Korea in dealing with Asian communist. For example, in 1947 Mao Zedung boldly explained to General George Marshall his strategy of "Talk-Fight; Fight-Talk" ("*Da-Da, Tan-Tan*") was his way to wage a long contested war. Da-Da, Tan-Tan, a strategy of deceit off the actually battlefield, would be mastered by the North Vietnamese against hood-winked U.S. war managers, who always seemed to take the communist at that word.

An early assessment of the communist insurgency in South Vietnam, and Diem's inability to effect positive change, caused the Kennedy administration pause. In the White House, colored pins on maps showed rural areas under Diem's control; colored pins that seemed to change only when Diem moved his soldiers.

Kennedy's reaction was to increase economic and military aid and send additional military advisers along with American helicopter units to transport and advise South Vietnamese troops in battle. This move necessarily involved Americans in combat operations. Kennedy justified the expanding U.S. military role as a means "to prevent a Communist takeover of Vietnam which is in accordance with policy our government has followed since 1954."

The nuances of this new way to word our involvement spoke volumes for Kennedy's justification for the U.S. military presence continuing in Vietnam. "We're doing this because that's the way it has been done since '54" was not effective foreign policy.

Even despite McNamara and Rostow and Taylor saying that we were doing good. We weren't. Not even from the start.

Karl von Clausewitz

Master philosopher of war Karl von Clausewitz emphasized almost a century and a half earlier that because war is controlled by its political object, the value of this object must determine the sacrifices to be made for it both in magnitude and also in duration. He went on to say that once the expenditure of effort exceeds the value of the political object, the object must be renounced.

Like Eisenhower's advice, none of this perceptive thinking was being considered during Kennedy's start-up White House.

Southeast Asia as a Piece of the Worldwide Geopolitical Puzzle

As Kennedy's administration started rolling, there was a political/military stand-off in Berlin. The East-West dialogue generally was adversarial and toxic. Then in mid-April 1961 the U.S.-backed Bay of Pigs invasion of Cuba failed, which caused international jitters.

To distract from the bad Europe and Cuba news and to reinforce U.S. commitments in SEA, in May 1961 Vice President Lyndon B. Johnson visited President Diem in South Vietnam and hailed the embattled leader as the "Winston Churchill of Asia."

Also in May 1961 President Kennedy sent 400 American Green Beret "special advisers"' to South Vietnam, to help train South Vietnamese soldiers in "**counterinsurgency**." But then their role expanded to include organization of the mountain men in western South Vietnam into irregular defense groups, although the employment of these groups had no apparent long-range objective. It was a knee jerk reaction to the increasing number of VC and NVA coming down the Ho Chi Minh Trail from North Vietnam.

There was no strategic connection to NSC 68 resolutions. The deployment of these Green Beret "A" teams was, however, an incremental increase in U.S. human investment in South Vietnam.

In Laos, under that "covert action" authorization for Laos that Eisenhower signed right before leaving office, two CIA case officers were assigned to work directly with mountain warlord General Vang Pao's forces to stop communist military advances around the PDJ in northeast Laos. More CIA advisers would follow. Weapons were provided. Bill Lair's PARU provided training. Lao operations – significant especially early on because they demonstrated how the North Vietnamese could be engaged and contained in Laos - were coded as "Top Secret" in Washington. War efforts in Laos seemed to belong to the State Department and to the CIA. McNamara showed no interest.

The most significant event in the month after the failed Bay of Pigs attack on Cuba was Kennedy's dispatch of Averell Harriman, his ambassador-at-large, to Geneva to meet with Soviet delegation to find a diplomatic solution to the continuing violation of the Lao border.

Harriman later said that his main official business in Geneva was to find some diplomatic alternative to war in Laos, because he thought that SEA was only a regional dust-up and almost an incidental sidebar to the nuclear armament threat to U.S. security posed by the Soviets in West Europe. He even speculated that the Soviets might be using Southeast Asia to divert U.S. attention from Soviet ambitions in and around Berlin.

Harriman had convinced Kennedy that to "deny" Laos to the North Vietnamese was doable in principle with diplomacy, especially because he was involved and had the necessary cachet with Russian leadership. It was worth a try, he said. The Soviets had agreed to the meetings. This tact had the potential, according to Harriman, to avoid loss of American lives halfway round the world in the Lao outback.

President Kennedy and Averell Harriman

Once on the ground in Switzerland, Harriman and his deputy, Ambassador William Sullivan, established a strong personal and working relationship with George M. Pushkin, chief Soviet delegate and almost immediately made significant movement in finding common ground to establish an international agreement on Laos' neutrality.

While this warm and fuzzy relationship was being established, in early June President Kennedy met with Premier Nikita Khrushchev in Vienna. This first-time contact between the two men did not go well for the West, as Khrushchev bullied the new U.S. president for most of the two day conference; often bellicose, he slammed Kennedy from pillar to post on almost every issue. The only thing they agreed on was the ongoing talks in Geneva on the possibilities of striking some accord on Laos.

In retrospect this encouragement on the Geneva talks by the duplicitous Soviets should have given the Kennedy team reason to worry that the net advantage might accrue to Khrushchev.

In the early fall of 1961 top Kennedy aides, General Maxwell Taylor and Walt Rostow, visited Vietnam for a first-hand assessment of the SEA situation. Rostow reported when they got back that, "If Vietnam goes, it will be exceedingly difficult to hold Southeast Asia." He advised Kennedy to expand the number of U.S. military advisers and to send 8,000 combat soldiers to South Vietnam.

On October 24, 1961, the seventh anniversary of the creation of the Republic of South Vietnam, President Kennedy sent a letter to President Diem and pledged that "the United States is determined to help South Vietnam preserve its independence."

The cost to America of maintaining South Vietnam's 200,000-man army and managing the overall conflict in Vietnam had risen in 1961 to nearly a million dollars per day. Also in 1961, South Vietnam received $65 million in military equipment and $136 million in economic aid, with an undeterminable amount lost to corruption and graft.

On the other side, Viet Cong had killed some 4,000 South Vietnamese officials during the first year of the Kennedy presidency. The SEA map in the White House showed that the communists controlled much of the South Vietnamese countryside, with safe sanctions for their military across the border in Cambodia/Laos and an elaborate logistic pipeline down to the South Vietnam battlefield though Laos. An unending train of supplies was entering North Vietnam from Russia and China. It was a South Vietnam battlefield that greatly favored the communist North Vietnam.

Going into 1962, there were almost no success stories of Buddhist peasants in the rural south being pacified and converting from communist control to Diem's control. Only boots or sandals on the ground made any difference. The colored pins on maps in the White House were more and more turning communist red.

Coordinated anti-war rallies began on U.S. college campuses. The fight for South Vietnam was worldwide news, and people, including the media, were taking sides. More and more people were supporting North Vietnam or what Vice President Lyndon Johnson called that "damn little piss-ant country."

PART III

The Diplomatic "Neutralization" of Laos to North Vietnam's Great Advantage

During his State of the Union address mid-January 1962, President Kennedy stated, "Few generations in all of history have been granted the role of being the great defender of freedom in its maximum hour of danger. This is our good fortune."

In early February 1962 the Military Assistance Advisory Group (MAAG) Vietnam, established in 1950, was replaced by the U.S. Military Assistance Command for Vietnam (MACV). This new command authorized U.S. military advisers to fire their weapons only "if fired upon." In a combat zone, this clearly represented Washington-driven political rules of engagement, rather than anything that helped the cause in South Vietnam.

By spring of 1962 U.S. Ambassador W. Averell Harriman's pursuit of Soviet support for accords on Lao neutrality was coming to a conclusion in Geneva.

The experienced senior U.S. diplomat was convinced that maintaining Lao peace through Western negotiations served U.S. interests best in its overall dealings with Russia. Europe still remained, to his mind, the industrial world's critical terrain and was the most important Soviet-U.S. equities were in play.

Sometime in the spring, the lead Soviet representative to the talks, Georgi M. Pushkin, said privately that the Soviet Union would take the responsibility to make

China and North Vietnam abide by any accords reached in Geneva.

Quietly, shortly thereafter, with hardly any press coverage, the Declaration on the Neutrality of Laos was signed by the United States and 13 other nations.

It prohibited foreign armies from operating inside Laos and gave 75 days for all foreign military to be out of the country.

The United States and the Soviet Union complied.

North Vietnam did not.

While there was a token, public exit of a few North Vietnamese soldiers from Laos, for the most part there was no interruption in the construction of the Ho Chi Minh road network by the 557th Transportation Group and movement of supplies and men down to the south.

Challenged on this again and again, North Vietnam either did not respond or denied their "troops" were in Laos. In 1963 Harriman went to Russia to ask after the promise he had received from Pushkin that Russia would be responsible for China's and North Vietnam's compliance, but Khrushchev would not discuss the subject. Pushkin reportedly had "died of natural causes."

The Geneva agreement provided the communists with means to protect their borders. This protection was guaranteed when William Sullivan, Harriman's deputy in Geneva, was assigned as the U.S. ambassador to Laos and famously prohibited U.S. DOD from any involvement in the country.

The 1962 Geneva Accords, "a good, bad deal" as Harriman called it, was very, very good for the North Vietnamese and very, very bad for the allied forces trying to keep South Vietnam free. Some military historians have suggested that with the Ho Chi Minh Trail protected from Western troops by the Geneva Accords – protection ensured by William Sullivan, the U.S. ambassador to Laos, and by Harriman sitting as the U.S. czar for SEA in the State Department -- the war in the south was unwinnable.

Meanwhile, nationally coordinated anti-war rallies were becoming increasingly popular on U.S. college campuses.

South Vietnam Heats Up

In South Vietnam "**counterinsurgency**" just was not working. For example, in March 1962 Operation Sunrise began the Strategic Hamlet Resettlement program in which scattered rural populations in South Vietnam were moved into fortified villages defended by local militias. However, over 50 of these new hamlets were soon infiltrated and taken over by Viet Cong who killed and otherwise intimidated village leaders.

As a result, Diem ordered bombing raids against suspected Viet Cong-controlled villages, which further eroded support for his administration. It also helped VC propaganda make the case that Diem was a puppet of the Americans so, in fact, the United States was responsible for the bombings, as well as the unpopular and badly run resettlement program.

Also at this time newly created battalion-size Viet Cong units were moving with impunity as a show of force in central Vietnam and in the delta.

Against this backdrop, Defense Secretary McNamara, during a South Vietnam visit in May 1962, reported to the press that, "we are winning the war." However at the time the VC, operating from bases in the Mekong Delta and Central Highlands, were controlling the time and place of most contact with South Vietnamese forces. Like the French before them, the ARVN was spending more and more of its time reacting to VC initiatives.

Beginning in early January 1963, ARVN went on the offensive in what would be its first big battle against the Viet Cong.

An American radio-intercept aircraft located a Viet Cong radio transmitter in the hamlet of Ap Tan Thoi in Dinh Tuong Province just below the Parrot's Beak on the Cambodian/Vietnam border. It was a small village that sat like an island in a sea of rice paddies and delta mud. A small farming settlement called Ap Bac was located on the only road into Ap Than Thoi from the southeast.

U.S. Lieutenant Colonel John Paul Vann, adviser to the ARVN 7th Division, opined the Viet Cong were using Ap Tan Thoi as a regional headquarters and his intelligence led him to believe the Viet Cong had deployed a reinforced company of about 120 men to protect the site. Vann worked with the ARVN 7th Infantry Division in developing plans to attack Ap Tan Thoi, initially with M-113 armored tracks from the southeast through Ap Bac, to be followed by ARVN attacks on Ap Tan Thoi from three sides with troops brought in close by American helicopters.

Lt Col John Paul Vann

The attack was launched at 4:00 am on January 2ND. The ARVN lost, beaten by possibly 350 VC who had dug in around the two villages. Eighty-three South Vietnamese were killed and more than a hundred wounded. Five U.S. helicopters were shot down; three American pilots were killed.

That night the VC defenders melted away into Cambodia, leaving nothing behind except ARVN and U.S. casualties. The battlefield was close to Saigon and was inspected by journalists the following morning. By that night the VC victory was front-page news in the United States.

Kennedy Rethinks Diem

In an assessment of the battle, Vann found that the 7th Division had orders from Diem to be cautious and to avoid casualties. This order created combat timidity that clearly contributed to the lack of forceful South Vietnamese military leadership on the battlefield around Ap Bac. It was also apparent that there had been a breakdown in communications between the different South Vietnamese units, which, among other things, resulted in late artillery support and an indecisive commitment of the M-113s.

Then this - on Jun 11, 1963, Thich Quang Duc, a 66-year-old Buddhist monk, sets himself afire in protest of the South Vietnamese government, its religious intolerance and its discriminatory policies. In the following months, other Buddhists would follow his example and self-immolate to demonstrate against the regime.

In a press conference at the time, President John F. Kennedy recommitted the United States to support South Vietnam. "To withdraw from that effort would mean a collapse not only of South Vietnam, but Southeast Asia. So we are going to stay there." But privately Kennedy was deeply affected by the horrific, continuing Buddhist monks' suicides.

Diem responded to the unrest by imposing martial law. Some South Vietnamese special forces controlled by Diem's younger brother, Nhu, waged violent crackdowns against Buddhist sanctuaries in Saigon, Hue and other cities. These crackdowns in turn soon encompassed other issues that sparked more anti-Diem demonstrations, loud protests that were heard in Washington.

As the overall situation worsened, high-level talks in the White House focused on the need for a regime change in South Vietnam.

On August 26, 1963, President Kennedy met with his top aides to begin discussions over whether the U.S. should support or initiate efforts to oust Diem. Those discussions came to a conclusion three days later when Henry Cabot Lodge, the U.S. Ambassador to Vietnam, sent a message from Saigon stating, "There is no possibility, in my view, that the war can be won under a Diem administration."

Walt Cronkite interviews President Kennedy

During a subsequent TV news interview with Walter Cronkite, President Kennedy laid out results of his recent deliberations on South Vietnam. He described Diem as "out of touch with the people" and added that South Vietnam's government might regain popular support "with changes in policy and perhaps in personnel." But also during this interview Kennedy was unequivocal about the U.S. commitment to stay the course of stopping the communist insurgency in South Vietnam.

On September 2, 1963, the CBS eye blinked open and *CBS Evening News with Walter Cronkite* became network television's first half-hour weeknight news broadcast. The first airing highlighted the Kennedy interview.

The program proved to be an enormous success, what with the exotic, catastrophic struggle in South Vietnam played out in front of Americans as they sat down to their evening meal. Live coverage of self-immolations made for absorbing TV.

A month later, U.S. Secretary of Defense, Robert McNamara told the press that the war was going well for the Allies in Vietnam and the Kennedy administration intended to withdraw most American forces from South Vietnam by the end of 1965. Unconnected to any other reporting, that statement demonstrated a significant credibility gap between information released by the U.S. government in Washington and what journalists were coming to know as the actual situation in Vietnam.

It demonstrated again how McNamara sometimes just talked and made up things as he went along. Lyndon Johnson also ad-libbed in talking with the press. Once President Johnson was addressing a group of young men getting ready to deploy to Vietnam and told them to fight hard, with great resolution, like one of his relatives who had fought at the Alamo. A reporter did some facts checking, which came to the attention of one of Johnson long-time staffers, who knew perfectly well that Johnson had no relatives at the Alamo. The staffer confronted Johnson with the problem, and although Johnson's comments were taped and audio recorded, Johnson insisted he had no relatives in Alamo, and defied anyone to find him wrong.

The Army of South Vietnam (ARVN), despite its poor showing in Ap Bac in early 1963, showed signs of improvement on the battlefield. In several later engagements handily beat VC in skirmishes. By all military accounts, there was an abundance of good commanders in the South Vietnamese military who were dedicated to the survival of the new up-start South Vietnam. They went to war every day, year after year.

In October 1963 Ambassador Lodge informed President Kennedy that a coup against Diem, discussed by some ARVN leaders months before, appeared imminent.

This scenario was well received at the White House, in that the generals would appear to be acting on their own without any apparent U.S. involvement. President

Kennedy gave his approval and the CIA in Saigon signaled the conspirators.

At 1:30 p.m. on 1 November the coup began as mutinous troops roared into Saigon, surrounded the presidential palace and seized police headquarters.

Diem and his brother Nhu, trapped inside the palace, rejected all appeals to surrender. Diem telephoned the rebel generals and attempted, but failed, to talk them out of the coup. Diem then called Lodge and asked, "What is the attitude of the United States?" Lodge responded, "It is four thirty a.m. in Washington, and the U.S. government cannot possibly have a view."

Diem Out; Kennedy Out

At 8 p.m., Diem and Nhu slipped out of the presidential palace unnoticed and went to a safe house in the suburbs. During the night one of Diem's aides betrayed this location and it was surrounded.

As the sun was breaking over the city, Diem and Nhu offered to surrender and were subsequently taken into custody by rebel officers and placed in the back of an armored personnel carrier. While en route to Saigon's center city, the vehicle stopped and Diem and Nhu were assassinated.

Saigon at first celebrated Diem's death, but it was short lived. The coup resulted in a power vacuum in which a series of pretenders to head the South Vietnamese government came and went under the existing military junta. Viet Cong used the unstable political situation to increase its hold over the rural population of South Vietnam to nearly 40 percent.

On November 22, 1963, three weeks after Diem's assassination, President John F. Kennedy was assassinated in Dallas.

Johnson Takes Over as Commander in Chief

Lyndon B. Johnson was sworn in as the 36th U.S. President.

Two days into office, Lyndon B. Johnson was quoted as saying that "**strength and determination**" must be used in the battle to stop communist aggression in Southeast Asia.

President Johnson promised Ambassador Lodge, while he was in Washington, that he would not lose Vietnam.

By the end of 1963 the junta that had assassinated Diem was itself deposed by the flamboyant Nguyen Khanh. The Americans would have preferred some form of a democratic transfer of power post-coup, but generally were pleased with Khanh's commitment to form a strong government and an effective military.

On March 6, 1964, Defense Secretary McNamara visited South Vietnam and stated that General Khanh "has our admiration, our respect and our complete support." He added, "We'll stay for as long as it takes. We shall provide whatever help is required to win the battle against the Communist insurgents."

Following his visit, McNamara advised President Johnson to increase military aid to shore up Khanh's recast of the South Vietnam military.

This "all-in on Vietnam" attitude had now replaced Harriman's contention that whatever happened in SEA posed no threat to U.S. security or our standing in the world.

On March 17, 1964, the U.S. National Security Council recommended the bombing of North Vietnam but President Johnson hesitated. Also in March, aides began work on a congressional resolution supporting the president's **"strength and determination"** initiatives in Vietnam. That petition was shelved temporarily due to lack of support in the Senate, but the language would be used later as the basis of the Gulf of Tonkin resolution.

Dean Rusk (State), President Johnson and Robert McNamara (Defense)

Many close to Johnson even pushed for the situation in South Vietnam to be "Americanized" to give the U.S. government greater control of how the war was actually being fought. The Joint Chiefs of Staff put forward a plan that included air and commando strikes into North Vietnam, flights over Laos and Cambodia for intelligence, and the use of U.S. combat forces. Gaining traction was the thought to just go over and win the thing – get it out of the way -- and come back home so that Johnson could focus on his "Great Society" domestic programs.

During the spring of 1964 some 1,000 students gathered in New York City to protest the Vietnam War. Twelve burned their Selective Service registration cards—draft cards—in a symbolic gesture of opposition to the war.

The cost to America of maintaining South Vietnam's army and managing the overall conflict in Vietnam under Johnson rose to $2 million per day in 1964, almost twice what it had been a few years before.

In mid-1964 Khanh declared a state of emergency and drafted a new constitution for South Vietnam. People gathered in the streets in protest. Not surprisingly, there was a coup attempt on September the 13thbut it collapsed within 24 hours.

The United States was now losing patience with Khanh and asked him to resign. Of course he refused, explaining to the U.S. government emissaries that he had the power to expel them, not the other way around.

Political instability in Saigon and the Khanh's administration frosty relations with the United States in its new "**strength and determination**" mode would continue for a year. In mid-summer General Maxwell D. Taylor, chairman of the Joint Chiefs of Staff, was appointed as the new U.S. ambassador to South Vietnam. During his one-year tenure, Taylor would have to deal with constant rumors of coups and five successive governments.

Reflecting the generally conservative mood of the voters, Senator Barry Goldwater was chosen as the Republican nominee for president at the Republican National Convention in July. A virulent anti-communist, Goldwater's campaign rhetoric would impact general White House war planning because Johnson did not want to appear to be "softer on Communism" than his adversary.

The Starter's Gun: Tonkin

North Vietnamese torpedo boats attacking the USS *Maddox*

On August 2, 1964, the U.S. destroyer USS *Maddox*, operating in the Gulf of Tonkin 10 miles off the coast of North Vietnam, was engaged by three North Vietnamese torpedo boats. In the resulting sea battle one U.S. aircraft was damaged, the U.S. destroyer was hit by a small rocket and the three North Korean torpedo boats were damaged, with one possibly sunk.

At the White House, it was Sunday morning. President Johnson, reacting cautiously to reports of the incident, decided against immediate retaliation. Instead, he sent a diplomatic message to Hanoi warning of "grave consequences" from any further "unprovoked" attacks. Johnson then ordered the *Maddox* to resume operations in the Gulf of Tonkin in the same vicinity where the attack had occurred.

Meanwhile, the Joint Chiefs of Staff put U.S. combat troops on alert and also selected targets in North Vietnam for a possible bombing raid. The United States was on a war footing.

Two days later, on August 4, possibly precipitated by false radar images, another "provocation" was reported by the U.S. Navy in the same area off North Vietnam.

The Joint Chiefs of Staff strongly recommended a retaliatory bombing raid against North Vietnam. President Johnson concurred and North Vietnam oil facilities and naval targets were summarily attacked by 64 U.S. Navy fighter bombers.

Two Navy jets were shot down during the bombing raids, resulting in the first American prisoner of war,

Lieutenant Everett Alvarez. He was taken to what would be called "Hanoi Hilton" by the nearly six hundred American airmen who would become POWs.

What was America's public reaction? Opinion polls indicated that 85 percent of Americans supported President Johnson's bombing decision. Numerous newspaper editorials also come out in support of the president.

With that public support in mind, Johnson's aides, including Defense Secretary McNamara, went to Congress to lobby for a resolution to give the president a free hand in Vietnam.

Senator Wayne Morse

During an August 6, 1964, meeting in the Senate, McNamara was confronted by Senator Wayne Morse of Oregon. Morse had been advised that the Maddox was not the victim of an "unprovoked" attack but in fact had been involved with South Vietnamese commando raids against North Vietnam at the time. McNamara responded that the U.S. Navy *played absolutely no part in, was not associated with, was not aware of, any South Vietnamese actions, if there were any.*

This may not have been entirely true.

On 7 August 1964, Congress approved what was called the Gulf of Tonkin resolution, giving the president authority *"to take all necessary steps, including the use of armed force"* to prevent further attacks against U.S. forces.

It passed unanimously in the House and 98-2 in the Senate. The only senators voting against the resolution were Wayne Morse and Ernest Gruening of Alaska, who said *"all Vietnam is not worth the life of a single American boy."*

Two months after the Gulf of Tonkin incident, China tested its first nuclear bomb on October 16, 1964. Probably they were assisted in its development by the Soviets.

Also, China had massed troops along its border with Vietnam, probably in sword-rattling response to increased U.S. military activity in the south.

With 61 percent of the popular vote, Lyndon B. Johnson was elected president of the United States in a land-slide victory November 3, 1964. Democrats also achieved big majorities in both the U.S. House and Senate. The Democrats considered the vote to be a mandate to remain tough against communism and firm in the face of challenges in a changing world.

To up the ante in South Vietnam, Johnson increased the number of U.S. military advisers to 15,000.

At the same time, 10,000 NVA soldiers arrived in the Central Highlands of South Vietnam via the Ho Chi Minh Trail, carrying sophisticated weapons provided by China. They shored up Viet Cong battalions with new soldiers and experienced North Vietnamese leaders.

At the White House, President Johnson's top aides recommended gradual escalation of U.S. military involvement in Vietnam to put teeth in Johnson's **"strength and determination"** policy.

On Christmas Eve 1964 Viet Cong set off a car bomb near an American officers' quarters in downtown Saigon. The bomb was timed to detonate at 5:45 p.m., during "Christmas Eve happy hour" in the bar. Two Americans were killed and 58 wounded.

Operation Rolling Thunder, a USAF bombing campaign into North Vietnam, was launched in retaliation for the Saigon Christmas Eve bombings targeting Americans in Saigon.

By year's end, United States had 23,000 military advisers in-country assisting the 200,000 man South Vietnamese army. They faced an estimated 170,000 Viet Cong/NVA fighters in the "People's Revolutionary Army" and untold thousands of civilian sympathizers in the South Vietnamese countryside.

In taking his oath of office on January 20, 1965, Lyndon B. Johnson declared, "We can never again stand aside, prideful in isolation. Terrific dangers and troubles that we once called "foreign" now constantly live among us."

Possibly alluding to Ho Chi Minh supporters in the United States.

National Security Adviser McGeorge Bundy and Defense Secretary Robert McNamara sent a memo to the president January 27, 1965, stating that America's limited military involvement in Vietnam was not succeeding, and that the United States has reached a 'fork in the road' in Vietnam. The United States must commit, either escalate or withdraw. One or the other.

Johnson pondered their comments without coming to a decision.

While this memo was percolating in Washington, National Security Adviser Bundy visited South Vietnam in early February 1965. In North Vietnam, Soviet Prime Minister Aleksei Kosygin coincidentally arrived in Hanoi at the same time. During his talks with the communist leadership, Kosygin promised to provide all military equipment the North Vietnamese needed to carry their fight to the South Vietnamese and the Americans in the south.

Viet Cong guerrillas attacked the U.S. military compound at Pleiku in the Central Highlands February 6, 1965, killing 8 Americans, wounding 126, and destroying 10 aircraft.

The next day President Johnson told his National Security advisers, "I've had enough of this." While he did not voice an inclination to go McNamara's "all in" he did approve Operation Flaming Dart, the surgical bombing of a North Vietnamese Army (NVA) camp near

Dong Hoi, possibly as a stalking horse to gauge public reaction to a more pro-active approach to fighting the communists in Vietnam.

<u>**Polls, Policy and Warfighting**</u>

Opinion polls taken in the United States shortly after the February 1965 bombing indicate a 70 percent approval rating for the president and an 80 percent approval of U.S. military involvement in Vietnam.

Oval Office 1965

Johnson by this time had a three-TV console built in the Oval Office and at night during network news, he would sit in front of the TVs watching with rapt attention, going from one network to the other. The preponderance of the TV reports fixed on his history-making emergence as commander in chief of the war in Southeast Asia. The commentators were his allies, or his enemies. Certainly Johnson considered their remarks his grades for his day's work. He also took the news anchors comments and national polls as the voice of the people.

The guide-on words for our military during the 20th century had proceeded

from	"Total War "
to	"Containment"
to	"limited war"
to	"flexible response"
to	"counterinsurgency"
to	"war of attrition"
to	"strength and determination"

Soon the guide-on words would change

to	"pacification"
to	"Vietnamization"

and finally

to	"You are on your own. Good bye."

On February 22, 1965, General William C. Westmoreland, military commander of U.S. forces in Vietnam, requested two battalions of U.S. Marines to protect Da Nang from 6,000 Viet Cong massed in the vicinity possibly with intentions of cutting South Vietnam in two parts.

The president approved his request, despite the "grave reservations" of Ambassador Taylor. The old general turned diplomat did not necessarily believe – at that time – in the escalation of United States field troops in SEA, warning that America may be about to repeat the same mistakes made by the French in sending ever-increasing numbers of soldiers into the Asian jungle quagmires.

Also about this time the first U.S. air strikes were launched against the Ho Chi Minh Trail. Throughout the war, the trail was heavily bombed by American planes, even though this bombing did little to halt the ant-like flow of soldiers and portered supplies from the north.

The majority of bombs dropped in South Vietnam were against Viet Cong and NVA positions but collateral damage included displacement of 3 million civilians.

U.S. Marines landing at China Beach

In early March 1965 two U.S. marine battalions of about 3,500 men landed at China Beach to engage the NVA in and around Da Nang. It was the same beach the French military had landed almost 100 years before.

The United States was now fully committed to a war at the cost of U.S. soldiers on the ground.

The Drums of the War Become Louder

Operation Market Time, a joint effort between the U.S. and South Vietnamese Navies, commenced on March 11, 1965 in an effort to disrupt the North Vietnamese sea routes used to funnel supplies into the south. The operation was highly successful in cutting off coastal supply lines and resulted in the North Vietnamese shifting to sea routes to Sihanoukville in Cambodia.

On March 29, 1965, Viet Cong sappers bombed the U.S. Embassy in Saigon. As if the communist were saying, "Tonkin Bay? Da Nang? Don't matter. Come on. Come on America. We aren't afraid of you!!!"

President Johnson delivered his 'Peace without Conquest" speech on April 7, 1965 at Johns Hopkins University. He offered Hanoi "unconditional discussions" to stop the war in return for massive economic assistance in modernizing both North and South Vietnam. Johnson was quoted as saying that "this offers Ho a deal he can't refuse," however his peace overtures were quickly rejected.

This should have been no surprise, because in March the NVA were marshalling west of Da Nang and its sappers had boldly attacked the U.S. Embassy in Saigon. Some observers said the sapper attack was like someone slapping someone else to start a bar fight. "Come on, fight me."

Unlike Johnson's thinking his "Peace without Conquest" offer was a "deal Ho can't refuse," it came so quickly after the NVA sapper attack on the American Embassy in Saigon that there was the appearance that Johnson was suing for peace. Certainly it seemed to the North Vietnamese war planners that they had grabbed the momentum and were on the right course to carry the fight to the U.S. in South Vietnam.

This even though - with Hanoi rejecting Johnson's "Peace without Conquest" offer - a thousand tons of bombs were dropped on Viet Cong positions by allied fighter-bombers on April 15, 1965.

On 17 April 1965, as the dust was settling, 15,000 students gathered to protest the U.S. bombing campaign in Washington, D.C. The protestors themselves were becoming the news as much as the war. Around the world, people were taking sides – for or against the war, for or against the protestors. In that sense the conflict had become a world war.

Peace demonstration in Washington, D.C., April 1975

In Honolulu later in the spring, Johnson's top aides, including McNamara, General Westmoreland, McGeorge Bundy, and even Ambassador Taylor, met and agreed to recommend to the president that he send another 40,000 combat soldiers to Vietnam.

Johnson advisers had taken the fork in the road that would lead to war.

The first U.S. Army combat troops, 3,500 men of the 173rd Airborne Brigade, arrived in Vietnam May 3, 1965.

On May 13, 1965, a bombing pause was announced by the United States in the hope that Hanoi would now consider negotiations. There would be six more pauses during the Rolling Thunder bombing campaign, all with the same intention.

However, each time, the North Vietnamese ignored the peace overtures and instead used the pause to repair air defenses and send more troops and supplies down the Ho Chi Minh Trail.

North Vietnam was not going to be distracted by peace offerings or psychological operations (psy-ops)... they were in to win... and world opinion was starting to side with them as the great under-dog to the God-almighty United States.

U.S. bombing of North Vietnam resumed May 19, 1965.

Nguyen Cao Ky took power in South Vietnam as the new prime minister June 18, 1965, with Nguyen Van Thieu functioning as official chief of state. There had been 10 separate governments in Saigon over the past 20 months.

This leadership of this newest regime was relatively stable and straight-forward with the United States but the old problems of an unresponsive and corrupt civilian and military hierarchy remained. U.S. in-country advisers suggested that Thieu and Ky adopt a **'pacification'** program to win the 'hearts and minds' of the people.

'Pacification' started to share space with the **'strength and determination'** language in Johnson's South Vietnamese program.

At this time, too, the CIA's covert Phoenix Program began targeting those people in the countryside collecting taxes to fund the VC. It was successful in and of itself but did not greatly affect VC popularity out in the countryside.

Then on July 1, 1965 the Viet Cong staged a mortar attack against Da Nang air base, destroying three aircraft.

President Lyndon B. Johnson

Finally, a week later, during a noontime press conference, President Johnson took a position in front of a single TV camera. His thinning hair slicked back, his floppy ears looking like butterfly wings on either side of his big head, his jowls sagging off his bulbous nose, his face somber, he drawled, "My fellow Americans... (The first part of his long speech, in essence, can be paraphrase : For me as your president and Commander in Chief of the U.S. military--to absolutely, no-kidding-around, militarily, put a stop to this communist aggression in SEA)... "I have today ordered to Viet-Nam the 1st Air Mobile Division and certain other forces."

Well Positioned at the Intersection of Destiny and High Adventure

Fort Benning was home to the U.S. 1st Air-Mobile Division. I was finishing airborne training there and was sitting in an Officers club auxiliary that night when Johnson's announcement was replayed on the evening news.

Everyone in the bar cheered. A colonel bought a round of drinks and the bar buzzed with excitement. Men came in from the dining room and were told the news. Others scurried out, some to make telephone calls, some, especially those from the Air-Mobile Division, left for their units.

I was taking airborne training at Fort Benning, but was assigned to the Big Red One Division at Fort Riley,

Kansas, and waited my turn at a public telephone to call my unit. I wanted to find if our division had been placed on alert -- as part of the "certain other forces" -- but couldn't get through. But I was sure in my heart that the First Division was going, it had been on alert for deployment for a month.

I went out on the Officers Club balcony and watched tanks move through areas of Fort Benning in which they never had been before. Trucks in the distance clogged the street. The whole base was lit and mobilized in the fading light of the day. Cheers continued from the bar behind me.

Two months since receiving my Infantry 2nd Lieutenant commission from Officer Candidate School - fit and proud - I knew I would be goin' to war as well and I felt privileged to be a part... smiling... confident... anxious for the adventure...

-- ONE --
Army Recruit

Cottonpicker didn't think it was a big deal. This was Christmas 1963 and I was home from college. We were sitting on his back porch drinking beer.

"You don't die if you quit school," he said. "We ain't talking about the future of the world here."

Donald Lawrence, dubbed "Cottonpicker" by my father several years before, was my best friend growing up. A big, brawny redhead, he was a paratrooper sergeant in the 82nd Airborne Division at Fort Bragg Army Base near my hometown of Southern Pines, North Carolina, and lived with his wife and children in an apartment behind our house. During my early teen years, we had spent many late afternoon hours tinkering with his old car under a nearby magnolia tree. On weekends, we had hunted and fished deep in the woods of the Fort Bragg reservation. He taught me how to stalk deer and gig frogs and light a cigarette in the wind and cuss like a soldier. He had always done most of the talking when we were together. "I'm da Chief and you da Indian" was his way of putting it. I was used to taking his advice so I listened carefully.

"You're what now, twenty-one? If you want to quit up there at Chapel Hill and just raise hell, well that's all right, I reckon. It's your life. Just don't go feeling guilty about it. Tell people, 'I ain't getting nothing out of college and what I want to do is get out there and holler, so get outa my way.'" He paused. "But, you know, you might want to have some plans, Jimmy. Just raising hell don't feed the dog."

He looked at me and smiled in that lopsided fashion of his.

"The Army ain't bad. Been good by me."

My father had suggested that I stay in college while I was making up my mind about my future because it was a better environment for decision making -- more educated counselors, better choices. I had already dropped out once for a semester.

"If you drop out again," he reasoned, "you'll never go back. But you are the family namesake. You have an obligation here."

James E. Parker, Jr.

When I returned to the University of North Carolina (UNC) after Christmas, I tried to study, but despite Dad's admonitions, I simply wasn't interested. Plus I felt alone. My friends had dropped out. That left me, along with maybe twenty thousand strangers at Chapel Hill, reading *The Organization Man* and in danger of becoming one.

I would sit at my desk in the dorm at Chapel Hill, a book open in front of me and stare out the window, bored. I had always been restless as a kid. Growing up, I'd watch a train go by -- or even a Greyhound bus -- wanting to be on it, traveling, "getting on down the road." The journey had always seemed as important as the destination.

My home was on the western edge of Fort Bragg. From a big tree in my front yard, I used to watch U.S. Air Force planes in the distance and daydreamed about flying those planes or jumping out of them. Cottonpicker had taught me the eight jump commands. Standing on a lower limb of the tree, I would recite, "Get ready. Stand up. Hook up. Check equipment. Check buddy's equipment. Sound off for equipment check. Stand in the door. Go." I would jump to the ground and do the parachute landing fall, just as Cottonpicker had taught me. I'd climb back up the tree and fantasize about life as a soldier or a world traveler. In my mind's eye, I could see myself clearly out there: Comfortable in some exotic setting, challenging death, living by my wits.

These thoughts might have passed in time and I might have had a more normal adolescence and a less troubling college experience if I hadn't taken a trip during the summer of 1957, between my freshman and sophomore years of high school, that forever changed my life. My parents had sent me to Mars Hill College, my father's alma mater, to take college-level summer courses in hopes of jump-starting an interest in academics. Instead, I made friends there with a rowdy group of college sophomores. Two were from Cuba, one from Lake Wells, Florida, and one from Wilson, North Carolina. At the end of summer school, we developed an elaborate ruse to excuse my absence from home for a few days. My friend from Wilson and I then thumbed to Florida and went to Havana, Cuba. Three days and two nights there in the tenderloin area near the harbor -- neon lights flickering off a Cuban bar at three o'clock in the morning, rumba music coursing the air, cigar smoke, fights, whores, rum were exactly what I had dreamed about in that tree in my front yard. I hated to leave, but we ran out of money. With a revolution going on in the hills, there were restrictions on just hanging around.

2

The Vietnam War Its Ownself

My parents were happy to see me when I arrived home, but in short order they sent me to a military school. This was a radical decision for them. They had grown up on farms in North Carolina and thought that only uncontrollably spoiled kids in California went to private military schools. They found it hard to believe that their son, raised in the rural heartland of the South, required special education, but they saw that unusual glint in my eye, the Cottonpicker influence, my total lack of interest in their goals, my trip to Cuba. I needed an attitude adjustment.

The structured environment of Oak Ridge Military Institute was not a bad situation, the instructors were more engaging and challenging than those I had known in public school. Also there were some real characters in the cadet corps, and living like a soldier had a certain attraction.

I fell in love with an old 1903 Springfield rifle that I was issued for the drill team. We practiced almost every weekday afternoon and I looked forward to getting into the armory and taking my rifle gently out of its place in the rack and twirling it in my hands. It was a handsome, no-nonsense war piece. I imagined that it had served our country in some previous war and had been retired to duty in a North Carolina military school. I had great respect for that rifle, and felt an uncommon rapport with it. In all the turns and twists required of us as the drill team marched along, that rifle never failed me. It was a solid weapon with a natural balance -- a war tool.

After graduating from Oak Ridge, I enrolled in UNC. During my sophomore year, a couple of friends and I dropped out of school and drove a beat up 1950 Willis Jeep through Central America to Nicaragua. We were looking for jobs there when we ran afoul of what would become the Sandinestas, and we had to get out. We flew to Miami, where I worked on the beach until the next semester of college began at Chapel Hill.

I still dreamed about "getting out there," living in faraway places. Hell, knocking around was a family tradition -- my father should realize that, I thought. His father had never settled down. Grandpa had been a rural mail carrier but somewhat irregular in his work habits. Once during World War I, he was supposed to be on his delivery route but he was holed up, drinking moonshine. Someone bet him that he couldn't drive his Harley motorbike up a nearby tree that was half bent over. He got up most of the way before he fell off. The motorbike was torn up pretty bad, plus the mail blew away and he lost his job. He and the family went back to Grandma's home place and he tried to farm the forty acres they were given, but he just wasn't cut out to be a farmer. Every once in a while, he left the farm and

3

traveled around. He worked at odd jobs, once selling Fuller brushes in the eastern part of the state. Living in rooming houses, sometimes under bridges, he was different from all the rest but happy in his own way.

That's my heritage, I thought. I had heard genius skipped a generation, and I figured that held true as well for wanderlust. Maybe, like Grandpa, I was meant to be out there knocking around. It was my destiny.

I shook my head to clear away those thoughts, looked down at my book, and tried to study. Then I thought about Cuba again -- that fight when two drunk sailors slammed into one another, knocking out teeth, breaking each other's noses, throwing blood over a group of whores standing nearby. The girls screamed and moved farther back, but no one tried to break up the fight. I looked back at my open, unread sociology book and yawned.

I didn't take many of my finals that January 1964. Midway through the exam period I packed all my clothes, left without saying good-bye to anyone, and drove my old junker station wagon back toward Southern Pines. In Sanford, I stopped at the Army recruiting office and signed up for three years in the infantry.

At home, I went into the kitchen and told Mother what I had done. When Daddy came in from the office, he stood in the doorway and smiled. Then he caught Mother's dour look and his smile froze.

"I've joined the Army, Dad." I tried to sound upbeat, but my voice broke.

Dad walked over and slumped into his chair. The last rays of sunlight coming through the half-drawn blinds did little to brighten the gloom. Finally he said, "That's dumb." After a pause, he said, "Dealing with you is like trying to push a rope." Then he just stared out the window as if a great calamity had befallen the family.

On February 4, 1964, Mother and Daddy took me to Little's Gulf Service Station on the edge of town and we waited in the car for a bus to take me to the induction center in Raleigh, the state capital. They both cried. I told them everything was going to be OK, wondering as I said it why the bus was taking so long.

It finally arrived, coming to a stop in front of our car with a hiss of its air brakes. I kissed Mother on the cheek and reached over the seat and shook Daddy's hand. After boarding the bus, I looked out the window and saw the car parked off to the side of the service station. Mother was in the front and Daddy in the back, a sad, out of the ordinary sight. As the bus pulled out, Mother waved good-bye and I could see her smile. Daddy had his head down.

Grandpa's departures were probably just as melancholy.

The Vietnam War Its Ownself

****

The boys and young men sitting around the U.S. Army induction center in Raleigh looked like they belonged in the lost and found. I spent the afternoon mindlessly leafing through crumpled sports magazines that lay on tables by the worn Naugahyde couches. Eventually I was called to a desk and signed my official enlistment papers. Later, everyone went into another room. An Air Force captain with a tired voice asked us to raise our right hands and officially swore us into military service. He then wished us good luck and added that he thought most of us would need it.

The next morning, we went by train and bus to Fort Jackson, South Carolina, where we were processed into the Army. On the morning of the tenth day there -- sheared to the skull, tested, vaccinated, wearing new ill-fitting fatigues, scared -- my group fell into formation in front of the barracks with our duffel bags and boarded Army buses for basic training at Fort Gordon, Georgia. No longer "INductees," as we had been called in the processing center, we were off to become "BOOTS."

At Fort Gordon the bus convoy pulled in front of our training company headquarters. "Company C" was painted on a brick-and-concrete sign out front. The doors to the bus opened, and I saw a "Smokey Bear" drill sergeant hat above a square-jawed black face rise over the two boys in the front row. Standing almost at attention beside the bus driver, the man slowly moved his eyes over the interior of the bus. Outside we heard the shrill shouts of other noncommissioned officers (NCOs) as they rushed recruits off the buses. There was a tense pause as the sergeant continued to look around. Finally he spoke in a low, smooth and slow, southern voice, "Welcome to Fort Gordon, Georgia, boys and girls. Ma name is Staff Sergeant Willie O. McGee. I am ya drill instructor. I'm going to make ya soldiers or ya'll find ya ugly asses run clean into this red Georgia dirt. Everyone stand up."

Everyone tried to push things aside and get to their feet. "Stand up, goddamnit." The voice suddenly became loud and frightfully mean. "Stand ya worthless civilian asses up, get off dis fucking bus and form four ranks in da company street."

The recruits in front tried to get off quickly, but Sergeant McGee was blocking their way as he climbed slowly off the bus. As he moved aside, we fought one another to get out and into a sloppy formation.

Standing before us, Staff Sergeant McGee was an impressive

figure. Ramrod straight and deathly still, he moved only his eyes. His voice carried easily to the back ranks. He advised us to respond quickly as he "learned" us how to soldier. The Army "weren't" patient, didn't cater to individuals. The "onliest" way to act was to do exactly what he told us to -- no more, no less. He picked one of the largest men, by the name of McDiarmid to be the recruit platoon leader and four other large men to be squad leaders and positioned them to the right.

He said that he would not attempt anything silly yet, like trying to make us march or even to fall out of formation in a military manner. He said, "Pick up ya duffel bags and go into da barracks behind ya, squads one and two on one side, squads three and four on da other and try to do hit without falling down."

Sergeant McGee followed us inside and paced the aisle while we claimed either top or bottom of the bunk beds. Calling us to line up at attention at the end of our bunks, he walked by and corrected the stances of most of us. I stared off into the distance when he stopped briefly in front of me.

Finished, he told us that he graduated the best soldiers in the company, possibly in the whole training command. "Nobody skates," he said, "not no greasy Puerto Ricans," as he bent down close to one of the Puerto Ricans, "not no angry Negroes," as he put his nose close to the face of a very large black man, and "not no educated molly-wolly shithead," as he moved farther down the line past me and bent in close to a skinny country boy from Tennessee.

"I think I have made myself clear about what I expect, but I knows from experience dat some of ya ain't understood me, gonn'a be slow, won't follow orders, gonn'a want'a fall out. But listen here. Dis is my platoon. I own ya ass. You'll learn to do it right or I will get rid of ya." He turned to leave and then turned back, "Oh, and one more thing. I do not like ya, any of ya, and I don't want ya for a friend, any of ya. Don't try to be nice to me. Stay away. Do not talk with me. Do not come close to me unless ya have to. I do not want to know ya first names, I do not want to know about'sa dog or ya Momma or dat ya girlfriend's pregnant. Stay away from me. See the Chaplain if ya want to talk with someone nice. I am Drill Sergeant Willie O. McGee. Stay da fuck away."

The recruit across from me made eye contact and bounced his eyebrows as Sergeant McGee left. I did not acknowledge him but turned to the task of making my bed.

Throughout that day and the next, McGee was with us constantly. Up and down the lines, shouting, cussing, correcting us in our dress and our drill. I stayed in the middle of the platoon, safely

6

out of his way.

The second night, I was brushing my teeth in the latrine when the recruit who bunked across the aisle, the one who had bounced his eyebrows at me, came up to the next sink and started washing his face. "McGee is a rather persuasive fellow," he said. "Direct. I like that in a man."

I turned and smiled, possibly for the first time since I had arrived at the induction center in Raleigh. He said his name was Van Pelt and he had signed on because he had lost interest in college. He was from Cape Canaveral, Florida, where his father worked as an engineer. He said he was doing fine in school until he got a little sports car and then something happened -- there were all those beach parties and hangovers. He forgot to go to class one semester, so he joined the Army. But he was finding the experience rather boorish and was considering asking for the papers he had signed to see if there was an escape clause. Possibly there was a legitimate breach of contract here. He sought a more casual routine.

Coming into the latrine about the same time was a large black man named Tate (alias), whom McGee had jumped on that morning for being too slow in reciting his serial number. Another black man going out the door bumped into him and Tate shoved him away, growling. He went in the shower room mumbling to himself. Several other people came out of the shower quickly, some still lathered with soap rather than stay in the shower with that very large, very black, very intimidating man.

The third day we were issued field web gear that we had to display over our lockers -- packs, canteens, ammo pouches, canteen belts, and suspenders. We also received helmets along with their protective steel outer shells, called "steel pots." I noticed one man was having difficulty putting his gear together properly and I watched him for several minutes. Even with his GI haircut it was apparent that he was balding. He had a large head, a skinny neck, no shoulders, a pudgy middle, big butt and short legs. He wore thick glasses which he kept pushing up his nose as he tried to adjust his gear. I resisted an impulse to help him. The chore was so simple, and the fellow seemed so helpless. I decided he was exactly the reason that Cottonpicker had told me to mind my own business during basic training. Van Pelt went over later and arranged the man's web gear for him. He also helped adjust the webbing inside the helmet liner and with the steel pot encasement in place, Van Pelt put the helmet on the head of the man to check the fit. It fit too low and the man looked silly. His big glasses barely showed underneath plus his neck was so skinny that he had trouble holding his head up under the weight of his steel pot. His head wobbled from side to side. He looked like a turkey. Van Pelt continued to make adjustments until he got the helmet to fit properly. The man sat silently as Van Pelt worked. Van Pelt finally left and, after going to his bunk for a moment, came over to my bunk. Looking the other way, he said that he thought the "professor," a draftee, was out of his element. He said the man smelt a trifle rank too.

Later we were told to put on our web gear and fall out into formation outside -- falling into and out of formation being a large part of our first few days. I noticed that the professor had his web suspenders twisted in the back. They were the least of his worries however, because he was having considerable problems as he tried to hold up his head under the steel pot.

Sergeant McGee came up to the formation from the rear and spotted the professor's twisted suspenders. He walked up to the man and said, "How do ya feel, Molly-Wolly? Don't shake ya head at me, recruit. Do ya hear me, quit shaking ya frigging head!" McGee's face was contorted in anger. "I said goddamnit quit shaking ya frigging head." I could see McGee's face soften after a while. "Is ya hat too heavy for ya, Molly-Wolly? Are ya so fucking weak dat ya can't wear a steel pot? OK, I can understand dat. I can understand." McGee stood there for a moment and looked the professor in the eye. "But ya know ya look like a smart young fellow to me. I gotta question for ya. How come ya fucking suspenders are twisted? Dat don't take no goddamned strength. Ya got to think, Molly-Wolly, think."

The professor turned his head to one side, still wobbling from the weight of the steel pot, and I could see tears welling up in his eyes. McGee continued to look into the professor's face, and he too saw the tears. I quickly turned my gaze to the front as McGee looked around to see who else was watching the man cry.

"Go inside now, double time, and get ya suspenders fixed, soldier, and come back out shere. Now, move out. Now. Go."

My first thought was that McGee was maybe a nice guy. A nasty individual, like he had pretended to be, would have embarrassed the professor about the tears. McGee told the squad leaders to check each member of their squad to make sure the equipment was on right, and he went into the barracks. The professor soon came out and regained his place in the formation.

That night at retreat, the professor fell out of the barracks with his shirttail out of his pants. McGee hesitated as he saw the man awkwardly run by to get in formation, but when he saw the professor fall in without tucking his shirt in, McGee walked up to him. He told him that he was a disgrace to the platoon, the U.S. Army, and the human race and, because of that, he was number one on McGee's list of people to watch.

Before lights out that night Van Pelt sat on my bunk and polished his shoes. He said, "Life's relative, you know. It's a proven scientific theory -- The Theory of Relativity. You are judged against your peers. Like, for example, two men in the woods, surprised by a bear, were running away, the bear at their heels, and one man said he sure hoped he was faster than that bear and the other man said, 'I only hope I'm faster'n you.' That guy understood the theory. Wasn't necessary to be the fastest man in the universe there, only the faster of the two of them. The bear got the slow one. You see what I mean, things are relative. Life's relative to the situation. Here at Fort Gordon, it don't help if you're smart or rich, look like a movie star, or got the greatest little sports car in the world back home. Not relative. Takes primitive instincts here. Semi-developed playground skills and the muscle tone of a marathon runner don't hurt either. Don't think the professor, relatively speaking, is packing the right gear here. He ain't playground material."

The professor was sitting on his bed, awkwardly bent over shining his shoes. He stopped often to push his glasses back up his nose. "You know," Van Pelt said with a smile, "it makes me feel better about myself here when I see how out of place the ol' professor is over there. Relative to him, I'm OK."

I told Van Pelt that it was because he was basically a blunt instrument -- primal man, comparable to Tate, the Neanderthal looking black man. Van Pelt said that was a clever observation. "Not correct," he added, "but a good comment anyway, about a three on a scale to five. Above average. Maybe you should be the one dealing with the professor, since you're so clever."

"No," I said, "you are the one with the mother instinct. I'm here to learn to kill."

"You, my friend," said Van Pelt, "are the blunt instrument, but I like you anyway."

The next morning when we fell out for reveille, Sergeant McGee inspected the barracks. He came out and addressed us from the top of the stairs before we marched off to the mess hall.

"OK, slimeballs, I walked into da barracks just now and hit smelt like a urinal. Like a goddamned piss pot. Ya hear me. A fucking piss pot. Someone peed in dere bed last night!"

McGee was talking so loud that people standing in formation by other barracks could hear.

"Then goddamnit made da bed up on top of da stinking piss!" He walked down the stairs and up to the platoon. "My fucking platoon. We got ourselves a bed wetter. In da fucking Army." Softer,

9

meaner, he asked, "Guess who it is?" He walked through the first squad line to the professor. "Who Molly-Wolly? Who?" McGee fixed a hard, steady look at the man.

"Me, Sergeant," said the professor softly.

"Ya go in dere while da rest of us are in da chow hall and ya get dat stinking mess and ya exchange it for clean stuff and ya have yar bed made before we get back. And ya take a shower. And, Molly-Wolly, I ain't finished." McGee grabbed his arm, "I am going to help ya get over dis. I'm going to stop ya from wetting da bed. Tonight. Ya'll stop. I'll show ya. I done it before."

That evening, Sergeant McGee walked into the barracks and everyone quickly braced to attention. The drill sergeant's footfalls were loud as he walked toward the professor's bunk. McGee scowled at him a moment, then went down the line to Tate's bunk. He told the man who slept on the top bunk over Tate to trade places with the professor.

Van Pelt was standing across from me. He pursed his lips and squinted his eyes, as if in pain, when he realized what McGee was doing. Tate was possibly the most ill-tempered individual in the world. Not only did people leave the shower room when he entered, they were reluctant to stand behind him in the chow line for fear they might accidentally bump into him and set him off. He was an animal. No one even tried to get along with him.

After McGee left, Tate grabbed the professor's t-shirt and told him in words that were hard to understand but whose tone was expressively clear what would happen to him if he peed in the top bunk. One of the black men suggested that Tate kill the honkey right now rather than later, because he was sure to piss in his sleep again.

The last thing we heard that night after lights out was Tate's muttered warning to the professor, "OK, mudder fucker, wet da bed and I'll knock ya fucking head off, ya hear?"

The next morning the professor was up and dressed before anyone else. He looked tired. Van Pelt guessed that he had not slept at all that night. And he did not sleep the next night.

The professor went on sick call the following morning after breakfast. When we returned from training before lunch, his equipment was gone. We never saw him again.

****

A couple of days later we drew our rifles, the venerable M-14s. As we gathered outside the armory, I inspected my issue and tested its balance. It was an older rifle that had probably been handled

10

by young recruits for years. Its stock had been restained and revarnished many times; the butt plate was scratched from hard landings in the manual of arms. The trigger mechanism was worn from a thousand training disassemblies and assemblies. The weapon looked like a tired old piece of rental equipment with no character and I remembered the love affair I had with the Springfield at Oak Ridge Military Institute. The shoulder strap was old, tattered webbing, and I tightened it as tight as I could so that the strap would slap smartly against the stock when I handled it.

McGee called us into ranks and talked about the value of the rifle, the main tool of our trade. He said that before we learned to shoot it, we had to learn to respect it and to handle it correctly. Our training for the next couple of days would be in the manual of arms -- moving the weapons from the ground at our sides, as we stood at attention, to "port arms" and then to "right shoulder arms" and "left shoulder arms" and finally back to the ground, "order arms." I stood in the middle of the platoon and thought about going through the manual of arms a hundred thousand times at Oak Ridge. This was like explaining the fundamentals of walking to an experienced hiker.

Taking a rifle from a man in the first squad, McGee demonstrated the movements. He gave himself the commands and brought the weapon up and then back to the ground again, with a bit too much waggle in his movement, I thought; he would have been reprimanded at Oak Ridge. Then he talked us through them slowly -- count one, port arms; count two, right shoulder arms; count three, back to port arms; count four, left shoulder arms; count five, order arms -- before giving the commands at regular speed.

The rifle movement felt familiar, and I slapped the rifle strap as I brought it up and down. I also snapped the butt plate with my thumb as I went to right shoulder arms so that it twisted quickly into the crevice of my shoulder. I was careful to move only my arms and to keep the rest of my body absolutely still, as we had been taught on the drill team. With some pleasure, I noticed that the men in front of me were awkwardly moving their shoulders and heads as they lumbered through the drill. McGee was counting cadence as we repeated the movement. He abruptly stopped counting in mid-movement, and the platoon finished with the random clamoring of metal butt plates on the company street.

Out of the corner of my eye, I saw McGee looking in my direction. Without a word, he came through the first two ranks and stood directly in front of me. He cocked his head to one side and eyed me quizzically.

My face flushed. I had been found out. I had not stayed out

of sight, and now I had come to McGee's attention. He looked at my name tag, then down at my M-14, and slowly up my uniform back to my face.

"Parker," he said, "do dat again."

I brought the weapon back to my right shoulder, but I did not slap the strap or snap my thumb on the butt plate. McGee told me no, do it again and make it pop, and I did. He told me to come out in front of the platoon and gave me the manual of arms orders there. When I returned the rifle to the ground he came around in front of me and got very close to my face.

"What's going on here?" he asked, "Where'd ya learn to do dat shit?" I told him military school, and he said "Huh."

He stepped away and ordered me to do a left face, right face, about face, and then the manual of arms again. I moved with precision. McGee moved in front of me and again said, "Huh."

It was altogether a grand moment, enhanced, I realized, by Van Pelt's explanation of "The Theory of Relativity." I forced myself not to smile. In the hot Georgia sun that day I had done a simple thing very well, and I felt good about myself.

"I would equate your little majorette act today as the high point so far in our little adventure here," Van Pelt told me. We were sitting on the barracks steps and smoking after the dinner meal. "Life will not be the same for you around here my friend. McGee actually said something nice to you. Who knows the consequences."

"What did he say? Tell me again."

"He said, 'Huh,' like in 'Huh, that's pretty good.' He's never said 'Huh' to anyone I know."

At the end of the second week, we received classroom instruction on guard duties and the eleven General Orders that applies. We were told that we had the weekend and most of the next week to memorize all of the orders. A test was scheduled for the end of the following week. McGee talked to us before we were dismissed that day and said that platoons in the company would be ranked against each other based on the test scores. The General Orders were just simple English sentences. He wanted the platoon to make the best scores in the company, and he ordered everyone to learn the General Orders perfectly. He walked up to Tate and said, "Even ya, fat lips, perfectly. I'm going to call ya out da morning of da test and ya going to recite ya General Orders. And if dis man can do hit -- and he's going to do hit -- each and every one of ya can learn dese eleven very simple little sentences."

It did not take long to memorize the orders and I sat on my bunk during study time over the next week and read other manuals. I noticed Tate slowly, painfully reading his General Orders, over and over again. He moved his lips and occasionally squinted his eyes as he focused on a particular phrase or word. After supper the night before the test, he returned to the manual with dogged determination, but his efforts remained the same -- slowly reading the orders over and over again. I walked down to his bunk.

"How's it going?"

He looked up quickly, angrily. "Ain't none of ya fucking business," he said? "Why ya wanta know?"

"I know that learning the General Orders can be tough but there are tricks to memorizing things for tests."

"Fuck ya," he said flatly.

"Listen." I sat down on the end of his bunk, which I got away with because Tate was desperate. "Number one, you got to play games with your mind, Tate. Take General Order No. 1 for example. I say to myself, what's the first thing I do in the morning? I charge -- Charge -- out of bed and take a shit on government property. First General Order? To take charge of this post and all government property in view. The second thing I do is to walk -- Walk back to my bunk by that post near the head and look at everybody. That's the second General Order: To walk my post in a military manner, keeping always on the alert and observing everything that takes place within sight or hearing. First General Order, I charge. Second General Order, I walk. First thing I do in the morning, charge -- government property. Second thing I do in the morning, walk -- observe."

Tate looked away, but he was listening to me.

"First General Order, to take charge of this post and all government property in view. Come outside in the back and we'll go over the rest. I'm going to smoke a cigarette anyway."

I got up and walked out by the latrine. The only light outside came through the door from the barracks. I sat on the stairs and lit a cigarette. Tate soon appeared at the door and walked down the few stairs to where I was sitting.

"What's the first thing you do in the morning?" I asked without looking his way.

"I charge out da bed for a shit on government property."

We went over each order, making nonsense out of them, but connecting them in sequence. Slowly at first and then with confidence he repeated them in order, then randomly as I called out the numbers. I told him he would do fine the next day and went inside and went to bed.

The next morning McGee called Tate in front of the platoon and asked him to give the fifth General Order. Tate hesitated a

13

moment, then spoke clearly and loudly, "To quit my post only when properly relieved, Sergeant."

McGee asked him the seventh and Tate responded quickly, "To talk to no one except in the line of duty, Sergeant."

McGee said, "Huh," as he backed away from Tate and looked at him. He sent Tate back into ranks and walked up to Van Pelt. "OK, Molly-Wolly, what's da fucking tenth General Order?"

Van Pelt hesitated. Then in a short burst, he said, "To give the alarm in case of fire or disorder, Sergeant."

"Asshole, dat's da eighth fucking order, you jack shit Molly-Wolly idiot" Out of the corner of my eye, I could see Tate smiling despite himself, as he rocked back and forth slightly on his heels.

At breakfast Van Pelt asked me if I thought being a "jack shit Molly-Wolly idiot" was hereditary.

The next week Cassius Clay was to fight Sonny Liston for the heavyweight championship of the world, and Tate and I decided that Liston would break Clay's smart-ass face. Liston was a three-to-one favorite, and it was hard to get a bet on Clay in our company. I offered five-to-one. Ten dollars on Clay would get fifty if he won and I had some takers. No money passed hands before the fight, but Van Pelt kept the books. I had almost five hundred dollars of my money at risk, having taken in one hundred dollars in committed bets on Clay. I was slightly overextended; we were making only $84 a month as Army privates. I would be about three hundred dollars short if Liston lost but I saw no problem. Liston was absolutely a sure bet. Tate promised to help me collect.

We listened to the fight on the radio. Liston did not answer the bell to the seventh round -- despite my desperate yells -- and I was suddenly surrounded by people who wanted to collect on their bets. I had to scurry around that night and borrow money from McDiarmid, Tate, and Van Pelt to cover my losses. Van Pelt said it was a typical low-life maneuver to lay long odds on a loser. He reckoned it did not bode well for my life as a risk taker, as in being a soldier or fighting a war or something. To do any soldiering, one needed to be lucky. He wasn't sure this line of work was up my alley -- "You lost five hundred dollars -- that's more than you make in six months, you dumb Molly-Wolly."

Tate became something of a shadow, sitting beside me in class and in the mess hall. He simply had no social skills, and I often acted as his spokesman. In turn, he provided security and an intimidating presence to others when we were together, an enhanced status not lost on Sergeant McGee. I was awarded "Outstanding Trainee" at graduation from basic training. As we were packing up to go to separate advanced infantry training (AIT) companies, I went down to Tate's bunk. He was reading a comic book. I wished him well in life. "Yea," he said, but he did not smile, as if our brief friendship was over and he was going back to his more hostile, antisocial nature, the only way he knew to meet the challenges ahead.

Along with many other recruits, Van Pelt and I put in for Officer Candidate School (OCS) during the last week of basic training. We were together in AIT and, during a slow training session, we began exchanging notes. In one convoluted, pseudo-intellectual analogy, I took the position of a weed in life, ugly by urban standards but durable and adaptive. Van Pelt claimed that if I was a weed, he was a flower, cultured and beautiful -- a more attractive standard. Our notes were crazy, surreal flights of fantasy, and we worried occasionally what our drill sergeants might think if they read them, especially when I found out my friend's entire given name and began addressing him as "Miss Elmer Lee Van Pelt the Third, the Flower Child."

Within weeks of starting AIT, people in our company began to get rejection notices on their OCS applications. The notices were form letters sent regular mail. This made mail call after retreat at night very tense. I looked forward to letters from home, but I hated to hear my name called for fear it would be the rejection notice. It was like Russian roulette.

One night after supper, I went over to Van Pelt's barracks. He was sitting on his bed and writing a letter. As usual, he smiled broadly as we talked about our planned weekend together in Augusta, Georgia, home of the Masters and blue-eyed southern belles who "luved" skinhead GIs from Fort Gordon. I was leaving when he said, "Hey, weed, this came in the mail to me tonight." He tossed his OCS rejection notice on the bunk. He went back to writing as I read the form letter. He looked up after a while and shrugged his shoulders. I left without a word.

When AIT training was completed, Van Pelt received his orders to an infantry unit. I did not see him when he came to my barracks to say good-bye; I had been sent on detail across post. When I returned the following note was on my bunk:

Jim,
You weed, you low, scummy, slimy, slob
of a worthless infectious grub. Despair ingrate,
the beauty and inspiration which you leaned on
like a crutch has left you, leaving you to wallow
in the crud of your mind, like a snake in the mud.

15

James E. Parker, Jr.

Crawl weed, wither and die. Love, beauty, fun,
happiness is gone. The flower has triumphed, herd
your miasmic children, change their pants, and tell
them their stories, you pimp, weed. Ugh? Leave
the world and all its charms to men, not nursemaids,
scouts.

Ha? I despise you, fool. Wilt weed, there is nothing left,
don't try to retaliate, it's too late. I tried to show you the
light, now you must burn. Weed, burn bright, and perhaps,
for once in your inglorious, dark, misery laden life a bright
spot might shine.

Burn Weed. Burn.

****

After AIT there were almost eighty of us, still awaiting disposition of our OCS applications, who were assigned to two barracks near my AIT training company. I was given temporary corporal rank, which I wore on a band around my upper-right sleeve, and assigned to a basic training company as an assistant DI (drill instructor) or "gopher," as in commands from the regular DIs, "Hey shithead, go for this, or go for that."

Almost every day, someone in our group received a rejection notice from OCS. When we came in at night a mattress would be folded back and the bed coverings gone -- like tombstones of the departed.

Five weeks after I graduated from AIT we heard that someone across post in another holding company had been accepted to OCS for the November 1964 class. Following this first acceptance, we all had new hope, but then came a spate of rejection notices. Our eighty-man group was reduced to twenty. One barracks was closed, and we finally moved down to a single floor. Every night, another mattress had been turned down. We continued to hear of other candidates receiving acceptance, but no one in our group had been selected.

I came in one night from a long march with the basic training company and found a notice to see the first sergeant at our holding company headquarters. He and I had had a run-in during the previous week over the weekend duty roster, and he had threatened to put a reprimand in my OCS application folder. He was an unlikable,

16

crass individual and I knew the message to see him was related to extra duty that weekend. He was in the company commander's office when I entered the orderly room. The door was open and the commander caught my eye and motioned me into his office. I was sweaty and dirty from the road march and regretted not cleaning up before answering the first sergeant's summons, but I walked in and saluted. The commander stuck out his hand and said, "Congratulations." I had been accepted for the November OCS class.

-- TWO--
Command Training

On November 15, 1964, after home leave, I drove my uncle's maroon 1949 Ford from Southern Pines to the Infantry Officer Candidate School at Fort Benning, Georgia. Parked across the street from the three-story barracks of the OCS company that I was to join, I sat silently smoking, as I watched new OCS candidates arrive. Immediately, they were set upon and summarily hazed by both the senior candidates in blue helmet liners and the more lethal commissioned officers assigned to the school as instructors. These officers, referred to as "Tac officers," were cool predators, hanging back in the shadows until they decided on a new candidate to attack. They walked up to a new man, called him to attention over some slight, got close to him and talked angrily -- sometimes fast but sometimes, for effect, very slowly. Even from where I sat it was apparent that the comments of the Tac officers were hard hitting, as they evoked painful grimaces from the candidates.

I resolved to ignore them -- that had been Cottonpicker's advice. Show no emotion, take nothing personal, find out what you are expected to do, and do it. "It's not a personality contest," he had said. "OCS is a six-month test to find the fuck-ups. That's it. Don't fuck up. You got it more'n half licked getting to the school. That's the hard part. Don't fuck up. Don't try too hard. They'll try to break you down, you're going to get tired and sometimes you're going to want to quit, just keep on. Don't show emotion. Keep on. Don't fuck up."

I put out my cigarette, got my duffel bag out of the trunk, and walked across the street. As I expected, I was immediately attacked by blue-helmeted upperclassmen. I stood at attention and responded to their loud orders to get my chin in, suck in my gut, straighten up my back, get my gig line straight.

"I saw you sitting in the car across the street, candidate."

Someone had come up to my right side and was talking into my ear. His voice was lower in tone but clearer than the voices of the upperclassmen yelling in my face about my shave and haircut. I could feel the man's breath.

"I do not know why you were sitting in your car for so long, but I do not like it."

The man moved in front of me, his nose a couple of inches from mine. The blue-helmeted upperclassmen moved aside, as if they were getting out the way so the big dog could eat.

"I do not like sneaky people. The Army wants its officers to be upright. Men of character." He continued to speak in a low, soft voice. "You, I am going to watch very closely. This is no joke, candidate. I don't like you. I am going to get you out of here. I don't like your looks, I don't like your sitting in a car spying. You are finished before you start because you're a sneak. You're finished, I guarantee it. I'm going to kick your sniveling little young ass out. I'm gonna do it. I promise."

I looked straight ahead into the distance and did not focus on the Tac officer in front of me. I tried to show no emotion. He stepped back.

"Look at me. Look at my face. Look at my name. I am Tactical Officer Lieutenant Taylor. Every time you see me for the next week -- every time you see me -- drop down and give me twenty push-ups. You understand? It's going to be my way of telling you to get out."

"Yes, sir," I shouted.

"Drop now, and count them out loud."

I did the push-ups. When I got back to my feet beside my duffel bag, Taylor was gone.

Eventually I made my way into the orderly room and was assigned to the fourth platoon on the third floor. As I tried to go up the stairs I was constantly assaulted by blue-helmeted upperclassmen yelling, "Up against the wall, candidate," or "Give me ten, candidate."

Later that first day, we were called out to formation, and the ever-yelling upperclassmen arranged us alphabetically, by platoon. Standing as still as possible to avoid harassment, I could see from their name tags that a Nesse was on my right and a Particelli on my left. I did not know or care to know the names of anyone else in the platoon.

After a time, the blue-helmeted men moved behind us and a slight, serious-looking young officer moved in front of the platoon.

The Vietnam War Its Ownself

"My name is Lieutenant Joseph C. Hailey," he said in a conversational tone. "I am the 4th Platoon Tactical officer. The U.S. Army has asked me to find out who among you isn't qualified to be an officer. And you know what, most of you aren't. Not," he said, with emphasis, "because you aren't smart. You are all smart. Not," he said, again with emphasis, "because you don't want to be officers. You all do. No, most of you are not qualified because of," he paused for emphasis, "need. The U.S. Army just doesn't have much room in the officer corps right now. It doesn't matter if you are all relatives of MacArthur or Eisenhower, the Army doesn't need us to manufacture many second lieutenants. They're going to take the West Pointer and the ROTC grads first, and this year there're plenty. So there are not many openings. Sorry," he said. "It's just the way it is. Most of you are going to be weeded out."

At the end of the first week, we were introduced to the most insidious aspect of the weeding-out process -- the infamous "bayonet" sheets, in which everyone ranked everyone else in the platoon. Every Friday each member of the platoon submitted, on a single sheet of notebook paper, names of all the other men in the platoon listed in order, according to the way we judged their individual officer potential. The man we thought would make the best officer was number one, the man we thought was least qualified, was last. The "bayonet" sheet got its name because of the knife job that one could do on his contemporaries. With thirty-five people in the platoon submitting a bayonet sheet every week for eleven weeks, a lot of evaluation was developed. The total process, called peer or student rating, counted for much in assessing the overall officer potential of each candidate.

There were exacting, almost impossible, housekeeping standards in OCS, certainly more demanding than anything I had known in military school, basic training or AIT. We lived in two-man rooms. My roommate, an older, former noncommissioned officer, and I spent our first weekend shining every square of our linoleum tile floor with hard wax and spit. We cut cardboard within a fraction of an inch to fit inside our clothes on display in our wall locker and chest of drawers. We used a ruler to get our boots lined up properly under our beds and to get the right distance between items of clothing in the closet. We brassoed the door hinges, washed the windows, polished our desks, and cleaned every piece of our equipment.

On Monday morning, Tac Officer Taylor came in and dumped our stuff in the middle of the floor. Despite myself, I pursed my lips and said "Shit" under my breath. Taylor whipped around.

"What did you say, candidate? Did I hear you say

19

something? This candidate cursed me, I do believe. I will see you in formation."

There, he called me out of ranks and ordered me to run around the company as it marched toward Building No. 4, where we had most of our classes. This was not easy, especially when I had to cut across the front of the marching company. Taylor called me back into the rear ranks of the fourth platoon before we reached the building. When we stopped, one of the candidates near me said, "I think that man out there likes you."

"You want an introduction?" I responded.

"Nope," he half-whispered back, "I don't want him to know my name."

When we received the order to fall out to class, I looked at the candidate who had spoken. His name was Larry ("Pete") Peterson and I learned later that he was from Lincoln, Nebraska. Before coming to OCS he had been the PFC driver for the commander of a medical battalion at the Fort Benning hospital. Of medium build, he was wholesome looking, straight-forward and he cackled when he laughed.

Tac Officer Taylor's attentions continued. Pete thought it was because Taylor sensed -- right or wrong -- that I had a cocky attitude. Pete worked with me on appearing humble, but he finally gave up, "You're just an asshole, I reckon, and Taylor seems to know that."

When I was assigned as platoon leader and had to march the platoon to an assembly area on the athletic field, Lieutenant Taylor walked briskly at my side. During most of the march, he yelled obscenities, particularly as I prepared to give commands to the platoon.

Early the following week, we had our first written test on leadership. Although it required reading during our study period at night, I had used my time surreptitiously to clean my equipment, that being Lieutenant Taylor's focus of the week with me. Just before lights out on the night before the test, I told Pete I wasn't ready; I was just going to have to wing it. Ten minutes after lights out I heard a "psssss," by the door to my room. It was Pete. He told me to get the blanket from the foot of my bed and follow him into the latrine. As we huddled under the blanket in the showers, Pete shared his notes.

Because of Pete, I passed the test the next day.

Sometime later that week we made a pledge to help each other get through OCS. There was strength in numbers, we said. Thereafter I made him number one on my bayonet sheet. Pete ran interference for me whenever Lieutenant Taylor was around and tried

20

to distract him. This often cost him push-up punishment. When Pete's roommate dropped out, I moved in with him.

We worked well together, Pete and I, though we both had a sense of fun and irreverence that was a liability. As the weeks progressed, we became more accepting of the traditional OCS hazing and no longer took the constant harassment personally, except with Taylor.

Classroom instruction was interspersed with field exercises, with emphasis on leadership training. According to our instructors, our effectiveness as future infantry officers depended on our ability to motivate and lead men. Respect, fairness, humor, poise, determination, confidence, and empathy were characteristics of good leaders. Vanity, laziness, and sarcasm were not. Smart-asses don't make good leaders, we were told. Peterson looked at me and shook his head.

Veterans of World War II and the Korean War spoke to us about the demands on a small-unit commander in combat. One old gnarled NCO said personal courage was essential in leading men under fire. A good combat leader had to be a natural risk taker or he had to summon the will to get in harm's way from within -- either way, courage appeared the same. Infantry officers must be courageous to do their jobs in war and South Vietnam was our likely testing ground.

"South what?" someone asked.

"South Vietnam," the veteran said, "is a small jungle country in the Orient and American soldiers are fighting and dying there."

I had heard Vietnam mentioned occasionally during basic and AIT training, but it was never discussed outside the classrooms that I remember. However it seemed more relevant now and we talked about it among ourselves during the next break. Everyone pronounced it differently.

"What are we doing in Vieeet-nammmm, really?" someone asked.

"Killing Commies," someone else said.

"OK, that's legal."

At the end of the eleventh week at OCS, all candidates faced an evaluation. Those who fell below a certain rating had to go before a panel, ostensibly to defend their records. In fact, candidates who were paneled were usually kicked out of the program or recycled to another company, regardless of what they said. It was the weeding-out process at work.

The panel was scheduled for Friday morning, January 29, 1965.

21

On Wednesday morning before the panel we fell out for a PT run, although the rumor circulated that it was to test endurance and would have a bearing on those selected for the panel.

Wearing t-shirts, fatigue pants, and boots, we left the company area and shuffled along in formation. A candidate at the side led us in marching songs. It was a warm morning and Pete and I were shuffling along side by side, singing. Occasionally we would windmill our arms. Ah, it was good to be young and in shape. We could take the run.

We trotted out to one of the rifle ranges along a dusty tank trail. The dust became more of a problem as time went on. As we approached the rifle ranges, the candidate singing cadence fell back into ranks because we expected to take a break when we arrived. There were endurance runs, and there were death marches.

Several Tac officers, however, were standing poised in the assembly area of the rifle ranges. An ambulance was parked in the shade next to a couple of deuce-and-a-half trucks. This did not look good. "Damn if it don't look like an execution squad," I told Pete. "Them trucks for the deal bodies, you reckon?"

The Tac leading us fell out. Lieutenant Taylor took the lead and told the guidon bearer to follow him. He made a big circle on the rifle range, then headed the company back toward our barracks, almost seven miles away.

Taylor came back to the middle of the company file and told us that we were not to kill ourselves. An ambulance was right behind us, and the deuce-and-a-halfs would take the dropouts back to the company. "No problem," he said. "If you can't go on, stop. No problem." And he smiled at me. "I'm talking to you Parker. Drop out, it'll be OK."

The formation began to break down. Some of the older candidates fell back as the young bucks moved to the front. Pete and I kept our places.

By the time we had run ten miles -- seven out and three back -- we were back on pavement again and the dust ceased being a problem, but we were thirsty and becoming more and more leg weary. "Keep going," Pete said. "We're almost home, more than half finished." Behind us, members of the company stretched out into the distance.

Taylor turned us off on a side road and then off onto a fire break, and we started shuffling up a long bumpy hill. Pete and I began to fall back -- save our strength, we told ourselves. We didn't have to finish first.

As we made the hill, Taylor and some of the candidates

pulled ahead, and we stumbled down the other side. Then we climbed another hill -- and another and another -- until we were on the paved road again. Taylor was five city blocks ahead of us.

Pete and I said we could make it. We could see the barracks. We could make it. We were not going to be paneled. We were going to make it.

When Taylor reached the company assembly area, he dropped out and fresh Tacs led the first of the candidates around the barracks and out toward a PT field in the distance.

We were not stopping at the company. We were not almost finished. My feet felt suddenly ten pounds heavier. Pete cursed under his breath. I glanced at him. He looked like death -- filthy, sweaty, bloodshot eyes, face contorted in fatigue, mouth open with dirt crusted around the edges. He started repeating, "We ain't quitting, we ain't quitting." I began to say it, but it took precious breath, so I stopped.

We stumbled through the company area to the PT field and around the quarter mile track and then back to the company area where the run mercifully ended. Pete and I fell out on the grass and gasped for breath. We came up on our elbows and smiled at each other. A deuce-and-a-half pulled up with the woebegone candidates who had fallen out.

After retreat the following day two Tac officers took their platoons off to the side of the company assembly area and read out the names of the candidates who were being paneled the next morning. Two other Tacs posted names on the walls in the individual platoon areas.

Lieutenant Hailey, our Tac officer, wasn't around, and we found nothing posted on the walls in our area.

During supper word circulated about the "panelees;" it was a massacre. Half of the 2nd, 3rd, and 6th Platoons were going and almost all of the young guys in the 5th Platoon. I looked around the mess hall and could easily spot them. They ate with their heads down or were not eating at all, just looking straight ahead. No one talked with them. Those of us from the two platoons who hadn't heard anything were afraid to offer condolences because this would challenge fate. Didn't want to get too close to the panelee -- bad luck. They were untouchables.

Pete and I finished our meal and went to our room. As we had always done, in order to protect the shine on the floor in the center of our room, we took one step in and then stepped onto my bed. Pete continued around the room by stepping on the desks and down to his bunk against the far wall without stepping on the floor.

Laying on our bunks, we stared at the ceiling and made wild comments ranging from the dark and negative to confident and optimistic. We remembered Hailey's comments that first day that few would graduate and agreed that we had to have an attitude about all this, something to cling to until we heard who was going.

"It's for the best, whatever happens, it's for the best, that's going to be our policy," Pete said.

At one point, we were convinced that one or the other wouldn't make it, so we resolved that whoever stayed in OCS would not say he was sorry to the other. If both of us got paneled, we'd be out of the place this weekend and we could get some girls, have some fun. It wouldn't be so bad. Cottonpicker would say that the world wasn't coming to an end. Some mighty good people from the other platoons were paneled. We would be in good company.

Pete's bunk faced the door. Suddenly, he yelled, "Attention!" He was unusually frantic in getting to his feet, and I followed quickly, wide-eyed.

Lieutenant Taylor stood in the doorway with the right corner of his mouth turned up in a humorless, mean half-smile. He looked me in the eye, turned and left.

I did not say anything for several minutes. My stomach hurt. Pete told me to lay back down, that it was nothing to worry about.

"Hailey makes up the list," he said. "This guy is just trying to make your life miserable. Forget him."

I wasn't listening. I was thinking that it was all I could do to keep myself upbeat about this panel thing anyway, and Taylor shows up. He probably knew who was going from our platoon, and his smile, his "I've got the last laugh," made it pretty clear to me that I was on the list.

When the bell sounded for mandatory study, Pete and I got up from our bunks and sat at our desks but we continued to talk. Where was Hailey?

We heard someone come in through the swinging doors off the stairwell and walk slowly down the hallway of the platoon area. Our door was open. We thought we recognized Hailey's casual walk, but we did not look up. He walked down to the end of the hall and back toward our door. We heard him address one of the hardest working but least personable of the candidates in our platoon and softly ask him to come down to the first floor. Hailey walked to the stairwell, opened the swinging doors, and was gone. We looked up when the dejected candidate walked by our door. He was gone for what seemed a long time, but probably no more than five minutes. When he returned, he walked slowly down the hall to the room next

24

to ours, told a candidate there that Hailey wanted to see him and then walked heavily to his own room. Next, we watched our neighbor making his way slowly past our door, and the process continued.

There were thirty-three men in our platoon when Hailey called out the first man that night. Pete and I agreed that the first ten men to go downstairs -- all upstanding young men -- probably were relatively low in the platoon ranking. The eleventh man to be called I had always placed toward the top of my bayonet sheet. Surely, I thought, he ranked higher than I did. If he's gone now, I must be next. A third of the platoon is gone. I'm next.

When he came back, he was crying. He walked quickly down the hall to a room near the end, and his voice broke as he called out the name of another candidate. Pete's face immediately contorted in pain. This guy, also from the Midwest, was a friend of his. They had known each other before OCS and Pete thought they stacked up somewhat equally.

Pete and I sucked in our breaths when we heard the swinging door open five minutes later. The candidate walked slowly. Pete noted, in a tense voice, that he was walking on our side of the hall. We looked at each other without moving. The candidate stopped before he got to our room. He didn't call for anyone, but just stopped. Then he started walking again, came up to our door, and stopped again. He was looking in at us.

"Pete," he said, sadly.

****

But Pete was not paneled. The friend had stopped to say that he had tried as hard as he could and he had no regrets.

We went on to graduate, Pete and I. In fact not long after the eleventh week panel most of the hazing subsided and we focused more on field tactics. South Vietnam and guerrilla warfare were mentioned more and more, though our training was never tailored to non-conventional combat. Only when we received training in patrolling did we get a firsthand account of what was going on in Vietnam. Our instructor had recently returned from a tour as adviser to a South Vietnamese ranger battalion. He told war stories, both in the classroom and during breaks and said that the Army did not train its troops to fight in the jungles of Southeast Asia -- he didn't know why.

A few days after patrol training we had the opportunity to put in for additional schools after OCS. Thinking of Cottonpicker, I asked for paratrooper training.

Our assignments were posted on a bulletin board the week of graduation. I got jump school and an eventual assignment to the 1st Infantry Division at Fort Riley, Kansas. Pete was also assigned to the 1st Infantry Division, or, as it was more commonly called, The Big Red One, because of its storied tradition as a bloody combat unit.

Pete and I danced a jig. We were together, going to a tough line outfit. Others around us suggested that we get married.

Mother, Daddy, and my little sister Kathy came down for graduation. Maj. Gen. John Heintges gave the commencement address. He congratulated us on our commissions and went on to say something to this effect: "You have been specifically, individually selected to protect our Constitution and the dignity of our country against all enemies. You do this -- you are charged with doing this, expected to do this -- without any reservation. You must be willing to die to do your job. Your commission has no meaning without that commitment."

As excited as I was, trying to keep up with everything going on that day, I heard the general's words clearly, as if he were speaking directly to me. I was oblivious to the hundreds of people in that auditorium. No one else was there -- only General Heintges on the stage, and me sitting alone in the middle of all the seats when he said, "You have been selected to protect the dignity of the United States. If necessary, die fighting ... You ... You."

Sitting in the auditorium, as if I were alone, I thought, "Yep, I'm your man. I'll take the risks. I'll do the job."

Later Dad pinned my second lieutenant bars on my shoulders. The words of General Heintges still ringing in my ears, I stood tall and felt a tremendous sense of self-worth and dedication.

As a graduation present, Daddy and Mother gave me $2,000. When I returned to Southern Pines on two weeks' home leave before jump training, I went out in search of a 190SL Mercedes convertible. Pete was a sports car enthusiast, had an Alfa Romero, and had made the case a thousand times that dollar for dollar, pound for pound, the 190SL was the best sports car on the road.

So I looked for a 190SL. A used car dealer in Raleigh had heard of one on a small lot in South Carolina and I drove down in one of Daddy's trucks that afternoon.

I came around a curve on the country road. There on the edge of a field ahead was a 1957 190SL Mercedes convertible. It was love at first sight. Graceful, continental -- what was it doing on a South Carolina dirt farm? The farmer/dealer said he had bought it at an auction and did not know its history. I bought it for $1,500, pulled it back to Southern Pines that afternoon, and was racing along

26

country roads near home late that night with the top down and a beer between my legs.

I went out most nights during my leave and usually didn't return home until early in the mornings, sometime after the sun had come up, but I hung around Mom and Dad and my sisters during the day. I took Mom shopping in the Mercedes. She squealed as we scooted along the streets and occasionally waved at the townspeople.

Returning to Fort Benning for jump training, I checked into the bachelor officer's quarters (BOQ) at the school and played poker that night with some of the newly commissioned officers from my OCS company. We were making now the unheard of amount of $242.42 per month. Some of the new officers lost a whole month's pay in the poker game. The following morning when we started airborne PT training, my former classmates and I realized that we were in better shape than anyone else. We ran the last leg of an endurance run backward, and the jump instructors criticized us, but we found it was hard to be humble and intimidated after a half year of OCS training.

We did become humble, however, when we started tower training prior to our first airborne jump. We became even more humble the first time out of a plane. I was in the middle of the "stick" of men along one side of the plane for my first jump. I ran out the door and do not remember anything until my chute opened, jerking me back to my senses. The ground came up so quickly that I froze and landed with a bone-jarring thud. The next time out, I had a sense of doom as I jumped. I felt little relief when my canopy opened because I knew that I still had the thud ahead.

The third time, unfortunately, I was the stick leader. As we neared the drop zone, the jump master went through the jump commands. When he reached "Stand in the door," I stood with my hands outside the doorframe, helmet hitched tight, loaded with parachute main and reserve plus combat gear, one foot slightly in front of the other, head up to watch the red light under the wing outside, ready to jump when it turned green and I waited and waited. I looked down and the sky was filled with chutes as other jumpers from other planes were descending to the ground and then I looked back to the light, but it stayed red and the jump master yelled that we were too far over the jump zone and had to come around again. I stood in the door as we flew over trees and a lone country blacktop road and some houses. My legs, tense from standing at the ready, began to ache and then they started to shake, so I relaxed them and continued to look down. I began to lose the feeling that anything could stop me from falling out of the door to the ground below and I suddenly lost

27

all enthusiasm for jumping. I stood there paralyzed with fear and the drop zone came into view and the jump master yelled for me to get ready but my grip on the door remained loose and I swayed back and forth. The light turned green, the jump master yelled "Go" and I just stood there and the jump master yelled again "Go, Go" and something hit me squarely on the butt. I was out the door, tumbling, then jerked up when the canopy opened and the ground rushed up and I landed with the most jarring thud yet. I hit so hard that my teeth hurt. Mercifully, no one ever mentioned my hesitation. Cottonpicker would not have been proud.

The Saturday after our third jump I was at the bar in the main officers' club when President Lyndon B. Johnson delivered a speech to the nation. Sitting at his desk in the Oval Office, he began by saying, "My fellow Americans, we have been called on to stem the tide of Communist aggression in Southeast Asia. I have today ordered the 1st Cavalry (Airmobile) Division at Fort Benning, Georgia, to Vietnam."

Some of the officers in the bar cheered. A colonel bought a round of drinks, and the bar buzzed with excitement. Men came in from the dining room and were told the news. Other men scurried out, some to make telephone calls, others, especially those from the 1st Cavalry (Cav), left for their units.

I tried to call Pete at Fort Riley to find out if the 1st Infantry Division was on alert, but couldn't get through. The next day, Fort Benning was alive with troop movements. Tanks moved through areas in which they had never been before. Trucks in convoys clogged the streets.

Monday started our last week at jump school. We had two more jumps to make, one at night, but they were anti-climactic. The real interest was in the buildup of the 1st Cav for deployment to South Vietnam. The base was on a war footing. There was a sense of breathless anticipation.

We made the last two jumps. Neither of mine were noted for artistic performance. Both hurt when I landed. I was proud to get my wings, but I was sure that I had developed a fear of heights and had no interest in future jumps. Graduation was on a Friday afternoon. By nightfall, I was on my way to Fort Riley and assignment to the 1st Infantry Division.

I went over again and again what I planned to say to the men of my platoon at our first meeting. Though we had had numbing hours of lectures on leadership at OCS, I thought back to conversations with Dad and Cottonpicker, and I remembered lines I had heard in movies and had read at college. As I developed phrases that seemed appropriately firm and yet reasonable, I remembered General Heintges' comments at OCS graduation and felt a sense of destiny.

I drove with the top down most of the way and the radio turned up. Occasionally I would just howl with joy and pump my fist at the moon.

Arriving at Fort Riley late Saturday night, I got Pete's BOQ room number from the post locator and woke him up. We went out to a seedy after-hours beer joint in nearby Junction City, Kansas, and talked. Pete said that the entire division was on alert, although most of the able-bodied men had been grouped into the 2nd Brigade which was being readied as the first for deployment to Vietnam. Pete was in the 1st Brigade and had asked an old enlisted friend who worked in division personnel to have me assigned to his battalion.

Early Monday morning I was not surprised to learn at 1st Division headquarters that I had, in fact, been assigned to Pete's battalion and by midmorning was checking in with battalion Sgt. Maj. William (Bill) G. Bainbridge. Friendly but firm, his look clearly said, "Second lieutenants do not outrank me, so mind your manners." Respectfully I asked him for a platoon beside Pete. The sergeant major looked at me for a long moment, shrugged, nodded his head yes and within minutes I was walking down to Company A, 1st Battalion of the 28th Infantry Regiment, 1st Brigade, 1st Infantry Division -- Capt. John (Jack) E. Woolley, Commanding.

The buildings in the company area were built during World War II. Four barracks, two stories each, on the right of the company street, orderly room and mess hall on the left. An old oak tree provided shade for the orderly room. Woolley was behind his desk when I walked into his office and saluted. He greeted me warmly and said that I had the 3rd Platoon, Peterson had the 4th, Joseph L. Duckett the 1st, and Ray A. Ernst the 2nd.

At sunrise the following morning, I stood under the oak tree and smoked as the men fell out for reveille. Captain Woolley, tall and tan, was already on the scene. At breakfast, Pete pointed out some of the men in my platoon -- they looked sloppy, undisciplined. My platoon sergeant was an old World War II veteran who was sleepwalking, according to Pete, and rarely spent time with the platoon. Pete thought there were only about a dozen sick, lame, or lazy men in my platoon. All the able-bodied soldiers had already been pulled out for the 2nd Brigade. Not much of a first command, I thought, disappointed.

I met the other platoon leaders over breakfast. Duckett was a large black second lieutenant from Philadelphia who had driven a cab to pay his college tuition. He was quiet but not shy. There was a toughness to his manner that was unfamiliar to me. Ray Ernst was a small, deliberate South Dakotan. He was, surprisingly, a natural companion to Duckett. They just went together, like a long-time married couple.

Woolley joined us at the head of the table and easily, naturally assumed the leader role. He expected deference to his rank and position, but he listened when we spoke and had a reassuring confidence about himself. He was a friendly, articulate man who led through the strength of his personality. I immediately felt privileged to be under his command.

After breakfast, as I walked down to the 3rd Platoon's barracks, I went over my introduction speech. I had added, since seeing them at breakfast, that I did not tolerate sloppy attitudes and expected close attention to military deportment. We faced the prospect of imminent deployment to a theater of war; beginning this morning, we were going to shape up.

I took a deep breath on the barracks steps. Another benchmark in my life, I thought, as I went in to "meet my men." Tough but fair was the image I wanted. I walked in with a stern expression on my face.

Loud music coming from a radio in the latrine competed with another radio on another station to the rear of the bay area. Nine men were lounging around. A few turned and gazed disinterestingly at me. A fat private got off a bunk to my right and called attention, but it produced little response from the others. One soldier lying on a bunk with the mattress folded back closed his eyes and made snoring sounds. Another, a cigarette dangling from his hand, continued to lean on a broom. A Latino, wearing a towel and combing his hair, came out of the latrine, looked at me and then around at the other men.

"My name is Lieutenant Parker," I began, "your new platoon leader."

"Who's this guy?" asked the Latino.

"Shut up, everybody," from the fat guy.

I turned to him. "You want to wake that guy up down there and go turn off those radios?"

He walked away, shaking the snorer first, then headed to the radio at the rear. I heard someone say, "Touch my radio and I cut your fat ass."

The Latino said, "Can I get dressed before you start talking, siirrr?"

It wasn't starting out the way I had in mind, but Manuel, the

30

fat guy, eventually turned off the radios, the Latino got dressed, the snorer got to his feet, and the man with the broom put it down and finished his cigarette. I asked them something about themselves. Each had a reason for not being sent to the 2nd Brigade. Some were finishing their enlistment and leaving service within a month or so, others were awaiting court-martial, some were sick and lame or claimed to be. Manuel was fat.

I had a speech ready, so I let it go, but it was lost on this audience, except for Manuel. I ended by saying that no one skates anymore in this platoon, even if they had only a week left in the Army. Until they received their orders, they belonged to me. As I turned to leave someone turned on a radio.

I told Pete that my group couldn't fight a cold.

--THREE--
Marshaling for War

Troops from U.S. Army units in Germany and Korea arrived at Fort Riley. The misfits in my platoon and throughout the battalion were sent to a holding company at the hospital. Sgt. Cecil W. Bratcher arrived and was assigned to my platoon as 1st Squad leader. Slightly stoop shouldered, he had a facial tic in which the muscles in his neck tensed and his jaw jerked to the right. He reminded me of Cottonpicker, however, when he walked up closer to me than was necessary, saluted, smiled, and introduced himself. Within days, I had Woolley transfer my original, timid platoon sergeant to company headquarters so that Bratcher could take over the job.

One morning after a load of new replacements arrived Woolley called me to his office.

"Got a new rifleman here that's I'm going to assign to your platoon, but, ah, he, ah, he's, I'm not sure how long he's going to be around." Woolley continued to look down at a paper on his desk as he talked. Not yet completely comfortable around the company commander, I stood awkwardly in front of his desk.

"He's scheduled for a Dishonorable Discharge. Just got out of the brig for shooting a man -- apparently he was dorking this man's wife and got caught. He's an ex-M.P. Sergeant E-5 before his court-martial. He's here, best I can tell, because of some administrative mistake -- all the bodies being moved around, he got out of a line to get kicked out of the service into a line of replacements for the 1st Division. His name is Pvt. Wiler Beck. Keep an eye on him until we decide what to do with him."

I called Beck off to the side shortly after Woolley assigned him to my platoon to tell him that he probably would not be around long, that as far as I knew his Dishonorable Discharge was still being processed. A big, burly man in his mid-twenties, he stood as tall as he could and with a stoic, implacable look on his face, said. "Sir, I bribed my way here from the holding company at Fort Leavenworth. I don't want a DD. I want to go to Vietnam with the 1st Division. I won't let you down."

Beck was, in fact, a very good soldier, though he was assertive by nature and tended to be the first and the loudest with an opinion. He was a Private with a Sergeant's attitude. He carried an M-79 grenade launcher like a war club.

A month after I arrived, the battalion was at full strength. President Johnson gave another televised talk, beginning with "My fellow Americans." Pete and I were at our favorite bar in Junction City that night and didn't hear the broadcast live. When we got back to the BOQ around midnight people gathered in the day room were talking excitingly.

"We're going to Vietnam," someone told us as we walked in. He was excited to be telling someone who didn't know.

"Who?" I asked.

"The whole damn1st Infantry Division. President Johnson just said so. We're going to join the 1st Cav. We going to war, boy." With his close cut hair and flushed face, the young officer looked a little zingy. Pete looked at me and said smiling, "War!" I repeated it, "Waarrrr!!"

The day after that announcement the battalion left for a planned cavalry exercise with the armored personnel carriers (APCs) assigned to the battalion. It was great fun racing across Kansas prairies kicking up a rooster tail of dust. Peterson peered out of the turrets of an APC on my left and Ernst and Duckett were on my right. We were all yelling "Yahoo" as the tracks took dips and then bound over the tops of rises. Vietnam in an APC wasn't a bad proposition, I thought. On our return to garrison, however, the APCs were turned in. We were going to Vietnam as "straight leg" infantry, not as a mechanized infantry battalion.

Robert M. Dunn from Portland, Oregon, and George McCoy from Munster, Indiana, other platoon leaders in the battalion, teamed with Pete and me on our nights out in Junction City and at the various officers' clubs on base. McCoy was quiet, but funny. He was a good listener and true to his midwestern roots, a man of his word, the type person you wanted at your side in combat.

Dunn was also good to have around. His loud laugh could burst street lights. He had a quick wit, but he was also quick to fight. His father had played professional football for the Green Bay Packers, so Dunn probably came by his physical nature honestly. Orphaned when he was thirteen years old, he went to live with an older brother who was also a minor. This arrangement actually worked out pretty well and gave Dunn a certain freedom in growing up that most other kids his age envied. Eventually, however, he ran afoul of the law for selling false IDs while he was in the tenth grade. This led the social service people to place him with an older married sister who insisted on more responsible behavior and he eventually graduated Seattle University ROTC. Because of his loud wit and the fact that he did not bluff, nothing was calm when he was on the scene. Though he probably would never hit one of his men, if a fellow officer irritated him, he'd hit the officer flush in the nose. He'd do it without a second's thought and that came across in his manner. We didn't mess with Dunn.

One night in a remote club, I went outside to pee and then staggered across the Kansas plains, more to keep my balance than to see the countryside. I ended up at a stable. When I turned around I could see the officers' club behind me in the distance. There were several horses in their stalls. No one was around, so I got a saddle and bridle from the tack room and had opened the door to the first stall when a strong right arm landed on my shoulder. A friendly, mustached sergeant told me not to mess with Chief, he was the Army's last cavalry horse, a local institution. "Ah, Chief," I said, having no idea that this was the most famous horse in the Army.

"Chief," the sergeant repeated. "I'll take you back to the O club."

In the club parking lot, Dunn was in the middle of a ring of other young officers pushing someone around. I broke through the crowd and tried to separate the two. One of them hit me square upside the head, and I fell to my knees. Dunn and the other man continued slugging each other above me. One of their blows came down on my crown like a club, and I fell forward, face down in the parking lot.

McCoy helped me to his car. When Peterson and Dunn joined us, Dunn looked none the worse for wear. I told him that sometimes it sure hurt having fun with this crowd.

More staff and equipment arrived every day. Our platoon received two very heavy antitank guns, which we assumed would be turned in with the APCs. Incredibly, we learned that we would take them to Vietnam, although we hadn't heard much about Vietcong tanks. Bratcher said that if we were taking the guns to Vietnam, they would be good for something. You've got to believe in the Army, he said, plus something about those heavy guns made him think they were going to be valuable.

Dunn left for Oregon to marry Linda Lowe, the daughter of a dentist. On weekends Pete and I raced north to his home in Lincoln, Nebraska. He pushed his Alfa Romero faster than I wanted to drive my Mercedes and he'd often go out of sight in front to wait for me sitting high on top of a ridge, ready to race down and pass me again.

Back at Fort Riley training intensified. I was pleased to see that most of my men were good marksmen, whether they came from the city or the country. A fair shot myself, I challenged the high scorer from the platoon for a shoot-off at the end of rifle practice. Sometimes I won, but usually the marksman of the day beat me.

We also marched across the Kansas prairies on field exercises. As we walked along, I had a chance to talk with the men in the platoon. Sergeant Bratcher's father in Tennessee had a business fixing jukeboxes, a business he planned to join when he retired from the Army. Jo Ann, his wife, had recently broken both her arms, but was moving the family from their last post back to Tennessee. "She's a good woman," he said. "Good soldiers have good wives. I see it all the time."

The majority of the NCOs in my platoon were black. On average the riflemen were eighteen years old. Most had bad teeth, many had tattoos, and few had graduated high school.

Sgt. Miguel Castro-Carrosquillo from Puerto Rico was one of the platoon clowns, PFC Gilbert P. Spencer was a tall black man from an urban ghetto who led the "Angry Negro Coalition." Pvt. Antonio De Leon, a college graduate, had been sitting out a year to make money for graduate school when he was drafted. PFC J. V. Patrick was a lanky Texan who had gone through a series of civilian jobs before joining the Army. Sgt. Roosevelt S. Rome was a burly squad leader who rarely spoke. Pvt. Harold G. Ayers was a large, barely literate eighteen year old from the Midwest. Sgt. Ray E. King was a red-headed non-com who led the 3rd Squad. Pvt. Warren J. Manuel, who carried a machine gun, had been in the platoon longer than anyone. He was the fat guy who was in the platoon when I arrived. PFC James E. Newsome carried my PRC-25 radio. Pvt. John J.(Jack) Lyons, Jr. from Pittsburgh, Pennsylvania, was a draftee, Pvt. Beck's best friend. Together Lyons and Beck formed an alliance that was seldom challenged in the platoon.

Most of the men had personal situations to settle prior to

departure and most requested leave to go home, except Ayers. Pay allotments had to be taken out, wives and families settled, cars sold, and personal equipment sent home or thrown away.

We received movement orders in mid-August. Our battalion was going by train to the west coast and by ship across the Pacific. Departure was tentatively set a month away, mid-September. Training activities increased. Lt. Col. Robert Haldane, a West Point graduate, was battalion commander. He had an intelligent, educated manner, spoke in a low resonant voice, and had that intangible quality usually referred to as "presence." By reputation, he was the finest battalion commander in the 1st Division. With his sidekick, Sergeant Major Bainbridge, he often led the entire battalion on PT runs in the morning.

Men continued to arrive, and most of them immediately went on leave to take care of personal business. Once a day, it seemed, I was called to the orderly room for a telephone call to exclaim, "You have to do what?" or "You're where?" It was hard to believe some of the twisted situations in which the men, boys mostly, of my platoon had found themselves. Some returned from leave with broken noses, or drunk or broke, in taxis, on buses, thumbing, with pregnant girlfriends or dogs, with chest colds or venereal disease.

"Is there something about going to Vietnam that makes people crazy?" I asked Bratcher.

"Yep," he said, "there is some of that, but most of these guys are crazy anyway." Bratcher smiled and the muscles in his neck tightened and his head jerked to the right.

The platoon was unanimous in its disapproval of war protesters. The men talked about them as we marched out to the rifle range.

"They don't have anything to complain about," Beck said. "Hell, we're the ones going to get shot at. What are they protesting about? Soldiers are real men, dope smoking hippies are slime."

But De Leon said, "That may be true, but those hippy girls do it with the lights on, sometime in groups."

Lyons said, "Hippies are pinko commies."

"They protest about this fucked up society, man," Spencer said.

"Shut up, Spencer," Beck responded quickly. "I get tired of your whining. Bitch, bitch, bitch. Ain't you ever been satisfied, man?"

"Yea," Spencer replied, "with your sister."

Beck shifted his M-79 and slowed his gait as he glared at Spencer.

"Tell you what," Bratcher quipped, as he walked up near

35

Beck, "if I hear any more bickering, I'm going to take your young asses out there and tan 'um. I'm looking for about ten minutes of quiet here. Don't nobody say nothing. No body. Shut the fuck up."

Even I was quiet, which I didn't particularly like. Bratcher had a way of taking over -- he was very strong willed. He had the respect of the men because he was tougher than they were. My problem was that platoon sergeants often usurped the authority of young officers and turned them into mascots. They had the network of sergeants in the platoon on their side. If it came down to a popularity contest, the platoon sergeant won. During those first few weeks, as we prepared to go overseas into God knows what, Bratcher and I had been sizing up each other. I liked the Tennessee sergeant, though. He reminded me of Cottonpicker and I believed that we could develop an effective division of labor in leading the platoon. But we kept an eye on one another.

Out of nowhere, I received orders to Little Creek, Virginia, for load master training, to help the battalion liaise with the Navy during sea travel.

I had decided to leave my car with Pete's dad. The weekend before I left for Virginia, Pete and I raced over the Kansas/Nebraska line to Lincoln. I opened up the Mercedes and for miles on miles we raced side by side, bumper to bumper.

While we were in Lincoln, Pete suggested that we visit one of his high school classmates, now an insurance agent. Each of us bought a $10,000 life insurance policy. The agent said that we could not name each other as beneficiaries because initially, in drafting the policy, the beneficiary had to be a family member. We could take out the policies with our mothers as beneficiaries, and after a period of time, say a month, we could change our beneficiary to each other. Fine, we said, that's the plan. We paid a nominal amount in the way of the first premium, got receipts and change-of-beneficiary forms, and went to a bar to discuss what we had done. In a back booth at the Diamond Bar and Grill, I said, "If anything happens to you, Pete, I will be surely sorry. I want you to know that I will be sad like I have never been sad before. But this $10,000 policy, I think, will almost make it all right."

"You know, Parker," Pete said, "You could have saved money on your premium, 'cause I would have been happy with a buck fifty if something happened to you."

After attending the ten-day naval training class I flew down to North Carolina to say good-bye to my parents. While I was there I took my old 12 gauge shotgun out of the broom closet and carried it to the back porch. Like I had done years before when I was preparing

36

to go hunting with Cottonpicker, I checked to see if there were any shells in the chamber. Then I bounced it in my hands, feeling for its center of balance. It felt comfortable. I brought it to my shoulder quickly and laid in on a distant tree. Dead center. No wasted movement. The gun knew where to go, like the .03 Springfield I had used at Oak Ridge.

A good weapon was important in a war. This shotgun and that .03 were the best that I had ever had in my hands. This gun was an extension of my body. I had been firing it since I was a kid. If I had a way of taking it to Vietnam, I would. And I suddenly remembered the antitank weapons. I could pack my shotgun with them. Bratcher was right. Those weapons were going to be useful for something, to carry my very own shotgun to Vietnam. I disassembled it and put it in my duffel bag without telling my parents.

Later I went out to Fort Bragg, home of the Special Forces and bought a jungle hammock from the post exchange. It was made for Vietnam and I wondered why the battalion hadn't been issued similar types. If I could pack a 12 gauge shotgun in those antitank weapon boxes, then I could squeeze in a hammock. I put it in the duffel bag along with the shotgun.

When I was ready to leave, my parents told me to be careful. I laughed and said, "OK."

"Come home," Dad said shaking my hand. Mom, with tears in her eyes, twisted her mouth to one side and looked off to the side. I put my arms around her and she looked at me, tears now rolling down her cheek. She kissed me and said softly, "Please come back."

I went to Pope Air Force Base to catch a space-available military aircraft hop to Fort Riley, but I was bumped and rerouted twice. In Chicago the morning after I was supposed to return to base, I finally got Pete on the telephone and he said, "You are where?" He said Woolley was pissed. Movement had been rescheduled and we were leaving within the week. Woolley himself had taken a forty-eight hour pass to go somewhere, and I had better be there when he returned.

At reveille the next morning I was back under the oak tree by the orderly room. The battalion was moving out to Vietnam in five days.

****

Railroad tracks ran beside the highway dissecting Fort Riley. For days passenger cars and engines came through the base to make up a train for transporting the brigade to Oakland Naval Base,

California.

In getting my personal equipment ready for Vietnam, I had the company armorer take off most of the barrel of my shotgun. It changed the balance, but I thought that it would have a broader shot pattern and I could point it quicker at close range, thus making it more effective. Bratcher, King, and I packed it with the jungle hammock in an antitank weapon box. King called it the "Lieutenant's survival kit."

There were surprisingly few problems in packing out the company. We did not have that much equipment actually; the infantry operates with what it can carry. The antitank weapons and the mortars were our biggest pieces and after we had those packed, we killed time, doing PT, waiting for the last of the men from the platoon to return from leave.

Captain Woolley and I were at battalion headquarters one morning doing administrative chores when the Sergeant Major motioned us into Colonel Haldane's office. "What are we going to do about this guy, Private Beck?" Haldane asked.

Woolley, in his usual good manner way with the battalion commander, said, "Well sir, Beck's a pretty good soldier according to Parker here. We think he'll do OK."

"The Sergeant Major says we can get him paroled to the 1st/28th. But if he proves to be disruptive or criminal, what's the point?" Haldane looked at me as he finished.

"He'll do fine, sir," I replied. I briefly considered telling the Colonel that the man had bribed his way to the 1st Division, but that sounded loopy as I thought about it so I continued to hold the Colonel's gaze without further comment.

"OK, we'll do what's necessary here. He's the only man in the battalion in this kind of situation. He's supposed to already be out of the service with a DD. How did he get here anyway?" Haldane asked. I looked at Woolley and he shrugged.

Later I told Beck that he was going to Vietnam because I had stood in front of the Colonel and had vouched for him. He better not make me look bad.

Trying to stand as tall as he could, Beck said, "I won't let you down."

When the train was finally assembled, formal movement orders were posted in the battalion area. We were to leave at 1500 hours on 17 September 1965.

Pete and I packed out of our BOQ the night before and left our gear in the orderly room while we went into Junction City for one last beer at the seedy bar we had gone to on my first night at Fort

Riley. Pete and I sat on the edge of a damaged pool table and watched the colorful mix of prostitutes, drifters, and other patrons going about their Thursday night business, which probably wasn't much different from any other night. About to start a trip halfway around the world, we had no idea what awaited us. The common night crawlers who frequented this bar couldn't have cared less, and we smiled about that.

"We gotta remember this scene," Pete said. "It means something. I don't know what exactly, but I think this is America, if we're ever going to wonder about that later. I mean if we're ever going to try and put our finger on what we're doing over there, who we fighting for, just remember this lineup at the bar.

A bum came over and begged a dollar to buy a beer.

After he left Pete and I agreed that we might very well be that guy in a few years. We were just going through a phase, our short-haircut phase. I wondered aloud what lay ahead -- the adventures to come, the danger.

"Any last minute things that we needed to do?" I ask Pete.

"Well, Pete said, "we'll mail those insurance forms on the way back to base and that's it. We're set to go warring."

Earlier that afternoon we had met in the company orderly room and filled out the change of beneficiary forms for our $10,000 policies. If I were killed, Pete would get ten grand, tax free. If Pete died, I would get the same amount. I had the change of beneficiary forms sealed in envelopes in my jacket. On the way back to Fort Riley, we passed a post office. I got out of the car and walked to the mail drop, but then the devil overcame me. I had not planned it, but I put Pete's change of beneficiary form in the drop and I put the envelope with my form back into my jacket.

If I died, Mother would get the $10,000.

There was something very rotten about this, I thought, but then I smiled. Naw. Walking back to the car, I figured the people back in that beer joint would have given me a hand. This was their kind of thing. Naw, I thought, this is rotten. Later. I'll mail it later. It made me smile, because we did not expect to die, neither one of us. We were doing it for bragging rights with Dunn and McCoy. Plus I could always say I was worried that Pete might shoot me for the money... I'll just give it some time to make sure he's honest. Then I'll mail it in.

Back in the company area I walked down to the barracks. All the men in my platoon had returned except Sergeant Castro. He had called from Puerto Rico the previous morning, and I had told him to be back by 1200 hours the next day or he'd miss movement. He had a heavy Puerto Rican accent and I had trouble understanding him, but I thought that he had only one thing to do and he'd be on his way. I said, "You're in Puerto Rico -- you're out of the country -- you've got just a few hours to get to Kansas and you've got something else to do before you leave?" There was no answer. "Castro," I said, "are you crazy?"

"I be there, I be there, I be there," he kept saying, sounding like the roadrunner cartoon character.

He still wasn't back by 1500 hours the next day as we started to assemble in the company street. I had Bratcher bring out his duffel bag out and put it in formation. The first sergeant called us to attention and took roll. Castro was the only man missing in the 3rd Platoon. We stacked arms, loaded our duffel bags in the back of trucks, and milled around. At 1600 hours, Captain Woolley called us to attention and said, "Let's go kick some ass."

We were marching out of the company area in rout step toward the railroad tracks -- and Vietnam -- when a taxi screamed up and Castro leaned out the front passenger window. Bratcher told him that his uniform was on his bunk, we had already packed his duffel bag. Castro ducked back into the cab and motioned for the taxi driver to drive on.

The train cars went out of sight in both directions. Steam hissed from brake lines. Everyone in my platoon was talking and laughing as we marched along the tracks. I stopped the platoon beside our assigned train cars and dismissed the men to climb aboard. From across a nearby, congested parking lot, Castro's yellow cab, speeding dangerously, made its way in our direction and stopped almost at the tracks. Castro was putting on his field uniform as he got out of the cab. Everyone in the platoon cheered. He paid the driver and waddled past me quickly to the train. I followed him up the train stairs. The men clapped their hands in unison and shouted, "Hey, Hey, Hey, Hey." Castro walked down the aisle and finally started stomping his feet.

"I told you I be here," he called out to me before he slumped down in a seat.

Civilian and uniformed well-wishers were standing beside the train on both sides. Children on the shoulders of their parents, old people, farmers, and businessmen lined the road. People in cars drove slowly by. Some late-arriving wives and girlfriends raced by us on foot and asked the soldiers leaning out of the windows what unit they were with. One soldier down the line reached out and kissed a girl for a long time. She finally stood back with tears in her eyes. Another GI reached down and took a small child into the train and played with him for a few minutes before returning him to his crying wife. We could hear the division band playing at the front of the train.

The sun began to set over the western prairies when, without warning, the train lurched and started to move. It went slowly at first, and the well-wishers easily kept up with it. Then it picked up speed, and only a few people could keep pace. As our section of the train pulled through the main post area, we saw signs that read, "God Save America," and "The Big Red One". Well-dressed civilians stood by large cars in the parking lot of division headquarters.

Some soldiers in the platoon stuck their heads out the windows and yelled at people. Others were asleep or playing cards. The train gathered momentum and sped across the flat farmland, as it headed west.

We stopped at Laramie, Wyoming, where the snow was two feet deep, for the men to disembark and stretch their legs. Back under way, we traveled over the Rocky Mountains. Somewhere east of the Oakland Naval Terminal, the train pulled to a stop again. Scuttlebutt sourced to battalion headquarters in the front of the train was that a large demonstration of peaceniks blocked the train tracks into the terminal.

"Hell," Lyons said, "put me on the top of the engine with some live ammo and I'll clear the tracks."

On Monday, 20 September, three days after leaving Fort Riley, the long train pulled into a railroad terminal inside the naval base. Sections of the train were pushed down a pier beside an enormous gray World War II troop carrier, the USNS *Mann*. We had to lean out the window and look up to see the deck. We had to wait for hours before disembarking and then in single file, with our duffel bags over our shoulders, we walked along the pier toward the gangplank. Grandmotherly-looking Red Cross workers stood smiling behind tables filled with pastries and coffee.

The endless line in front continued up a gangplank to the deck, across a passageway and down into the bowels of the ship. Once we arrived at the fifth level down, we found the company's area in a large compartment with bunks stacked five high. There was barely enough room to pass down the rows of bunks. The men were happy about leaving the train, and they began settling into the smaller spaces of the ship in good humor. A card game, started on the train before we left Fort Riley, picked up again in the latrine. I noticed that there wasn't much air circulation. I was thinking that it was going to be a long Pacific crossing for me down in this hold, when a Marine told me that the officers' quarters were above. I wished Bratcher well, told him it was better he than me down here and left. Pete, McCoy, and Dunn had already secured a four-bunk stateroom off the main officers' mess. I stood inside the hatch and looked at our plush, spacious cabin.

"Goddamned if I don't feel a little guilty about this," I said. "Those men are crammed together like cattle down below."

Dunn reminded me that in the U.S. Army, a second lieutenant took what was given to him and said, "Thank you."

Troops boarded the ship all that day and throughout most of the night. The single file was rarely broken as train sections continued to arrive. Eventually 2,800 soldiers of the 1st Brigade, 1st Infantry Division boarded the *Mann*.

Around two o'clock the next day, the ship's horn blew and I went out on the deck. Halfway down the pier, a military band stood at the ready. The Red Cross women were cleaning up around their tables. Longshoremen disengaged heavy ropes from cleats on the pier. Fewer than a dozen civilians stood below looking up at the huge ship. Another whistle blew, and the band started to play. The women stopped picking up trash and looked up. One in the front waved, and then the others joined in. The longshoremen heaved the ropes away, tugs moved the ship from the pier, and, under her own power at last, the *Mann* headed into San Francisco Bay.

McCoy joined me on the deck as we sailed by Alcatraz. We watched in silence, lost in thought about the sights around us and what lay ahead. George finally said, "It's like the movies. Going to war is just like the movies."

We sailed under the Golden Gate Bridge and headed out to sea.

--FOUR--
Sea Voyage

The second day at sea I began preparing and delivering training classes on small-unit tactics and field hygiene to the company. Later, support personnel from brigade headquarters delivered a series of lectures on Vietnam and its history. These were held on the open deck where movies were shown at night. The movies were better received. No one seemed to care much about the history of the place we were going.

When they were not involved in training, the men waited in line for meals, for the PX, for the latrine, for space on deck. If one of the soldiers wanted to see a movie he had to get in the mess line for dinner at 1600 -- everyone was supposed to go through the chow line for every meal whether or not they ate it -- so that he would be finished in time to get in line for the limited seats on deck for the movie. The card game in the latrine never stopped. No one interfered and I often stood and watched. Conversation between the players was biting, with much bragging, much bluffing, and some shouting. There were few friendly smiles. Stakes were high. New players came and went, leaving their money behind with the regulars. Not a game for sissies.

I often used Bratcher's bunk for my office/couch when I was in the hold. Once I was sitting with him wondering out loud what kind of operations we were going to be involved in.

"It's no big deal," he said. "It's a police action. Stopping cars, checking ID cards. The U.S. Army, the U.S. Navy, the U.S. Air Force, the U.S. Marines against one little pipsqueak country. Come on, Lieutenant, get serious. We'll blow 'em away." He smiled and his jaw jerked to the right.

The officers' mess had clean starched tablecloths at each meal, and Filipino stewards served us. There were plenty of seats for our movies, and coffee, soft drinks, and sweet cakes were on a table in the rear should we want refreshments. We had the run of most of the ship. At night Dunn, Peterson, McCoy, and I often climbed to one of the uppermost decks to talk and joke. Dunn was the master of ceremonies. One night after dinner, he was late coming up because he had to meet with his company commander. McCoy suggesting rigging coin tosses in the future, any two of the three of us against Dunn. If the object was to be the odd man -- odd man wins -- then all we had to do was to make sure that one of us had a heads and the other a tails. Dunn, getting either heads or tail would have to pair with one of us and the other would win. If the object was not to be odd man out -- the odd man lost -- then our two coins would be the same. If Dunn tied -- had the same as the two of us -- then we'd flip again, and again until he lost. George said that if he was around, he'd make the call, telling Pete or me whether to make our coin heads or tails depending on whether George scratched his head or put his hand on his tail. That night shortly after Dunn joined us, we flipped coins to see who would go to the officers' mess and get some sweet cakes. Dunn lost.

Late in the morning of the eleventh day at sea, I went down in the hold to see Bratcher but he wasn't around. I picked up the platoon roster from his bunk and went over to Spencer's bunk to read it. Spencer was reading an old dog-eared letter.

Directing his comments to no one in particular but speaking so that only I could hear he said, "Da man is coming down to the slave quarters to look after da field niggers, huh?" He smiled faintly. Although not educated or well read, Spencer was probably the brightest man in the platoon. Aware of what was going on in the States in the mid-1960s, he was angry that his country had tolerated segregation for so long and he felt that the law of the land was still stacked against him -- that he didn't have the same opportunities that the white man did. "Discrimination is as American as apple pie," was his phrase before something like that became part of the national black/white dialogue. Spencer was angry and sassy and was, in our platoon, the king of jive.

"Spencer, you know I didn't make the reservations for this cruise. You've got a right to complain, I reckon, but then so do a few thousand other good men on this boat."

"It seems strange to me that it's never anyone's fault. It ain't the man's fault, he was born white, it's his society, his laws. Problem sure ain't the black man's fault, he ain't never had nothing. Don't have no stuff, don't have no voice. We got ourselves a society that is fucked up, dude, and there ain't no one to blame, no one to fix it. White man likes it like it is. Negro ain't got no power. Nothing ever's going to change. You understand what I'm saying? In our society Negroes don't get due consideration, though I note we're more than well represented in this group being sent to some god forsaken place to get shot at 'cause it's what some white man has decided to do. Ain't nothing in it for me or my kind. Understand, Lieutenant?"

"Nope, Spencer, I don't," I told him. "It ain't my job. You'd be surprised all the things I don't understand. All I know for sure is that, for whatever reason, we're on this boat together, going somewhere where we have to work together. Shit you're talking about don't matter. I didn't ask to be born white, you didn't ask to be born black -- you just supposed to make the best of what you given. That's what I know."

Bratcher walked up and sat down on Spencer's bunk with us. He and I talked for a few minutes about a class coming up, and then I left. Later I told Bratcher in passing that Spencer had made some point about our changing social consciousness and I understood his frustrations.

"What da fuck is that, Lieutenant?" Bratcher exclaimed. "Spencer is a private E-3. Rifleman. Period. That is all you should think of when you see that person. Rifleman. Do not let him talk to you about nothing that doesn't have to do with him being a rifleman and you being the platoon leader. Not now on this boat and certainly not in Vietnam. Don't be his friend. Don't listen to his shit. Let another rifleman listen. Don't make this any more complicated than it is. Sitting on that private's bunk talking some intellectual sounding bullshit don't help you do your job, and it don't help me and it don't help him. You understand the concept here, Lieutenant?"

I looked at Bratcher who was glaring at me, his jaw twitching. His points were well taken, but he was testing the limits to our relationship, telling me that he knew the score and I didn't. He might have been right about Spencer, but I couldn't let him take over.

"Sergeant," I said, mustering as much authority as I could, "let's understand each other. If I go down and hold that man's hand and talk about poetry, that's OK. Because it's my fucking platoon. Not yours. I set the standard. I talk about whatever I want to talk about. You don't tell me what to talk about. Be careful giving me advice when I don't ask for it. You understand this concept, Sergeant?"

Things were chilly for a couple of days with Bratcher but they returned to normal, without a winner or loser, by the end of the first week at sea, when we heard about the 1st Cav's first skirmishes in the A Shau valley.

Rumors began circulating over breakfast that some news had come in overnight regarding an operation by one of the 1st Cav brigades in the central highlands of South Vietnam. It was the first big engagement of an American unit in the war. Some companies, we heard, had taken heavy casualties.

Later in a briefing to the officers and senior NCOs, we heard that the 1st Cav had "gotten their noses bloodied," which was an understatement. That afternoon we read the stark and sobering dispatches. Whole units were wiped out. All of the officers in one company were killed in the first few minutes of a firefight. The North Vietnamese had surrounded some units and had attacked in waves. Weather was bad and air support limited. Under the jungle canopy, it was apparently difficult to fix exact positions of the ground forces and artillery fire support was imprecise. When it was on target, overhanging foliage often dissipated it. The battle evolved into hand-to-hand combat, and with the American units separated, the North Vietnamese moved against the smaller straggling units and wiped them out.

"So much for your opinion that the U.S. Navy, and the U.S. Air Force, and the U.S. Marines and the U.S. Army can whip up on this little pipsqueak country," I told Bratcher. "This doesn't sound like any police action I've ever heard about. This sounds like combat. And I want to look at those men of ours again and think about who's going to handle the heat, who's going to get the job done, and who's going

James E. Parker, Jr.

to break and run."

"A lot's going to depend on you, Lieutenant," Bratcher said. "The men are getting the word about this 1st Cav thing through the grapevine and it's loaded with bullshit. Every soldier's going to make it sound worse. Don't let our men start off thinking they're going to get their asses shot. You need to go down there and tell 'em the 1st Cav was suckered in them mountains. Tell 'em we ain't going to be no one's sucker. We ain't going to walk into no traps. We're going to keep our head on our shoulders and we're going to kick some ass. Doesn't matter exactly what you say, you just gotta say something with confidence. They're down there now and don't know what to think. You've got to step in and give them an attitude they can believe in, live by, fight by. 1st Cav fucked up, but we're tough. Dinks attack us, we're going to kick their asses. If you say it with enough conviction, they'll believe you."

We were on the deck off to ourselves. Bratcher wasn't looking at me as he talked. He was looking out over the ocean, his neck tightening up and his jaw twitching. I'm thinking this guy is right, but hell oh mighty Pete, who's going to lead this platoon, me or him? I had told him not to give me advice when I didn't ask for it. But then I'm thinking again, he's right, the men need to be reassured. And it's my job. We'd have to work out the command and control thing later.

We walked down into the section of the compartment where my platoon was bunked, and Bratcher called the men together. He moved aside, and I recounted the dispatches we had received on the 1st Cav. Then I started winging it.

"We're going to do just fine," I told the men, " because we aren't going to make the same mistakes. The 1st Cav screwed up, but we are going to cover our asses and we're going to be tougher. And when you're more determined, you're luckier in battle. It's a well-known fact, you can will victory. You can beat 'em with a tough attitude. And I ain't just whistling through my teeth -- the officers in the 1st Cav died faster than anyone else, and I personally am looking forward to my chances out there. Y'all should be looking forward to what lies ahead. We are going to walk through the valley of death and, like the Captain said when we left Fort Riley, we were going to kick some ass. You have nothing to worry about."

As I finished I looked around; Beck, Spencer, Castro, Manuel, Patrick, Lyons and Ayers were standing close by and they believed me -- I could see the trust in their eyes. I heard Bratcher behind me tell the men that now was a good time to clean their weapons and he wanted every man to bring his weapon by his bunk

46

for inspection before going to chow. On the way out of the compartment, I noticed that the poker game was still going in the latrine, the players nonplused about the 1st Cav reports.

After supper, Dunn, McCoy, Pete, and I went to the top deck and talked about the 1st Cav reports and what we were getting into. Without giving Bratcher any credit, I repeated parts of my speech about the probably clumsy execution of the 1st Cav in the mountains but that we were tougher and would survive.

"Well that's just hogwash," Dunn said. "You have no idea what went on out there. Fact is, people get killed in combat. You just accept the fact that it's not going to be nice and live with it. Some of our men are going to live and some are going to die. Maybe one of us ain't coming back. You just accept that and you don't misrepresent the situation with some kind of double talk."

McCoy agreed. He said, "War isn't so difficult to deal with really when it comes down to the basics. You make the best of it day to day. Learn as you go. What can happen? One, the worst is you get killed. But hell, you get killed, you're dead. It doesn't hurt anymore. Somebody else has a problem with that, then it's their problem. You're dead. You're at peace. And the next worst, what's that, you get wounded and you get sent back home. Not too bad there, getting sent back home. Hell, you can get on with your life. What does that leave? You don't get wounded or killed. You finish your tour, you go home. It's that simple. One, you die, but dead you're in no pain. Two, you get wounded, you go home. Or three you don't get wounded. But no matter what happens, it's OK."

"The important thing isn't living or dying," Pete said. "None of us think we're going to die anyway. The important thing is how we handle ourselves over there. We platoon leaders are the ones who have to get the men moving when bullets are flying and bombs are going off, when there is noise and confusion. That's the time. Right then. Will we have the presence of mind, the good judgment, the courage, and the luck to do the job? Or will we freeze and hug the ground? Can we hold ourselves responsible for the death of our people and keep on going? What's it like, really, to get shot at? To give orders that get people killed?"

We were lost in thought. I looked up at the stars and thought about freezing in the door of that airplane during jump training. Would combat be different? I had started this conversation by saying we were going to get through the next year's walk thought the valley of death by just being tough, but I
sat now and worried about my personal courage.

"You know what?" McCoy finally said, "I think the worst
47

here is not knowing exactly what to expect. I think we're going to be OK. What we should hope for -- and there ain't nothing more to do right now but hope, 'cause we can't change shit -- we should hope that we got what it takes to be strong and that we are courageous in front of our men and that we have good judgment. That we just get it right, regardless of the consequences." He turned to Dunn, "But as for who's going die -- since we don't know -- you want to flip a coin and see who might likely be first."

We laughed, even Dunn, and lapsed back in silence.

As I sat there I could see clearly in my mind's eye some of the skirmishes that I had read about in the dispatches. I tried to imagine what I would do, what my platoon would do, if we were surrounded by drum-beating, whistle-blowing, Oriental fanatics crawling forward in the jungle. No air force, no artillery, no mortars -- us and them in dense jungle at night. My stomach tightened and began to hurt. Don't get in the fix in the first place, I thought. Think tough. Cover your ass. I was right to start with. We can will victory here. Tough is a state of mind. Stay tough. Think tough. And hope, like George said, that we're lucky.

****

Nine days out from Oakland, we passed near Midway Island. Rumors began to circulate that we would stop at Guam to refuel, we would be allowed off the ship for a day on the beach, and that the Guam National Guard was going to host a beach party for the ship. Snorkeling, Polynesian girls, bonfires, free beer, clean air. Vietnam could wait. Guam was ahead.

The mood below deck was jubilant, but the poker players were unaffected. Guam came into sight off the starboard bow early on the morning of Sunday 2 October. Men abandoned the chow line in a rush up to the deck for a glimpse of the approaching island, green and lush in the distance. Native fishermen in fishing boats passed close by the ship and the men on deck waved. Some yelled, "Where're your sisters?"

The port was now in sight and tugs had come out to guide the *Mann* to the dock.

The commandant of troops, speaking over the PA system said that, despite the rumors, we would be allowed no shore leave. Repeat, he said, no shore leave. The ship was docking only to take on fuel and supplies, and we would be on our way the following morning.

Suddenly a low, angry rumble drifted up from the hold. I

48

was on deck watching the tugs work and did not turn when the commandant spoke. What he said was not surprising. It seemed improbable that the thousands of men on board the ship could be allowed off on this small island, entertained, and returned to the ship in any reasonable amount of time. They would overwhelm the island.

The men, however, were not understanding. The rumors about shore leave had been detailed, some aspects even discussed by the Navy crew. The troops thought Army brass had decided among themselves against letting them off. The rumbling grew louder. Some men came running up the steps from the troop compartments. Clusters of soldiers stood on the deck and talked in conspiratorial tones. Somewhere below, a soldier slammed the butt of his M-14 into the side of the ship. The noise increased as more and more men grabbed their weapons and started thumping the bulkheads.

Pete came up, and we stood together waiting, listening. It was mutinous. The banging of weapons continued as the tugs pushed the ship into place beside a long concrete pier.

A gangplank was lowered from the ship. We watched the commandant and Sergeant Major Bainbridge leave with an entourage of staff officers. When some of the men on deck saw them leave, they yelled that the top dogs were going ashore, leaving the troops to rot on the ship. Men ran below to spread the word. The banging got louder.

The sergeant major soon returned and a meeting of all officers was called in the officers' mess.

The banging stopped.

An officious lieutenant colonel addressed the group. Without reference to the previous message over the PA system, he said that the Port Authority had offered some old dry docks, a few miles from the pier so that the men could stretch their legs and drink some beer. But he said everyone had to be back on board by midnight because we sailed for Vietnam at first light. It was then almost 1300. As he was giving instructions for off-loading, we heard a roar from below. The men apparently had heard through their own sources that they were going ashore.

Disembarking by companies, almost three thousand soldiers marched off the pier and down the island road toward the dry docks. Four abreast, they sang, waved their arms and clapped their hands as they marched. They gave the impression that they were following some pied piper from the land of Anheuser-Busch.

The dry docks, four large wooden bulwarks, three stories high and in varying degrees of disrepair, stood amid a variety of smaller buildings. Once inside, the men fell out from the column to

49

explore or stood around in groups and talked. An officer climbed on top of a shed near the gate and announced that the Guam National Guard would arrive in a few minutes with beer on the back of flatbed trucks. The beer was ten cents a can, and each man could buy twelve, no more. After giving further instructions about what the men could not do, he said that the opportunity for the men to stretch their legs was done on the authority of the troop commander who wanted the men to form up at 2200 and march, by companies, back to the ship.

The men were milling around as he spoke. Peterson opined that not everyone had paid attention. He guessed that before the day was out there would be a few violations of the rules.

Captain Woolley gathered his platoon leaders -- Peterson, Duckett, Ernst, and me -- and said that two of us had to stay with the men at all times. The others were allowed to go to a nearby officers' club. Duckett and Ernst agreed to take the first shift. Pete and I would return by nightfall.

As we walked out the gate, two dump trucks laden with beer pulled into the compound. The men behind us let out a roar and began to form up in lines. McCoy and Dunn were in the officers' club when we arrived. They had staked out an area overlooking the beach and had their drinks on a side table. We thanked them for thinking of us, ordering ahead, and they said, fuck you, these are our drinks. Hard to get service, they said. Need to stock up. Pete and I eventually got a starter set of drinks and downed a couple quickly before we settled down to more reasonable drinking. We became boisterously happy and made preposterous toasts. Larry Moubry [alias], the battalion supply and transportation platoon leader, came over and loudly joined us in making toasts. He had a reputation for being very religious and we found his drunken behavior unseemly, maybe because he was a little drunker than the rest or because he wasn't funny or clever or invited. He was, in fact, obnoxious and his mood turned morose quickly after we had gone through a series of toasts. He imagined that many of us would die in Vietnam, a sweltering, Oriental hell-hole. He said the Vietcong were godless demons, who killed without mercy, had no regard for life, and ate their dead.

He finally stumbled off and after watching him barge into another group Dunn commented that he was a righteous son of a bitch.

Dunn noticed Woolley, carrying several drinks, across the room and called to him to join us. Woolley made his way through the crowd and placed his drinks on a nearby piano. Dunn said it was fair to tell him that Parker and Peterson didn't think much of him. Dunn said the good captain looked pretty damn good in his uniform and everything, and Dunn liked him a lot personally, and that was why Dunn was going to tell him something in confidence. "Keep your eye on Parker," Dunn said, "especially when we get live bullets."

Woolley threw back his head and laughed. Dunn reached over and got one of Woolley's drinks from the piano.

"Mr. Parker's going to be in front of me most of the time, pulling point, I think," Woolley said.

"Pulling point?" I asked. "Odd sounding phrase."

Dunn explained that I had joined the Army because I couldn't hack college and was still somewhat confused about military terminology; plus he'd noticed lately that I just stood around not exactly understanding what was going on. Dunn figured the reason for this was that I hadn't expected Army duty to be anything substantive, just a couple of years of KP or something like that; when I realized that I was just hours away from the hostile work environment of Vietnam, where I was expected to be decisive and responsible, I had become confused. So he asked Woolley to go easy with me. Woolley said he appreciated the advice.

Suddenly Ernst burst into the room and ran over to Woolley. "They're rioting at the docks," he yelled. "They are out of control. They've turned trucks over, burnt buildings. They've gone crazy. Crazy, Captain, crazy. It's a riot."

Maj. Robert J. Allee, the battalion executive officer, came in and talked with the troop commander. The commander stood up and said everyone was to return to the dry docks and begin policing up the men. He was canceling shore leave as of that moment.

Not far from the officers' club, groups of men were wandering off in all directions. The gate to the dry docks was clogged with people trying to get out. Most were heading toward the ship, but many hundreds were making their way inland. In the half light of dusk, we could see some small buildings on fire inside the dock area. I found a few of my men and told them to go back to the ship. Down by the gate Moubry was telling men who appeared to him to be heading away from the ship to drop down and give him fifty push-ups and then go on to the ship. To their credit, most told him to fuck himself and walked away as he screamed, "Give me fifty, give me fifty, soldier." Dunn told Moubry to go to the ship or he was going to break his nose because he was giving all the officers a bad name.

Sergeants Bratcher and King were sitting on top of some lumber inside the gate. They had a couple of cases of beer between them.

"I thought twelve beers a person was the limit," I told them.

"King can't count good." Bratcher said. "Want a beer,

Lieutenant?"

I sat down beside them and opened a beer. The scene resembled Sherman's sacking of Atlanta. Some buildings were on fire, and others had been torn down. King said that too many men were standing on the roof of one building and it just collapsed, so the men built a bonfire.

High up on the off-limits bulwarks, men were happily walking about. Others were sitting with their legs hanging over the side and drinking. Some men were swimming in the lagoon. Hundreds of beer cans were floating in the still water.

Bratcher said, "It was the lines. They made the men form up in lines and they have had a lot of lines lately, weren't that interested in more lines. Plus it was the ten-cent beer and the twelve-beer limit and the fact that not everyone had the right change and it took a long time sometimes for one person to get his beer and get his change and then, maybe the most important, was the fuck-you attitude of the National Guardsmen, who weren't hardly going on to Vietnam themselves. They didn't show enough respect. Not necessarily smart on their part, when you consider that they were inside a barbed-wire enclosure, outnumbered a thousand to one or more."

He shook his head sadly and drained off the remaining half of his beer. Immediately he reached for another. "It was crazy," he continued. "Truck came in blowing its horn and the men just swarmed over it and quick as a flash there was no more beer on the back of that truck. And then lines started breaking down at the other truck. I had to confiscate these two cases myself from men who stole them. Stole them, Lieutenant. Bad sign for this unit, I tell you. Bad sign -- going into a police action and no respect for the law. Hard to predict what the outcome is going to be if this night is any indication."

A soldier, fully dressed with his boots on, jumped off one of the dry docks into the water, producing a painful sounding "wack." A couple more men walked out of the lagoon from swimming. They were wearing their full fatigue uniforms, including boots. Came walking up on shore like creatures from the black lagoon.

I told Bratcher and King to stay behind at the dry docks while I went to the ship and made a head count. They were to send any stragglers from the platoon down and come back themselves when they were convinced that none of our people remained at the dry docks.

King said, "Good plan, Lieutenant." He opened another beer.

By midnight, my men were all back on the ship. This was not the case everywhere; men staggered back all night. Two swam up to the ship from the sea side. Several got on the wrong ship. A group tried to board a submarine. The local police returned another group that had crashed a local high school football game, run out on the field and stolen the game football. Policemen also found 1st Infantry Division soldiers on people's roofs, under cars, and in churches.

The ship slipped her mooring at midmorning the next day, and the tugs pulled her to sea. Under her own power, the *Mann* continued her westward journey toward Vietnam. As Guam disappeared behind us, the holds were awash with puke. The Navy stopped issuing sheets. Everyone stayed on deck for as long as they could.

The men regained their sea legs by the second day out, and the platoons began to organize their equipment. That night battalion officers met for a briefing on what lay ahead. Our mission after landing at the port city of Vung Tau was to move to a staging area north of Saigon for outfitting and then overland to an area further north where we would set up a battalion-size base camp. When that was built, our battalion would join other division units securing the area north and northwest of Saigon. We received maps and intelligence briefings about known or suspected enemy activities in our tactical area of responsibility (TAOR). Small Vietcong units were active in the coastal and central regions, Main-line North Vietnamese units were on the Cambodian border. Some friendly Army of (South) Vietnam (ARVN) units were scattered throughout our TAOR, although irregular forces that had U.S. Special Forces advisers comprised the principal Government of South Vietnam (GVN) presence along the Cambodian border. Our area was primarily jungle, but it included a number of rice fields and rubber plantations. We would go ashore on U.S. Navy landing craft. The beach area was reported to be secure, and no hostilities were anticipated.

"Reported to be?" I whispered to Pete. "Anticipated? Sorta vague, don't you think? You reckon we ought to call him on it?"

"Everything's going to be OK. Cool it." Pete whispered back out of the corner of his mouth. "This is a good briefing."

"Good my ass," I said as I leaned toward Pete as if I were retying my boot laces. "We're heading into a combat zone and this guy doesn't 'anticipate' hostilities. I don't think he knows what he's talking about."

"Just shut up. There'll probably be a brass band playing when we arrive."

****

53

James E. Parker, Jr.

We arrived off the coast of Vietnam on 8 October, eighteen days after leaving Oakland. The next morning at first light we would go over the rail of the ship and down rope ladders to the Navy landing craft.

I was up long before dawn, packed my gear, and went down into the hold to wait with my platoon until we received orders to go on deck. We were among the first out, with Vietnam before us and the sun coming up behind us. Still some distance from shore, we couldn't make out many details there. The fading night lights from a coastal town were visible to the north. I asked about the ammo and was told that it would be in the LSDs (landing ships, dock).

Looking over the side of the ship, I could see small landing craft bobbing on the ocean. Some were tied up to the *Mann*, and others waited in the distance. Alpha Company, amidships, would be in the first wave over the side and among the first to reach the beach.

Word came over the loudspeakers to board the landing craft. I hitched my helmet strap one last notch tighter and slung my leg over the rail. The loose rope netting jerked around as men all along the side of the ship climbed tentatively down to the waiting LSDs. The *Mann* moved up and down as if she were trying to shake us off. We were laden with equipment. Anyone who lost his grip would fall backward to his death in the landing craft below.

Reaching the boat, I was helped aboard by Rome. In turn I helped Ayers. The landing craft bobbed up and down in the water like an empty paper cup. Men continued to board our small craft, but there was a breakdown in unit integrity. Not all of my men were in the LSD with me. Men from Peterson's and Ernst's platoons were there, plus other soldiers I didn't recognize. I was considering an attempt to make contact with the crafts on either side to find the rest of my men when we cast off. For a time, the *Mann* loomed large above us and then disappeared. We couldn't see over the side.

The ammo was in boxes in the middle of the LSD. Bratcher and I discussed whether we should obey the order not to break the cases. He was in favor of doing everything possible to protect our asses, such as issuing some ammo, but I didn't comment. I was afraid to say yes or no -- bad sign. My first decision and I couldn't make up my mind. So we left the ammo crates unopened.

Most of the men held their weapons close to their chests to protect them from the spray. Some looked around nervously; others kept their eyes down. No one talked. The pounding of the waves on the bottom of the landing craft increased. We were coming through the surf, I thought, and would be landing soon. I looked at the big door ramp in front, which would drop into the water at any minute.

54

We were getting ready to make our entrance into the war zone. I had a flashing recollection of John Wayne and *The Sands of Iwo Jima*. The Navy driver yelled something. As I turned to look at him the locking latch was disengaged and the ramp fell forward. Beck was the first soldier off, bravely running down the ramp into waist-high water. Surprisingly, Spencer was right behind him.

On the back of a U.S. Army flatbed truck ashore the 1st Infantry Division Band was in mid-stanza of "God Bless America." Several U.S. military officers were standing in a group off to the side and waving at us. Vietnamese civilians were further away. Some of them smiled, but others appeared to be apprehensive. A column of deuce-and-a-half trucks were parked on a blacktop nearby. My platoon gathered around me on the beach, looking confused.

And the band played on.

Later I told Peterson that, all in all, I was disappointed.

--FIVE--

First Firefight

We were trucked to a staging area near Bien Hoa and off-loaded near medium-sized tents inside a concertina wire enclosure. Wet and sandy from the beach landing, we had dried out in the truck ride. When we moved our equipment into tents, we burst out in sweat and our uniforms were soon drenched again -- our first taste of the "now-you're-wet, now-you're-not" cycle of life in the Vietnam countryside.

The staging area was on a hill near some local government buildings. To the south, sectioned rice fields stretched almost out of sight. Grazing water buffalo dotted the green landscape. This peaceful, bucolic scene, with a cooling, earth-scented breeze coming up the hill from the rice fields made it hard to believe that this country was the site of so much turmoil and fighting.

A paved, heavily traveled road was to the east. In front of huts scattered along the roadside produce was displayed for passing motorists. To the west were office buildings and to the north was jungle.

The heat was suffocating. As we acclimated, we drew special jungle equipment that included claymore mines and, for night firing, starlight scopes. Not only were the scopes cumbersome and heavy, but they didn't work because the oddly shaped batteries were missing. Not believing the Army would issue us incomplete equipment, we tried without success to make them work and became frustrated. Moubry thought that it was irresponsible of the men and officers to make such a fuss over something so small. When he said that the Army would provide in time, McCoy told him that it was entirely possible the Army could be fucked up. Woolley sent a sergeant from company headquarters into the large supply depot at Bien Hoa to barter for the batteries that we needed and Bratcher came up with a half dozen for our two scopes on his own. Moubry reported to Haldane that men were going outside channels to get material.

During our fourth afternoon in the staging area Woolley ordered me to take my platoon on an ambush patrol behind a village across the paved road that night. Before leaving we test-fired our weapons and drew grenades. In planning the route to the ambush area, I decided to take the men down a stream that led away from the staging area to the north, then over the road to the east, and back along a hedgerow to the high ground behind the village, where we would set up the ambush at a trail junction.

My platoon was up to its full strength of forty-five men. In addition to Bratcher and the radio/telephone operator (RTO), Newsome, I had three eleven-man rifle squads and an eight man heavy weapons squad. Each rifle squad had two five-man fire teams and a squad leader. The heavy weapons squad had the squad leader, two-man machine gun teams, and three men carrying disposal antitank rockets, or LAWS, in lieu of the heavier and more impractical antitank weapons that had come over in crates. This platoon organization was suited for a conventional war, but, as I prepared the platoon for the ambush patrol, it was apparent that the four-squad structure wasn't appropriate for the jungle work that lay ahead. Castro was one of the best fire team leaders, so I had his team lead the patrol. Ayers, a rifleman in Castro's fire team, would be at point. He would be followed by another rifleman, then Castro. I would be midway in the single file, just ahead of my RTO. Bratcher would be at the rear.

That evening, Bratcher stood by the concertina fence and checked that each man had his weapons locked and loaded before he stepped through the wire. There was a steady clamoring of bolts as rounds were loaded into the chambers. We were armed, ready for combat -- our first patrol.

We walked cautiously along the zigzag path through the minefield of the staging area and out into the jungle. Avoiding trails, we cut through the jungle until we reached the stream that I wanted to follow. It began to rain softly as we waded into the water. We passed several houses and could hear the Vietnamese talking inside. Occasionally, a baby cried or we heard someone laugh or cough. We got to the road and crossed it without detection; we were in position on one side of the trail behind the village by 2100. From where I was, halfway down the platoon, I could see the lights from the village. It was supposedly friendly, but, in fact, we didn't know who the friendlies were and who they were not. What we knew for sure was that the Vietnamese had a 2100 curfew. Anyone moving around after that could be taken for a Communist, either a Vietcong or a Vietcong sympathizer. We were to shoot to kill, which didn't leave much room for error.

Lying on my stomach I looked down at the village and wondered if any innocent schoolboy ever came along here at night after seeing his girlfriend or delivering something for his mother. What if a woman, or child, came down that trail? What if a family appeared? Could we tell the difference? It was such a peaceful looking village below. There was no sense of danger here. Just quiet, friendly night sounds. Please Lord, I prayed, don't test us tonight.

A Vietnamese walked into the rear of the ambush sometime after midnight. He saw us, turned and was gone before anyone fired a shot.

In the morning, on the way back to camp, we passed the village near the highway. The villagers, up and going about their early morning farm chores, stopped what they were doing and silently watched us pass.

I thought that everyone had been lucky the previous night -- the men in the platoon and that guy who stumbled into us. No blood, no foul, no harm done.

The men expressed regret as we walked along, however, that we did not get the gook. I didn't tell them how relieved I was for fear they would think I wasn't tough enough for the job ahead.

McCoy and Peterson were waiting for me near my cot. I gave them a detailed report of the patrol. Peterson suggested that he cut off the tail of my shirt, as was done in hunting parties to men who missed a shot.

****

A few days later the entire battalion moved out of the enclosure in single file down the highway, past a few villages, along a side road, and across a rice field. We were going to "sweep" a wooded area between two villages. As we walked alongside the highway, cars slowed down and people looked at us. If there were any Vietcong out here we weren't going to sneak up on them, I told Bratcher.

We crossed the open field and the men lined up along the wood line, shoulder to shoulder. On order from Haldane, we chambered rounds in our weapons and moved into the jungle. We were to stay spread out all the way to the next village, 3.5 kilometers away.

This was not my idea of releasing the dogs of war.

A dozen steps into the jungle, my RTO fell in behind me.

"This ain't the way it's supposed to be," I said. "I ain't breaking trail."

Then, some men fell in behind the radio operator.

"OK," I said, "none of this. You men get out there on the flank like you were, and let's get back on line."

"What if we just looked over at the flank, Lieutenant. Ain't that enough. I mean we don't have to actually walk every step of this goddamn jungle, do we?" This came from Beck who, unfortunately, had a good point.

I told him to get up in front of me. Off to the left, Ayers, strong as a horse, was breaking through the jungle. Several men had fallen in behind him. Bratcher was leading some men on the right. "Who's fucking idea is this anyway?" he asked.

Peterson called on the radio and asked where I was.

"How in the hell do I know where I am? I'm in the Vietnam jungle somewhere. That's all I know," I said. "And my platoon's all over the place. You see any of my people, send them my way. Over."

"I don't know where you are, so I wouldn't know where to send your people if I came across them. I want to know where you are because I hear some people moving up ahead of me. Is it you or the bad guys? Over."

"Assume it's me. Don't shoot. Over."

Shortly afterward Woolley asked for my location. I gave him my best guess. If I was right and if Peterson's guess was accurate, he was on the opposite side of me from where he had been when we started. Then shortly I saw one of Duckett's men beside the group behind Ayers. They should have been on the other side of Ernst, who was to my left. Bratcher's group moved closer to mine. The jungle was so thick that we couldn't see ten feet in any direction.

"I think this is going to be a long year," Beck said.

Suddenly, off to the left came the sound of movement through the undergrowth, crashing, charging toward Ayers' group. Ayers fired a burst from his M-14 fully automatic. As he fired he yelled that we were being attacked.

Whatever, or whoever it was, turned and began making its way to the right. Spencer joined Ayers in firing at the retreating sound.

I got on the company radio and was warning the other platoons that we had contact with something when a group opened up on the right. Some of the stray bullets zipped over our heads. We hit the ground. People opened up to our left, to our right, in front of us, behind us. Rounds were going everywhere. My radio operator kept repeating, "Holy Shit, Holy Shit, Holy Shit." Grenades went off. M-79s went off. More automatic fire.

Then someone started yelling, "Hold your fire, Hold your fire, Hold your fire."

And everyone stopped.

Woolley came on the radio and said it was a deer.

I told Bratcher that I thought it was World War III.

It was absolutely miraculous no one was hurt.

The battalion staggered out of the jungle over the course of the afternoon in twos and threes and sevens and eights. Haldane was the first to admit that we needed to staff out that tactic before we tried it again; it was a reasonable idea, but it needed work.

A week after arriving in the staging area, the battalion moved by truck convoy to Phuoc Vinh, the area selected for the battalion base camp. The town and airfield were considered to be pacified and the men lounged in the shade without much concern about security. I joined the command group moving up the hill north of the airstrip to reconnoiter the area where we would build the battalion base camp. Bratcher was with me, and we tied handkerchiefs to jungle vines to mark our area of the perimeter and then returned for the men. As the sun set the platoon cut down the underbrush to our front and cleared fields of fire for the platoon's two machine guns.

It was quiet that night. I washed down my C-rations supper with warm iodized water from my canteen, checked each position after dark, and slept hard, even though it poured rain toward morning.

For the next four days, we cut the trees and scrubs in front to improve the fighting positions and to connect them with a trench. Three bulldozers arrived on the scene the following day and graded circles around the entire battalion perimeter. We received the crates of antitank weapons that contained my shotgun and jungle hammock. I hung the hammock in a small cleared area behind the command bunker. The men ran radio land lines from the platoon area to company headquarters. Truckloads of concertina wire were stretched and connected in three strands in front of the area. The men worked hard, mostly with their shirts off, sweating in the Southeast Asia sun. Morale was high and there was much friendly banter.

We posted a lone sentry out by the wood line as we worked, causing Spencer to say, "Man, I feels like I'm on a Louisiana chain gang, whacking weeds and a guard sitting over there with a gun."

"Spencer," Beck said as he stretched out a strand of wire, "I've been on chain gangs. This is good work here. Plus, look'it. We're making $9 a day, got all the grub we want to eat ... dry hootch, air mattress, smokes, mail. Shit man, this is fine."

Spencer began singing in a good baritone voice, "Beck's been working on the chain gang, all the live long day, Beck's been working on the chain gang, just to pass the time of day ... "

Beck, off-key, joined in, "Don't you hear the whistle blowing, rise up so early in the morn... "

Lyons, from across the field, "Oh my bleeding ass, shut the fuck up, you two."

"Fuck you, Lyons," from both Beck and Spencer.

The next day the mines arrived.

Medieval, ugly, they smelled like death. Appropriately the wooden boxes they came in were marked with skull and cross bones. We were issued three types: Bouncing Betties that jumped up and exploded above ground to maximize casualties, foot jammers that blew feet apart, and swarthy, lethal antitank mines.

We dug row upon row of potholes between the concertina wire loops in front of our positions. The following morning, we placed the mines by the holes and marked them on a map. At midday King, Rome, and I, laying on our stomachs started laying the mines on the row of holes nearest the concertina wire. We lifted the mines, one by one, put them in the holes; covered them with dirt; tied out trip lines; and, finally, removed the safety pins.

I had Castro replace me when we finished the first row. I sat on top of Spencer's bunker the rest of the day watching the men as they slowly and carefully laid the minefield. The following afternoon, they placed the last mine. We were the last platoon in the battalion to finish. A safe lane was marked through the field with reflectors that could be seen from the inside looking out. If a friendly patrol arrived back at the outer concertina strand, someone from inside would have to go out and act as an escort into the area. Our safe lane came down right in front of the M-60 machine gun.

There was nothing funny or cute about laying a minefield. It lay like death at your front door.

The Vietnam War Its Ownself

For meals we had C-rations which included a canned meat, such as boned chicken, turkey loaf, ham and eggs, bean and franks, roast pork, chipped beef, or ham and beans; a dessert, such as fruit cocktail, fruit cake, or chocolate; peanut butter and crackers or jelly and bread; plus chewing gum, cigarettes, matches, salt and pepper, coffee and cocoa, powdered cream and sugar, and toilet paper. Altogether it was not a bad box lunch. We all had our favorite meals. I always got first pick, so I took what I wanted. Lyons once told me that wasn't necessarily fair. I told him to fuck himself.

Castro, who had been in the Army longer than anyone else in the platoon, knew how to turn regular C-rations into gourmet meals. Two days after laying the minefield I invited him to my command bunker to fix a communal stew. He propped a steel pot half-filled with water between three rocks and put several boxes of heat tablets beneath it. He lit the heat tablets; while the water was coming to a boil he put in several portions of different meats. From his pack, he brought out some Tabasco sauce, garlic, onions, and red peppers and put them in the pot along with some greens he had cut as we cleared the area. After adding salt and pepper, stirring the stew with a wooden spoon from his pack and spitting in it for real Latin flavor, Castro ladled out rich, aromatic portions.

It was so hot my eyes watered, but it was, all in all, the best meal I had had in Vietnam.

I had a cigarette and beer later when Bratcher and Castro had gone to their bunkers, unlaced my boots and leaned back against a tree. Night was falling, the moon was out. With the bunkers built, the land cleared, and the barbed wire and mines laid, I felt safe. Everyone in the platoon was becoming more acclimated to the heat and more accustomed to living in the jungle. It's not such a bad place, I thought as I put out my cigarette, crushed my beer can and threw it toward the trash hole. I stood up, stretched, and walked over to the jungle hammock. After unzipping the side, I bent down and inward, turning so as to sit on the hammock inside. I took off my boots, and put them on the ground, put my belt inside one of the boots and reached out for my pistol inside the holster of my web gear. My shotgun was on a peg nearby under my poncho. I zipped shut the mosquito netting, put my pistol under the clean set of fatigues I used as a pillow, took a deep breath, and fell asleep.

A couple of hours later, a Vietcong sniper crawled up behind an anthill on the edge of the wood line beyond our last strand of barbed wire. Kneeling, he rested his rifle on the top of the anthill and scanned the bunkers along the perimeter. Other Vietcong were taking their positions around him. They intended to wait until their companion in the middle drew the fire from the different positions so that they could pick out individual targets from the muzzle flashes of my men. The Vietcong gunman in the center continued to scan the line. He finally focused on the command bunker and then at the irresistible hammock to the rear. The moon glistened off the rain roof.

He aimed for the center of the hammock and fired. The first bullet went through the rain roof over my head and the second through the mosquito netting beneath me.

I woke from a dead sleep when the first bullet whistled by and was desperately trying to get out when the second round passed under me. Frantically, I clawed at the zipper, and the hammock rotated 180 degrees as another round zipped by. The Vietcong in the middle ducked behind the anthill after firing his three shots, seconds before men in the bunkers opened up on the anthill. I heard automatic fire from a dozen M-14s and a long burst from the M-60 machine gun punctured by explosions of M-79 grenade rounds.

Frantic, I couldn't find the zipper to get out of the hammock. Upside down, I literally didn't know which way was up. Outside, it sounded like a full-scale attack by hundreds of Vietcong, and there I was suspended in the air, captured in a hammock death trap. Where was the frigging zipper? Which side was up?

"Aaauggggggg." My yell was not heard over the din of battle.

One of the other Vietcong, watching the reaction along the perimeter to his companion's three shots, debated between firing at the machine gun in one of the bunkers or at the strange bag jiggling wildly in the middle. He would have time for one shot, or at most two, before he would have to duck. The machine gun or the hammock? The hammock was so conspicuously attractive, the way it wiggled invited a pop shot.

Captain Woolley was calling on the radio to find out what was happening. Newsome, my radio operator, crawled over to my hammock and yelled out that Woolley wanted to talk with me.

I was still thrashing around inside, my hands wildly searching, legs pumping. The hammock flipped on one side, then the other. The pistol hit me in the head. Mother of Jesus. WHERE IS THE ZIPPER?

Then incredibly one end of the hammock dropped to the ground and I tumbled down to the bottom.

Another round zipped overhead.

Newsome reached over from the base of a tree, unzipped the hammock, and pushed the handset toward me, as I squirmed out. He had cut one end of the hammock down rather than chance standing up.

"Hate to wake you up like that sir, but we got a shoot-out going here and the captain wants to know what's going on," he yelled.

I told Woolley that we were under attack, did not know about casualties and I'd get back.

Bratcher yelled out, "No attack, just probing. We're OK."

"Hold your fire, goddamnit, hold your fire," I yelled.

Gradually, the firing stopped. No more rounds came in. It was absolutely quiet, although my ears continued to ring. My heart seemed to be beating in my ears.

I radioed Woolley that we had been probed, but the enemy had pulled back. I didn't think we had any casualties (hoping this was true) and promised to report if we discovered any wounded.

As I finished my radio transmission, Peterson's platoon fired mortar flares and the whole area was illuminated. The wood line beyond the concertina looked eerie, but unoccupied.

Everyone had been looking toward the front when the firing started, and no one in the platoon saw me wrestling to get out of the hammock. I had no comments the next morning when the radio operator put his fingers through the bullet holes in the rain roof.

"Close, man," he said.

Peterson, Dunn, and McCoy dropped by the next morning.

"You know, Parker, it's people like you who keep the average high on second lieutenant casualties in combat," Dunn said.

McCoy looked at me for a long moment and just shook his head. "Correct me if I'm wrong here, but weren't you the one saying you were going to be the meanest bastard in the valley of death?"

"All right, all right. Anyone want to buy a hammock?" I asked.

Colonel Haldane found no humor in the incident and chastised us for opening up with all of our weapons against an unseen enemy. Because he felt that we had given away our position, he had us relocate every foxhole and bunker. He issued an order that we could not initiate counter fire at the perimeter unless we clearly saw a target.

The order specifically talked about rifles. It did not mention the large 106mm antitank weapons.

A few nights later, Duckett's men thought that they saw Vietcong out on the edge of the woods and Duckett conferred with his platoon sergeant. Soon there was this "Kabooooooom!" as the 106 mm fired, then "Whaaaammmmmmm," as a large tree fell over, dead.

The next morning Haldane came to the perimeter. "Duckett,

look at me," he said. "When I say you don't fire your individual weapons, I'm also talking about that 106 millimeter. You hear?"

Pete came out later, fuming. He said, "Duckett, we used that tree to register and adjust our mortars. What we going to do, now you've blown it away?"

At lunch Duckett told me, "You know, you can sure get in trouble shooting your gun in this war."

--SIX--

Rookies

Two nights later, the group of Vietcong returned and sniped at our position. Some of the men saw them clearly, and we returned a tremendous amount of fire. Peterson's platoon fired flares more quickly this time. Interdiction rounds from our mortars flew over us and landed in the jungle well beyond the perimeter. The noise, the tracers, the fluorescent half-light from the flares were surreal, like Halloween.

Woolley was yelling on the radio, "What's going on? What's going on? Red Cap Twigs Alpha November Six?"

I hollered to the men to stop firing. In the rear, we could hear fresh mortar rounds *whoof* as they left their tubes, whistled overhead, and exploded in the jungle in front of us. There was no other sound except low half-whispers from our men discussing the attack.

"We were probed again. It's quiet. Nothing more. No casualties," I reported to Woolley.

The next day, we went out to the anthill on the other side of the concertina wire. There was no evidence that anyone had been there the night before. We could find no expended cartridges; the grass was not matted down. When I talked to Woolley later, I found myself defending my platoon's actions. Why were we the only ones probed, Woolley asked. "Well, maybe," I suggested, "because there's that trail that comes near my part of the perimeter from the village. Maybe that's it."

Bratcher and I later decided to put some men in the jungle in front of the perimeter for a few nights in hopes of catching the probers. There was a point of honor here. Had we been firing at ghosts? Spencer and Beck were drafted to man the listening post. At midafternoon I took two squads for a small patrol out to the trail leading from the village. I carried my shotgun with the sawed-off barrel. Woolley knew about the gun. In fact, he had smuggled a shotgun himself to Vietnam -- a Browning 12-gauge automatic.

On the way back to the perimeter, near the anthill, Spencer and Beck dropped off into a thicket where they would spend the night in hopes of catching our visitors if they came calling. Spencer gave me a resigned look as he disappeared into the bamboo.

That night, I sat on top of my bunker and suddenly felt a breeze. I remembered Cottonpicker talking about spooking game when the wind was in his back. Creatures living in the woods can smell creatures that don't. The wind was blowing away from the perimeter, taking Spencer and Beck's scent into the jungle. How good are the Vietcong, I wondered. Then, it started to rain. Beck cursed the next time that he called in. He was cold, wet, and sleepy. I told him to shut up and do his duty.

When the rain stopped, I went back out and sat on the top of the bunker. Clouds covered the moon. I squinted to make out images in front and listened closely. Focusing on the jungle, I strained to hear any possible footfalls of Vietcong moving behind Beck and Spencer. Rain dripped off leaves and branches, and a slight breeze caused some of the foliage to sway. I could almost make out images of people along the wood line and hear footsteps. Once, I was sure I saw a man holding a gun across his body as he stood by a tree between us and my two soldiers. I asked the RTO if he saw anything. He looked for a long time but could not see anyone. When I looked again the image had changed into a tall bush.

Beck and Spencer were at the wire at first light. Patrick went out through the safe lane to escort them in.

Later that day, we went out by the anthill and cleared away some bushes that I had imagined to be Vietcong the night before. Bratcher hid two directional claymore mines behind the anthill, and ran wires along the safe lane to the machine-gun bunker. If someone climbed up behind that anthill and fired, we could just mash a button to detonate the claymores and the entire area behind the anthill would be a killing zone.

Bratcher was in the machine-gun bunker that night. I instructed the men not to fire for any reason until the claymores went off. If the sniper came back and fired, Bratcher would take him out.

Showers continued on and off all night, with the moon breaking out of the clouds periodically. Several times, I thought I saw movement by the anthill. The more I watched, however, the clearer it was to me how the eye can be fooled.

There were no sniper attacks that night. The next day, most

of the men in the platoon worked to clear an area where we were going to build a tent city for the battalion. It would include an aid station, an ammo dump, a supply area, latrines, showers, and mess halls. After we staked out the streets the area began to resemble a Wild West frontier town.

Bratcher manned the detonators for the claymore that night and the men had instructions again not to fire until the mines went off. Near midnight, a single round zipped over the perimeter. I was instantly wide awake and expected to hear the mines. After a few minutes, I called out to Bratcher. He said he was waiting. He hadn't seen where the shot had come from, and wasn't sure that it was the anthill. Somebody down the line thought he saw a muzzle blast off to the right. The moon was out, and the anthill was clearly visible on the edge of the jungle.

Fire again, you son of a bitch, I thought. Fire.

There were no more rounds during the night. Ayers, Castro, Bratcher, and I went out to the anthill the next morning. Ayers stood guard near the jungle as Castro, Bratcher, and I looked around. At first, we saw no signs of anyone having been there the night before.

"Lieutenant," Castro suddenly said, "look at this." He was standing by the area where we had hidden one of the claymores two days before. It had been moved, turned, and aimed back at our machine-gun position at the end of the safe lane.

The other claymore was missing. The wire had been cut.

"Very cute," Bratcher said, his neck tightening. "If I had detonated the mine we would have gotten splattered. As it is, the guy still got one of our mines."

"Clever little bugger," I said, although there was some gratification in knowing that there were VC operating outside our lines and we weren't shooting at shadows.

That same day, we received orders for a battalion-sized patrol operation twenty kilometers to our north. My platoon led the battalion north and at dusk, four hundred infantrymen of 1st of the 28th Infantry were in position along a VC supply trail.

Around three o'clock in the morning, Lyons crawled over to the tree where I was sleeping. He shook me awake and said that he thought some men were carrying things down the trail. I couldn't fathom what was going on. Lyons didn't see things that weren't there and it hadn't been raining. If Vietcong were walking down the trail, units on either side should have fired at them. The whole battalion was near the trail. I told him to go back to his position and if he saw anybody else walking down that trail to shoot him. Lyons crawled away and disappeared in the dark jungle. I had just decided to follow him and see these men on the trail for myself when he started firing his M-14 on full automatic.

The night was suddenly filled with tracers and the thunderous sound of automatic rifle fire. It finally died down and then stopped completely as the word circulated: "Hold your fire."

In the quiet that followed, we heard a man groaning. He called out in Vietnamese. Around him, from my platoon and from down the line, men fired toward the sound. I yelled to stop the firing. There was quiet. Then I heard the man groan again. A long painfully wail. Some men fired again. I yelled again to stop the firing.

Colonel Haldane and Captain Woolley crawled up with a Vietnamese interpreter. Out in front the man babbled Vietnamese. Haldane asked the interpreter what he was saying.

"He says he is shot and he says he hurts. He asks us to help."

Woolley and Haldane exchanged looks without comment.

"I think ... I think, maybe trap. Maybe other Vietcong around. He has gun for sure," the interpreter offered.

"Yea, well what's he saying?" asked Haldane.

"He says he hurts a lot," the interpreter said after a pause.

"Continue talking to him. Try to find out if he is really alone," Haldane ordered in a hushed voice.

In the jungle to our front, the groans had no accent, the tremor in the low wails were an international human expression of pain. But could that be faked? Were we being baited to come out of our perimeter?

The moaning continued for an hour or so, but became gradually weaker. It stopped before the sun came up.

At first light, my platoon moved out toward the area where the sound had come from. The young Vietnamese man was dead. He had taken off his watch and tried to hide it in some bushes near his outstretched hand. A bag of rice lay some distance away. The man was unarmed. The first Vietcong killed by the battalion was an unarmed porter. We had come halfway around the world to kill a laborer.

"Ain't war fun," Spencer said, standing near the dead man. Surprisingly, I did not feel much remorse, although I had listened to the man as he died. It had been frightening in the darkness, not knowing if other VC were around us, getting ready to attack. Plus I had been frustrated by our lack of catching the VC who had probed our part of the perimeter at the base camp. Last night, in the dark, we had reached out to get the enemy and had only gotten a porter, but it was a start. We had much to learn about jungle fighting.

I walked away from the dead man without looking back,

saying under my breath, "Don't probe my perimeter anymore."

The battalion swept the area from the trail down to the river and uncovered a large store of rice. Some of the bags had the sign of clasped hands across the ocean on them, which indicated that the rice was part of U.S. aid to the region.

While burning down a hootch near the rice cache, Patrick was standing by, lighting a cigarette, when suddenly he heard a shot. He dropped to the ground, brought his rifle to his shoulder, and looked around wildly for the enemy. The rest of the men in his squad did not react.

"The bamboo," De Leon said. "It's the bamboo burning. Sections popping. Get up. Nobody's shooting at you, sweetheart."

The bamboo continued to pop as Patrick got to his feet.

Later when we broke down into platoon patrols for the move back to the base camp, a grenade on Manuel's web belt came unscrewed and fell to the ground. The firing pin was still on his belt.

"Grenade!" he yelled, as he dived away.

He lay there, his mouth wide open and his eyes shut tight, waiting for the explosion that would take his life. After a minute the men around him got to their feet. Bratcher walked up, saw the fuse, pen and handle still on Manuel's belt, who continued to lay on the ground with a confused look on his face.

"Good God Almighty," Bratcher said, "how can we be expected to fight in this war when we got dumb-bells for soldiers. Get your fat ass up, Manuel. You ain't going to die. Fix your frigging grenade and move out."

Over the course of the next few days, the platoon was assigned to work details to fix up the company area, erect tents, dig latrines, and string wire. Ernst, Duckett, Pete, and I moved into a tent next to company headquarters, near the mess hall. My platoon was in two similar-sized tents down the company street. We changed our routine from having the whole platoon on the line each night to posting a small twenty-four hour guard detail.

****

Periodically at night, the mortar platoons, including Pete's in our company and the 4.2-inch mortars at battalion, shot harassment and interdiction (H&I) fire at randomly selected road junctions or trails. The purpose was to keep the Vietcong, if there were any out there, on their toes and wary of mindless wandering near our position.

One night, one of the battalion's mortar platoons misfired an H&I round into a group of huts northwest of the friendly village of

Phuoc Vinh. The local ARVN unit advised our battalion about the accident early the next morning. Company A was sent out to investigate.

The huts were separated from the main part of the village along a river, and the mortar round had landed directly on top of a hut in the center. A woman and two men had been killed and several other people wounded, including some children. The dead were lying in the shade by the side of a hut when we arrived, their bloodstained night clothing only partially covering the gaping holes in their bodies from the shrapnel. The villagers were wailing and crying. Most of the wounded had been evacuated to a hospital in town, but a few of the lesser wounded were standing around, displaying fresh bandages. Through an interpreter, we took information about the time of the accident, the number of casualties, and the exact location of the huts.

The hit occurred at approximately the same time that an H&I round was fired by the battalion 4.2-mortar platoon at a road target near the huts. Our unit had killed the civilians. It was a mistake, and everyone was sorry.

"Things like these happen in wars," Bratcher said, twitching his jaw. "We just got to hang in there and learn how to do it right. War ain't never been easy. Or error free."

Two nights later to the west, near the huts we had accidentally hit with our mortar fire, several rockets were laid in wooden V wedges and ignited by a small group of people, probably Vietcong. The rockets soared up and into our base camp. They landed in Company B's area. The west side of the perimeter was probed at about the same time.

Within ten minutes from the time of the first rocket explosion, everything became quiet. I reported to Woolley that there was no activity in my sector but I continued to stand in the command bunker and scan the edge of the jungle line. There was no conversation on the radio. Finally the field telephone rang. My RTO said Lieutenant Peterson was on the telephone.

"Dunn's wounded," Pete said. "He's at the aid tent."

I took a flashlight and made my way to the aid tent near the center of the base camp. Haldane and Allee were just coming out through the blackout curtain. Haldane said Dunn was going to be all right. Inside the tent, three men were lying on stretchers on the floor. Dunn was on the operating/examination table. He was talking fast to the battalion surgeon, Dr. Isaac Goodrich, and the corpsmen attending him.

"Goddamned that hurts. Quit it. Goddamnit. Quit it. Quit it."

"Lieutenant," said Goodrich, "if you don't shut up, we are

69

going to quit it and leave you alone to sew up your own mess. Shut up."

Dunn had shrapnel wounds on his chest, arms, stomach, and legs, but they did not appear to be life threatening. The corpsmen probed in the open wounds to find the shrapnel, occasionally extracted bits of metal and dropped them in a stainless-steel pan on a nearby table.

"Owweeee," Dunn moaned, though not very seriously. "Don't you have some laughing gas or opium or something? Aren't there supposed to be some female nurses around here? Owweeee."

"Bob," I said, "I just talked with some of your men. They did it. Threw grenades at you. Don't like you. Tried to kill you. They're standing around outside, some of them, taking bets on whether you live or die. Only no one wants to take bets that you live."

"Owweeee, Jimmy, Ohhhhhh, Jimmy, I don't like this. You gotta help me."

I took out a .45-pistol round and put it in his mouth. "Bite on this," I said. "It's the way they do it in the movies."

Dunn was flown out to the 93d field hospital in Bien Hoa the following day. The doctor opined that he would be back in the unit within weeks. He had lost some blood and had some nicks, but he was going to be all right.

Shortly after Dunn left, the battalion received orders to provide protection to a truck convoy traveling between Phuoc Vinh and Bien Hoa. We were deployed along the road in advance of the convoy and spent several days in relaxed platoon-size positions as the trucks sped by. We received mixed reactions from the civilians in the area. Some of the older men and women ignored us and stayed out of our way. Others, especially the children, were fascinated and watched as we approached, smiling when we smiled. Rumors circulated that we should not buy drinks from the locals because glass and poison had been found in Cokes sold by children in other areas.

After the convoys passed, we were trucked down to the edge of Bien Hoa, where we were to camp while the trucks were loaded. We expected to be in the bivouac area for several days. The day we arrived there, Pete, Duckett, and I borrowed a Jeep and went into Bien Hoa. I went to a furniture maker and placed an order for a bar for our tent at Phuoc Vinh. The furniture maker promised to have it finished by the next afternoon.

We wandered from the furniture maker's shop down to a strip of bars and noticed that we were dirtier than most of the U.S. soldiers we passed, who we assumed worked at the Bien Hoa logistic command.

The Vietnam War Its Ownself

"It's like the Wild West movies, you know," Pete said. "These here are townies and we're just in from the range, covered with trail dust."

An Armed Forces radio station was on in the bar we finally entered, reporting on an upcoming Bob Hope concert. We envied the way the local GIs seemed to know their way around the bar, playing darts and talking with the girls. One of the soldiers came up to Duckett and asked if he had any souvenirs for sale.

"Beg your pardon?" Duckett said.

"Vietcong stuff, flags, AK-47s, hats," the soldier clarified. "Big price for it at Bien Hoa, though they make VC flags in some of the shops better than the real thing."

"Nope, we ain't got none of that," Duckett said as McCoy came in the bar and joined us.

"I tell you what," he said. "This is the way to do the war -- inside work, light lifting, air conditioners, bars, girls, cold beer."

"You're going candy ass, George?" I said.

"Ah, the romance had gone out of being in the infantry," George said. "A little logistic command assignment, two or three months down here -- I could do that."

We noticed a drunk soldier, with pressed fatigues and shined boots, groping at a bar girl.

"Well, I don't know," George said. "Maybe it is better out in the boonies. The beer tasted better when you can get it cold. You're thirstier, you know what I mean? Didn't have to worry about dressing up for any Bob Hope concert."

The next day I commandeered an empty deuce-and-a-half truck and, with Manuel driving, returned to the furniture make. The bar was all I had expected. Nicely curved on one end with adjustable shelves behind. A water-resistant top. We took it back to our bivouac area and put ponchos over it, more for protection against the possibility of rain than to hide it. When the convoy was assembled the following day, I located a driver who was taking supplies to our battalion, and he agreed to put the bar on top of his load. I assigned Manuel as the bar guard and told him to ride in the back and to protect that bar with his life.

I was standing by Woolley as the convoy passed. Manuel was on the back of one of the first vehicles. The bar, obvious to me because of its shape, was under wraps. I waved to Manuel. Woolley put his head to one side as he looked at me, quizzically.

Manuel had the bar in our tent when we finally arrived three days later. Woolley came in and asked where it came from.

"Damned if I know, but it sure is pretty," I said. "Something

71

to come home to from those long camping trips we take around here."

An hour later Colonel Haldane and Major William E. Panton, the battalion G-3 (operations officer), walked into the tent, looked at the bar, then at me, and walked out without comment.

I wrote to several liquor companies at the addresses on their bottles and asked for bar accessories, napkins, shot glasses, anything to give our bar a professional touch. Within weeks I began to get packages. Each liquor company responded and was generous with gifts. Our bar soon had all the accommodations of a first-rate neighborhood gin mill.

Mail call was the most important part of the day to most of the soldiers. Late in the afternoon, Bratcher picked up the platoon's mail from the company clerk. He called the men into the company street and yelled out the names on the packages and letters. Ayers was always in the front, but he never seemed to get any mail. Bratcher said that it was painful for him, when he had to tell Ayers that he got no mail; the big lug always looked so hurt. It wasn't that Ayers didn't write to anyone. Every couple of days, he gave the company clerk a painfully addressed letter to someone in the Midwest. As far as we knew, no one ever responded.

Ray Ernst also had a man in his platoon who didn't receive mail and, like Ayers, stood in the front during each mail call. Ernst wrote to a preacher friend, who organized an Operation Alpha Company. Members of his congregation sent personal letters to men in the company, including Ayers. Bratcher was also careful to call out Ayer's name for boxes addressed to "Anyone in Alpha Company, 1st/28th Infantry." We were soon receiving care packages from other churches, civic organizations, and grammar school classes. We got a lot of Kool-Aid; some newspaperman somewhere must have written, "Those boys over there need Kool-Aid to win this war," 'cause we got Kool-Aid packages by the hundred. No one ever used them.

Dunn returned from the field hospital within a month. We had a "welcome home" party for him at the bar.

We continued to widen our area of operations in November and December, sweeping farther and farther from our base camp. In late November we had returned from a battalion-size sweep when we were visited by a congressional delegation led by Senator Jacob Javits. The officers and NCOs of the company were standing in a loose formation near the company headquarters when the senator arrived. As he came down the line, he asked me if I needed anything or if there was anything he could do for me back home. I told him that we had a bar in our tent, but we needed a picture of a nude behind it.

The Vietnam War Its Ownself

"I am trying to upgrade the ambiance of the place," I added.

"A nude?" the senator asked hesitantly, as though my request was slightly uncongressional.

"Yes sir," I said.

I did not look at Woolley or Haldane because I knew they were glaring. Second lieutenants should not be forward with congressional delegations. Certainly, they shouldn't ask for pictures of naked women. Javits smiled and wished me well.

****

In late November 1965, my platoon was on patrol south of the base camp. Private De Leon and Sergeant Rome were on point. As they broke out of a bamboo thicket De Leon dropped to one knee and Rome lifted his arm in the air, stopping the platoon. Rome turned, made eye contact with me, and called in a loud whisper, "Lieutenant."

Rome moved off to one side behind a tree, and I joined him there. We looked through the jungle toward a small Vietnamese village in front of us. Off to the side of the village near an open field, several women wearing straw cone hats were sifting rice, separating it from the chaff. Several old men and a few children were moving around among the huts. Smoke from two cooking fires drifted up.

"No men," De Leon observed. "Don't look right."

A chicken crowed from inside the village and then, closer to us, some pigs snorted.

I leaned against the back side of the tree, wiped my brow, and pulled a map from my side pocket. Sergeant Bratcher walked up. When he took in the scene and saw me studying the map, he turned and motioned for the platoon behind us in the thicket to get down and rest.

The village was clearly marked on my map, as was the nearby rice field where the women were working. The map indicated that a path ran from the village across our front to a road five kilometers distant to the west. On the other side of the village from us was another rice field.

We had been in Vietnam now for seven weeks. Although my men had killed the VC rice porter -- and had been probed at our base camp -- the platoon had not been fully engaged by the enemy. We were coming together as a unit, however, and becoming comfortable in the jungle, more sure of ourselves, as we gradually expanded our patrols farther away from other friendly units. We looked jungle tough. Because we carried our weapons with us every minute we were in the field, they were extensions of our bodies. Our field

73

uniforms and web gear were becoming faded; the coverings to our steel pots were personalized with identifying marks -- girlfriend names, personal mottoes, etc. Most of us carried our C-rations in extra socks hanging off the backs of our packs. Although we looked like pack mules with all of our gear, we did not clank when we walked. On patrol, every day, we moved more silently as we learned to traverse jungle obstacles, but we were tired of trudging endlessly through the jungles. We wanted to engage the Vietcong, and we felt that we were getting closer. Newsome, my radio operator, in fact, had remarked during our last break that he felt like we were being watched.

It was midafternoon but still hot. We heard no sounds from the women, old men, and children in the village, only the distant steady thumping of thrashing rice and the whirring of nearby insects.

I reached for the handset to the PRC-25 radio. "Red Cap Twigs Alpha Six, this is Red Cap Twigs Alpha November Six, over," I said, calling Captain Woolley in a soft voice.

There was a short pause. Then, "Yea, November Six, this is Alpha Six, what's your location, over?"

After giving a coordinate from the map, I turned to look at the Vietnamese people working to my front and said, "We're near this village, and there ain't no men that we can see. Maybe twenty women, children, old people. I think they know we're here, but they ain't looking this way. Just going on about their business. Don't like it. What you want me to do, over?"

During a long pause, I stared at the back of an old man in black pajamas, who was sitting in the shade of a hut, stiffly staring away from us. I sensed he was listening intently. He probably had heard the distinctive squelch sound from the radio.

"Alpha November Six, this is Alpha Six. Go on around the village; don't go mixing it up with civilians. You're out there looking for VC. Go on, you got another few clicks to go anyway to tie up with Alpha Mike Six before sundown. Circle the village and continue on. You copy, over?"

I acknowledged the order and handed the hand set back to the RTO as I pushed myself away from the tree. Sergeant Rome had also heard the company commander's order. He raised from his squatting position and turned to me. I motioned with my head to stay well in the jungle and pass the village to the left. As Rome and then De Leon started moving, a dog in the village began barking. I stood by the tree and watched the village as my platoon slowly filed by. The dog continued to bark loudly. The old man sitting in the shade did not move.

The Vietnam War Its Ownself

Falling in near the end of the patrol I walked alongside PFC Joaquim S. Cipriano for several minutes, although my attention was still on the village we were passing. Cipriano had not been feeling well lately. "I'm sick," he said. "Stomach, plus I'm hacking up some crud. Feel like I got bugs or worms or something. Really, I ain't making this up."

I heard him, but my focus was to our right. Finally I looked in his direction and we made eye contact.

Cipriano smiled. "Back home feeling the way I do, my momma would make me some soup."

Smiling at him, I made no comment and moved up the patrol line to fall in near Newsome with the radio. Ahead, De Leon and Rome cautiously came to the path leading across our front to the village. De Leon stuck his head out into the pathway, looked both ways, and took three quick steps to the other side. Rome followed and then a few more soldiers. I crossed the path, and one by one, the rest of the platoon began to cross. Up ahead, De Leon was approaching the second rice field, and I strained to see if there was anyone working in the field.

With fearful suddenness, a sharp sound cracked through the air. For a second, an enormously loud blast consumed us. Shrapnel shredded the foliage around us, and everyone hit the ground.

"Owweeee," someone in great pain yelled immediately. De Leon began firing his M-14 on full automatic. Falling to my knees behind an anthill, I couldn't see anyone between us and the rice field.

"What the hell's happening, De Leon?" I yelled.

Behind me, near the path I heard again, "Iiioooooowwwwweeeeee," and then, "Oh Mother of Mercy, oh God, oh God, oh God I'm dying. Iiiioooooooowwwweeee."

"Nothing just yet, but I ain't letting no one come up on me," De Leon answered. Behind at the path, more screaming. "Medic, medic, medic. God, where's the medic?"

Quickly moving back, I saw Cipriano lying face down at the side of the path. He had a large, bloody wound in his back, above his pack, near his neck. He kept yelling for the medic. Nearby on the path was a hole surrounded by fresh dirt blown away by a mine. Two wires sticking out of the hole led back toward the village. Someone had touched off the mine as Cipriano passed. A patrol member applied a bandage to the wound. I told Cipriano to be still and it would be all right.

Crazed with fear and pain, he kept looking around as he said, "I'm dying, doc. I can't feel nothing. I can't feel my legs or my arms or nothing, doc. And goddamn it hurts. Don't let me die. Please don't

75

let me die."

Newsome had followed me back to the path. He had called in a medevac helicopter, and I took the radio to report to the company commander. As I finished, the air ambulance chopper was arriving; it must have been very close by. I sent men to surround a nearby clearing and throw purple smoke into the field. Within minutes, possibly less than fifteen since the mine had exploded, Cipriano was on the chopper heading for a hospital. He was still conscious, but he had bled a great deal and bloody bandages covered his back. Lying on his stomach in the back of the helicopter, he looked in our direction with eyes glazed in pain. As the helicopter rose out of the field, the corpsman on board was clearing Cipriano's weapon. Helicopter gunships buzzed the tree lines on either side.

Then, it was quiet again, and we went into the village.

I sent some of the men to the far side, and they herded the women from their rice chores back into the center of the village, while the rest of the platoon searched the huts. Shortly, all the villagers were collected near me in front of one of the cooking fires. There were no young men -- just women, old people, and children standing in a huddle as they fearfully looked around at us. But I knew that one of them had set off the mine that had wounded my man, or perhaps killed him or maimed him for life. Or, if one of them had not set off the mine, they were hiding the person who did.

Rome, Bratcher, De Leon, and the others had stopped their noisy search of the small village and gathered around to look at the Vietnamese. The loud dog, beaten off by one of my soldiers, continued to bark at the side of a hut.

To let the Vietnamese go free would certainly mean that they would shield attacks on other Americans patrolling their countryside, looking for their Vietcong brothers, fathers and sons. Allowing them to go without punishment would not further our ends here or vindicate the attack on Cipriano. They were the enemy -- directly or indirectly. I felt something needed to be done.

None of us in the platoon spoke their language. We could not threaten or interrogate them or make them understand why we were here. What could we do?

De Leon walked up with a VC flag that he had found in a tree on the edge of the village.

Beck picked up the old man who had sat silently in the shade of the hut and shook him. The old man did not show fear and I told Beck to release him.

A few moments later, I ordered the men to move out and we left the villagers alone, unhurt.

It is not pleasant to be the conventional force in a guerrilla war -- maintaining high moral standards of conduct when the enemy is engaged in total war. It is a hard war to win.

--SEVEN--
At Home in the Jungle

Peterson was transferred out of the company to take over the battalion reconnaissance (recon) platoon when we returned from the field. Expected to be the eyes and ears of the battalion, roaming in the front and on the flanks during conventional field operations, the recon platoon had been heretofore in Vietnam no more than battalion staff security and the colonel wanted more aggressive leadership. I hated to see Pete go. He was my best friend and I wanted him at my side in battle. Pete, however, was eager to get out of the mortars and into a maneuver element. Plus he wanted to work directly for Colonel Haldane. So I was happy for him, but sad to see him go. I thought about the insurance policy, remembering that I hadn't ever sent in the change of beneficiary form. I looked for it, couldn't find it, and then let it go. Helping Pete move his gear over to battalion, I started to mention the insurance, but I was embarrassed and told myself I just had to find the form or to write the company for another.

During the next battalion operation, Pete's first as recon platoon leader, we went across a large river to the west of our base camp and broke down into platoon-sized units. Battalion staff officers, assigned to spotter helicopters, looked for signs of VC fleeing in front of the platoons.

From their elevated vantage the spotters could not see men moving on the ground as well as they could see trails, villages, and clearings. They had never served on the ground themselves and did not realize how difficult it was to move through the jungle. Sometimes, we faced swamps and deep crevices beneath the jungle canopies, so the observers often miscalculated the time that it would take us to move through a particular area.

"OK, Red Cap Twigs Alpha November Six, you, ah, you, ah, are where? Throw smoke?" Pause. "OK, I got it. What are you doing there, you're supposed to be another click ahead. They're waiting on you up there."

Down below, Bratcher would say, "I think I am going to

shoot that REMF, next chance. Next opportunity I have at that clean, good smelling, staff shithead, he's dead."

Ayers and Beck, stinking from their sweat, would be out of breath from breaking trail in the dense jungle, and we'd hear the helicopter way off in the distance. The static on the radio would break, and the staff officer would come back on telling us to double-time to meet up with the other men. Once Moubry told Duckett's unit that they were off line. Duckett ignored him and soon thereafter called Woolley with a request to stop for the night. His men were exhausted. He invited Moubry to come down with some supplies, such as cold beer.

For the most part, we were not successful in initiating contact with the VC during that operation. We did have one encounter, however, when Bratcher was at the head of our column. The platoon was walking down a trail. We often avoided trails because of the chance of mines and ambushes. Breaking new trails through the jungle was safer, but we had been beside this path earlier in the day and we were not going to stay on it for long. As he was looking down for trip lines Bratcher almost ran into a couple of VC who were coming in our direction around the bend in the trail. He dropped to one knee, but by the time he got his rifle to his shoulder and fired, the VC had turned on their heels and were gone. Beck was running after them when I ordered him back.

Although we were unsuccessful in finding the VC during the day, they came at us at night, probing our positions. As we lay in a tight perimeter, tired and wanting to sleep, they crawled in and threw grenades or sniped at us. They also tried to steal our claymore mines; however, we planted trip flares around them so that if a VC slipped in to steal them, the flares went off. One night, a work detail of VC crawled along the perimeter, figured out how the trip flares were planted, and stole the flares and the mines. The next night, McCoy planted flares beneath the claymores. At midnight, he heard movement out by the claymores just moments before a flare went off. One of his men squeezed off the detonator. In the morning, McCoy guessed that there were three VC, but it was hard to tell from the mangled bits of flesh blown over the area.

My platoon suffered no casualties in the operation. Duckett was not so lucky.

Duckett was a stern taskmaster. He told his men that he expected them to get out there and fight. He pushed hard at the enemy whenever we had contact, and he was the last platoon leader to call in dust-offs (medevacs) for his wounded. This was different from some of the other platoon leaders. When there was contact and we took

78

casualties, some of the platoon leaders stopped everything to look after their wounded. Duckett's first job always was to kill VC. Duckett did not wear socks or underwear. This made his early weeks in Vietnam painful, but, after a short time, his feet and his crotch toughened up and he felt no discomfort from the lack of underclothing. He also wore a flak jacket he had picked up from a cavalry friend. Because he was Duckett, people did not question this. Most of us would not have worn a flak jacket if they were available. They were heavy and wore down the body. But, like no socks and underwear, Duckett got used to the weight of his flak jacket. He never left base camp without it and it eventually saved his life.

Early in the operation, he and his platoon deployed some distance from the company in an area north of a village thought to be sympathetic to the VC. After dark he posted a two-man listening post (LP) among some rubber trees halfway between the village and the thicket where the platoon had dug in. Soon the listening post reported hearing movement off to their right. In a low whisper, they suggested that a small group of people might be moving from the village toward Duckett's position. Duckett alerted the platoon, and everyone waited quietly.

A light rain began to fall. Suddenly out of the dark, a shot zinged in.

As the men tensed, Duckett's platoon sergeant hissed loudly, "Don't fire." He thought that other VC might be waiting in front for the muzzle flashes to give away their positions.

He was right. The VC in front, soon tired of waiting, began firing at the platoon. Duckett called for mortar flares as his men returned the fire. Illumination rounds burst over the rubber trees, and the VC pulled back. Within minutes the listening post reported the VC running back toward the village.

Everything was quiet until early morning when the two men at the listening post reported hearing movement all around -- the VC had returned. Duckett told them to calm down; it could be the rain dripping off the trees. They did not acknowledge his call but quickly, breathlessly reported seeing men maneuvering directly at their position. Before Duckett could answer, he heard small-arms fire to his front. The listening post yelled in the radio that they were pulling back to the platoon.

Duckett called down the line to his men, "Get ready, the LP is coming in. VC in the front. Be careful, don't shoot the LP."

The men lay silently in their holes as they scanned the jungle toward the rubber trees. Duckett, who shared a foxhole with his RTO, ducked into the hole, called for more flares over the radio and drew his .45-caliber pistol. As he came back up, he aimed it over the top and took a deep breath. Woolley came on the radio and asked about the situation. Duckett bent down into the hole again to talk with Woolley.

The RTO saw movement in the front. He had a grenade in his hand. Men were running toward him. He pulled the pin on his grenade. The footfalls came closer in the dark. Gradually, but quickly, forms began to take shape into men, running headlong toward the foxhole the RTO and Duckett shared. The RTO pulled back his arm to throw the grenade. He saw the distinctive steel pots on the heads of the men. He stopped his motion to throw the grenade and yelled down the line, "LP coming in. Don't fire. Don't fire."

The men from the LP were running as fast as they could in the dark, eyes wide, scared, afraid that VC guns would open up on them at any moment. They heard the RTO yelling.

A shot ran out behind them, and a round whistled through the trees over their heads. They put their heads down and ran harder. Another round zinged through the jungle. The men lunged toward the hole as Duckett came up after talking with Woolley. He barely avoided a head-on collision.

The radio operator, with the grenade still in his hand, ducked into the hole. As more rounds from the pursuing VC passed overhead, the two men landed on top of the RTO, the grenade was knocked out of his hand, and it fell to the bottom of the hole. The radio operator tried to get out of the hole, but the LP men forced him downward as they desperately sought cover from the enemy fire. The handle flew off the grenade and it was armed. The radio operator yelled and became frantic. The two men, also excited, continued to worm their way into the hole.

Duckett was trapped on the side of the hole. As the three men wrestled beside him, he fired his .45 into the dark, toward the VC.

And the grenade went off.

The radio operator and one of the men from the LP were blown apart. The other man from the LP had shrapnel wounds over most of his body. Duckett was covered with bits of clothing, web gear, and flesh, but his flak jacket had protected him. Although he was not wounded, he was blinded by the blast and could not hear anything except a ringing in his ears. By morning, he had regained his sight but had lost the hearing in his right ear.

Duckett and the wounded LP man were evacuated, along with the remains of the other two men. After a night at the field clearing station, Duckett was sent to a U.S. Army hospital in Japan.

****

When we returned from the operation, a Specialist 4th Class Burke, who carried one of Colonel Haldane's radios, sought me out. He said that he had heard, although he could not confirm it firsthand, that an oil painting of a nude had arrived at division headquarters in Di Ann. It was from Senator Javits' office in Washington, D.C., and was addressed to the unidentified 1st Infantry Division field officer who had built a bar in the jungle. A division support officer, a REMF, had it in his office, but he was not, as far as Burke knew, making any effort to find the intended owner. I thanked Burke and went looking for Captain Woolley, who had not been pleased when I asked Senator Javits for the painting. He might not approve any effort on my part to retrieve it. I found Woolley behind his desk in the company headquarters tent and asked him for a day's leave to go down to Di Ann on a personal matter of some importance. He smiled. I smiled.

"And?" he asked.

"And what, sir?" I replied.

"What is the personal matter?" he asked, not smiling as much as he had.

"I'd rather not say, sir, exactly, other than to say it is important to me."

Woolley gazed intently at me for a moment or two and then said, "OK, but this better not have any blow-back. You understand me?"

At Di Ann I first went to the post office and talked with the NCOIC (noncommissioned officer in charge) who remembered the package. It was addressed the way Burke had described, so he sent it to G-4 (logistics). The NCOIC was there, in fact, when the personnel officer opened it. The painting was hanging on the wall behind the officer's desk when the sergeant had last seen it. "Damned nice piece of work," he told me.

I thanked him and went to the Quonset hut where personnel records were held. I was clearly aware of the difference in my appearance from that of the staff people whom I encountered along the way. My fatigues were worn, and I had a strange tan - my forehead was white from wearing my steel pot, but my cheeks were ruddy and showed briar scratches.

As I made my way toward the rear of the Quonset hut, I looked into each office as I went, sometimes interrupting conversations and work activities. Finally, in a major's office I spied an oil painting of a nude woman, looking out a window from behind a curtain, as if she were waiting for someone to come home. I was staring at the painting when the major looked up from his paperwork at me, then at the painting and back at me.

"Senator Javits?" I asked.

"I beg your pardon," the major said.

"Did that painting come from Senator Javits to an unidentified 1st Infantry Division field officer?" I asked as I walked into the room.

"Who are you?" asked the Major.

"That officer," I said.

There was a pause. Then, the major asked, "How am I supposed to know that?"

"I just told you, that's how you know. Last month, Senator Javits visited our position at Phuoc Vinh -- I'm with the 1st of the 28th -- and I asked him for a picture of a nude. That one. So I'm here to pick it up."

"No, you're not," said the major, leaning back in his chair. "You are going to have to get me some proof from your battalion commander or someone who can verify the fact that Senator Javits was sending you a painting. How am I supposed to know this is actually meant for you? You just think it does. Maybe you aren't right. Maybe you've just heard it's here and are trying to talk me out of it. I've got a responsibility here."

My first thought was that I didn't know how Woolley or Haldane would react. But then I thought, that isn't the point; this REMF major is a horse's ass, sitting here in an air-conditioned office with my painting hanging on his wall.

"Major," I said, "I don't know about your responsibilities, but I know that's my painting and that I've only got one day down here. I'm a little hurt you don't want to help me with this."

The major continued to lean back in his chair; I wasn't going to win any war of words. Without thinking it through, I changed tone and said, "So listen here. I'm just going to take MY painting off YOUR fucking wall and if you so much as touch me, I'm going to hurt you. And I'm still going to take it."

With that, I walked over, took the painting off the wall and left. I didn't look at the major again, so I did not see his reaction. He did, in fact, file a report which eventually reached Woolley, saying that I had threatened him and stolen a painting off the wall of his office. By the time the letter arrived, the painting was a fixture behind our bar and the story of how it came to be there was part of Alpha Company folklore. Woolley destroyed the letter.

Map 13

1st/28th Battalion, 1st Division arrived in Vung Tau and moved overland to set up a base camp in Phouc Vinh. In January 1966 the battalion cleared the Iron Triangle for the 25th Infantry Division. In the course of that operation we ran into the Cu Chi tunnels and Pete and I were both wounded. In July the battalion led the counter ambush on the Minh Thanh road. Notice how close the road ran to the Cambodian border. Also note how close the Cu Chi tunnels were to Saigon.

S.Sgt Donald "Cottonpicker" Lawrence
My hero and best friend in the 1950s.
He advised me to go into the Army.

Elmer Lee Van Pelt lll, Basic Training
Buddy. He said he was a flower
I was a weed.

Lt Taylor OCS Tac Office who told
me the first day I was not Officer
material and he was going to
kick me out.

Larry Peterson, my OCS roommate,
who insisted I'd make it, and pulled
me through

OCS Color Guard. I'm on the far left next to the saluting officers.

My 190 SL Mercedes at Pete's house in Lincoln, Nebraska

Band playing as we left Ft Riley, Kansas heading for Vietnam Sept 1966

**Last passenger car in the troop train taking us to
Oakland Naval Station to board a ship for Vietnam**

Boarding the USS Mann at Oakland

On Board deck the Mann

USS Mann troop carrier

Me, Bob Dunn, George McCoy and Pete en route

Vietnam four months after Pete and I graduated OCS

3rd Platoon section of the base camp defensive
Perimeter at Phou Vinh. Notice the vegetation
growing in front of the bunkers. Mines planted
there were occasionally tripped by growing
vegetation. This led to George McCoy's death.

With my platoon getting ready for a patrol out in

front of the platoon section of the perimeter. Notice
we still have the venerable M-14s and leather boots.

1st Division 3.5 rocket launcher team on patrol. These weapons were designed
to kill tanks, though our division had no contact with enemy armor. They were
used as enemy bunker busters. On the ammo bearer's back pack is bed roll
with his air mattress wrapped on the inside so as not to get snagged in the
rough jungle. Insect replellent in the stretch band around the helmet.

1st Division soldiers moving down a stream. What with monsoon rains and
movement through jungle rivers soldiers would often get wet and dry out a
couple of times a day.

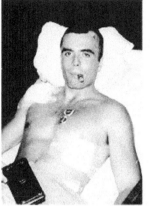 

Bob Dunn after being hit by shrapnel.   Spencer
(photo taken 2015)
.Purple Heart on his chest

1st Division Soldier in a Cu Chi tunnel which is much
larger than the one I was in chasing the wounded VC.

Helicopter lift of 1st Div soldiers near the Michelin Plantation

**Bob Dunn, me, George McCoy and Pete behind the bar we had made
in Ben Hoa**

3rd Plt: Beck left, Lyons middle and Fondren right.

My first radio operator Newsome (left) Ayers (middle) and "Doc"
Klimmel (right). Newsome rotated home, Ayers was KIA and
Kimmel suffered paralyzing wounds.

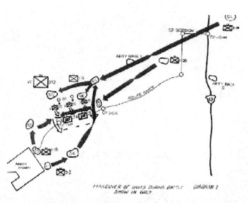

Minh Thanh Road counter-ambush

Slippery Clunker Six led the convoy, the bait, codenamed Task Force Dragon, south from An Loc. 1/28th Battalion was waiting nearby, monitoring the Task Force's progress. When it passed Check Point Dick, the PAVN 272nd Regiment hit from both side. Immediately the 1/4th Quarterhorse Cavalry in the convoy returned fire, plus artillery fire from FSB 1 and 2 shot pre-set coordinates on both sides of the road. USAF jets also responded with bombing runs of napalm. The 1/28th Battalion was the first on the ground, landing near Check Point Dick and then moved west through the napalm scared battlefield. 238 dead NVA were lying in piles from the USAF jets and from the artillery.

Destroy 1/4th Cav APC near the Minh Thanh ambush site.
Dead VC lying in front

Me and Dunn heading out on operation with Battalion

In the Officer's Club, sitting beneath the oil painting "For
This We Fight" Senator Javits sent me after
he visited the unit..

Front of house in the Carmel Highlands, California where Pete and I
lived on return from Vietnam. Grand panorama of the Pacific
from this deck

Back of the Carmel Highlands house. Kim Novak lived two houses
down.

6th Army area Drill Sergeant's school cadre.

Big Red One   1st/28th Battalion

My colors that I followed in Vietnam

The Vietnam War Its Ownself

Ernst returned from an operation in December with what was diagnosed as dengue fever. Over the next few days he became gaunt and tired easily, but he did not go on sick call. He couldn't do it, he said. Some "dingy fever" wasn't manly enough to call him out of the field. Now cancer and typhoid, they were lethal sounding. He'd leave if the medic said he had typhoid fever -- but not dingy. "Get outa here," he said. "It's just Jimbo and me to help the good captain." Peterson and Duckett were both gone.

He had in his platoon one of the world's all-time leading chatterboxes, a young man who never stopped talking. And, he was funny. Shortly before picking up the dengue bug, Ernst and his platoon were on patrol south of Phuoc Vinh. He and the comic were walking close together when the platoon was ambushed. A bullet hit Ray in the hand. The young man was splattered with shrapnel. They had to be moved several kilometers to a clearing for a medevac. Although he was wounded in dozens of places, the young man walked most of the way out. He was lying by a tree when the medevac helicopter arrived. A corpsman walked up with a bandage in his hand but paused because the man had so many wounds. "Just put a bandage on me anywhere," the young man said. "You're bound to cover a wound." As the corpsman worked, the youngster borrowed a cigarette from someone standing by and lit it himself. Exhaling, he asked the corpsman, "You know the names of any nurses in the hospital where we're going?"

Ernst, on the other hand, had to be carried on a makeshift stretcher all the way from the ambush site to the open field. He was in great pain. Eyes sunken from the dengue fever, his hand torn open, he looked like a corpse. He was a good man, popular with his men. They knew that he was leaving them, and they feared that he would have to have his hand amputated. At the least it would take many months to graft bones and skin to make the hand functional. As the corpsmen were carrying Ernst to the helicopter, several of his men grabbed the sides of the stretcher. When they lifted the stretcher to put him inside the helicopter, it came apart and Ernst fell through it to the ground. He landed on his head.

The youngster, already on board, said, "Not necessarily the helping hand the lieutenant was looking for."

Ernst was finally righted and put on the helicopter. With his good hand, he gave a thumbs-up to his men standing in the waist-high saw grass as the helicopter lifted up.

He was eventually evacuated back to the States and we never saw him again.

James E. Parker, Jr.

For a short while I was the only platoon leader left in the company and then a new second lieutenant, named Brad Arthur [alias], arrived. Woolley gave him Ernst's platoon. Arthur was loud. When some other replacements whom he knew dropped by, he repeated the stories he heard about Ernst's medevac but he had the wrong emphasis, I thought. He hadn't earned his spurs yet and didn't have the right to laugh.

****

The new M-16s assault rifles arrived and like Arthur, they did not make a good first impression. I had handled guns all my life, but I instantly disliked that light aluminum and plastic toy with its designer lines. It didn't feel right, made silly little sounds when a round was chambered, no recoil when it was fired, didn't come up naturally to the shoulder, and had a handle on the top. A handle for God's sake! For what? It made sighting awkward. I told the men I didn't know about this thing that looked like it was made by Mattel. Didn't look like the kind of gun that would win wars. Didn't want any of my men holding it by the handle, like a woman's pocketbook.

I told Bratcher I was keeping my shotgun. He nodded and asked when I had last fired it. I figured about three or four weeks before. Bratcher said that he had noticed a lot of rain and wondered how waterproof that gun was, how well it might be able to handle, say, firing all seven rounds without jamming.

Newsome, my RTO, had covered it with oil, and I had cleaned it religiously every time we returned from an operation. It seemed to be in good shape. I told Bratcher that I had had this gun for a long time. It would last me. It'd do the job. It was a good gun -- fit my image.

On Bratcher's suggestion, however, we took it down to the perimeter. Standing on top of Spencer's bunker, I put it to my shoulder and fired. The gun jammed after one round. I tried to clear it and heard something break inside. The bolt stopped working altogether. Bratcher looked at me with his eyebrows raised, his disingenuous way of saying, "Hey, that's strange." I tore the gun down as much as I could and found several pieces, weakened by rust, that were broken or bent from firing that one shot.

"Not many spare parts around here for a Stateside rabbit gun," Bratcher said.

I threw the shotgun and the parts into the minefield, then went back to the company armorer and drew a M-16. I tried to like it, but the more I handled it, the cheaper it felt. Where was the wood, the

84

The Vietnam War Its Ownself

weight? Sure, we could carry three times the amount of ammo, but everyone would fire the thing on full automatic and no one would aim. This was not a woodsman's gun.

And the magazines? The guns might be high-tech but those magazines were mass produced and cheap. I asked everyone to look at the springs. The wires were smaller than coat hangers. I could bend them with my finger.

I raged against those M-16s and the magazines, but no one listened seriously.

"Parker," McCoy said, "you don't like nothing much. You don't like Moubry, Arthur, mines, staff officers. Lighten up."

So, I resigned myself to life with the M-16. Like everyone else, I put twenty rounds in each magazine, as we had been told to do, and then one more for Mother. If we squeezed down tight on that thin wire spring, we could get twenty one rounds in. For many people that last bullet was a tragic mistake because the springs in the early-version magazines rusted together. Also, because they were so light, men taped two, sometimes three magazines together so that they would be at the ready in a firefight. This extra weight on the light latch that held the magazines in would allow the magazines to droop just enough to cause misfires. Plus, the guns were not hardy and would not function with any dirt in the workings. And there was a lot of dirt in the jungle. We had to give up the durable M-14 and got a light, faster, cheaper replacement. Initially we certainly suffered more from its disadvantages than we gained from its lighter weight and speed.

At about that time, Mother and Daddy sent me wire spectacles and a commode seat. I had asked for the latter item because the company latrine had uncomfortable holes cut in flat wood. I took great pride in my ass, I told my friends. The civilized man looked after his toilet facilities. It was what separated us from the animals that crapped in the jungle. Woolley said that he wondered about me sometimes -- the bar, the toilet seat. He wondered if I was queer.

I kept the toilet seat near the bar and took it with me on each visit to the latrine. No one made any catcalls. That might have been because I usually carried the toilet seat in one hand and a .45 in the other.

One day, I was walking down the company street toward the latrine with the commode seat. I saw Spencer sitting in front of his tent. He looked at me and the seat and then smiled. I tried to look ahead and ignore him. I was wishing I had my .45. As I walked in front of Spencer, he followed me with his smile. I passed by.

85

"I can't think of a damned thing to say, Lieutenant. Goddamned I'm trying hard and I can't."

Just before Christmas, Jim Newsome, my RTO from Fort Riley days, rotated back to the States. I went down to his tent to say good-bye. I picked up his PRC 25 radio and walked over to Spencer. Bratcher, Castro and Rome were standing by the entrance to the tent.

"No sir, goddamned, no sir, goddamnit, no. I ain't carrying no fucking radio. I ain't. I don't have to." He appealed to Bratcher, "Tell him, platoon sergeant."

"I don't care what you think about this thing, Spencer. Learn how to use it right. Get the freqs and call signs you need from Newsome before he leaves." I had a half smile on my face, but my eyes were serious.

Spencer looked at me and said, "Ah, shit."

****

For months I knew that Newsome would be leaving the Army not long after we arrived Vietnam and had often considered who to replace him. It was an important position to me and to the platoon. Generally in the field if Captain Woolley called to give instructions or ask questions, the radio operator would hand me or Sergeant Bratcher the radio to respond, but as was often the case both Bratcher and I would be involved otherwise – and the more urgent the call, the more likely Bratcher and I would be otherwise busy. In these times the radio operator, or RTO as he was called, would have to speak for us. And too, there were times I needed artillery or coordination and would yell out to the RTO to call someone with this request or that. The RTO needed a cool head under stress, who could think for himself.

And more than that, I looked for someone to spend "after hours" with in the jungle... because at night if we were not out in an ambush or alone forward of the battalion, the men in 3rd platoon would dig holes along the defensive perimeter... and just to the rear Bratcher, I and the RTO would dig a small hole, hunker down and spend the night side by side... and those two foxhole buddies would be the first I'd see in the morning, to share a cup of coffee with and join me hacking and coughing as we took our individual pisses and scratched our asses.

The RTO would be family in a closer way than others in the platoon. He would be at my elbow 24/7 and if we weren't necessarily friends than at least we had to be of the same mind when it came to reacting to combat situations.

86

The Vietnam War Its Ownself

Plus there was something else. The RTO was from the ranks and although he might be in my shadow most of the time, his asshole buddies were in the infantry squads. If the RTO didn't respect me, he would promote discontent in his network of friends.

And also this. It was 1965 and the U.S. was just stepping away from the shackles of segregation. Many of the white boys in my platoon had never carried on a conversation with a black man before. They looked on the black members of the platoon awkwardly, with color lenses. And maybe 50 percent of the NCOs in my platoon were black. They bonded amongst themselves - and cooperated with the rest - but always looked on me and Newsome and Bratcher as people from another universe. We worked together out of necessity in the platoon, but there was the constant sense that we were made of very different parts. Had different points of reference in life.

But come on ... Spencer? He led the angry black delegation, could be sassy, that was true ... but he thought clearly under fire and had the intangibles of good judgment and courage. He was always around it seemed when things starting happening, and he was deliberate. And he was smart, could process new information quickly. And I liked him, sassy ass and all.

In theory, having Spencer as my RTO was a good choice - that's why I told him to get a brief from Newsome before picking up the platoon radio.

Though there are times things in theory don't work out in the real world. But in this case, things worked just fine.

Some of the other white, college-boy radio operators at Battalion had trouble understanding him at first, but that problem went away after a short time, I don't know why. Woolley initially questioned his selection because of Spencer's irascible reputation. But that smart-aleckness just went away. And Woolley found that when Spencer spoke for me, he always got it right. Never a time did he misunderstand or misspeak.

Every morning - pissing, scratching, coughing – we were comfortable together. And our platoon was stronger.

****

We stayed in the base camp from shortly before Christmas through New Year's. Each night different platoons were sent out on ambush patrols. Woolley told Arthur that he had the patrol for Christmas Eve night.

I told the captain how much I appreciated that, "I'll be able to spend Christmas in camp, probably because I'm your favorite, been around the longest."

"Nope," Woolley said. "It's because I want you on patrol New Year's Eve. If there is any man I want out away from the base camp New Year's Eve parties, it is Red Cap Twigs Alpha November Six, the proprietor of the Company A bar."

Christmas was pleasant. The company cook made a wonderful, holiday meal. We cut down a small shrub for a Christmas tree and put homemade ornaments on it. On Christmas Eve Peterson, McCoy, Dunn, and I opened presents together. Just like home, we opened them in turn, one at a time, so that we could comment on each gift, and stretch out the evening.

On New Year's Eve, I was lying on my belly in the jungle by a bridge south of town. Around midnight, the soldiers on the perimeter of the base camp behind us began firing tracers in the air. I started singing "Auld Lang Syne" softly and the men on both sides of me joined in. With the tracers still going off in the distance our voices carried over the water and into the village on the other side. The locals must have wondered.

Ten days later, Colonel Haldane and his staff went to division headquarters to receive new operational orders. They had left in the morning, and we expected them back by early afternoon; the trip had never before taken them more than a couple of hours. They didn't return until after sundown, and all officers and top NCOs were called to the operations tent at 2100. Bratcher and I stood at the back.

Colonel Haldane began by saying that during the twelve weeks we had been in-country, we had learned how to fight in the jungle, had engaged elements of every VC unit operating north of Saigon and disrupted their ability to control the territory. This had come at no small price -- we had also taken casualties. In addition, we had lost men to disease and through termination of service. Only 50 percent of the men who had left Fort Riley for Vietnam were still here, but we had received replacements. We were still an effective fighting organization.

"Operation Crimp will launch in three days. It will test our ability to live up to the 1st Infantry Division tradition," Haldane said. "We are going to attack an area the VC and North Vietnamese have controlled for decades. It is the Ho Bo woods north of the town of Cu Chi. It is where the Ho Chi Minh trail ends inside South Vietnam. We will be up against hard-core Vietcong combat units supported by local villagers. The VC own this territory. The only significant South Vietnamese military presence in the area is inside the town of Cu Chi. Turn the first bend in the road west of town and you are in territory of the VC's 7th Cu Chi Battalion, a unit that has never lost a battle. We know from the French that their tactics are to bend away from frontal attacks but slap back on the sides and attack from the rear. They do not run away. They fight. Our mission is to attack the center of the area, secure a base, and clear it from the inside out. Once we have pacified the area, the 25th Division, presently en route to Vietnam, will move in and control it."

The plan was to move by Caribou airplanes from our base camp to Phu Loi, a staging area some distance east of the operational zone. On 7 January 1966 we would conduct a helicopter assault into Landing Zone (LZ) Jack in the middle of the Ho Bo woods. The landing zone area would be prepped by artillery and then Air Force fast movers (jet airplanes) and finally Air Force prop-driven slow movers. Leading the troop-carrying helicopters ("slicks"), would be helicopter gunships. 1st/16th Battalion would go in first. We would be in the second wave. My platoon was to be in the third, fourth, and fifth helicopters of the second lift into the LZ.

The briefing went on until midnight. We picked up new map sheets on the way out.

As we walked back to the company area, Bratcher said, "It looks like we got ourselves an operation here. We're going to get after them Commie bastards, rather than just hanging out the way we been doing, acting a lot like bait. You want to do business, go where the customers are. Am I right or what?"

The following morning, we loaded onto the ugly Caribous for the short flight to the staging area. Dunn's company had already arrived there and had set up poncho shelters at the end of the runway, near where Alpha Company was assigned. The next day more units came in. Helicopters and planes were flying overhead constantly. Round rubber bladders of aviation fuel were positioned at the end of the runway. Fresh ammunition, medical supplies, and batteries arrived. The whole assembly area was alive with activity.

Before dusk, Dunn and I went over to an old building built by French plantation owners. A basketball hoop was attached to the back of the building and someone had found a basketball. We joined a half-court game and wore our fatigue pants, combat boots and t-shirts. Dunn played basketball the same way that his father had probably played no-faceguard football for the Green Bay Packers. Very tough. One guy, who was much quicker than Dunn, was driving around him when Dunn hooked him around the neck, throwing him to the ground. He was angry and getting up in a hurry, when Bob pushed him down again. Dunn moved quickly to stand over him and said, "Get up asshole and I'll knock your fucking head off."

I grabbed Dunn and said, "Hey man, save it for tomorrow.

89

James E. Parker, Jr.

That's a good guy. You gotta know the difference. This is just a game."

--EIGHT--
The Tunnel to Hell

The following morning we were up before sunrise. The mess units flew in hot breakfast. After eating, we were standing in groups of ten along the runway when we heard the first rounds of artillery fire in the distance. Not long after the sun came up, we watched a large formation of helicopters, in seven groups of ten helicopters each, heading our way carrying the first wave of the 1st/16th. Ahead and below them were the gunships.

As the helicopters came closer, I followed them through my binoculars. Crammed on board were soldiers in olive drab. Some were sitting with their legs hanging out, and most of them were clutching their M-16s in both hands. Artillery fire increased as the helicopters passed. We heard the jets before we saw them, streaking by toward the west. The artillery stopped, and the jets began working the area. More explosions came from the west, then the ground shook as B-52s bombed the fringes of the operational zone.

We figured that it would take twenty minutes for the helicopters to fly from our area to the LZ. In forty minutes, they should be back to pick us up. I was anxious to get started. The waiting reminded me of the ride on the landing craft when we arrived in-country. This time, we would not be greeted by a brass band. The lead gunships came back first. Two moved off to the bladders of fuel. Others landed at the end of the airstrip and picked up more ammunition. Shortly, the first lift of ten transport helicopters came in low over the tree line.

I got the men up and in line. My platoon would be boarding the second group of helicopters.

Only seven came in. Where were the other three? I had not imagined that some of the helicopters would not return. Maintaining their original positions, the helicopters landed. The third, ninth and ten helicopters were missing. I had been standing at the head of the line to board the third helicopter, but it wasn't there. Unsure of what to do but anxious to get going, I told Spencer to follow me and went to the fourth helicopter, telling two riflemen there to get off.

90

The Vietnam War Its Ownself

As we crawled onto the helicopter, I noticed bullet holes in its side. The pilots sat in front of the controls looking forward, shaking with the vibration of the blades, their faces impassive behind their helmet visors.

When the helicopter lifted off the ground I got Woolley on the radio and reported what he already knew about the helicopters. A third of my platoon was still at the airstrip.

The helicopters stayed low. Some distance in the front, we could see jets strafing the ground. Clouds of smoke drifted up from an area on the horizon. The small, gnat like gunships moved in and out of the smoke. As we got closer, we saw bombs falling from diving planes. The napalm tanks tumbled and exploded into fireballs when they hit the jungle.

As the large, open LZ finally came into view, the gunners on both side of the slicks began firing into the jungle. I had the impulse to sit on my M-16 to give me an extra measure of protection from bullets that might come up through the floor of the helicopter.

In the field ahead, I saw soldiers moving around. Several downed helicopters were seen lying on their sides. Fires were burning in the nearby jungle. I felt myself breathing faster. I grabbed and re-grabbed my M-16.

Get on the ground. Get on the ground. Why are we moving so goddamned slow, I thought angrily.

The helicopter finally flared out to brake its forward speed and settled down in the field. Everyone in the platoon knew that we would be landing south to north and that we had to move to secure an area along the wood line to the east. As the helicopter settled to the ground I was looking for a point of trees extending out in the field that was to be the platoon rallying point. I did not see the litter detail standing on the ground until the helicopter touched down. With adrenaline pumping, we barely avoided the soldiers carrying the stretchers as we jumped to the ground. Some of the soldiers on the stretchers were dead.

With the wounded loaded quickly, the helicopters took off behind us and as the bat-bat-bat of their rotary blades began to fade, we heard the popping of automatic fire to the north and to our front. Rounds zinged over our heads. Rockets landed among us.

High-stepping through the tall grass, we finally made it to the wood line and then to our rally point. Once established, I sat down behind a tree and contacted Woolley. Bratcher took a head count. Twenty-one of the men had made it. We had not seen anyone hit in the field. The missing men must have been left behind in the staging area. Woolley told me to hold my position until the remaining men

91

arrived.

Taking a deep breath, I stood up to light a cigarette. Rome yelled at me as I had the match halfway to my cigarette. I dropped it and fell to the ground.

"Napalm. You're standing in some napalm that didn't ignite," he said.

I looked down. Napalm jelly was on my fatigues and all around on the bushes. My match was still smoking on top of a glob and I quickly stepped on it.

By late afternoon, all of my platoon had come in. Most of the fighting to secure the 1st/28th's part of the LZ had been done by Dunn's platoon north of the field. My platoon had no contact with Vietcong ground forces that afternoon or that night.

At first light the next morning, we moved straight out into the jungle. Duckett's platoon, now being commanded by the platoon sergeant, was on my left. Woolley was with Arthur's platoon in the rear. We were heading toward our TAOR, a two-day movement through the jungle, and hoped to reach a midway point near a small village by nightfall.

Duckett's platoon began to receive sniper fire from its left front during the late morning. Yelling out to the platoon sergeant that I was maneuvering my men around to his front, we soon saw enemy small-arms fire coming from a clump of trees. Manuel fired a long burst of rounds into the trees and the enemy stopped firing. We slowly walked into the strand of trees as we reconned by fire.

No one was there. Strange. I had seen the firing. We would have noticed anyone leaving the thicket.

Beck found two spider holes close to the forward edge of the thicket, partially covered by fallen debris from our fire. The openings were smaller than a basketball rim, barely large enough for a man to squeeze out. A cool, earthy smell emanated from the openings.

"Are the VC at the bottom of these holes, or do these go back to some room or tunnel?" I asked Bratcher as Woolley came up.

I sent men out to the front as security and looked back at the spider holes. Spencer stuck a long bamboo pole down one. It hit bottom after about five feet and then, when Spencer pushed, it went down another four feet. We shined a flashlight down the holes. Both holes curved out of sight to our front.

Yelling "Fire the hole," we threw in grenades and ducked behind trees. The explosions were muffled, and only a small amount of dust came out and blew away. We walked carefully back to the holes and looked down. I said, "Damn. We either send someone down or we leave and keep on toward our TAOR."

The Vietnam War Its Ownself

Woolley told me to send someone down. I called one of the Puerto Ricans, PFC Fernandez-Lopez, the smallest man in the platoon, and told him to take off his web gear because he was going on a little trip. He looked around at us, shrugged, dropped his gear, and started walking toward the hole barehanded.

"Hold it," I said. I gave him my .45 and Woolley's radio operator gave him a flashlight. We told him just to go to the bottom of the first hole, see what was there, and come back. He said something in half-Spanish and half-English that I couldn't understand, but it was a question. He looked at me for an answer. I asked him to repeat it, but I still didn't understand. Finally, he put his hands over his head like he was diving. "Yes," I said, "head first. We'll hold your feet."

Fernandez crawled on his stomach to the nearest hole and stuck the flashlight over the side. He looked down for what seemed like a long time. Then he turned around, and said something to Castro in Spanish, crossed himself, and crawled over the edge. The .45 and the flashlight were in front of him. Bratcher grabbed his feet and began pushing him. Yelling, "Slow, amigo," Bratcher gradually pushed him down until his feet were the only thing out of the hole.

"What do you see," Bratcher yelled. Fernandez's comments were muffled.

Woolley told Bratcher to pull him out.

When he came out and got to his feet, dirt was caked on his fatigue jacket and on his face where the sweat had run down. Someone gave him a cigarette and he talked quickly to Castro.

Turning to us, Castro said Fernandez didn't like going down the hole.

"Well fuck him, what did he see?" Bratcher asked.

"A lot of hole. Just hole. Some spent casings, but just the hole going on out that way," Castro said pointing to our front.

"They are ahead of us," I said. "Waiting."

"They're tunnels here. Maybe that's why they've been so successful in this area," Woolley said.

We ate lunch before moving out. A short time later, we received sniper fire. At midafternoon, one of Arthur's men, behind us, stepped on a mine and blew his foot off. He was evacuated, and we were on our way again within the hour.

For two days, we patrolled west. We encountered more mines and snipers; sullen, men-less villages; and more spider holes leading down into tunnel complexes. There was a different sense to the jungle here than we had experienced in other places. It was quieter, and it seemed more deadly. When we stopped occasionally to

93

get our bearings or to rest, we heard no sounds -- no birds flying or chirping, no insects humming. We felt that someone was watching us all the time.

As we moved into a company defensive perimeter around a small field the third night of the operation, Major Allee arrived on the supply helicopter with small revolvers, field telephones, and spools of wire. He told us what we had already realized -- we were walking over an extensive network of tunnels. They were unexpected and had not been part of the intelligence package for this operation. The spider holes were openings to these tunnels, and Allee told us to investigate them wherever we found them. They were enemy sanctuaries. We were to send down a small man, a tunnel rat, with a pistol, flashlight and telephone. Someone was to feed the wire down as the tunnel rat explored. The man in the hole should send back situation reports every five minutes or so. He could find his way back by following the wire.

Pete led his recon platoon by our area the next morning on their way to a village off to our south. He stopped for a cup of coffee and said that a group of men from the colonel's battalion headquarters group had gone down a hole the previous night. They had run into VC in the tunnels and had a running battle. They got back by following the telephone wire; however, one man had not returned. Pete had no idea what had happened to him.

"Tunnel ratting, is that infantry duty?" I asked.

Pete stood up after finishing his coffee and told his men to saddle up. I told him to be careful. He turned toward me and smiled.

"Your mother said that, be careful, I heard her," I said. "Me, I'd rather have it the other way. You die, I'm a rich man."

"There's something on that insurance I need to talk with you about, when we have a chance," Pete mumbled.

"What?" I asked, suddenly uncomfortable. I was the one who needed to talk about the insurance; I had yet to find the change of beneficiary form.

"I'll tell you later," he said, and then he was gone.

Company A continued sweep operations that morning. Snipers pinged at us, and we encountered mines, and more tunnels. Cu Chi was not friendly.

****

The battalion came together at midafternoon with plans to dig in and spend a couple of days licking our wounds. We had been on the move almost constantly for three days and had slept very little.

The Vietnam War Its Ownself

The men were grouchy with fatigue. We welcomed the opportunity to rest, receive mail, and eat hot food.

When my platoon tied up with Arthur's on the left, Spencer, Bratcher and I sought a central position in the rear to drop our gear and dig a small hole. Woolley came up as we were removing our packs and asked me to take a few of my men and do a "clover leaf" patrol -- make a short circle out about five or six hundred meters from the perimeter -- to ensure that we hadn't inadvertently camped next to a VC position.

The men grumbled as they dropped webbing that was not needed for the patrol. I left a few men behind to begin digging in and the rest fell in behind Lyons, who was followed by Beck and King. We moved out to a small clearing a hundred meters to our front. The setting sun cast long shadows and made it hard to see the opposite side clearly, so we skirted it.

The jungle woods were not thick and Lyons walked along briskly but cautiously. We were all anxious to get back. Suddenly, Lyons stopped and raised his hand. Because the area was so open, most of the men dropped to one knee. Beck with his M-79 at the ready continued to walk forward beside Lyons. I remained standing several men back in the patrol, but I could see the two men squinting ahead in the jungle.

Finally, Beck turned around and said in a loud whisper. "Looks like a plane."

I scowled as I walked to the head of the column. However, I could see something metallic reflecting off the setting sun in a bamboo thicket ahead. It was long and cylindrical and covered with vines. Incredibly, but clearly, it was a small plane, minus the wings.

Lyons, Beck, and I approached the thicket one slow step at a time. The plane could be the bait to a trap. When I could read the number on the tail, I called it out to Spencer to report that we had found an old spotter aircraft apparently shot down some time ago, but we were moving on and would come back and check it in the morning.

We saw no signs of the wings, wheels, or propeller. Beck guessed that the plane had crashed somewhere else and had been hidden in the ticket. I pointed out that the fuselage looked intact and there didn't appear to be any signs of a crash landing.

Beck said he was going to look inside, but I told him no -- too much of a chance that it was booby trapped and we had only a few more minutes of daylight. If we didn't move on, it would be dark before we got back to the perimeter. I motioned the patrol around to the right of the thicket. As King came by, Beck and Lyons fell back

95

in at point.

A small clearing was behind the thicket, and a berm ran out of the jungle along the east side of the field. Spencer was coming up the column to walk behind me. King was turning around as he walked and asked me what the hell was a berm doing coming out of the jungle like that, when an automatic weapon opened up from our right. Rounds zinged between King and me.

Everyone hit the ground. Manuel was carrying the machine gun, and I yelled at him to start shooting. Short bursts of fire continued to come at us from over the berm. We crawled forward. Bratcher was at the end of the patrol. As I reached the berm I yelled for him to move out, flanking whoever was firing to the right, we'd cover him.

Bratcher yelled for Sgt. Ollie Taylor, Jr. to follow him. I told Manuel to bring the machine gun up to the top of the berm. He stood up and fired from the hip. The rest of us slung our guns over the top and fired.

Beck fired his M-79 grenade launcher. The round hit an overhanging tree limb and bounced back. It landed squarely in his lap. Beck screamed, expecting the grenade to go off.

Bratcher was maneuvering in from the right. He yelled for us to stop firing. He and Taylor advanced, firing as they went. Bratcher yelled, "We got him. I saw him go down."

As I was waving the men over the berm, King turned to look at Beck. His mouth open and eyes wide, Beck was staring at the grenade in his lap.

"You lucky motherfucker," King told him scornfully. "The round has to travel fifteen yards to arm itself. It didn't go fifteen yards. It ain't armed. It ain't going off. Pick it up and put it on the ground beside you."

From the other side of the berm, we could see that the firing had come from beneath a couple of shelters, each just four posts holding up palm-frond roofing and no sides. Bratcher and Taylor were moving in from our right, and the rest of us came straight in, with Manuel occasionally firing the machine gun.

We saw that the ground under the roof of the larger shelter had been excavated, leaving a pit perhaps five feet deep by fifteen feet wide by twenty feet long. A trench led from the main shelter to a similar pit under the smaller one.

Expecting to see the VC lying in the bottom of the hole, we covered the last few feet very slowly, guns at the ready.

Behind us, Beck was telling King, "Maybe, maybe, maybe, the round's only gone fourteen yards and something. Maybe I pick it up and, and, and, that's enough." He was trying not to breathe hard for fear of disturbing the round lying on his stomach. He took short breaths and talked as he exhaled.

"Help me, Sergeant, help me move it." Beck looked up at King.

"Nope," King said, leaning against the berm. "You can do it as well as I can. You either slap it off and roll out of the way quick, or you reach down very carefully and lift it off."

"Tell the lieutenant to come here," Beck said.

King looked over the berm in my direction. I was easing up to the shelter. The sun was almost down, and it was hard to see into the hole. Bratcher and Taylor reached the edge first.

"He's gone, the son of a bitch, down a fucking hole," Bratcher said.

A pool of blood lay next to the forward edge of the hole under the main shelter. An AK-47 assault rifle was nearby amid some empty casings and dark green cotton pouches holding AK-47 magazines. A blood trail led over to a spider hole located in the corner like the drain in a sink. Taylor, standing by the smaller shelter, said that he saw another spider hole there.

"He's down in that hole, probably down in a little room between these two shelters. Wounded. Without his gun," I said.

The radio on Spencer's back squawked as Woolley asked what all the firing was about. From the far side of the berm, I heard King call out, "Lieutenant, you got a minute?"

I told Spencer to tell Woolley that we wounded a VC and that we were going to try and ferret him out of a hole. Didn't know how long it was going to take.

King called again, insistently, "Lieutenant."

I told Bratcher to see what King wanted and told De Leon and Ayers to move out to a guard position near the small field. After sending some other men to protect our other flank, I walked over to the smaller shelter, where Taylor was shining his flashlight down the spider hole. It led down and away. We tied a small piece of nylon cord to the flashlight and lowered it down the hole.

Meanwhile, Bratcher had walked back to the berm. King nodded toward Beck, who was sitting awkwardly with the M-79 grenade round in his lap and a sick look on his face.

"Lift it off, Beck," Bratcher said firmly. Like King, he saw no value in putting two men at risk.

Beck's hand shook slightly as it moved slowly to the round. When he lifted it with two fingers, the head of the round rotated downward. Beck opened his mouth as wide as he could, as though he

97

were going to yell, but he didn't drop the round. Moving it slowly to his right and then toward the ground, he rolled out of the way as he set it down. Quickly, he got to his feet and looked down at the small metal ball.

"You son of a bitch. You goddamned son of a bitch. You nasty little son of a bitch," he kept repeating as he climbed over the berm.

Beck borrowed Patrick's M-16 and went back to the berm. He fired most of a clip of ammo at the M-79 round until he finally set it off.

Thinking we were being probed or attacked, I turtled my neck and started to jump into the pit when Bratcher said, "No problem. It's just 'Bad News' Beck."

Spencer had finished sending the radio message to Woolley and was looking down the spider hole under the main shelter. He mentioned that he could see the light from Taylor's flashlight shining at the bottom of the hole. Woolley came back on the radio and said that battalion wanted us to take the man alive. They wanted a prisoner. I told him we'd do what we could.

Convinced that a dying VC was beneath us, I told Fernandez that it was time for his starring role again, to get a pistol and to get ready for a trip down the mine shaft.

Fernandez did not take it well. He was angry and mumbled in Spanish under his breath. I told him that I was sorry, but he was the smallest, and he had to go. He pretended not to understand me.

By now, the sunlight was almost completely gone. I told Bratcher to ensure that the men were set up in good guard positions all around the shelters. As I went under the small shelter, we started to receive small-arms fire from across the field.

We ducked down. Looking closely at the spider hole, Fernandez started saying, "No, no, no."

Sitting with my back against the side of the larger hole, I was suddenly very tired. I wanted to be back with the battalion -- eating my C-rations and maybe drinking a cup of coffee. I did not want to be beside the entrance to this hole that led to God knew where. We knew only that at least one wounded VC soldier was down there.

We received more probing rounds from the area near the plane and then some rounds to our front, from deep in the jungle. The VC were all around us.

I grabbed Fernandez by the collar of his fatigue jacket and told him not to get me angry. He kept saying, "No, no, no."

Finally I said, "Ah shit." I told Spencer to throw a grenade

98

down the hole under the large shelter, and I took a grenade off my web gear, pulled the pin, and dropped it down the other hole where I was standing. It wasn't necessarily going to give us a live prisoner, like battalion wanted, but my reluctant Puerto Rican tunnel rat wasn't going down the hole until we did something.

The grenades went off with muffled thuds. We lowered Taylor's flashlight down the hole again, and Spencer said that he could see the light shining dimly from the other area.

I looked at Fernandez and said, "OK, friend. Time to go to work. Go down the hole."

He gave me a long, angry look. Then he took off his web gear, retrieved Taylor's flashlight, checked the magazine in his pistol, crossed himself, and crawled over to the spider hole. After looking inside it for several moments, he went over the edge and was quickly gone, head first.

Almost immediately Spencer said that he could see the tunnel rat's light. I kept expecting to hear a shot.

Fernandez popped back up near me. He said something I couldn't understand and then disappeared down the hole again. Within a minute he appeared in the spider hole under the large shelter where Bratcher and Spencer were sitting.

Occasionally, bullets whistled through the shelters from all sides. They made startlingly loud sounds when they crashed through the palm fronds.

I crawled over to Spencer who was holding a flashlight as Fernandez began drawing a diagram in the dirt of what he had seen underground. The spider hole under the small shelter was connected to the spider hole in the large area and from there the tunnel led away to the west. The blood trail led down this tunnel. Fernandez said that the tunnel curved and he had not been able to see how far it went, but there was a lot of blood in the tunnel.

The VC probably had sat near the spider hole, perhaps to put a bandage on his wound. He had probably been there when we were talking with Woolley. Maybe he had stayed until we first dropped the flashlight down the hole. Even now he could be right around the edge of the bend.

I told Bratcher that I was going down. About then, Beck came crawling up to the shelter and asked if we had gotten the VC in the hole. I told Bratcher that Beck would go with me. Beck said OK.

Taking off my web gear and steel pot, I took the flashlight and the pistol from Fernandez. I crawled over to the spider hole and shined the flashlight down. It was about four or five feet to the floor of the tunnel. I could see the opening on one side back to the small

99

shelter and, on the other side, the opening as it went down and away.

I went over the side head first and caught myself with my hands on the bottom. Shining the flashlight down the tunnel, I could see the blood trailing out of sight around the bend. I came back out of the hole and went in feet first. Going down to my knees, with my feet back inside the tunnel toward the small shelter, I bent down and into the tunnel. I was suddenly enclosed in a solid earthen tomb. The sounds from above were muted. I felt as though I were in another dimension. Everything was quiet, cool, and very confined. With the blood trail and bend ahead, I faced the real prospect of a deadly, subterranean confrontation at any moment. Holding my finger on the trigger of the pistol in one hand and the flashlight in the other, I crawled slowly forward. Beck landed with a thud behind me and clawed ahead quickly until one of his hands grabbed one of my feet.

When I came to the bend, I inched around it, pistol first. I expected to see the wounded VC at any moment but about thirty feet ahead, the tunnel came to an abrupt end.

There was no VC in sight.

I laid down and looked at the end of the tunnel. It looked as if people had maneuvered around the area often, coming and going, their bodies wearing off the loose dirt and rounding out the sides. My first thought was that a hole at the end led up and out -- the tunnel must be an escape route away from the shelters. Once I reached the end, I might find myself coming out of the tunnel into a nest of VC, or coming out near one of our guard positions and being shot by my own men.

"Where da' fuck did he go?" Beck said behind me.

"I think up and away," I said as I got back to my hands and knees and inched further down the tunnel.

The air was stuffy. I could smell my own body odor and Beck's. I did not like the confinement and wished as I inched along that I had not invited Beck. He blocked any escape and seemed to close off the tunnel behind me. As I moved along, my world became smaller and smaller.

Every few feet, I stopped crawling and laid down to study the tunnel end. As I came closer, I saw that there was no hole going up. The end was a round circle, with no opening at the top. On the floor I saw what looked like a toilet seat, but it proved to be a hinged door.

"No," I said to Beck, "I don't think he went up and away, I think he went down."

I continued to look at the trapdoor, in the hope of divining a course of action that was safe. Why a door? What was underneath?

100

Was it filled with VC? Was it booby trapped? In the flashlight beam, it looked like the gate to hell. I wished I had more air to breathe.

"What are we going to do?" Beck asked.

The trapdoor was covered with bloody fingerprints, and smeared blood was on the front of the wooden base. Our wounded VC had indeed gone through. The blood was not dry, he was only minutes ahead of us. I felt very close to my prey.

"Beck," I said, turning to look at the burly soldier behind me, "I'm going to turn on my side, and you're going to crawl by me. There's a trapdoor in front at the end of this tunnel. I think you can stand over it. You're going to take the pistol and the flashlight and I'm going to open that door. You shine that light in and be prepared to shoot."

"OK," Beck said with his usual cheerful willingness.

I turned on my side, and Beck squeezed by on his hands and knees. When he got close to my outstretched hands, I handed him the flashlight, but I said I'd hold the pistol to cover him until he was in place. It was a well-intended idea; however, when Beck passed by me, all I could see was his butt. I would have little chance to fire around him if any VC suddenly appeared out of the hole.

When Beck reached the end of the tunnel, he came slowly to his feet. His back was against the top of the rounded-out area overhead, he was standing with his feet on either side of the door. There was a small handle on the top of it.

"You want me to pull it open?" Beck asked.

For a fleeting second I thought about telling Beck to come on, we were going back up. We were still alive, but we might die if we opened that door. My face was only inches from the wet blood.

"No," I said. "Here, you hold the pistol. I'm going to open the door with my bayonet. You keep that flashlight and gun pointed inside."

Lying on my stomach, I got the bayonet off my belt and extended the blade forward. After a second thought, I turned the bayonet so that I was holding the blade and tapped the handle on the door to see if the tapping in the eerie quiet of the tunnel would draw fire. Nothing. Nobody home. Sweat dropped down from Beck's face. Above us, we heard more small-arms fire, a few single rounds as the VC probed and then the return fire from the platoon.

I turned the bayonet around and stuck the point between the trapdoor and the base. Stooping over the hole, Beck had the flashlight and pistol inches above the knife. I lifted the door slightly and Beck moved the flashlight forward to shine in the crack. Lifting the door wider, I raised up on my elbows to look down inside.

James E. Parker, Jr.

The room below was narrow and long, three times the size of the tunnel and filled with olive drab boxes. I saw a pool of blood on some clothes at the end of the flashlight beam.

There was no VC. I was suddenly angry. Relieved, but angry.

"Lieutenant, my back is killing me. Let's do something," Beck said.

Taking the flashlight from him, I lifted the door all the way and bent down into the room. The blood trail went to the end of the room. Bloody handprints were on the rear wall. I figured that the VC had made his way up the wall to the hold above.

I dropped into the room and could almost stand up. Old carbines and mortar tubes were stacked in one corner. I told Beck to go back and get Fernandez and a couple of more men because we were going to clear all the stuff out of the room. When Beck dropped the door, I suddenly realized I didn't have a weapon. I opened the door and told him to leave the pistol. I left the door open and went back to the other end of the room. As I suspected, there was a trapdoor in the ceiling above the bloodstains. Aiming the flashlight at the door, I eased it open with the barrel of my pistol.

There was nothing but more tunnel on the other side. I opened the door completely and stood up. With my head up through the door opening, I shined the light down the tunnel. It went to a dead end, but I thought I could see openings off to each side.

Fernandez soon appeared, and I sent him down the tunnel after the VC. He went reluctantly.

Beck joined me in the lower room, and we began to hand out items to Lyons, who was waiting in the tunnel above. They included medical supplies, textbooks, mine parts, clothing -- civilian and military -- ammo, weapons, maps, letters, pots and pans. The room was the supply cache for a VC cell. On the side of one wall in the dirt was a square area that had been hardened with water and some cement like agent contained several lines of Vietnamese writing and a small American flag. I had Beck write the Vietnamese as best he could.

When the tunnel rat returned, he said that he had gone down the tunnel to the dead end, taken a right and followed the blood trail until the tunnel got so small that he couldn't go any farther. The tunnel that led off to the left continued to what appeared to be a cave-in.

Still no VC.

Back aboveground, I leaned against the wall of the hole under the shelter and breathed deeply. The moon was full and the

102

night was surprisingly bright. Bratcher and Spencer were nearby. Spencer handed me a cup of coffee, and, hiding the match in my cupped hands, I lit a cigarette. The pile of material from the underground room lay in the middle of the hole. Occasional rounds whistled overhead.

I called Woolley to report that we had lost the VC down a tunnel but, in chasing him, had come across a small VC supply cache. We were being probed, but I thought we could hold our own until sunrise. No casualties -- we were hungry and tired, but OK.

When I finished my report, I leaned back against the dirt pit wall.

Bratcher pointed at the spider hole in the corner and asked, "Do you want us to wake you up if any VC come out of that hole tonight, or do you just want to sleep through it."

More rounds zinged overhead.

Kiss my bejesus, I thought. Will this ever end? I was so tired that it was difficult to focus on the problem with the hole, but it was clear, once Bratcher mentioned it, that the tunnel was unprotected and the VC could come in during the night and attack us from the inside out. It would be hard to find all the men and move away from the shelter at this hour. Plus everyone was tired and we were surrounded by VC. The easiest thing would be to protect the hole.

I looked at it in the corner and thought that, at any second, a VC could jump out like a jack-in-the-box and start shooting. I noticed that Spencer and Bratcher held their weapons pointed toward the hole.

More rounds zinged overhead. I borrowed Spencer's bayonet, took a couple of grenades off my web gear, picked up some tape, a trip flare kit, and went down the hole feet first. After crawling to the trapdoor at the end of the tunnel, I banged on the door with the handle of the bayonet before opening it, but I saw no signs of anyone being there since we had left. I shut the door again and drove one bayonet into the ground on one side of the door. Repeated attempts to get the other bayonet into the ground on the other side failed, so I impaled the blade on the bottom of the doorframe. I taped the grenades to the bayonets, attached the wire from the trip flare kit in the ring of one grenade, and ran it across the trapdoor to the ring of the other grenade. My shoulders were tired when I finished. I laid my arms on the tunnel floor and then brought them back to cushion my head. I closed my eyes and was drifting off to sleep when I heard more gunfire above.

I looked at my booby trap, knowing that I hadn't straightened out the safety pins. If I hit that wire after I straightened

103

the pins, I was dead, because I couldn't back out of this tunnel in time. Carefully thinking through every movement before I made it, I straightened the two pins and moved my hands back in front of me. My face was covered with sweat, and I was breathing heavily. Slowly I backed out of the tunnel and joined Bratcher and Spencer.

We were constantly probed for the next few hours. Sometime after midnight, the firing stopped. Then about 0200 VC opened up from all sides. I thought that they were attacking and called in mortar flares. A tracer round hit the straw roof of the smaller shelter, and it started to burn.

The mortar flares went off. Woolley asked if I wanted mortar rounds fired around my position. I said yes, but I wondered if he and the mortar crew had our exact position plotted. Within minutes mortar rounds began crashing around us. We stopped firing and hugged the ground.

There was no more fire from the VC when the mortars stopped. I called the company commander and thanked him. He said they would get a relief column out to us at first light.

Around 0500, the first rays of the morning sun began to seep into the jungle around us, and it was light by 0530. From across the hole under the shelter, Spencer said, "Hell of a night."

I told Bratcher that I wanted us up and moving soon. If each man carried some items, we could take everything that we had brought out of the underground room.

Bratcher yelled out to the men that we would be moving out at first light. I looked at the spider hole in the corner and thought about the two-grenade booby trap over the door. I could leave them there. No one would know. But the VC would certainly get the grenades when they came back and eventually use them against us. I thought about sending Bratcher or Beck to recover them, but only I knew how the trap was set.

I told Bratcher and Spencer that I was going to get the grenades and picked up a pistol and flashlight. Down in the tunnel, I saw that the wire between the two safety pins had been bent upward. During the night, someone from below had pushed the door up but had stopped before the wire across the top pulled out either of the pins.

I smiled to myself, but I was suddenly unsure how to bend the safety pins back. One of the safety pins was slightly out the detonator. I backed out of the tunnel and asked Bratcher for the pliers he carried to crimp claymore detonators. They had wire cutters on one end.

Back in the tunnel I crawled to the trapdoor and caught my

breath before reaching up and cutting the wire between the safety pins. Then, one at a time, I bent the pins back. I was backing down the tunnel when I heard small-arms fire from above. It started slowly, then a full battle erupted. I backed out furiously and was almost to the spider hole when I heard Bratcher yelling for everyone to hold their fire.

Coming out of the hole, I saw Bratcher running off to the side with Spencer on his heels. I heard loud, frenzied talking in the bush ahead of them.

Castro was yelling, "Ah shit, man, shit, shit."

I recognized Peterson's voice yelling for the medic and telling his men to spread out. Wondering why Peterson was here, I rushed forward.

Ten or fifteen feet from the shelters Castro was holding Private Patrick in his arms. Patrick had been shot in the chest and shoulder. The medic was on his knees. Patrick's arms were lying loosely at his side, his eyes roaming around the faces of the men standing above him. Castro helped open his fatigue jacket. Blood was gushing out of a number of holes, and his eyes started to lose their focus. Castro yelled for him to hold on. He told the medic to hurry. Patrick coughed, and blood came out of his mouth. I dropped to my knees beside him.

"Goddammit, don't you die, Patrick, don't you die, don't give up," I said, helping to rip open his shirt.

Blood was everywhere. Patrick closed his eyes and his head rolled to the side, and he died.

We stopped what we were doing. The medic shook his head, took a deep breath, and stood up.

Castro was still holding Patrick and rocking back and forth on his heels. Then Castro laid him down on the ground. I stood up and looked at Pete. His eyes were moist. He had his hands out with the palms up.

"I left as soon as I could this morning to get here and help you," Pete said. "Colonel wouldn't let me come last night." He paused. "Patrick must have fallen asleep, lying here in these bushes. He fired at my point man. Just jerked up and started firing. He and my point man just fired at each other. I'm sorry."

I looked down at Patrick, then at each man who stood around him in slight shock -- Castro, Bratcher, Spencer, Beck, Pete's point man and finally Pete. Tired, it took a while for me to understand what happened. Then, more quickly, I sought some meaning. I couldn't yell at Pete or his point man. It certainly wasn't their fault, nor was it Patrick's. I felt a mindless rage, like I wanted to cry and scream at the same time.

"Goddamnit," I heard myself say, as random thoughts drifted through the fog of my mind. Death is so ugly. War is so unfair. Why Patrick? What's the use? Who's to blame? No answers and my mind turned numb.

Without comment, we built a stretcher out of ponchos and bamboo and gently rolled Patrick's body onto it.

Pete's platoon would stay in the area and try to pin down the VC who had attacked us during the night. As I began to walk away with my platoon, Pete fell in beside me, and we walked along together for a short distance. We didn't look at each other or talk. I was exhausted. Pete didn't know what to say. He stopped and I walked on.

--NINE--
Phoenix and Fate

We delivered Patrick's body to Specialist 5th Class Heyekiah Goss, Jr., the company medic, and then slept most of the day under shady makeshift shelters. Soon after I awoke, Pete's recon platoon returned to the battalion perimeter with the bodies of two of his men killed during the day.

A hot meal, cold beer, and mail came in by helicopter late in the afternoon and the platoon slept through the night. The following morning, 15 January, the battalion swept toward a village west of our bivouac site that was suspected of harboring VC. Alpha Company's route was just inside a wood line by a large open rice field. The company would follow a small trail, with Duckett's former platoon on the left and mine on the right. Ernst's platoon, now commanded by Arthur, would ride on armored personnel carriers and bring up the rear in reserve.

Several units were moving on the village from different directions to contain the VC. As we were getting on line that morning and preparing to move out, Pete's platoon moved by on my right to reconnoiter in the front of our advancing line. When Pete and I saw each other, we smiled and nodded our heads in greeting. Pete looked tired. He raised his M-16 up in the air and then went out of sight.

As Alpha Company moved out, gunships passed overhead and buzzed the tree line by the rice field. Random artillery rounds landed across the field. We heard occasional bursts of gunfire around us as the men fired into suspicious bushes and tuffs of bamboo. In my platoon, Ayers was at the front of one file, Beck led another, and Sergeant Rome was off on the right.

Far off to our left across the field, Charlie Company was pinned down by fire from a VC machine-gun bunker. Arthur was ordered over to help. The VC gun crew retreated when they heard the tracks coming through the jungle. After sweeping the area, Arthur was ordered back behind us again as reserve and he fell in somewhere to our rear. We overheard Woolley talking with him by radio. According to the coordinates that Arthur gave, he should have been directly behind us, but no one could hear any noise from the tracks. Woolley was walking down the path that separated Duckett's old platoon from mine. His point man spotted a trip wire running across the trail. We slowed down while the company first sergeant cleared the brush around the wire. When he found it led to a flare, we moved out again. Woolley went back to the radio and began talking with Arthur again. Duckett's platoon encountered some heavy brushes, and Beck yelled for us to slow down so that we would stay on line.

Suddenly, an automatic weapon opened up on the company to our left front. Everyone dropped to the ground. I looked at Spencer and lit a cigarette. It was 0915, and I noted from my map that we were at the coordinates XT 637177. For no particular reason, I made a dot at that location on my map.

To our front, perhaps five hundred meters away, we heard a couple of shots fired, than a pause before a tremendous blast. The violent sound of a dozen automatic weapons followed the blast. Grenades went off. There were long sustained bursts of fire.

Peterson's platoon!

Breathlessly, I scrambled back to Spencer's radio and turned it to the battalion frequency.

Up ahead, the grenades went off one after another -- boom, boom, boom, boom -- amid the continuing small-arms fire.

I recognized Pete's platoon sergeant talking on the radio, "They're on both sides, all around us, no place to go."

He went off the air. I started to get up. The battle continued in front. There was no letup in the firing.

Why wasn't Peterson on the radio?

The platoon sergeant came back on, "Almost every man's hit. I ain't got no one. Give us some fire. Help us! Give us some fire! Give us ..."

I stood up. Pete was in trouble. His platoon was pinned down.

107

Someone came back on the radio, "This is the 1st Squad leader. We're almost wiped out. The radio operator's dead, the platoon sergeant's been shot in the head, the lieutenant's dead. Help us! God give us some help!"

Yelling for the men to get ready to move out, I crashed through the bushes to the trail where Woolley was listening to the radio. I told him I had to go help Pete.

"OK," Woolley said. "Let me coordinate with Battalion."

I had taken the captain's arm as I talked and was pushing him along the trail. We had passed other men in his company headquarters group and were now well ahead of even the two platoons on either side. He and I were leading the company down the trail. I kept looking off to the right front, where the firing was still heavy. There had been no letup since the first blast. Hand grenades, M-79s, automatic rifles, machine guns.

With one hand still on Woolley's elbow I turned around toward Woolley's radio operator and yelled angrily for him to catch up, "Come on, goddamnit, I got to go."

Then, the whole world exploded.

A mine went off beside the trail, midway back in the company headquarters group. Shrapnel flew by my head.

"Goddamnit to hell, goddamnit!" I dropped to one knee and was still looking back at the blast as dirt and debris fell around me. I was intent on getting to Peterson -- all this struck me as just another delay.

The firing was still intense in front. Dust continued to settle as I looked back and tried to spot the radio operator. I thought it might have been a mortar round, short.

Then, out of the dust, Beck walked up with blood streaming from his ears. Bratcher, who had blood oozing out of his fatigue jacket near his shoulder was behind him. They had followed me over to talk with Woolley and had been caught in the blast.

I turned and saw several other soldiers, dead or wounded, lying along the trail. A round zinged down the trail over our heads. Bratcher and Beck, both in slight shock, quickly regained their wits and dove to the side of the trail.

Some men from Duckett's platoon started firing.

Goss, the company medic, was still on the trail, lying on his back. His fatigue jacket was shredded from shrapnel. He was laboring for breath, his eyes open wide as if in surprise.

I knelt beside him and yelled for another medic. I took a bandage off my belt, opened it, and tried to remember what to do with a chest wound. Put the plastic from the packing next to the wound, I thought, when Bratcher yelled from the bushes, "The man's dead, Lieutenant, get off the fucking trail."

"He ain't dead," I yelled, as I placed the bandage on his chest.

"He ain't breathing no more," Bratcher said right above me.

Dirt and dust were settling on Goss's eyes, but he was not blinking. He stared vacantly off in the distance, his mouth open. I knew by the smell that his bowels had emptied as his body relaxed in death.

"Get off the trail, Lieutenant," Bratcher insisted.

I stood up and turned to look at the radio operator, who was laying half on and half off the trail. A bullet zipped by in front of me. Out of the corner of my eye, up the trail, I saw a VC rise up out of a hole.

I had reached a point where nothing was making much sense. I had been absorbed in moving out to help Pete -- and then the mine blast and Goss dying and the radio operator lying dead and rounds coming down the trail. Everything seemed to be happening in slow motion as adrenaline surges overloaded my mind. Trying to focus on each separate event, I saw things in flashes, as if my surroundings were illuminated by a strobe light. The VC was still coming out the hole. I started to turn and look at him, but then I thought about Pete and getting to him and I looked down at Goss and I turned back to see the radio operator's feet lying out on the trail and I started yelling at myself: Think, Think, Think.

Another round whizzed by in front of me. I turned back around so that, for a fleeting moment, I was looking up the trail. Then I clearly saw the VC standing up in the hole near a ditch and aiming his rifle at me. Bratcher was in the bushes beside the trail, and I dove toward him. I saw the muzzle flash from the VC's gun.

A searing pain in my buttocks brought me to my senses. In mid-dive, I knew that I had been shot. Bratcher grabbed me by my fatigue jacket and pulled me into the bushes, while Duckett's men opened fire down the trail.

A medic crawled up. Bratcher said he was OK, to look after me. Lying on my stomach I took some deep breaths, pulled off my web gear and undid my belt. When I pushed my pants down, I felt blood collecting between my legs.

Woolley knelt down beside me. "We're going to move out, Jimmy, and try to get to Pete's platoon. I've called a medevac. You're going to be all right. Sergeant Rome will take your platoon." There were heavier mortar explosions now, in the distance to the front of us.

"Get to Pete. Hurry," I said as I looked up, unashamed of my

109

exposed, bloody rear.

The medic worked on my buttocks. I could not see what he was doing. He moved off soon without a word and started treating other wounded, including Bratcher and Beck. I lay on the ground and felt weak as adrenaline faded. My butt felt like a knife had been plunged into it.

Later, the less wounded in my ragged group carried the more serious wounded to the edge of the field and went back for the dead. Beck carried Goss in his arms.

In time, a medevac helicopter came down and landed near our purple smoke. It was almost completely loaded with other casualties when it landed and could only take the two most seriously wounded from our group. Bratcher and I were the last to leave, with the dead, a couple of hours later. As we lifted off, we could see rows of men in body bags by the edge of the field, close to where Peterson's platoon had been hit. I knew that Peterson was in one and I felt like crying.

****

At a medevac clearing station, Maj. Gen. Jonathan O. Seaman, commander of the 1st Division, came through and passed out Purple Heart medals to us. Later, at what must have been the most impersonal, the most insensitive aid station in Vietnam, I had my wound cleaned and stitched. Beck and Bratcher had their wounds treated and were discharged to return to the battalion base camp. I was admitted to the convalescent tent next to the operating room.

The next morning, I was aware of the trucks before I opened my eyes. The air brakes hissed as the tractor trailers came to a stop. When the trucks started out again, they whined in first gear and then, after a pause, more whining as the driver shifted into second.

I shared the tent with six men who were talking amongst themselves, undisturbed by the trucks. The sides to the tent were raised and only the mosquito netting was between me, lying on a cot in the corner, and a busy intersection of two dirt roads. Heavy olive-drab transfer trucks were passing, one after another, throwing up billowing clouds of dust. It was barely past sunrise and I was already covered by a thin layer of dust.

"Get used to it, man," said one of the soldiers from the other end. "It goes with the territory here. But look on the bright side, it's better than the fucking field, right?"

I lay on my stomach most of the day and thought about Peterson. I remembered when we first met in OCS, Pete's exhausted face during the eleventh-week run when he kept saying, "We're going to make it, we're going to make it, we're going to make it," and then a few days later when Pete's friend scared us into thinking Pete was going to be paneled. I could see Pete's shock as the man came to our door and just stood there. For days thereafter, we said, "Oh no, Mr. Death, get away from our door. Get away!" Other memories flashed through my mind -- our nights drinking in that honky-tonk bar in Junction City, laughing together, racing our sports cars over the prairies of Nebraska, sitting on the top deck of the USNS *Mann* on the way to Vietnam, talking about the past, wondering about the future. Ours had been a rich, robust, and trusting bond. He was my best friend, ever. Now, he was dead.

Then I thought about the insurance policy, and not sending in my change of beneficiary form. I felt tremendous guilt. Pete had been so trusting and I had been such a heel. "Pete," I said under my breath, "I promise to you, wherever you are, that when I get that check, that I'm sending it to your Momma. Please forgive me."

More trucks hissed and whined outside and dust continued to settle on my bed. The men joked and talked loudly among themselves at the other end of the tent.

I felt so terribly lonely.

I recalled how Pete and I had silently shared the sorrow of Patrick's death a few days before, how we had walked alongside each other as my platoon headed back toward the perimeter, and the pain in his face later that same day when he came back in with his dead. The last time I saw him, he was lifting his M-16 in the air as his platoon went out of sight to recon in front.

Every word that I had heard over the radio when I switched it to the battalion frequency came back to me. Pete's platoon was wiped out. "The lieutenant's dead," the platoon sergeant had said. The platoon sergeant, himself to die within minutes, had eulogized my best friend with the noise of battle in the background: "The Lieutenant's dead." Pete was so proud of his commission. Maybe it was the way he would have wanted to go, but for me, I had never felt such sorrow.

I tried to write a letter to his parents that day, but it was blubbering nonsense. I crumbled it up and threw it toward the trucks outside.

That night after supper, the medic came down the aisle of cots. He was humming and had a gigantic needle in his hand. "Needle time, Parker, show me your fanny."

I reacted angrily, without thinking, telling the medic to stick the needle up his own ass.

111

The man walked away but he soon returned with a Medical Corp major.

"Specialist Wallace says that you are very uncooperative," the major said with a frown, "that you refused to let him give you your tetracycline shot. It is not helpful if you act like a child. You can understand that, can't you? We won't stand for any more outbursts. We have too much to do to hold the hands of everyone here."

He was right, of course. After he left, the medic jabbed me with the needle and I yelled.

About midmorning the next day Terry Mulcay, the Battalion Headquarters Company commander, walked in. I yelled out a greeting, happy to see a familiar face from my old battalion.

He sat on a nearby cot and handed me some mail. He told me that the battalion had secured the area around Cu Chi before being replaced at night by the 25th Division. Some VC had popped up in the middle of the substitution of forces and fired off a couple of rounds. The 25th Division, new to 'Nam, returned fire with everything they had. It was a hell'va show there outside Cu Chi that night, he said.

Our battalion was now located in a defensive position near the Cambodian border. It had taken heavy casualties, and he named some of the men who were killed. I waited for Peterson's name but sensed that Mulcay would name Peterson last, out of respect for our friendship, or so that he could offer his personal condolences.

He didn't mention Pete.

"Pete? Pete wasn't killed?" I asked incredulously.

"Nope," he said.

I knew before the word was completely out of his mouth that Pete was alive. Happiness surged through me -- incredible joy. Peterson, that son of a bitch, wasn't dead. He's alive. That son of a bitch.

"He was one of the first ones hit in his platoon," Mulcay said. "Took a round in his right shoulder. It knocked him back and as he was spinning around, he took another round in the same shoulder from behind. The first one took out most of his shoulder bone, and the one in the back took out a lot of meat and muscle, but he's OK. He's going to live. I just saw him in the 93d field hospital. He's heading back to the States tomorrow or the next day. No more war for him."

Peterson was alive. That son of a bitch.

Later that morning on the way back from the latrine, I shuffled down to a Jeep ambulance parked in the shade at the rear of the tent. Behind the wheel, Private First Class Richardson [alias] was reading a *Playboy* magazine.

"Howyoudoing?" I said in my best "good ol' boy" tone of voice.

The driver looked first at my face and then down at my gown. "OK," he said.

"Where's the 93d field hospital?"

"It's about twenty-five miles from here. Nice, very nice-looking nurses there. Round-eyed beauties. Got me some lady friends over there. Why?"

I said, "I got a friend there, too, who's heading back to the States tomorrow. We've gone through a lot together."

Richardson continued to look at me.

"No problem in driving over? You can just get on the road and go? Can you go there, Mr. Richardson?" I asked.

"Well you're supposed to have an armed escort. When we're carrying people back and forth, we get an MP (military police) detail to come along, but it's no problem. Only once in a blue moon does anyone ever get shot at."

"What do you think about us going, you and I, over to the 93d. Who you got to ask? You got to ask anybody, Private Richardson?"

"You got any war souvenirs? VC flags, guns, that kind of thing?"

"Nope," I said, but I had hope. This guy had a price. This guy would go.

Suddenly, I had a thought and left without a word. The Purple Heart medal General Seaman had given me was still in a pocket of my fatigue pants. In the ward, I bent over awkwardly and pulled my fatigues from under the bed, took the medal out of my pants pocket -- dried blood was on the box -- and carried it outside to Richardson.

"General Seaman gave me this Purple Heart," I said, opening the box as if it was very special, "and I'll give it to you if you take me to the 93d today. Twenty-five miles there, I'll spend an hour with my buddy and twenty-five miles back. No problem. You'll have an interesting day, I'll have an interesting day, and you'll get a real trophy for the rest of your life. What do you say?"

Richardson examined the medal closely. He finally looked up and around to see if anyone was looking.

"OK, go get dressed, we'll go."

"Get dressed?" I asked.

"You ain't going like that, with your ass sticking out of that gown, are you?"

"No, I reckon I'm not," I said, knowing that the only clothes

113

I had were the bloody fatigues I was wearing when I was wounded.

Specialist Wallace, the needle man, watched me as I came back in and shuffled to my cot. I smiled at him, the fatigues at my feet. He must have noticed a change in my attitude and thought something was up. He started toward my cot.

"I wonder," I asked in a friendly tone, "if there is a shuttle that runs from this aid station to the 93d field hospital? You know, a bus or something?"

"You can't just check into any hospital you want to, you know. You're here, you belong to me, I'm going to make you whole again. You can't make no reservations at the 93d."

"No, you don't understand. A friend of mine is there, leaving tomorrow for the States. Got shot up pretty bad. Need to see him. Just over and back, that's all. Shuttle?"

"No shuttle. The doctor has ordered bed rest for you until your wound has healed. Even if there was a shuttle, you couldn't go. You can't even sit down."

"What if I were to catch a ride? Say, a helicopter ride over and back? What do you think? Would the major go along with it?"

"No," he said, crossing his arms over his chest.

"Would you please go ask him? Just ask him if I could get a pass to go to the 93d. That's all."

"He's going to say no," he assured me, but he turned and walked out of the tent.

After dressing in the latrine and slipping on my boots with the laces cut to shreds by the hospital staff when I arrived, I shuffled down to the ambulance. The stitching hurt when it occasionally caught in my pants. Richardson started his Jeep and I walked around to the passenger side. Suddenly, I realized the corpsman was right, I couldn't sit down. I went to the back and painfully climbed up. Some of the stitches came loose and blood ran down my leg. As I crawled onto a stretcher behind the passenger seat, the bleeding stopped.

Richardson jerked the Jeep in gear and I grabbed the stretcher like a rodeo rider. On the open dirt road he floored the accelerator and whipped around the first turn without breaking. My legs flew off the stretcher and I ended up half on and half off of it. Screaming in pain, I yelled for Richardson to stop while I got myself back on the stretcher.

"Personally, my friend, I'm not that interested in getting there, you know, real, real fast. Fast is good enough. So you don't need to speed just for me, and the VC weren't that good a shot anyway, they only got me in the ass," I told him as I crawled back up on the stretcher.

The Vietnam War Its Ownself

Back moving again, we did not go slower, however, and we hit bumps with jarring thuds. Passing a slow-moving truck, Richardson whipped out to the left and I was slung off the stretcher again. Finally he stopped and tied a strap around my legs. Back on the road, he went as fast as he could, playing chicken with oncoming traffic, bouncing wildly over bridges, and missing farm animals and people by inches. He remained nonplused and slowed the Jeep only when we arrived at the 93d field hospital. He parked, asked for my friend's name and went into the administrative building.

Richardson was gone for what seemed like a long time. I tried to reach down and undo the big, broad strap holding my legs, but I could just barely reach it. The buckle was on the other side from the way I was reaching, and as I turned around and stretched out my right arm, a stitch popped. I yelled from the pain and jerked my arm back, which threw the stretcher off balance and my upper torso fell to the floor. The stretcher turned on its side although the foot end stayed on the bracket because of the strap around my legs. I was trapped, tied upside down in the ambulance.

"Aaaaaauuuuuuugggggg," I was moaning when Richardson returned.

"You're dangerous, you know that," he said quietly as he stood at the rear of the Jeep and looked down at me. "You sure you didn't shoot yourself?"

He helped me out and gave me the number of Pete's ward. He was going to see some friends and said he would meet me in Pete's Quonset hut in a couple of hours.

I found the right building and straightened my bloody, dirty fatigue uniform as best I could. Smiling, I walked in.

****

Classical music was coming from speakers on the wall. Concrete floors. Bright lights. Clean sheets. Metal bed frames with thick mattresses. Pretty nurses. Air conditioning. Smiling people.

I saw Pete halfway down the aisle on the right. A nurse was sitting on the edge of his bed writing a letter for him. His right shoulder was covered with thick bandages. He had his left arm through the sleeve of his pajama top. Sitting propped up, he was watching the nurse as she wrote. His hair was wet and combed.

"You son of a bitch," I said softly.

He looked up, his face expressionless and then he smiled.

"Well goddamn," he said after a moment. "You look like hell."

115

"I'm alive, though," I said and I shuffled around the bed to grab his left hand.

"This guy is a good friend of mine," Pete said to the nurse as he continued to look at me. "Can you look after him?"

They brought in a rolling dolly and put it between Pete's bed and the man next door. When the nurse helped me up, she noticed fresh blood. She insisted on looking at my wound. I told her that could cause me some embarrassment here in an open bay with all these people looking on. She wasn't listening to me and had my pants down to my knees in a matter of seconds. I told her that I thought she had undressed men before.

While I lay there talking and laughing with Pete, she called for a couple of corpsmen, and they re-stitched my wound.

Pete showed me the bullet taken out of his shoulder, which he kept on a bedside table. Someone produced some champagne, and we drank it from bedpans, even though glasses were available.

A doctor came in and wanted to know if I was registered in this ward. I explained that I had just come over for the day from division, which he took in stride and then he left.

Pete and I talked without stopping.

"It's going to be hard at times, telling people I got shot in the ass," I said.

"Couldn't have happened to a better guy," Pete assured me. "There is that irrepressible conceit about you, Parker -- getting butt shot'll be good for you."

"Well, fuck you. I got shot 'cause I was all atwitter about you."

"Appreciate the thought," Pete said.

"Hell, I'm just sorry I missed out on the insurance," I said.

"Yea, well, about that insurance ..." he said in a sober tone.

I broke in, "Pete, I have something to say about that insurance, something that I'm terribly, terribly embarrassed about -- sorry about."

"What?" Pete asked.

"I, ah, I, ah ..." I couldn't get it out.

"What the hell is it? I know it's something 'cause every time that insurance came up, you'd look away, or you'd change the topic. What is it?" Pete asked.

"I never sent in my change of beneficiary form. If I died, Mother would get the money."

Pete looked at me without expression.

"But I want you to know, Pete, I want you to believe me on this, that when I thought you were dead, I made a solemn oath to send the insurance money to your mom. I swear. And I am so glad that I won't have to do that." I looked away. "I am so glad you're alive."

"You know, Parker, that's why I like you. You're a shit. You'd steal the pennies off a dead man's eyes ... but you'd get your ass shot up trying to come help me."

"I'm glad you're OK, Pete."

We looked at each other for a moment, and Pete said, "I ain't OK. I hurt."

"But you ain't dead."

Pete smiled and looked away. Finally he said, "I got a letter from my friend -- the insurance agent -- right before we left base camp. He said our policies were canceled. War zone clause or something. His company doesn't write policies on people who swallow swords or go fight wars."

"Why didn't you tell me?" I asked.

"Never had a chance."

I was honestly very glad the whole insurance thing was over.

"I'm really, really glad you're OK, Pete," I said as if to purge any lingering guilt.

"You've already said that. Don't change the fact that you're basically a mulky, lousy ne'ar do well -- you really do belong there with those bums in that honky-tonk bar in Kansas."

I looked him deep in the eyes, hoping to convey how sincerely I cherished his friendship. Then thinking about what he just said, I asked, "Mulky?"

****

Richardson came back late in the afternoon. He said that we had to be leaving soon so that we could get back before dark. By this time, most of the people in the ward were around Pete's bed -- telling stories, laughing with the nurses, drinking champagne.

I told Richardson it'd only be a few more minutes and invited him to have some champagne.

We continued with the bedside fellowship until Richardson said that he was leaving in five minutes. I could come or not. Either case the Richardson freight left in five minutes.

I grabbed Pete's left hand and we shook, nodding, not talking. I bounced my eyebrows, he smiled, and I crawled off the dolly.

As I started shuffling down the aisle, Pete said, "Be careful. Your mother told me to tell you. Be careful."

"Thanks," I said. "Take care. See you in the States."

"Hey, by the way," Pete said suddenly, and I turned around. He reached under his bed, "Take this back with you."

He pulled out a box and, with a grimace, put it on the part of his chest that wasn't covered with bandages. I returned to his bedside, and he extracted a bathroom scale.

"Momma sent this. Maybe she was thinking I was getting out of shape." Pete handed me the scale with his good hand. "Put it by the bar."

"Yes, sir," I said, trying to think of something silly to add, but nothing came to mind and besides, for some reason, the scales were nothing to laugh about.

Outside, Richardson strapped me in, and I grabbed the stretcher. Racing the setting sun, we took off for Di Ann.

We arrived about dusk. The MPs were putting the barricades across the road at the perimeter's main entrance and we just squeezed through. Specialist Wallace and the doctor were standing in front of the tent when we approached. The headlights from the ambulance passed over the tent as it came to a halt at the rear, near my cot. Both men walked toward us while Richardson was unstrapping me and helping me to the ground.

"There are several things here," the major said. "that we need to about. Like AWOL. You were ordered to bed. Corpsman Wallace told you that you couldn't go to the 93d and you went anyway. No one authorized the dispatch of that ambulance. You've been nothing but a problem since you arrived."

"Sorry," I said, but my tone and the set of my jaw probably indicated to the two that I didn't care.

"I am going to discuss your case with the adjutant general. You can't just take a vehicle like that and go out on unsecured roads. You can't do it. You are in my hospital ward and you answer to me. You understand?"

As I walked by them with Pete's scale in my hands, I said, "Yes, sir."

I put on the fresh gown lying by my bed. One of the men from the other end of the tent said in the half-light, "Man, you are in some heavy shit. These people are mad."

I didn't respond as I awkwardly crawled on my cot, sliding the scales under the cot and went to sleep.

When I woke up the next morning, I put on my fatigues and jungle boots with cut laces, picked up Pete's scale, and shuffled out the rear door of the tent. Ignoring the looks from other people, I crossed the busy intersection near the hospital tent and shuffled to the division helipad. I located the dispatcher and told him I was looking for a ride to the 1st Battalion 28th Infantry base camp.

Midday I was back in the company and ate lunch standing by a table in the back of the mess hall. The scales sitting on the table beside me.

Summary orders of some kind came down to the Battalion from the field hospital about my insolence, but I had already told Woolley the story, so he wasn't surprise. He filed the orders in a campfire out behind his tent.

****

For the next ten days, as my wounded healed, I worked at battalion operations. Standing by a battery of radios, I followed the movement of the battalion as it completed its sweep of the area near Cu Chi. On the night of 27 January, the VC attacked my platoon as it lay at rest in a defensive perimeter. Sergeant Rome was killed, blown apart by shrapnel.

Two days later the battalion returned by truck from Cu Chi. Woolley was the first off. I thanked him for getting to Peterson as fast as he did but he said that Colonel Haldane and Sergeant Major Bainbridge were the first to get there. Pete was in the hospital at the 93d within an hour after he was shot.

"Pretty fast," Woolley said and then added with some suspicion, "like your return to battalion."

"Sir, on that, ah, there may be some paperwork on the way," I told him.

He shook his head, "I'm not surprised."

My platoon clamored off another truck and walked by me making comments about my wound. Spencer came by with the radio, "We been talking. That toilet seat you are so famous for, I think that VC knew about that toilet seat. Pissed him off. Someone carrying a toilet seat around ought to be shot in the ass. You know what I mean?"

Bratcher came over to me. The hospital staff had told him to go back to the base camp, but instead he had rejoined the platoon in the field. He was the acting platoon leader the night Rome was killed.

"What happened?" I asked.

He jerked his jaw to the right a couple of times. "I don't know, a round came in on top of us, could have been ours, could have been theirs. Landed by Rome. He never heard nothing."

That night when McCoy and Dunn came by the tent, we talked about the randomness of war.

"It is altogether a proposition of chance," McCoy said.

119

James E. Parker, Jr.

"Remember when we were talking on the USS *Mann* about courage and presence of mind and that kind of shit. War for us grunts is none of that so much as it's just pure luck. War -- this war -- has no heart, no rhyme or reason." We got drunk that night, toasting our men who died at Cu Chi and to Pete's safe exit to the States.

During the next few weeks, as my wound continued to heal, I stayed in the base camp and occasionally helped at the battalion S-3 (operations section), manning the radios. Someone had bought a chess set and McCoy and I would play a game most evenings when he was in the base camp.

After Operation Crimp, my platoon was down to twenty-one men. Some of the wounded had been sent to the States, others had left because their enlistments were up. We had gotten few replacements because the limited reserve of infantrymen in the United States were used to filled out new units for deployment to Vietnam.

We collected Rome's personal effects and sent them to Division so that they could be forwarded to his next of kin. In preparing Patrick's effects, however, Bratcher and I realized that his billfold and some other personal items must be with his body, which we assumed was in the morgue at Bien Hoa. I took a day trip down there to pick them up. Starting out by the brigade helipad at sunrise, I caught an early flight for Bien Hoa and was standing in front of the MACV (Military Assistance Command, Vietnam) field morgue later that morning. There was an unusual smell about the place -- antiseptic and forbidding. When I walked into the reception area, I told a young corporal that I had come for the personal effects of one of my soldiers killed mid-January and gave him Patrick's name and service number. The corporal looked off into the distance for a moment and then reached for a field telephone on his desk. He was soon in lengthy conversation about what was Patrick's and what wasn't. He hung up and suggested that we go in the back.

We walked into the working area of the morgue. Six dead, nude GIs were laid out on marble-top tables. Other, unprocessed body bags lay in the rear. The concrete floor around some of the tables was covered with blood. A man was calmly hosing down the area. The morgue operators, wearing rubber boots, were talking among themselves as I walked through. One or two apparently noted that I was trying not to lose my breakfast. My muscles froze, and I walked awkwardly.

The smell in the midday Vietnamese sun was putrid: excrement, alcohol, and another atrocious odor, akin to rotten oranges. Trudging along behind my escort and stepping through water, blood, and slime, I felt the stark image of the room etch itself

120

into my brain. Dark blood dripped from the cold marble tables. Some of the men had lost limbs; the mouths of some were open, as if gasping for breath. Some stared wide-eyed, vacantly at the ceiling. The black men so colorless, the white men so chalky. All quietly, patiently waiting to be processed.

The scene assaulted my senses. Time stood still as my mind involuntarily examined every detail. It was too ghoulish, too sudden, too unexpected, too macabre -- the most horrible sight I had ever encountered.

When we arrived in the supply room, the receptionist asked whose effects I had come for, but I could not speak. Patrick's name was finally mentioned, and some personal items were put on a table in front of me. I went through them as though I were hypnotized -- taking this, discarding that, not sure why. When I finished, I looked at the supply sergeant and said, "That's it."

He put the items in a plastic bag. I signed for them and walked out without a word, away from the working bay, around the building, and out to the road in front. I jogged to get away from the place. Finally, a quarter of a mile away, I stopped and looked back, still afraid. What a godless, deadly place. The gateway to hell.

****

We heard that General Seaman was being replaced by Maj. Gen. William E. DePuy, called "Peppy" by some of the men who had served under him. He did not like sedentary troops and immediately began launching extended field operations: "Rolling Stone," "Lavender Hill," "Quick Kick II," and "Silver City," came one, right after the other.

I went on the first operation, but, because of my healing wound, Woolley was easy on my platoon and we were held in reserve. Just a casual "walk in the woods," said Spencer. He suggested that I get wounded more often.

Between operations, we received replacements. The base camp had a rough-hewn battalion officers' club and when we came back for refitting between operations, Dunn used it as his private venue to instruct new officer replacements on the history of the 1st Battalion 28th Infantry Regiment, 1st Infantry Division, United States Army. The history was his lead-in to a welcoming toast that had a typical Dunn ending.

He'd get to the end of the bar and say something like this, "OK there, you clean-smelling, unscratched, undented newcomers, come over here. Come here, come on."

121

James E. Parker, Jr.

I used to marvel at how he took command like that, how those replacements responded to him.

"You have been assigned to the 1st Battalion 28th Infantry Regiment in III Corp, Vietnam," he continued, "though by the looks of you, you're hardly deserving, because this unit, youngsters, is one of the finest fighting units in the world -- we have fought and died for our great country since 1813. Our colors have flown wherever America has needed strong, courageous men, willing to die. That's what we do; we fight, we die. We are called the Lions of Cantigny 'cause in World War I, after we took the town of Cantigny, we held off five German counterattacks. This unit, this one you're assigned, took more 'an five thousand casualties in World War I. In World War II this regiment landed at Utah Beach in Normandy and fought its way across Europe. We never, never, never backed up. We don't do 'dat. We fight, we die. We are, you are, the Lions of Cantigny. You are the newest in a proud tradition of officers in a storied battalion. Gentlemen, you need to buy some drinks here. Champagne. We're going to make some toasts."

With glasses charged, he'd say, "Here's to the President of the United States -- the Commander in Chief," and he downed his drink and insisted that the replacements do the same. When the glasses were refilled, Dunn said, "Gentlemen, here's to the Chairman of the Joint Chiefs of Staff," and everyone downed their drink. He went all the way down the chain of command until he got to the battalion commander, Haldane. The bartender, who had one champagne bottle filled with gin, poured gin into the replacements' glasses.

Bob then said, "And here's to the best damn battalion commander of the best damn battalion in the whole history of the United States Army," and he downed his champagne. The replacements downed their drinks, not knowing that it was gin.

The reaction was always the same -- the replacements' eyes bulged, they opened their mouths, slammed their glasses down on the bar, and said, "Aaaaaaauuuuuuuggggggg,"

"Replacements are so dumb," Dunn always said as he walked away from the bar, leaving the replacements gasping for air.

Because we had been wounded and returned to duty, Dunn and I were among the first two officers in the battalion to be selected for a week of out-of-country rest and recreation (R&R). Bob arranged to meet his bride Linda in Hawaii, and I picked Hong Kong.

The day I left, I was surprised to see Moubry, the supply officer, dressed in his best, also on the way out for R&R. "Extra billet," he said, "came in at the last moment."

122

The Vietnam War Its Ownself

Yea, right, Moubry, was all that came to mind. A celebrated incident had occurred several weeks before when Moubry had flown into the battalion forward base on a resupply helicopter that took enemy small-arms fire when it made its landing approach. An enemy round came up through the fuselage and hit Moubry in his seat; the spent bullet lodged in his wallet. On the ground he rushed up to Colonel Haldane, dropped his pants to show how he was bruised from the round and asked about a Purple Heart. Haldane eventually said no, but everyone remembered Moubry running after the battalion commander with his pants down to his knees as he pleaded for a medal. He was hard to like and I had to share my R&R with him. Didn't seem fair.

On my first night in Hong Kong, I took the Star Ferry from Kowloon to the Hong Kong island. I paid something like ten cents for the ride in passenger class. It was a grand voyage -- Chinese junks sailing by, a huge freighter sitting at anchor, barges being moved around, and the lights of Hong Kong going up the side of the mountains on both sides -- how majestic and grand. Getting on and off were thousands of people, young and old, stooped and tall, beautiful and exotic, dour and ugly, richly dressed and in rags.

I stayed on board when we reached the island and sailed back to Kowloon, then to the island and back again for a total of five round trips. No one could have been more enthralled, more captivated with Hong Kong and I vowed to come back.

In a small bar, I spent hours talking with a bar girl who had a Dutch-boy haircut. She did her job well and kept me entertained. Her English was perfect. How strange, I thought, for an Oriental to speak the Queen's English.

I had suits, sport coats, and silk shirts made to order. After living in holes and eating out of cans for six months, I had never been so fit and trim. The clothes looked smashing.

On the third day of my R&R, Moubry ambushed me in the lobby of my hotel. He said that he was running short of money and wondered if he could stay in my room with me. He'd share the cost of the single.

I could have said, "No, Moubry, I don't like you," but I didn't. I said OK and went out and rode the Star Ferry.

Over breakfast the next morning, Moubry wondered aloud what was happening back at the battalion. He said he had a feeling in his bones that something tragic had occurred. We were here having a grand time, and those poor slobs back there were facing danger every minute. He hoped he was wrong and said he was going to pray for the men in the battalion.

Two days later, Moubry and I walked back into the battalion perimeter. I had the tailor-made clothes in bags under my arms. R&R had been altogether too short, but it was good getting back to the unit.

The battalion was in camp, getting ready for an operation scheduled to kick off in the next couple of days.

I waved to Woolley, who was down the company street, as I ducked into my tent to drop off my new clothes. I was on the way out to tell Woolley about my R&R when he came in.

"Jimmy," he said, "I've got some bad news." He paused. "McCoy was killed by a mine two days ago."

I stood perfectly still. "No he wasn't."

"George was here at the base camp. He went out to do some maintenance in his minefield and something happened and a mine went off. He was dead before he hit the ground. There was nothing the medics could do."

I was stunned. McCoy. Dead. Gone. I stood absolutely still --- only my eyes blinked --- sinking into shock, thinking about nothing at all.

Woolley left, and Dunn soon arrived. He sat down at the chess board where George and I had played so many games. He didn't say anything.

I lit a cigarette and sat down in a chair by him.

"What happened?" I asked, my voice breaking.

"Well, one of those things. The trip lines to the mines around the perimeter have gotten tangled in undergrowth and a couple of days ago one of the mines went off in front of George's positions. Someone said a dog had gotten into the minefield, someone else said they saw some villagers near the concertina. George went out to check. He was walking down the safe lane and he took a little half-step off to one side and a mine went off. He never knew what hit him. No reason. There is no great combat story here. Our friend was just walking along and he took a misstep and he died. No moral. Nothing gained. Just one of those things."

George's death was constantly on my mind for days. I could not shake the sense of loss. The only consolation was George's contention that if we die in combat, we're at peace. If others get upset, it's their problem. Be that as it may, my attitudes changed. I did not make friends with the replacements but kept to myself, relaxing only with Dunn, Woolley, and the men in the platoon.

--TEN--

Lavender Hill

The operations around Phuoc Vinh continued. Dunn was wounded again when a bullet grazed one of his legs. He was not medevaced and was out of action for only a few days.

During "Operation Lavender Hill" we were searching for VC supply caches in an area near the Song Be River. On point in my platoon was a young soldier who had recently arrived as a replacement. He came to a clearing, took a couple of steps out and dropped to one knee. Beck, coming up behind him but staying inside the wood line, said, "Get your ass back here. You goin' to get shot."

I was walking forward up the platoon file as the new man stood up to move back. Suddenly a VC automatic weapon opened up from across the clearing. The point man yelled out, grabbed his stomach and lunged forward and to his right behind an anthill out in the clearing. Other VC began firing at us from around the field. The point man was hit again in the leg and screamed. He pulled his legs up as far as he could behind the anthill and continued to yell.

I called Manuel to come up with the M-60 machine gun and told the rest of the platoon to get on line and put some fire on the enemy positions. As our counter fire increased the VC sought cover and their fire died down. The point man was still yelling and I went to the edge of the clearing and looked out at him. He appeared lightly wounded in a couple of places but seemed to be in fair shape otherwise.

"Hey, shut up," I said over the din of the firing. "You're all right. Just keep your head down. You'll be OK."

He continued to yell, and I dived out beside him.

This encouraged the VC and they began firing again -- at me.

There wasn't enough room behind the anthill for both of us, so I rolled to my left behind another anthill. I brought my knees up to my chest as rounds began to hit the ground on either side. Then fire from an automatic rifle began to saw down the anthill gradually. As chunks of the rocklike structure were shot off, pieces fell on my helmet. When I looked up, I saw the top of the anthill coming down.

"Shoot that son of a bitch with the machine gun. Shoot him," I yelled to my men.

More VC rounds came in and hit the ground on either side of me. The top of the anthill was getting lower and lower. Trying to roll

125

myself into a smaller ball, I looked back at the wood line where my men were firing past me.

I had a clear thought: if I were to get out of this alive, I'll never worry about the small stuff of life again. Then I had another clear thought: I hope no one in my platoon shoots me.

Firing continued back and forth, but we were gaining the edge in volume. Finally, the gun that was cutting down my anthill stopped as the VC pulled back and disengaged. I got slowly to my feet. The medic was treating the point man, as other members of the platoon moved around the clearing to chase the VC.

Later, I told Bratcher about my promise to myself not to worry about the small stuff if I survived the anthill attack. "Naw," he said, "you'll forget about it."

Back in the battalion area after the operation, Specialist 4th Class Burke, Colonel Haldane's radio operator, sought me out and told me the colonel wanted to see me. Strange -- this had never happened before. Maybe, I thought, a court-martial order had come through from the division aid station. I could take the heat, I thought, because I had no guilt about the aid station problems.

Dunn also had been summoned and was waiting outside the colonel's tent for me. We went in together and saluted the battalion commander who was sitting behind his desk. He told us that we were good officers, good platoon leaders, and we were lucky. Of the twelve line platoon leaders in the battalion who had arrived in-country, only five remained. New replacements were coming in, and the colonel had decided to rotate some of the staff officers at battalion headquarters into platoon slots. He asked if Dunn and I would like to leave our platoons and join Major Panton in battalion operations.

Dunn and I said together, without hesitation, "Yes, sir."

I would be replacing 1st Lt. Paul Trost in operations. Dunn was replacing a man who had left because he had finished his commission commitment.

Smiling, I asked Haldane if he thought he could live with Dunn and me underfoot, all the time.

He did not smile. "Yes. Can you live with me?" he asked.

Colonel Haldane was best known for his quiet confidence -- he always seemed to know what to do. Even if he didn't, he never showed indecision. He was the boss and he was right; Dunn and I were going to have to mind our manners in our new jobs. The relationship between the colonel and us would be straightforward -- friendly but professional. We were not assigned to battalion operations as court jesters.

I found Trost packing his things inside the operations tent. A serious, studious man he said that our exchange of duties was fair, although he had mixed feelings about taking my platoon.

"Bratcher is a well-known, popular personality in the battalion. He's used to working with you," he said as we walked toward his tent, which he shared with Moubry. "Will he turn surly if I do things differently? Plus it's going to be hard to replace someone who is still on the scene."

"Don't worry. Just don't feel the need to assert yourself," I suggested. "Things will take care of themselves."

After Trost gathered up his few things, we walked to Alpha Company. On the way, he said, "OK, I'll not try to get out ahead of Bratcher, and you resist the temptation to judge how I'm doing with your old platoon. It's mine now."

"Deal," I said.

I went down to the platoon area and gathered together Bratcher, Spencer, and the squad leaders to tell them I was changing places with Trost. For the most part, they shrugged, but their faces indicated to me that they were wondering how this change would affect them. I said I appreciated working with them. They were the best men in the world. I walked through the platoon and shook hands -- Ayers, Castro, Beck, King, Lyons, De Leon, Manuel, Taylor, Spencer, Bratcher. They were tough combat veterans. We had been together for less than a year, but it was as if I had known them all of my life. They were so familiar, so dependable. If, instead of saying good-bye, I had told them that we were going on a dangerous patrol, they would have turned to their equipment and put it on without question. Spencer would have bitched, Beck would have told him to shut up, and Ayers would have been the first out the tent. No one would have wanted to be left behind.

Outside, I told Bratcher to work with Trost, bring him along.

"Ain't no sweat, Lieutenant," Bratcher said as the muscles in his neck tightened. "You always thought overly highly of yourself. Trost'll do all right."

"Don't be a wise-ass, Bratcher," I said. "I'm telling you, Sergeant -- listen to me, look at me -- don't let that man get blown away or get someone else blown away. You hear me?"

Bratcher was a born leader. All through his Army career, his biggest problem was serving under less talented, less experienced officers, especially young lieutenants. Actually, the best situation was to let Bratcher handle the platoon by himself -- he didn't need Lieutenant Trost or any lieutenant for that matter. But that's the way this war was managed; there was a constant rotation of the chain of command in the field, and the combat efficiency of the U.S. Army suffered.

I said good-bye to Woolley, packed my personal equipment, and walked back to Moubry's tent. Dunn, already there, was surveying the accommodations. Moubry had built up one end of the medium-sized tent with sandbags. He had a metal hospital bed and a thick mattress; a desk with a Bible open in the center; a wall locker; and three lights, one over the desk, one over the bed, and one over the middle of his area. Moubry's area was neater and more comfortable than a dorm room at UNC. Behind it, a step below Moubry's lovely sandbag floor, was the area for Dunn and myself. It was marshy, with a layer of mud from side to side. A shipping pallet was near the cot where Trost had slept so that he wouldn't have to step out of bed directly into the mud. A duffel bag suspended from one of the inside guy wires served as a dresser.

"Now, what's wrong with this picture?" Dunn asked as he motioned first to our muddy end and then to Moubry's neat, dry end.

Moubry came in about that time and said gaily, "Hi, guys."

"Moubry," I said, "I don't like my accommodations here. I had a bar in the other area and the same sleeping stuff that everyone else had. I want a metal bed and a wall locker and a desk, and I want lights and a sandbag floor."

"But you people are out on operations all the time. What's the use?"

"The use, Moubry, is that you'll be our friend. And if you don't, we'll kill you. We want a nice bed and a nice desk just like yours. We don't want a packing crate and a duffel bag and a cot on a muddy floor. You're the supply officer. And our friend."

"Well, put in a requisition. I'll do everything I can. I promise."

When Moubry left, Bob turned to me and expressed his doubts about the man's sincerity and general character.

Burke came in through the back door. "Welcome to Headquarters Company. Nice place you've got here. You guys like it muddy? I am, as you know, Specialist 4th Class Burke, and you will be seeing me off and on. You will not see me when you are looking for someone to help you clean this mud up or, say, when you need money or when there is make-work to do. You will see me, you lucky devils, when Colonel Haldane or the sergeant major asks you to do something and you don't know what they're talking about. Because I do. And I will tell you, but I remember, and after a while you owe me. Big time."

"OK, Burke," Bob said with a big smile. "Tell me how we get some equipment here, a bed and a wall locker and a desk."

"You go downtown and you buy it or you get someone in one of the other battalions who knows the supply officer to get some stuff for you."

"But we live with the supply officer here."

"Right," he said.

"So?" Dunn asked.

"As far as anyone knows, he hasn't done anything for anyone since he's been here. Except the colonel. And the sergeant major. You have to respect him for that. You can't threaten him or coerce him, or intimidate him, or blackmail him, and it's very difficult to steal from him. He thinks if you don't get it, the world's a better place. It's part of his religion, I think. You can't beat him. Hell, even I can't beat him, and I am good. He is the quintessential support officer."

"I'll break his scrawny neck," Dunn said.

"Not bad thinking, Lieutenant. I think I am going to enjoy working with you," Burke said. "Good to have you aboard."

"Right, Burke," Dunn said. "You got a first name?"

"Nope, not in this job. I'm Burke, or as the colonel likes to call me, 'Hey you,' or when he's in a hurry it's 'you.' And that ain't bad. Makes me everyman. I'm 'you, dude'"

"Wait, can you call me dude?"

"Yes I can."

"OK, I'm good with that."

****

Two days later, Dunn and I accompanied Colonel Haldane to division headquarters, where we received orders for "Operation Birmingham." Like Operation Crimp to clear Cu Chi, the next field exercise was a heli-borne assault into a VC area close to the Cambodian border. Also, like Crimp, we were going in force.

Preparing for our first operation as liaison officers, Dunn and I studied all of the maps for the battalion and memorized the radio frequencies for medevacs, artillery, Air Force, division, brigade. (We didn't have to, we learned later -- this was the battalion RTOs' responsibility.) We plotted objectives and routes of advance, known enemy locations, villages, and depths of rivers. The comedian Burke helped tremendously, as he had said he would. He knew everything. He also carried the colonel's radio.

The battalion was airlifted to an air base west of Saigon by C-130 transports. On the day of the operation, we were standing by the airstrip there in groups of eight. I was to travel in the helicopter with Colonel Haldane, and Dunn would be with Major Panton in the helicopter behind us.

The helicopters arrived in flights of ten, a swarm of giant mosquitoes. As we boarded, I saw two choppers behind us as they descended toward the airstrip. Still twenty or thirty feet off the ground, they were swaying as the pilots brought them down and then they came too close to each other. Their rotor blades hit first and the impact jerked the helicopters around in strange new directions. One chopper dropped out of the sky straight down. The other, with the pilot fighting to gain control, veered off to the side and then began to pinwheel toward the ground. It landed with a thud near some men who were running to get out of the way.

The incident occurred within the few seconds that it took our chopper to gain altitude. We changed directions, and the scene was lost from view.

I was watching the dozens of helicopters around us and thinking how much they reminded me of pictures that I had seen of Allied planes on bombing missions during World War II when Burke hit me on the shoulder and handed me a radio handset. He said the colonel wanted me to monitor the Air Force net.

Over the "battey-de-battey" of our helicopter, I heard the cryptic conversations of the Air Force jets who were prepping the LZ. This wasn't so bad -- I felt like a spectator. I looked out of the chopper to our front and tried to see the jets working the area, but it was hard to associate what I was hearing with the streaking planes ahead.

I heard one of the jet pilots say that he was receiving small-arms fire, and I asked Burke to relay that information to the colonel. "Yep," he said, "it's a hot LZ."

We landed in waist-high grass. After helping to off-load the chopper, I picked up the maps and fell in behind the colonel. We made our way to a line of trees extending out into the field, and Panton said that we would set up headquarters there. Dunn was on duty first to monitor the radios and plot the maps. I went out to ensure that the men with the heavy mortars knew where we were and that the Headquarters Company guard element was in place to protect our western flank.

Later, I was sitting on commo equipment near Dunn when reports started to come in about contact with the VC, who were all around us and were staying to fight. A couple of times, Dunn was reminded to get the "body count."

The heavy 4.2-inch mortars came on line and began firing over us in support of a unit across the field. Nearby, to the west, a machine gun began firing, then two, then three or more. They were so close that we all ducked. The guns did not sound like our M-60s; their sound was deeper, more throaty.

Panton yelled at Dunn, "What unit is that? Who's over there?"

Burke, leaning over a map, yelled back, "Alpha Company."

My old unit.

The firing increased. Some rounds zinged over our heads. The colonel asked Dunn to find out what was happening. Panton got on another radio and told the mortars to support Alpha.

Dunn got Woolley on the radio, while Burke turned to a frequency that brought up the platoon in contact with the VC. Bratcher was talking. He said that the platoon was ambushed. They had taken casualties, both killed and wounded.

"Press on," Haldane said in an even voice. Then louder, "Tell Woolley to have his men press on. Attack. We'll get someone out to look after his wounded. We're close by."

Picking up my M-16, I trotted by the heavy mortars that were being moved around 180 degrees to support the A Company engagement. I came up beside the guard unit digging in and told the sergeant in charge to come with me. We moved through the trees to the back edge of the field. Down the tree line I saw Beck leading a party of men in my direction. At the end of the field behind him, I could see tracers coming from the jungle. There was some return fire from the field, but not much. Then the mortars behind me began firing with the swoosh of the rounds overhead, followed by the poof from the tubes, and then the crash in front as the round exploded in the trees. Ahead, small-arms firing continued.

Beck was followed by Ayers and Castro, both of whom were carrying men in a fireman's carry. Behind them were other 3rd Platoon stragglers. I motioned for everyone to get into the woods. A medic came up and we made our way down to the group. Beck, Ayers, and Castro all had flesh wounds. PFC James A. Livingston and Staff Sgt. Julian Willoughby, both recent replacements, were dead.

I asked Castro what had happened. He said that when they came to the edge of the field, Ayers started to go around it inside the wood line. The lieutenant told him no, to go straight ahead, that they had to get to a rally point. They were caught in the middle of the field with no place to hide. Everyone in the front was killed or wounded.

Goddamned Bratcher, I thought angrily, why did he let the new man send the platoon out into the field? Trying to get to a rally point? What was this, hurrying to a rally point?

More men came from the guard unit. Some body bags

appeared, and I helped to put Livingston and Willoughby away.

When I got back to battalion headquarters area the colonel was at the center of the activity. To his right, Dunn and Burke were busy taking his orders and relaying them on the radio. Panton, on his left, was plotting a map. I was sitting on the commo box when the wounded men from my old platoon came in with the two body bags. I told Bob that we needed a dust-off. Burke looked over and gave me a thumbs up. Soon Bob told me to take some purple smoke and go out into the field near where we had landed. A medevac helicopter was on the way.

I led the group out, threw smoke, and stood aside as the chopper landed and the men boarded. Castro and Beck waved from the helicopter as it lifted off, bent its nose down, and gained altitude. Both would be back in a couple of days.

Ayers' wounds were light and he stayed. I sent him to join the battalion guard unit until we linked up with Alpha Company again. I slapped him on his broad back as he walked away.

The various units of the attacking force maneuvered in the area for three days and then moved out into separate tactical areas. The division killed 119 VC and wounded many more, in addition to capturing five hundred tons of rice, one hundred tons of salt, mortars, bombs and mines. We were becoming better at our jobs, but at a price. Even very good units have casualties in war.

On the fourth day, my old platoon came by the battalion area. Trost stopped in to see Panton. Ayers was leading the column and I nodded to him as he passed. Bratcher was midway down the column. I made eye contact but did not smile. I blamed him for letting the platoon walk out into that field. He dropped out and came to stand in front of me, his neck tightening occasionally.

"Goddamnit, you told me to let the man alone."

"You dumb fucking asshole. Don't come over here with any fucking excuses. You don't let people walk out in an open field like that."

"We were told the other side was secure."

"Who said that, Sergeant? Goddamnit, all the time we were together, we didn't trust anyone else. We took nothing for granted. Someone says the other side's secure? Fucking show me." I paused. "You don't go putting your people at risk trying to get to some fucking staff officer's rally point on time."

Trost walked by, and I looked away. Bratcher turned and followed him.

That afternoon, we received mail, cold beer, and hot food. I had a letter from Pete, who was convalescing in a hospital near his home of Lincoln. He was in the same ward with Ray Ernst and they both sent their regards. Pete said being wounded wasn't all bad. Some of the nurses loved wounded GIs.

Haldane asked some of the staff members who had previously stayed behind in the base camp to join us. The deputy S-3, Capt. Robert Wardell, was short and stout. He arrived with his air mattress wrapped around his bedroll. The mattress had snagged on the seat of the helicopter when he got off, and unknown to the captain, had developed a hole.

As usual that evening, a duty roster was drawn up to monitor the battalion's radios throughout the night. Each man had two hours. I had 0200 to 0400. Dunn had 0400 to 0600.

As Dunn and I had done every night in the field, we untied our bedrolls from our web gear at dusk and began to blow up our air mattresses. After twenty puffs or so, a mattress is semi-inflated, the way I liked mine. Taking my entrenching tool, I went over behind a bamboo thicket, dug a small hole, crapped in it, covered it up, and returned to my air mattress. I took off my boots, put my watch, billfold, cigarettes, and lighter inside the boots and put my steel pot on top. My M-16 was lying beside me with the barrel on top of the steel pot. I balled up my fatigue jacket for a pillow and wrapped myself in my poncho liner. When I had been with the platoon I fell asleep within seconds, but there was too much activity here.

Across from a pile of radios the deputy S-3 had been blowing into his air mattress for a while. His face was red, and the mattress was still limp. I thought back to basic training and the professor who was so out of his element. I should have stopped thinking then and gone to sleep, but I got up and told the captain that the mattress probably had a hole in it. He had blown enough air into it to fill a blimp.

"You won't be able to find the hole in the dark," I said, "and even if you could, those repair kits don't work."

I suggested that whoever had guard give up his air mattress to the man he was relieving. The deputy S-2 was on duty at the time. He said that that sounded reasonable, and he tossed over his mattress. The captain blew it up, pulled his poncho liner over him and went to sleep.

At 2300 the mortar platoon fired a short round that landed in the area where Company B was dug in. Several men were wounded. The battalion surgeon, another of the staff officers ordered into the field that day, worked on them to keep them alive. He said they had to get to a hospital soon or they would not make the night.

We got the men in Company B on their feet and moved them

to a clearing a half mile away. After they secured the tree line, we stood in the field, with the monsoon rain falling, and shined flashlights at the sky to guide in the medevac helicopter. We put the three wounded men aboard and retraced our steps to the battalion perimeter. By then it was almost 0200.

I fell on my mattress but had not slept for more than fifteen minutes when I was awakened for radio duty. Giving up my air mattress, I went over to the radios and made a note in the journal that I had taken over radio duty. There were sitreps every half hour from the various companies in the battalion. The mortars continued to fire H&I periodically. I labored to stay awake. At 0400 I went over to Dunn and told him he had duty. He grunted and went back to sleep.

I bent down close to his ear, "Wake your ass up and give me your fucking air mattress. It's your time with the radios." He opened his eyes and looked at me, without expression, without moving.

Behind me the 0400 sitreps started to come in. I pushed down on Dunn and went over to answer the radios. As I was finishing, Dunn stumbled over, his poncho liner thrown over his shoulder, dragging his air mattress. He fell down in a heap near the radios, rolling onto the air mattress.

I spent the rest of the night sitting against a tree, my arms folded on my chest, glaring at Dunn on his air mattress. He's more of an asshole than I am, I thought.

After fourteen days in the field, we were heli-lifted to Tay Ninh for a C-130 flight back to Phuoc Vinh.

Dunn and I were the last to leave the LZ. We had to coordinate on the heli-lift out and make sure that the men were lined up in the right numbers and no one was left behind. The sergeant major had found several sets of tanker goggles for keeping debris out of our eyes that were perfect in the turbulence of the helicopters.

As we trudged up the road from the airfield at Phuoc Vinh, our goggles pulled down to our necks, we looked like raccoons, with clean rings around our eyes. Our fatigues were dirty and sweaty from the two week operation, plus all the debris that they had collected from the dozens of helicopters in the lift. Our hair was matted down from dirt and grime. We were tired to the bone and we trudged along with our heads down.

When we arrived at our tent, we found devastation. A river from the monsoon rains had run through our section of the tent. Bob's cot had been swept to my side. Our clothes, hanging on the mosquito netting of the tent, were mildewed. A package of cookies from home that had been ripped opened and destroyed by rats was lying on top of my cot. Mud was six inches deep across the floor to Moubry's

The Vietnam War Its Ownself

elevated section.

Moubry had added an easy chair and a rug. The light over his desk was shining down on his open Bible.

Still carrying our guns, we walked around our area of the tent in mud up to our ankles and tracked it across Moubry's new rug, out into the company street, over to the supply tent, and behind the counter. Moubry saw us and went out the back. Going down the line of supplies, we pulled out new fatigues, new skivvies, new socks, new sheets and new pillows. We went back to our tent and put our supplies on Moubry's bed. On a revisit to the supply tent, we picked up shipping pallets to put on the floor of our tent section.

After showering, shaving, and dressing in our new fatigues, we went to the mess hall and persuaded Cookie to make us some sandwiches, even though he had long since closed the line for supper.

Later at the officers' club, Dunn and I were joined by 1st Lt. Frank Bradley, who had taken the recon platoon from Pete. We sat by ourselves and stacked beer cans five levels high until Dunn knocked them over. Then I went to my old tent in the Alpha Company area and retrieved the picture of the nude behind the bar.

Arriving back at the battalion officer's club, I put the painting of the nude in a position of honor behind the bar. I proposed a welcoming toast to her. Bradley, drunk, stood up, staggered to get his balance, saluted the lady and left. He stumbled down the battalion street as he tried to light a cigarette. He was so intent in lighting his cigarette that he lost his way and weaved off between two tents. Finally getting the cigarette lit, he found the tent that he shared with the communication officer, 1st Lt. Larry Lingel, who was in bed but not yet asleep. With the cigarette still in his mouth, Bradley stumbled to his cot and pulled up the mosquito netting. He turned around, sat down heavily, and reached forward to undo his shoes. He couldn't. He came halfway back up and fell back on the cot, his legs still off the side.

Lingel had seen the cigarette in Bradley's mouth, but he didn't know what happened to it, so he turned on a small bed light over his head.

Bradley started to breathe deeply. A couple of seconds later, the cigarette rolled off his chin and landed on his neck.

A couple of seconds went by.

Suddenly, he jerked forward and became entangled in the netting. He swung his arms around and became more ensnared -- fighting, twisting, kicking. The cot turned over and he fell over backward, with his upper body completely wrapped in the mosquito netting. He thrashed around on the floor for a few more seconds and

135

then he lay still.

Lingel, propped up on one elbow, looked down without expression.

The cigarette began to smolder inside the mosquito netting at Bradley's back. He lashed out again, jerking and struggling, and rolled across the floor away from the overturned cot. Coming to rest in a ball in the middle of the tent, he lay silently.

Finally, from inside the netting, came a faint voice, "Lingel, Lingel, save yourself, I'm done for. Can't get away."

After Lingel told me the story the next morning, I sought out Bradley.

"I think your friend Lingel and my friend Dunn heard the same bedtime stories growing up," I said. "They are not nice people."

--ELEVEN--
War Is What It Is

Within a couple of days, we received orders for "Operation Adelaide," a search and destroy mission in the VC-held Ong Dong jungle. The operation began with an overland move down the road south of Phuoc Vinh with armor from the 1st/4th Cavalry attached. 1st/4th, always referred to as the "Quarterhorse," employed medium-sized M-48 A3 tanks and armored cavalry assault vehicles (ACAV) outfitted with a .50-mm machine gun in the commander's cupola and two lighter 7.62-mm machine guns at the top rear. Additionally, M-113 armored personnel carriers modified as flame-throwers, referred to affectionately as "Zippos," were included in most cav formations. A Quarterhorse unit of combined tanks, ACAVs, and Zippos was an awesome fire and maneuver force, unlike anything ever deployed in war before.

Because we were moving to a forward position on all-weather roads, the battalion would use the command van for the first time in Vietnam. Mounted on a standard deuce-and-a-half chassis, the van itself looked like a refrigerator container. The only door let out to the back. Inside on the right was a console for eight or nine radios, with two tables beneath these radios. A walkway on the left led to a large map board fastened against the front wall and an area large enough for a half-dozen men to stand before the map.

Burke drove the van. Dunn and I were in accompanying

The Vietnam War Its Ownself

Jeeps behind the colonel.

Halfway to our objective, we drove by Alpha Company, which had moved south the previous afternoon to help secure a bridge. Bratcher was sitting on a berm with Castro. I gave them a thumbs-up as we passed. Bratcher smiled back and gave me the finger. Infantrymen did that to staff officers in Jeeps.

We turned off the main road and traveled down a smaller dirt road past several clusters of huts, where stone-faced villagers stared at us. Ten miles down the secondary road, we arrived at a large field that had been secured by advance elements of the battalion. We drove across the field with Panton, who was responsible for locating and setting up the battalion CP (command post). Dunn and I were drawn to a large tree with low, sprawling branches inside the far tree line, and we convinced Panton to set up the command van nearby. We dropped our web gear and went back to the edge of the field. Dunn motioned with a big wave of his arm for Burke to drive the van over to the tree.

Because Burke was not large, he was flung around behind the wheel of the van as it bounced across the field. He looked out of place, overmatched, and the van was traveling too fast. Dunn and I jumped out of the way as Burke passed us heading into the woods.

"Hey," we yelled, "hey, slow down."

Burke stopped the van near the large tree, but not before it had rolled over our gear and mashed most of it into the ground. It almost seemed as if running over our stuff was the reason for his haste.

"Sorry," he said when we came up beside him, "couldn't stop."

Other members of the command staff, seeing the van stopped inside the wood line, figured that's where the CP would be set up. They began to unload nearby trucks parked in a semicircle in the field.

Dunn told Burke that he almost killed us. Besides, he was in backward. We wanted him to back in so that the entrance to the van would be under the tree.

Burke said, "Okey-dokey," and tried to find reverse. He finally popped the clutch, and the van jerked quickly backward. Dunn and I jumped out of the way as it ran over our gear again. Burke looked somewhat confused. He almost impaled himself on the steering wheel when the van hit a tree. We saw him grab his chest and shake his head. Suddenly the van lurched toward us again and ran over our gear for the third time.

"Hey," we yelled.

137

Burke was crashing through the jungle when the colonel came up. Like a rampaging rhinoceros, the van rumbled through the trees and passed us as it went out into the field. It almost ran over some of the men who were getting out of their vehicles.

"Why is Burke in that van?" the colonel asked. "He's from New York City. I don't think he can drive. He's going to crash."

Burke did a turn in the field, and the van headed back toward us.

"Holy shit," I said, "he's coming back."

The men who were trying to form the battalion perimeter looked up and scattered. Burke ran over some commo gear and finally stopped, well out in the field. I climbed up on the running board.

Burke looked at me calmly and said, "Is this OK?"

"Crash Burke, you are a piece of work," I replied.

The squadron of cavalry that had provided security for our move appeared across the field. Several tanks and accompanying ACAVs spread out and raced in our direction. The lead tank came to a stop near the wood line, and a short, square-jawed tank NCO jumped out. Pulling down his goggles and smiling, he said that he was "Slippery Clunker Six," and his Slippery Clunker boys would be with us through the night. The name tag on his fatigue jacket read Bretschneider. Despite his friendly, cavalier manner, he looked rock solid. His diction was crisp and precise, and his eyes -- prominent in the clean circles where his goggles had been -- were bright and intelligent.

Panton pointed out where the cav commander could put his tracks and asked if he could dig a hole for our command vehicle. Slippery Clunker Six said, "Certainly, it would be our pleasure," and ordered one of his tanks with a dozer blade on the front to dig a wide trench.

We watched the elephant-like tank turn its turret to the rear and move back and forth near the large tree as the blade dug a trench. When the job was finished, the tank lumbered off to the side and I backed the van into the hole.

I told "Crash" Burke -- a name that seemed to fit him -- that I had better back up the truck, to prevent more damage, plus, we didn't want the infantry to look too bad in front of the Quarterhorse. He said that was OK because he figured he had done all the command van driving he needed this tour.

By dusk, all of the battalion units were in place and the command van in operation. A mess hall with lights from a small generator had been set up. Dunn and I built a small rain shelter under the large tree. Sitting on our air mattresses after supper, we looked around at our surroundings and said this is the way to go to war -- You got your mess tent, your shade, your rain proof, bug-free, air-conditioned office. It was almost civilized.

"But I don't know," I said. "Over there, that tank looks like a big metal building, looks like it would draw fire. And it's loud. You hear that thing today? How you going to sneak up on VC in a tank?" From our position on the ground, the tank appeared monstrously large.

Dunn said, "Ah, the American man and his fighting machines. One good thing though, lucky Crash Burke wasn't assigned to armor."

Slippery Clunker Six walked purposefully over to us and asked if we'd like something to eat. He had a little cooler in his tank where he kept some very good sausage and pate and wondered if we wanted any? I said that we'd just taken supper in the local diner, but I added quickly that, of course, we would like some sausage and pate; we hadn't been asked things like that nearly enough since we'd been in 'Nam.

"You got any wine?" I asked.

"Of course," he said.

We walked over to his tank. He had a folding table set up, and we sat on boxes and ate exotic food out of several containers. Dunn compared it to what he thought it must be like going on a safari, certainly not what we were used to as grunts in Vietnam.

As we ate and drank, the cavalry NCO said that he and his men had it a little easier and were a little more distant from this jungle war than the infantry -- maybe it was the noise or the tracks they left.

"You guys aren't in harmony with the jungle," I suggested.

"There you go," he said. "But you know, the VC stay away in droves. 'Course there are those damn mines which take all the fun out it. But it is not supposed to be fun, is it?" He paused a moment to give us a chance to respond. Dunn shrugged and he continued, "Ours is a noble endeavor here. We are crusaders, the fortunate ones in our generation. 'Far better it is to dare mighty things, to win glorious triumphs, even though checkered by failure, than to take rank with those poor spirits who neither enjoy much nor suffer much, because they live in the gray twilight that knows not victory nor defeat.' That's from the late great Teddy Roosevelt, who knew about war and noble causes."

Eloquent quotes from former statesmen were seldom heard on the battlefields of Vietnam, but they did not seem out of place

139

coming from Sgt.1st Class Hans Karl Bretschneider. Maybe that was because he was so self-assured. Confidence writes its own rules.

"Ah," he continued, "but I'm afraid Kipling also knew about fighting, especially war in this part of the world. He said:

> "At the end of the fight is a tombstone white
> With the name of the late deceased.
> And the epitaph drear:
> 'A fool lies here
> Who tried to hustle the East.'"

"Something which we fools might be trying to do here in Vietnam, don't you think? Aren't we trying to hustle 'em? I think if we are, there is a tombstone out there with our names on it."

Dunn laughed. "You think so?"

"Yea, I think so," the tank commander said, "but, you know, for us that shouldn't matter. We're soldiers. 'Ours is not to question why, ours is to do and die.'"

"Now there you've almost got it," Dunn said. "We fight, we die, but damned if we don't kill a bunch of them son'bitches too."

Slippery Clunker Six smiled slowly and said, "There you go."

****

The cavalry left the next morning to provide security for elements of the 1st Engineer Battalion which was improving the road to Phuoc Vinh, but we saw Slippery Clunker Six occasionally throughout the operation. For several days, small-sized units patrolled around the battalion CP and then company size forces moved out to protect engineer work parties that were cutting pioneer roads through the jungle. There were occasional firefights, but the VC avoided contact.

Then on 2 June, the third platoon of Alpha company was sweeping through deep underbrush and bamboo when the point man came to what looked like fire breaks cut in the jungle. He stopped and Trost came up to the head of the patrol. The fire breaks had marks or intersecting breaks along the way. It was nothing like Trost had seen before and he called Woolley to explain what the platoon faced.

Not sensing any danger in Trost's report, Woolley told him to move ahead, that they were starting to fall behind the others. Trost, laying on his stomach, told the point man to move across the

140

ten foot cut in the jungle.

With the gear on his canteen belt and on his pack rustling, the point man ran a short distance and dove into the bush on the other side.

No reaction from anywhere. Everything was quiet.

Trost motioned for the other men to follow, and inside the thicket on the other side the point man began moving again.

As men moved quickly past Trost, the point across the way came to another fire break in the jungle. He looked both ways for a moment and ran across.

Other men followed.

Near the end of the platoon crossing the first break, Trost got to his feet and jogged across. The point, some distance away now, came to and crossed another break... when suddenly the afternoon was rent with the sound of Viet Cong machine gun fire that turned the fire breaks into killing zones.

The 3rd platoon had walked in front of a VC position that had cut firing lanes through the thick jungle... that the men took for unexplained fire breaks.

The platoon was cut into three parts.

Trost radioed back to Woolley – he had replaced Spencer on the radio with someone of his own choosing who was hugging the ground. Woolley and Haldane called in mortar support and then fast movers, that finally suppressed the enemy fire.

The third platoon pulled back, carrying its dead and wounded, to a safe cleared point to receive the medevacs.

****

We had been in the position, with the command van under that beautiful tree, for five days. Dunn and Crash had the 0700 to 1500 shift in the van. I had the 1500 to 2300 shift that day with another NCO. Colonel Haldane left by Jeep for an early briefing at brigade headquarters. At noon, I was sitting on the step of the van. Inside, Dunn and Crash were taking down the radio messages on a clipboard. When the messages were about firefights, enemy sightings, or movements of friendly units, they plotted the positions on the map board. With the colonel out of the area, Dunn was singing as he worked the map board.

I left for lunch and a short nap and returned around 1430. Dunn was sitting on the top step of the van. Crash, on the ground in front of the van, was talking about all of the great Fred Astaire movies that he had seen. Settling on the step below Bob, I asked him

141

what was happening, referring to the battalion patrols, and he said that everything was quiet.

Crash was absolutely grand entertainment. He had energy, enthusiasm, and the ability to tell a good story. Skinny, in his big combat boots and t-shirt, he reminded me of Bugs Bunny as he danced around, held an imaginary Ginger Rogers, did a soft-shoe, handled an invisible top hat and cane, and swayed back and forth. He talked about one scene where Fred Astaire did a soft shoe-number with two other men. He said he knew the whole routine -- it was marvelous and simple. He invited us down to the ground and said he'd show us.

"Not on your life, my friend," I said.

"In the van," Dunn said.

Crash climbed up the steps around me. I looked both ways. There was nobody around, and I followed them inside. Crash had his arm over Dunn's shoulder near the map board.

"OK," he said, "we got on spats, straw hats, and black canes with solid gold caps on the top. The music is 'Dun de dun, de doddle de doddle do.' Got it? It's that simple, Dun de dun, de doddle de doddle do,' over and over again. Two steps and then three steps. We go left -- come on, Lieutenant," he said to me, "join us, we go left two steps. 'Dun de dun,' then we shuffle three times, 'de doddle de doddle do,' then go back to the right. OK, now bounce your canes in step. Here we go. 'Dun de dun, de doddle de doddle do.'"

We practiced until we had it down -- Crash on one end, Dunn in the middle, and I on the other end. We were working on the finish, in which the two of them would spin me off to the right. I would do a pirouette and land on one knee as I raised my hand, holding an imaginary hat, into the air and say "Da Dum." Mine was the showcase move, the grand finale. At first, I had trouble facing in the same direction as the others when I came out of the spin onto one knee, but we practiced the whole set several times, and I was getting it down. I came out of one spin -- the whole routine had been perfect, our best performance -- and I put gusto into my "Da Dum."

Colonel Haldane was standing in the door of the van. He was looking at me.

Dunn and Crash were standing at attention.

"Who's on duty?" he asked quietly and slowly.

I got to my feet and turned toward the clock on the wall. It was 1520. Theoretically, I had been on duty for twenty minutes.

Dunn and Crash both said, "He is," and pointed at me.

The colonel took a step in and put his map case on one of the tables below the radios. He continued to look at me, very seriously.

142

The Vietnam War Its Ownself

Dunn and Crash said, "Excuse us," and walked out. Standing behind the colonel, Dunn had an exaggerated smile on his face, his eyes wide and twinkling, as he closed the door to the van.

Inside, the air conditioner and the lights came on. I stood at attention. There were only two people in the whole world -- me and the colonel.

"What's happening?" he asked, seeking a briefing on the movement of the various units in the battalion. His battalion.

The clipboard was beside him on the table. Sweating, I figured if I could get to the clipboard and read the messages maybe I could get through this.

I got the clipboard, walked to the map, and read the last entry on the clipboard about an enemy sighting. It wasn't plotted on the map. I read the next entry. It wasn't plotted either. Nothing on the clipboard had been plotted since 1400. And it was past 1520.

The colonel cleared his throat, and there was a pause -- like those last few seconds before an incoming rocket explodes. Then he began talking to me in a low, even voice, his eyes hard.

When he finished, I wanted just to be by myself, to walk alone down a quiet country road.

He said he would be back in fifteen minutes and he wanted a complete briefing. He opened the door and left.

Dunn and Fred Astaire Crash Burke were standing in the distance. They waved and did a soft-shoe to the right. It wasn't funny.

The colonel had received orders from General DePuy, the division commander, to bring in the battalion and prepare the men for a heli-borne move to the Michelin rubber plantation, near the Cambodian border. We would support the brigade's attack on a suspected VC command center. Thankfully, for the rest of the afternoon and evening, I was busy calling in the companies and coordinating how they would tie in around the battalion CP.

A lone helicopter brought in replacements the next morning. Jumping off the helicopter in their new uniforms, some held their rifles by the handles and bent over more than necessary to get away from the blades. When the chopper lifted off, I noticed a black man who had gotten off on the other side. Standing erect, taller than the rest, he started walking toward us behind the other replacements who were jogging our way.

Duckett.

Smiling, I stood up, and met him halfway. We hugged. I asked how he was doing and pointed at his bad ear. He said, "Say what?"

"How's the ear?" I asked. "How you doing?

"Say what?" he said again, then he smiled. "It's OK."

I told him that it was good having him back, and we went to find the colonel. Although I was still in trouble from the previous day and the colonel ignored me, he smiled broadly at Duckett and welcomed him back. Haldane told Joe that he would like to put him in a staff job, but we were low on platoon leaders. We were losing one a month. Only two officers, Woolley and Trost, were left in Alpha Company, Arthur had been wounded and evacuated to the States. Duckett said that he wanted to work with Woolley again, wanted his own platoon back.

As we walked away I told Duckett not to be surprised if he didn't see too many of the old guys around.

The next day the entire battalion was heli-lifted in one flight of helicopters. Dunn and I were on the last chopper. All of our trucks, included the van, had already moved out for the battalion rear camp. I looked down at that very good hole under the old tree as we gained altitude and headed west, leaving the Fred Astaire stage behind.

Our battalion landed at an old airstrip near the Michelin plantation. We established a battalion CP just inside a forest of rubber trees near the airstrip. The four companies in the battalion, Alpha, Bravo, Charlie, and Delta, were deployed to secure individual TAORs.

Alpha Company broke down into small units. My old platoon, on a patrol during the third night of the operation, walked into a North Vietnamese position and Ayers and Castro were killed.

Bratcher led the party that brought back their bodies to the battalion CP. Covered by ponchos, they lay at the edge of the CP in the shade by the runway for a long time. Tags on their boots sticking out from the ponchos identified them and their unit.

I tried to go about my work that morning, but, from deep inside, thoughts of the two soldiers kept interrupting. A picture of Ayers would come to mind, and I would remember that he was an eighteen-year-old boy from Tennessee. As strong as an ox, he stayed on point until he dropped. Never complained. Bad teeth. No one wrote to him much. Quiet most of the time. No rough edges. Responded to praise. Did everything asked of him. Dead now -- over there under the trees.

I would shake my head and try to focus on the staff work. Then, I would see Castro, laughing, getting to the train at the last moment and once aboard, stomping his feet in a circle, like he was doing a Mexican hat dance. He was in his late thirties, twice the age of most of some of the other men. He made good, hot stew out of C-rations. Friendly, humble. A sergeant E-5 from the old Army. Over there under a poncho, with his boots sticking out, tagged with his name and his unit. Dead.

Suddenly, I had trouble breathing, I took a deep breath every few minutes, but I finally had to get away from my work. I walked across the airstrip and sat down. Looking back at the CP, I worked on thinking about nothing. Don't moralize, I said to myself, my lips moving. Nothing to do, nothing to say. Just sit here quietly, everything will be OK.

Then clearly, in my mind's eye, I saw Ayers and Castro moving quietly through the jungle that night. The sudden, deadly firefight. I saw Ayers fall. His finger still on the trigger of his M-16, he fell backward without expression, his M-16 firing into the night. Then Castro, moving forward, caught in a deadly hail of fire with bullets, one after the other, going through his chest, getting knocked around by the impact, coming to rest finally on top of Ayers. The sound of battle fading as they died.

I could no longer keep from looking at the two lumps lying under the ponchos, and I stared, transfixed, running the imagined nighttime engagement over and over again in my mind. Finally I focused on the peacefulness that was surely on their faces. I remembered McCoy saying on the boat over that we either live, get wounded, or die. Either way, it's no problem. If we die, maybe others have a problem with that, but, for us, we're dead and at peace. It isn't bad. It's simply the way things worked out.

Sadly, I constructed a compartment for Ayers and another for Castro in the back of my mind and I put their memories in baskets there.

A medevac helicopter came in sometime later that morning and took away their bodies. Emotionally paralyzed, I watched from a distance.

I would never be the same again.

Occasionally their memories would escape their compartment and leap out at me in my mind, along with others, but I would put them away and go on. In time, with practice, I kept them securely in the back compartment, under control.

****

Several days later, Bravo Company engaged an enemy unit. The battle raged throughout most of the morning in an area that the VC had not previously controlled. It was possible that a new North Vietnamese outfit had moved in, which would affect the security of Saigon. Because the enemy troops were staying and fighting, Haldane guessed that they were not guerrillas but were, in fact, from a main-line North Vietnamese unit. We could hear the firing from the CP.

At midday, a Bravo Company platoon leader reported that he had a prisoner. I was on duty. The colonel had walked away, and I sent Crash Burke to find him. Haldane soon came back and told the Bravo Company commander to bring the prisoner out. We searched on a map for a clearing near the company's location where we could get in a helicopter and I notified the air controller in the area that we would soon have a priority requirement for a slick and a gunship or two. The company commander came back on the radio and said it was useless, the man was shot up too badly. He wouldn't live another ten minutes.

We could not find a clearing large enough to get in a helicopter close to the fighting, so Haldane told the commander to start moving overland toward our location. If the prisoner died en route, then it was too bad, but he wanted to talk to the man if possible.

Less than an hour later, a group carrying several stretchers broke through the tree line across the airstrip. I called for Colonel Haldane, the medics, the battalion intelligence officer and the Vietnamese interpreter, "Jose," assigned to our unit. Dunn walked up, and I asked him to call in a dust-off for the Company B soldiers who were wounded. He picked up a radio and jogged onto the airfield toward the group coming our way. A couple of medics slung their bags over their shoulders and joined him.

Dunn pulled on the PRC 25 radio and talked into the handset. Looking up he yelled at me to get some purple smoke for the medevac.

By then, the colonel was at the CP. He picked up a smoke canister and handed it toward Dunn and the medics. When they reached the group in the middle of the airfield, the medics began frantically working on the men on the stretchers. Finally, two men picked up one stretcher and started walking toward the aid tent beside the CP. Haldane fell into step beside them. I told Crash to look after the radios, and I followed the interpreter and the colonel inside the small tent. The soldiers had just lifted the Vietnamese prisoner onto the operating table. They moved away and began unwrapping their ponchos from the two bamboo poles used to make a stretcher.

The Vietnamese prisoner had one arm blown off above the elbow. His right leg was cantilevered at a crazy angle, and his left leg was torn open at the thigh, with a jagged piece of bone sticking out. His olive-green uniform was matted with blood, dirt, and slime, and the jacket had several bullet holes in it. Half of his face had been blown away. Some of his teeth and lower jawbone were exposed. Most of his left cheekbone was missing, and his left eye was dangling by a few strands of muscle and tissue.

But he was breathing -- deep heavy breaths. His good eye was moving and making contact with us as we looked down at him.

How could he be alive? Blood was oozing out of him everywhere; with each breath, he gargled blood.

Haldane told the interpreter to ask the man what unit he was from. Jose leaned close to the man's ear and said a long sentence in Vietnamese. The prisoner's one dancing eye continued to scan us. Jose raised his voice and repeated the sentence. The prisoner turned his head and looked at Jose. As the prisoner tried to talk, he spit blood on Jose and on Haldane's hand, but he managed to say something in Vietnamese. Jose leaned forward quickly as he listened. He said something in Vietnamese. The prisoner responded with a few fractured words.

"What did he say? What did he say?" Haldane asked. "What's his unit?"

The man on the table continued to mumble.

"Don't know," Jose said shaking his head. "He calls his mother, father. He says Vietnamese names."

"Ask him, please, what is his unit?" Haldane, a good and moral man, was having trouble keeping his focus on the job at hand without lapsing into pity for this mangled boy, still alive, calling out the names of loved ones.

Jose repeated his question, but the prisoner was losing ground. His eye stopped roaming and he looked straight up at the top of the tent. I noticed that blood had stopped seeping from the wound on his leg. His breathing became weaker.

One of the medics came in hurriedly and broke through the crowd of men around the table. He looked with some disgust at us because no one appeared to be helping the man. The medic had been opening a bandage package as he moved, but when he looked down at the mess lying on the table, his hands dropped to his sides. He said, "Ah, shit."

Dunn, apparently finished with medevacing the wounded soldiers from Bravo Company, came in and stood beside me. Two more medics walked in.

The man on the table was barely breathing. Then, he gathered some energy from somewhere and started to babble. He blinked his good eye. His raised his arm slightly. Jose repeated his sentence. A medic reached down and put the man's whole arm on his stomach and wiped his forehead. His breathing became slower again, irregular.

One of the medics said, "The man is dead, he just doesn't know it yet. His whole body's in shock. He can't think. He doesn't know who he is."

I remembered when Goss died. It wasn't sudden. Most of him was dead while his heart was still beating.

But this boy -- any one of his wounds should have killed him. Tough son of a bitch, I thought, but give it up. Go on. Give it up. You're blown apart. You'll never be whole again. There is no hope.

Most of the men around the table began to slip away. Dunn and I remained at the end of the table. Bob's platoon had suffered as many casualties as had mine. He had held some of his men as they died. We hated the VC for causing so much pain, for killing so many good men. This one, in fact, might have killed Castro and Ayers, and here he lay. The enemy. Castro and Ayers had been avenged. This enemy was dying in front of us.

But I kept saying to myself, give up, please give up. You must hurt. Die and it will all end. You'll be OK. Your mother will be sad and those other people you called out to. Your father, if he knew, would be proud. You are so strong. You must have stayed to fight when the others pulled back, and now you still won't give up. Give up and there's peace.

Bob and I were alone in the room with the man when he stopped breathing.

You were a good soldier, I thought. You did your duty. How noble to have lived and died doing something as well as you did. You should have been in my platoon. You have my respect. You, Castro, Ayers. I shall always remember your sacrifices, one against the other.

Then we heard a loud gasp. The prisoner suddenly bent forward at the waist and sat up straight, reaching out his arm toward us. He looked at us with his good eye, his other eye bobbling around like a bloody ball on a string. His mouth was open. He was gargling, and blood splattered over us, but his eye remained focused on us, on both of us at once. Then, Mother of Jesus, one leg moved off of the operating table. He garbled again, louder. His weight followed the leg that was draped over the side of the table. His whole arm moved across the front of us when he turned--as though he wanted to get off the table.

His body twisted around, and he fell to the floor. There, thankfully, he died.

Dunn and I had jumped back to the far side of the tent. We were holding each other's arms, our eyes and mouths wide open. Maybe we yelled. One of the medics came running in and around the

148

table to the man on the floor. Bob and I walked out.
"Goddamnit, that was a tough son of a bitch," I said.
"I think I poop-pooped in my pants," Bob said.

****

Two days later we received word that Gen. William C. Westmoreland, commander of MACV, would visit our unit for an awards ceremony. To Haldane's credit, he didn't break a sweat over receiving the highest-ranking American general in Vietnam. Instructions about security, timing, and ceremony arrangements came in gradually. Throughout the day before Westmoreland's arrival, Haldane said that we were not going to stop the war or fall down dead because one man was coming for a thirty-minute visit. He was upset, however, when he received word that Westmoreland would be handing out Silver Star medals.

"Well just who do we give them to? Sorta getting the horse in front of the cart, isn't it," he asked no one in particular when he received the message. "I don't remember recommending anyone for Silver Stars."

Major Allee thought that perhaps Westmoreland was upgrading the level of decorations for combat bravery. He remembered that we had about eight recommendations in the works for lesser medals and suggested that we line up the people who had been recommended for awards and think of the general's visit as a dry-run ceremony.

Westmoreland's party arrived exactly on time, as if the U.S. Army and the whole Vietnamese war were running on his schedule. We saw the covey of helicopters coming in long before they landed. Gunships making passes along the tree lines looked like advance body guards, eventually landing at either end of the runway. Westmoreland's command helicopter arrived near our CP right on the smoke that Crash threw. Photographers jumped off a following helicopter and focused their cameras on the general as he stepped to the ground. They swarmed around him like gnats and took pictures of his every move.

The general had a regal manner. With silver-gray hair and a square jaw, he stood taller than those around him. I noticed that he had his arm in a sling. Assuming that he had been wounded I asked one of his aides about it but his answer made no sense. The aide wasn't very friendly, in fact. I had shaken his hand when we first met. He had small, dainty hands and manicured fingernails.

The visit turned out to be pure public relations for General

149

Westmoreland. We were props. He trooped the line and smiling warmly, presented medals to the assembled men. And then he was gone, back on his clean helicopter, with the escort gunships lifting off first. The newsmen hurried to get on a trailing slick.

Panton went along the line of men as the helicopters lifted off and took back the medals, an awards ceremony in reverse.

Within hours, Crash learned that Westmoreland had fallen on his elbow while playing tennis in Saigon and had suffered a sprain.

I told Dunn and Crash later, "I'm a little sick of this war. There isn't much to make me proud. Platoon leader, at least I had the men and it was us against them. Being a staff officer -- I don't know -- Ayers and Castro dying. This is one useless fucking war. Westmoreland handing out medals. Show time. We got all this stuff, helicopters, medals, hot meals. What's Charlie got? He ain't got shit. Death's a blessing. What's the use of it all? Nothing, one big fucking waste." I was not making sense, nor was I trying to. I was just mouthing thoughts coming into my head. My voice trailed off.

"What exactly are you talking about, Parker," said Dunn, never a sentimentalist. "There ain't no great truth here. This ain't the first war man's ever fought. This is all you have to remember: 'Ours is not to question why, ours is to do and die.' It's just W-A-R, as simple as a three letter word. Some people die, some people live. That's it. Some people win and some people lose. Winners are right and losers are wrong. It's no more difficult than that, so don't agonize over it."

"Screw you, Dunn."

"If you ever did, you'd never go back to girls." Dunn refused to be drawn into my despair. "Don't moralize, Parker. Forget about it. Kill them before they kill us, and fuck the reasons why. Win. Survive."

--TWELVE--
Minh Thanh Road

We returned to the base camp later that week. Bob had a calendar above his cot. In seventy-six days we would be eligible for rotation, after being in-country for one full year. That night in the makeshift battalion officers' club, I sat with Dunn, Duckett, and Bradley at a rear table. Bradley, a replacement, would be around for several more months. Duckett's convalescence time counted toward his year, and he would rotate home with Bob and myself.

We were talking about what we would do when we got back to the States when Dunn mentioned that Colonel Haldane was returning to the States through Europe.

Bradley said we all could. Any active-duty person could book passage on a scheduled round-the-world U.S. Air Force charter called the Embassy Flight. It was used primarily by Defense Department attaches, diplomatic personnel, and couriers, but seats were available for military personnel with legitimate reasons for travel, like us. He suggested that the three of us try to go home on Air Force One, like Haldane.

In our typical, grateful fashion, we told him he was full of shit. Haldane's a colonel. We're second lieutenants. There's a little difference there.

"Fine," he said, "don't believe me. But the next time you're in Saigon, go to the Travel Section at the U.S. Embassy, and ask about seats on Air Force One."

Dunn, intent on getting back to Linda in California on the fastest plane going, had no interest in traveling through Europe. But Duckett and I liked the idea, we just didn't think it was available.

Later that week Haldane authorized in-country R&R and Duckett and I took off for Saigon.

We stopped off at division headquarters on the way down and I sought out a friend of Crash's at the Administration Section and we asked him about our exact departure-from-Vietnam date and orders.

"Ah," he said, "the magic ticket. DEROS orders. The Date of Estimated Return from Overseas orders. Very, very valuable. The keys to heaven. You don't leave 'Nam without it. I have yours here. Burke told me you were on the way and to look after you, so I have taken the liberty of running off a couple of extra copies for both of you."

I was authorized to leave 13 September 1966. Joe was authorized to leave on the 14th. Signed, stamped, mimographed, in duplicate, everything. Legal. Some people didn't get their orders until the day they left and we had ours two months early. Crash Burke, I thought, you and your friend are very good people.

On the afternoon of 2 July, we were standing in front of the Marine guard post by the main entrance to the U.S. Embassy in Saigon. Throngs of people were coming and going. We felt out of place. We looked out of place. Our uniforms, though clean, were not starched and tailored like others that we saw, and we were leaner than most military personnel on the streets of Saigon. I had a funny steel-pot tan -- my forehead white and my cheeks tanned. And we must have looked unsure of ourselves.

The Marine said that the Travel Section was in a Quonset hut to the side of the Embassy building. Walking along tentatively, we stepped out of the way when busy Embassy people hurried by us. A Vietnamese receptionist in the front of the Quonset hut did not act surprised when we asked about signing up for the Air Force One flight on 14 September. She gave us some forms to fill out and a mimeographed sheet explaining what was required -- DEROS orders, passport, military ID, uniform while traveling. Although I was authorized to leave 13 September, we decided that I would stay over in Saigon until the 14th so that we could leave together, if this actually was for real. We finished filling out the forms and were directed to an Air Force sergeant in a rear room. He said that everything looked in order. We nodded.

"What's this going to cost?" I asked.

"Nothing," the sergeant said.

"That's it, then?" I said, still not sure that this was for real.

The sergeant looked at me hard, curious about my hesitation. "Let me see your DEROS orders again," he said.

He examined the one I offered for a moment, shrugged, and said, "Everything's all right. You two are the first signing up for the 14th and unless something extraordinary happens and you get bumped a day, that is when you'll be on your way to Europe."

We left the Embassy in a more confident manner.

We went down to Tu Do street in downtown Saigon and had some photos made for our passport applications. That night, we practiced our international bar room skills. We liked the feel of being out together. Duckett was six feet four, and I was six feet two. Maybe it was the look in our eyes from our experiences in the field, maybe it was our size and our smiles, but people treated us with deference. When we walked into bars, people noticed us. And we had Europe right down the road. Hold on continent, here we come.

In the coffee shop of our hotel the next morning we heard that Tan Son Nhut airfield had been bombed during the night. Rockets had landed in the departure area and killed several soldiers from the 1st Cav who were due to leave country that day. After surviving a year of combat, they were killed in their sleep in the departure area in Saigon, the night before they left country.

"Fortunes of war," Duckett said.

"Yea, and I ain't staying one more night here than I have to, my friend. I'm leaving on the 13th. I'll meet you in Bangkok or

Europe or Philly, but I ain't staying here one extra night."

We went back to the Air Force sergeant and I made the change without problems. Duckett and I would meet in Bangkok, Thailand, 14 September; depart on Air Force One on the 15th for New Delhi, India, where we would overnight, and then go on to Afghanistan, Athens, and Madrid. We were on our own there to rent a car for a drive up to Germany where we could get a military hop to the East Coast of the U.S.A.

****

On our return from Saigon we found the battalion going through familiar preparations for another field operation. Two days later, Haldane asked the entire battalion staff to division headquarters for a briefing. Representatives from every battalion in the three brigades were on hand.

Dunn and I stood at the rear of the room before the briefing and greeted other staff officers whom we had met previously. Colonel Haldane was talking with the cavalry commander, Col. Leonard L. Lewane. When Haldane went to the front of the room, Dunn and I asked Lewane about Slippery Clunker Six. The colonel said that call signs had been changed, but the man whom we knew as Clunker Six had volunteered to lead this new operation.

After Col. Sidney B. Berry, Jr., the 1st Brigade commander, took the stage an officer called us to attention as General DePuy walked in through a side entrance and up the stairs to the stage. Speaking in a surprising strong voice, his comments went something like this: "In this war, we have to kill more of the enemy than they kill of us in order to win. It's that simple. It is a war of attrition. They try to get us; we try to get them. They have advantages we don't have; we have things they don't have. The monsoon weather has been on their side for the last three months, and they have operated in some of our area with impunity. We haven't been able to use our Air Force, our cavalry gets stuck, rivers are swollen, men get foot rot. But the rains are almost over, replacements are in, we know where the enemy is, we know his weaknesses, and we are going on the offense. We are going to use our advantages, and we are going to kill a lot of the enemy. And we are going to win. I have worked on this next operation with Colonel Berry and it is good. We have borrowed from the Air Force, the Navy, and the Marines and all the U.S. Army units around us and we have all we need." He paused. "Now it's up to you. Be tough. Be aggressive. Do your job. This is the 1st Infantry Division. We have a reputation to live up to." He paused again. "I'll

153

turn the briefing over to Colonel Berry. I want all battalion commanders to remain after the briefing and join me for lunch."

General DePuy left the stage. Colonel Berry pulled aside a curtain behind him to show a map blowup of the area along the Cambodian border north of Parrot's Beak. The following is a paraphrase of what the colonel told us that day:

"Because we are not allowed to attack the Vietnamese inside Laos and Cambodia, they have developed, as you know, a highway that originates in North Vietnam and comes all the way down, inside first Laos and then Cambodia, to this area, north of the Parrot's Beak, here [pointing to map] northwest of Saigon. At the terminus is their forward field headquarters, called COSVN.

"The VC unit that operates between COSVN and Saigon is the 272d Regiment of the 9th Division. Because of our operations in January near Cu Chi, 272d Regiment forces do not stay inside South Vietnam for very long now. They move across the border, attack a target, and move back to their base sanctuaries in Cambodia. It is an ideal situation for them -- we cannot follow them into Cambodia. Do not ask me how they arranged this with our Congress.

"During the recent monsoon rains, elements of the 272d Regiment came into South Vietnam to attack American and ARVN positions in the following locations: [He used his pointer to indicate a dozen points on the map.]

"I now call your attention to this area. [Berry replaced the first map with a map showing the South Vietnamese/Cambodian border to the left and Highway 13 dissecting the center. On Highway 13, at the top of the map, was the town of Loc Ninh; farther down was the town of An Loc. Near An Loc was a spur road running west toward the South Vietnamese/Cambodian border and ending at the Minh Thanh rubber plantation. At the bottom of the map was the Ho Bo woods and the town of Cu Chi.]

"During the rains, the Vietcong attacked Loc Ninh three or four days a week. It was difficult to give the Special Forces unit there fire support, and it was difficult to airlift in supplies. We dropped ammunition and food when we could, but the enemy located rockets in close and our resupply planes had to fly high when they dropped. Fifty percent of our supplies landed outside of the wire and were recovered by the enemy.

"These two engagements [he pointed to two marks along the road] were the result of Quarterhorse efforts to open the road into Loc Ninh. On 8 June, Troop A of the 1st/4th Cavalry was ambushed by elements of the 272d here south of An Loc, and, on 30 June, Troop C with the 1st of the 2d Infantry conducted a reconnaissance in force and engaged elements of the 271st Regiment here south of Loc. Ninth. The Quarterhorse, as some of you know who participated, took heavy casualties but killed close to four hundred VC.

"The VC 272d Regiment has been hurt but not destroyed, and we think it will engage our units operating in this area again, if it has a chance. We want to give them that chance. We have told local Army of South Vietnam forces -- for the sake of the known VC agents in their ranks -- that, on 9 July, we are going to send a convoy composed of an engineer bulldozer and several supply trucks from An Loc to Minh Thanh. We expect word to reach the VC 272d Regiment and we expect that they will ambush this convoy for its supplies. They think it will be lightly guarded, and it will be traveling down a road only ten miles from their sanctuaries in Cambodia.

"What we will send down the Minh Thanh road on 9 July will be Task Force Dragoon, commanded by Colonel Lewane. It will be composed of Troops B, C, and D of the 1st/4th Cav, augmented with Company B, 1st/2nd Infantry Battalion. Plus, on standby, we are going to have three heli-borne battalions of infantry and all available artillery and Air Force/Marine fast movers waiting to spring a counter ambush -- a vertical counter ambush.

"This is Operation El Paso II. We're going to have a deception move on D day minus 1 to put the standby infantry and the artillery in position at LZs near the road. ARVN units will be told this deployment is for a sweep south toward Cu Chi, a goodly distance away from Minh Thanh. Artillery will be deployed at the same time to co-locate with the infantry in the staging areas.

"At 0530 on D day, the three battalions with artillery will move from their deception ops staging areas to launch positions. These launch positions, which are within artillery range, are located here, here and here. [He pointed to three points on the map in vicinity of the Minh Thanh road.]

"At 0700 D day, Task Force Dragoon will depart An Loc. There will be radio silence except necessary communications between Colonel Lewane in the command and control (C&C) helicopter and the lead elements of the task force. We have established checkpoints on the road; please mark them on your maps. The first, as the intersection of the spur road and Route 13, is Checkpoint "John." Approximately four miles farther is Checkpoint "Gordon." Four miles farther is "Hank," then "Dick," and finally "Tom," four miles from the Minh Thanh plantation.

"If -- when -- the VC 272d Regiment takes the bait, the artillery will began immediate fire. They will be tracking the movement of the convoy -- turning their tubes as they get location reports -- and when the VC bite, they will lay down a blanket of fire on the south side of the road. The fast movers will be on station. They will drop napalm and high explosive ordinance on the north side of the road. Artillery has the south. Task Force Dragoon has the inside. The cavalry will sustain a high volume of fire during the counter ambush; they will not split up; they will use flame-throwers -- their Zippos -- as offensive weapons. We will have the first flight of infantry counter ambush forces on the ground within ten minutes to relieve pressure on Task Force Dragoon and to mop up along the sides of the road. We will put one battalion of infantry in blocking positions near the Cambodian border.

"If the VC 272d takes the bait, we will destroy them."

In outlining the responsibilities of the various units, Colonel Berry said that the 1st/28th Infantry Battalion would be the first to respond if the ambush was sprung at checkpoint Dick or Tom, near the Minh Thanh rubber plantation.

There was a flurry of movement by groups of officers as each unit's responsibilities were announced. Many had questions.

"Before I take your questions," Berry said, "the deputy division commander has something to say. Sir," he nodded to a one-star general at the side of the stage.

Gen. James F. Hollingsworth rose and picked up a pointer from the map board.

"We are going to kill gooks in this operation," he promised us. "We're going to take some casualties. Goddamnit, it's a war, But I don't want the war to stop when we take casualties. We don't have time." He said each word in the last sentence slowly, loudly. "We gotta keep going, like a good fighter, we keep going. These son'bitches are going to be surprised all to hell. We don't get 'em like that often. We will be in control, and goddamnit I want to think we're pushing a mean pointed stick out there against those son'bitches. Get your men ready, get 'em mean. There are times to go slowly, and there are times to lock and load -- kick ass. This is that time, won't be a long period. Gotta get in there fast and move fast. Kill fast. The ambush could take place less than ten miles from a line we cannot cross. That doesn't give us much time to muck around. Don't stop because one of your men gets hurt. Press on. Leave a medic behind or a guard and push on. Those son'bitches aren't going to stay around long."

Hollingsworth stopped and walked to the front of the stage. "You're good soldiers, in the finest tradition of the 1st Infantry Division. Good luck. Remember: Kill 'em, kill 'em fast." He paused. "Kill 'em," he added for good measure, then turned and left the stage.

The Vietnam War Its Ownself

"Damned fine plan, Bobby," I said to Dunn as we left the briefing and started our trip back to the battalion. "Damned fine."

"You know," he answered, "The cav commander said ol' Slippery Clunker Six's leading this thing. I bet this isn't the last month of Slippery Clunker Six's tour here. He wouldn't be doing something like this if it were."

I said, "Maybe this is his last month here -- on this earth. He must feel invincible. He volunteered, too, you heard that. Volunteered? Can't imagine that from someone who appeared so -- so balanced. So perceptive. Seemed like such a smart fellow. Why you reckon he volunteered, Bob?"

"I don't know. Maybe it's the fumes inside those tanks. I wish him luck. He's the best we got, and as a poet, he's going to be stage center here pretty soon."

****

Dunn and I were busy fourteen hours a day as Haldane and Panton directed our battalion's coordination with artillery, Air Force, the Division G-3, the other battalions, and the helicopter units. Every new unit with which we had to liaise was a problem multiplier.

I sought out Duckett and told him to keep his head down. "Europe is right out there, right where I can see it, at the tip of our fingers, Joe, don't get yourself blown up. This is important. Stay low, you big black lug. You hear me, you half-deaf son'bitch?" I went by his platoon sergeant and told him to protect Duckett with his life.

On D day minus two, we moved by C-130 to Quan Loi and were deployed to a rubber plantation off the runway where we would bivouac for the night. As we were walking along the road to the plantation, a cavalry troop came up behind us and, with their tracks clanking and clamoring, slowly passed. Slippery Clunker Six was in the lead tank. He touched his hand to his tanker's helmet as if to tip it when he passed Haldane and the command group. He recognized Dunn and me and gave a "V" sign with his right hand. He did look invincible -- bigger than life.

Behind him were several ACAVs filled with cavalry troops. Our two groups exchanged taunts, the likes of which probably have been shared between the cavalry and foot soldiers since wars began.

I had the feeling that after a year in Vietnam, we were all coming together somewhere out there, going full speed, us, the cavalry, the artillery, the Air Force, the enemy.

We carried mountains of material in the command group and had extra radiomen assigned. Crash, loaded with gear, looked like a

157

Sherpa mountain guide from Katmandu.

The following day, D day minus one, we were to be heli-lifted to the staging area to the south as part of the diversion operation. Except for the men we put out on guards, the men stayed in their groupings for the heli-lift to the launch site at first light.

I woke up about 0430 the next morning. It was 9 July 1966. Crash was already up. He had made coffee and was looking over the colonel's map, which he carried. Talking to the colonel as he gave him a cup of coffee, but loud enough for everyone in the command group to hear, he said that he thought the North Vietnamese would attack in our area. It was the closest point to the Cambodian border, and there were river valleys between the road and the border for the VC to use. Also, according to intelligence, elements of the VC 272d Regiment were reported near Minh Thanh as recently as the previous day. "It's going to be our nickel, Colonel," Crash said.

The transport helicopters and their accompanying gunships came in low over the trees at first light and were on the ground at the staging area by 0530. The men were onboard within a matter of minutes, and the helicopters lifted off for the forward launch site, ten minutes flying time from Checkpoint Tom.

Dunn went in the first chopper. I went in the last, after ensuring that no one had been left behind.

When I arrived at the forward launch site about 0630, Panton had already set up the battalion CP near a tree on a berm at the side of the field. The field itself was a half-mile square. In one corner, two artillery batteries, a 105-mm and a 155-mm, had arrived, and the artillerymen were running around in organized chaos as they uncrated ammunition and prepared the guns for action. The thirty-one helicopters that had moved our battalion were in two files down the center of the field. The gunships, looking like a group of thugs, were off to the rear. All of the aircraft were in the process of shutting down. Most of the men from the battalion had disembarked and were lying around. Some of the pilots were walking around and talking to each other, while others remained sitting in their seats. The doors to the choppers were open.

Panton had laid out a map on the ground under the tree. He had a round rock, representing the convoy, on top of An Loc. Clearly marked along the road to Minh Thanh were the checkpoints: John, Gordon, Hank, Dick, and Tom. If Crash was right, the attack would come near Checkpoint Tom. We had six radios set up around the map on the ground. Haldane stayed close to the division command net radio, but we were most interested in the radio monitoring the cavalry's frequency.

D hour of 0700 came and went. Finally, at 0710, Slippery Clunker Six broke static on the cav frequency and reported that the 1,200 meter long convoy was on its way -- he was moving out. We recognized Slippery Clunker Six's voice, which had the casual, reassuring tone of a friendly airline pilot.

Colonel Lewane in the C&C confirmed. We knew from the briefing that Slippery Clunker Six would be leading the task force in his tank, followed by another tank, then two ACAVs filled with troops, and then another tank. The remaining elements of Troop C would be dispersed within the convoy. Troop B would bring up the rear behind a wrecker. Colonel Lewane soon reported that the entire convoy was on the road and moving.

Shortly before Checkpoint Gordon, Slippery Clunker Six said that he would begin to recon by fire as he went along. As he passed Gordon, he called out his position. We could hear the booming of a .50-caliber machine gun in the background.

Panton moved his rock. We drank coffee and smoked -- waiting and listening. Birds sang in the distance. Flies buzzed around. Time dragged. I reread letters from my parents and from some children at a Nebraska public school.

Between Checkpoints Gordon and Hank was the first of the three areas from which Colonel Berry thought that the Vietnamese might attack. Lewane reported that he saw people moving across the road around the bend from the lead tank. On the cavalry net, we heard Slippery Clunker Six alert his troops and tell them to tighten their chin straps. Their Great Adventure might be coming up soon. He said that he was going to recon ahead and told the ACAV behind him to follow. Everyone else was to hold back. We could hear his .50-caliber machine gun firing in the background. Then there was silence on the radios. All U.S. forces involved in the operation stood by and waited.

Finally, the Quarterhorse colonel came back on the radio and said that the people he had seen must have been hunters or farmers. He found no one in the area. The convoy moved on.

On the other side of Checkpoint Hank, the road left the sparse prairie grass and entered a dense jungle forest. The convoy would travel under the canopy of the forest for more than two miles. It was the most dangerous area of the operation. If the convoy were attacked here, the closest place where reinforcements could land would be on either side of the forest.

Slippery Clunker Six said, on the cavalry net, that he was going into the Enchanted Forest and God be with anyone who tried to stop him before he came out. Lewane told him to be careful, he'd see him on the other side.

James E. Parker, Jr.

Ten minutes into the forest, Slippery Clunker Six reported, "There are some logs across the road three hundred meters to my front. Hold the convoy."

Panton asked Colonel Haldane if we should alert the men and possibly start the helicopters. The colonel said no, not yet.

On the Quarterhorse radio frequency, the cavalry platoon leader -- several vehicles back from Slippery Clunker Six -- said, "This could be a VC tax point. If it's an ambush it's not very subtle. I'm going to send a tank down with a blade on the front to act as a battering ram." He told Slippery Clunker Six to move ahead and clear the road. He told one of the ACAVs to follow shooting.

We waited, looking around at each other.

Slippery Clunker Six came back on the radio and said, "OK, we're moving out again, the road's clear. No Charlie, but we sure scared the hell out of some trees."

The sun was climbing in the morning sky, and it began to get hot. Down by the artillery, we could hear one of the NCOs in the fire direction center of the 155 battery yell an alert to the gunner. Apparently the convoy was coming into range of its guns. We saw a man climb over one of the traces to the gun and put his eye into a sight.

Colonel Lewane said that the fast movers orbiting on standby were running out of fuel and would be replaced by new jets.

Panton pointed out that the convoy had not received any sniper fire, which proved to him that something was planned. The VC operated all along the road. Unless they were told to keep down because a big attack was planned, they would have been sniping.

The convoy approached Checkpoint Dick and the 105 battery in our area went on alert. The gunners turned the tube slowly as their fire direction center plotted the movement of the convoy.

Haldane sent Dunn and me to tell all the company commanders to have their men take a piss and get ready. We walked down the line and spoke to each commander. Woolley was, as usual, full of good cheer. Our relationship had not changed since I had moved to battalion. He was a fine officer and a gentleman, and I did not try to become familiar. I would have followed him to hell.

Dunn started back to the battalion group, and I told him I'd be along soon. I walked over to my old platoon. Bratcher was sitting in a helicopter with his feet dangling over the side. Propped up on his radio, Spencer was laying on the ground close by. Lieutenant Trost had contracted dengue fever during the previous operation and was back at the division aid station. Bratcher was acting platoon leader.

Beck came out the crowd of men and stood beside me. I sat

160

down next to Bratcher, who offered me a cigarette. Spencer stood up, and Manuel, Lyons, and King walked up to join Beck in a semicircle around us. Bratcher asked if I knew anything they didn't about this upcoming operation. "Nope," I said, "you know about as much as I do. But I know this -- we got less than a couple of months to go in-country. You don't have to be a hero to catch that plane out, just alive."

"Yea," Bratcher said, "we'll be OK."

Returning to the battalion CP, I noticed that Panton's rock on the map was near Checkpoint Tom. I looked back at the helicopters and saw that most of the pilots were in their seats. The gunships started up with their individual swooshes and whines.

Slippery Clunker Six came on the air and said that across the field ahead was Tom, the intersection of the road and a tree line. He was moving out front as point.

Trees came down close to the road for about a half mile and then the road went through a marshy area and up a short incline. The road had been built up in the swampy area and had steep banks. Crash had a stick in his hand and tapped the map just beyond Tom.

Slippery Clunker Six said that he was approaching Tom and was going to move ahead through the woods at a good pace.

After telling Panton to motion for the helicopters to crank, Haldane stood on the berm and raised his hand -- his signal to the company commanders to load.

I picked up the satchel I was to carry for the colonel and helped Crash put on his radio. The entire command group packed up and started moving toward two helicopters near the front of the column. Haldane had insisted that he get on the ground as soon as possible to coordinate the counter ambush. If an attack occurred now, we would be the first in. We would be going in on both sides of the incline near the marsh.

Crash had the division radio. The RTO behind him had a radio on the Quarterhorse frequency and as we walked along to the helicopter, we heard the Quarterhorse commander in the C&C saying that he spotted some people ahead of the convoy. Slippery Clunker Six, on his net, reported the same thing and said that he was taking the people under fire.

Then, suddenly – at 11:30 - from Capt. Steve Slottery, commander of Troop C in Task Force Dragoon, "We're under attack! All around us! My lead tank's hit. They're all over us ..." In the background, we heard catastrophic, violent firing and explosions.

On the Air Force spotter aircraft frequency, a calmer, businesslike pilot's voice said, "Bingo, Bingo, Lead 42 come down on my smoke."

The artillery at the end of the field began firing before we reached our helicopter. As I jumped on, it began to lift off. The gunships were already in the air and heading toward the convoy.

The artillery behind us began to fire at a steady, deafening rate, the concussions pounding off our chests one after another. All around us, helicopters were gaining altitude and heading toward the road. I was sitting beside the Air Force radio and tried to make out the indistinct messages between the spotter aircraft and the jets. From the radio to my left, I could hear the sounds of battle on the Quarterhorse frequency above the noises of the helicopters and the frantic messages among the cavalry leaders as they fought for their lives in the middle of the ambush.

In the distance ahead of us, I saw a jet streaking down from the heavens and, after it pulled up, a giant ball of fire. Nearby, within seconds there was another ball of fire from an unseen jet.

I caught myself whistling, looking ahead, tense. Faintly, from the distance, we began to hear explosions on the ground. The helicopters moved off the tree tops and gained altitude so that they could get a diving run down into the LZ. The higher they lifted, the more fires we saw in front of us. Off to the southeast, I could barely make out the end of the convoy still out in the field. Some of the vehicles were ablaze.

The road through the woods was clearly marked by the Air Force and artillery fire. Some of the gunships already on the scene came into sharp contrast as they streaked past burning napalm.

Ahead, I saw the incline and the marshy area as the lead chopper landed in the clearing by the marsh. The lead vehicles of Task Force Dragoon were on the road to our left. Some were on fire. In the distance, I could see flames from the snout of a Zippo spray the roadside with a hellish flame. In the jungle, napalm had burned long black splotches along the north side of the road. Some trees stood naked.

Amid more explosions and more fire balls we began to hear the clatter and heavy thumping of machine guns. Tracers from some of the tanks were still streaking into the woods.

Men from the lead choppers raced for the wood line. Several fell. People were moving about hurriedly on the road. It was hard to tell whose side they were on. For a fleeting second, it appeared that most of them were Vietnamese running across the road from the south. We were landing in the middle of the battlefield.

On the ground seconds later, I laid down until the helicopter lifted off, then moved under its skids to join the command group running through the waist-high grass for the trees. I could see the turret to the lead tank off to the side, near the marsh. It was at a crazy angle. The tracks on the tank were blown askew.

Panton had a simple map of the area between Checkpoints Tom and Dick in his hand and was plotting the locations of the companies with a grease pencil. I walked past him and joined Dunn, who was staring into the woods.

The area smelled like spent gunpowder and burnt wet weeds. Bushes were burning everywhere. Suddenly, to our right, a Vietnamese got up and started running through the woods. By the time Bob and I got our rifles up, other men in the battalion had cut him down. He was dressed in olive-green fatigues, but he did not appear to have a weapon.

Haldane came up behind us and told us to move out. Most of the battalion was on the ground.

I took the point for the command group as we moved cautiously by the burned-out area on the tree line into dark jungle. We could see sunlight ahead where napalm had burned through the foliage and I headed in that direction.

Firing continued all around us. Occasionally, a round zinged overhead. The slow-moving, heavily armed Skyraiders came on station, and Haldane asked the company commanders to have each platoon throw smoke to identify their forward positions. He told them to hold up until we got a fix from the forward air controller (FAC).

Company C was beside the road, Company B was beside them to our left, and Company A was to our right. The lead elements of Company B suddenly began firing. Grenades went off. The commander came on the radio and said they had run into Vietnamese.

Some walking wounded from Company A had approached our group and were being treated by the head corpsman when the FAC came on the air and said that he had our smoke. We were even with the cav unit at the head of the convoy, more or less on line. He told us to hold up for five minutes while the Skyraiders worked the area in front of us. General DePuy came on and said four minutes -- we had to move on.

The slow-moving Skyraiders came from behind us. Suddenly, their firing drowned out everything else around us. Then, off in the distance, we heard other explosions, and the ground shook.

The Skyraiders' fire cut down whole trees. One wave of two planes was followed by another wave and another.

General DePuy was on the radio yelling for us to move out, mop up.

Haldane passed the order.

163

Another bomb went off somewhere in the distance, and the ground shook again.

Company B sent a gravely wounded man on a poncho stretcher to our area. Haldane told the two soldiers carrying the stretcher to stay with us, take point for the command group, and move out. We left the wounded man behind with the head medic. Haldane told the corpsman to make it to the road with his wounded when he got him patched up.

Company C called in to report they were stepping over Vietnamese dead. Did Haldane want a body count? Haldane said that he wanted the company to move ahead.

About this time, the two soldiers leading our group stopped in their tracks. Haldane asked loudly, over the din of noise around us, what the delay was about. I told him I'd check and I moved up by the men. They were looking down at a ravine that went straight across our front. It looked like a dried-up river. Beside us, Alpha Company came on the radio to report the ravine.

Down in the bottom was a trail -- a "super highway" through the forest that the ambushers were certainly planning to use as an escape route away from the road. I sent the two men across. As they reached the bottom, an automatic weapon opened up from the left and the lead man recoiled from a hit, but he gathered himself, dived to the side, and hid behind a log.

Company B soldiers were behind the Vietnamese gun. They threw grenades into the position and two Vietnamese soldiers were blown partially out. The other Bravo Company soldier in the ravine got across and up the other side. The command group followed. The remaining medic helped the first man up and treated his wound. Down the ravine, some of our soldiers were investigating the Vietnamese blown out of the machine-gun position and yelled up to us that one of them was still alive. Haldane told them to take him to the road.

Charlie Company continued to report that it was coming across a lot of bodies and taking some prisoners. Haldane told them also to move the POWs to the road.

Firing picked up as we approached the heart of the ambush, where the bulk of the Vietnamese had been hiding as they waited to be used as porters to carry the supplies back to Cambodia. Rounds continued to zing over our heads.

Alpha Company reported that it was wading through the carnage left by one of the Skyraiders that had hit a Vietnamese group broadside with its .50-caliber machine guns. I heard Duckett say that it was a Philadelphia mess. Spencer was on the air and said that

Bratcher and my old platoon were coming across individuals and pairs of VCs trying to make their way north away from the ambush.

The small-arms fire subsided, and two more men from Company B came our way with a soldier on a stretcher. Their charge -- only a boy, a small, youngish eighteen looked up at me and said he didn't want to die.

"Hell, man, I can't see where you're wounded," I said.

He pulled up his fatigue jacket and I could see a small bullet hole near his navel. There wasn't much blood outside, but it was clear that he had extensive internal bleeding. His skin was bloated around the bullet wound.

Haldane walked up. The boy continued to say over and over again that he didn't want to die. He was going into shock.

"Gut shot," I said to Haldane. "He'll die unless we get him to a medic soon."

"We don't have any," Haldane said.

I suggested that we could send the litter detail to the road but Haldane said the men with the stretcher were needed where they were. He told me to get the man to the road, find a radio and tell him what was happening out there.

"Rog," I said.

Haldane directed the two Bravo Company men to return to their unit and told Dunn to move out on point. I stood beside the boy on the stretcher and watched the battalion group follow Dunn.

Firing was picking up, some of it coming from our rear as if we were in the middle of fight now.

At the end of the battalion group, an Air Force forward observer came along with his radio operator and another soldier who had fallen in with us. I reached out and grabbed the soldier as he walked by and called out to the Air Force officer.

"Hey, I've got a man here that has to get to the road. I got me a man here to take one end of the stretcher. Can I borrow your radio operator for the other end?"

The Air Force officer, who had not been in Vietnam very long, looked confused. "What about the radio?" he asked.

"You carry it," I said flatly.

"OK," he said.

I helped the radio operator take off the PRC-25 and put it on the back of the officer. The battalion group had moved ahead, and, still adjusting the radio, the officer quickly followed.

Too soon, we were alone. Motioning the soldier to the front of the stretcher and the radio operator to the rear, I began moving toward the road with my M-16 at port arms.

James E. Parker, Jr.

The boy on the stretcher continued to cry out. After a half-dozen steps, I went back to the stretcher and bent down on one knee, I grabbed the boy by the chin and said, "Shut the fuck up. Moaning don't help. It gets on my nerves. And it gives our position away. We're all alone, fellow. Shut up, and I'll get you out of here." I twisted his chin back and forth and smiled.

We went on, but we had to stop every few feet to listen. We were standing still at one point when I saw someone darting between some bushes to my right front. I extended a hand back and motioned for the litter detail to drop to the ground. Putting the gun to my shoulder, I aimed at the bushes. A Vietnamese with an AK-47 in his hand came from behind a tree. He was looking away from me and heading toward the ravine. As he started to break into a trot, I had a clear shot and fired a short burst of rounds. The Vietnamese fell backward and disappeared into the undergrowth.

I suspected that there would be other Vietnamese ahead, so I turned and started toward the ravine. The two men with the stretcher followed me.

Nearing the ravine, I saw where the battalion CP group had climbed up the side. I knew that off to my right would be the machine-gun position destroyed by Company B. Small-arms fire zipped over our heads from below.

"Ah, shit," I said as I dove for the ground. Vietnamese were in the ravine, but they did not attack. They had probably fired and run, I thought, as I lay on the ground. After a few minutes, I got up in a crouch, came back around the stretcher, and started off again straight toward the road.

Near where I had shot the Vietnamese, I saw movement in the bushes ahead. Whoever was there was moving awkwardly. Far to my front, a Vietnamese moved out into a small clearing. He was carrying another man on his back. Although I could barely make out the pair, I knew that both men were Vietnamese and the shirt of the one being carried was bloody. As they went out of sight, I could see his head roll around as if he were dead or unconscious.

More Vietnamese appeared to the right. Three or four, I couldn't tell. Jesus, I thought, as I dropped to the ground again, I'm making my way across the migration route of the whole North Vietnamese nation.

Do I stand up and shoot or let them pass?

The boy behind me moaned. I began to sweat. I listened. There was firing in the distance. I strained to hear what was happening in front of me. Two or three minutes went by. The boy moaned again.

The Vietnam War Its Ownself

I got to my knees. There was no one around. Where the fuck had they gone? The men behind me picked up the stretcher and waited in a crouch. Walking along, I looked quickly from one side to another. Where were they?

Suddenly, through a bamboo thicket ahead, I could see a Vietnamese standing, as if he were waiting for us. I stopped and went to one knee. Then, off to my left, the three men whom I had seen earlier bolted for the ravine. We had been hiding from each other. None of us had fired out of separate fear of not knowing exactly what we were up against -- two opposing three-man groups, avoiding each other on a spent battlefield.

Except that the man ahead had not moved. I waited for him to turn and join the others, but he stayed his ground. Finally, I was afraid of waiting any longer. With sweat dropping in my eyes, I fired toward him and fell forward. Lying on the ground, I wiped my face with my sleeve and waited. There were sounds all around me, but I could not identify any as belonging to the man ahead. I came back up to my knee and stared straight ahead. The man was still there. He was dead, I realized, hung up on some vines. He had been dead before I fired.

We moved by the thicket, past the dead man, then through a burned-out area, through more jungle, and finally onto the edge of the road. At a distance of about two city blocks down the road, I saw the lead cavalry elements of the convoy. In front of me were trucks. Some of them were burning.

Men were standing around near the cav vehicles. Wounded and dead littered the shoulders of the road. We climbed up to the road and walked toward the cav vehicles. We passed a truck with the driver hanging out of the half-open door. The next truck was untouched. Off to the side, a patch of woods had been burned by napalm and a cluster of burnt Vietnamese corpses lay in a ditch. A truck was half in and half out of a crater near the first Quarterhorse vehicle, an ACAV. Quarterhorse troopers were in the process of removing some of their dead still draped over the top of it. Many had tanker goggles pulled down to their necks, their bulletproof vests hanging open. Two of the tanks at the lead were maneuvering in the road. As we approached, someone yelled for them to stop because there could be more mines.

I could see a medevac helicopter taking off from the road near the incline past the marsh, and we walked in that direction. Black smoke, with the putrid smell of burning flesh, swirled from some of the burning vehicles.

The lead tank, off to the side of the road, was out of

commission. Smoke was coming from an open turret near the front.

One of the Quarterhorse troopers with a radio was at the very head of the column. Some helicopters were landing in the field where we had first come in. I told the man with the radio that I needed to call for a dust-off. Without waiting for an answer, I reached down and turned to the right frequency, gave my position, and requested a medevac. A medevac chopper came on the air. He was in the area and coming down. I threw smoke, and, within a matter of minutes, the helicopter was on the ground. We put the young boy aboard.

I went back to the radio and called the colonel to tell him that the action was in front of him. The battle back here was over. As I was talking, I saw photographers coming up the bank from helicopters in the landing zone. They were taking pictures of everything. I moved off to the side as they clustered around the lead Quarterhorse vehicles. When they moved on, I walked over to the lead tank to look for Slippery Clunker Six.

I turned a complete circle as I looked at everyone standing around. There was no one familiar. A tanker walked by.

"Where's Sergeant Bretschneider?" I asked.

He nodded toward a body bag lying on the bank. A short distance away were five more bags. Some cavalry soldiers brought over another body bag and laid it beside the rest.

Shit, I said under my breath. Don't think about it. I sat down, suddenly realizing how tired I was. The adrenaline was draining away. I lit a cigarette and looked at my hands. No shake. I looked back at Slippery Clunker Six's body bag. Don't agonize, I said again to myself and I stared at the body bag without reflection. I noticed all of its lumps and its smell and I remembered Clipper Clunker Six eating pate and reciting poetry. I heard his voice just within the past hour on the radio. I put all those thoughts together, slowly and I put them in a basket at the back of my mind.

More wounded were coming along the road. I got up and started to walk down the line. The photographers were ahead of me. Up ahead, a soldier was bringing a Vietnamese prisoner in our direction. As they came by one of the burning tanks, a photographer moved around for a good angle. The soldier was Moubry.

I avoided the supply officer as he posed for the photographers, continued down the line, past the burned-out trucks, trying to get even with my battalion in the woods.

By nightfall, the 1st of the 28th had swept the wood line along the north side of the road. It pulled back to the road and then down near the area we had come in on the helicopters. The 1st/16th and the 1st/18th Infantry battalions had been put in blocking positions near the Cambodian border. They continued to report that Vietnamese main-line forces were straggling toward them all afternoon and night.

The next day, we watched mine-sweeping teams clear the road above the incline. Tank recovery vehicles were still hauling out the tracks damaged or destroyed by the ambush.

Peppy visited the troops and congratulated everyone for a damn good operation. A total of 240 Vietnamese had been killed. Our casualties had been light, 24 killed in action. We got 'em ten to one. Slippery Clunker Six would have been proud.

I could almost see him smile and say, "There you go."

****

By nightfall of the second day, the road had been cleared and the convoy headed on toward Minh Thanh.

We were lifted out the next morning. As usual, Dunn and I were to be the last ones out. The battalion had the same helicopters assigned to it that had been used in the heli-assault, but some had mechanical problems and others had suffered battle damage. Fewer than thirty helicopters showed up for the move.

When they left, Dunn and I had an oddball collection of fifty men around the LZ. The road was deserted. Although the 1st/16th, augmented with cav, was going to stay around and help bury the dead Vietnamese, they were on the other side of the forest. Enemy soldiers, some wounded and some looking for wounded, were still around us.

Two helicopters that had just dropped off supplies to the 1st/16th arrived and took out twenty men. We were down to thirty men scattered around the LZ and we pulled them in close. It was quiet. Alert, Dunn and I sat by our radios in the shade near the edge of the field. We strained to see into the forest.

Three partially filled helicopters came in about thirty minutes later and we began moving out the last of the men. Two loaded and left. As the last helicopter was loading Bob and I were standing by the radio. We indicated that we were the last two by holding up two fingers and pointing to one another. The kicker shook his head and waved the palm of his hand back and forth to say, "No more."

I picked up the radio and talked with the pilot, "We're the last two people here," I said.

"Sorry," he said, his voice shaking from the vibration of the helicopter. "Maxed out. Other helicopters in the area. We'll get you soon."

169

"Shit," I said to Dunn and turned back to look into the woods. I tried to focus on the shadows inside but, for some reason, the noise of the helicopter behind me made it more difficult. I told Dunn that it was coming down to this. I had been alone in this Enchanted Forest, as the late great Slippery Clunker Six had called it, once before and here we were again. Dunn didn't respond. I continued to squint into the woods.

When I gradually turned my head in Dunn's direction, he wasn't there. He was high-stepping toward the helicopter in an exaggerated effort to move quietly. The kicker was holding up one finger, as if they could take one more.

"Jesus Christ," I said. I picked up the PRC-25, sprinted by Dunn, and dove onto the helicopter. He was laughing so hard that he couldn't keep up. When he got to the helicopter, he climbed aboard, even though the kicker was telling him that he couldn't get on. Sitting on the floor beside me, he was still laughing as we took off.

THIRTEEN

Heading Home

We were back in the base camp for only two days before deploying to Bear Cat, southeast of Saigon near the Mekong Delta.

Duckett was able to get to Saigon once. He learned that our seats had been confirmed on Air Force One on 13 and 14 September.

We received a letter from Pete. His convalescence was continuing successfully, and he had his orders to Fort Ord. He said that he had had indirect contact with an old OCS buddy who was working in the Pentagon. He had asked his buddy to try to get Dunn and me assigned to Ord, as well, but he added that it was a very long shot. Fort Ord on the Monterey Peninsula of California was one of the U.S. Army's most sought after post.

I was promoted to first lieutenant. The same day, I received orders for my next assignment, Fort Ord, California. Dunn also received orders to Fort Ord.

Colonel Haldane's replacement arrived. Two first lieutenants, who had arrived in the battalion as replacement platoon leaders several weeks earlier were assigned to take Dunn's and my positions. We had a two-week overlap. Seemed awfully easy, they said about our jobs.

The Vietnam War Its Ownself

The new battalion commander was an uncommunicative, sullen man. After Haldane left, Panton was offering advice on means of reacting to a VC contact when he became angry. He told Panton that it was his battalion now, and he would decide what needed to be done.

On 1 September 1966, I asked the angry colonel if Dunn and I could go back to the base camp at Phuoc Vinh to tie up some loose ends before we left. "Yea," he said, without further comment.

I went by to see Woolley who had been transferred recently to brigade headquarters. He showed me his recommendation to battalion that I receive the Bronze Star with V award. He said that I had set the standard in the company. After our first contact on the perimeter at the base camp, he knew that I was a first-rate soldier, he said. He thought that I was a natural and, under fire, I had a voice as calm and cool as lemonade on a hot summer day. I thanked him and said that his comments were a very high compliment to me because I respected his judgment. I saluted and we shook hands, but I didn't tell him that, during our first contact, I had been caught in my hammock like a monkey in a cage.

Bratcher, Spencer, King, Beck, and Manuel were still around, and each expected to receive their DEROS orders any day. None of them wanted to go on operations.

"Beck," I said, smiling. "What'd you get? Three, four Purple Hearts? You have a death wish here or something?"

Beck stood as tall as he could, raising his head high on his shoulders. "I told you early on I'd make you proud. Plus you said one time that you could WILL victory. On the boat coming over, you said that. And that's what I've believed in. That's what I was doing. I weren't backing down from no little slanted eyed dink. Fuck'um. Here I am, take your best shot."

Beck had wanted this war. He had bribed his way into the Big Red One when he was released from the brig at Fort Leavenworth. A lesser man would have accepted a Dishonorable Discharge and gone on with life. Beck, a throwback to proud gun-toting frontiersmen out of the wild-west, had set about to restore his honor. In doing that, he proved to be a hell'va soldier. A hell'va American. And I told him as much.

Leaving the platoon area after saying my good-byes, I had my arms around Bratcher and Spencer and we took a few steps together. As I took my arms down to walk away, Spencer reached up and ruffled my short hair. Smiling, he said, "The man."

Duckett said that he was leaving for the base camp on 9 September. We confirmed where we would meet, either at the base

171

camp or, if that didn't work out, at the BOQ in Bangkok. Get the women and children off the streets. Watch out Europe. Here we come.

Dunn and I went back to Phuoc Vinh on different helicopters. The one I was on skimmed the trees the whole way. I was looking out the front between the two pilots. Power lines appeared to come up across our front and head straight toward us. The pilots waited until the last moment, it seemed, to go over, and then we were back at treetop level. We almost skimmed the sides of large trees sticking up above the rest.

After landing at Phuoc Vinh, I leaned into the cockpit near the helmet of the pilot and asked him if Dunn had put them up to this wild trip.

"What?" he said. "Who?"

"Never mind," I said and walked up to the base camp.

I wrote letters, separated my personal items into giveaways, throwaways and take-aways, turned in my equipment and hung around with Dunn for the next few days. On 8 September, I told Bob good-bye and said I'd see him at Fort Ord. Carrying my Hong Kong clothes in a Phuoc Vinh bag I left the battalion for the last time. I took a scheduled flight to Saigon but then bummed helicopter rides out to Vung Tau, an in-country R&R site. I stayed in a cheap hotel there away from other military people, and spent most of my time lying on the beach, trying to get rid of my infantryman's tan, reading, or looking out across the South China Sea, with bottles of local beer buried in the sand beside me. For most of two days, I didn't talk with anyone.

Occasionally I would think about the jungle sweeps, the firefights, the tunnels of Cu Chi, the dead and dying on the spent battlefield along the Minh Thanh road and I would take a deep breath to relieve the tension in my stomach.

I remembered the bar with the nude painting and the toilet seat and Dunn's air mattress and Crash Burke and Fred Astaire and I would smile.

I thought about my deep devotion to the men with whom I had served and the circumstances that caused some of their deaths. Staring out across the water, I took the clear images of Patrick, McCoy, Ayers, and Castro out of the baskets where I had them stored in the back of my mind and I examined them. Not searching for answers why, because Dunn was right, there is imponderable morality to war. I just looked at the images calmly, detached. But I also felt a deep sense of loss because I loved them in a way only soldiers at war can know. Going through the outer perimeter of our base camp on night combat patrol, as I chambered a round in my weapon, I knew that it was not me against the dangers out there in the dark jungle, it was the platoon against what laid ahead. A fraternal bonding, based on mission, fear and survival, tied us together. My platoon - Patrick, Bratcher, Ayers, Lyons, Castro - was my only chance of survival. When I went to sleep in the jungle, I gave my life to Spencer to protect till I woke. And in firefights, I faced live bullets, dodged grenades, moved ahead, because the platoon expected it. We had an obligation to one another. To fight. To die, even.

For a soldier, war is a proposition of doing your duty to your unit and surviving if you can. And winning.

I had won, I had survived.

This beach -- Vung Tau -- was where I had arrived a year ago. To my right, I could see the area where the band had been playing on the back of the flatbed truck, where my platoon, confused, had collected around me in the surf. We had come here to fight and we did, out there, behind me in the jungle. And now I was back, ready to go home. That's all there was to it.

****

On 11 September, I bummed a ride to Saigon and checked into the Out-Processing Administration Section on the following afternoon. I had dinner alone at the local officer's club and was back in my assigned Quonset hut by early evening. A group of soldiers, who had just arrived in-country, had gathered in a corner. They were talking loudly while a tape recorder played at high volume. Two of them were playing cards and sharing a strange-looking and strange-smelling cigarette. After complaints about their noise, an officer asked them to turn down the tape recorder, but none of them looked up or moved. The officer was unable to determine who owned the recorder, and he left. The soldiers gleefully went through a hand-slapping, elbow-knocking, chest-thumping routine. Their raucous behavior continued until a group of MPs arrived and threatened them with the brig unless they knocked off the noise.

I watched it all, propped up on my elbow, and thought, good I'm getting out now -- different cast of characters coming in. Different standards and attitudes that I wasn't sure I knew how to deal with.

Around 0200 the next morning, I was awakened by a familiar voice in the bunk below me. Bratcher. Drunk.

"1st Battalion of the fucking 28th Infantry Regiment is the best fucking battalion in the whole fucking country. Last operation we killed them son'bitches by the hundreds. Hundreds, goddamnit.

Had 'em piled up. Crispy Critters. You know how we did it? We did it because we had a goddamned good battalion that's how. You talk to anyone, anyone, anyone, anywhere who served in the field in Vietnam and you goddamnit won't find a better fucking battalion. Most of the shits in the battalion were wounded at least once. Every man I knew had killed a gook. Lions of Cantigny. Goddamned Lions of Cantigny. Lions of Cu Chi and Phuoc Vinh and Minh Thanh. Best fucking fighting unit in the whole fucking country, the whole fucking Army."

I jumped off the bunk and smiled at Bratcher. Unbelievably, he seemed lost for words, but just for a moment.

"I'll be a son'bitch," he said. "Where'd you come from." He stood up and laughed.

From down the Quonset hut, one of the black replacements said, "Shut the fuck up."

Bratcher turned around quickly and swayed in place as he tried to locate the person in the half-light of the Quonset hut. He had a disbelieving look on his face, as if it was not possible that someone was talking to him that way. The old lanky sergeant from Tennessee stumbled down the line of bunks, came up to one bunk, and turned it over. He kicked the man inside as he fell to the floor. There was viciousness in Bratcher's actions that was unlike normal garrison shuffles, probably unlike anything that young man had ever experienced before.

"Don't you tell me to shut up, you chicken-shit asshole. I'll break your skinny black ass."

Getting to his feet, the boy yelled, "It wasn't me, man, I didn't do nothing."

Bratcher pushed him in the chest. "Don't you fucking say anything to me, asshole." I came up beside him and grabbed his arm. "Let it go," I said. "I want a cigarette. Let's go outside."

The black boy said, "Hey man, you're crazy, you know that."

I turned to the black boy and took a step so that I was inches from his face. "Crazy? After a year in Vietnam? Crazy, yeah, crazy, so don't fuck with us 'cause we'll show you crazy," and I dragged out the words, "like ... you ... ain't ... ever ... seen. Want some? Say something."

We stared at each other in the half-light of the barracks. I felt unusually fearless and calm. Never before in my life and never since have I felt the way I did then. I was ready to kill him, anxious for the fight -- adrenaline pumping, elbows protruding slightly from my sides, my weight moving forward toward the balls of my feet -- angry, quick, and strong. Without looking away from his eyes, I took

174

the measure of his neck and groin. I waited for something to trigger my reaction -- a movement, or a word.

He did not move. After a moment, I relaxed. Only after Bratcher and I went outside did we hear his low mumbling.

Bratcher said, "Last night, shit, go out fighting, that's all right. Wanta go back in there and whip his black ass?"

"No," I said. "What do we have to prove? Time to go home. Plus, you got the wrong guy in the first place. I think that kid was just lying there, minding his own business. It was some other guy lipping off." And we laughed.

We talked about our first meeting in Fort Riley, about the different men in our platoon, Trost, Woolley, the last operation, small, recent stuff. People inside probably heard us. I suggested that it was all over for us, we'd done our duty, so we could sit back and smile.

"Naw," he said, "this war will be around for a long time. We'll be back."

"Not me," I said. "Back to school when my tour's up."

"You'll be back," he said. "You like the action."

He and I had sat side by side so often. The fact that it was our last night -- that we had Vietnam almost behind us -- didn't make much difference. I had been afraid of him early on -- afraid that he would take the platoon from me -- but it had worked out. Luck plays a big part in war. I had been very lucky that Staff Sgt. Cecil Bratcher had been assigned to my platoon, that we had gone to Vietnam together. I slapped him on the knee, got up, and went to bed.

He was still sleeping in the morning when I woke up to catch my flight to Thailand.

****

I was in Bangkok that night. Joe arrived the following night, and I showed him some of the places that I had found. They compared with the Tu Do bars of Saigon and the harbor area of Hong Kong and Havana. For me, there was much to like about Bangkok.

The next morning we boarded Air Force One, a C-141, for New Delhi. Our overnight in the Indian capital was memorable for the filth, the cows, the people living on the streets and the smells.

We stopped at Kabul, Afghanistan, and Athens, Greece, the next day, and landed finally at Terrihone Air Base near Madrid, Spain. We went to a BOQ when we arrived and slept for ten hours. The next morning we ordered a rental Volkswagen convertible from a base concessionaire for drop-off in Germany, picked up the car and drove into Madrid. We got lost and ended up in the old town, where we rented a room in a hotel near several bars that featured flamenco dancers. The next day, we went to the bullfights. Several horses were gored and several bulls were killed, but we missed the point. Too ethnic, we decided. We bought some playbill posters and called it a day.

The following morning, we loaded our convertible and made Barcelona, Spain, by nightfall, then on to Nice, France, the following day. There, we checked into a pension and had a late sidewalk-cafe dinner with a couple of carafes of wine. Very continental. We felt conspicuous, however, often looking up to see French men and women looking at us.

"Salt and pepper," Joe said. "They're not used to us blacks and you whites being so -- so familiar."

"Yes, they are," I disagreed. "They had colonies all over Africa. There shouldn't be anything strange about us sitting here. Maybe it's the way we're dressed? Or because we're so tall."

"OK," he said, "if it isn't the black-white thing, then it's the eyes. They're looking at my eyes. You've never noticed them, have you?"

"No," I admitted. "I hadn't ever really looked into your eyes, Joe. What about them?"

"The ladies," he said, "like them very much."

"How come so many men are looking at you, then?"

"Ah, the French. Quiem sa ba?"

"What the fuck is that?"

"French. Means 'Who knows?'"

"No, it don't. You don't know French. Sounds like Spanish anyway."

"The French would know it means 'Who knows.'"

Later in a smoky bar not far from the beach, we were nursing beers when a group of locals came in. In the middle of the group was the most beautiful woman I had ever seen. She was tall and buxom, with blond hair and a deep tan. Her white blouse was tied under her bust to show off a flat, tan stomach above the red skin-tight toreador pants that encased sculptured legs. And her face -- strong, yet soft, exotic, sexy. In the half-light of the smoky bar, she appeared to be perfect. She looked at us as her group walked toward tables in the rear.

"Oh, my God, Joe, I'm in love," I said, my mouth agape.

The chattering from the group continued as they walked along, punctured occasionally by laughs. The woman held our gaze as she walked, quietly distant from her friends.

176

The Vietnam War Its Ownself

Turning on my stool I saw her sit down so that she faced back toward us at the bar. The others fell into chairs around her. She lit a cigarette and when she inhaled the glow lit her face, her hair shining in the dark.

"She is absolutely the most gorgeous woman in the world. The sexiest. She is a goddess sitting over there. I have to meet her. I have to have her."

"Not your type," Joe said.

"I know what my type is, my friend. And that lady, that wench is what I've been looking for all my life. Oh, my God, she's coming this way."

She came up and slid between Joe and I on our bar stools and said something to the bartender in French. Her perfume was musky. She turned to look at me -- her eyes wanton, smoldering, intense, like an animal's. Her breast rubbed against my arm.

"HellohowyoudoingWhatsyourname?" I mumbled as I slicked my short hair back with my hand.

She didn't respond but examined my face closely. Then suddenly, she looked into my eyes.

Those eyes! They had no shame. They were predator's eyes.

Finished with me, she turned and looked at Joe.

"Bon jure, madomessel," Joe said in fractured French. I couldn't see his face because the woman was between us. All I could see was the back of her beautiful head.

She put one arm around Joe's neck and turned his face and body toward her with the other hand. Then, with both arms around his neck, she leaned in and kissed him.

For "bon jure" he gets this?

Had to be something more than "'bon jure."

Later, Joe said it was his eyes.

We went on to Monte Carlo. The first night there, we put on our tailor-made clothes and went to the casino. Because we didn't have much money and didn't know how to play any of the games except blackjack but we weren't so sure how to play it in French, we decided just to get some chips, say $100 worth each, and walk around the gaming tables and look smart. After much dickering with the French bank teller, we managed to get the two $100 chips, which he initially offered us, broken down into ten $20 chips. We wanted something that we could shuffle together as we walked about looking smart. It was such a simple transaction, we thought, and we became frustrated when the Frenchman didn't cooperate. Plus a long line collected behind us. Finally with our five chips each, we walked into the gaming room.

177

Jingling the chips in a way we hoped looked practiced we walked over to a baccarat table where a guy had a paddle. We stood behind a velvet rope and watched, but we had no idea what was going on. When people looked at us, we smiled knowingly. The club was not unlike the Tropicana in Havana, but it was more reserved, cleaner, and quieter. The women were dressed the same, but the men were whiter, more haughty than I remembered from Havana. There were more sideways glances, more appraising looks.

We were having drinks at the bar and looking over the crowd when a woman at my left asked, "Are you a spy?"

"Pardon me?" I asked.

"*I Spy*," she said and smiled.

Duckett and I looked down at her. Maybe this is the way they talk in Monte Carlo -- in catch phrases that everyone else knew but us.

"You look like the characters in a U.S. television program," she explained, "*I Spy*. You are Americans, aren't you?"

"Yes, ma'am," I said.

"And you know about the program, *I Spy*, don't you? It began last fall."

"No ma'am. We're just coming back from Vietnam. We haven't watched much television lately."

"Oh, this is almost as good. We thought that you were associated with the program, *I Spy*, but Vietnam veterans, that is something. Will there be many of you coming back this way?"

"I don't know. What is the program *I Spy* about?"

"Two Americans, a black man and a white man, traveling around the continent, spying for the U.S. A very dashing pair. Like the two of you."

My first reaction was to say, "Ah, go on now," but then I thought that was not quite right for someone who had been taken for a movie star playing an international spy in the Monte Carlo Casino.

"Do say," I said.

We met the woman again the following morning while we were eating breakfast at a sidewalk cafe. In her early sixties, she was a well-to-do widow who spent half the year on the Riviera and the rest at her home in the United States.

She said that the French did not approve of our involvement in Vietnam, but in fact, the French did not approve of much that the Americans did. But she was curious about how it was over there. Joe and I told her it wasn't bad, we would prevail, we had more stuff. We were the U.S. of A.

Refusing to believe it was so simple, she said that more

complex forces of good and evil were at work. The war, she said, will not be won on the battlefield. Attrition was an insignificant variable in the long run, and it was going to be a long war. She wished us well and thanked us for serving our country so well.

That afternoon, we drove into Italy. Then, we headed back into France and arrived in Paris three days later. We picked up college-age Americans when we saw them thumbing and learned that they were against the war in principle, although not against us personally. They expressed outrage easily and sometimes asked naive, leading questions in the hope of uncovering our involvement in mass murder. Joe especially enjoyed responding to their queries. He unashamedly altered his accounts from session to session to fit the audience. He told me that a black man can use his blackness sometimes if he wants to. Liberals will not challenge a black man on anything, especially an articulate black man. Plus, he reasoned, no matter what he said, these college kids would hear what they wanted. "That's the problem with the morally outraged youth of today," he said, "selective understanding."

Our money was running low when we reached Paris, so we looked at a tour map and decided on the one place, above all else, that we wanted to see in Paris. Not the Arc de Triomphe or the Eiffel Tower, but the Crazy Horse Saloon, with its topless chorus line. We went there, drove around town later, and headed for Germany.

The most pleasant part of our trip through Europe was just driving along, with the top down, the two of us sometimes talking, sometimes with the radio on, one of us sometimes snoozing. We drove through clean and beautiful villages, along vineyards in the country, along the Mediterranean, in the mountains -- sometimes with hitchhikers onboard. Laughing, lying, looking up at the sun and feeling its warmth. After the hardships of Vietnam, Europe was heaven. For some reason the words, "Nothing could be finer than to be in Carolina, in the morn...ing," got caught on the end of my tongue and I sang the song off and on all across Europe. We talked about what awaited us in the States. Joe said we would not have had a chance of true friendship there.

"Why?" I asked.

"We come from two cultures. The American culture and the Negro culture. If you are a Negro, you can only play white. Black stands out on a white background."

"Get off that black-white shit, Joe."

"Hard to, Jimmy," he said. "I will always be a black man in a white man's society. We are friends here, but you're from North Carolina. You won't want me to date your sister, would you?"

179

"You know my sister?" I asked.

In Frankfurt, we turned in the car and changed into our dress uniforms with our medals. We were more decorated than anyone else we saw. Singing "Nothing could be finer ..." we marched into the terminal and got first priority standby tickets to the States. Within an hour, we were on our way to McGuire Air Force Base, New Jersey.

There, on 30 September, Joe and I said good-bye. We didn't have much money left. He took a bus to Philly, and I took a bus to New York City to see an old girlfriend.

****

No one noticed me in the bus terminal. Everyone seemed busy with their own lives. I took a seat toward the back of the bus and felt insignificant, lost. The urban New Jersey countryside appeared dirty and in disrepair. The weather was chilly, especially to someone coming back from a year in the tropics. The bus rattled through the bumper-to-bumper traffic and crossed the George Washington Bridge into New York City, where I knew one person.

I took a taxi from the bus terminal in New York City to the apartment house of my friend. It was midafternoon of a weekday, and she was working. I didn't have her office telephone number, so I stood on the sidewalk in front of the building and wondered what I was going to do. When the bellman asked if I was waiting for someone, I told him that I was but had timed my arrival a couple of hours early.

"Betsy Nottingham," he said. "You're the soldier boy Betsy Nottingham talks about. I thought you were kilted once."

"Wounded maybe," I said, glad to find someone to talk to in this city of millions. "Is Betsy's roommate around or someone who can let me in?"

"I'll let you in. Betsy would want me to. Come on, follow me."

He showed me up to Betsy's door, opened it and told me to relax. She should be in around six. I sat down on her couch and fell asleep. She was kneeling beside me and crying when I woke.

The next afternoon, I left on the train for Southern Pines, North Carolina. When the train hissed to a stop at the train depot in downtown Southern Pines, I saw Mom, Dad, and my youngest sister Kathy and the Lylands, a couple from the church, waiting on the platform.

It is a special time for a young man when he comes home from war. The anticipation, the explosion of emotion, the touching, the feeling, the crying, the stories, the old news, the new news, and then the comfortable regular routine. My Bronze Star had arrived in the mail. After dinner, my mother pinned it on my tunic and then ran her trembling fingers across my lips. Daddy read the citation aloud. Kathy applauded. My other two sisters, Judy and Joan, came in the next day and we held hands as Daddy said grace at supper. He thanked the Lord for looking after me and returning me home.

I looked up old friends. The person I wanted to see most of all, Cottonpicker, was, himself, in Vietnam, assigned to the 173th Airborne Regiment. He had influenced much of what I had done in Vietnam and I wanted to report to him, to get his approval.

Most of my other boyhood friends did not know what questions to ask about my experiences, and I did not volunteer much. Public energies during this war were spent on moral hand wringing. There was little understanding about what was going on in the jungle of Indochina. American soldiers were not the war's heroes. Actually, they played a minor role in everyday reporting. The principal characters in this country were the politicians and media opinion-makers.

The media was a powerful influence in the war. Comments from everyday Americans tended to be reframed television and newspaper reports. Each day, the media rearranged their words to deliver the same message: "bad war." The TV video clips of the fighting were not balanced. They were impersonal, catastrophic, horrible imagery of a losing army -- intentionally cast that way, it seemed to me. My memories of our Army in Vietnam were of dedicated men doing dangerous work.

I stop reading the papers and at home we did not watch the evening news.

After two weeks of home leave, I flew to Lincoln and picked up my car for the drive to Fort Ord. Pete's parents met me at the airport and listened carefully to my version of the stories about Pete and the action on the day he was wounded. Mrs. Peterson held my hand in the car as we talked and said how fortunate that we came out of that chaos alive.

We went down to the filling station where my Mercedes was garaged. As we drove up, I saw it parked off to the side, cleaned up, and serviced for my arrival. How handsome it looked. I thought about the day that I saw it sitting on the edge of the farmer's lot. It still looked as good a year later. They also serve who sit and wait -- this car had soul. I had the feeling that it was glad to see me too, as it jumped away from the service station -- like a young kid, I thought, happy to be on the road again.

Though winter was setting in, I put the top down, turned the radio up loud, and streaked across the wheat lands. I felt great. "Nothing could be finer than to be in Carolina, in the morn...ing."

I passed through Cheyenne, Wyoming, where we had stopped for a rest during our train move to Oakland en route to Vietnam. I'm lapping the world I thought. Small place.

--FOURTEEN--

Best Job in the World

Pete was asleep in his BOQ room when I arrived in Fort Ord. We embraced but Pete said that was generally frowned on between two men alone in a BOQ room. I had brought along a six pack of beer and we sat talking, laughing.

Though late, we decided to visit Bob and his bride Linda, who lived in a Monterey apartment. We bought a bottle of champagne on the way and jumped over the back fence of the apartment house. The sliding glass door was unlocked, and we barged in, catching Bob in his shorts. I said that only six weeks out of the combat zone and already Dunn had dropped his guard. He promised to sandbag the patio over the weekend and post Linda guard. She said, "I can do that. Got my broom and my hair spray, they'll never take us alive."

We liked Linda right away. Perky, bright, personable and attractive, she filled out the group. We sat around their living room and out by the pool of the apartment house that evening. Finally everybody had to show their battle scars. Pete's shoulder looked terrible, with lacerated, pink skin stretched over what looked like the end of a coat hanger. Bob had been wounded in so many places, we tried to count all the scars, marking them with a ball point pen. For me, Pete and Dunn held me down and pulled by pants to my knees. There isn't much honor in getting butt shot in war, although Linda said, "Well, Jimmy, at least you weren't facing the other direction."

I officially signed in at Fort Ord the next morning. Within the month, I was officer in charge (OIC) of the 6th Army Area Drill Sergeant School, the boot camp for drill sergeants in the Northwest. Sergeant Vick was the noncommissioned officer in charge (NCOIC). There were seventeen senior NCOs on my faculty, all impressive soldiers. Each carried a riding crop as a special symbol of authority as a Drill Sergeant School instructor.

The Vietnam War Its Ownself

The school was a showcase for the post commander when VIPs toured and the staff and I were called on almost weekly to conduct 6th Army Area award and retirement ceremonies. As the OIC, I sat on NCO promotion panels, prosecuted summary court-martials, and was a mainstay on OCS review boards.

I taught two classes, conducted Saturday morning inspections of the drill sergeant candidates, and had the final word on who graduated.

It was the best job in the Army, at one of the most sought after posts, and my closest friends were nearby. Pete and I roomed in the same BOQ. He was assigned to a line unit that went to a field garrison every Monday through Friday. On the weekends we spent time with Bob and Linda, playing bridge and doing the Monterey Peninsula. Carmel and Big Sur were incredibly beautiful and we were particularly enthralled with the area in between -- the Carmel Highlands -- where we could drive to scrub-lined vistas high in the hills and look out over the rocky coast littered with rafts of seals, otters and herds of sea lions, far out into the Pacific where migrating gray whales passed. Late one afternoon, Pete and I, with dates, were on an overlook when a storm came in from the north. Under the threatening sky the waves broke angrily on the rocks and lightning flashed in the distance. The old evergreen trees in the Highland swayed in the wind. There was salt in the air, the smell of nature.

"This is what we were fighting for, this is America," I said.

"Boy," Pete said, "how times change. We used to say America was those people back in that honky-tonk bar in Junction City, Kansas. Remember?"

"Aug," I mused, "fuck 'em, I hadn't seen this yet."

My sister Judy, now married with a couple of kids, lived in the San Francisco area. Pete and I occasionally drove up to the Bay area on the weekends and hung out, at Judy's and in the Fisherman's Wharf area.

Pete Javit, another OCS graduate and Vietnam vet, told us the ins and outs of off-post housing. We applied, got pre-approved for a substantial allowance and started looking for a place -- with what we would be given, the three of us could live almost anywhere on the peninsula. I was for something along Cannery Row in Monterey because I was a John Steinbeck fan. Javit wanted something near Pebble Beach.

Pete, however, found the best place -- a furnished three-bedroom house in the Carmel Highlands owned by a local professor on a year's sabbatical somewhere. To reach it we had to turn off the ocean highway and climb a winding road halfway to the top of a hill and then down a small one-lane road behind an Episcopal bishop's house. The house faced the ocean and jutted out over a ledge so that standing in one of the front bedrooms there was nothing but ocean to the front. Below, the distance of five or six football fields, was the rocky coast where seals and otters and sea lions played. The sound of waves crashing on the rocks was a pleasant background to the noise of birds in the trees behind the house. It was as near a perfect setting as three boys in their mid-twenties could hope for. On the weekends it became "party central" to all levels of the local community, although there was a tendency toward Vietnam veterans and zingy, hippy girls. One on one, the braless wonders of northern California got along with the short-haired GIs of Fort Ord, especially when they found out some of us had war wounds. Linda Dunn did not approve of most of the girls who hung around the house, however.

"Look 'it, Linda," I would say when she and Bob visited, "just look 'it. Look at this house, look at this view, think about what I have been through. Isn't a little tender kindness appropriate? Here, let me turn on some music. Would you like some wine?"

"Jimmy Parker, and over there, you, Larry Peterson, you both are bad. Bad. And Bob Dunn, you listen to me, you are never, ever allowed up here without me."

Kim Novak lived two houses down from us. Everyone I knew had seen her in *Picnic* with William Holden. She lived by the ocean in a compound with a gate. Almost every day, we stood on our terrace, looked down toward her house, and quoted William Holden's lines to her. Sometimes at night before going to bed, we went outside and said, "Good night, Kim."

I often had to dress to the nines in my best uniform with all my combat ribbon plumage to do VIP escort duty, or ceremonies or inspections or panels. Coming back on those looking "as-military-sharp-as-I-can" days I usually put my hat on the passenger seat and lit a cigar. Most often I was in Winston-Churchill-cigar-clinched-in-jaw mode by the time I got to the left turn in Monterey that shot me south along the Pacific highway, pass Carmel to our house in the Highlands.

One day when I was wearing my finest, with that day's cigar on the dash, I started home. After I left the main gate I put my hat in the passenger's seat, took the wrapping off the cigar and put it in my mouth.

No lighter. Not in my pockets, not on the dash, not in the glove department. No lighter, no matches. Just a new cigar in my clenched jaw. Pissed, because I like this routine, I idly pushed in the cigarette lighter on the dash, which just shows how futile all this was, 'cause that lighter didn't work, never had, not since I owned the car.

Or that's what the guy said. But you know what, after a while it popped back out, from where I had pushed it in.

I was right at the turn south in Monterey at the time. So I had to stop, shift to first gear and then when the light changed, turn the wheel in lane to keep us goin', while shifting into second before getting through the intersection.

I had, almost unconsciously, pulled the lighter out of its place in the dash as I started all this shifting gears and turning the wheel and keeping in my lane... I put my thumb at the end because I knew the lighter didn't work.

I was shifting gears with the heel of that hand....that hand... that held the thumb that was on the business end of the cigarette lighter that had never worked.

I smelled my finger burning before I actually felt it. Hard to believe but it's the truth. That red hot coil at the end of lighter had branded the end of my thumb in the "Many Circle" stupid brand. And then like an explosion it started to hurt.

Hurt bad, because I had burnt the shit out of my thumb. First degree or third degree whichever is worst.

My thumb glowed where the lighter had tried to light it. And the hurt just kept on coming.

I stopped the car – in the middle of the intersection – and got out and held my right hand and jumped around and yelled. YELLED...

Damn that hurt.

Pretty soon cars that were backed up started blowing their horns and I got back in and drove through the intersection to park along the side of the road and wave my thumb as if the wind would cool it off.

That some major league hurt. And you know what? Found the lighter later under the passenger seat. Never found my hat. Haven't a clue how it got out of the car or where it went.

****

Our mailbox was near the cutoff by the bishop's house. The mailbox for the house across the street hung on the same board. The woman who lived there often worked in her garden and she would wave at me. Occasionally, we met at the mailbox or in the local supermarket. One day, I was coming in from the Drill Sergeant School in my dress uniform. She hailed me from her yard as I checked the mail.

She was in her late forties or early fifties and looked bookish, like a New Englander, I thought. Obviously she had been working in her garden for some time that day; she was dirty and rumpled. After she asked me about the plumage on my uniform and I explained it briefly, she told me that she was having a garden party that weekend and wondered if I would be able to come. Possibly, the other men in my house would also attend. I said I couldn't speak for them, but I'd be there. She asked if I would wear my uniform because, she said, I looked so handsome in it.

Pete and Javit had no interest in garden parties. Bob and Linda said they would go with me, but then something came up and I went by myself, still dressed immaculately from Saturday morning inspection at the Drill Sergeant School. About thirty people were gathered in the side garden. A bar stood under a small tent in the rear.

The Episcopal bishop was standing near the lattice entrance portal, and we spoke. He did not seem as warm and engaging as the ministers I remembered in North Carolina, but rather of the arty sort. Beyond him, I saw several people moving in our direction, drawn, I was sure, by my uniform.

"These medals," one woman said to me, "what do they mean? What did you do to receive them?"

I began explaining the campaign medals, and the bishop asked to be excused. As he was breaking through the crowd around me, he looked back in my direction and nodded, smiling sweetly.

"Tell me about this ribbon," said a woman. "What did you do, personally?" She wasn't friendly. Her tone was hard, her gaze steady and accusing. I looked around, surprised to see that the other people were glaring at me.

"Did you kill any women and children for that?" someone asked.

"Be quiet, Helen," said the first woman, turning quickly to the new questioner. "I have him first. He answers to me first. What did you do that got you that medal?"

I scanned the crowd again for one friendly face. Finally, I looked at a man standing behind some women on my right. He had a round, happy face and looked a little drunk. I continued to look at him until he spoke.

"Did you carry a bayonet?" he asked with a slight lisp.

Where was Duckett when I needed him? They wouldn't attack a black man like this.

I talked about some of the personalities I knew -- Pete, Dunn, Woolley, Bratcher, Spencer. It wasn't what they wanted to hear. One woman told me that she had heard we gassed whole villages, the Air Force bombed populated areas with napalm and we had body count quotas on operations.

Smiling at her, I said the public perception of the war in Vietnam was distorted because it had been sensationalized by the media. They had an attitude when it came to coverage -- get as much blood in the frame as possible -- and they always ended with the message that it's a bad war. It seemed to me that they never ever had a feel for the GI. One reason, I guessed, was the men doing the reporting could not relate to the poor and the black from our society who were doing the fighting and the dying over there. I also guessed that no one here knew anyone fighting on the ground in Vietnam. No one they knew, knew my war.

"War," a scrawny little man said, "corrupts the human experience. Failures in statesmanship lead to war. It is an enormous waste."

"It is disconcerting," a woman close to me said, "your contention there is a separation between us and the soldiers over there. That's what happened with the Nazis. No one knew what the soldiers were doing in Treblinka. It's a government gone mad. Leads to things like the Holocaust where mass murder was sanctioned. Body-count murder in Vietnam is very similar, it seems to me."

I looked around. My way out of the gate was blocked. Perhaps they sensed that I might try to make a break for it. I stood there, like a bear in a bear baiting, nodding to the people who were talking, but it was hard to focus on one person. So many were talking in a breathless frenzy.

Finally noticing a path open toward the bar, I excused myself and made my way to the rear of the garden.

"Very mean scene, man," said the smiling young bartender. "They were on you like a mob. Like they were waiting for you. Why did you wear your uniform, for Christ sake?"

"She asked me," I said, looking at the guy with eyes wide, "the hostess asked me to wear my fucking uniform. Jesus, I didn't know that she was an antiwar piranha."

I took a deep breath and asked the boy for a beer. Someone walked up beside me. A woman. I could smell her. She placed her arms on the counter. I looked at her wrist to see if there was anything I recognized about her jewelry to tie her to the women behind me. Nothing was familiar, but I decided not to make eye contact anyway to avoid any further confrontation. The woman asked for wine. She had a soft, cultured voice, not harsh and raspy like the voices in the crowd by the gate. I fingered the rings of water on the bar and debated whether to look at her. Acting on a sudden impulse, I turned my head at the same time that the woman turned hers. We were no more than ten inches apart.

Kim Novak.

Honest to God, Kim Novak. I looked at her eyelids, at the pores of her cheek, at her full lips. She smiled, warm and friendly, and said softly, "Hello."

Kim Novak.

My mind froze. I couldn't think of anything to say. I didn't even think about thinking about something to say.

Kim Novak.

We were so close that I couldn't even tell if she was beautiful. I looked at the forehead and the eyes and the nose and the lips, but I didn't know what the whole face looked like.

Except for my eyes, my body was rock still. Saliva collected in my mouth, and a little drained out and ran down my chin. Kim lowered her gaze but continued to smile. She looked up at the bartender when he handed her the glass of wine, thanked him, turned to look back at me quickly, and then walked away.

I stood there in shock, my head still turned to where she had been. First the screaming liberals and then Kim Novak. Get me outa here, I said to myself. I turned, walked through the house, passed the hostess without comment, and went out the front door and down the road to my house.

That night, I told Javit and Pete about the party and meeting Kim Novak but I did not tell them that I had been frozen speechless. What I said was that we had a little chat, and she was nice, very soft, very different from the other hard cases there. I told them that I thought I had made an impression. She knew where we lived, I wouldn't doubt that she might someday just pop in for a drink. Or invite us down. Whatever.

Several nights later, Javit and I were at the Matador Bar in Carmel. We were sitting at a table for two against the wall, near the front. Javit looked up and said that Kim Novak had just walked in.

I said, "Yeah, sure. I bet she'll come over and hug my neck when she sees I'm here." Shortly afterward I was walking near the row of bar stools on the way to the men's room. A woman swung around as if to leave. I was close, and she looked at me.

Kim Novak.

Veering off to the left away from her, I walked right into a table and spilled all of the drinks on it. Fortunately, apologizing and righting people's drinks gave me something to do, so that I didn't have to turn back to Kim. No one at the table understood how I could have "accidentally" walked into their table -- it wasn't like they were in the middle of the aisle.

****

Kim Novak notwithstanding, it was a very good year. In March 1967, a representative from the Army's Personnel Section at the Pentagon visited Fort Ord and told an assembly of company-grade officers that most of us would be going to Vietnam after our Fort Ord tour. We were infantry officers, and the Army needed infantry officers in Vietnam. Pete put in for helicopter school. Dunn said he was getting out.

Betsy wanted to visit the Monterey Peninsula. I told her that if I got out of the service, she could fly out and we'd drive back across the states together. A grand idea, she said.

But I told her I hadn't decided to get out yet. I'd let her know.

I wavered for days.

I did not want to go back to Vietnam as a replacement. If I had been offered a proposition to take my Drill Sergeant School staff to Vietnam, I would have gone. If I could have gone back and taken over my old platoon with Bratcher and Spencer and Rome and Manuel and Ayers and Castro and Lyons, I would have gone. Neither of these was a possibility.

I also considered the soldiers who had been in that Quonset when I left. And the news. It was not a very good war. The United States was not winning on anyone's scorecard and, more important to me, did not appear intent on winning. There was no ground swell of public support for the fighting GI.

Plus, Dunn said there were bullets with our names on them over there. As long as we stayed here, we were OK, we were out of range. Dunn knew I felt an unusual strong sense of duty -- I told him in Vietnam about the personal way I took the OCS graduation address, how I accepted responsibility to protect the dignity of the United States for all of time. Bob's comments at the time had been, "It was just gas. You were excited, all pumped up, Momma and Daddy and your little sister in the audience. Had some champagne I bet. Just gas. It does that... distorts your thinking. Besides, Parker, like Pete and I have told you often, you are one of the most unashamedly self-serving individuals we have ever known. You are not one to go into the priesthood, or to be believed about dedicating your life to some principle, other than 'Jimmy first.' So I don't know where all this comes from. Forget it. Do what's expected. That's enough."

When I told him in Monterey that I was thinking about

getting out, but I felt guilty about forsaking my duty, abandoning my obligation to country at a time of war, he said, "Listen, my friend, you have served one tour in Vietnam. That's enough. You wanta die, go back. You wanta live, get out. Remember when Haldane ordered us to Battalion Operations from our platoons? Remember? Did you say, no, my duty is to my men? Of course not. You said, 'Yes, Sir.' Went with the flow, right? Plus you ain't got your college degree, because you're stupid. You stay in the military, you'll get to about captain and they'll say, OK go stand over there, you ain't going to get promoted again, because you're stupid and don't have a college degree. That's the way it works. There is no question in my mind about this. Get out and go home."

I agreed with him for the most part. But there was in me a compelling notion about the flag, about duty to country. So I wavered, feeling guilty. Then Betsy said she really wanted to come out, and I said, OK, I'm getting out.

It came down to that. Bigger decisions have been made for lesser reasons. Plus the lease was up on our house, so if I stayed, we'd have to find a new place. So like Dunn said, I went with the flow. I put in my discharge papers.

I went through the giveaway, throwaway, and send-away selection of personal stuff and was down to a suitcase when Betsy arrived.

On my last day in the Army, 2 May 1967, I cleaned out my desk at the Drill Sergeant School. Vick had the seventeen staff NCOs standing at attention when I was ready to leave.

A very fine honor guard for my leave-taking, I said. As I stood in front of them, I remembered when I had joined the Army, three and a half years before -- just a faceless "INductee," shaven-headed, in an ill-fitting new uniform, scared out of my wits.

It had worked out altogether better than I could have ever imagined. I was fortunate to have served in Vietnam when I did and to have led 1st Division soldiers in combat. And I ended up in charge of these seventeen NCOs standing in front of me -- among the best in the Army. I would have liked to work with them for the rest of my life. I told them that I had learned most about life from my father, who grew up on a North Carolina farm. But I had also learned from Cottonpicker and Willie O. McGee and Bratcher -- all three of them Army sergeants -- and I had learned from this staff. I saluted them, wished them the best and left.

Unfortunately I forgot my hat. Couldn't very well go back and get it, however. Last impressions are important in benchmark events like this. I left it and drove off base as a civilian.

The Vietnam War Its Ownself

I said good-bye to Pete and Bob and Linda that night. Nothing would ever be the same with us again. We were on different tracks now. There would be new situations, new friends, new places. We told each other that we were thankful that our lives had crossed and that we had spent some time together when we were young and full of energy, hope, and humor. Bob, Pete, and I had fought a war together.

We were all over the place with our comments that night trying to say it all. It was as if we were back on the top deck of the USNS *Mann* trying to figure where we were going based on where we'd been.

Bob finally said, "Be happy, nothing else matters much. That's what I've learned. One little word is the key to a successful life. And that's, Be happy."

Pete, drunk, said, "Pardon me. Pardon me, please. But, ah, ain't 'be happy' two words?"

Betsy told me later that it was obvious that we three loved each other. I told her it was just gas.

****

Three weeks later, I reported to work for Dad at a North Carolina timber mill he had just bought with turn-of-the-century equipment. Despite our best efforts and the long hours of our thirty-man workforce, we had trouble competing with new, high tech mills that were also suppliers to the North Carolina furniture industry.

I started work for a $100 a week, enough to pay for room and board in the small town of Sanford, where the mill was located but not much else. I worked ten to twelve hours a day, first manhandling logs in the yard, then behind the lathes and finally in the splicing and grading room.

At Christmas, we were down to a few weeks' worth of orders. Money was slow coming in. We stopped buying logs so that Daddy could give each man in the mill a Christmas bonus. The plant was not making a profit. In our efforts to keep up with the lower prices offered by the modernized mills, we were not meeting cost.

I drove up to New York City to spend the holidays with Betsy. Bravely she introduced me to her friends at a neighborhood restaurant and at a party in her apartment house, but she was obviously uncomfortable when I told people I managed a veneer mill in Sanford, North Carolina. The New Yorkers would invariably asked, "VAneer?" and I said "VEneer" and nodded. It seemed to me everyone was very opinionated and loud. Different cultures, Betsy

191

said, different ways of interacting.

Our time alone was pleasant. Briefly I forgot about Sanford and the problems with the mill, but after a couple of days I was ready to leave. I was out of place.

Betsy was not surprised when I said I was going back home before Christmas. She said that she understood. Our parting was tender, and final.

--FIFTEEN--

Transition

Driving south with Betsy and New York City very much in my rearview mirror, I listened to country-and-western music and occasionally sang, "Nothing could be finer than to be in Carolina, in the morn...ing," but the tune was melancholy that night. I didn't have much to look forward to. The orders at the mill were good only through January, I was out of touch with most of my friends, the girls I dated in the Carolinas were of no interest, and a return to college was a difficult proposition.

I would have liked just to turn the car west to find my place in life by chance, if it weren't for Mom and Dad. Dad was overwhelmed by the mill but he wouldn't just walk away from his investment. He needed help.

With the dark winter highway stretching out ahead, I felt alone in the little two-seater. I was twenty-five years old, maybe time to take stock. Let's see, I thought, what do I have? Two years of college, Army, no conspicuous talents or well-placed friends. This veneer plant venture had no future and I was getting beyond that point where I could rationalize that I was still growing up, kicking around. Shouldn't I be seeking a career, something stable? What do I do?

Cottonpicker had told me to do what comes natural.

Looking back on Vietnam, I liked the dangers and I missed the patrols, the comradeship, and leading men into combat. For a fleeting moment, I wanted to be back in the jungle with my platoon. I thought about Cecil Bratcher, my platoon sergeant, and Pete, Dunn, McCoy, Duckett, Captain Woolley. How I missed them and our times together. I remembered the rush of adrenaline when a round zinged overhead and how I crouched, all senses alert, when a sudden exchange of gunfire erupted nearby. I remember the smell, the taste of fighting in the jungle. That was my element, I thought. Great risks, great rewards. My element.

Bratcher had told me the last time I saw him that I would be back, that I liked the action.

I thought when the mill had run its course, I would move on. I had liked Havana, Monte Carlo, and Bangkok. Maybe I'd head to Thailand and look for work. Something would turn up. Just keep on keeping on...

"Nothing could be finer than to be in Carolina...... in the mooooornnninnnng."

By midday on Christmas Eve I was back in Sanford. I stopped at the mill to ensure that the steam was up in the boiler before heading to Southern Pines, thirty miles away. On the way out of town I stopped at Lee Drug Store on Main Street, the only store that was open. I hadn't bought presents for my parents or sisters. The day was dreary, cold and wet. I was tired and had no idea what presents to buy.

A bell rang as I came in the door.

"Merry Christmas, can I help you?" The young lady who approached was tall, lanky, and wholesome in a freckle, fresh way, though if she had freckles I didn't notice. The southern twang to her voice was such a welcomed change from the last people I talked with in New York City that I smiled. And she smiled and I wasn't so tired any more.

You hear how it was "love at first sight"... Well I don't know about love, but I had flirted with hundreds of girls over the years, and this one I could tell in seconds was different. Out of the ordinary. Her smile, the twinkle in her clear brown country eyes, her sense of ownership of this spot where we were standing, but especially her sincere welcome, was very becoming. She was classy and self-confident, but approachable and she was very attractive. I tilted my head to the side, taking her all in. What was it about this girl? This aura about her?

"Really, can I help you?"

"You are beautiful."

"Well, thank you," she said in a calm, matter-of-fact voice. Smiling she asked, "You need a last minute gift?"

"It is Christmas Eve. What are you doing working in a drugstore on Christmas Eve?"

"It's what I do on Christmas Eve. Work for Mr. Lazarus here in his drugstore. Been doing it since I was in high school. It's become part of my holidays ..."

"Lazarus' sounds Jewish."

"Shhh," as she put her right index finger to her pursed lips.

"He's Jewish." I interrupted in a whispery voice. "This is Christmas. Selling gifts for the baby Jesus. In the South. Is this legal?"

"Yea! It's OK by me. So?"

"So." And I was stumped. "It is good to meet you."

She looked off in the distance for a moment then back as if she wasn't sure about me. Was I a customer or not?

"My sisters. I need to buy some gifts for my sisters." I said nodding, trying to assure her that I did have business in this drugstore. "What do you have for sisters... in their late twenties... but my youngest is a teenager... we're not sure, maybe she's adopted. Just showed up at our house one morning. What'sha name?"

"Brenda. Here let's look at this body lotion..." As she turned to go behind a counter, I watched her walk away. I was looking at her butt when she turned back to see if I was following her, saw I was staring at her backside, frowned a little, than smiled in a professional drugstore clerk way and nodded for me to join her at the counter.

Despite her confident way when I first came in, as time went on she acted flustered.

But she did not lose her smile. As she gathered things from around the store, she explained why she thought that each one would be a great gift for my sisters.

"Mother is hard to buy for. So it's going to take your best effort."

"Hard to buy for? Why?" Brenda knitted her brow.

"Well, she's big. Mother is. And she has these tattoos on her arms. Comes from her days in the circus. She really doesn't need much... these toilet things, I think she would take offense that my sisters wouldn't. Like I don't think she's clean or something. Got any power tools?"

Brenda smiled, "and your wife?" She asked. "What kind of gift would she like?

"Not married."

Brenda looked down at my left hand, back in my face and nodded her head as if in thought.

When she had gathered things that she thought were good gifts, I really had little idea what she had selected. I told her I had to write a check for my purchases because I didn't carry much cash. I was trying to maintain eye contact, then looked away, regretting being so flippant. This girl deserved more. There was a great sense

1957 Mercedes 190 SL, white with black interior and a working cigarette lighter. "Rocinante." Travelled the North Carolina back roads, the Kansas prairies and the Carmel Highlands of California.

Cool Spring Baptist Church, Sanford, NC 25 May 1968.

Brenda and I on the Washington Mall during a break
in my CIA intelligence training.

**"Jim Pendy" and Brenda's enter-on-duty picture
with the CIA**

Jerry F., Larry R and "Jim Pendy"

of goodness about her. It was her gift. That and poise and beauty. But especially goodness. Flippant didn't seem appropriate. I just didn't know how else to act.

After scanning my check, she asked me to have it approved by the owner in the back.

He initialed the check and I returned to the counter. The girl smiled and asked to be excused for a moment. She was very nice.

She went back to the owner. "Mr. Joe," she said, "See that guy up by the cash register? Did you just approve this check of his?"

Mr. Lazarus, a portly, balding, gentle man looked at it briefly and said, "Yeap."

"I'm not so sure it's a good check. I've never seen this guy before. Said he just drove down from New York City but works here in Sanford at a mill. Acts like he's God's gift to women."

"He looks okay. It's all right," he said and went back to work.

The girl came back, smiled sweetly, and asked if she could gift-wrap the presents. I said, of course, and as she wrapped them I asked about her other Christmas plans and she told me a little about her family and opening gifts, eating a big Christmas meal. She reluctantly gave me her telephone number. I tried to memorize it, but got some of the numbers reversed. She hesitated and gave me the number again. This time I intentionally mangled the number.

"Yea, sure," she said.

As she helped me take the gifts to the car, she noticed that I had a Carmel, California, city tag on the front bumper. "California," she said, "you do get around, don't you?"

I told her how much I appreciated her help. I leaned forward and kissed her lightly on the cheek, "for Christmas," and left for Southern Pines.

****

Coming home so many miles through the night, the mill, the holidays, Betsy, New York, my future, suddenly that lanky, sincere girl in the drugstore was all I thought about. And I smiled.

Back in the store, Brenda quickly walked to the pharmacy in the rear and stood beside Mr. Lazarus, watching my car turn the corner. "Mr. Joe," she said, "I have been working here for several years and I have had my share of bad checks and I know that guy is a con man. He didn't fool me. He's got charm he can turn on just like that." She snapped her fingers. "New York, huh, and, and, listen to this, his car is a white convertible sports car, with California tags. California. In Sanford, North Carolina? Works at a mill? No. That check is going to bounce. Yes sir, he's a crook. I can tell. It was the way he smiled, like a carnival barker. He's as shady a character as I have ever met."

Brenda Joyce Denton accepted my proposal of marriage on Valentine's Day, February 14, 1968, fifty days after we met.

****

The mill continued to do poorly. With our old equipment, we had no reason to hope for a reversal of fortunes in an industry that was becoming fully automated. Our principal customers began to cut back on the orders and it was becoming a problem to make the payroll.

I had always had a competitive, defiant – almost unemotional -- relationship with my father. We often competed for Mother's attention -- but I cared for him and was concerned about his health. Once he went up to our biggest buyer to ask for orders to keep the mill going. He came away with nothing, and on his drive back to Sanford was pulled over by a highway patrolman for driving erratically. The patrolman didn't smell any alcohol and while talking with him about his driving, Daddy had trouble talking, choked up and his eyes watered. He said over and over that he didn't get any orders. The patrolman told Dad to get in his car and that he would follow him back into Sanford. It was where the patrolman lived and he was going home anyway. They arrived at the plant as I was coming out of the office, and I thought that Dad was under arrest or was in some trouble. He got out of his car, the patrolman out of his and I joined them with a puzzled, concerned look. The patrolman explained that Dad was upset over something about "orders" but was otherwise OK. The patrolman wasn't writing a ticket, or anything, just wanted to make sure Dad got home. I thanked the patrolman for his kindness and concern for my father. He saluted, patted Dad on the back and left.

Brenda and I had dated the day after Christmas 1967 and we were together thereafter almost every weekend. She also noticed that Dad seemed to be struggling under the load. If there was no hope of things getting better, she reasoned, we should cut our losses, close up the mill, and go on to something else.

She suggested that I go back to school. "You qualified for the GI Bill, you liked to know stuff," she said. She would help me make it work. The bright side was always clear to Brenda. Whereas I often struggled to find a way forward, I felt that she just knew. She had uncommonly clear vision and sense of direction.

And like my Mother, she always saw the best in people. We would meet some old lady and walking away I'd talk about the person's bad teeth and Brenda would talk about her smile.

I would daydream about us going to Central America and Brenda would say, "OK," and I'd say, "You want to go?" and she'd say, "Sure, I just said OK." Then I would say, "We'd really have an exciting time and a better opportunity to make a future for ourselves than here, you know?" "Yes, I bet so. We'll have so much fun."

Then somehow -- she wasn't leading me, I don't think -- I don't know how, but we would get back to the subject of UNC and I'd be talking about going back to school. She'd say, "We'll rent an apartment, and you can read to me and I'll help with your studies, I will. I'm so excited. Chapel Hill is very good stuff. It is the best place I know. It is the right answer to so many questions."

After one late night discussion with Mother, Dad also came to the conclusion that there was no hope to keep the mill going. On April 1, 1968, we shut down. We let the fire in the boiler die out for the first time in decades, laid off the workers, and locked the gate.

Admission officials at the University of North Carolina said I could return to Chapel Hill in the fall if I made up my grades during the summer sessions. I signed up for summer school and paid my tuition.

My future held great promise and it was because of this sincere, beautiful, intelligent lady I met in a small town drugstore. She was a wonderful listener, with a quick wit. And did I mention gorgeous? I got shivers when she would reach out for me when we were in a crowd, to touch my arm or to hook a finger in my pants pocket as if she didn't want to lose me.

Sometimes we spent the evening talking. We could talk for hours. She kept asking questions. I'd say sometimes that she was playing with me, that no one could be that interested in someone else. And she'd say, yea, I was on to her tricks, she handled all her guys this way. But, really, if I didn't want to talk anymore that was OK, she just felt happy being with me.

All our initial contacts couldn't possibly have been so swooning, that wouldn't have been natural, but that's the way it seemed.

Once Friday night she had driven down to Sanford and had fixed dinner for the two of us in my small apartment. We ate on the floor in the living room, our plates on a coffee table.

She asked what was important to me and I pointed at her.

"OK, before me, what was important?"

"Well my Dad told me to make something of myself, and although I tried not to pay any attention, I do. It's my guilt thing. But other than that, I don't know. I'm not one of your big planners. I sorta do life on impulse. Like I liked you a lot that first time we met. Something from the gut. Like I loved my car since the moment I set eyes on it in farmer's field in South Carolina. I love that car now to the core of my being... but you're getting there."

"Are you comparing me to your car? Really?" She was smiling as she looked down to butter a biscuit.

"No, I'm just stupid. Saying jerk things without thinking... but I do like my car a lot. You, maybe I love. My car doesn't serve me a cold beer when I come in. I've tried to train it. I've said, Car, go get me a beer and it just sits there. And it doesn't laugh like you. You are easy to like, you know."

"Because I bring you cold beer? Well don't get so used to it, big pants. I'm auditioning to be your girlfriend here. But I give you fair warning. When I think I got 'ya, thing's get different, you'll get your own beer. You goin' be toast."

"What's important to you?"

"You, now. My family. The idea of a good marriage is important to me. Sharing, supporting. Finding a good pace. .. Not big stuff. Personal happiness. Family."

There was a pause as if there was something else she wanted to say, but then she asked where did I come from? Really....what made me? I told her about my Aunt Wilma telling me for as long as I could remember that I was special and about the looks Mom and I had shared my whole life, and how I believed her prayers had kept me safe.

I asked her why she never went to college. She was the smartest lady I had ever met, and just high school? Twisting her mouth to the side and looking at my empty plate, she asked, "Finished?"

"Yep, I sorry, maybe, like I was saying I'm not always ..."

Brenda was carrying the dishes to the sink and she was talking loud enough for me to hear, but she did not turn and make eye contact.

"Dad works at Fort Bragg. In maintenance. Our house. He built the house. Still... he's still working on it. He had a rough childhood ... raised in an orphanage ... never had anything ... well neither did Mom, really, but she had a lot of love. Dad never did. As a family we are close ..."

She was standing at the sink, washing the dishes off.

"I've got BJ my younger sister and Larry Ray, my younger brother. Dad's always paid cash for everything he's owned. There wasn't money for us to go to college. And he wouldn't borrow. He's never been in debt any time his whole life. Plus my family ... what we want ... what's important to us ..."

I had gotten up and was standing behind her.

"What's important is family. I mean I like to laugh. No, now stop. You ask. Stop it, now. Listen. I like friends... don't kiss me on the neck, now. Listen... I like travel, and friends, did I mention friends, and family... and family... and....ooohhhhh."

Other times we would talk about politics, entertainment, music – we always tended to agree on things. But she'd always say, tell me more about you. And I'd tell her about Daddy and his life growing up. About the way he put me to work at the plant. About the way he let me wander unlike other fathers I knew. About Cottonpicker and Pete. And boyhood friends growing up, Henry Turner and Bob Somers. Their influence. And unlike Betsy I told her about my deep fears in Vietnam – the tunnel to hell and that morgue at Bien Hoa. About leading the carrying party with the wounded soldier through that spent battlefield. How I had suffered over the loss of Patrick and McCoy and Castro and Ayers and that crazy cav NCO. But how -- despite that wrenching hurt -- I had liked the danger and adventure. How seeing Mom when I came back was the most wonderful thing that had ever happened to me. I also told Brenda about how lonely and lost I felt before meeting her. How she gave me hope. How she made me feel blessed. And she would reach out and run her fingers over my mouth. And smile.

"My man," she would say.

Brenda really liked to laugh. Sometimes when things struck her funny, she would laugh this deep, throaty laugh. Almost a man's laugh. She told me once that I was a keeper because I was funny. She wasn't looking for money or looks. She wanted my humor. "Don't lose it," she said. "Bring it every time you come."

"Yea, I like to laugh too. Tell me something funny..."

"Well," she said, "You've met Myrtle, she's one of the girls who lives in our house in Raleigh. She's always been anxious about finding a husband. A handsome, quiet, considerate man who worked in her office was her first choice, although he gave no signs that he was aware Myrtle existed outside work.

"Until one day out of the blue he asked her out to a movie and Myrtle's world was suddenly never so bright or so challenged. She wanted to knock this country boy off his feet. This plan called for buying a state of the art wig.

"The night of the date we helped Myrtle with her shoes and the dress and finally the new wig. To make it fit right we rolled her hair into dozens of flat little curls and bobby pinned them down. Though scary the way she looked before putting on the wig, with it on, Myrtle looked like a North Carolina million. We just 'euwed and awed.'

"The guy arrived and after a polite greeting he escorted Myrtle out to his car. It had begun to rain, you know, and – we were looking out the window of my bedroom - the man held an umbrella over her head and then reached around her when they got to the car to open the door and still protecting her from the rain with umbrella, stood considerately by as she got in.

"They left.

"Thirty minutes Myrtle came bursting back in the house. She was a mess.

"It had been a dreadful half hour, she said. They arrived at the movie theater, it was still raining, and the man got out of the car and went around with his umbrella to open the door for Myrtle. As she was getting out, the man hit the button on the shaft and as the umbrella sprung open one spoke caught Myrtle's wig and flung it off her head into a nearby puddle.

"It happened so quickly that Myrtle froze trying to understand what was happening, why her head suddenly felt so breezy. The man, so quiet and considerate, was suddenly nervous and he momentarily froze too, the rain now beating down on them both.

"Their eyes fixed on the wig in the middle of the puddle, looking very much like road kill, and they couldn't think of anything to do, until finally the man walked over, reached down and picked it up gently with two fingers, water dripping off it and he looked back at Myrtle, her make up running, her hair tightly bobby pinned to her head. He walked back with the wet wig and, because Myrtle was still in shock and could not speak, he tried to put the wet wig back on her head, getting her new dress wet and muddy.

"And she started to cry.

"That's my story. That's what makes me laugh."

The Vietnam War Its Ownself

****

My high school friend Kenny Reid was working for a petroleum company and visited Sanford occasionally. I told him I was thinking about proposing to Brenda. He thought that I was a victim of circumstances. Here the New York trip hadn't gone well, and I was tired from the drive, the plant wasn't doing well, then this country girl appeared on a dreary Christmas Eve, of all times, and relative to my mood, she was an upper. But you cannot make a decision like marriage on first impression, he reasoned. Give it time, he said, and you'll see this thing is all a mirage.

But as we got to know each other better, I loved this girl more. I was impulsive, Brenda was methodical. I had a rambling curiosity, she was stable. I could be abrasive. She had no rough edges. I lived a lot for the moment. She planned. I was a talker, she was a listener. I was a sprinter, she was a marathon runner. I enjoyed everything about being with her.

I took her to Southern Pines and introduced her to Mom and Dad. This was not usual, me taking a lady friend to meet them. A few years earlier, during the hellion days of my freshman year at Carolina, I had dated this married woman off and on and she had insisted once that she take me back to Chapel Hill. So she arrived and stayed in the car in front of the house as I lugged my suitcase out of my parents' house and threw it in the back seat. Mom and Dad strained to see who this person was but she was wearing big sunglasses and didn't turn her head toward them or offer a smile or a wave.

But now Brenda. It was that combination of her country innocence and poise that got them. And her attention to me. That sincere goodness in her manner.

As we were leaving the third time I brought her home, I noticed in saying good-bye, that Mom gave Brenda that I-love-you look I knew so well. That had sustained me all these many years. It wasn't a long sappy look. Just a brilliant flash. I love you, Mom said clearly with her eyes and that smile. And that pretty much sealed the

deal with me. Mom approved. She was passing me on to another woman. Everything was very right. I had never been as happy.

Mom went with me to pick out an engagement ring.

For Valentine's day 1968, Brenda and I had reservations at a Durham steak house. I had the ring in a box in my coat pocket.

When I got to her house in Raleigh, we started talking in the living room about our week. At a pause in the conversation I asked her to marry me. This was supposed to occur later at the restaurant, but there I was, hearing myself ask her to be my wife. My hand was shaking as I brought out the ring.

"Oh my God in heaven," she said. "You know what you are saying? You thought this out."

And I was lost for words. I was so very happy. Don't know why my eyes watered like they did. All I could think to say was, "Yep."

"Oh, my. MY, MY, MY ..." and, her hands shaking a little, she tried on the ring and then she kissed me and kissed me and kissed my neck and my forehead and my head and my lips.

Then she leaped up and ran into the other rooms where her roommates were. Brenda began screaming, "LOOK. LOOK. LOOK. Jim asked me to marry him. Just you LOOK AT THIS ... RING!!! Jim, oh Jim ..."

And she came running back into the living room and jumped into my lap to tell me that I had made her the happiest woman in the world. Then she got pseudo-serious and said that first I was going to have to ask her father if it was OK. It was the southern thing to do, you know, she said.

So rather than go to a restaurant that night, instead we drove back to her home in Sanford, North Carolina.

It was fairly early when we got there, but her parents were already in bed. Brenda went into their bedroom and told her Dad that I was in kitchen and wanted to talk with him a minute. She stayed with her mother, while Mr. Denton came out, and sat at the kitchen table listening without expression as I said that Brenda and I wanted to get married and I was asking him for her hand in marriage. In that particular way about him, he looked off in the distance and said, "Well if it is what she wants, it's OK with me and her mother ..." or something like that. I know he said that as long as it was something his daughter wanted then he'd certainly go along.

I sort of knew Brenda was going to be happy with the offer, and Mr. Denton would go along with it. But like everyone who's just had the woman he loves accept his proposal of marriage, I felt pretty damn good.

The next morning first thing I called Mom from my apartment in Sanford and told her that Brenda had accepted and that ring was actually a pretty good fit. She was wearing it and the last I saw of her she seemed OK with the deal. Didn't have to threaten her or anything.... I could feel Mom smile through the telephone wire.

The Vietnam War Its Ownself

It rained that day and there were problems at the plant and I got back to my apartment after dark. I was fixing a sandwich for supper in the little kitchenette when the front door bell rung.

It was Brenda standing in the rain outside... crying.

****

I pulled her inside and hugged her, completed confused by all this – it was the end of the work week, but I knew that Brenda was working the next morning in Raleigh. What was she doing here at my place, crying the night after she had accepted my proposal of marriage?

She cried and cried – her body shaking with sobs – and I moved her to the couch where she cried some more. Finally she stopped shaking from sobbing and though still crying she looked up in my eyes, her hair a mess from the rain, and her make up running from the crying, and she said, "I can't marry you."

And I almost died.

"I've lied to you," she said. "And we can't get married."

I couldn't think of anything to say... I was numb. "Lied?" Can't marry me? What!

She said... in a rush of words... that the whole meeting and dating and then the friendship and the love that developed... had happened so fast, it was so wonderful, just so perfect in her mind, but there was something she never told me that would take away from this most wonderful time for her and she realized last night after the proposal, the drive to Sanford to see her parents and then back to Raleigh and our finally long kiss that night... after all that, her guilt building... she realized in bed that she couldn't - for sure – go through with the marriage. She never told anyone at work today about the proposal, and the ring.

She tried to say more and couldn't ...

"I love you," I said, "and there is nothing you can say that will change that, nothing that you could possibly have done that will

ever matter.... I promise you, nothing could change my commitment to you."

She said when her mother was pregnant with her, she took some drugs, maybe the doctor had prescribed, maybe not, or maybe there was something else, no one knows for sure, and she said she has seen doctors since she was a kid. Her ovaries never developed. She cannot have children. There's nothing there in her to make babies.

She's infertile... she never told me, she said. That we'd never have kids. She deceived me...

I didn't pause. Never hesitated. I said, "I don't care. I love you. And I want you for my own forever... I promised I don't care about this other thing. I want you the way you are."

And she looked at me wanting so badly to believe what I said, you could see the great hope I was telling the truth in her eyes, and I said again that I loved her and I desperately wanted her to marry me....

And then she was shaking when she hugged me, and then she started babbling about how she was goin' make me the best wife there ever was, ever, ever. And she was kissing my ears, and my nose and my mouth and my neck and the top my head...

"Oh," she said, tears streaming down her cheeks, "Oh.... Oh.... Oh."

****

Brenda and her roommates would often go as a group to one of several clubs in the area that played music to the beat of the Myrtle Beach shag, a Carolina jitterbug that had gained popularity at the beach. As couples held hands, they would do a lot of shuffling of their feet -- while keeping the upper body still -- and do coordinated turns. The woman would usually swing her free hand at her side with the rhythm of the music. The guy would do the same thing with his hand although occasionally – if he was cool – he'd be snapping his fingers.

I think it was that look that I objected to, that snapping of the fingers, trying to act cool on the dance floor. I had worked at Myrtle Beach as a kid and had danced the shag for hours at the Beach Club near Ocean Drive Beach and had danced the shag for hours. Now, older, that dancing seemed affected, put on. Kid's stuff, and here I was a war vet. Snapping my fingers while my lady did a skirt-twilling turn behind me, was for others. Not me. Not anymore.

But Brenda didn't know this.

She knew about my Myrtle Beach days. She was excited to invite me out with her house mates for a night at the club. I agreed to go, but Brenda noted later I had not shown a lot of enthusiasm for the outing, and had not in fact actually said I would dance. I had just said I would go to the club.

The Vietnam War Its Ownself

So we got there – maybe six, seven couples. Got a table, and the band started up with "Under the Boardwalk" and Brenda said, "Oh my Gosh. Come on... Let's go." And I said no, let's sit here for dance or two and just watch the others. And Brenda, of course, said, "OK."

So we sat there and I noticed that several of the guys were swinging their free hand and snapping their fingers and I thought, "that ain't me."

And the next song was "Sixty Minute Man" and all of Brenda's buddies were still on the dance floor and Brenda said, "Oh, Jim, that's my favorite, we have to get out and dance. We have to."

And I said, "Please, no. Let's just sit here and watch for another song or two."

And Brenda said, "OK."

And then the next song was "Carolina Girl" and Brenda's buddies were still on the dance floor, waving to her. Brenda turned to me, raised her eyebrows, and with a pained smile, said, "Oh, Jim, now, please. Please. For me"

So we got up from the table and went out on the dance floor. Brenda was so excited. She smiled broadly at her buddies as she grabbed my hand and started to shuffle her feet. And I started to shuffle and darn if my feet didn't remember the steps and I was matching Brenda's feet shuffle for shuffle and then I pulled her to me for her to pass to my backside - she expecting me to turn - and I did and there we were now shuffling in a different direction and Brenda was smiling at me, when I slipped and fell. Just my feet went out from under me and I was on my belly on the dance floor. Brenda was immediately at my side, kneeling to see that I wasn't injured, and then helping me to my feet. Not concerned that most everyone had turned to look at us, but worried that I might have hurt myself. I apologized and then we started dancing again, as did others, and I pulled Brenda to me for her to pass, in the way this dance is done, and as I was turning to face her my legs got tangled up and I fell again. This time with a loud slam to the floor. Everyone all around turned, stopped and looked as Brenda knelt down beside me, again, to see if I was hurt. And I wasn't, although as it turned out I had a dirt spot on my cheek. As she helped me to my feet, she kept looking at my face. And I tried not to smile, but I think, ever so slightly the ends of my lips were turning up. But we started to dance again, and the others all around started back dancing. But Brenda was more wary now, and her head was cocked a little to the side and she watched me as we shuffled the shag. And I could not get my smile off my face. I tried and tried, but I kept smiling and then I slipped and fell again. And Brenda left me on the dance floor as she turned and walked back to our table.

When I eventually joined her, she did not believe me when I that I was that clumsy... but she also did not ask me to dance again that night.

****

My car, that beautiful, white, faithful 1957 Mercedes Benz 190SL, seemed to sense the rapid changes in my life. It certainly knew that it wasn't squiring around the ladies anymore. It wasn't out running the roads at all hours of the night nor was it the extension of my personality that it once had been. One Friday night on the way to see Brenda in Raleigh, it overheated. I was late and anxious to get back on the road. When I filled the radiator with cold water, I heard the motor block crack and the sound of steaming water running to the ground below the engine. My car died like a tiger, hissing and blowing as though it was angry because I was more concerned about something or someone else.

It was probably best. A convertible sports car was not right for a struggling young married couple. Plus, it held too many memories of a different time. I had often felt a little guilty about this wonderful moral woman I was going to marry, slipping into the passenger seat of my little car where so many painted ladies of lesser virtue had once ridden.

I sold it to a collector for $500, and watched sadly as a wrecker pulled it away. That car had soul and personality. Men are seldom so well served by their machines.

Cool Springs Baptist Church was filled to capacity for the wedding. Dad was my best man. Brenda's oldest sister, Betty Jo, was maid of honor.

We honeymooned at Hilton Head, South Carolina, for five days. On the way back to North Carolina we stopped off at Myrtle Beach. Even though it was early June, the young man sitting at my old stand was tanned and altogether too healthy looking. Too cocky.

I walked up with my new bride of less than a week and introduced myself as the guard who sat in that seat for three summers.

"I'm Jim Parker. You've probably heard of me?"

"No," he said, "can't say as I have."

****

With part of the money we received from Mom and Dad as a wedding present, we bought a trailer and had it moved to a trailer park south of the Chapel Hill campus. It was my idea, and Brenda said having our own place was a good way to start. We chose colors and accessories, the way young people in love enjoy doing that kind of thing.

Brenda had been working for the state of North Carolina in Raleigh. Her boss there was able to arrange a job in the Education Department at UNC and Brenda began work as I started the first session of summer school. We drove to the campus together every morning. Down the road in the other direction from campus was a large chicken farm, and trucks loaded with crates of chickens came past our trailer park every night to catch the interstate near Chapel Hill. Occasionally, some chickens got out of broken crates and fell to the road. We saw bloody chicken carcasses along the road every day as we drove to school.

One morning Brenda remarked about how gory the scene was, like driving through Gettysburg the day after the battle. I said the real problem was with the chickens that got away and then, in my most sincere voice proceeded to tell her the story of a chicken I called "Redleg." It was a warm, beautiful morning, a good time riding along to tell a story.

"Those on the side of the road are dead and gone," I said, "but some of the chickens survive the jump. There's a herd of the wild chickens now, west of the road, deep in Chatham County. Grow to be three and a half, four feet tall. Leader of the pack is called Redleg, must weigh thirty-five, forty-five pounds. Three times as big as the biggest turkey there ever was. He and some of the chickens in his pack killed a baby down near Pittsboro a couple of weeks ago. Pecked that little baby to death. Wild chickens of Chatham County."

Brenda was looking out the window at the carcasses as we passed. She had stopped breathing and had a frightful look on her face.

It wasn't nice to exploit the trust of a loved one, but I smiled to myself. Like falling when I'm supposed to be dancing and Pete and the insurance years before -- sometimes, I am not a nice person.

Brenda let me have my jokes and, for the most part, allowed space for me to be my own man. She was never demanding... she was always complimenting, always proud of things I did. But she was her own woman. She was no push over. She had intelligent ideas, always gave good advice. Was grounded. Had no highs and low. Monday's Brenda was also Saturday's Brenda. She was always good company. Someone once asked her about her job and she said, "My main job's my man over there."

I pulled in $125 a month under the GI Bill, and Brenda made little more than $100 a week as a secretary at UNC. At the end of the first month, we figured how much we needed to pay for tuition and books and how much to put aside for gas, food, mortgage for the trailer, and a Christmas fund. We had something like $13.50 for the rest of the month. Brenda said that would be enough and it was. We met others on the GI Bill and had BYOS, bring your own steak, parties although it sometimes turned out to be chicken.

"Road kill!" we all yelled.

Classes, mostly political science, were exhilarating, challenging, interesting. I enjoyed going to the library and doing extra reading. I made all A's during the summer. It would have been difficult to go to Brenda, who was working to send me through school, and explain anything less than good grades. She wanted her money's worth.

We were getting gas in the car one day on our way home. Brenda saw a box filled with small puppies at the side of the service station. The lady behind the cash register said we could have one, they were free. Some were furry, some had short hair; some were larger than others. The lady said it was the damnedest litter she had ever seen, looked like there were three or four different daddies. Brenda picked out one of the small furry males and we headed home to the trailer. Getting a little puppy was right for our situation.

I had been talking about former President Harry Truman's famous 1951 confrontation with Gen. Douglas MacArthur over the Korean War when we pulled into the service station. We decided to name the pup "Harry."

He peed on the floor for a few days before getting the message that even a small puppy was expected to do his business in the woods, where the Wild Chickens of Chatham County lived.

While I studied at night Brenda and Harry played on the floor and on the bed and in the backyard. The dog slept on the foot of the bed at night. At first light he woke Brenda, and she would take him to the sliding glass door in back and let him out. She left the door ajar for him. She returned to bed for another thirty minutes or so of sleep.

One morning, Harry returned with a farm dog friend that had been rolling in cow manure. The smell prompted Brenda to wake up. Within three inches from her pillow as she opened her eyes, was a huge, black, smelly dog looking at her. She screamed and, using her elbows, the back of her heels, and her butt muscles, shot toward the ceiling and landed on the other side of me.

What was happening? My wife was screaming, and at least two animals were spinning in place, their feet trying to make traction on the linoleum floor. A hell'va racket.

For a second I was sure that ol' Redleg and his Chatham County wild chickens had gotten in and were coming after us.

****

On my way to class one morning, I was walking past the administrative buildings where the resident war protesters usually congregated. A pimple-faced youngster was dragging the American flag behind him at the rear of a demonstration.

I had stood, bemused, on the edge of campus demonstrations before as protesting students marched around in tight circles chanted such things as "Hell, no, I won't go," and "Ho, Ho, Ho Chi Minh." Simply street theater, I thought. I considered the U.S. government policies in Vietnam well founded – although they obviously weren't popular -- but our government had served us well over the years, and we went to South Vietnam to stop that country from being overrun by its neighbor to the north. A noble endeavor, and I felt no regret for my part in it. I was powerfully proud, in fact. Plus it was my war, those baskets in the back of my mind that held the memories of friends who had died in that far-off place, made it personal.

Why do these youngsters take such issue with my war, I wondered? Probably because it was all the rage across the country. It was very hip in the summer of 1968 to be anti-war. As a popular song of the times proclaimed, this was the Dawning of the Age of Aquarius and moral outrage over pre-Aquarius traditions was acceptable. Alternate lifestyles were encourage. Plus these youngsters were not invested in our society... someone else paid their tuition and their gas home. What part of this freedom to demonstrate had they earned?

As I was getting my infantry commission in the Army I had taken a vow to uphold the dignity of our country and I had been faithful to that promise. I understood fidelity. I had sweat equity in upholding my country's honor. So, only five or six years older than the Carolina protesters, I felt like I was made from different parts. Like an old codger, I would stand, watch and smile at these kids playing in the streets.

But, to my mind, that young man – the one dragging the American flag -- went beyond hip Age of Aquarius free love and expression. To me, the red of that flag represents the blood shed by me and my friends in Vietnam. That kid dragging it on the street denigrated our noble sacrifices. Ahead of him other students were cheering, "Ho Chi Minh." Without thinking, I yelled out, "Hey Shithead," and the boy turned in my direction. He had a smirk on his face.

I dropped my books and charged after him. He bolted away, collecting the flag as he went. I followed him, but he was too far ahead. I lost him in the crowd. Standing in the middle of the demonstration, with my fists balled up, wearing my old fatigue jacket, angry -- indistinguishable from those around me -- I shouted profanity, which added to the hue and cry of the crowd. People near me were supportive until they saw the look in my eyes and then they moved away. When I stopped yelling and walked back to my books, the crowd was quieter than before.

Later, in a speech class, I try to articulate my thoughts. I pointed out that the war is being fought on our side by people too stupid to get out of the Army and, once in the Army, too stupid to get out of the infantry. They smell bad and have rotten teeth, tattoos, bad grammar, and no future to speak of. They are on the point out there, doing their duty, and if we appreciate the traditions of our country, then those American soldiers deserve our respect. They are the most honorable people on our side of this war -- those young men in harm's way, in that foreign jungle. They answered their country's call, and in the years ahead they will take great pride in that. It will give them sustenance. I had been there, I know those men love their country, respect its laws and traditions in a way all Americans should. No one should drag around the American flag.

A glib senior from New York dissented, respectfully, presenting a sophistical argument against the war based on the premise that all people are well intending. He proposed that we give world peace a chance. It was a far more noble thing to do, he intoned, for our government to wage peace rather than war. He quoted Senator Church that the protestors were maybe more patriotic than the soldiers heading mindlessly over to war.

My final comment was that peace is a good idea - in concept - but the communist won't buy it until they get what they want. The North Vietnamese didn't want peace. They wanted South Vietnam. The only truly peaceful communists I had ever seen, in fact, were dead communists.

The Vietnam War Its Ownself

By a voice vote, the class decided that the peace position was stronger and I lost the argument.

****

The owner of the trailer park where Brenda and I lived gave me an old Morris Minor auto some college student, long departed, had abandoned. Only we didn't have any keys. Brenda's father came up and we installed a new key box, but the car still wouldn't start. We worked on it for days and the engine finally cranked, but it needed several replacement parts to make it road worthy. We found the best place to get parts for a Morris Minor was in England or some no-name mail order warehouse in Oakland, California. In addition to being hard to get, they were expensive. It was like the Polaroid camera recently put on the market. It was cheap but the film cost an arm and a leg. So I had a free car that needed expensive parts. Cute looking little car though.

Brenda suggested that we tie it to our Plymouth and drive around. We'd look like a two-car family.

One Friday on my way back home from Raleigh after finishing my after school job, I spotted a junked Morris Minor sitting on the edge of a pasture near an old farm house. I stopped along the road, climbed over the fence and went out to the car. Surprisingly, most of the engine parts were still intact and were not bad looking for equipment abandoned in a farmer's pasture.

I knocked on the farmer's door and asked the black man who answered if I could have the old Morris Minor junker out in his pasture. And he said, "Which one?"

"How many you got?" I asked.

"Well one, I reckon. Just want to be absolutely sure that's the one you're talkin' 'bout. Don't want to give away the family car. But you can have that there'un in the field there if you can get it out y'self. What d'ya want an old car like that fer?"

"For parts," I said. "I have a Morris Minor someone gave to me that needs parts and maybe the one out there has things I need. I want to take it back to my trailer and cannibalize it as I need to."

"OK, it's you'rn. But what do you mean about a cannibal?"

That evening Brenda's nine-year old sister, Kim, was dropped off for a weekend visit. On Saturday afternoon I borrowed some rope and the three of us went back to the farmer's pasture. I backed the Plymouth through a gate in the fence out as far as I could into the pasture. With one end of the rope tied to the rear bumper of our car I walked across the pasture and tied the other end to the front of the Morris Minor. And I drove the car out to the road, maybe twenty yards, untied the rope, backed the car out into the pasture again, retied the rope and drove back out to the road. I did this four times before I got the old car across the pasture.

Brenda and her sister were sitting on the front porch with the farmer and his family watching me.

I had noticed as I had pulled the old car out that the wheels were out of round, because it had been sitting so long.

Brenda and her sister, in the Plymouth, were going to pull me in the Morris Minor, which I had tied so it would be fifteen feet behind them. Before we started I asked Brenda to drive slow until it was clear how towable the old Morris Minor was.

So we pulled out and went by the farmer's house, with his whole family waving good-bye from their front porch, going five/six miles an hour. The yard dog trotted along beside us, barking as we gained speed from four to five to six miles per hour.

It was a lumpy ride for me, jarring, but safe. I was in control.

At five/six miles an hour we would never get home, however, so I leaned out the window and told Brenda to speed up to say ten miles an hour.

And she did.

The country road we were on went through some open fields. Straight and level. The rattle and shaking increased, but things were under control. And I yelled out for her to speed up more.

And she did.

I held onto the steering wheel with two hands as our speed got up to twenty/twenty-five miles an hour. It was actually a smoother speed than the ten-mile pace, which had seemed to maximize the bumps and lumps. Maybe the centrifugal force had pushed the rubber out of the tires, making them more round. If twenty/twenty five was better than ten, then thirty/thirty-five might even be better, so I waved Brenda to go on a little faster.

And she did, as the road left the open fields and snaked its way down into a little swampy valley, across a narrow bridge and up around a bend.

Brenda, possibly tired of looking in the rear view window, looked ahead as she navigated down to the narrow bridge. She also became involved in a conversation with her sister. And she seemed to forget about me.

The Morris Minor swung across the road as we picked up speed making the first turn going down into the swampy valley.

Inside, my eyes wide, I suddenly realized I had no control, and the rope was too long. I was like a water skier holding onto the line of a rapidly turning boat. And then the road turned the other way and the little light Morris Minor was whipped at the end of the rope back across the road, on to the shoulder. Rocks were flying. The two right wheels were off the road, the two on the left were on the road. I was bounced around inside with my head hitting the top, every three, four seconds. And then another turn and I was out in the road and there was a car coming and then another turn and thankfully I was pulled directly behind Brenda.

And she looked in her rearview mirror and I looked just fine, with my two hands on the wheel. I could see her looking and I started to take one hand off the wheel to wave for her to slow down but we were approaching another curve and by the time I got my hand up Brenda was back looking at the curve ahead and she was still talking with her sister. I was suddenly half on, half off the road and there was a road sign ahead and I was going to hit it square on and I tried to turn the wheels to get me back on the road away from the sign and the road curved again the other way and I was flung across the road, faster because I had turned the wheels. The narrow bridge was up ahead and I was heading for the abutment on the other side but as we straightened to go across the bumpy bridge I was pulled in behind Brenda. She looked in her rearview mirror to see how I was doing and I lifted one hand off the steering wheel and gave her the infantryman hand signal to stop. A raised fist. I had her attention. I could see she was looking back at me in the rearview mirror and she nodded.

How-some-ever, I was bouncing so much that she thought I was pumping my fist in the air like a trucker blowing his whistle, and she took it that I wanted to go faster. I had asked her to speed up twice before. That's why she nodded.

So as we came across the bridge, she accelerated, now going maybe forty/forty five miles an hour as we started winding our way up the other side.

I was off the road charging straight on to the back side of signs one second and the next out in the middle of the road, whipping back and forth.

Yelling for Brenda to slow down. Occasionally balling up my fist as the car swung behind the Plymouth on its way to one side or the other. And Brenda was gaily chatting with her sister.

James E. Parker, Jr.

At one point I had been jerked so fast from off the road to the middle of the road, that I thought I was going to break the rope in a catapulted move past the car.

Kim, bless her heart, happened to look behind at me as Brenda negotiated the last few turns out of the swamp and noticed that I had a frantic expression on my face as I was whipped from one side to the other. She suggested that Brenda might want to slow down and go back and see how I was doing.

She stopped soon thereafter and walked back to where I sat, shaken. She could not understand why I was so disheveled and mad.

"What is wrong with you?" she asked.

****

The 1968-1969 University of North Carolina basketball season began with the inter-squad Blue/White game on Thanksgiving. Bill Bunting, Rusty Clark, and Charlie Scott, among other notables, were playing for the Carolina Tar Heels. Every home game night, I met Brenda at her office and we walked downtown to Zoom-Zooms, a pizza/steak house. We ordered "The Special," a strip steak served on a sizzling platter with a mountain of fries and all the ice tea you could drink for under three dollars each.

There was a sense of revere and fun, like a tailgate party, game nights at Zoom Zoom. Newly married, UNC was special in the fall of 1968.

Brenda and I walked across campus and took our seats in the student section long before the junior varsity game began. We liked all the young Carolina freshman players, every single one, and we knew all their names. They were good at the game and usually beat the opposition, sometimes doubling the score, often reaching a hundred points. Carmichael Auditorium was small. No matter where we sat, we had good seats, close to the floor, in the middle of the noise and the action. We were enthusiastic about the freshman games, as lopsided as they often were, because of the players' enthusiasm and their promise.

The varsity games were more serious entertainment. ACC (Atlantic Coast Conference) basketball is high drama. At that time, Lefty Driesell was coaching for Maryland, Bones McKinney for Wake Forest, and Vic Bubbas for Duke. We believed all the lanky, tow-headed players on opponent's teams to be evil people with awkward moves. Our Carolina team -- Bunting and Scott and the others seemed so clean looking -- had a certain sweetness about them.

And they were very good, especially when they played in Carmichael.

In one game, for example, Bunting slapped the ball away from a Duke player, grabbed it in the same motion, and threw it over his head down court in front of Scott, who had broken toward the other end. Chased by Duke players amid the deafening roar in the auditorium, Scott came to the top of the key and stopped. Running hard on the fast break, he stopped dead. And jumped in the air to shoot the ball. Out in the open. He didn't want to go in for a lay-up, maybe, because he would be lost behind the backboard. He wanted it out there, in the middle of the noise, at the top of the key -- sure of himself. The ball arched perfectly and swished cleanly through the net, without hitting the rim. With his fingers sticking forward like chicken feet in his follow-through, his white Carolina uniform so perfect on his dark skin, his feet landing lightly back on the floor, the Duke players running by him, he was framed in our minds for all time as the perfect Carolina athlete, and we adored him. Charlie Scott. Gave up a sure lay-up and shot it from the top of the key. How audaciously grand. Jumping into the air and pumping our fists, we felt pure joy. "Nothing could be finer than to be at Carolina ..."

****

One day, while waiting for Brenda to get off work, I visited the student placement office and noticed a man leaning on the door to one of the interview rooms. I told him he looked like a prostitute, scanning the crowd for customers. He said he often felt that way; it was a competitive business. I asked who he represented. He said the CIA, the Central Intelligence Agency. You don't meet that many CIA people during your normal day in North Carolina and I told him so, guessing that his work must be interesting. He said it was a good job for some people, maybe me. We went into his office where I summarized my background. The Agency had openings, he said, for young men who had served in Vietnam and might consider working on contract, to go back to Indochina.

"For the Phoenix program?" I asked, alluding to the ongoing TV and newspaper stories about a CIA operation to assassinate Vietcong leaders. "Terminate with extreme prejudice," was a term I had heard the media associate with the work.

He smiled, shaking his head as if he had heard that comment before. He wasn't at liberty to discuss the particulars of the job, other than to say the work would be interesting, and challenging, especially to someone who knew something about soldiering. He cautioned that anyone who did drugs, had committed a felony, was a homosexual or had a disreputable character would not be hired. Scoring well on Agency tests was also necessary. Many applied, very, very few were taken. One in a million.

"Wanta take a shot?" he asked.

"You aren't like a prostitute at all, and don't go telling people I said that... but you do remind me of a carnival barker!" I smiled as I said that.

I took the twenty-page application he offered, filled out most of it that night and sent it in within the week. A notice arrived a few days later from a CIA administrative office in Washington advising me that my application had been received. An invitation soon followed to take a battery of tests at the Carolina testing center. I took the tests and then heard nothing from anyone. Months passed. Finally I received a telephone call from an Agency administrator who said that I was still being considered for contract employment in Indochina. Although I did not have a job offer yet, she said my application looked good.

The CIA.

The more I thought about it, the more it was exactly what I wanted to do. The CIA. I tried to remember everything the administrator had said on the phone, how she said it, the inflections in her voice, what she had really meant. She said my application looked good. She wouldn't have called and said that if there wasn't reason to believe I would be hired. A CIA paramilitary case officer. That's me, I told Brenda, that's what we're going to do.

James Bond movies were all the craze at the time and we saw them all. I knew the action was Hollywood and the dialogue invented, but intelligence work was interesting, no doubt. And James Bond was sort of paramilitary. He used guns. And in a certain light, from a certain vantage I could pass for Sean Connery. I knew guns. I could drive fast. I had said words like he said. I could learn to look sexy like Connery did to all the chicks in evening gowns. People around me saw the movies as entertainment. I saw me up there.

"That's not like the CIA, Jimmy," Brenda said after we saw *On Her Majesty's Secret Service.*

"Yea, little bit."

"No it's not, and if it is, you aren't taking the job. James Bond isn't married. You are." But she would smile. "But listen, Jimmy 'James Bond' Parker, I think you would make a pretty good spy. At our wedding, you looked good in that tux. And I know you can do the bedroom scenes. But it isn't like that, really."

The Vietnam War Its Ownself

I followed all the news on the CIA. Went to the library at Chapel Hill and got books. CIA! What did the guy say, "one in a million chance." Well I'm still in the running. I've bought my ticket. Put in my application. Maybe. Just maybe. She had said my application looks good. CIA. Damn ... "Parker, James Parker," I would say, mimicking the very British "Bond, James Bond" line.

****

I graduated from the University of North Carolina in January 1970 with a bachelor of arts in political science. Brenda and I decided to find temporary work as we waited out my CIA application.

Another Vietnam vet, Dennis Myers, graduated from UNC at the same time. He was accepted to UNC law school in the fall and was also looking for temporary work. Our first idea was "Myers and Associates, Private Investigators and Bodyguards." We advertised in several North Carolina newspapers.

Didn't work. No one responded to our ads. Mighty safe state, we assumed.

We heard that volunteers were needed at Duke Hospital for experiments. We did not particularly want to work for Duke, the evil empire, Carolina's arch enemy. But the pay was good, something like four dollars an hour. Dennis and I signed up. Our first session was a Pavlovian-based drill that tested concentration. A technician taped little wires to the ends of my fingers and told me to indicate the different colors that would be projected on the wall.

"OK," I said. "What are these little wires taped to my fingers?"

"Oh," said the technician, "if you make a mistake you get a little shock. Just a tiny, little prick."

This was not good. They knew I had gone to Carolina. We were in the basement of the Duke hospital, and a Duke person was strapping me to a chair -- big, no-nonsense straps -- and the chair had wires running to it and the Duke person was saying that I was liable to get a "tiny, little shock." I imagined cadavers upstairs who had been Carolina graduates had received some of those shocks.

It was the longest hour in my memory. I was shocked every minute for a total of four dollars.

That was enough for me. I quit, but Dennis continued. He obviously had a higher pain threshold. This was found most often, I told him, among primates. Sensitive people avoid situations where they regularly receive electrical shocks.

James E. Parker, Jr.

I managed to get a job at a garment mill in Sanford through the help of the assistant manager, Don Harding, an old friend. Sam, a tall, very likeable, very funny black man, was king in the washing/drying room where I was assigned. He had been working in the mill since before there were blueberries, he said, and before there was sin. Teg was another member of the washing/drying room gang. They said that no one with a high school education, as far as either of them knew, had ever worked in the room, much less a white boy who had just graduated from college. The job was simple. Trolleys delivered yarn dripping wet to the back room from the dying vats. We grabbed handfuls of yarn and loaded first the large washers and then the dryers with the clean yarn. The dried yarn went into clean trolleys that we pushed into the processing room.

Teg and Sam sang, laughed, and danced all day. Most of the others in the room, about eight people altogether, were quiet. Teg and Sam were often moved by the spirits and did little dance steps, especially when they knew the songs coming from the radio that sat on a high windowsill. It was a hot, wet, happy, and honest workplace.

The workers brought me documents occasionally that I read. When they asked, I made recommendations. They were mostly tax forms, alimony payment requests, voter registration forms and other legal-like documents. Once, Sam received a personal letter from a union representative in New Jersey, asking Sam to meet another representative who would visit the area to contact people willing to form a union of the mill workers. I told him that was risky business; it wouldn't make his life much happier either. It would cause a lot of confrontation. Something like that ought to be left to people who liked confrontation.

A garble of our conversation reached the front office. Later Don called me outside. He said word was circulating that I was talking with Sam about unionizing the mill. The mill manager was so angry he couldn't talk; he was just standing in his office and mumbling. Don said he was on the block for hiring some college fellow and putting him in the back to stir up union sentiments. I finally convinced him that he had bad information but the front office was never completely convinced. Everyone in the front office stopped talking and just stared at me whenever I walked in. The management of garment mills in the South had a paralyzing fear of unions. I finally just kept to the back room. Front-office people had different priorities from us in the back. They weren't nearly as much fun either.

In March I went back to Washington for more tests, including a polygraph examination. I met with a CIA representative whose office was interested in hiring me as a contractor. Meeting in

218

the lobby of CIA headquarters, we sat on a marble bench as he asked about my combat and college experiences. He had a friendly, congenial manner. It was not an interview as much as it was a conversation, mostly about me. He didn't take notes, didn't seem to have an agenda. We just chatted. Finally after a surprisingly fast forty-five minutes, he quit asking questions. There was a pause and he said that barring unforeseen difficulties, I would know whether I would be hired by early summer. He told me to hang in there, the Agency liked people with "hang," especially for this job.

On the drive back to Chapel Hill, my thoughts raced over a hundred scenarios of how my application would work out, and what I would be doing if I were hired. I thought about the James Bond movies but they didn't match up with the job as the man had described it. I remembered from my reading that the CIA was well represented in all provinces in South Vietnam, working with the South Vietnamese intelligence service, the police and the military, in a variety of jobs. The Agency was also running a "secret war" in Laos, but there was little reporting on how they were doing this. The rules of engagement in Laos did not allow for U.S. ground troops, so maybe the Agency put civilians like me in the mountains to work with the hill tribes. The Agency liked men with "hang," my CIA interviewer had said. I assumed that meant men who could "hang in" when things were tough out in the wilderness.

I also worried about the polygraph examination that I had taken. What a terrible, intrusive test. Was it exacting? Could it misread reactions? There were so many shades of meanings to things I had done in my life. The examiner had asked if I had ever been involved in a felony. Growing up I had been rowdy and done a number of things. Had any of those "things" been against the law? Well, maybe, yes, a little bit. Were they felonies? I didn't know. The obvious answer that they wanted was, "No, I haven't committed any felonies." So that's what I said, and then I worried about my answer during the rest of the test. Did the fact that I worried indicate on the polygraph machine that I was lying? Please let them know that I am a good citizen, a God-fearing, non-felonious patriot, and that I would make a good employee.

I thought that the interview had gone well. Also the polygraph operator hadn't said anything out of the ordinary about the test. He was very friendly, the whole time.

Please Mother, I prayed, let your Lord look after me here.

When I stopped worrying I started to feel good about my chances. So I told Myers and others that I was most probably going to work for the CIA. Sure you are, they all said. The CIA was not an everyday employer.

Then Brenda said that she didn't think I was supposed to tell people that I was going to work for the CIA if, in fact, I had planned to do so. So, I told people that I was going to work in the government, maybe the State Department. Sure you are, they said. I was not known for having a diplomatic style.

In mid-June, I received a telephone call. The CIA offered me a job starting 2 August 1970. I hung up and yelled, pumping my fist in the air. Then I started jumping around. I jumped up and down, up and down, up and down -- through the kitchen, down the hall, into the bedroom. Jumping and yelling, "AAAAAAAHHHHHH." In the bedroom, I calmed down, stood still for a minute to regain my composure and walked casually back into the kitchen to call Brenda.

We quit our jobs, sold the trailer, and packed our few remaining items in the back of the smallest rental trailer available. With Harry riding at Brenda's feet and the back seat of the car loaded with houseplants, we left North Carolina in late July. Shortly after arriving in Washington, we found a small, unfurnished two-bedroom suburban townhouse, rented some furniture and moved in. Two days later, wearing my best suit and a new pair of shoes, I reported to work for the Central Intelligence Agency in Langley, Virginia.

--SIXTEEN—
CIA Training and First Assignment

Uniformed CIA officers at the outer gate took my driver's license. They checked my name against a list of authorized visitors that day before admitting me into the fenced compound. I was met in the front lobby of the main building, processed for a badge and escorted inside. There was a stillness to the building, cathedral-like, holy and mysterious. People walked by looking intense and purposeful, their footfalls echoing down the wide, sterile halls. I was taken to meet my new boss, the chief of the Special Operations Group (SOG) of the Directorate of Operations in his small, cluttered office in the basement of the building. (The CIA SOG section should not be confused with the U.S. Army Special Operations Group that saw extensive action in Vietnam. Although the Army's group had some similar paramilitary missions, the two were different organizations.)

The chief welcomed me into the CIA's SOG, created to provide the Agency with an enhanced para-military capability. I would be in all CIA clandestine corps and special operations training for about a year. If I completed it successfully I would be sent somewhere in Indochina, depending on need, to do paramilitary chores. The Agency had been given these types of duties since its inception and people like me had been hired to service them. I was following a proud tradition. I was to focus on the training that lay ahead, learn Agency rules of conduct and tradecraft and keep my personal affairs in order.

I was given a cover legend to hide my CIA employment to outsiders and an alias to be used within the Agency during training: Jim "Pendy." I was not assigned to any class group; SOG training programs were structured individually. Get to know the training officer, the chief said, and help plot a course through the training cycle and get out to the field.

I was scheduled for all nonconventional warfare training the Agency offered plus a full curriculum of traditional clandestine service tradecraft instruction, a training regimen akin to what former OSS (Office of Strategic Services) officers received during World War II. This was in 1970. The Agency was created in 1947, twenty-three years before and many of my instructors had been influenced by OSS instructors. Their way of doing field ops was passed on to my generation.

Over the course of my first few weeks in the CIA I met several SOG officers hired, like myself, specifically for assignment to Indochina. All were athletic, intelligent and personable people; all had Vietnam combat experience.

One of my first paramilitary courses was a small-arms familiarization course. Given driving directions to a clandestine training facility out from Washington, I arrived late one Sunday afternoon for a week's indoctrination to pistols and machine guns from around the world.

Guards at the front gate checked the name on my driver's license against an access list, gave me a map of the installation and pointed out where the barracks were located. I arrived at the housing area, received military fatigues which had my training alias writ large – PENDY - already sewn military-like above my left shirt pocket. I changed into my military togs and joined other special operations new hires at the installation restaurant/bar. A short, smiling, balding Jerry F. emerged as the quickest and most clever among us. He was ex-Special Forces/Vietnam and naturally cunning, a lawyer by education.

Lounging outside smoking a cigarette that night after supper,

Jerry told me that he had grown up in a tough Catholic section of Philadelphia. When he was about ten his mother insisted he take special lessons at the local parish on how to "give confession." At the conclusion, the class lined up in a side aisle of the church to go into one of several booths for their first official church-sponsored confession of sins.

Jerry was well back in the line, waiting for the others to find the pitfalls in this exercise. He knew out on the streets kids didn't squeal if they knew what was good for 'em. Jerry wasn't so sure this wasn't a set up, plus it was very dark in those booths. Talking with extreme authority figures was not an inviting prospect for Jerry. He watched as each boy ahead of him entered a booth as it became vacated.

He could faintly hear the high-pitched whisper from the boy's side of the partitioned booth, "Forgive me, mumble, mumble, mumble." Next, on the priest's side of the booth, there would be a lower-pitched, inaudible response. Except in the booth of Father O'Riley, who was hard of hearing. After each boy whispered his opening, the voice from the priest's side could loudly be heard, "YOU DID WHAT? TO YOUR BROTHER, YOU SAID WHAT? WHAT?"

Jerry hoped that when he came to the head of the line that he would not have to go into the good Father O'Riley's booth. The priest responded loudly to every boy, "YOU DID WHAT? YOU SAID WHAT?"

When Jerry's time came as if by fate he was sent to Father O'Riley's booth.

Inside it was warm. And it was dark. He could hear Father O'Riley breathing through the opening of the partition that separated them. He began, "Forgive me father for I have sinned." He paused. The priest said in an even tone. "Yes. And?" Jerry continued to sit quietly, remembering his street wisdom, so he said, "Actually I haven't sinned."

Father O'Riley yelled, "YOU WHAT? WHAT?"

Everyone in the church could have heard. "YOU WHAT? DON'T WASTE MY TIME. LYING'S A SIN." Outside people walking by the church surely stopped when they heard the shouting.

This made an impression on him, Jerry said, and he didn't go into dark rooms with strange men ever again.

This guy was very funny, I thought, and I sought him out the next morning when we went to the pistol range.

The instructor, a former Special Forces NCO (noncommissioned officer), had dozens of foreign handguns spread out on a long table. He spent an hour going over each weapon, discussing its country of origin, its caliber, what it could and couldn't do, where they were being used around the world. We were then offered the opportunity to take any one of the weapons to the firing line and, on command, fire them at targets mounted in front of an earthen berm fifty feet away.

We had worked our way through several of the weapons, with Jerry at the firing position to my right. One trainee in our group said something dumb about keeping up our proficiency with foreign weapons. Jerry thought it was a waste-of-time question, asked in a stupid way. He suggested to me that the person needed a reality jolt. Needed to be humanized. With the morning sun up, many of us had taken off our fatigue tops and were in our t-shirts. Jerry suggested that we get the dumb questioner's shirt, take it down range, put it behind our targets and shoot it full of holes. We could then put the shirt back and no one would be the wiser, until the fellow went to get dressed for lunch.

So I walked over to the fellow's area. Distracted by firing a weapon, he didn't notice me picking up his shirt and walking back to my place on the firing line, next to Jerry. The next time we went down range to check our targets I took the shirt and placed it on the berm behind my target. When we got back on line I began to fire the foreign weapon I had at the time, through my target, into the shirt. Time and time again I fired. One magazine, two. Jerry had put his gun back and was beside me, watching, laughing and laughing and laughing. He fell to the ground and curled his knees up to his chest in the fetal position as he laughed. Tears were running down his cheeks, he was laughing so hard.

I started to have second thoughts about my new friend Jerry because this was funny, shooting the shirt and seeing it bounce around behind my target, but it wasn't that funny. You don't fall down laughing over this, do you?

The next time we were allowed to go down range and check our targets, I went down and found I had been shooting my own shirt. Even the PENDY nametag had bullet holes in it. Jerry had switched shirts on me. I had shot maybe fifteen holes in my own shirt.

I had to wear it to the mess hall for lunch. An instructor came up and told me I looked stupid. Jerry laughed and laughed.

****

The main intelligence operations (ops) course was scheduled

early in my training regiment. It was the core tradecraft training for CIA new hires into the clandestine service. It addressed the fundamentals of the spy business, how to recruit and handle agents, even in denied areas. We were told at the orientation that intelligence work took nerve and discipline. Professional tradecraft was complicated. Covert communication (covcom) was difficult. There were basic principles that applied during most case officer assignments, but every situation, every assignment, was different. In an imperfect world we had to try and make our work exacting and structured. Sources and methods of handling agents had to be protected. The intelligence we gathered had to be reported to our U.S. government customers. Agent reports were nothing until they was disseminated. Nothing happened in the field until it was reported. Getting the story was half the job. Getting it right and getting it reported with clarity and alacrity were of equal importance.

New to American intelligence, I had little to say initially. I was in awe of the program and the training. I took good notes. Studied late into the night. Worked hard to adapt to the Agency way of writing. Picked up the language of the business and the tradecraft.

Some intelligence officer new-hires (called Career Trainees or CTs) were aloof and pedantic, although my SOG officer friends helped make them aware that they existed in a workplace of people with varied personalities. Our efforts were not always welcomed and SOGers were referred to as "knuckle draggers," alluding to our possible close kinship with the gorilla family. Outgoing, extroverted personalities were the stock in trade for case officer trainees and repartee between our two different groups tended to be lively and caustic.

My mentor at the training facility was Dr. Carroll; his discipline outside Agency tradecraft was in English. We held daily conversations about my writing style. I tended to write in a conversational way. He looked for more nouns and verbs. Contractions and adjectives had their place, but they were not his friends. Often too flashy or familiar or too accessorizing.

And Dr. C did not like the passive voice. There were people in the Agency who, I found, did not like communists. There were people, I found, who did not like cold weather. Or collard greens. Dr. Ed Carroll did not like the passive voice and he graded everything I did.

Now one of the problems with this is that I had no idea whatsoever what the passive voice was. In the intelligence business, there's a lot of writing, and his great hate for this particular "voice" was somehow rooted in the way I wrote training reports... but I was never sure and no one I asked was particularly sure either.   Dr. Carroll gave me a clue once early on when he said "… using action verbs indicate a strong command of our language."

But then after that session when he made the telling "action verb" comment, he had some papers I had written out on his desk during a counseling session, and he was reading them, when suddenly he slowed his pace until he came almost to a stop, pronouncing each of my written words carefully. They sounded OK to me.

Finally he lowered his head. This very dignified older, college professor look alike. Then got up from his desk and walked over to a wall and banged his head on the wall and came back and sat at this desk, and said, "Mr. Pendy, is English your first language?"

****

It always makes you feel better to see someone having a tougher time than you are. I think there's a word for it. Whatever, during my ops course, that would be Larry R. Another SOGer. Larry had been a Marine officer in Vietnam. Before that he was a starting guard on the U of San Francisco basketball team. But he hated – absolutely got faint of heart -- over one-on-one instructor/role player exercises. Before going out for training meets, he would start to sweat and his shirt by the time he launched would often be soaked. His eyes wild.

My situation, as I said, seemed better by comparison, but this ops course was not easy. Dr. Ed Carroll was seriously tough. And I remember clearly that the Remington typewriters had no spell-check.

You ask anyone I grew up with, "Parker, a brainiac?"

They'll say, "I don't think so."

But you needed some of that to do this CIA ops training work. I didn't know if I had what it took to do this. CIA clandestine crops new hires in 1970 were alpha animals and pretty quick-of-mind. This was the major leagues, as it was. Training was in fact like spring try-outs in baseball. There was doubt in my mind if I had what it took to make the team.

But then I don't know, midway through the course Dr. C did in fact smile or least nodded at something I wrote. Then one sunny afternoon I had a one on one training session with a kick-ass instructor/role player. Part of his role was to come to this make-believe meeting as an agent who had not done what I asked him to do.

I listened to his prepared patter about why he had failed me, and I said to this instructor/role player, leaning in, motioning for him to lean in too, speaking slowly, almost in a whisper, "Listen, shit for brains, don't you fuck with me, I'm trying to do good here ..."

Maybe it was the moment, or the innocent southern twang in our little "time-out," or the conspiratorial tone to my voice, but he broke up laughing. He wiped the smile off his face, looked away, got serious, and turned to me to say something else and started laughing all over again.

And I knew, "I can do this..."

A hole didn't suddenly appear in the skies and no angels started playing harps and singing or anything like that. But it was a special moment, an epiphany ... an "Ah, HA," realization that yea, I can do CIA intelligence training work... this agent acquisition and handling thing is learnable/doable.

****

The tradecraft instructor staff was composed of experienced field case officers. Some had been assigned to the training facility to cool off, having been suspected or exposed doing Agency work abroad. Some were called back from overseas assignments because of threats to their lives. Some had been living under deep cover overseas and took a training assignment to be with their own and talk about their experiences.

We learned as much about the intelligence business in casual conversations with the staff as we did in the classroom. We learned that the business had its share of drudgery. All would remind us that at the end of the day we worked for a U.S. government bureaucracy. Plus operations did not always happen the way they were planned, in fact they rarely happened like they were planned.

Agents were capriciousness and could not be taken at their word. Always we had to be aware of counterspy efforts by foreign services. Our agents would often be from the underside of humanity, with questionable hygiene. We were going to have to put our personal feelings aside and work with them professionally, dispassionately. Our organization was staffed with some big personalities and we had to understand that within the boundaries of our mission statement, sometimes field ops were driven by personalities.

Clandestine service officers pull eighty hour weeks. They do their cover work during the day, using their evening hours and weekends to do espionage work. Two jobs. One paycheck. Time management was important. Get rid of clutter. Focus. Watch what you say. Listen hard. Write fast. Small things like developing good summaries for long cables separated first tour officers from experienced case officers. Develop a thick skin. Intelligence collection is a tough business. Expect surprises. Spies are a breed apart.

After training, the knuckle draggers would be off to do intelligence and paramilitary chores in the Indochina war. The traditionalists, the CTers, were going to the far reaches of the world to fight the U.S.-Soviet cold war. The Soviets, Cubans, North Koreans and East Germans had aggressive spy agencies and were very active especially in the third world. Often CIA operatives were the only U.S. resources in play. In 1970 thousands of nuclear warheads around the world were aimed at the United States and the CIA traditionalists in our training course were going to be sent out there to find the people who controlled those weapons.

We were usually up late into the night working on our training assignments and typing our reports on electric Remington typewriters. All reports were due a 0800 in the morning. There was not much down time.

But if you got it, spy training was enormously interesting. We all grew. For example, listening. Someone said early on in the training that you are not learning anything when you are talking, a point well taken when trying to start up training relationship with instructors playing foreign targets. We wanted to be chatty and engaging to the point the instructor/target would want to meet us again, but at the same time we had to be manipulative with the chit chat to elicit information on the person. We'd ask when he graduated college to give us a rough idea when he was born, and we always asked for a calling card so that we could get the right spelling of his name. Family information might tumble out of his mouth at any time, or something about his boss or his car or his hobby, and we had to listen and remember.

This focus on listening was important in agent handling training. As a rule we did not want to carry electronics with us out to agent training meetings, because they incriminated us if discovered. Same with notes. Plus if we went with a small tape recorder or with a note hiding briefing case, they had to be transliterated later and we were up to 1 and 2 most nights anyway. They just added time. Easier to remember what the training agent had to say. And with practice we could. By the end of our training we could meet with an instructor/agent, handle the entire meeting with maybe a half dozen words and numbers scratched on a piece of water soluble paper, and that was all we needed to go back to our Remington electrics and type out a five page report.

We all came away from the training better listeners, better writers. And we were grounded in the techniques of the business.

At the end, some of our classmates were not certified, and did not attend our last session, a mini informal graduation. A senior official came down from CIA headquarters to speak. His message was that it was a dangerous world out there and our job overseas was to maintain a watchful presence. We were expected to use the training we had received during this tradecraft course to go out there, in all that danger, and do our job. He said he would be reading our dispatches, and he wished us well.

On the way back to my room to pack for the ride home after the intel course, I saw all my underwear up in a tree by my housing building.

Now probably that was because of this: We wore military uniforms during our training and part of that get up was a black tie knotted at the collar and tucked into the shirt two buttons down. Sometimes around the classroom building I would get a pair of scissors and cut the tie of selected trainees because I liked them or I didn't, one or the other. I became known for this. No one threatened to beat me up, and in fact some of the spies-in-training liked it. I certainly did. After I came to realize that I could do this, I reverted to my obnoxious way, like cutting ties, and got particular pleasure when an instructor, interacting with one of my cut-tie classmates, who notice the short tie and then turn to look at me. Sometime I'd get a smile. Most often not, but I liked the attention.

My underwear up in the trees was done by committee, all previous cut-tie victims.

But how did they get my drawers all the way to the top of the tree?

As it turned out, it was a problem for local maintenance, because I left 'um.

I could imagine Dr. Carroll coming by that tree the next day or so, looking up and saying, "Pendy. Had to be Pendy."

****

Shortly after I graduated the tradecraft course, I went back to SOG and its rigorous escape and evasion (E&E) training, a welcome change that allowed me to get out in the sun.

E&E training was divided into three phases. During phase one, we were taken to one end of a valley in the Sonora desert of Arizona, broken down into teams of two and released. We were only given three canteens of water and had three days and two nights to make our way to the other end of the valley, avoiding paramilitary instructors who were on patrol in front of us twenty-four hours a day.

When we were released, my partner, Ches J., and I decided to sleep for the rest of the day and begin our trek at night. The weather was a dry, sweltering heat during the day and cold at night. When we started our trek across the valley floor we ran into snakes. Every ten steps it seemed. Rattlesnakes.

Worse than a Vietnam minefield, I told Ches.

We were undetected that first night. The next day we endured in holes on the side of a dry river gulch, though the midday sun was absolute torture. Our eyes hurt and our skin burned and we were thirsty.

We moved at night again, having to go far out of the way at one juncture to avoid an instructor. Resting by a road that ran through the valley, we watched three Mexicans stop nearby to pee. At first light the next morning, we arrived at the rally point, the second team to come in.

Ice-cold orange juice, milk, coffee, eggs and bacon were served by instructors turned cooks. Throughout the morning our hallow-eyed compatriots dragged in.

We slept like babies that night in a downtown Holiday Inn. The following day we boarded four wheel drive vehicles for a ride up into the mountains to begin the second phase: mountain survival, repelling and land navigation. Escape and evasion in the mountains caused different pain from what we experienced in the desert, but pain was pain. E&E training was not comfortable.

My good friend Jerry F. went through the mountain phase in a different cycle. At dusk one evening another trainee, Larry R., came in to his group campfire at dusk. Like all of the rest, he was exhausted after a long day of mountain climbing in severe weather to secure buried caches. He fell to his knees, leaning over the fire to warm his face. We watched quietly as the trainee bowed, with his face in the smoke, as if he was genuflecting to the fire gods. He was big, tall and lanky; he had in fact played basketball for a large western university. Finally he leaned back on his haunches and looked around. Everywhere he looked people began laughing. His face was black from the smoke.

He kept repeating, "What're you laughing at? What's so funny?"

Sitting around that fire was one of the most intense SOGers in the program. Born in Cuba and an immigrant to the United States after Fidel Castro came to power in 1957, Amado G. had been a soldier in the Bay of Pigs invasion force. He was captured by Castro forces and spent a year in a Cuban prison before being released in exchange for tractors. Returning to the United States, he joined the U.S. Army, served with distinction in Vietnam, and was subsequently hired as an SOGer. He was the intellect of our group. Even during the mountain phase of the training he pulled out a dog-eared book on Plato and read it during rest breaks. He was reading that book the night by the fire after the black-faced trainee wandered off to find shelter for the night. Jerry F., sitting nearby said, "Amado, you know you reading that book all the time has come to the attention of the instructors and Joe, the chief instructor, doesn't like it. He doesn't like you." Amado looked up into the fire and then slowly around at Jerry. He smirked, saying clearly by his look that he wasn't going to be fooled into getting angry at the instructors. He knew a set up when he heard one. So he went back to his book. For ten minutes he stared down at the book. But he didn't turn a page. Looking back toward Jerry, he said in his heavy Cuban accent, "So he doesn't like me to read Plato? I try to improve my mind, to make me a better person and a better Agency officer and he doesn't like this. On my free time. I do what I like."

During a training session the next day, Amado sat near the front staring up at Joe, the chief instructor. Finally he got up and started walking off into the woods. Joe said, "Hey, mac, where do you think you're going in the middle of my class?" Amado said, "You have been talking for three hours, three hours and I have to take a piss. A piss. I have to take a piss." Joe said, "Sit down. Shut up. I'll tell you when to piss and when not to piss." Amado glared at him but he finally sat down, right beside Jerry. "You know," he said with his accent, "you were right, he really doesn't like me."

My four-day mountain survival training was especially noteworthy due the beating our hands took. The rocks and ropes and fires and briars laid them open. "Do these look like the hands of government employees?" someone asked.

After we came down from the mountains, we boarded a commercial flight for Miami, heading toward the third phase of our training. The jungle phase. In the Everglades.

Ches and I were partners again. This phase of E&E training had two parts. The first was a two-day simulated exfiltration (exfil) through the swamps. When we reached our objective near the Tamiami Trail, we were to board canoes for the second part, a waterborne exfil down Everglades rivers into the Gulf of Mexico and out to an offshore island.

The Vietnam War Its Ownself

For two days, Ches and I were up to our chests in the swamp, holding our handguns and our packs over our head, trudging along, trying to be quiet, watching out for instructor-aggressors.

The bullets issued for our handguns had the projectiles extracted, leaving only the cardboard to hold in the powder. This cardboard, our instructors had promised us, was more than enough to kill a small dog. It would certainly kill any animals we might happen upon in the Everglades. Except for alligators. They didn't tell us what to do if we ran into alligators. Ches suggested that was part of the training.

Our guns were primarily for signaling. If we came upon something and absolutely had to shoot, we were told to aim carefully and use only one shot. In a real escape and evasion situation, when you were being hunted, one shot will not give away your location. The hunter, without any warning, has no reference to fix the location of a single shot. He wouldn't know if it came from the front or the rear. It wouldn't help if there were two hunters. But if you were being chased and fired two shots, you gave your position away. One shot the hunter would be alerted; the second shot, he would fix the direction.

So we knew one shot was all we had. Two shots and the instructors would be on our necks. Three shots meant that someone was hurt and the training was suspended until the instructors or other students could get to the area.

One shot. I knew this wading along in the swamp. Late the second day I was leading, wading along with the water up to my waists. I noticed some high ground off to the right. I turned toward it. Coming out of the water, it was down to our thighs when I saw a giant snake laying on a rock outcropping. Coiled. Pointed head. Poisonous. It made eye contact with me. Its dark little snake eyes seemed to be saying, you don't belong here. This is my place in this swamp. Get out of here.

Lifting my .45, I aimed it at the snake's head. I found it disconcerting that I covered half the distance to the snake when I extended my gun out. That snake could probably strike and get me before I could get my hands away.

But I aimed carefully right between its eyes. I only had one shot.

And I squeezed the trigger slowly until the gun fired.

And the snake did not move, no flipping and flopping around like I expected from a mortally wounded snake. It lay back a little more in its coil and hissed. That was about it. I looked into its eyes. It was pissed.

But I couldn't fire anymore. Maybe the snake knew this? It started to arch its back. Slightly. Time was of the essence.

So I fired again.

And again, and again and again and again.

That monster snake never flinched.

"OK, you win. We're gone."

Ches and I started running in the swamp, as fast as we could. Which was pretty fast.

The instructors never did find us.

Oh, they fixed the location of the shots and they were there in a matter of minutes. But we were in the next county. Snakes can do that to you.

Later that day, after we had stopped running, we came up on a railroad spur through the swamp. Built to harvest cypress around the turn of the last century, the railroad workers were given oranges to eat. Some seeds took root and orange trees grew. Ches and I got all the oranges we could carry. We hid off in the swamp and ate everyone. We talked about the training, which seemed to be going on without end, and what laid ahead in Indochina. It was a common topic, our anticipated field work. We tried to imagine what we would be doing, where we would be sent. Ches, looking like a renegade sitting out of the swamp on a cypress limb, said it didn't matter, as long as we had some oranges every once in a while. They did have oranges in Indochina, didn't they?

After arriving at the rally point near the Tamiami Trail, where the instructors had positioned air boats, we began classes on survival. A part Seminole Indian, our instructor "Speedy" said that if we were striking out into the wilderness and had to carry only one item, carry a knife. If we could take two items, take matches with the knife. If we could take three items, take a fishing line and hooks. Even in the woods, fishing line and hooks could be used to snare small game. Around water you could use them to fish, of course, and to catch ducks.

"Catch ducks?" someone asked.

"Yep," Speedy said. "You get your pond where you got your ducks and you get a log and you tie one end of your line to your log and you get a rock and you run your line from the log to the rock, leaving a little line free on the other side of the rock to tie your hook. Then you get corn from a field and you put it on your hook. You put the rock on the log, the hook with the corn on the rock and you push this balanced trap out into your pond were your ducks feed. And some duck will come along, swallow the corn, with the hook. When he pulls away, he'd pull the rock off the log, it will sink, pulling the duck under and he will drown, quietly. Later, you pull your log in and you've gotten yourself a duck."

I told Ches it wouldn't work. I didn't know why it wouldn't work but it wouldn't work. Too clever. Sounded like something someone from Newark, New Jersey, would dream up. Well, Ches said, I don't know about them Indochinese oranges, but I know they got ducks over there, so I'm paying attention.

We left later that day for the last phase, the canoe exfiltration down Everglade rivers.

And we met the mighty sand fly. The God Almighty, Florida Everglades Sand Fly!

We had recently beat the rattlesnakes and heat of the Arizona desert, repelled off the tops of high mountains, walked waist deep through snake-infested swamps. Small training challenges we beat handily.

But not the sand flies.

The Everglades sand flies were as small as a grain of dirt, crazy with lust to get up your nose and into your ears. In their element they were impossible to get away from. Even mosquito netting didn't work. Submerging yourself in water and breathing through a straw seemed to be our only option.

Unknown to us that afternoon as we slipped our canoes in the water, there were eight hundred zillion billion quadrillion sand flies waiting for us.

You couldn't see them if you were moving. They weren't there. But stop. For a second. And suddenly you were breathing in sand flies. They were down your shirt, in your eyes, up the crack of your butt, in your ears, in your food.

In the desert, in the mountains and in the first part of the jungle phase moving overland through the swamps, Ches and I rarely bumped into the other teams. We rarely heard them.

But the sand flies changed that.

Within just thirty or thirty-five hours of total emergence in sand fly hell, every one occasionally heard someone yell, off in the mangroves.

"Auggggggggggggggggggggggggggggg."

Quietly drifting along in canoes, scouting for instructors around a bend, moving slightly above sand fly speed. Over some saw grass to one side would come a scream of hope for release from the torture, "THESE GODDAMNED, WORTHLESS, FILTHY, INSECTS ARE DRIVING ME CRAZY. CRAZY. I CAN'T

BREATHE." Then quiet. Then off in another direction, "Oh God take me now, give me some peace, get me out of here. These flies, these insidious, insects are, are killing me. They are EVERYWHERE."

We finally reached the island and the ocean breeze kept the sand flies away. Oh, that was a wonderful day!

****

For reasons no one could make clear to me I had to take three months of French language. Only one other SOGer I knew had ever been scheduled for French. I told the training officer I did not want French. I thought if you spoke English loud enough in foreign countries everyone could understand you. But I had to take it.

The instructors were lovable little old French ladies who smothered me with their language. It was mostly tutorial training although it seemed like there were thousands of those little ladies around. Reminded me of the sand flies.

But I had no aptitude for languages. Had ears of stone. One little French language lady may say something like, "Now Jim, listen to me...

Vu bastee comino pleslet, nes pa?
That means in French, "Why is there air?"
But now listen when I say this:
Vu bastee comino pleslet, nes pa?
That means "The pope wears holey underwear.
Got it?
Vu bastee comino pleslet, nes pa?"
But not
Vu bastee comino pleslet, nes pa?
See? Now, Jim, in French ask me, why is there air?"
And I'd say, of course,
"Vu bastee comino pleslet, nes pa?
And the nice little French woman's eyes would get big, and she'd say almost in a whisper, "You know what you just said, 'Bears shit in the woods.'" Did you know that?
No, I didn't.

****

After a reports writing course, I rejoined other SOGers at another downstate facility for special training in interrogation, sabotage and explosives. I elected myself the bus driver, the de facto leader of the group. For lack of any other reason, I told them that I drove the bus because I spoke French and they didn't. Now springtime, we were in the woods most of the time so I drove with the doors open to enjoy the nice breeze. Once I came too close to some trees; the doors got banged up so that they couldn't be shut. I didn't mind that.

One Friday morning we went for training at a site some distance from the main facility. A few of the SOGers drove their cars so that they could leave directly for Washington, D.C., after class. The class for some reason was postponed until the early afternoon, so we had time to kill. I was driving the bus back to the cafeteria for lunch when we came upon a beach along a wide river. I asked if anyone would like to go swimming, skinny dippin'. Jerry F. and another man, a former SEAL, said OK. Stopping the bus along the river bank, the eight or ten people aboard got off. Some grumbled because they wanted to go on to the cafeteria. I was driving so I didn't care what they wanted -- they couldn't speak French. Jerry and I and the other guy took off our clothes and waded into the river. And we waded and waded and waded. We went the distance of two football fields out in that wide river and the water was only mid-calf. You never feel as naked as when you're out two football field lengths into a river and the water is just a little bit above your ankles.

We had just turned to look back at the beach as one of the most evil SOGers drove up, jumped out of his car, a batmobile-looking Corvette, ran out on the beach, picked up our clothes, ran back to his car and sped off.

High-stepping back into shore the three of us were yelling, "HEY, HEY, HEY, DON'T TAKE OUR CLOTHES, DON'T TAKE OUR CLOTHES, PLEASE, PLEASE DON'T TAKE OUR CLOTHES."

Fortunately I had the keys to the bus with me so the people we left on shore couldn't drive off without us. When I reached shore I ran to the bus and jumped behind the wheel and started chasing the guy with our clothes. There was a SOGer still on board the bus who kept saying, "Oh shit, oh shit." The door to the bus wouldn't close, of course. As we sped through the facility, we occasionally had to stop at intersections to let cars pass. At one intersection a lady in a station wagon stopped beside me, on my open door side. I didn't look in her direction so I do not know if she noticed whether the bus driver was naked or not.

Catching up with the clothes snatcher as he pulled into the parking lot of our residence hall, I tackled him before he got inside. He was laughing so hard he didn't put up much of a fight to keep me from my clothes. Sitting on the lawn I put on my fatigue pants and drove back to the beach.

Jerry F. and the other guy had dug out little holes in the river bottom and were sitting submerged just to the top of their butt cracks.

A gale wind blew through the training facility the next week, forcing suspension of training. We battened down the hatches at the residence hall and prepared to weather the storm there. When it hit, we went outside and played hurricane football. Rain was coming down in sheets and the wind was blowing so hard at times that you had to lean into it to stand up. This often made the forward pass difficult. The field was muddy. Deep into the game, the score was something like six thousand to four thousand five hundred; we had our own scoring rules tied loosely to the force of the hurricane. I went out for a pass to the side of the playing area, got lost in the storm, slipped and fell on a rock, cutting my right knee to the bone. Play did not stop, however. I began yelling over the noise of the storm. Some players found me and helped me to a medic inside the hall. I was stitched up and waiting at the "hurricane central" bar when the game ended. "Man has no hang," some compatriots said to me as they walked in from the gale force outside and bellied up to the bar. They were so covered with mud that they all looked like creatures from the dark lagoon. "How's this individual going to work out in the field if he can't operate in a little bit of rain?" someone asked. "Think he's heading for indoor work," someone else suggested.

After the storm passed training resumed. In one class the instructor gave a historical briefing on sabotage techniques from the Second World War. He said a commercially available product had been used behind enemy lines to contaminate drinking water. One small container could contaminate a water reservoir. He held up a milk cartoon size container of the chemical, telling us this could make all the drinking water for a large size city unpotable, poisonous even. He passed the carton out to the class. A trainee, the one who had put his face in the fire during the mountain phase of E&E, was looking at the container with the same amazement I felt. Maybe we were thinking the same thoughts. He pressed the top of the container and it opened so he looked inside. Sitting several rows behind him, I was curious about what the stuff looked like and watched as the trainee reached in and got a little bit, a tiny little bit on the tip of his finger. He put the tiny little bit to his mouth.

And he exploded out of his seat, yelling, sticking out his tongue and grabbing his throat. His eyes wide, he stumbled from the bleachers and made his way to a water fountain behind us while he continued to moan and gargle and yell.

"Our friend just helped me make the point about the potency of this material," the instructor said.

But for my back-of-the-class seating assignment, I thought, but for the grace of Mother's God, I would have too.

****

Brenda also got a job working with the Agency. Since most of my training was out away from Washington, I was generally home only on weekends. She developed a friendship with a neighbor whose husband worked in New York City. The neighbor, who I referred to as Silly Susan because she didn't have an ounce of common sense, moved in with Brenda during the week when I was away. I would leave for training on Sunday afternoon or early Monday morning and Silly Susan would come in from New York on the shuttle early Monday morning and go directly to work. She would come in each night through the week, and on Friday she would leave work and go directly to the terminal for her flight to New York. I would arrive home Friday evenings. We did this for months yet I saw Silly Susan no more than a half dozen times.

Actually there was a changing of the guard every time I left for training. Brenda would make our townhouse "girly" with flowers and scented sprays. I on the other hand would be getting into Fred Brugger's car. Another SOGer, he and I commuted to most of our training over the course of a year in Fred's big old car. We spent hours together. He was from Ohio of German stock and grew up on a farm. Said one of the most poignant days in his life came when his dog starting chasing the farm chickens and killing them. Father told him that you couldn't change a chicken killing dog, had to kill him. Fred pleaded, not his dog. And his father didn't push the point then, but then the dog killed another of the chickens and his father insisted Fred take his dog out to the edge of the woods, dig a hole and shoot him. Only he couldn't. He put the dog in the hole he dug, raised the gun. Couldn't pull the trigger. Went back to the house, the dog at his heels. His father didn't understand so he took the dog, went out to the edge of the woods and soon there was a shot and there was no more dog. Fred never liked his father that much thereafter.

Fred was great company. I greatly enjoyed our commutes, would often start singing. "Nothing could be finer ... than to be in Carolina..." We often stopped for breakfast if we left for training early on Mondays. I taught Fred to enjoy grits. One of my greatest accomplishments.

James E. Parker, Jr.

****

Brenda and I bought our furniture for the townhouse at garage sales. At first, our weekend garage sale hunting was casual. As time went on, we developed a routine. We came to know the higher-class neighborhoods, where senators and diplomats lived, where we were more likely to find better stuff. We would go over the ads in the newspaper on Friday night when I got in. We were up and out on the road by 0700 on Saturday mornings. We got a classy couch and a breakfast table and end lamps and books and knickknacks. At one very swanky house I bought a chair for twenty-five cents. A quarter! The most comfortable chair in the world. I would sit in the chair and all the troubles of the world would go away. Only it didn't look so good. Brenda made me put it in the basement of our townhouse. I would go sit it in down by the furnace sometimes with Harry, the dog, and read the paper.

One weekend Brenda and I went to a Washington Senators baseball game at Kennedy Stadium. The game was decided in the last inning and we left with everyone else. The parking lot exits were clogged. We waited patiently for our turn to move out in traffic only to find as we inched forward that a car on our right was trying to cut us off. Slowly, one turn of the tires at a time, our front bumpers moved toward each other. I tried to intimidate the driver of the other car with a fierce look. He was animated inside his car, talking with another man in the passenger seat, looking back at me, pointing. When our bumpers finally bumped, the other driver shot me the finger.

That was it. This was the time to take a stand. So I got out the car, walked in front, hiking up my pants and yelled at the other driver. He got out of his car. So did his passenger. So did his buddies in the car behind him. Seven drunk men stumbled in front of my car to challenge me.

Jesus. This was not exactly what I had in mind.

Out of the corner of my eye I saw our car back up, slightly, to get around the bumper of the other car. Brenda had gotten behind the wheel.

Traffic in front had cleared out. Our cars were blocking the traffic behind us.

Brenda gunned the car and the men jumped out of the way. I jumped on the hood and rode along for possibly a city block before we were stopped in traffic again. The men behind us scurried to get back in their cars.

238

I climbed off the hood and got behind the wheel.
"Not bad, hon," I said. "But don't tell the guys, OK?"

****

In August 1971, a year after I had joined the Agency, I received my overseas orders.

The war in Vietnam continued, although it had exhausted the patience of the American people. We appeared to be losing on every front. There were individual, unpublicized CIA victories, however, and the SOGers assigned to Vietnam looked forward to working in programs that brought them into contact with the South Vietnamese police forces or out in isolated provinces where they would have opportunities to develop their own sources that could provide information on Vietcong and North Vietnamese plans and intentions. If American forces were withdrawn and the fight was left completely to the South Vietnamese, which looked more and more possible, then the Agency would stay and its role would be increased. There were uncertainties and challenges for the men heading to Saigon station. It was the destination of the majority of the SOGers with whom I had trained.

Laos was the promised land for CIA paramilitary officers, however. There wasn't much discussed about the program other than it was the largest, the most dangerous and the most successful covert operation the CIA had ever run. Wasn't much of a turnover of personnel; SOG officers tended to stay for years. The rear base for the Lao program was at a joint Thai Air Force and U.S. Air Force base in Udorn, Thailand.

The chief of the CIA paramilitary branch called me to his office to give me my orders to Udorn.

He said there were rumblings of a big upcoming battle in Laos that could decide the future of the program, maybe change the balance of power in Indochina. He wished me luck.

That night Brenda and I went out to a classy restaurant and ordered a bottle of good wine to celebrate. The next day she put in her papers for a leave without pay from the Agency, standard with working wives following their husband to the field. Life just could not have been more exciting. We had our own garage sale -- for the most part re-selling things we had bought at garage sales. We put other stuff in storage, packed Brenda's ol' Plymouth Barracuda, and at the end October 1971 left our rental townhouse to travel to our parents' homes in North Carolina. In early November Mom and Dad

James E. Parker, Jr.

took us to the Raleigh/Durham airport for our flight to the secret war zone in Southeast Asia.

--SEVENTEEN--

Shadow War

As Brenda and I were settling into our seats on the plane leaving North Carolina, North Vietnamese General Nguyen Huu An stood in the shadows of a mountain outcrop east of the Plain of Jars (PDJ) in Northeast Laos, hidden from the view of United States Air Force (USAF) forward air controllers in their small observation planes hovering overhead. From his position he could take in the entire 250 square miles of the PDJ... from the northern savanna plains down to the marshy tapered southern tip. He had been assigned here in 1963 as an adviser to the Lao communists and had walked the PDJ from one end to the other.

It was occupied now by the CIA army of Thai irregulars and Hmong guerillas. An artillery base camp was off to his right in the far north of the flat land, with surrounding defensive positions guarding the avenues of approach. Between An's position hidden on top of the mountain and that northern most Thai irregular artillery outpost, was a scattered gathering of local hills tribesmen. They were not dug in and obviously were being used as a mobile defense and early warning force.

Further to the south, on the western side of the PDJ, was another smaller Thai irregular artillery base with surrounding fighting positions next to a dirt airstrip. And then across the PDJ on one of the highest peaks on the southwest crescent was another artillery position with bunkers of Thai irregulars surrounding the site. To the south right off the southern nipple of the PDJ was another fire base.

But this afternoon he focused on the two artillery positions nearest him on the east side of the PDJ near the foot of the hill where he had his observation post. Around each of the positions the Thai irregulars had dug formidable fighting positions.

He knew the artillery position at the base of the largest east/west finger ridge was called "Lion" and that the major fighting positions on the protecting ridgeline above it had originally been built by the Japanese during World War II and reinforced with concrete. The other artillery position was called "Mustang" and was protected by fighting positions surrounding the artillery.

The irregulars in the two artillery base position complex

were all wearing new uniforms, probably indicating their lack of field experience. Rookies or not, they occupied the commanding terrain and Hmong warlord Vang Pao's soldiers were known to be tough.

Forty-five year old General An was one of North Vietnam's most experienced field commanders. He had studied battlefields many times before as he made up his attack plans; in May 1954 he was the 174th Regimental commander who took the Elaine 2 position at Dien Bien Phu, which was the key terrain overlooking the French headquarters. In 1965 he had studied the terrain of the area around where Lt Col Harold G. Moore would land his troops in an effort to secure the Ia Drang valley. His division's subsequent fight with Moore's battalion was the first major engagement of North Vietnamese against the American forces, and he was recognized by General Vo Nguyen Giap afterward for showing that the North Vietnamese could fight Americans soldiers man to man.

An's style was first ... to know the battlefield: every hill, every concealed wash, every road, all avenues of approach to the targets, and avenues the enemy might take in trying to escape.

An also knew that he shouldn't start a fight like this unless he was sure of victory. You either knew you were going to win, or you didn't attack.

Back in the spring General Giap had called him from a seminar he was attending in Hanoi to Giap's home. There the North Vietnamese military commander ordered An to drop what he was doing and go to the PDJ in Laos to ensure that pending attacks there would be successful.

Calling the Lao operation "Campaign Z," Giap said it was to attack and kill all of the CIA forces under the command of Vang Pao, and to occupy the CIA headquarters in the Long Tieng Valley -- twenty miles southwest of the Plain of Jars.

General Lee Trong Tan would be the overall Campaign Z commander, but Giap was depending on General An to make sure the North Vietnamese carried the day. Giap wanted a victory against Vang Pao and the CIA at "all cost." There was no margin for error, or defeat. He wanted to completely eliminate this enemy force, would accept nothing less.

Tan and An would have at their disposal more than 27,000 North Vietnamese soldiers as follows: The 312th and 316th Divisions augmented with two additional infantry regiments (the 335th and the 866th) plus twenty-six tanks, three sapper battalions, AA gun crews, 130mm field gun batteries, engineers, medical corps, signal corps, porters... plus North Vietnamese MIG jets would be used.

After meeting with Giap, An traveled here to the PDJ and had sat on this mountain top in making his final battle plans. Once he even went with some of his commanders, including the ill-tempered PAVN 165th Regiment commander, Colonel Nguyen Chuong, to reconnoiter the Thai positions defending fire support base (FSB)Lion. They had crawled up to the outer defensive wire of the eastern most position to take a close look at avenues of attack up into the entrenched bunkers.

The battle plan to capture the PDJ and kill Vang Pao's army was developed in two phases.

Phase I:

➢   *Massive artillery bombardment of all Vang Pao positions on the PDJ.*

➢   *Followed by frontal assault on the primary targets - FSBs Lion and Mustang - and the secondary target - FSB King Kong - and then up to four days in siege, to allow PAVN artillery to continue pound the FSBs and the defensive positions while at the same time developing breech points into the Thai defensive positions.*

➢   *Much emphasis was placed on PAVN AA gun placements in tight to the FSBs to shoot down aircraft brought in to resupply and provide fire support to the Vang Pao defenders.*

➢   *Colonel Nguyen Chuong, commander of the NVA 165th Regiment, 312nd Division, would lead the attack on primary target FSB Lion and the three major fighting positions on top of the finger ridge. Two other 312nd Division Regiments would attack FSB Mustang with the use of tanks.*

➢   *316th Division would attack the secondary target, FSB King Kong, also with the use of tanks.*

➢   *Other elements of the 316th and the 312th divisions would be pre-positioned behind FSB Lion, Mustang and King Kong to (1) occupy the poorly defended FSB in the center of the PDJ, (2) to kill or capture the Vang Pao irregulars if they tried to abandon the forward FSBs, and (3) to stop any reinforcements from the FSBs far across the plains and then to the south.*

➢   *Because 95% of the CIA army was deployed on the PDJ, most in/around the first and second priority targets, the goal was to destroy it with a final push after a four day siege. With Vang Pao's army finished, his headquarters in the Long Tieng valley would be left virtually unprotected.*

Phase II:

➢   *866th and 148th regiments and the 27th Sapper battalion were to pre-position north of Skyline Ridge which protected the CIA and Vang Pao's headquarters in the Long Tieng Valley.*

➤ *This force would be joined by 165th and 174th Regiments (after their successful PDJ assaults) for attacks over Skyline into Long Tieng Valley. (141st PAVN regiment in reserve.) Because minimal resistance was expected, men would carry on their back the ammunition and food they would need for the few days required to breach Skyline and occupy the valley beyond.*

An had thought at the time that the 27,000 men Giap had made available to do this job was more than was needed. He had done more with less before.

He liked the battle plan. He did not like the lack of discipline he found in some of the units when he came down to the battlefield, but he had become more optimistic about their ability to destroy the ragtag guerrilla army they faced. He thought that the CIA's defense plan was flawed because they had no fallback position. If the irregulars were knocked out on the PDJ, then the fight, as An saw it, was over. They won. All left was to occupy Long Tieng.

Timing was not right yet. They waited for more artillery munitions to be brought in, and for the weather to change. Bad weather was part of the North Vietnamese plan – it would hinder USAF support to the CIA positions on the PDJ. Once the prevailing winds in the mountains brought in smoky clouds mid-December, the time would more right.

An continued to look down at the Air America choppers bringing in supplies to the different positions. Bad weather would keep the support fleet of helicopters out of the sky too.

He remembered what one of his sub-commanders had told him after a planning session in which An had said something along the lines that they had 27,000 strong soldiers to handle the handfull of local riffraff, and he knew they would achieve an easy victory. "I request that you not be too enthusiastic, my young general," An's officer had said. "We are attacking Vang Pao's army, not...the South Vietnamese puppets."

With the wind ruffling his thinning hair, An continued to scan the PDJ below. He thought about the promised use of North Vietnamese MIGs in this campaign. He had never fought using aircraft and tanks on his side. Victory, he thought, would surely be theirs. Just wait for the smoky season. Wait. We attack. We win. Laos is ours.

243

James E. Parker, Jr.

--EIGHTEEN--
The Eagle Has Landed

We arrived in Bangkok, Thailand, early evening and took a taxi from the airport to a downtown hotel. Brenda's enthusiasm for the travel and what lay ahead was gushing, though she was startled by the chaotic traffic on the ride into town. And she noticed an earthy evening scent coming in through the open windows of the old taxi. She was surprised to realize that this country was not as orderly or as sanitary as the one she had grown up in and her excitement began to wane.

The next morning, walking outside the hotel, she came across Thai women squatting by their charcoal grills in the shade of alleyways, cooking meat on wooden skewers and she was further taken aback. These people are not clean, she explained to me with her eyes wide. Their food is out in the open, just a few steps from where people walked, near open car exhausts. Plus the bustling street people in Bangkok tended to have different attitudes about personal space and Brenda felt crowded. It was very strange, very foreign -- much more of a culture shock than she imagined it would be. She was tired and said late in the afternoon that she wanted to go home.

Twenty-four hours in Thailand and she wanted to go home.

I asked her to give the country time, to understand that this was Bangkok, as far from the states as you could get without starting to come back. People just did things differently on this side of the world. I asked her for a little bit of "hang" as they said in the Agency. She agreed but continued to be very tentative in her dealings with the Thai people and their food.

Following instructions we received at a small commercial office building in the downtown area, we went back to the airport after two days in Bangkok and made our way to a private terminal used exclusively by Continental Airlines Service (CASI) and Air America.

Late morning, after a short wait, we were called to the ramp to board 50-Kip, a regularly CIA-chartered CASI flight north to Udorn. The plane, an old C-47 aircraft, would go on to Vientiane from Udorn, and then down to the two southern cities in Laos - Savannakhet and Pakse - before returning to Bangkok. The two pilots knew many of the passengers and the chatter from the cockpit was neighborly as we boarded. The co-pilot looked around the cabin after the plane was in the air and we made eye contact. "Hey," he yelled out, "we've got some folks making their maiden 50-Kip. Welcome aboard."

Although the old plane was noisy, people talked and moved around as if it were a community outing. We banked slowly as we approached Udorn and could see the U.S. Air Force base south of town. The small commercial downtown district and the airfield stood out in the middle of a vast expanse of sectioned rice fields. A small urban oasis in a neat, bucolic Asian farming landscape. Brenda said, "Now, we are as far from North Carolina as we can get."

After landing we taxied beside a repair hanger where planes and helicopters with the distinctive Air America logo were in varying stages of disassembly for repair, overhaul and inspection. Leaving our luggage at the waiting lounge, we walked to a two-story block building off the tarmac. We announced ourselves to the Thai receptionist and in short order the inside door clicked open and Jim Glerum, the deputy chief of base, walked out. A tall neatly dressed, well-mannered man, he greeted us in a rather formal manner and escorted us inside. We went into the first office off the reception area and were introduced to Pat Landry, aka "the Stick," the base chief. A squat, hard, square-jawed ex-GI, the Stick had been in Indochina most of his adult life. He was well-liked by the Thais, the Hmong, and the men who worked for him. He lived by himself in the upstairs area, had no known interests outside of work and was not particularly comfortable in small talk with people he didn't know. As a boss he had a reputation of being blunt and having the capability to make hard decisions and sticking to them. He carried a variety of sticks around with him, thus his moniker. One lay on his desk. He welcomed me to the program, saying there was a lot of work to be done and deferred to his deputy to get me settled.

Outside of his office, there was constant movement of people from room to room in the mostly windowless rear headquarters building for the Lao program. Radios scratched and chattered in the background. In the center room, maps, hinged on boards, were moved back and forth by a variety of men and women as they plotted positions, posted overhead photography, and added to lists of call signs and other number/name combinations along the sides. No one was idle. Occasionally someone would shout out to someone in another room or yell a profanity, especially a young lady in the center room who operated like a traffic controller. Except for Jim Glerum, dress was casual, what you'd expect clerks in an Army/Navy store to wear. People would pass and look us in the eye. Though they were friendly, no one stopped to talk.

James E. Parker, Jr.

The general atmosphere was that things were happening and they were being dealt with straight on. It was a lean, no-nonsense workplace.

We calmly moved through the flurry of activities and Brenda was introduced to a clerk who was answering her questions on housing as they moved off to a side room.

Jim introduced me to the chief of operations in his small office behind the center room. Cordial, he was retired Special Forces Colonel George Morton, one of the first U.S. Army officers sent to Vietnam. Jim said I had just arrived as a new paramilitary case officer and asked the ops chief to give me a short over view of what was going on.

Morton said something along the order of, "We're the Lao program rear base, here at Udorn, Thailand. The two main jobs of the program are to engage as many of the North Vietnamese soldiers in Laos as we can - to keep them from South Vietnam - and – just as important - to protect the sovereignty of Laos. We do this – the CIA does this – because the Geneva Accords of 1962 prohibit the deployment of U.S. troops inside Laos, and we are signees of that Accord.

"We divide the country into four military regions or MRs. MR I is here to the west," he said pointing to a map of Southeast Asia on the wall beside his desk. "There are several Groupe Mobiles - we call them GMs - battalion size units of local guerrilla soldiers, committed to fighting the local communists and monitoring the construction of the road the Chinese are building south through Laos. Our officers in this MR just lost their base camp and have pulled back close to Luang Prabang, the ceremonial capital of the country.

"In the south are MR III and MR IV. They also fight the local Pathet Lao communists there, plus the North Vietnamese who defend the Ho Chi Minh Trail. Their main job is to do road watch work, watching traffic on the trail goin' south and north. There's a lot of seasonal shifts in control. In the dry season we'll have people in the forward areas, near the border of Vietnam, but when the rains come, and we can't provide resupply or fire support, the irregulars pull back. Those southern MR areas you'll find are quiet most of the time, but during the changing of the seasons when we don't know who is exactly where, there are violent clashes, sometimes hand-to-hand. Often whole units are wiped out."

"MR II," Morton said, "is the big show. We have six GMs of Hmong, plus over the course of the past two years a Thai military regiment was deployed there and lately we sent Thai mercenaries. This army of Hmong, Lao and Thai is commanded by General Vang
246

Pao, or VP as he's called. The Hmong guerrillas work on the ground, patrolling, maneuvering. The Thais sit on mountains and hold ground. Right now they are defending positions on the PDJ, right here," he said pointed to a distinctive, well-marked flat area on a map of mountains.

"We have about 4,000 Thais and another, I don't know, 800 Hmong guerrillas defending this key terrain. PDJ. Plain of Jars. Mountains of Laos are some of the roughest in the world... but it's level here, and it's goin' be a battlefield very soon.

"Hmong GM 23 is located here in the northeast of the Plain and operates as a mobile defense force. Their job is to impede the movement of any enemy onto the PDJ from what we call the Ban Ban area, the junction of Route 6 and 7 coming from North Vietnam.

"Then here, at the main east/west junction on the PDJ, is GM 21. Hard to pin down exactly how many Hmong irregulars are with this group, about three or four hundred. But it's getting on close to Hmong New Years. They come and go. It's their homeland you know. But GM 21, like 23 up in the northeast, are to provide mobile defense... and stop enemy patrols from moving around on the PDJ.

"Here to the north is Fire Support Base (FSB) King Kong with both 105mm and 155mm artillery guns and 4.2 mortar tubes. It is protected by Battalion Commandos (BC) 606 and 608, about a thousand Thai irregulars, positioned on top of the Phou Keng mountain here, and on positions that overlook Route 7 coming north off the PDJ, here."

As Morton was talking the Stick walked into the center room. Morton called out to ask if he needed anything. The lady who was doing the loud talking before yelled back that he was trying to track something, a thread of conversation I didn't understand. George shrugged and went on.

"Then below that is FSB Panther, with a couple of 105mm and three 4.2 mortar tubes... but it's lightly protected with only a company of Thai irregulars. But there's the Hmong GM 21 nearby. It's set up near this long dirt fixed-wing airfield. Lima Site 22.

"Then on the hilltop here is FSB Sting Ray protected by about 500 men. It's the location of the command group because it's got a full view of all the FSBs on the PDJ.

"In the far south, here, on the first ridgeline south of the PDJ is FSB Cobra with a couple of 105mm artillery guns... and maybe 500 Thai mercenaries around the perimeter.

"But look here... Mr. New Guy... what's your name again?

"Jim Parker."

James E. Parker, Jr.

"OK, Jim, see all this on the map... it is our most forward complex... FSB Lion in the shadow of Phou Teung, the long finger ridge that extends out from the edge of the PDJ, near the road that goes down to Xieng Khoungville – used to be the biggest settlement in the area. The province headquarters. French were headquartered here.

"On top of Phou Teung we got BCs 605 and 609, again about 1,000 men. FSB Lion has two 105s and two 155s and a huge ammo dump. You walk that area and you gotta think, it's impregnable... we've certainly tried to make it that.

"Right next door's another finger ridge that we call the Ban Thon hill... got FSB Mustang here on the low ground near FSB Lion and all around, on top of Ban Thon and then out to the front are BCs 603 and 607, close to another thousand men.

"So you see, Mr. New Guy, of the about 4,000 plus men defending this area we got about 3,300 or so on this upper northeast crescent around FSBs King Kong, Lion and Mustang. We can hold out, we can defend these positions with protecting artillery fire from Panther, Sting Ray and "Cobra," and – this is important - USAF support. We need close tactical air. And we got the USAF word they'll be there for us, weather permitting.

"You with me on all this?

"Yea," I said, "They didn't have much to say back at Langley before I left, but they did talk about the Thai commandos defending the PDJ.... that a big battle might be in the offing.

Taking me by the elbow, we went out to the big maps. "This is Route 6, and over here this is Route 7," he said pointing to one of the prominent maps, "which run from North Vietnam to the PDJ. As we speak elements of the North Vietnamese 312th and 316th Divisions are bringing troops and supplies for what looks like a major push against our positions on the plateau, probably in early December. We know the North Vietnamese are serious about the campaign this year because they have assigned one of their most senior officers to the attacks on our PDJ positions. It's always been pivotal, strategic terrain. It's where we've drawn a line in the mountains. It's our best effort to stop the North Vietnamese from moving on the Lao capital and taking the country outright."

That was where I wanted to go to. "The big show." The PDJ. With the mountain guerrillas and the Thai irregulars. To hold the line against pending attack from the North Vietnamese, with our artillery, and our irregular troops and the USAF.

Jim Glerum, standing beside George, told me I would be working MR II. I smiled and said, "Thank you."

He said I would be working MR II as a desk officer in Udorn.

"What?" I said, "I don't want to be a friggin desk officer."

Jim smiled and continued, "Your duties in Udorn will be to collect the information on the hour-to-hour situation in MR II and collate it for dissemination to our stations in Saigon, Vientiane and Bangkok and to Headquarters in Washington, D.C. You will join this motley crew here to make sure the maps and boards are current and you will be prepared to brief. There is a lot of responsibility in this job," he said, "especially with the North Vietnamese offensive about to begin. There are enough agency officers in MR II at the moment. If you want an assignment upcountry after you have done your duty here, then I will try to arrange it. You should know however that we rarely send married case officers to MR II. It's very dangerous and the separation is hard on the wives."

As Morton went back into his office he patted me on the back. Jim told me to draw a car from the support officer, check into the hotel on the edge of town, help my wife get settled, and report to work in the morning at 0600.

Brenda took my assignment to Udorn base as good news. I would be around most of the time and it was safe. She missed the point, I told her. I had come so far, and I wasn't on the playing field. I had to sit on the sidelines, at a typewriter all day. And give briefings. That is no fun. I want to be out there, where the North Vietnamese are massing and our men are digging in. Where there is action and adventure. "In due time, my dear," my wife said in a motherly fashion.

The Charoen Hotel was the best in northeast Thailand but it was not luxurious by American standards. Our room was a sparsely furnished twelve-by-twelve cubicle with a bed and dresser and a bathroom heavy on white industrial tile and exposed plumbing. It was oppressive and we spent the first evening sitting in the lobby, Brenda a little unsure of what we were actually getting into and me very disappointed over my desk assignment.

--NINETEEN--

Recon North

I read reports, studied map boards, memorized unit

designations and call signs, and acquainted myself with MR II during my first few days on the desk. I sat in on scheduled and impromptu briefings about the developing situation on the PDJ, some delivered by "Buck," the officer I was replacing, and others by Jim Glerum. Both had extensive knowledge of the area. Jim was especially gifted as a briefer. He spoke in a low monotone but with authority. A Princeton graduate and former intelligence officer in the Air Force, his reasonable, cultured nature left visitors assured that the prosecution of the war here was in good hands. His briefings were comprehensive and erudite, well received by those visitors from the United States who had spent previous hours in U.S. military briefings, the types I remembered that had sometimes sounded like half-time speeches by high school coaches.

On 10 December Buck took me on a familiarization tour of MR II. We left Udorn on an Air America cargo plane while it was still dark, crossed the Mekong River into Laos as the sun was coming up, flew high above the rugged mountains of the northeast and landed early morning on the airstrip in the Long Tieng Valley, designated Lima Site 20-A in aviation handbooks though it was known by many names. "The Alternate," in Air America pilot parlance. "The Sky headquarters in MR II," by the U.S. Embassy staff. "The CIA secret base, Spook Haven," by the newspapers. "Shangri-La," by the Raven forward air controllers (FACs), the U.S. Air Force pilots living in Laos who flew small, single engine Cessna O-1 aircraft.

The CIA men who worked out of the Long Tieng Valley were referred to as "Sky" by the locals - for unknown reasons, maybe because they descended from the Sky, or because the early CIA people were mostly responsible for sky resupply. Whatever the reason, Sky became the local term the Hmong used to describe their rounded-eyed allies, CIA, Ravens, Air America.

The runway ran inside a bowl-shaped east-west valley. Tall rock formations, or karsts as they were called upcountry, jutted straight up 300 feet out of the earth at the north end of a 4,400 foot long macadam runway limiting all takeoff and landings to be performed over a steep mountain at the south end. No runway lighting. No night or instrument approach capabilities existed at Twenty Alternate. Flight operations were conducted only during daylight, weather permitting. There was no road south. The only way in or out was by air or down small foot trails. Isolated, it helped provide the anonymity for the program. Visitors were flown in, by invitation only.

To the north a switchback mountain road led from the valley floor up the side of the towering Skyline ridge. The road was the main artery to Sam Thong, a previously thriving mountain village two ridgelines to the north. The abandoned village overlooked a river valley that snaked its way from Skyline north-northeast through the Ban Hin Tang pass the entire fifteen miles to the PDJ.

Vang Pao's stone house, surrounded by a barbed wire fence, was on the south side of the runway in the valley, surrounded by the thatched shacks of maybe 20,000 Hmong. The headquarters for the Thai mercenaries was at the east end along with several batteries of 105mm and 155mm artillery. The Sky compound was on the west end situated hard against protecting karsts.

Buck said LS 20A was one of the busiest airports in the world with more than 500 takeoffs and landings a day, more than Chicago's O'Hare International. The loading ramp where the plane parked was about the size of a city block and it was teeming with activity. Supplies were being off-loaded from some planes, riggers were loading other aircraft with bundles to be air dropped, helicopters were coming from the ammo dump with pallets of ammunition slung below, hills tribe villagers with animals in bags and baskets sat among wounded soldiers waiting for rides to outlying regions. There were dozens of Hmong and Thai soldiers standing around. Jeeps and trucks moved among the planes, supplies and people. A few Americans, mostly pilots, sauntered to and from the Air Operations building and to the rigging shed off the ramp in the shadow of Skyline.

Two Sky case officers, who I had met in Udorn earlier, came out of the Air Ops building and walked across the ramp with a pair of Air America helicopter pilots. They were discussing locations on a mangled map that one of the case officers extracted from his back pocket. We passed close by but it was hard to hear what they were saying because of the roar of cargo planes and helicopters taxiing in the area.

A middle-aged, smiling man emerged from Air Ops and Buck introduced him as the chief Sky air controller, jokester and king of the skies in MR II. A Hmong came out of the building and joined us. Throwing his arm around the shorter Asian, the large American air controller introduced the Hmong as the chief laugher at jokes in MR II and his able assistant. We joined them in a short Jeep ride around the karst behind Air Ops to the Sky headquarters. The gates, made of cast iron fencing and barbed wire, were open and Hmong walked up and down the compound street. It was not necessarily like the guarded field compounds I remembered as a GI in Vietnam.

Past the gate was a two-story block building on the right, the

251

James E. Parker, Jr.

sleeping quarters. To the left was the mess hall and beyond that the bomb-proof concrete headquarters building. The front and side entrances to the headquarters were large bank vault doors. The Hmong Air Ops officer jumped off the Jeep when we pulled in and walked across the road, past the sleeping quarters to the Hmong ops assistant building in the rear. Buck and I went into the headquarters bunker, passing a 260 pound plus muscle man who introduced himself as "Tiny." Buck said that almost everyone who worked out of the valley upcountry had a call sign and whether it was for security or had just become the way things were done, everyone was addressed by his call sign.

Inside we met "Bamboo," "Digger" and "Ringo" who were finishing a conversation with Dick Johnson, the CIA base chief. With the exceptions of Dick Johnson and the chief air ops officer, all the Sky people were my age. They wore mismatched civilian/military clothing and jungle boots. They carried nine millimeter pistols with escape and evasion (E&E) bags and canteens on pistol belts. All had white twine tied loosely around their wrists, placed there by the Hmong for luck. All used the palms of their hands to write down notes. Their faces were weathered with crow's feet in the corners of their eyes. They greeted me cordially - all were surprisingly well spoken for as rough as they looked. Like the people at the base office in Udorn, all appeared seriously intent on what they were doing and no one made small talk. As Digger and Ringo walked out, and Bamboo went over and began rummaging around boxes of supplies, Dick Johnson crouched over a typewriter and began pounding on the keyboard. He looked up saying he had an immediate precedent cable to respond to, shook hands without getting up and welcomed me to Long Tieng, suggesting that we go out to the PDJ as soon as possible. Turning to the air ops officer, he told him to make sure we got a pick-up late in the day. I told him thanks, and he said, with a slight smile, that wasn't necessary. Ringo from across the room said that the boss didn't have time to keep up with the "FNG" and smiled.

As he was talking a man walked in the small office and stood silently by the door. Buck said, nodding to me, "FNG, meet Hog." Standing across the room, Hog looked at me without offering his hand. He had the dark handsome looks of a Valentino movie star and like the others he was weathered. With his dusty, dark clothing and his dour expression he reminded me of cowboys I had seen in old, turn of the century black and white photographs.

All SOGers heard about Hog their first day in the Agency. He was a teenage smoke jumper for the U.S. Forest Service in Montana when he was recruited by Air America to come to the

252

mountains of Laos for work as a kicker/flight mechanic on Air America planes. He eventually moved into the Sky ranks as a contract employee, like myself. His first Sky job was to monitor an isolated region of MR II and he would spend weeks out away from other westerners, working with the Hmong. He was criticized at first by his Agency supervisors for going "native." There was the implication that he was a little crazy, at the very least he was feared to have divided loyalties. But when he was reassigned to Long Tieng and stayed in daily contact with other Sky officers, his unassuming nature, clear thinking and devotion to the Sky mission became obvious. He had no pretensions. No rancor. He was intimidated by no man though he had little in common with east coast bureaucrats. He absolutely did not care what others thought about him. He stood by his word, expected others - Hmong, Thai, Sky, Air America - to stand by theirs. He did his job taking the minimum of risk, but even at that, he ventured daily out into the fighting and was shot at often. His manner never changed. He never became excited. He put getting the job done above any personal consideration. He did not like people with an attitude or strident point of view.

On the other hand the chief, Dick Johnson, was not a hired gun, like Hog, employed to work specifically in Laos. He was a career Agency staffer who had held a variety of intelligence postings around the world before, including a paramilitary assignment during the Korean conflict. He understood regulations and the moral responsibilities of CIA field work. He was trusted by our Headquarters to make sure that the Long Tieng operation did not turn into a rogue elephant, that it maintained Agency standards of propriety. But Hog – despite no military background - was chief of operations. He knew every mile of the area, every commander. He had special rapport with the Hmong, knew the capabilities of the small little mountain fighter, knew what they could be expected to do, and what they wouldn't do. And he knew the enemy. He rarely left MR II, staying in Long Tieng for weeks on end. Every two months or ten weeks he would go to Vientiane or Bangkok and stay drunk for several days, coming back to the Stick's quarters above the office in Udorn to dry out before returning to the valley. He had been doing this for ten years. He put the concept of "hang" into the work of MR II and into the jargon of the Agency. He was the definitive SOGer.

Hog didn't talk to strangers and he didn't talk to me. He just nodded ever so slightly, turned to Dick Johnson with a comment and left.

As we drove back down to the ramp later, the air ops officer radioed a helicopter that was coming in for a landing to take a couple of passengers out to the PDJ after he had off-loaded and taken on some fuel.

I asked Buck what an FNG was. He said, "Fucking New Guy."

Nice touch, I thought.

Standing in the shade of the Air Ops building we watched our helicopter discharge its passengers and then taxi over to the fuel tanks I asked Buck, "OK, I understand why we came to work with the Hmong here. It is their homeland. And Vang Pao's the warlord. And the other units recruited and trained by the CIA in other regions of the country that come in periodically... I understand. The bad guys got to come through this area to attack the Lao capital. But now what's with the Thais? What are they doin' here? They work for us, right? No one was ever clear about this at Headquarters. They just said we got some irregulars from Thailand."

To be understood over the loud ramp noise, Buck turned and talked directly into my left ear.

"Back last year ... 1970, the Cambods were having their problems and Lon Nol – the boss Cambod - agreed to our offer to send him locally recruited and trained multi-national commandos. I reckon it was our offer, I don't know where the idea came from. So the Thais were OK with it, and helped recruit some men from that area of east Thailand that used to be Cambodia, where they still speak Khmer... our U.S. Special Forces trained 'um – 'bout a thousand I think, in two 550 man groups. 50 men in the command cadre were mostly former RTA officers and NCOs. Other 500 were right out of the rice fields there in northeastern Thailand... some just out of prison.

Two groups, BC 601 and BC 602, were trained up , and when they were getting ready to go, hell Lon Nol said, nope, he had since thought it wasn't a good idea... so what you goin' do?

"We asked the prime minister of Laos if he wanted 'um, and he said hell, yea. Keep 'um out of sight, keep 'um away from the capital and sure, we want all the help we can get."

The pilots of the helicopter we were going to use were walking into Air Ops, but gave way to a C-130 fixed-wing airplane that had landed and was taxiing through to the back of the ramp. Buck didn't speak until it passed.

"So," he finally continued, "we deployed these 1,100 men in southern Laos, out on the Bolovens plateau and I reckon the NVA thought they were another piss-poor Lao unit and attacked... and lost 150 of their men killed in the wire. You know how many of the Thai irregulars were hurt. One killed and one wounded... and the guy killed, hell it was an accident. Sure was a good first sign about the effectiveness of these new guys. 150 to 1 is a pretty damn good score.

"A few months later - earlier this year - the Thais sent up one of their regular Thai army battalions here to Long Tieng to help stop North Vietnamese attacks and... they got their shirts ripped by attacking North Vietnamese infantry... one unit of the Thai army was almost completely wiped out up at Ban Na.

"So the next two units of these newly recruited and newly trained Thai irregulars were sent up here. They were BC 603 and 604... 601 and 602 were the two forces in the south.

"And shit... 603 and 604 bailed out the Royal Thai Army guys. They kicked some ass... and eventually pushed the North Vietnamese back to the PDJ and then beyond. 605, 606, 607, 608, 609 and 610 were recruited in Thailand for us, and trained by US Special Forces this past spring and over the summer and they're the units now out on the PDJ. All newly flung together. All pretty much untested as far as real combat's concerned... except for 603 and 604. They're feeling pretty spunky. Morale's high. Look like shit, some of 'um. But with the CIA, we ain't after looks."

"What do you call 'um, these Thai? CIA soldiers?

"Well there you go, I think they call themselves "Tahan Suae Pran" or "Tiger Soldiers." Others I hear call 'um 333 soldiers after the Thai Army group that helps recruit and supports this effort. We call 'um, mercenaries sometimes, but mostly Thai irregulars. They work for us. They aren't called CIA soldiers, but are part of the CIA army of Asian irregulars. Vang Pao's the warlord. But really I reckon they consider themselves Thai Tigers. You ask 'um, who are you, they'll say Tahan Suae Pran.

The Thai guy that runs the shop that allows us to recruit these guys in Thailand is called General Dhep. One no-nonsense sumbitch."

The pilots came out of Air Ops and waved to us, so we followed them across the ramp. Their helicopter was filled with rations inside so Buck and I had difficulty finding a place to sit. The Filipino kicker/mechanic handed Buck a radio head set, the "customer set," and as we taxied back out onto the airstrip for the take-off, Buck began what was obviously a friendly conversation with the pilot who sat in front and slightly above us. We gained altitude as we left the valley to the east, swinging back over Skyline for the twenty mile ride to the PDJ. As we flew north we passed rows and rows of east/west ridgelines. Sticking my head out the open door I could see the PDJ in the distance. It looked absolutely level, an incredible sight among the mountains. It was a freak of geography or as someone suggested, a monument to what your ancient slave labor could do for you.

As we began to make our approach on the PDJ we could see dozens of aircraft - fixed wing and helicopters - buzzing around, like bees during pollination season, servicing different sites.

The supplies on board were destined for the northern most site – King Kong -- and our helicopter descended toward the LZ used by that position, marked by white cloth pegged to the ground.

Standing near the open door of the helicopter we could make out the faces of the men on the ground.

Suddenly the helicopter dipped quickly to the left and we were slung up against the far bulkhead. Buck took off his headset and pointed out the open door to one of the artillery batteries behind us and yelled over the noise of the helicopter that the battery had suddenly started firing, had gone "hot", through our approach pattern.

The helicopter righted itself and came into the LZ low from the west. We jumped off when the wheels hit the ground to get out of the way of the Thais who had run up to unload the supplies.

"Greek," a former Marine helicopter pilot who worked Sky air operations in the field, was off in the grass beside the LZ yelling into a radio, telling a Thai artillery officer that someone was going to get killed if they continued to fire when aircraft were landing. Greek said he had to know when the guns went hot again. The Thai said quickly, "OK, OK."

As we stood beside Greek an Air America helicopter pilot came up on another radio saying he was returning to LS 20A until the guns stopped firing. Greek and the pilot argued for several minutes. The pilot said he was dropping off the 105mm shells he had at a 155mm position and leaving. Greek said, "if you do that you low life, scum-sucking, asshole sumbitch, I will rip one of your ears off the next time I see you."

As Greek was yelling in the radio he was looking south in the direction of a helicopter with ammo crates suspended below, hovering near an artillery position. It finally moved some distance to one side and came down gently, released its ammo, put its nose down

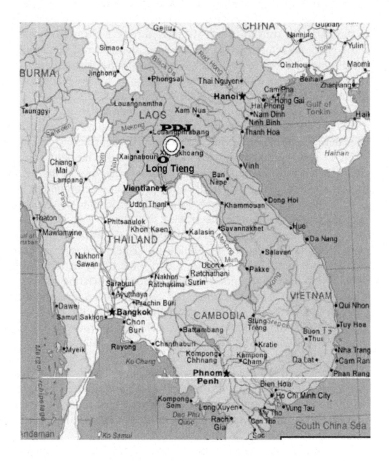

PDJ/Southeast Asia

Not shown is the 200 mile French-built road between
Hanoi and the PDJ

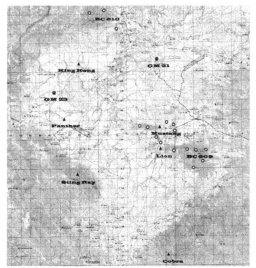

The PDJ with the location of the six Fire Support Bases. With their surrounding defensive positions and Hmong mobile defense units, there were about 4,000 irregulars under Vang Pao's command on these positions on 18 December 1971. Almost 3,000 were located at or near FSBs King Kong, Lion and Mustang.

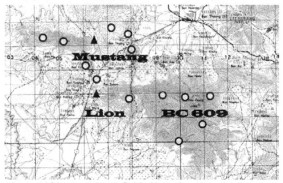

The Lion and Mustang battlefield. Note the steep incline up to the Thai irregular BC 609 positions, that the PAVN 165th Regiment charged on the afternoon of 19 Dec 1971, taking enormous casualties. The tanks came down route 5 and then up on the top of the ridgeline northwest of Mustang that night, to finish the conquest of their main objective.

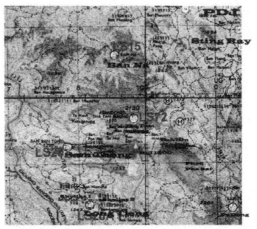

The battlefield between the PDJ and the Long Tieng valley. Note the tall Phou Pha Sai and Tha Tam Bleung mountains on either side of Ban Hin Tang Pass. Also note Hill 1800 that the PAVN tanks could not climb, forcing the main PAVN tank charge inMarch just north of hill 1737, where the Thai irregulars were dug in.

Helicopter pads on top of Skyline Ridge surrounded by defensive fighting positions. Note road that GM 30 climbed from Long Tieng to get to CE, then to CB to attack PAVN sappers around CW. Also note the angle Thai irregulars 75mm gunners had from CE down on the PAVN tanks climbing the road up the north slope. CW, CA and CT were on the highest point of Skyline, which the PAVN. The dark area north of CA was known as "VP's farm."

Two weeks after adopting the kids

Coming in from work upcountry

Long Tieng Valley, aka LS 20A, or most commonly, the "Alternate." Location of CIA and Vang Pao hqs in NE Laos. Skyline ridge dominates the north.

Bill Lair standing in the middle of the back row of Thai "PARU" cadre that he trained as an all-purpose vanguard against communist aggression in Southeast Asia (SEA).

Hmong trained by PARU to fire carbines and M-1s

Vang Pao as young war lord and mountain tribe leader

Thai irregulars brought up in 1971.   "Spotlight" a CIA FAG

The Plain of Jars (PDJ) a spectacularly beautiful 250 square mile plateau in the mountains   of NE Laos near the North Vietnamese border.

Thai irregular volunteer position near FSB "Mustang," being resupplied by Air America.

Bouam Long (LS 32) north of the PDJ. C o n s t a n t l y
a t t a c k e d . Never occupied by the North Vietnamese

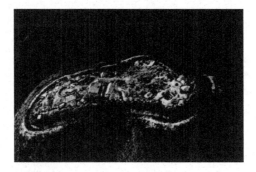

A Hmong defensive position on a Bouam Long hill top; like
the one Mule visited

CIA COS Hugh Tovar and Ambassador Mac Godley.

Hmong War Lord Vang Pao   Thai General Dhep, Thai
                            irregular commander

Dick Johnson, CIA Chief   Hog and COS Tovar
w/ Vang Pao

PAVN General An   PAVN Colonel Chuong

Thai volunteer BC 609 on graduation from US Special Forces training in Thailand.
Most would be killed or captured on 18 December 1971 defending FSB "Lion"

Attacking NVA soldiers   Whiskey 02 who died in
                                defense of "Lion"

Artillery firing from FSB "Cobra"   Twin ottor delivering two
                                     parachutes of ammo

NVA captured all PDJ positions by 20 December 1971. These Thai
and Hmong irregulars are being led towards POW camps in North
Vietnam. Most never to be seen again.

Skyline Ridge. The high peak on the left was called "CC" after the Air
America helicopter LZ designation. In the ridge saddle just to the right of
the "CC" pad a road crossed the ridgeline. NVA tanks would eventually
try to climb that road in their attacks. "CW" is the LZ at the very crest of
the long ridgeline to the right. It was the focus of much of the fighting.
Changed hands several times in the course of the fighting.

and gained altitude off to the west.

The artillery starting firing again. Greek threw down the hand set and said everyone tried to make his life difficult as he reached in his pocket for an anti-acid pill.

Walking up a dirt trail to the position we were met by the Thai commander. He spoke colloquial American English in welcoming us to his "campus," saying he was the dean of students at this location. He led us to the center of the position. Standing on top of his command bunker we looked out over the defenses. The perimeter had three inter-connected rings with firing ports. Well-fortified mortar pits were behind the command bunker. In front for a hundred meters the saw grass had been burnt to the ground and strands of barbed wire overlapped circling rows of concertina wire. The commanders said the whole area to the front was laced with mines; in some sections mines were two deep.

"Impregnable," the commander said, and I agreed. I had seen nothing like it in Vietnam.

He said he slept soundly at night and although his was the northern most position on the PDJ and he was probed often, he had not lost a man since the North Vietnamese began their buildup. He considered the probes a welcome diversion in fact and did not doubt the ability of his men to hold off against any type of full-scale attack. In addition to his own
interlocking fire, local artillery could be brought in within seconds, plus flare and gunships -- "Spookies" and "Spectors" - were usually on station. "I can turn the whole area in front into a killing zone. A Coney Island shooting gallery," he said.

Standing on the bunker, helicopters could be heard behind me to the south. In front there was complete quiet. No bird sounds, no insects humming, nothing. As a youngster hunting with Cottonpicker, I knew if you listened, the woods and forest were noisy with the sound of living things growing, breathing, their sound carried by the wind blowing in the trees.

But there was no sound in front of me. It was because of the thousands of North Vietnamese soldiers hiding out there in the woody ravines and mountains, some less than a half mile away, waiting to attack.

The silence was deadly, ominous. The quiet before the storm.

From the reports I had filed in Udorn I knew that truckloads of new recruits had been brought in to make the attack. The North Vietnamese used the same tactic in South Vietnam, bringing in young recruits for human wave assaults, holding out veteran units for occupation duty. The hundreds and hundreds of young men hiding in front of me now were going to be cannon fodder within a matter of days.

In my mind's eye I could see them storm this position, yelling, whistles blowing, artillery landing around them, running headlong into the barbed wire in front of me, through the mine field, until so many had died that they had cleared a path. The Thais would shoot until the barrels of their guns were hot and they would pick up new weapons and fire until the enemy stopped attacking or they had used up all their bullets.

Were there more Vietnamese in the woods in front than the Thais around me had bullets? How strong was their resolve? How much support will we be able to provide the Thais when the attack comes?

Still standing exposed on top of the bunker imagining what it would be like when the attack came, I suddenly had the feeling someone was looking at me. Some North Vietnamese patrol hunkering down in the weeds to the front or some North Vietnamese staff officer perhaps, with binoculars. Maybe, although I didn't know it at the time, North Vietnamese General An was looking at me from his perch on top of one of the mountains to the east.

I climbed down to join Buck and the commander in his bunker where a very feminine looking young Thai soldier served us hot tea.

In leaving, I told the commander - "the dean of students" - that it looked like tough exams ahead. "Ah shit, sir," he said, "we'll pass. My people will make the honor rolls."

Greek called in a helicopter working the area to pick us up and he joined us for the ride to Long Tieng for the night.

We were among the last to return. As the pilot was shutting the chopper down we walked into Air Ops for Greek to drop off his radios and for Buck and I to pick up our overnight bags. The man who was running the rigging shop, "Shep," came in and accompanied us as we walked around the karst into the Sky compound. Buck and I put our bags in an empty room in the
sleeping barracks and went to the mess hall where the Air America pilots and a few Sky officers were eating. "Bag," Hog's deputy, came in and asked Greek if "Kayak" had come in off the PDJ. Greek said that as usual Kayak was the last man out; the last chopper off the plateau had gone into a Hmong position near FSB Panther to pick him up. As Greek was saying this, Kayak came walking in with a

toothbrush in his mouth.

Lean and hard like the other Sky officers, Kayak was also high energy. He took the toothbrush out and immediately started to explain to Bag about his request to Hog earlier that day to lead a Hmong patrol out to cut off a North Vietnamese reconnaissance unit. Bag listened for a few minutes and told him to come into the Sky bunker next door. As they were leaving Kayak was saying he didn't go on the patrol, but he had waited until it returned before he left the PDJ.

Before in Udorn, Buck had gone over some of the case officers I would be meeting in my trip north. He talked about Hog, of course – his stoic manner, effectiveness and the love the Hmong had for him. He also talked about Kayak, who he said is a freak of nature, because he's genius smart, but got bigger balls than he's got brains. When the Thai unit was up at Ban Na getting the shit knocked out of them, Kayak was assigned as their Sky officer and he would go out every day - if he could find an Air America helicopter to take him - to dodge incoming and land in the middle of the surrounded Thai position. All day long this site would be under attack, and all day long Kayak would be there calmly coordinating USAF support, and resupply and advice to the commander about how to maintain the defense, and counter North Vietnamese breaches of the defense. An absolute hell-hole, but clearly Kayak's element.

Buck and I followed Bag and Kayak out of the mess hall, leaving Greek in testy conversation with an Air America pilot. Other Air America pilots in the mess hall, especially the younger ones, ate with relish reminding me of football players eating at a training table. Most were ex-military. They were drawn to Air America because of the money and the action. They were first of all mercenaries but the Air America pilots were also American patriots; each had lost many friends in Indochina over the years and they were not a sentimental group. Frenchy, B.J., Cliff, George, Hubie, Izzy, and Greenway among others in the mess hall that night were aggressive, hard-living, gnarled, tough, in-your-face Americans. There was nothing phony about them in the way that people who constantly make decisions with life and death consequences are not phony. They were as a group blunt but calculating. They risked their lives every day and wanted fair compensation. And, they might say, "Fuck you if you don't like it."

They were as happy in their dangerous work as farmers in the dell.

When Buck and I walked in the Headquarters bunker Dick

Johnson, Hog, Bag, Moose and Kayak were talking beside a stack of C-rations in the open bay area. Close by, Cobra, Electric and Hardnose, three Sky case officers who worked exclusively with the Thais, were talking with two senior Air America pilots.

Dick Johnson told Kayak that he was to never, ever again to think about going out with the Hmong on patrol. "We don't do that here. The Hmong do that, you understand me." Kayak said, "I know, I know," and went on quickly to add that the Hmong patrol reported the North Vietnamese were wearing new uniforms and he walked to a map and plotted the route the Vietnamese had taken along the west side of the PDJ.

Electric suggested they were looking for an approach route to the middle Thai positions. He said another Hmong patrol reported earlier today that more North Vietnamese troops had been brought in east of the PDJ overnight – near Xieng Khoungville - plus their convoy included heavy trucks loaded with what may have been tanks.

For the next hour, as Sky officers came and left and returned, the discussion continued about the buildup and ways to blunt the pending attack. Bag suggested that the best defensive was a good offensive and that we should move Hmong north toward Ban Ban, to put pressure on their rear and flanks, maybe to pre-empt their attack plans. "A good defense is a good offense," he said. Because we simply sit and waited, the Vietnamese were able to mass their forces at will. Dick said the North Vietnamese were being bombed every day and night by artillery and the Air Force. Digger countered however, that nothing substituted for the little guy on the ground. He agreed with Bag's suggestion to send the Hmong north behind the Vietnamese and push them into the Thai defensive positions. Hog was sure Vang Pao wouldn't go for it, that a similar plan was discussed last night and Vang Pao said there would be too many Hmong casualties. The North Vietnamese could just put in another call home for more replacements. Where was Vang Pao going to get more soldiers? Plus VP was convinced the Thais could hold off anything the Vietnamese threw at them, and he said the good Hmong general has stared at many North Vietnamese forces gearing for attacks over the years.

Cobra and Bag both opined quickly, loudly, that Vang Pao didn't give a hoot about the Thais and he hadn't faced tanks before. The Thai positions had been built to hold off attacks by ground forces. If the Hmong road watch patrols and Sky special intelligence was right and tanks were being brought down – and especially if they were used at night when our USAF couldn't hit them - that altered the balance of power, tilted the advantage to the Vietnamese.

Hog said that he would talk with Vang Pao about some type of preemptive maneuvers by the Hmong forces and he left to go to VP's compound. "Dutch" came in and said it was time for all the good young Sky men to come to Jesus and give him some good coordinates. Dutch, a Texan, had a number of duties, among them to develop target information for B-52 bomb strikes. He pulled out an acetate-covered map that had strike boxes plotted from the previous day, erased them with an old rag and started to plot new targets. Many of the officers read coordinates off the palms of their hands that they had jotted down over the course of the day. Others pulled out dog-eared notebooks and called out number groups. Dutch plotted them all on the map. After considerable discussion about some of the plots, the ridgeline north of the PDJ and the mountains just east of FSB Lion was covered with dots... some just north of where I had been earlier in the day.

Moose was one of the last people to offer coordinates for B-52 attacks. His job was to maintain an intercept program and he had incept-radio operators with both GM 23 up in the northeast of the PDJ and GM 21 near the Panther airstrip. They sent in audiotapes each day to Moose's shop in the Sky compound where three Vietnamese worked through the night to translate North Vietnamese conversations captured by the field teams.

Dutch added Moose's information and then quickly drew rectangular boxes around the target dots, "arclight strike zones," and wrote down the corner coordinates for transmission to the Air Force. They would be hit tonight or tomorrow.

Hog came back and said VP had taken a hard position against moving the Hmong out on attacks, saying again the Thais could hold, especially with U.S. Air Force support. Bag said, "Yea, U.S. Air Force. The Vietnamese will not attack until the whole area is socked in by bad weather. Guarantee it. We don't need a divining rod to predict the time of attack," he said, "The weatherman will tell us. And anyone in this room can tell you how effective the U.S. Air Force will be in bad weather in these mountains. Or when the smoky season starts… you know smoke from the slash and burn farmers up as far north as China drift down our way about the time the rains start." Except for B-52s and flare ships that can operate above the weather, close support fighters didn't go below the clouds because they would hit mountains or run into small-arms fire. "Nope," Bag continued, "Charlie's going to come when the U.S. Air Force can't. The smoky season's coming any day now. Goin' be like the referee blowing the whistle, 'Game On!' And when those bastards start coming, it's going to be them against the Thais, an Asian affair, hand-to-hand. Forget about the U.S. Air Force." Like Hog, Bag was a former smoke jumper from the mountains of Montana. Though – like Hog - he had not served in Vietnam, he had many years experience in the nonconventional warfare of Laos and he knew what lay ahead.

Dick Johnson said that the Stick also discounted using the Hmong to go north of the Vietnamese. Too late. We hold what we got with what we got. Cobra said as he was leaving that he'd bring in some bulldozers from Udorn at first light the next morning to dig tank traps forward of FSB Lion and Mustang at least cut the road going down to Xieng Khoungville.

Greek walked in complaining about the Thais shooting through our landing pattern that afternoon. He went to the map board and began discussing his suspicion that the Vietnamese were going to move all their forces along the west side of the PDJ and attack coming up on the soft underbelly of the Thai positions, hitting the artillery first and then working their way back across the plateau from south to north. This thinking tracked with Kayak's unit spotting North Vietnamese units wearing new uniforms moving along the west side of the PDJ.

Hog, Bag and Electric joined him at the map and began debate on possible means of protecting the west flank. Electric didn't think they could sneak large numbers of troops along the west PDJ without being spotted. He said they're coming head on from Ban Ban and Xieng Khoungville.

By nine o'clock that night most of the men had drifted away from the office, either to the bar in the mess hall or their rooms.

I turned in around ten but woke up in the middle of the night. Walking out on the balcony of the building I could hear radios squawking in the Hmong ops assistant building. Buck had said each of the Sky officers was assigned a least one interpreter/ops assistant, a Thai or a Hmong depending on which unit they worked with. The Hmong ops assistants were among the brightest, best educated young men in the Hmong nation. They were translators, note takers, liaison officers, gun bearers and anything else the Sky officer might call on them to do. They also maintained the radio network at night to the GMs and to some of the outlying Hmong villages.

As I listened to the radios squawking in their radio room below I heard the unmistakable background sounds of small-arms fire in one of the transmissions. It was a foggy night and I thought perhaps the major attack had commenced on the plateau.

I walked downstairs and into the building as "Glassman," one of Hog's several ops assistants, was yelling into a radio. He looked up and said the caller was a Hmong man, still living with his family on the western edge of the PDJ. Glassman translated the man's message as it came in.

"Flare ship on station."

"Big Light."

"ENEMY IN OPEN. ENEMY IN OPEN."

"They're pulling back. Fast. Running."

"Artillery coming in. Spooky working."

Later, "OK now. Everything quiet. Good night."

I walked out into the street of the compound and then around the headquarters building. There was a jail or stockade built into the karst in the rear. My first thought was that it was for prisoners while they were being interrogated, but I had never seen any reports where Sky had personally interrogated any Pathet Lao or North Vietnamese. Maybe it was a holdover from years past.

There appeared to be a freshly beaten path to the front gate and I peered in to see if it was occupied. There was something under a blanket in the corner and as I looked in the blanket stood up.

And a bear walked to the bars, snorting.

"Holy shit," I said, jumping back five feet.

In the morning I found out the bear had been caught as a cub and was a local pet, though he was never let out of the cage. He liked beer and expected a bottle from late night visitors. Once during a lull in the fighting Bag wandered out to the cage and sat drinking with the bear for hours. Late into the night Bag opened the cage and wrestled with the drunk bear. Or that's what he told people later to explain the scratches all over his arms.

The valley was socked in the next morning with low hanging clouds and Buck and I sat in the mess hall drinking coffee to stay out of the way of the regular Sky officers preparing for their day's work. I had learned in the Army that no one liked loud, chatty replacements. And this was very select company here. I was the FNG and my place was silent and to the side. I had nothing to offer, nobody wanted or needed my comments about anything.

The first chopper that got out of the valley left midmorning to pick up two Thais wounded the previous night in the probe attack on the PDJ. The air ops assistant came into the mess hall not long after the first chopper left and told Buck and me that we had a ride to Bouam Long, LS 32, with Digger if we wanted to go. We gulped down our coffee and made our way to Air Ops.

Most of the Sky officers were on the ramp when we got there. Some were busy getting supplies together or talking with Air

America pilots, though others were sitting, waiting. Waiting was part of the job and all the officers carried paperback books. Most would read a couple of books a week: fiction, nonfiction, the classics. Except for Kayak. He read the thickest, dullest tomes ever written - mostly about economics and the stock market but also books titled *Calculus as Art* and *Labor Union Considerations of Dental Plans*. Things like that. And financial journals and curious articles like "The Effects of the Industrial Revolution on Italian Emigration Patterns." Greek pulled Kayak's book out of his hands as we walked into Air Ops and told him that he was crazy. Either he was crazy for reading stuff like this or this stuff made him crazy. One or the other. Kayak, sitting on the floor, leaning against the back wall with his knees up, reached up, got the book back out of Greek's hand and went back to reading without comment, swirling his toothbrush from side to side in his mouth.

When our Twin Pack was loaded Buck and I joined Digger in walking across the ramp and climbing aboard. Several Hmong soldiers were already aboard, heading back to Bouam Long with boxes of batteries, cloth, food and radios. We lifted off and headed north, staying well west of the PDJ.

Bouam Long was an oddity. In Laos generally there were clean lines separating areas controlled by the Pathet Lao/Vietnamese and those controlled by the Sky forces. In MR II the Vietnamese with their Pathet Lao hosts controlled all the area from North Vietnam down Route 6 to the PDJ. Except for Bouam Long. Twenty five kilometers north of the PDJ it was the homeplace of one of Vang Pao's fathers-in-law, Cher Pao Moua, and he was not moving. The outpost itself was in a valley at the top of the highest mountain in the area. Surrounding mountains were rugged with sheer drops to lowlands densely covered with trees and foliage. The only way in was by air. North Vietnamese and Pathet Lao had been trying unsuccessfully for years to dislodge Cher Pao Moua and his people. Even now Bouam Long was under siege and there were attacks almost every day on the position, which produced casualties on both sides. The Hmong at Bouam Long tended to their wounded and buried their dead in a corner of the compound. Villagers slept in bunkers and were rationed food and water.

We climbed up through clouds west of the PDJ and turned northeast. Digger said that some Air America helicopter pilots wouldn't fly over the clouds all the way to Bouam Long because if they developed any mechanical problems and had to make an emergency descent through the clouds, there was almost no chance of survival. Chances were not good in any case, but it was possible to bring in a crippled chopper by auto rotation if there was room and time to find a landing spot. Even when the weather was good, flying to Bouam Long was dangerous because all the territory north of the PDJ was controlled by the Vietnamese and Pathet Lao. Plus Bouam Long was always under attack.

This Twin Pack pilot, one of the best in the business according to Buck, made the trip without argument because "Red Coat," the Sky officer assigned to Bouam Long, had been trying to come down for several days, prevented by the weather. Digger was going to replace him for a couple of weeks. A former Marine officer who had led long-range patrols in Vietnam, Digger also had a masters in psychology and was a clear, objective voice in any discussion about tactics in MR II. He was not as sympathetic toward the failings of the Hmong guerrillas as others, including Hog, and thought the Hmong forces should be on the move more, patrolling, engaging the North Vietnamese. He was frustrated when the Sky forces were outmaneuvered. Bouam Long was a perfect place for him. He was one of the toughest officers in Long Tieng, going up to work with the toughest Hmong.

As we headed northeast the clouds dissipated and one of the Hmong soldiers on board pointed out a mountaintop he recognized, which helped the pilot get his position. Soon "Spiderman," a LS 32 ops assistant on board, began to get radio transmissions from Bouam Long and the helicopter was guided in. It was the highest peak in the area. When the helicopter got overhead the position it descended in a tight spiral. It was like landing on the head of a needle.

Red Coat was waiting for us as we jumped off the helicopter in the middle of the compound. After introductions we joined Cher Pao Moua in his bunker for a general orientation briefing on the area and to expand on Red Coat's radio reports on enemy activities north of the PDJ. Later Digger and Red Coat went off to work on a generator and Spiderman asked if Buck and I would like to visit one of the outposts around the compound, pointing to a position on top of a mountain peak to the north that looked like a turret position for a castle.

We walked up a narrow winding mountain trail north of the runway and went up and up and up and up. I finally had to stop and rest. As I sat gasping for breath I looked off to the edge of the trail at a defensive way-station where seven or eight young boys squatted, looking at me. They looked like dirty boy scouts, but they held their rifles like they were extensions of their own bodies, like they had been handling weapons all their young lives. Their smiles were friendly; they apparently thought it was funny that I was so winded.

Getting back to my feet I caught up with Buck and Spiderman as they approached the top-most position. It was protected by a moat that had been dug out of the mountainside rock. Some ten feet down at the bottom of the moat I could see concertina wire and clusters of mines tied on the wire, amid panjii sticks. There were so many mines I thought that if one went off, there might be a sympathetic explosion of the whole lot.

The moat looked like the valley of death.

In front of me inside the position a dozen young boys had gathered. One was lowering a hinged drawbridge made out of six large bamboo poles.

"What is this," I asked Buck, "my initiation rite? You brought me all the way up here to see if I can cross the bridge?"

I weighed 220 pounds, Buck maybe 150 and Spiderman, maybe a hundred. The bridge was made for the youngsters inside, smaller than the ops assistant, certainly not for me, King Kong Junior.

I didn't want to go into the position that badly and I didn't need to prove myself to Buck. Hell, he was leaving, so I don't know why I started to follow him and the little ops assistant across the valley of death on that tiny little bamboo bridge, but I did. I was the FNG just going along. Tentatively I put one foot on the bridge and tested its strength. It seemed secure enough and I put my other foot on the bridge and it swayed slightly but it steadied as I stood still. The rope that pulled and lowered the bridge was the only thing for me to grab on to but I couldn't reach it until I got more than halfway across. So with my arms out to my sides like a tightrope walker, I took another very small step forward and behind me the bamboo bridge began to eat into the side of the moat. Another small step and the bridge began to sway again. I could either stand perfectly still and wait for the bridge to stop swaying or, because my knees were shaking too much to stand perfectly still, I could take one more giant step and hope to reach the rope in a lunge to the other side. This I decided to do because the bridge was swaying more, rather than less. Stepping to the middle, I leaned forward, grabbed the rope and used it to catapult myself forward and up so that I jumped to the other side, but not before the bridge dipped very low toward the concertina and the mines. I landed with a thud as the bamboo bridge behind me bounced up and down several times.

I asked Buck just how the hell did he expect me to get back since going back I didn't have the rope to grab. "Don't worry about it," he said, "you'll think of something."

I thought, I'm trapped in north Laos, not far from China. A

prisoner in a tiny little outpost way up on top of a mountain. I thought, Brenda, this is the furtherest you can get from North Carolina.

I looked around at the position. It was much more littered, less organized than the Thai positions on the PDJ. The young boys who defended it looked half the age of the Thais I had seen, some not much taller than their rifles. Weren't we in violation of some child labor laws here I asked Buck. "Common observation by FNGs," he said. "We gotta fight an unconventional war here with the forces that are available to us. The average life expectancy of a Hmong male is probably not over forty. This is an almost stone age society, you know. People don't live long. They grow up fast. These young men," Buck said as he settled down on an empty ammunition box, "number one, are older than they look and two, the Hmong respect their elders and are not the child worshippers we tend to be in the States. The young men around us are fourteen, fifteen years of age and haven't any established value in their society. Now someone forty or fifty or fifty-five even, he's got experiences and grandchildren and personal debts - substance, respect, value - and they do other things. The young men - these boys here - have to man the barricades. The bullet leaving their guns can do the same job as the bullet leaving the gun of someone older. And we can't change the Hmong culture to fit ours. These boys are all volunteers, ask them. `Course they don't have many alternatives. Their fathers and their older brothers have defended this little outpost for a long time and in time their younger brothers will work here and eventually their sons will defend it, God willing, while these boys will have a chance to sit back in the compound by the fire. And if they die before they get that chance, they'll be buried in the corner of the compound and the older people will make another boy."

"Ah," I said, "you bring all the FNGs up here and tell them the facts of life in MR II and give them the trial by the bridge over the valley of death and then you give them their Sky pin. Very CIA."

"No," he said smiling, "it's just the way things are. You'll understand better after you've been here a couple of years. Let's go back down and see Red Coat and Digger."

And he and Spiderman walked back to the draw bridge and crossed it. I walked to the edge and asked the ops assistant to ask the young soldiers around me if they had more long planks to give the bamboo bridge some support.

They did not.

Was there another way across the moat?

267

There was not.

Were all the mines below armed?

They were.

Did anyone have any idea how I was going to get across?

They did not, and everyone laughed except me.

I spotted a rope off beside a bunker and told the ops assistant to tell one of the young defenders to take this rope to the middle of the draw bridge and to tie it to the rope that lowered and raised the bridge and then to go to the other side and hold the rope. Because when I got to the middle, the bridge was going to sway down and I had to have something to hold.

One of the young defenders walked casually to the middle, nonchalantly tied the short rope he carried to the drawbridge rope and walked casually to the other side. The bamboo bridge did not strain to hold him up. On the other side he, Buck and Digger's ops assistant dug their heels in to hold the rope taut.

I took one step out. And then another. And the bridge started to sway down and then side to side and I jumped, landing in the middle of the bridge with one foot and I grabbed the rope and I pulled as I pushed down on the bridge which was dropping anyway because I had jumped on it. And I fell off to the side, screaming.

But I did not let go of the rope.

And thankfully the three people on the other end did not either. They yanked me toward them. I landed with a thud on the rim of the moat, my feet scant inches from the closest mine. I had the breath knocked out of me and as Buck and the others pulled me to the top I was gasping for breath.

Everyone was laughing as I turned on my belly and peered back over the edge of the moat at the grenades and mines below. I continued gasping. When I got my breath, I said that it wasn't funny.

We walked down the trail to the airstrip and went into Red Coat's bunker. It was a man's place, stark, dirty, drab. In the entrance was a 55 gallon drum filled with water and an immersion heater - the bathing trough. Inside radios sat on an earthen shelf near the back wall. On a table was a propane gas camp stove, some empty C-ration cartons and candles. Rifles, pistols, binoculars and other assorted military equipment lay around in disorder. A couple of boxes of books were near a metal wall locker. To the side were steps that led down into an underground bunker. We heard Red Coat and Digger talking below and went down. Two cots were in the corner. Digger's duffel bag lay near the steps. Red Coat, stuffing things in a pack, said that he was always glad to leave and always glad to get back. Tough duty, I suggested. "Yes indeed," he agreed. "It isn't safe here. Every night I go to sleep thinking this may be it. Look at this," he said walking over to a piece of plywood leaning against one of the earthen walls. He pulled it off to the side, uncovering a man-size hole that went out and down. "That tunnel leads out to a rock quarry by the edge of the runway," Red Coat said. "It is my only escape route and it doesn't even get me out of the perimeter. I spend many of my nights there. I sleep better in the hole because we get rocketed a bunch and you never know where that first round's going land."

"Why do you stay?" I asked. "What happens if you ask for another job? Not that I'm asking for it you understand."

"What would these people do if I weren't here? It's my job. It's where they told me to go."

Digger came up and said we needed to get in the air; a helicopter sitting too long on the ground here drew fire.

We walked down to the airstrip ahead of Red Coat. There were several Hmong waiting to board and several others standing around saying good-bye. I asked the pilot if anyone had ever tried to stow away or jump aboard as he was taking off and he said, "No, this place is where they were born, it's their home.

We were back in Long Tieng by midafternoon and on a flight to Udorn within minutes, saying good-bye to Dick Johnson by radio.

Flying south I thought about the difference in the way the US military was running the war in Vietnam and the way the Agency was handling its tasking in Laos. Keeping the American army in the jungle of Vietnam took an incredible support structure. I remembered that it took seven U.S. servicemen to keep one U.S. soldier in the field. Using local forces in Laos the Agency needed only one Sky man for about every five hundred soldiers or so in the field. Inverse pyramid. Plus it was obvious to me in my orientation visit that there was a bond between the local soldiers and the Agency men. The Hmong were taken for who they were and there was no effort to make them oriental Americans. We did not corrupt their values to accommodate ours. The Agency had good men working in the program. No one had rigid, self-serving attitudes; the whole workforce was experienced, intelligent, adaptive, dedicated, with strong work ethics. Everyone was involved, felt they were making a contribution. The impetus for planning and for execution came from the field, not Washington. People tended to stay year after year. There was no bureaucracy. The Agency field headquarters in Udorn was away from the politicized centers of government.

With all those positive factors, could Sky keep the PDJ? I

didn't know, but then no one working our side of the line seemed to know for sure either. Except that Thai mercenary commander. He was sure we'd hold.

--TWENTY--
D-Day: Campaign Z, Phase One

The next morning I went into Jim Glerum's office and told him about my trip. I ended by saying again that I wanted to be assigned to Long Tieng. He told me to talk with the Stick. Later that day the Stick was walking by my desk and I asked him about a reassignment upcountry. He stopped, tapped my desk with his stick and in an even, but annoyed voice, said, "Hey listen, do your job here. This here is what you're supposed to do right now. This here's your fucking job."

That night over supper at the hotel I told Brenda that I felt I hadn't learned anything in my trip up north. Nobody gave a damn what I wanted to do. Thrill seekers weren't going to jerk the program around. I hadn't earned my spurs and I was asking for special consideration. Patience, I said. Patience. I have to have hang, even in Udorn though it's more terrible in ways than Bouam Long.

Get up to Long Tieng, with the fight coming up on the PDJ, I'd just be the FNG, my job was in Udorn... but damn-it.

Brenda said she didn't understand me sometimes, why I wanted to go get shot at. Peer pressure she thought. I looked at her without comment.

****

At work I struggled to get my mind around the many new places, names, units and weapons for both the irregulars under Vang Pao's command and the enemy, as best our intel and order of battle shops could provide. And I learned Air America and USAF terminology and rules of engagement.

I was tremendously impressed with situation briefings given by Jim Glerum to a never-ending cycle of U.S. civilian dignitaries and regular military liaison contacts. A Princeton graduate and former Navy intelligence officer, Glerum was probably the most widely known face of the CIA in Udorn. His briefings for the most part were the only information available in the local U.S. military community on the situation in the secret war to the north. Reserved and cultured, he would brief without use of military lexicon or acronyms. Always clear in sparse, direct everyday language, Glerum's military audience usually listened slack jawed and quiet. Jim Glerum ran shut-down briefings and most visitors would walk away knowing they had not been the smartest person in that room. Politicians and bureaucrats he briefed from Washington tended to come away thinking the Lao program was in capable hands.

In his briefings Jim suggested several possible tactics the North Vietnamese might employ to capture the PDJ from laying siege, to a methodical move to capture one position at a time, either north to south or south to north.

By mid-December the smoke from slash-and-burn farmers clearing new land from China to the Gulf of Thailand would begin covering the area and we would find out what was planned, Jim said. He was confident in the defensibility of the Thai positions and hoped that the pending battle would engage the North Vietnamese force for a long time. He often made the point that soaking up their resources on the PDJ improved the overall U.S. government position in Southeast Asia. But job one for the CIA here was to protect the sovereignty of Laos. If we lose in the mountains - if the CIA force was destroyed - there was no opposition between the North Vietnamese and the Lao King's court in Laung Prabang and the Lao government capital of Vientiane.

What struck me time and again as I listened to Glerum's briefs, was that I had no idea the importance of the Lao program when I was back in the States. And as a CIA covert ops it was secret, which meant that almost every American citizen didn't know the critical importance of its spy organization's work. I would catch myself at the end looking at Jim and the map board he had just used, and thinking what a great story the world was missing... the drum beats of pending combat between the fanatic Asian army from North Vietnam and the Asian army under command of mountain hill tribe warlord Vang Pao. CIA running things way the hell and gone out in the Himalayan foothills, in the shadow of China.

****

On 14 December we received overhead photography of large covered trailers coming down the road toward the PDJ from North Vietnam. In an effort to cut them off, B-52s and U.S. Marine and Air

271

Force jets, "fast movers," were targeted on the road that night and the next day.

There was a disquieting report from Hardnose that large-caliber rounds were landing randomly around all FSBs. Loud, with a tremendous payload, they had inflicted only minor damage; Hardnose opined that they were registering their guns as a final prep to the attacks. He was on the PDJ once when one of those monster rounds landed and it sounded like the mother of all artillery rounds. Tanks and now these big guns; the bad guys were coming with big weapons this time.

There was light ground activity on 15 and 16 December. The Stick would often come into the center ops room and stand in front of the map of the PDJ occasionally slapping the side of his leg with one of his sticks. Late on the afternoon of the 16th after he had stared at the map for fifteen minutes, he said, "Come on, come on, you dirty commie shits. Come on."

On the 17th resupply on the PDJ was cut short when the whole area was enveloped in low hanging smoke. The smoky season was starting. Greek was the last American off the plateau that day.

That evening in Udorn, Brenda and I had just arrived in Buck's compound to attend his going-away party when the beeper on my radio went off, signaling me to return to the ops building.

Most of the staff was on hand when I got there. Intercept from all sources indicated that the North Vietnamese were on the move. Our forces on the PDJ had been alerted.

We had three radios set to monitor the traffic through the U.S. Air Force "ABCC" radio platform that was circling high above the clouds over the PDJ. Their chatter filled the background of the ops room. Communications to the Hmong net and to the Thai nets were monitored and piped through speakers.

Grabbing a chair, I turned it backward, straddled it, and leaned up beside a desk near the map board.

No small arms fired. No enemy was sighted yet. Thais irregulars fired harassment fire on all avenues of approach to the PDJ.

We waited. And waited.

Some of the staff went home... with promises to return in hours. I left shortly after midnight, but was back in the center room by 4 a.m.

****

At 0530 hours on 18 December as the sun was just coming up... when ground fog and a low cloud ceiling had the PDJ socked-in.... all the Thai fixed positions and the Hmong mobile positions suddenly came under ground and artillery attack ... simultaneously.

Most units were reporting B-52-like bombs/rounds hitting with accuracy. The background noise in the radio transmissions was deafening. One of the northern most BC positions overlooking Route 7 went off the air in mid-sentence. A neighboring position reported that the Vietnamese appeared to have breached the perimeter and enemy ground troops were swarming over the defensive bunkers. All surrounded Thai positions were ordered to fire on the overrun outpost. Artillery was told to fire air bursts over it. A flare ship came on station and began dropping flares through the clouds.

The commander of the northern-most position, who had introduced himself to me as "the dean of students," came on suddenly to say tanks were approaching his wire. He said they were spreading out, some moving south toward FSB Panther.

More USAF gunships arrived but could only circle the area because they could not get through the clouds.

North Vietnamese infantry were reported to be following tanks as they plowed through the mine fields and concertina toward FSB King Kong.

Artillery from the FSB Sting Ray, Panther and Cobra, were redirected to support the northern-most position. The radio operator there, who had replaced the commander, was too excited to adjust fire. No one could get him off the air. He kept screaming in Thai and English that Vietnamese sappers were outside his perimeter.

Midmorning, Ed Reid, flying an Air America helicopter, flew Hardnose in under the clouds of haze to FSB Sting Ray so that the Sky officer could make an on-the-ground assessment of the situation.

Reid landed and Hardnose jumped off. The flight mechanic on Reid's helicopter held off some of the Thai soldiers, who were trying to get aboard the helicopter. They did take on two seriously wounded mercenaries. Soon after Reid lifted off, the position began taking heavy mortar fire. Inside the command bunker Hardnose surveyed the PDJ through binoculars. He was looking at the FSB Lion and Mustang positions, talking to some Thai mercenaries there, when the ammo dump was hit by enemy artillery. It blew up and Hardnose could feel the shock waves from the explosion inside his bunker. Debris was blown out for hundreds of meters and a huge dust cloud slowly enveloped the area. The few surviving Thais inside the gun position were seen breaking out of the dust, running off the position to join clusters of other Thais retreating off the plain to the south.

Outside of Hardnose's bunker, incoming mortar rounds continued to pound the position. It was obvious that all the other Thai positions on the PDJ were surrounded by North Vietnamese - there seemed no realistic hope to marshal the Thais moving south off the PDJ to make a counter attack.

Since the North Vietnamese had launched their attack at 0530 hours there had hardly been a let up in the incoming artillery fire – and some of the rounds coming in were enormous, sounding like large aircraft delivered ordinance. Hardnose called in Reid, who carefully picked his moment to land amid the mortar barrage. Hardnose scrambled aboard, rounds landing around him.

After gaining altitude Reid flew along the western edge of the PDJ as Hardnose talked with Thai commanders and interpreters/forward air guides, some still in fighting positions, some fleeing the fighting. They suddenly came under heavy 12.7 mm machine gun fire and Reid took evasive action, dipping and sliding around in the air. Just as suddenly, large bombs started raining down beside the helicopter. Right at the end of the rotary props. Reid, and Hardnose sitting in the back, would see them only for a fraction of a second as they fell by the helicopter. They were from a pack of Hmong T-28s, flying overhead that had seen the 12.7mm firing position and were bombing it, despite the fact the Air America helicopter was between them.

"JESUS H. CHRIST," Ed Reid said as he continued to slide his helicopter to one side to get out of the line of fire, from above and below.

In Udorn the Stick left late morning for the 333headquarters, the Royal Thai Army unit that facilitated the Thai irregulars program. He came back late in the afternoon to say that they were sending the three battalions of Thai irregulars currently in training up to Long Tieng as reinforcements. Some had just entered on duty recently, but they were all that was available to throw into the fight.

Midday on the 18th most of the Hmong guerrillas in GM 21 and 23 were heading to the southwest. Digger in a helicopter found the GM 23 commander leading a column of his soldiers through the central area of the PDJ. Digger had the helicopter land near the Hmong guerrilla commander. He jumped off and caught up with the stubby Hmong commander with the thought in mind of getting him to return to the fight. They had talked before about how GM 23 would fight and maneuver. The Hmong officer would hear none of that -- his unit had been hit with the large incoming artillery, so they had left their poorly defended mobile position when they saw tanks on the edge of the battlefield heading in their direction. And he continued his forceful retreat, leaving Digger standing alone on the trail. He scurried to his helicopter when he called it back in and left the area. No need to stay on the battlefield without troops willing to stay and fight.

One unit of Lao hills men from GM 23 was Lao Theung and they did not follow the GM 23 commander across the PDJ. They moved south toward FSB Mustang. They came up on the large NVA force launching attacks on Mustang, who took them for Vang Pao soldiers trying to cut off their attacks. They were taken under heavy fire, killing many and capturing others.

The Thai artillery positions continued to report that enemy was near their outer perimeter, amid the different defensive positions, and that they were receiving heavy incoming rounds. Big rounds, they said. Two 155mm guns were knocked out.

But as of midday all FSBs held.

The position along the ridgeline overlooking FSB Lion said they were being attacked by what looked like hundreds of enemy, plus they were under constant indirect fire.

At 3 p.m. on 18 December 1971 a USAF F-4 - Falcon 66 - was shot down near the PDJ by a PAVN Air Force MIG-21 firing an Atoll Aa-2 missile.

Two USAF F-4 responding to the SAR (search and rescue) for the downed F-4, fixed on two MIG-21s flying the Lao/North Vietnam border and took off in pursuit. One of these two F-4s broke off pursuit because it was running low on fuel. And heading back to its base, it did in fact run out of fuel. The pilots ejected before the plane crashed. (They were picked up the next day.) The other F-4, Falcon 75, headed for the South China Seas and was not seen or heard from again.

Later in the afternoon a T-28, flown by a Lao or Hmong pilot, was lost to ground fire. An hour and half later, near dusk, another T-28 was shot down near FSBs Mustang and Lion.

Total TacAir losses for the day were three F-4s and two T-28s. An all-source theater-wide effort commended to recover the downed pilots. This necessarily took TacAir resources away from protecting Thai irregular positions on the PDJ. Additionally, bad weather hindered effective close support.

With the aerial platform reporting of the loss of aircraft, one after the other, the confidence of the Udorn staff around me eroded. There was much consternation over the USAF pulling all their planes off for the SARs, because our defense of the Thai positions on the PDJ depended on U.S. TacAir. But who could we blame for the weather?

Late in the day a 105mm battery soldier came on briefly to say hand-to-hand fighting was in progress and he went off the air. I surmised that message was probably from FSB Panther.

By nightfall, all FSB were still in the hands of the CIA army except for Panther, which had been abandoned.

The North Vietnamese had taken severe casualties running head long toward the fixed positions of irregulars, but they had the momentum.

Throughout the night the North Vietnamese sappers and infantry kept snuggling in closer to the FSB perimeters and to outlying defensive positions. Enemy indirect artillery fire kept pounding primary targets without pause.

"It was hell in a mighty small place."

Taking in the bad weather and lack of covering U.S. TacAir, plus special intelligence from Hanoi that three battalions of fresh Thai replacements were being deployed up to the battlefield, the PAVN 165th Regiment's commander, Colonel Nguyen Chuong, argued to forgo the planned siege of Lion/Mustang FSBs. NVA Generals Tan and An and regional headquarters concurred. Sometimes during the night Chuong ordered his regiment to take out the Thai irregular commandos holding the three positions on top of Phou Teung - the tall hilltop protecting FSB Lion – the next day. Plans for this all-out assault were tentatively set for midafternoon.

In the north, the 316th Division units attacking FSB King Kong were told by regional headquarters during the night to put aside its plans for a three or four day siege and attack to occupy Thai FSB King Kong afternoon of19 December 1971.

****

Fighting on the morning of 19 December was not as intense because the NVA was maneuvering for its major assault in the afternoon.

Whiskey 02, the CIA's Thai forward air guide (FAG) on the center-most position of Phou Teung reported a large force of NVA to his front and, in as much as he could, he directed in artillery fire from FSBs Cobra and Sting Ray. There was some support from T-28s, but enemy AA fire was intense, prohibiting close strafing runs.

At 4:45 in the afternoon of 19 December 1971, the BC 609 positions on Phou Teung came under renewed intense indirect fire from almost 1,500 rounds of artillery fire.

At 5:10 two USAF F-4s, Falcons 82 and 83, guided by FAC Laredo 17, were overflying the FSB Lion area when Falcon 82 exploded in mid-air, possibly hit by PAVN 23mm or 37mm AA fire, or by indirect artillery fire. There were no chutes.

On the ground the PAVN artillery shifted from the Thai irregular positions on the top of the hill to the rear and – in attacks similar to the Dien Bien Phu battle - more than a thousand PAVN soldiers from Chuong's 165th Regiment attacked en masse up the hillside.

The Thai irregulars fired their weapons until the barrels of their guns were too hot to handle. Ammunition began to run out. The commander of the irregulars on the ridgeline, saying his positions was untenable, asked for permission to withdraw. The ranking officer with the Thai irregulars, Colonel Saen, denied the request; he told the irregulars to hold for as long as they could.

Hardnose received a radio call from Whiskey 02, reporting that the enemy was within their perimeter and they were down to throwing grenades and hand-to-hand combat. He said the PAVN infantry was attacking in waves, those at the front were waving red flags and running straight into Thai irregulars fire.

Whiskey 02 also reported that they were running out of ammunition. Hardnose contacted the ramp and asked air ops to try and parachute boxes of grenades into the three Thai irregulars positions on Phou Teung.

Knowing that there was a 23mm AA gun on the north side of the hilltop, a CASI Twin Otter took off from Long Tieng loaded with two parachute bundles of grenades. Once on the PDJ it approached Phou Teung at high speed and low from the south. At the last moment the pilot pulled the nose up to avoid hitting the hill and turned sharply to the west away from the AA gun. In the back, the ammo was kicked out as the plane strained to make the high-speed turn.

Hardnose got back on the radio to see if Whiskey 02 had gotten the grenades, but the old FAG did not answer the call. Smallman, Hardnose's ops assistant and close friend of Whiskey 02, said in Hardnose's absence that Whiskey 02 was making adjustments to the artillery he had called in on his own position … when he frantically reported enemy swarming his bunker. Small arms firing could be heard in the background.

Whiskey 02 abruptly went off the air, not to be heard from or seen again.

James E. Parker, Jr

****

Part of the 312th Division's report on the Phou Teung attack reads:

At 4:45 afternoon 19 December) The explosions came so fast, one on top of another, that they sounded like thunder in the middle of a violent storm. 120mm mortars, 82mm mortars, recoilless rifles, pounded the three [Thai Irregulars] strong-points and they disappeared beneath billowing clouds of smoke and flame. [That was followed by] our 130mm, 122mm, and 85mm guns pounding the hilltop.

The sound of the explosions suddenly changed. Our artillery had shifted fire to the rear. Signal flares flashed into the air over our command observation posts. Company Commander Nguyen The Thao leapt up out of his fighting position. The assault troops of 9th Company, 165th Regiment rushed forward, ignoring the steep slope of the mountainside and the enemy hand grenades thrown down to block their advance. Thao and Dan led the company forward, striking right into the center of the enemy strong-point. In the rear, a 12.7mm heavy machinegun barked as it provided support to 9th Company.

The red flag held by Squad Leader Vu Duc Thanh was unfurled and flapped back and forth like a flame as Vu Duc Thand advanced. The enemy troops who had been forced to keep their heads down by our artillery barrage now began to resist.

The entire 9th Company makes its way inside the enemy strong-point. Individual combat cells crept down the trenches. Exploding hand grenades and hand-held explosive charges shook the ground. The air was rent by constant bursts of AK-47 fire. The Thai soldiers utilized their solid fortifications to fight back.

10th and 11th Companies attacked up the hillside from the west and the southwest. Courier Hoang Minh Tri planted 10th Company's flag on top of an enemy bunker, where it flapped in the breeze. An enemy hand grenade exploded next to Tri. The pressure of the grenade explosion knocked Tri down and made him lose consciousness. His left arm was hit by a piece of shrapnel from the grenade. The soldiers behind him rushed forward, picked Tri up, and placed him in a shell crater while they bandaged his wound. After he regained consciousness, Tri returned to the fight. Wounded a third time and with blood soaking the leg of his trousers, Tri continued to stick right beside Deputy Company Commander Hieu to carry orders for him. Deputy Company Commander Hieu himself had been wounded at the very start of the assault, but he continued to command his company in the attack.

After several minutes of fighting, the soldiers of the 6th Battalion had captured half of the Strong-Point 1. On the other half of the strong-point, enemy soldiers used the cover of bunkers and fighting trenches to form pockets of resistance. Deputy Battalion Commander Bach Xuan Buong was hit and killed by an enemy bullet. The battalion had to halt to reorganize before it was able to resume the attack.

Meanwhile, Company Commander Nguyen Nhu Kim and Political Officer Nguyen Xuan Xien led 1st Company forward through a breech-point on the east side of Strong-Point 2. As soon as our artillery bombardment shifted fire to the rear, the deep penetration platoon charged forward. The red flag held by Deputy Platoon Commander Le Thanh Ngat was unfurled and waved in the air in front of the charging platoon. An enemy gun suddenly opened fire, raking the platoon's flank. Ngat, who was out in front of the platoon, fell dead to the ground.

Squad Leader Hoang Trung An grabbed the flag from Ngat's hand, but after charging forward a few steps a bullet ripped right through An's chest.

Private Quyen ran up from behind and took the flag. The problems in front of the breech-point in the enemy's perimeter fence brought 1st Company's assault formation to a halt. After taking a few minutes to spread out the assault formation, the B-40 and B-41 gunners began firing rockets at the enemy gun position. The enemy 12.7mm machinegun continued to deliver heavy blocking fire against our troops. The deep penetration platoon had only half of its original strength left. Company Commander Kim and the commanders of 1st and 2nd Platoons were all wounded.

A bullet hit Private Quyen. The flag, now soaked with the blood of our courageous soldiers, was passed to Squad Leader Nguyen Xuan Quy.

Enemy aircraft swept in and dropped bombs around the strong-point's perimeter fence. Smoke and dust rose into the air like a wall and enveloped the battle-site.

The situation inside Strong-Point 1 at that time was difficult. Both 9th and 10th Companies were out of B-40 rockets, B-41 rockets, and hand-held explosive charges, and they had only a very small amount of AK-47 ammunition left. The enemy survivors had retreated back into four underground bunkers to hold out. These four underground bunkers had been built at the time that the Japanese fascists had occupied the Plain of Jars. Later, the French had rebuilt

James E. Parker, Jr

and strengthened the bunkers.

Thirty minutes later the attack on the underground bunkers where the enemy survivors were holding out resumed. Enemy bullets were fired from the bunker openings and the enemy tossed out grenades as well. Five minutes later, our troops fired B-40s, B-41s, 75mm recoilless rifles, and 12.7mm machineguns at the enemy firing points, then our assault platoons carried the large packages of explosives forward. The massive explosions shook the ground. Blinding clouds of smoke and dust rose into the air. Our 6th, 9th, 10th, and 11th Companies simultaneously charged forward, tossing hand grenades and explosive charges while at the same time using bullhorns to call on the enemy to surrender.

At Strong-Point 2, even though Company Commander Nguyen Nhu Kim and all of his platoon commanders were wounded, none of them left their combat posts. Their actions induced a number of the wounded to stay with them and hold onto the ground in the breech-point of the primary attack sector.

After a barrage of heavy weapons fire against the enemy firing positions, our troops launched another assault, but the attack again failed. More soldiers were cut down in front of the breech-point.

The battle continued as fiercely as ever. Another assault wave was organized. Deputy Squad Leader Nguyen Dinh Nhi charged forward and hurled a satchel charge that destroyed a dangerous enemy firing position. The assault surged forward.

Enemy bullets shattered both of Squad Leader Nguyen Xuan Quy's legs, but Quy never let the flagpole fall from his hands. Company Commander Kim ran over, took the flag from Quy, and waved it back and forth to signal for his unit to assault and annihilate the enemy survivors.

After throwing an explosive charge into a trench and then raking the trench with a burst from his AK-47, New Recruit Luong Ba Son suddenly collapsed to the ground. An enemy bullet had gone right through his chest. Son gave his AK-47 to his squad leader before he took his final breath.

The last minutes of the attack were very active. Soldiers popped up into view and then disappeared again as they cleared the trenches. The pace of the attack accelerated.

Meanwhile, 3rd Company had launched a powerful attack deep into the interior of the enemy strong-point to support and facilitate the 1st Company's primary attack. Company Commander Ngo Truong Do and Political Officer Tran Van Tuc led their company in attacking BC-609's command post from the southwest.

280

The soldiers of 1st and 3rd Companies planted their tradition flags, now full of bullet holes and stained with the blood of their comrades, on top of the BC-609 battalion's command bunker. The attack formations of the two companies merged together atop the peak inside Strong-Point 2. The wonderful images of the division during the Dien Bien Phu Campaign were reenacted once again. More than twenty years later, the division's tradition of "Solidarity – Courage – Victory" had been maintained and enriched in new ferocious battles.

The battalion ordered that the siege ring be tightened even further in order to totally annihilate those who continued to stubbornly resist. Not a single [Thai irregular] soldier was able to escape through 5th Battalion's siege ring.

At FSB King Kong, Thai Artillery commander Pichai lowered the barrels of his 105mm artillery and fired point blank into attacking PAVN until he ran out of ammo. He then slipped out the back side of the position for eventual pick up by an Air America helicopter the next day.

By early evening FSB Lion and all the Thai irregulars positions on top of Phou Teung had been overrun. Still the irregulars on top of the ridge line protecting FSB Mustang held out ... until – in the early evening - North Vietnamese tanks came up the road from Xieng Khoungville, through the tank traps that had been dug earlier and smashed the last lingering positions. Some of the last reports from Thai irregulars above FSB Mustang was that enemy tanks were on top and crushing their positions. By midnight, small-arms fire had almost ceased and the North Vietnamese were consolidating their control of the eastern side of the PDJ.

With FSBs Panther, King Kong, and now Lion and Mustang overrun, Cobra and Sting Ray were abandoned.

By morning of the 20th, the PAVN owned the entire plain; all Thai positions had been captured or abandoned.

Some Thai irregulars made their way southwest toward Long Tieng. Others moved toward Ban Na (LS 15). Some collected on the other side of the second ridgeline south of the PDJ, near Pa Dong (LS 05).

Sadly, other captured Thais, Hmong and Lao Theung were being led away by the NVA east to North Vietnam, most never to be seen again.

****

General Vang Pao flew down from Long Tieng late on the 20th. It was the first time I was to meet him. He had a warm, wide smile and had a more cultured look than most of the other Hmong I had met. Rather than a fierce-looking mountain man, he looked like a serene, congenial Asian college professor. The Stick was waiting for him and they went into his office with Jim Glerum and closed the door. Later they moved to the briefing room and I joined them along with George Morton, the chief of operations.

VP contended that neither his forces nor the Thai could defend that ridgeline south of the PDJ. There were no protected airstrips or landing zones for resupply. Plus artillery fire, from the big guns that the Vietnamese had used in the attack on the Thai positions, could be fired and adjusted from across the PDJ.

The place to make our next stand was Skyline.

Stick thought we would be giving up too much territory without a fight.

VP said we could defend Skyline. "We cannot defend that ridge south of the PDJ. How can we? Come up, we go up together, like old times. You'll see. Cannot defend that position. Skyline. We can fight from Skyline."

The Stick said he wanted to think about it. He knew wherever the remnants of our forces went, the NVA would follow with their troops and tanks, big guns and jets. Skyline was next to our headquarters. Better to fight some distance away, because if we made our stand on Skyline, then we had to hold there or all was lost. Maybe around the Ban Hin Tang pass area between the PDJ and Long Tieng would be better.

Latter VP and the Stick went over to the Thai rear headquarters. The commanders there regretted the loss of their countrymen and the positions on the PDJ but they were willing to facilitate the recruitment and training of additional mercenaries to stop the advancing North Vietnamese. They said the North Vietnamese should pay for every inch they moved south.

The Thais and the Vietnamese had been fighting one another for centuries. Cambodia had been the most frequent battlefield, but the Thais also fought the Vietnamese in what is now Laos. Their natural inclination had always been to attack the Vietnamese at the head of their advancing columns. They wanted Vang Pao to make a stand on a ridgeline south of the PDJ. The Thais facilitated the recruitment and training of the Sky mercenaries because it was in their interest. Their borders and national security were at risk. They wanted to stop the Vietnamese in the mountains before they got to the

Mekong.

Where to take the next stand was partially decided that night, however, when the NVA big guns opened up again and the new positions on the other side of the second ridgeline were blown apart.

The Vietnamese had to be stopped at Skyline. Pa Dong and the Ban Hin Tang pass were dropped from consideration.

****

Early on 21 December, the three newly organized Thai irregular battalions – BCs 616, 617 and 618 –began arriving in Long Tieng on Air America C-130s from the U.S. Special Forces training site in Thailand. BCs 616 and 617 were immediately ferried by helicopters to the peak of Skyline and were in place by nightfall amid a rag tag collection of other Lao irregular units strung out along the ridgeline. BC 618 was kept in the valley on the east end of the runway, near the Thai headquarters.

That same night PAVN sappers infiltrated the Long Tieng Valley and hit the ammo dump before all were killed by Hmong, Lao Theung, and Thai irregulars. Some, who ran into the area where Hmong villagers lived, were killed by civilians. To their great credit the newly arrived mercenaries did not start firing at shadows and more or less let sappers die in situations of their own making. There were no friendly casualties.

Next morning some Hmong packed their belongings and left the valley. NVA attacking their families in their homes was more than they wanted. Other Hmong watched, but did not strike camp. Some stayed because they had turned into merchants working the Long Tieng market and had too much merchandise to haul away, others refused to be pushed around by the hated North Vietnamese and stayed just because it was part of the Hmong character to fight outsiders. Those that stayed were comforted by the fact that the full Sky contingent arrived for work every morning – just like as before. The enemy may be massing on the other side of Skyline, but if Sky stayed, then they would stay too. They knew that Hog and the others always spent the night up in Vang Pao's bunker on the southern ridge. They trusted Sky, and stayed because of their dedication to Vang Pao.

Air America became very selective about landing fixed-winged aircraft, though work in the valley and on Skyline to fortified the fighting positions continued cautiously. Aerial photography of the PDJ showed heavy tank tracks going south, first to the road leading around the first ridgeline where the Thais had initially fallen back and then generally to the southwest in the direction of the Ban Hin Tang pass.

Air America helicopters continued to fly in, but as time went on some of the fixed-wing pilots refused to work the area because of the potential threat of the big, big guns the PAVN had used with such deadly accuracy on the PDJ. The Stick and Jim Glerum talked with some of the senior pilots, asking them to take reasonable risks. He was sure the Vietnamese could not adjust the fire of those guns because they did not control the high ground, were firing at maximum range, and did not have forward observers in position. Plus to bring the guns out in the daytime when Air America was asked to fly in would expose them to strikes by the T-28s or, if they were close enough, to counter battery by the VP's 155mm artillery. The big enemy guns were a psychological terror weapon and posed no real threat to aircraft on the ground, the Stick said. Air America continued to bitch about the risk but, as always, did the job.

Some Hmong GMs not involved in the defense of the PDJ were ordered to interdict the North Vietnamese as they moved southwest toward Skyline – particularly at the Ban Hin Tang pass, although the majority of the hills tribesmen were put at the east end of the valley to close that off to an end around attack by the North Vietnamese.

Hmong GMs patrols out in the area between Long Tieng and the PDJ reported large numbers of the enemy moving southwest, but not through the river valleys, as much as up and over the tall mountains. But all reports indicated the North Vietnamese were coming in significant numbers.

Bulldozers and construction materials were sent to Long Tieng to help make the bunkers on Skyline as strong as Agency engineers could make them.

Air America helipads were built to support concentrations of bunkers. On the far east was the CD pad, then going along the razorback ridgeline to the west was CT, built in a slight deflate off the south crest, then CA to support the forward-most fighting positions. Some of the most dominant bunkers were built on the west side of CW, the highest peak on the ridge. Down the ridgeline was the isolated CB helipad; the terrain on the north slope in front of CB was the most severe, the steepest, and the least attractive avenue up to the top of the ridge. Then at the lowest point of Skyline was the CE pad that was well positioned to defend the road that came up and over the ridgeline from Sam Thong. Across the road and on top of the next crest was the far western helipad, CC.

Hugh Tovar, the CIA's chief of station (COS) in Vientiane,

tried for several days to located Vang Pao after he returned from Udorn. He finally found the sick/dispirited warlord hunched over a fire in a desolate Pa Dong field position. Tovar rousted him from his funk and sent him to the USAF hospital in Udorn where he was diagnosed with pneumonia and exhaustion.

Thai irregulars continued to stumble into Vang Pao's forward positions east, northeast and north of Long Tieng. Sometimes they came alone, sometimes in twos and threes. Many had fought their way through PAVN ambushes.

Morale dipped among the new arrivals as the ragged and sometimes bloody stragglers were collected at rally points to be sent to Thailand for medical examination and reorganization.

On the morning of the 27th, as a Hmong T-28 was taking off from Long Tieng, the pilot spotted a group of soldiers on top of a karst toward the east end of the runway. Shoua Yang, Vang Pao's deputy, sent Hmong commandos up and they kills the entire group. They recovered maps, compasses and binoculars plus notebooks with "130mm" written prominently on several pages.

Also about this time two PAVN regiments – 148th and 866th -- and several sapper units, overran Hmong positions on top of Phou Pha Sai mountain and began arriving north of Skyline to prepare for the assault over the ridgeline and down into the Long Tieng valley. They joined other PAVN units in the shadow of Skyline including the 19th and 27th sapper battalions.

****

On December 31, 1971 (New Year's Eve) most of Sky left the valley early. Only Hog in the Hmong command bunker on the south ridge, overlooking the valley, and Hardnose, in a bunker near Bounder Control (the Thai command center), remained.

Just before midnight the PAVN 130mm field guns - re-located to well-hidden positions on the southern PDJ - began to fire a massive, teeth rattling, shock and awe artillery barrage into the Long Tieng valley.

The mop-up Phase II of Campaign Z to occupy the Long Tieng valley had begun.

James E. Parker, Jr

--TWENTY-ONE--
Joseph

Brenda was on her own most of the day and early evenings as I worked up after-action reports and helped with development OF new ops proposals. We often got together for lunch. She bought a car, made a trip down to Bangkok on 50-Kip to get Harry, our dog, from quarantine. She did not like the house Buck had lived in and on her own located a nice bungalow near the edge of town. Our closest neighbor would be Izzy Freedman, an Air America pilot.

As Christmas approached, we had been in the Charoen Hotel for almost a month and were anxious to move out. However, there were too many things that had to be fixed at the house first. It became painfully evident that we were going to have to spend Christmas in our twelve by twelve hotel room. Along with the presents we received from North Carolina, I bought my wife a dozen gifts, had them gaily wrapped and put them around the tiny plastic tree we had bought at the base exchange and placed in the corner of our hotel room.

On Christmas, after having breakfast in our room, we exchanged presents on the bed. It was a hundred degrees outside by midmorning. Brenda didn't want to go to the pool - "indecent on Christmas to go to a swimming pool" - and refused to go to the lobby and read - "I'd feel like a refugee" - so we decided to go to the local Catholic orphanage near the air base. After buying two large baskets of fruit from the open-air market downtown, we headed out to Saint Mary's School and Orphanage on the Sakon Makhon road. Pulling into the parking lot in the back, we were immediately surrounded by dozens of kids in clean, pressed clothes, some jumping up and down outside the car. "All this for fruit?" I asked.

We got the baskets out of the back seat and gave them to some of the larger kids who led us into the orphanage. Some of the children reached up and grabbed our hands; there were many little hands competing for our fingers. The kids were talking excitedly in Thai, pulling us along. Smiling, some showed missing teeth. We were brought to a Sister sitting behind a desk. Apologizing because we had so little and there were so many, the Sister said it didn't matter... merely coming was the best gift. Besides, she said, the U.S. Air Force would be here soon with bags of toys. She invited us to go in the back near picnic tables where the kids ate and wait for the Air Force.

286

The Vietnam War Its Ownself

As our small parade was making its way through the orphanage to the back we passed the nursery. There was only one kid there. Standing on his small legs, his head steady, he gripped the bassinet, using his weight to sway it from side to side. He wasn't smiling. His dour expression, standing all alone in his metal bassinet, made him look like he was serving time in jail. Brenda and he made eye contact. She walked on a couple of steps, but then leaned back into the doorway and saw the boy standing still, more forlorn as the crowd moved past. Brenda straightened up and asked the nun about the sad-looking little waif.

The nun at the head of our column said he had always been sickly. Didn't expect him to live, really, but he had survived. Recently he had a growth surgically removed from his stomach and had been standing up now only a couple of days. My wife asked if she could carry him to the back and the nun opened her palm toward the little runt. Brenda swept in. As she approached the boy tilted his head back to follow her and his eyes got very, very big. When she picked him up, his immediate response was to push away. At his arm's length he continued to look at Brenda with very serious, little boy doubts.

Out back, however, he came to like his position on her lap. Once when she went to put him to the side so that she could play with some of the other kids, he reached his two scrawny little arms out toward her and she picked him up again.

And suddenly there wasn't anyone else around my wife. Sure, the other kids were there, still vying for her attention, but for Brenda there was just this scrawny kid who seemed to respond to her in a special way. The look in his dark eyes was of intense awe.

The Air Force's sweating Santa Claus and attendants soon arrived with gifts and ice cream to an explosion of noise among the kids. Some of the gifts were simple, yet to the kids they were the most wondrous things. Everywhere you looked kids were laughing and jumping around. Some of the GIs got on their hands and knees and the kids crawled over them, riding them like horses. Off to the side, two of the Fathers stood smiling.

And Brenda fell in love with the little boy on her knees.

"Isn't he the grandest thing?" she said. "Oh Jim," she said, "Look at him laugh. Look at him. He's laughing."

She went back to see him the next day, of course, and then a few days after that. She said that he seemed to recognize her when she came in that third time. And she said he seemed to like being with her as much as she liked being with him. They had something, the two of them, that crossed age lines, gender, culture, language. Something you felt in your stomach, she said. And in your heart.

There was much going on with my job so it was shortly after New Year's Eve and the startling happenings up at Long Tieng that I went with Brenda back to the orphanage. By this time she had seen the boy maybe four times.

This was visit five.

She wanted to ask if we could take him home overnight. When she stopped by the front office to talk with the head nun, I walked on back to the nursery.

Off to the side, hell I didn't know which of those dozens of kids was the scrawny kid Brenda was after. They all looked pretty much the same to me, dark hair, big diapers; all in the same style of bassinet.

When, down the hall you could hear Brenda talking and laughing with the nun and clearly you could hear her footfalls. There in the middle of that nursery one little boy stood up, suddenly energized. Eyes wide, standing as tall as he could, he leaned to one side of his bassinet so as to try and look around the corner of the door where Brenda's voice was coming from, anxious, straining to hear, waiting to see... and then Brenda turned the corner...

I think an American kid would have yelled or maybe jumped up and down, I don't know.

But this kid just stood tall and still there in his bassinet looking at Brenda... but he had the greatest expression of love on his face I have ever seen. Not two years old, his face showed enormous joy... with a glowing smile and dancing eyes. Without a sound, his happiness just took up the whole room. It was an amazing picture. This kid had nothing to call his own just days before. Barely had a life. And now he had this wonderful woman who seemed to like him, not anyone else. Just him. And he was so happy, he so loved this woman. He held out his arms to be picked up, beaming. Happy times a thousand.

--TWENTY-TWO--
D-Day: Campaign Z, Phase Two, Part One

Back in Long Tieng on 31 December the enormous 130mm rounds began to land. Hog established contact with all the Hmong units to ensure that everyone stayed protected and prepared for ground assaults. While the message itself wasn't important, what was important was the Hmong knew Hog and Sky were still with them. Hardnose, having first contacted Hog to make sure he was alright because many rounds were landing near him on the south ridge, made contact with all Thai irregulars positions on the ridgeline to warn of impending assaults up the other side.

The initial rounds, landing one and two at a time, were soon followed by a steady bombardment, one monster round after another. Hardnose scrambled out of the headquarters bunker to another site dug into the side of the south ridge. Rounds were landing so quickly and were so deafening on impact that he had trouble talking on the radio.

Alerted to the bombardment in Vientiane, Digger was sent up in a Twin Otter aircraft to post over the valley and maintain communication with the two Sky officers in the valley below.

The two new Thai irregulars battalions on Skyline took the blunt of the ground attacks that followed the first incoming 130mm rounds. The attacks were more of a probing effort, rather than all-out assaults as had been seen on the PDJ on 18 December.

In Washington, when the National Security Advisor, Henry Kissinger was advised that attacks had commenced on Long Tieng, he ordered changes in the organization of USAF Operation GOOD LOOK. B-52s to support Vang Pao forces at Long Tieng could now be approved at the local COMUSMACV (Saigon) level. It was great news to us in Udorn, which meant that targeting the all-weather B-52s in defense of Skyline would be greatly expedited with communication possible between Long Tieng to the B-52 people rather than through two or three additional levels of USAF bureaucracy as was the case before.

On 2 January 1972 Hog and Bamboo stayed in Vang Pao's command bunker on the south ridge of the Long Tieng valley. Cobra and Hardnose stayed near the Thai command headquarters with their Thais ops assistants off the east end of the runway.

The large North Vietnamese guns opened up again after sundown and shortly before midnight the Long Tieng ammo dump exploded. U.S. Air Force planes tried to locate the enemy 130mm guns in the hazy, moonless dark of the Lao mountains south of the PDJ but they could not; the 130mm North Vietnamese guns fired at will.

Air America Volpar planes equipped with photographic equipment flew the river valley daily looking for the gun positions.

289

We knew they were firing at maximum range because the trajectory of the rounds were almost flat, barely skimming the positions on top of Skyline before impacting in the valley below, and the south ridge beyond. Although the Volpar crews did not locate the 130mm right away, they photographed a road the Vietnamese were clearing south to advance their artillery and their tanks.

Dick Johnson looked for an area to set up a rear headquarters to support the fighting on Skyline. He found a good airstrip near Ban Song, LS 272, at the terminus of the road leading north from Vientiane into the mountains. Proprietary interests were involved. Vang Pao argued against making this airstrip a permanent Sky facility because it was out of his area of control. The government of Laos had influence there, as did the Pathet Lao, the communist guerrillas.

At daybreak CIA paramilitary case officers – Ringo, Digger, Greek, Kayak, Moose, Electric, Tiny, and others -- would come up from Udorn and Vientiane, check in with Dick at LS 272 and then proceed the last forty miles north to Long Tieng, usually on Air America helicopters.

At night the case officers would clear with Hog and Hardnose in the valley and fly straight down to Vientiane where Ambassador G. McMurtrie Godley and COS Tovar held no-nonsense nightly meetings. Each Sky officer – in addition to the USAF reps and support people - would quickly brief on the activities of their units during the day, and answer Godley/Tovar/Johnson questions. Coordination/problems were resolved on the spot. The next day's activities would be planned before the meetings were adjourned. After the meeting case officers pulled a rotating schedule of flying, with their ops assistants, in an Air America Volpar airplane as an aerial platform over the Long Tieng valley, staying in contact with the CIA officers on the ground to ensure there was no break in CIA radio communications and that all serious enemy contact was reported to USAF TacAir first responders.

It was only forty miles but the relocation from 272 to the Skyline battlefield added much "getting to the battlefield" time for the Ravens, at the expense of "time on target."

On the night of January 4th, B-52 bombers hit north of Skyline on targets coordinated with Hog in the valley.

The night of 6 January Team 4 of the PAVN 24th Sapper Company overran a Thai irregulars position on top of Skyline between the CA and CW pads.

The next night - 7 January - forty PAVN sappers from the 27th Dac Cong Battalion attacked in the valley. They destroyed two O-1 planes, part of the CIA compound and the restocked ammo dump. Rounds cooked off for two days. Hmong, protecting their family huts, took no sappers captive. One killed near the ramp had his privates cut off and stuck in his mouth. Other dead North Vietnamese sappers probably had their stomachs cut open so that the Hmong could determine what they had been eating. Vang Pao was known to do this to dead enemy after an attack. He would see if they were well fed, which probably indicated they were well rested and supplied, or if the stomach were empty, which might mean they were desperate.

An estimated hundred rounds of 130mm field gun rounds landed in the valley on 7 and 8 January. Thai irregulars were suffering casualties from both ground probes by small enemy units and from incoming artillery.

On 8 January Vang Pao returned to the valley from the USAF hospital in Udorn. It was a day of great activity in the valley. Some of the Thai irregulars from the new units – both those on top of Skyline and others held in reserve – deserted. Many collected as much food as they could, and then just joined the Hmong villagers who were moving out to the south. One group got as far as a road forty miles southwest of Long Tieng, commandeered a truck, and in their subsequent drive south were ambushed by bandits. All were killed including a Thai woman who had joined the group.

While the number of Hmong civilians moving out of the area was a continuing concern to Washington, deserting Thai irregulars also got Washington's attention because it sounded to some like the North Vietnamese were fighting irregulars way south of Long Tieng. That was the wrong read, which led Washington to put importance to the incident that it did not deserve.

When newly arrived Thai mercenaries would just summarily walk off their positions we came to accept it as part of the difficulty in running a volunteer, unconventional, irregular army. If they wanted to quit, they just said as much, and headed south. It became an accepted part of the program that after a while weeded out the faint of heart, leaving a dependable irregular fighting force. The units were made better for what we thought at first was a bad thing.

Triage centers set up near the Thai ramp in the Long Tieng valley handled the Thai wounded on Skyline, pending their medevac to Nam Phong, Thailand. Thai mercenaries killed were put in body bags and placed off to the side of the ramp. They would be sent south at the end of the day to eventually be escorted to their home of record, where their families would receive significant death benefits.

****

With the sappers still in control of the one isolated irregulars position between CA and CW, the Thais set up around that position to prevent enemy reinforcements to the site.

On the afternoon of the 9th soon after CIA case officer NoMan and his ops assistant were picked up from the CA pad by an Air America helicopter, the BC 617 Thai battalion commander was killed by an enemy sniper. The battalion gave up its positions en masse, including positions near the CW pad. As the 617 irregulars made their way east and south off the ridgeline, PAVN sappers quickly moved up and took most all the CW positions, giving them control of the Skyline high ground.

****

It was now more than three weeks since the large PAVN attack force swept the PDJ. Time, U.S. officials thought, for most of the PAVN thousands to have moved the twenty to twenty-five miles southwest to Skyline. Most assumed the PAVN sappers who occupied the middle of Skyline was the advance elements of this large enemy force intent on occupying Long Tieng.

With NVA sappers holding the CW pad, the only Vang Pao forces in defense of Long Tieng were BGs 121 and 122 of Hugh (Greensleeves) Murray's Lao GM (Groupe Mobile or battalion) from MR I on the far west pads of Skyline – CC and CE. CB was unoccupied. There were some 400 men of Thai BC 616 around the CA and CT pads and one Hmong commando unit was on the far east of the ridgeline near the CT pad. There were two Lao GMs from Savannakhet on the outskirts of the valley, with two Thai irregulars battalions in reserve, the remnants of BC 617 that had abandoned CW and BC 618, which had never been deployed forward. Hmong GMs were holed up in the east end of the valley and to the north as far as Romeo (aka Zebra) Ridge. They were in contact with other Hmong forces through the commandos at CT on Skyline.

Not many troops and not particularly well placed to withstand expected PAVN assaults.

In Washington, Kissinger told President Richard Nixon that there were almost no friendly forces defending Long Tieng. Nixon replied that maybe Laos cannot be saved.

Documents taken from a dead PAVN soldier, corroborated by debriefing of a PAVN prisoner, indicated PAVN plans were to take Long Tieng by 14 January 1972.

Pathet Lao radio announced on 12 January that Long Tieng

has fallen.

And then on 14 January the headlines on two Hanoi newspapers read "Long Tieng has Fallen," including the official military newspaper, *Quan Goi Nhan Dan*, which published a detailed, front page account of the "great victory."

****

Understandable why most thought the war in Laos was over

But that wasn't the case.

--TWENTY-THREE--
Mary and Joseph

Joseph's afternoon outings with Brenda were stretching to overnights at our home and eventually into long weekends. It was getting more and more difficult for Brenda to return him to the orphanage. One night over dinner she asked if we could initiate adoption procedures. Because I didn't know what was involved I went to the Judge Advocate General's office on base the next morning and spoke with an Air Force lawyer who had some experience in dealing with officials from the Thai Ministry of Interior, which had partial, but not complete, responsibility in adoption matters. He said according to Thai law, for an in-country adoption, the adopting parents had to be at least thirty years old, the natural mother had to sign an unconditional release form, and the Ministry of Interior had to do a six-month home study. He added that it was a bit more complicated and more difficult than that. He advised me not to try it, I was only asking for heartache. Maybe, he said, we should wait until we got ready to leave the country and apply for overseas adoption, which was easier. The Pearl Buck Foundation in Bangkok supposedly helped.

Brenda was crestfallen when I told her that night. We always knew that we would adopt because Brenda could not have children. However, we had not talked about that when we went to the orphanage on Christmas Day. There was something cosmic about Brenda's contact with Joseph that day and now, with their time together, they had developed a loving bond. There were so many kids at that orphanage, no one would miss that scrawny little runt, she said. I want that boy and he needs me.

And the U.S. Air Force lawyer asked us to wait for a couple of years before doing anything? Come on, Jim, she said, do something.

In bed that night I told her I'd get a Thai lawyer the following day. Since I was only twenty-nine, Brenda, twenty-eight, I suggested that perhaps the orphanage would allow us to be foster parents until near the end of our tour when we would be old enough, according to Thai law, to adopt.

Early the next day, a Friday, I drove over to the headquarters of the Thai mercenaries and sought an interpreter I had gotten to know when he had been called to our office as a translator. I asked him to recommend a local lawyer for a personal matter, like adopting a kid. He suggested we go see the province chief who, because the area was under martial law authority, was the final approving official on something like that. The interpreter said we ought to ask that man directly about what we needed to do, and not some lawyer. Getting a lawyer was the American way. You go to the people making the decisions here and get the job done yourself.

We drove to the province administration headquarters and were admitted to the province chief's office after a surprisingly short wait. There I sat silently while the interpreter explained the situation to the province chief, an army colonel. When he finished, the province chief spoke for a few minutes in fast Thai and then he stood up, extending his hand, ending the meeting. Walking out of his office I said, "Good? Bad? What?"

The colonel had said to forget the Ministry of Interior's home study. If the orphanage and the natural mother say it is okay for me to adopt the child, then he'll go along with it. He suggested that we check with both the orphanage and the mother - and see him again next week.

My first thought was this was better than I hoped. We could get it all done, maybe, in a week rather than the two years we were talking about yesterday. We had something here!

Then I thought we don't have a chance in hell to find the biological mother. All we know is that the boy was brought to the orphanage when he was one day old, probably not by the mother because she would have been too weak. And that was two years ago.

I expressed these concerns to the interpreter and he agreed that we probably had little chance to find the exact person we were looking for but we could hire some lady to sub for her. He said that's the way things like this are done in Thailand. I said I couldn't do that. He said he could and that if it reached a point where this was our best option, then he suggested that I back out and he would generate a mother. "Can do easy, GI," he said, mimicking a barroom phrase popular with Udorn Air Base camp followers.

When the translator and I arrived at the orphanage late morning, one of the nuns said Brenda had been in earlier and had taken Joseph for the weekend. We asked if, when Joseph was brought in at one day old, was there an address given for the mother. The sister thought so and led us into the administrative offices of the church where old orphanage records were kept. The sister rummaged through a file of 5 x 9 cards and finally extracted a card on Joseph, Yongyut Daimuphuang, according to his birth certificate paper clipped to the back. The sister said that the Bishop was the final authority on adoption, but if we could find the mother from the address listed on the card and she consented to our adopting Joseph then she was sure the Bishop would approve. She handed us the card and wished us Godspeed.

The interpreter whistled as we walked back to his Jeep, saying the address was in the worst area of town, occupied mostly by squatters in lean-to shacks.

It was, indeed, a hovel. After walking down a dirty alley on the edge of town, we entered a maze of shanties. Jumping over open sewers ditches, balancing ourselves on catwalks, turning sideways at times we moved in toward the center. The smell almost took my breath. The interpreter kept asking people directions as we moved along. They answered quietly while gawking at me. Possibly other Americans had been into this part of town before, but not many. I was an alien, out of place.

We eventually found the house we were looking for. It was a relatively nice-looking building, compared with others we had passed. Possibly it was one of the original structures before the squatters moved in.

Standing in front the interpreter yelled the mother's name. There was no answer, though neighbors gathered around. He called the mother's name again and several people came out on the small front porch. The interpreter, who had gone to school in Australia and considered himself above the squatters around him and on the porch, spoke in a condescending tone, noticeable even in Thai, which I did not understand all that well. He talked loudly and the different people on the porch responded, quietly, as if they were guilty of some crime. The exchange went on for minutes. The interpreter asked questions loudly and different people on the porch responded with short subdued answers.

Finally the interpreter stopped talking in mid-sentence and turned to me, saying, "The short chunky one is the mother, but she said she's leaving this weekend, tomorrow, Saturday, and isn't coming back. She won't be available to go to the province chief's office. But, in fact, she's not going anywhere. She's just saying that because she's ashamed of leaving the boy, of not ever going by to see him. She'll just hide the next time we come back."

I looked on the porch at the only stout girl there. She was young and attractive, but very uncomfortable with us standing in front of her house, bringing up something about her past that she wished to forget.

"OK," I said, "tell her she has to come with us now to the province chief's office, he wants to see her. She has to go." The interpreter said "Right" and walked up on the porch, talking to the girl as he went. He pointed inside the house, turned over his shoulder and told me to wait a minute, they would be right back. Everyone on the porch went inside and I was left to look around at the crowd of people who had gathered around me.

The interpreter and the girl came back out of the house shortly. She had put on some make-up, had on a different outfit and was soon accompanied by a friend.

The interpreter said he went into the house with them because he didn't want the girl to run out the back.

The province chief was in when we got back. He met with the mother alone in his office. When she came out, the interpreter and I went in. The province chief said that he thought he could finalize everything that afternoon. He said he had the mother's consent, he needed the birth certificate, the orphanage's release, and my wife to sign some forms. The interpreter handed him the birth certificate and said the sisters at the orphanage had given us approval for the adoption. "Fine," the chief said, "go get your wife and we'll have things ready."

Outside the office I saw the girl and her friend going down the stairs to the front entrance. I asked the interpreter to follow and I chased after them, catching up to the pair on the street in front. I told the interpreter to tell the mother that what she had done, what was happening was maybe God's will and she should know that Joseph was going to have much love and a good home. The interpreter repeated what I had said. The girl continued to look away, still very uncomfortable. I asked if I should give her anything and the interpreter said, "Taxi fare home, that's all, she lives amidst thieves

296

who would take anything more as a sign of weakness and they might come after you for more money. I'll give her taxi fare, that's enough."

The interpreter gave her some change and I put my hand on her shoulder as she turned and walked away.

It was only early afternoon when I pulled up in front of our house. Brenda was on the front porch with Joseph and waved as I unlocked the front gate and walked in.

Five minutes later she was crying and laughing and hugging Joseph so tightly that he cried out. She couldn't talk. Stamping her feet in a little circle she kept saying, "WOOOH, WOOOH, WOOOH."

Leaving Joseph with the maid we went to the province chief's office. Within fifteen minutes we had signed the forms that had been prepared. Brenda went in and thanked the province chief and we were back in the car, with the adoption papers. I dropped Brenda off at the house and I went to the American consulate where the papers were authenticated. As far as the Americans were concerned Joseph was officially adopted and we could request a U.S. passport.

Back at the house Brenda could not keep her eyes off Joseph. She would say out loud occasionally, "He's my son. My son." He was almost two and could not walk because he had spent so much time on his back in a bassinet. On Sunday when he kept his balance in making a two-step trip from me to her, we yelled and shouted, and he was afraid, so we calmed down and just looked at him a lot. Brenda said he was the most gorgeous boy in the whole world. "Our son is the most gorgeous boy in the world."

****

On Sunday afternoon, two days after we adopted Joseph, there was a knock at the front door of our bungalow. A tall, older American man who we had never seen before was standing on the porch. He said that he was a USAID staffer preparing to return to the United States. I stuck my head out the door to look past him to see if anyone else was around, possibly explaining why this stranger was on our porch.

He said he had heard about our success with the province chief in adopting our son and that was the reason he was here. A year ago he said he met a beautiful Thai girl in a bar and within the month they were living together in his large USAID-provided house. She had a daughter by a previous common-law arrangement with an

American soldier at the Air Force base and she asked if she could bring her daughter to live with them. Of course, said the USAIDer, and the next morning a beautiful blond-haired child came into his life. She was the most intelligent, the most energetic, the most affectionate child he had ever known. His voice softened as he said this. She was almost three, but the man said she acted like the lady of the house. He enjoyed his role as surrogate father. He loved coming home to that little girl more than anything else in his life.

Her name was "Mim," he said.

After a fight one night, Mim's mother moved out, leaving the little girl behind. The mother still came by periodically, the man said, but Mim had lived in the house as his daughter now for more than eight months and it was their home.

The man said he had expected to stay in Thailand for the foreseeable future and his transfer to the United States was sudden and unexpected. He loved the little girl and he was intent in finding a loving, caring, situation for her. He said he had a family back in the States and could not adopt her himself. He asked if we would be interested.

"What about the mother?" Brenda asked.

The man thought she had moved to Bangkok or that was what she told his housekeepers she planned to do two months before, the last time she came by to see Mim. The man said the mother was an exotic beauty, but was very focused on her own life. She looked on Mim as competition, perhaps, or something that aged her.

I thought the whole thing was almost bizarre, although we were in fact excited as we put Joseph in his car seat and followed the man to his house. In short order Mim was escorted into the living room by the maid. She ran to the man and hugged his leg.

She was so incredibly beautiful that she was startling. Holding on to the man's leg she looked at us, in an appraising manner. First Brenda holding Joseph, then Joseph, then me. And then she smiled, lighting up the room. As we tried to talk with her, she toyed with us by running behind the furniture and peeking out, smiling. She didn't speak English and didn't understand our poor Thai.

I loved that child. She had that about her, to make people love her on sight. She had a magnetic presence, even as a three year old. She looked mature, intelligent. When she wasn't running around she would boldly look us in the eye. She welcomed our attention, as if it were her due, as if she had been looked at with awe all her life. She was a special, out of the ordinary child.

The next day, on Monday, I called over to the Thai

headquarters and asked the interpreter to meet me at an off-post restaurant after work. There I told him what had happened the previous day and our interest in following through on adoption procedures, first in trying to find the mother. On his suggestion, we went to the USAIDer's house. While I played with Mim he talked with the house servants. They said the mother frequently made reference to a bar downtown. Possibly someone there knew where she was.

I wondered on the way down to the bar if Mim was aware of how tenuous her situation was. How her future was being decided by strangers. She was so precocious that it occurred to me that we ought to ask her what she wanted, but then she was only three, what did she know?

When we arrived at the bar, one of the customers inside said the mother was next door eating.

The interpreter rolled his eyes and said I lived a charmed life.

The customer described what the woman was wearing and we walked into the neighboring restaurant and sat down at the table where Mim's mother was eating noodles. She and the interpreter talked for a few minutes. She turned to me. "Are you trying to take my baby away?" she asked.

"Not if you don't want me to," I answered.

"I don't."

I was not put off and through the interpreter told her how much love and attention we would give Mim. Good schools, travel. She would have the very best. The girl seemed to soften, but said as she got up to leave, "No, no, no, a thousand no's."

Brenda was disappointed that night when I got home, but this time I told her there was nothing I could do.

On Wednesday night the USAID man reappeared at our front door. He said he was leaving in a week and he wondered what we were going to do about Mim. When I told him about talking with Mim's mother in the restaurant, he said the mother hadn't been by and he was at a loss. Brenda said, "She didn't come by after Jim talked with her on Monday? Not that night, or the next day or the next night? Knowing that you are leaving the country? That is irresponsible." She turned to me, "Do something."

The next morning on the way to work, I went by the orphanage and talked with the sisters, asking for their suggestions. One said they would discuss my situation during the day and they would pray. She told me to come by that evening.

Midmorning Brenda came to the office and called me out to the reception area. She was standing beside a young, American Catholic priest. He said he administered a church some distance away in the country and when he came into town this morning on routine church business the sisters had told him about Mim. He wondered if he might do some good by talking with the mother.

I stuck my head in Jim Glerum's office and told him that I had some personal business to attend to. The priest and I drove down to the bar. The mother was sitting outside. She and the priest, who spoke fluent Thai, talked for some time.

At one point she turned to me and in English said, "What if your wife has a child. Maybe you won't love Mim as much."

I said my wife cannot have children.

Finally the priest said that God's will be done, the mother had agreed and would meet Brenda and I at the province chief's office the next morning at nine.

We were standing in the front of the province administrative building with the interpreter the next morning, but nine o'clock came and went and there was no sign of the Mother.

At 9:30 a taxi pulled up and the mother and the priest got out. He said that he thought she might forget or would need moral support so he went to the bar and picked her up.

Within an hour, we had completed the procedures and Mim was ours. I told the Province chief that I would not be seeing him again, but we were forever grateful.

Outside the priest wished us well. He cautioned us about the mother, saying she was unpredictable. One of God's beautiful children, he said, trying to make the best for herself outside an Air Force base. We assured the priest that we would be the best parents we could to Mim and we thanked him. We shook the woman's hand and promised her that Mim would be happy. She said she was on her way to see her daughter to say good-bye.

We decided that we could not let one of the maids bring Mim over to our house because we did not want the mother to find out where we lived. The interpreter volunteered to get her but I said I would. It was going to be a family affair.

In the early afternoon I pulled in the back of the USAIDer's house and the USAID man came out. He said Mim's mother had come by and had told him that we were adopting her daughter. She was crying, he said, and he did not know what she had to say to Mim.

He asked how we were going to get her home. I explained why we didn't want one of the maids to come, which he understood, and said I would be taking her alone. He told the maids to get Mim's clothes and toys together and they filled up my back seat. Though Mim acted excited when I arrived she was against having her things put in my car. She became scared.

She was crying when the USAIDer hugged her. When the maids, individually, said good-bye, she began to cry harder. When they tried to lead her to the car she began screaming and she grabbed at things to stop from being put inside. She was almost hysterical when I got behind the wheel and we pulled away. She pawed at the windows and screamed. In that small car I was also traumatized and I thought a thousand times that we should have done it differently.

At our house, exhausted, Mim jumped into the arms of our maid when I opened the door. But she sat at the table with Brenda, I and Joseph that night at supper.

In time she and Joseph settled in. They came to understand that their new situation was not altogether that bad. It was different though, and there were some adjustments to be made.

For one thing Mim, for as long as she could remember, had lived a privileged life. She knew she was beautiful, she had been told that every day of her life. She had been told that she was special, American-Asian. And although only three, for almost eight months she had been the woman of her house. It had been her kingdom. If one of the maid's children was playing with a toy Mim wanted, she walked over and got it. No problem. The child knew Mim could do that and Mim knew she could do that. Sometimes she probably did it just because she could.

Joseph, on the other hand, grew up in an orphanage, where the rules of the jungle prevailed. Might made right. If he was lucky enough to get a stick to play with in his bassinet and an older kid wanted it, then that was simply okay by Joe; the bigger kid got it. Made sense to him.

We bought toys for both kids at the Udorn base exchange and gave them out evenly. When Mim suddenly became interested in one of Joe's toys and walked over and ripped it out of his hands, Brenda would say, "Mim, you must give it back to your brother." Initially this confused both children. Joe looked just like all the other little Thai kids Mim had always dominated. What's the new concept here, she'd wonder? For Joseph, Mim was larger, acted like she knew what she was doing. Why did he suddenly have rights?

Joe picked up on the nature of the new rules probably before Mim and he began to fight loudly over his toys. Mim always acted as if this was unseemly behavior on his part. Ill mannered.

Within a few days, I came home, unlocked the gate, and

Mim ran out and hugged my leg, welcoming me home. I tossed her in the air and squeezed her.

Mom and Dad visited from the states. Brenda, in a state of bliss because of the kids, showed my parents Udorn like it was her hometown. One afternoon I was telling Daddy that we were in the process of putting in for Joseph and Mim's U.S. passport and we had to give Joseph a middle name. I asked if he had any suggestions. He said no one was ever named after his father, whose first name was Joseph. I asked what his middle name was. He said Elijah. Brenda said, "No." He was too small a boy to carry around such a heavy name.

We compromised. She could name Mim anything. I was going to name my son after my grandfather. And we did. And it made my father proud.

But that little boy from the Thai orphanage did not look like your average Joseph Elijah Parker.

Mim looked like Miriam Kristen Parker.

--TWENTY-FOUR --
Spartans at Thermopylae

The story on what happened on Skyline in January 1972, when most assumed Long Tieng was being lost to the vastly outnumbered North Vietnamese, we reported faithfully from Udorn to a disbelieving limited audience in Washington and to some local USAF officials at Udorn.

At the time we did not always understand why things happened the way they did.... until the North Vietnamese published reports on their Campaign Z in the 1990s. And then the story became clear.

Following is a composite, all-sources explanation of why the North Vietnamese did not win the battle for Skyline in January 1972.

Reason One When the 165th Regiment commander, Colonel Nguyen Chuong, on 19 December committed his men on the PDJ to take out the Thai irregular BC 609 in their hilltop fortifications, he decimated his forces. The initial plan was to lay in siege and take the three positions in four days. Chuong moved the attack up because

Hanoi intelligence advised that Thai replacements were being called up from Thailand and he certainly knew that the lack of USAF TacAir support was temporary due ongoing SARs. It was reported in the White House three days later that 200 bodies were seen on the wire in front of the three main 609 hilltop positions following the attack.

Plus, later, the 165th was sent from the PDJ to the Skyline battlefield, not through the Ban Hin Tang pass, but over Phou Pha Sai. It took them four days to climb over the mountain, with some units sent through rugged mountain areas without trails. Most had to scale cliffs. Decimated, tired when they finally got to Skyline, they had no oomph for all-out attacks. The 174th came to the Skyline battlefield via way of Ban Na/Sam Thong and was late. They had been delayed, some of them, by the successful actions of the Hmong combat patrols in and around the Ban Hin Tang pass.

Reason Two   After talking with Hmong Colonel Shoua Yang, VP's deputy, on 3 January CIA case officer Hog requested and received significant, timely, pinpoint TacAir.   Here's what Lucky, Hog's Hmong ops assistant, said:

Hog and Shoua Yang put in a request for B-52s to hit in the valley just north of Skyline. Shoua Yang especially was familiar with the whole area and knew the only place where a large group of PAVN could hide just north of Skyline was in what he called "VP's farm." The area was also known as Bang Kalong. So in putting in for the B-52 strike they asked that the bull's eye to be the center of VP's farm. Next night they got a message that the coordinates for the farm were too close to friendly positions. Hog insisted that it was absolutely necessary. The response that came back was "Maybe yes, maybe no."

[It is important to note here that this coordination between Hog in the valley and the B-52 targetters would not have happened without Kissinger's timely move to allow field approval for B-52 strikes.]

Two nights after they put in the request, early on 5 January a three big-belly B-52D sortie dropped their bombs just a few hundred meters north of the Skyline ridgeline. This sortie would have delivered 108 individual 750 pound bombs per plane or for 3 planes, that's 122 tons of explosives dropped directly on the massed enemy. The whole Skyline ridge and Long Tieng valley area shook and rumbled during the bombing. Greek was flying in the Volpar that night and reported the bombing was an awesome display of air power.

James E. Parker, Jr

The next day some Hmong commandos were dispatched down to VP's farm and found it blown completely apart. All types of mangled enemy weapons and web gear and body parts were lying around. The B-52s had scored a direct hit on a large enemy unit. From the 866th's and the 312nd Division after-action reports, we know the 866th was marshaling in front of what the PAVN called Phou Moc (the crest of Skyline). By all accounts this was the unit that was hit, because the unit did not participate in any of the subsequent attacks and toward the end of January and was pulled back to "reorganize." FAG Spotlight reported that the PAVN 148th regiment was attacking up toward CC on the west end of Skyline the day before the B-52 attack. After the attack on the night of 5 January some Thai irregulars patrolled down into the valley north of the west end of Skyline and found bomb-destroyed web gear and weapons. This would have been the 148th and the unit was ineffective and rarely heard from thereafter.

Reason Three The only supplies the PAVN had for their initial attack on Skyline was what they carried on their backs. Their mortar crews and their DK-82 field guns did not have much ammo when they got all the way forward. Eventually resupply brought in by the 209th and 335th Regiments and transportation coolies caught up with them with more bullets, but not initially. Not by mid-January.

General Nguyen Huu An reported later, "It was a seven or eight day march on foot from the Plain of Jars to Long Tieng, and all supplies and preparations for this next phase of the battle had to be carried on the shoulders of our soldiers. The units participating in the battle would be completely responsible for carrying and organizing their own supplies and logistics support. Because of the distance that had to be covered, if the battle lasted two weeks or more, the units would run out of food and ammunition, and all of our plans would become completely bogged down. At the time, however, no one thought that the enemy would put up stubborn resistance or that the enemy had enough strength to resist, because at the time enemy forces (from the PDJ) were disintegrating in terror, like twigs caught in raging floodwaters."

Reason Four The Thai irregulars proved to be stout fighters or, in the word of Sky case officers to mean strong resolve, they had "hang." Credit must go to Thai and Hmong leadership, who were committed to holding Skyline. In all instances where there was strong leadership, the Thai irregulars acquitted themselves in a determined fashion. Also the Hmong guerrillas backed to the wall,

304

were some places the only force between main line Vietnamese invaders within a thousand meters to their front, and their families, a thousand meters to their rear.

Credit certainly goes to Hog whose presence was known to every Hmong in the valley. If Hog – who the Hmong revered – was still around, they'd stay.

And credit goes to CIA case officer Doug Swanson, aka Cobra, the chief Thai case officer at the time. FAG Wild Bill was with Thai irregulars on the PDJ and on 8 or 9 January 1972 he was working in the Thai irregulars command center in the valley. He reported, "The battle for Skyline was not going well... and on the radios in Bounder Control there were some of the same frantic transmissions that I had heard on the PDJ. All around in the command center and up on the ridgeline Thai soldiers were excited, and talking about escape routes out of the valley. Incoming was landing randomly in the valley. We had lost the CW pad. Everyone was afraid.

"And then Doug Swanson walked outside to get a clear view of Skyline – incoming still hitting here and there. And he stood there unafraid taking everything in – and he called Colonel Saen outside to stand with him and they stood there, the two of them, and talked about what was happening on the ridgeline and what they could do next.

"And the FAGs in Bounder Control noticed that their commanders were unafraid and in charge. And everyone seemed to calm down. It all happened within the course of thirty minutes. Everyone was excited, ready to run, then word circulated out from the command center that everything was under control. And people calmed down."

And finally the man they called Dhep who ran the shop that facilitated the recruitment of Thais and handled their deployment north after Special Forces training deserves credit. A man of lesser resolve would not had stood up to the enormous challenges of making a stand at Skyline.

Reason Five   PAVN reports indicated that their sapper units who made it to positions around the CW pad early on indicate they ran out of water and, completely dehydrated, were almost physically unable to fight. Also, the PAVN 148th Regiment commander reported that his men trying to climb the north side of Skyline came to a stop because their thirst prevented them from moving on.

Reason Six On 13 January "Groupe Mobile" (SGU or GM) 30 recently sent up from Savannakhet marched up the road on the south side of Skyline to the CE pad and then over to unoccupied CB. On 14 January 1972 the commander Lao Colonel Chanh Nasavanh, the commander, got his GM got on line and attacked toward positions at the CW pad held by the PAVN sappers who were thirsty almost beyond human endurance. The area between the two pads was narrow – barely half a block wide – with steep sides. It had been denuded by bombs, so there was no cover. Thai irregulars commander Colonel Saen, FAG Spotlight and Captain Chat Pron, a company commander at the time in the Thai irregulars unit that was also on Skyline (BC 616), report that Lao GM 30, despite taking heavy casualties, with Ravens overhead providing air and artillery fire support, moved slowly, under constant heavy fire from the east end of Skyline and took the positions around CW before nightfall on 16 January.

All observers described GM 30's attack as "heroic." Included in this strong effort were Air America helicopter evacuations of wounded from the CE pad. Five Lao women nurses in the GM were conspicuous for their bravery under fire. Spotlight in particular had a good view because he was on CC to the west and looked down at the attack as it was taking place. GM 30 suffered 30 percent casualties as they took CW.

The thirsty PAVN sappers were expecting reinforcements ... and they got a very determined GM 30 instead.

PAVN reports, usually critical of the fighting spirit of southeast Asia anti-communist forces, all reported VP forces were unexpectedly "tough" on Skyline.

Reason Seven The PAVN sappers did not strike fear in the heart of the Hmong villagers in the valley, causing the Hmong to rout south, as was expected by North Vietnamese battle planners. Some of the Hmong civilians stayed because they had accumulated too much stuff to carry out of the valley and with an increase in looting of the abandoned huts, they feared they would lose their hard-to-obtain merchandise. Plus some Hmong were just defiant; refusing to be moved by the hated Vietnamese. And some heeded Vang Pao's encouragement to stay, and took comfort from the fact the Americans had not left. Upwards to 5,000 Hmong civilians remained, and the North Vietnamese presumed they were all armed and dangerous... part of the Long Tieng defense force.

Reason Eight And then there was U.S. TacAir and "Moose." A tall, quiet, non-assuming mid-westerner, Moose had been in south Laos for a couple of years doing CIA reports-officer work before coming to Long Tieng in late 1970. Dick Johnson gave him the PAVN communication intercept program, though Moose had no prior experience. He started with the basics of putting out dependable Hmong teams with equipment that worked to capture radio signals from PAVN forces in the area. He also used a C-47 out of Udorn for some of his intercept Hmong operators to use in overflights of the area.

Every night the Hmong in the intercept teams would take their cassette products and give them to Air America pilots working wherever they were. Moose didn't have to interfere with this much; he didn't send up Air America choppers just to get the cassettes. It just sort of worked. The Air America guys would bring the tapes down and give them to Air Ops, Greek or someone there, and Moose or one of his people would police them up and deliver them around sundown to three co-opted Vietnamese who were with the intercept group in the valley when Moose arrived.

He had no idea if these Vietnamese were locally captured POWs, or were brought in by the Udorn base. But they did a superb job. Moose had them stay up all night working on the translations so that when Moose showed up at their hooch (next to the radio repair shop) at dawn the next morning they would have all the tapes translated, with the product typed in English and translator notes appearing in parentheses.

They found PAVN forward radio operators informally talked and bitched on the radio all the time. Every time they went on line to chat, Moose's people listened and learned. Plus one of the three Vietnamese working for Moose was especially good at breaking codes and he soon was taking note of PAVN plans and their SOPs.

Tracking PAVN SOPs was corroborated by the senior Raven at Long Tieng, USAF Major Scott. They knew that when the PAVN company commanders were called back to the rear for sandbox drills on coming attractions, and when medics were being deployed forward an attack was imminent.

Moose's Vietnamese translators/analysts also were able to follow the movements of some of the PAVN radio operators because of their signature radio operations MO. And they were able to identify PAVN positions by inference in comments they made. Moose would take these reports every morning to the Raven shack and pass them to an USAF intelligence NCO and the different Ravens.

Hal Smith, a Raven who arrived Long Tieng January '72,

remembers the "Moosegrams" well. He said they were in at first light and reported on things that happened the previous day, sometimes along lines of a PAVN radio operator saying some unit to his north rear was really getting hammered. Hal could go to the map board to see what area was bombed the previous day, and then trace that back to possible areas where the radio operator and his unit might have been hiding and then go out that day and bomb that area - to sometimes receive feedback the following day by the radio operator saying that "holy shit" they got hit all day long.

There is also another case where Red Coat, the case officer at LS 32, was going out on the Long Tieng ramp to get on a STOL Porter for a ride back up to Bouam Long. He was intercepted by Moose who said that he ought to read something they broke out the previous night...and it was a report from a PAVN unit that had secured a vantage of the LS 32 airstrip with plans to hit the Porter when it arrived the next morning - the plane Red Coat was heading out to get on. (The PAVN unit was in "the gray rocks at the end of the airfield awaiting the arrival of the 'little white plane.'") Red Coat took a helicopter up instead, went to see the LS 32 commander, Cher Pao Moua. They figured where the PAVN were hiding and Cher Pao Moua sent up a unit to flush them out. Sure enough, they had crew-served weapons that could have reached out there and touched that Porter plane Red Coat was going' arrive on.

Moose, as much as any other individual in the allied force, provided the means to close with and destroy the enemy. He greatly enhanced the effectiveness of U.S. TacAir.

****

But the battle was not over. The PAVN had come to win "at all cost." Like Pork Chop Hill in Korea and Dien Bien Phu in Vietnam, negotiations were under way elsewhere to decide a "peaceful" future. The communists looked for ongoing successful battlefield activities to provide them advantages at the negotiation tables.

At midnight on 14 January a PAVN Air Force MIG 21 overflew Long Tieng in an effort to draw off USAF aircraft flying in support of the fighting on Skyline, to give PAVN ground forces the same break they had on the PDJ. The PAVN jet intruder was engaged by two USAF F4-Ds who fired nine missiles. They did not pursue when the MIG returned to North Vietnam.

****

As Lao irregulars in GM 30 were taking back CW, Thai irregulars BCs 601A and 602A – the reorganized original two Thai irregular units - were flown into the Long Tieng valley and deployed by helicopter to the eastern and western ends of Skyline. As soon as the units got to those Skyline's bookend helipads, they began to move toward each other and shortly joined up with BC 616 and GM 30 in the middle of the ridgeline. Some NVA sappers remained near the top hidden in small spider holes or in isolated fighting positions.

Fighting continued all day on the 15th around CW and CA pads as the combined Thai irregulars and the Lao unit from Savannakhet rousted out the North Vietnamese hiding on the ridge. By the 16th Vang Pao forces controlled all the fighting positions from the CC to CT pads.

The international press believed the Hanoi newspaper and the Pathet Lao radio that the North Vietnamese had in fact occupied Long Tieng. Although general rumors that Vang Pao forces, against all odds, still held Long Tieng circulated in Vientiane, Laos, and Bangkok, Thailand.

On 19 January 1971, breaking a decade-old policy that newsmen were not allowed up near the fighting, COS Hugh Tovar escorted representatives of the international press to the CW pad on Skyline to show that the valley had not been lost.

At the time the newsmen visited, Vang Pao forces owned the high ground, but there were four PAVN regiments within two miles to the north. All were pretty chewed up except the 174th, which, like the 209th and 335th, didn't have much fight. The press group left hurriedly when Colonel Chanh, the GM 30 commander, was wounded in the head by a PAVN sniper.

President Richard Nixon, who had been following developments, wrote a message to the CIA in the margin of a situation report on the fighting in Laos: "Long Tieng must not be allowed to fall."

The day after the international press was on the scene, two PAVN battalions make a fresh assault on Skyline. GM 30, holding the CA pad high ground, took forty-five casualties before retreating to the CW pad. In their place, a lone Hmong SGU, BG 224 led by Sky officer George Bacon, aka Kayak, moved atop CA and held off continuing PAVN attacks.

On 24 January GM 30, together with BG 224 and Nam Yu's BG 103 surged east and cleared the next Skyline chopper pad, CT, which had been temporarily occupied by NVA forces.

James E. Parker, Jr

More important on 24 January the reconstituted Thai BCs 603A and 604A, arrived on Air America C-130s from Thailand. The next day BCs 606A, 607A, 608A and 610A joined them. (The "A" designated that the units were reorganized)

In Udorn we did not know exactly how Long Tieng survived the month, but we knew for sure that they had – Hog and Hardnose would say as much every morning... and it was our great privilege to report their valiant stand in our briefings and in our reports to Washington.

****

PAVN forces pulled back and regrouped some distance away from the foot of Skyline; their hopes to take Long Tieng by mid-month long since dashed. Efforts to re-plan for continued attacks on Skyline run afoul of PAVN Commander in Chief General Giap's insistence on keeping to the approved original thinking, which did not seem workable anymore, what with the depleted capabilities of the 165th and the 866th. The 335th Regiment was brought in and replaces the 148th and the 165th in front of Skyline. The 141st was moved forward.

PAVN continued to build the new road through the mountains from the southern tip of the PDJ down toward Sam Thong. Hmong T-28s flew bombing missions along the new road. B-52 strikes were called in. Hmong combat patrols were sent in. U.S. fast movers with laser-guided bombs worked the road and the Ban Hin Tang pass. But road construction continued. Enemy tanks were coming to the battlefield.

****

One of the Volpar photo reconnaissance planes finally caught one the 130mm field guns in the open near the point where the new road left the PDJ. With its long rifled barrel, the piece looked like an old German railroad car gun. It looked enormous sitting beside its smaller truck tractor and other vehicles carrying ammo. This ponderous weapon rightly put fear into the hearts of the Sky people who had to work within its range. And the North Vietnamese had more than a dozen of these giant guns aimed at Skyline and Long Tieng.

It was bombed and bombed and bombed until the big gun lay on its side, busted... its ammunition cooked off. It looked like a dead dinosaur.

--TWENTY-FIVE--

Reassignment: Long Tieng

Toward the end of January, as the fighting ebbed and then picked up again on Skyline, Vang Pao offered up the preposterous proposal to move his Hmong guerrillas back to the PDJ. His argument was that while they might be able to actually interdict some PAVN supplies coming down to Skyline, the real value would be that the low-land PAVN near Skyline would feel trapped deep inside the mountains of Laos and would have to fall back to protect its egress and lines of communication. Vang Pao knew the terrain and the mind of the North Vietnamese enemy and was sure the tactic would work to relieve pressure on Skyline.

No one else was so sure. Vang Pao said he'd have his soldiers walk overland from Long Tieng and down from Bouam Long; he wouldn't need Air America so much. His local fighters, he said, would go back to acting like guerrillas, rather than fight as SGUs from fixed positions on top of mountains.

Some said he was just trying to get his forces out of the Long Tieng valley to avoid what most thought was the inevitable Vietnamese hordes sweeping over Skyline and down into the valley.

Nope, said Vang Pao to all critics, it's a good military move. Positioning the Hmong to the PDJ will make the North Vietnamese pull back from Long Tieng. He said he knew for sure. When Tovar seemed to agree, somehow the notion that he just might just be right began to get traction in Udorn.

Morton drew up an ops proposal to send back to Washington – he had an amazing talent to write complicated, convincing war plans with great ease and alacrity. COS Tovar briefed Ambassador Godley, who concurred with the plan. On their OK, the plans went back to the Washington for final approval. In a Defense Department response a civilian war planner said it was the dumbest ops proposal he had ever read. He went on to say Tovar ought to go out there and yank a knot in Vang Pao's head – put the Hmong in positions on Skyline, he said.

But the COS and the ambassador stood by their support of Vang Pao's mission.

And it was approved by the National Security Council in Washington – who, as a group, didn't like the idea but deferred to the field.

In early February five of Vang Pao's six Hmong guerilla

battalions deployed toward the PDJ – northeast from the Long Tieng valley and south from Bouam Long. They maintained radio silence and at first didn't get any aerial resupply. However, the PAVN quickly got word of the movement and, after consultation with Hanoi, decided to send eleven battalions - half their Skyline attack force - back to the PDJ to interdict the Hmong and Lao... exactly like Vang Pao had said they would.

For the entire month of February, the Hmong, going back to basic guerrilla tactics, eluded main line PAVN forces on the PDJ and its environs, while the Ravens had much success in finding and killing PAVN who were in the open, trying to chase down Vang Pao's elusive hills guerrillas.

While the PAVN focused on unsuccessful efforts to kill Hmong threatening their supply routes, Thai irregulars BCs 605A and 609A were brought into the Long Tieng Valley and then deployed out to positions on Skyline and around Sam Thong, joining other BC units there. By mid-February – two months after being routed from the PDJ - the CIA army was larger than it had ever been. More than 5,000 Thai irregulars and 2,000 Hmong and Lao irregulars from other MRs of Laos were in the fight now to protect Long Tieng.

****

By mid-February early markings indicated that the road being built coming down from the PDJ was going to run alongside the Ban Hin Tang pass, to end near the base of Romeo ridge, which fronted the deserted village of Sam Thong much like Skyline fronted Long Tieng.

If the road was to provide a pathway for their tanks to the Skyline battlefield, then the PAVN avenues of approaches around Romeo Ridge were limited. Either tanks had to go around the ridgeline to the south or over it. And going up and over didn't seem feasible because the only possible place to drive anything up on Romeo ridgeline was a hill that was at 1,800 feet of altitude. Vang Pao did not think tanks could get over Hill 1800 – its slope was too steep - which would mean they would have to go south around Romeo ridge and attack through Sam Thong from the low river valley uphill. However, if the tanks were able to go over Hill 1800 they could plow through the abandoned town of Sam Thong and be at the base of Skyline in one night. With the cover of bad weather, they could be up and over Skyline into the Long Tieng valley in a day's time. Only the CE pad stood in their way.

In Udorn we spent hours staring at map boards. We took

Vang Pao at his word that Romeo ridge couldn't be breached by tanks. Too steep.

Believing Vang Pao, the new Thai irregulars battalions were positioned in eight new bunkers, expecting tanks to have to come around Romeo ridge from the south. Vang Pao had no doubt this funneled the PAVN tanks to his advantage. In Washington there was heightened concern, because on maps there, it was obvious if the PAVN tanks climbed 1800 they would own the high ground over-looking those positions, to either fire at them at their leisure or to go around them, in effect, trapping the approximately 1,500 irregulars in the mountain valley east of Sam Thong.

Overhead photography and FAC reports clearly showed PAVN engineers making a major effort to lower the grade on Hill 1800 to make it passable for their tanks.

PAVN AA gun crews were brought in to keep nosey USAF FACs away from the major engineering work.

We spent hours every day in Udorn, taking intelligence reports on PAVN engineering efforts and comparing them to new bunker construction of Thai irregulars positions.

****

Late one afternoon in mid-February, I was sitting at my desk staring at my typewriter. I had just finished reports on the previous night's action on Skyline and had dispatched them to Washington. I was working on the monthly "bullet report," a summary of ammunition on hand at end of February, which was a week overdue, when an Air American helicopter let down on the tarmac near the ops building. I looked out the window near my desk, one of the few in the building, and saw Hardnose, sitting with his legs out the door, his feet resting on the skids. When the chopper landed, he jumped off and was followed quickly by a half dozen Thai mercenaries - his interpreters, radio operators and ops assistants. He carried his AR-15 rifle comfortably at his side like a large handgun. Turning to the helicopter pilot he gave the fingers across the throat signal to cut the engine and pointed to his watch and flashed three fingers and an 0 to say he would be a half hour. He pointed to the ops building and turned and started walking in our direction. He was wearing jungle boots and camouflage fatigues, which were dirty and torn. A nine-millimeter pistol and ammo pouches were on his pistol belt. A map was sticking out of one of the lower side pockets of his fatigue pants. Even in the distance I could tell he hadn't shaved in days and I knew

313

he was going to smell bad.

He looked beautiful.

As he approached the front of the ops building he tossed his AR-15 to one of his ops assistants and with a wave of his hand, all of the Thais squatted down to wait for him in the shade of a nearby fence.

Two minutes later he was sitting on the edge of my desk. He smelled worse than I expected, but there was something of the outdoors to the scent - dirt and wind and sunshine and nature - in addition to the spent sweat. His eyes were bloodshot but his voice was firm and had resonance. He said he had just come in from the valley where he had spent the night trying to break up an all-out North Vietnamese attack on Skyline. Supplies were good, the bunkers were good, leadership was good, but Hardnose worried that we weren't doing everything we could... why hadn't the North Vietnamese attack en masse like they did on the PDJ? Was VP's deception really working? And when were the tanks coming in? Could they scale 1800?

He left to talk with the Stick.

I sat looking at my typewriter. Goddamnit, I thought, that's it. I have to go upcountry. I can't miss more of this fight. I didn't sign on to do any God damned bullet reports. To be a war reporter. I wanted to be upcountry. I wanted Skyline. To hell with being patient. If I waited I might never get there.

Before leaving that night I went into the Stick's office. He was leaning back in his chair with his feet on his desk. He watched me walk in front of his desk without comment.

I said that I had asked him before about going upcountry and he had told me to do my fucking job here and I understood and I had tried to do a good job.

"But," he interrupted, "you want to go up to the valley." He reached for a stick on his desk and began slapping his leg. "You're fucking stupid, you know that? You want to get your ass shot. All the problems I've faced today and you come in with some personal fucking problem. No one cares what you want."

I didn't take my eyes of him. I didn't want to be turned away again but I couldn't think of anything else to say.

"Okay," he said after a pause, "I'll see what I can do. Get out of here."

Two days later an officer who had not been in MR II long came down to Udorn to take over the MR II desk and I was reassigned north, to Long Tieng.

The Vietnam War Its Ownself

****

Before dawn the following day I was on the tarmac in front of the ops building in Udorn with the other Sky officers who had commuted in from MR II the previous night. We boarded a small cargo plane and arrived in the vicinity of LS 272, the new rear base, as the sun was coming up over the mountains. A low morning fog covered the area and we had to circle overhead for some time before the pilot could find the runway and land.

The first Sky contingent on the ground that morning, we were greeted by the local guards who were coming out of their bunkers around the airstrip, stretching and yawning. Two Quonset huts and four collapsible trailers sat along a meandering river on the north side of the runway. On the south side was Poppa Chu's mess hall, a supply area, the rigging shed and the ammo dump.

In the rice fields around the runway Lao farmers were already at work. Monkeys and birds chattered in the surrounding mountains. There was a musty outdoorsy smell in the air. Upcountry Laos. I started humming "Nothing could be finer than to be in Carolina in the morn........ing."

I was just coming out of Poppa Chu's with a cup of coffee when a CASI Twin Otter broke through the clouds and came to a stop near one of the Quonset huts. The chief, Dick Johnson, was the first off, followed by other Sky officers. They went into the hut. When I joined the group, several of the officers were at the map board hanging along the rear wall. Dutch was drawing new enemy designations in the river valley north of Skyline, which I assumed meant that intelligence gathered overnight indicated the presence of more North Vietnamese joining the attack force.

Digger was discussing resupplying the Hmong patrols out on the PDJ and talked about their hit and run tactic when they spotted bad guys... which appeared to Digger to be big on run and little on hit.

Lumberjack, one of the new Sky officers with the Thais, said that having most of the Hmong out at Pa Dong and on the PDJ left no home-grown reserve... the Thai were feeling exposed. They knew they were being deployed east of Sam Thong as North Vietnamese tank breaks. Some were soldiers swept from the PDJ, and they were not so sure they could withstand another all-out attack by NVA with field guns and tanks. Plus they saw the possibility that the tanks could come around Romeo ridge and fire at their new bunkers until they were blown away.

A couple of Air America pilots came in with coffee and sat at the rear, listening.

Some FACs came in talking about their planned day's work around Hill 1800. Steve Wilson had been shot up twice reconnoitering that site. The last time an enemy AA bullet had killed his engine and he had to glide back in to Long Tieng without power... the most eerily silent ride of his life.

An Air America helicopter kicker walked in and asked one of the Sky officers working with the Thais for help in prioritizing the delivery of supplies. He added that all the choppers were on the ground and the pilots were in Poppa Chu's.

Gradually the officers left, leaving Dick and I in the Quonset hut.

He expressed some mock surprise over my interest in coming up north when I had such a cushion job in an air-conditioned office, but he said he was glad to have me on board. Some of the case officers were due for reassignment this summer, including Ringo, and he would eventually move me to a GM. In the meantime, he said he wanted me to be an out-rider to the battle on Skyline. Drawing arrows west, southwest and south away from the PDJ, he said, "When we were run off of the plateau in December, Hmong families who had been farming and trading in that area moved away," pointing to his arrows, "and are now scattered in the mountains."

"Find them for me, make contact, debrief them on Vietnamese and Pathet Lao movement in the area, give them radios, weapons, ammunition and training. Encourage them to move back toward the PDJ, to patrol, to find the enemy, to fight 'um."

He pointed to several areas of known concentrations of civilians and he said there were many more. Vang Pao had a loosely organized militia force, the Armer Defend D'operaton (ADO), headquartered southeast of Long Tieng, which provided security to Hmong villagers. "Meet the Hmong commander of the ADO and get him involved. Help wherever you can out there to engage the Hmong citizenry in our efforts. Use fixed-wing planes - Porters and Twin Otters - we need the helicopters for Long Tieng. Most villages have airstrips, you don't need much ground to land Porters."

"Va Xiong will be your ops assistant. Plus there are a couple more I don't know their names, Khu Sao is one. You'll have a couple or three Hmong working for you. Hire more if you need them. Check out what you need from supply. Let me know if you want anything else. Take one of those AR-15s over there or nine millimeters or whatever you're comfortable with."

He went to the door and yelled for Va Xiong. The young

Hmong man, who would have to stand on his tiptoes to reach five feet tall, came bouncing into the Quonset hut toward me with a wide smile. He stuck his hand out before we were introduced. Dick threw me a map and told me to go out and do good.

My short, friendly ops assistant and I went out to the supply area and took stock of the equipment on hand. There were crates of carbines, assault rifles, mortars and 3.5 inch rocket launchers and tons of ammunition on pallets. In one of the shelters were radios, mostly old PRC-25s though there were a few handheld walkie-talkies. In another shelter were uniforms, ponchos and web gear. There was no one around who looked in charge, though Shep was nearby in the rigging shed preparing supplies for delivery to the Thais. I yelled over to him, asking what I had to do if I needed any of this stuff. He looked up, looked around curiously as if he didn't understand my question and shrugged. Va, at my side, said Sky people just went in got what they wanted, or they told Shep what they wanted and he got it together. There was nobody to ask. Va also looked as if he didn't understand for sure what I was asking.

Not like K-Mart or the U.S. Army I thought.

Va and I walked over to Papa Chu's. Laying out a map of the area around Long Tieng, we began talking about what we were going to do. He said we would have to use a carrot and stick approach with the ADO. They did not have a good reputation - some young Hmong joined the militia to get out of duty in the GMs. When ADO forces were called on in the field they were not very aggressive and were often reluctant to attack the enemy. The ADOs Va had been working with before my arrival were from villages due south of the PDJ. The villages west of the PDJ were not well identified, were not organized, had few radios and old weapons. But Va knew the area well because he grew up in the region. Pathet Lao and North Vietnamese forces operated throughout the mountains in this area west of the PDJ and we had to be careful where we landed. We had to be careful where we flew too, he added.

The previous week Va was in a small fixed-wing aircraft helping in the search for 555, an Air America C-123 plane that went down on a resupply mission and had not been found. The plane Va was on came through some clouds at Site 37, near a friendly village, but as he and the pilot began to search the ground for signs of the downed plane they got caught beneath low cloud cover in a dead end valley and started taking AK-47 fire. Rounds were whizzing through the wing and coming up through the bottom of the fuselage. They had to bank inside of a cloud to turn around and get down-valley. Va said we had to be careful of situations like that in the entire area west of the PDJ.

We went back to the airstrip. Dutch, who was running air ops at LS 272, assigned me a Porter for the first of my many flights to locate and organize the local Hmong villagers.

The Porter aircraft were built in the United States under license from Pilatus, a company in Switzerland. It had a single prop with a dependable engine and long, wide wings that allowed it to glide effortlessly among the mountains. They were referred to as STOL planes, short take-off and landing, because they could come in softly on short strips; by reversing the engine, the pilot could stop within forty or fifty feet. Almost on a dime. They were versatile with a parachute drop hole in the middle of the cargo section. Single pilots were used in working the planes in MR II and the co-pilot chair was turned around to face the cargo section in the rear.

That was the seat I took as we left LS 272 and soared up above the clouds. Because it was clear over Long Tieng and to the west of the PDJ, we took our initial reconnaissance there.

Skyline ridge was clearly visible in the far distance. The reinforced bunkers on top, though low to the ground, had hard corners and stood out in contrast to the cleared, rugged terrain around them. Because of the rain, the dirt excavated in their construction had drained down both sides of the ridgeline, like teared mascara. As we flew by to the west, the battle continued to rage for the ridgeline and we could hear the radio transmissions of the Thais as they reported on enemy movement and adjusted artillery fire. Air America, CASI and Sky were busy on other frequencies coordinating on the delivery of supplies and the evacuation of wounded.

We flew further north by the abandoned village of Sam Thong and north of that to LS 15 where VP had suggested moving some of his GMs. Scattered about between these two points were small clusters of huts. Off in the distance to the east lay the PDJ.

Slowly we crisscrossed the area. Occasionally Va would get a radio transmission from the huts below and he would identify the settlement usually by the name of the village chief, or "Ni Ban." Some of the villages had small airstrips cut into the side of mountains, some did not.

The Air America pilot, sitting beside me facing the front, pointed out areas Air America considered hostile. He thought some of these villagers changed their spots when the communist, or Pathet Lao, move in. The area could be friendly one day and the next they'd shoot you out of the sky. Va was quick to say no; he'd never heard of that. He added that sometimes the Hmong would move out when they were threatened, leaving the area open for Pathet Lao to move in. But Hmong didn't change their allegiance.

We were flying over one area when Va received a call that was different from the rest. It was louder and the person on the ground had a different accent. Va turned to me and said Father Bouchard asked for my call sign. He wanted to talk to me.

I didn't know what my call sign was and I didn't know Father Bouchard, but Va handed me the radio anyway. The caller said in a Boston accent, "Hello Sky. Welcome. I'm down here on a trail heading north to a little place I haven't been to in some time and it sure is nice to look up and see that ol' A.A. on the side of that bird. Nice to see you." I asked if he needed anything. "Oh no, no, I've got everything I want, right here. Just wanted to say hi. Hope to meet you soon. Good-bye now."

Va said Father Luke Bouchard was the best man in the world. He had lived among the Hmong since the early 1950s, spoke their language and had become an expert in treating people with leprosy and in helping women through difficult deliveries. Whenever it was felt that a pregnant woman was about to have an abnormal childbirth, Father Bouchard was called. He was known to have walked along mountain trails for days without stopping for rest to be at the bedside of some simple Hmong woman, often arriving to find that the delivery had gone without problems or that there had been problems and he was too late. He was the most loved and respected American in the mountains of Laos.

I told the pilot the good Father put things a little more into perspective. I was beginning to think I was going to be the Marco Polo of the region, but I was a Johnny come lately, still an FNG.

Because Va had grown up in the area, he kept up a running narrative on the background of the different settlements, some of which were abandoned. The Hmong were slash-and-burn subsistence farmers in that they moved into an area, burned acreage to plant their field rice and homesteaded until the ground no longer nourished new growth, and then they moved on. This slash and burning coincided with the changing of the seasons and brought on the smoky season haze. It was the bane of Air America because it increased the dangers of flying in the mountains over contested areas. The enemy, however, welcomed it because, more than the rainy season, the smoky season was more dependable cover for their activities on the ground.

Returning to LS 272, I asked Va about himself. He said his father was a well-known "Ni Khong," appointed by Vang Pao to

319

coordinate the regional activities of the Ni Bans southwest of Long Tieng. Va would have had a chance to follow as a headman in due course but he had elected as a young man to go to school in Vientiane, the political capital of the country, where he studied French and then English. He graduated with honors but rather than pursue employment in the capital he returned to the mountains to help his people. Referred to Hog by another Hmong who lived near Long Tieng, Va accepted the offer of employment. The Hmong considered it a high honor to work for Sky and as a result, Va's father's prestige among his followers increased. Va had recently married the daughter of a Ni Ban in a village south of Long Tieng.

For the next few days I would leave Udorn at first light, returning at nine or ten o'clock at night. If the Air America shuttle van was not around when we landed I would have to walk to the edge of the air base to get a taxi, arriving home about eleven. On almost every flight south at night there would be body bags filled with Thai mercenaries killed during the previous twenty four hours. The body bags were gruesome cargo, grim reminders of the ultimate cost of war.

During the days Va and I continued our reconnaissance of the countryside with a variety of Air America porter pilots, trying to fix the friendly and hostile areas. We found the villages south of the PDJ more settled and less responsive and spent most of our time to the west of the PDJ, where most of the new settlements were.

Plus with Vang Pao's deception ops there, Hmong soldiers overran my areas.

We were flying south of the PDJ one afternoon when Hog called and asked if we would go up to LS 15 and pick up a Hmong commander needed for a planning session and bring him back to the valley. Though fighting continued along Skyline ridge, Porters landed regularly and parked in the protective shadows of rock karsts around the Air Ops building. Larger resupply planes, the C-130s and the C-123s, did not come in, however, because of the occasional 130mm gun fire.

On landing in Long Tieng with the commander, the Porter taxied over behind a karst and I commandeered a Jeep for the ride up to Hog's bunker on top of the south ridge.

Surprisingly, on the ride I passed village huts occupied by Hmong families. When the GMs had pulled out some villagers returned to look after family houses. Still it was mostly a ghost town. The Thai artillery fired irregularly as I drove up the hill. As I got closer to Hog's bunker I noticed more bomb craters, testimony that the Vietnamese had attempted to hit this prominent position with their

130mm guns.

Inside, the bunker looked similar to Red Coat's at Bouam Long, dirty and cluttered with weapons and smoke canisters and C-rations and bunks and maps and radios. I laid out my map and was pointing out to Hog the different concentrations of Hmong civilians in the area west of the PDJ. Va stood behind me. Hog made comments about a few Ni Bans he knew, saying that Va's father was a Romeo in the area, had a slew of wives, some younger than Va.

Suddenly, in the distance we heard the heavy whine of a large incoming shell followed immediately by a tremendous explosion. Dust drifted down from the top of the bunker. The round had landed on the eastern end of the runway, away from where our Porter was parked.

As I looked out of the front ports of the bunker a dust cloud was rising off to the side like the mushroom of a small atomic bomb.

Bamboo came in from another earthen room off the main area of the bunker. "Damned nuisance," he said. While Hog was on one radio talking with a Thai ops assistant on Skyline about counter-battery fire, Bamboo picked up the binoculars. After looking at the site where the round landed, he went to another radio and asked someone to check on casualties. Bag was up in a helicopter and called in the coordinates where one of the pilots spotted what might have been a muzzle flash from the Vietnamese 130mm gun that had fired the round.

Hog turned to me when he had finished and asked, "What's your call sign?"

"I haven't got one yet," I said.

Hog continued to look at me. "Well?"

"Well, what?"

"Give me one. Who do you want to be?"

I had, of course, thought about my call sign, although, I had assumed Hog or Dick would have assigned something. Like the supply at LS 272, I expected things to be issued. The only name that came to mind was Cottonpicker, my boyhood hunting partner, but here with these people, it suddenly sounded too silly. Shouldn't have been. I was looking at an individual called Hog and over there was Bamboo and Bag was just on the air. What was wrong with Cottonpicker?

"I'm just a small town boy from North Carolina. Never wanted to be much," I said with a heavy southern accent, hoping for an opening to suggest Cottonpicker.

Bamboo bayed, "MULE. He's a MULE. The MULE."

James E. Parker, Jr

"MULE it is," said Hog turning back to the radio.

Later in the Porter after we left the valley, I had the opportunity to use my call sign and I blushed, hesitant. I had to repeat it several times before I made myself understood. I was more than a radio call sign - I had been Red Cap Twigs Alfa November Six with my Army platoon in Vietnam - that was a call sign. Here your call sign was your name. In MR II, I stopped being Jim or Parker or the FNG. I was Mule. To Air America, to the Hmong, to other Sky officers. Getting your Long Tieng name was proof of residence. It was like getting my badge when I first joined the Agency in Langley and later my in-house alias.

Mule. Forevermore.

Within the week I flew with Va to LS 353 to meet the ADO commander, Colonel Youa Va Ly. He was a venerable old Hmong commander who started out with Vang Pao working for the French. He was known as a brave man who had taken to drink, a failing that affected his judgment, which made him dangerous. He had also become ruthless, which made him a liability with Sky, which did not condone unnecessary force. Thus he was assigned to the ADO and not a line GM. Among the many stories Va told me about the man was the incident many years ago when he landed at Long Tieng - then a rear base - and saw a Hmong workman on a bulldozer clearing an area beside the runway. The colonel became excited. When the plane stopped he jumped off and walked up to the dozer, pulled out his .45 caliber pistol and shot the driver dead.

Unfortunately the bulldozer driver, following someone's instructions, had been clearing an area that was part of the colonel's family burial plot.

He was sober the day we arrived but his face showed the ravages of a life in the mountains. His voice was raspy, his hands shook.

We sat in his straw-thatched house most of the day talking about the Hmong civilians around the PDJ. We decided that I would give him a radio that would net with Va at LS 272. He would contact the different villages south of the PDJ every day and call in a situation report to Va at dawn. I was interested in any sightings or any contact with the enemy - Pathet Lao or Vietnamese. In the area west of the PDJ, Youa Va Ly agreed to provide ADO soldiers who would travel north out of the west end of the Long Tieng valley - away from the fighting at Skyline - to contact the southern-most village. This patrol would ensure that the landing strip near the village was clear of mines and the area was secure enough for a Porter to land and I would visit. We would contact neighboring

322

settlements by sending out men from that first village and continue until we netted all the villages west of the PDJ.

As it turned out Va found the ADO soldiers we needed in Long Tieng; we didn't have to rely on the colonel's men. Two days later we dispatched them with radios, new weapons, maps, marking panels and smoke canisters to contact a village about ten miles north of Long Tieng. Once they arrived and determined the area was safe, they were to call us and lay out panels I provided to form two letters: LL. These panels were the safety signal, because, as I explained to them, if they arrived and were captured by less than friendly villagers who wanted to do us harm - people who might be beside them when they made radio contact with us to guide us in - this would be their chance to tell me that regardless of what they are saying on the radio, that in fact it was not safe. It was our secret. They were to lay our "LL" only if it was absolutely safe for us to come in.

I had just landed at Long Tieng the first time I checked on the patrol's progress when Father Bouchard came across the ramp and shook my hand. He said I was a person he wanted to get to know, because he was out there everywhere. Sometimes I might be able to pick him up if I was going his way and he could get to where's he was going faster, which might do someone some real good. He looked willowy and frail, not what you would expect from a mountain climbing saint. Oh it's a wonderful place here, he said, and the Hmong, they're good people, hardy and strong. He wished me well and went on past the Air Ops building into a Hmong's hut.

The patrol made it to the village without problems and radioed back in a couple of days that it was safe for us to fly in. That day I happened to draw a helicopter because all the Porters were needed to make drops for the Hmong GMs. Frenchy Smith was the pilot.

I should be so lucky I get Frenchy Smith, the original Mr. Smart Ass.

I walked up to his chopper that morning at LS 272 and briefed him on the mission. He said, "Fuck you, Mule, I ain't going into no site that ain't secure."

I told him it was.

"How the hell do you know?" he asked.

"My patrol said it was."

"Patrol worked for you a long time has it, that you bet your life on what it says? Maybe I think more about my life than you do yours. Maybe I've been up here longer than you have and I know the questions to ask."

James E. Parker, Jr

I said, "Let's go up to the site and if you're not sure it's safe, don't go in. I don't want you to do anything you don't want to do."

And he agreed. As we got over the settlement and I was looking for the "LL" panels, our secret code that the area was safe, absolutely safe, I saw something like "TI" near the edge of the village. I had told Frenchy about the safety signal, something I seriously regretted now that we were overhead. Va talked to the patrol over the radio and they put out "IE" and then "II." While they were doing this I looked at the airstrip, because the patrol expected us to come in by fixed wing and two rows of villagers were walking down the strip shoulder to shoulder. Frenchy said, "Polish mine detectors." Va said they were having trouble with the panel markers because they couldn't spell "LL." Super, I thought. Nothing like your first field operation getting off to a good start. Va said the settlement was in fact safe and secure, he'd bet his life on it.

Frenchy, living up to his reputation of being testy but effective, was slowly spiraling down, as the team continued to make two letter combinations below. We noticed Hmong standing on top of all the karsts and mountains peaks in the area, like Indians in a grade B cowboy movie, and we landed near what had become "TL." As I started to take off the customer headset Frenchy said, "Don't worry partn'er, nothing ever happens here exactly the way it's planned. You just gotta hang in, as they say, and keep on planning. You are lucky, ain't you?"

"I got a lucky dog," I responded.

"That's good enough," he said, turning and smiling. He promised to be back to pick us up midafternoon. I took off the headset, Frenchy lifted off and after his noisy helicopter was out of hearing I noticed how quiet it was here on the edge of this native village and how alone I as with all these Hmong.

Va was standing, talking with the patrol members, who were proud of the job they had done, unconcerned that they couldn't spell LL. Wasn't their fault. Letter wasn't in their alphabet.

Va knew the Ni Ban. After he introduced us we were lead to the largest thatched hut in the village where the Ni Ban lived with his several wives and dozen or so children. The Hmong are polygamous, brought on at times out of necessity - if a head of family dies, his widow and children are usually taken in by a brother - though it was a common show of prominence for the leaders or chief merchants of a villages to take several wives, often marrying young girls of fourteen and fifteen.

The village chief's hut had a large center room lit by the front opening, with a cooking room and several lean-to sleeping areas

324

off to different sides. It was dark and drab inside with a poignant, arresting smell of cooking/heating fires in the air. But it was warm and there was a sense of community. The Ni Ban had prepared a feast by his standards and the food was laid out on a bamboo table in the center room. Although I had never seen some of the dishes before, I ate gamely. I had managed a portion of blood pudding when the head of the chicken, the main dish in the meal, was placed on my plate. As I looked down at it with a blank expression Va, sitting beside me, said the guest of honor got the chicken head. I smiled weakly, looking around the table, and got at some of the meat on the neck, though I didn't attempt the head.

After the meal we talked about the local situation. The Ni Ban said that there were no friendly Hmong to the east, though settlements to the north supported Vang Pao. The closest friendly settlement was another ten miles north, at the base of Red Mountain.

The Ni Ban said he did not have a radio and his weapons were a collection of old assorted French, Chinese and American rifles, though people hunted with the traditional Hmong muzzle-loaded muskets. He had limited ammunition. He said the settlement at the base of Red Mountain also had no radio and few weapons. I told him I would supply him with new equipment if he would send some of his people to the next settlement, to give them a radio and help arrange for our visit there. I also wanted him to send in regular radio reports to Va at LS 272.

He agreed and through Va we went over the information I wanted him to provide. I said we were going to win the war; he said no, there was always war. In other conversation as we waited for Frenchy to return, the Ni Ban asked me about rumors they had heard that some Americans had flown to the moon. Everyone standing around suddenly looked at me hard as if they expected me to say, naw, didn't happen. They listened with rapt attention as I explained how we did that, taking my word that things like that really were possible for man.

As the days progressed, while I pursued my relatively calm civic affairs work, the battle raged for Skyline. As I flew near the valley I would be able to see dust clouds as incoming rounds hit around the Thai positions, and hear cryptic radio conversations, "Incoming," "Fire counter battery to point XL," "We have wounded. We need Air America medevac or they die for sure." "We are out of grenades, we fight them with our hands, OK, no sweat," "Ten, twenty bad guys moving up that draw between DD and FD helipads, fire artillery, fire artillery."

James E. Parker, Jr

--TWENTY-SIX--
Skyline, March 1972

At night Sky officers alternated duty in a Volpar that circled overhead the valley to augment the U.S. Air Force radio platform and ensure that we maintained contact with our officers below. Also the Stick wanted Sky people coordinating communications to the Thai and Hmong positions. Whether Vang Pao forces could hold Skyline was still in question.

All officers not on duty in the Volpar or staying in the valley were still going through Vientiane to brief Ambassador G. McMurtrie Godley, nicknamed the "Field Marshal," and Hugh Tovar. While they did not advise us on how we should do our jobs better, both expressed continuing concerns that we not lose Skyline. Especially the ambassador would say every night that we were doing remarkable work. Just amazing.

In early March we got in a new GM from Savannakhet to help with the fight. Sword was their CIA case officer. His men got off troop carriers in the valley and were soon moved up to the top of Skyline to a place previously unguarded to find some PAVN waiting in hiding. This unit had to fight for every yard as they advanced forward.

Heretofore our briefings had been short, lean, direct. We did not dissemble, we answered the ambassador's questions completely, but we were brief.

The Sword did not pick up on this tone. He was dramatic. He and his GM had saved Skyline. According to him the whole of the war in Indochina had turned on the arrival of his people to the ridgeline. He briefed as if he was auditioning for the lead in a war movie. He spoke louder than the rest, used more hand gestures, paused more for effect and implied in his closing statement that the next day his GM would rouse the Vietnamese from every spider hole and would pursue them down the north slope of Skyline and up the river valley to the PDJ in all expectation of seeing them running, scared, for the North Vietnamese border.

The ambassador looked around at the rest of us as if to ask, why couldn't the rest of you do this? There was some small sense of guilt among us in MR II because, in fact, we couldn't do that; we lived in a harsher, less giving environment, apparently. But we knew the sacrifices, the casualties our Hmong GMs had incurred in fighting the enemy every day for years. They would still be needed in the area after the battle for Skyline was won or lost. The GMs from the other MRs, and the Thai mercenaries, were fresh. Bringing them in was part of the chess game aspect of the war in Laos. The Vietnamese would move and we would counter move. Or we would move and the Vietnamese would counter move. We built bunkers on the PDJ to withstand the Vietnamese units traditionally committed to our theater and they brought in more troops and tanks and 130mm to gain the advantage. They sent enough troops and ammunition down the river valley from the PDJ to Skyline to take the ridgeline defended by the soldiers we traditionally kept in MR II and we brought in the soldiers from the other GMs to give us the advantage. They were building a road to bring in tanks.

Move, counter move. Battlefield management. General An verse General Vang Pao. CIA verse PAVN.

The next day Sword's GM was pinned down and could not maneuver. He did not go down for the briefing. Others explained to the ambassador that the Savannakhet GM was pinned down and could not move. Concise. Good briefing. Forty words maybe total.

The ambassador was disappointed.

The following day the Savannakhet GM in retaking a lost position suffered casualties and Sword briefed that night with a flourish, explaining how his men maneuvered under murderous fire to the door of a lost bunker and there, after throwing in grenade after grenade, they charged the door and beat the remaining Vietnamese inside in hand-to-hand combat.

Better than T.V., Digger said on the way out. He hadn't realized before there was so much entertainment value in our work.

****

The PAVN continued work at the terminus of their new road. But we did not know which way they were goin' to go... over Hill 1800 or south of Romeo. Their reports, which we read years later, gives the details:

Yes, we had to be able to move our tanks forward to Sam Thong-Long Tieng, but the biggest obstacle we faced was how to get the tanks over a ridge that was 1,800 meter high with a very steep slope, a slope that in places was so steep that the gradient exceeded the stated technical capabilities of our tanks.

The 195th Armored Battalion was equipped with two types of armored vehicles: K-63 armored personnel carriers (APC) and T-34 tanks. The T-34 was a very old tank that was manufactured

327

James E. Parker, Jr

during the Second World War, and these tanks had been operating on the battlefield for a long time, so they were no longer in good condition from a technical standpoint. In addition, because it was an "antique" vehicle, its tracks were simple and could not obtain as good a grip on the soil as could the tracks of T-54 or T-55 tanks. For that reason the maximum gradient it could climb was only 300, and even that was only for medium-grade roads that would provide traction, but here the tanks would have to climb a rough, quickly-made military road so its ability to gain traction was even lower.

26 February 1972 the road to Ban Hin Tang has been completed. Last night we escorted and supported the tanks to the foot of Hill 1800 so that we can again attack Sam Thong-Long Tieng.

The primary attack sector would be an attack from Hill 1800 straight down into Sam Thong to overrun and destroy the strong-points held by the Thai BC 606, BC 610, and BC 608 battalions. The division's 141st Regiment, supported by tanks and artillery, would conduct the attack in this sector.

At that time we tankers were determined to overcome all terrain obstacles so that we could participate in the attack on Sam Thong-Long Tieng. In addition to this being a demand by our infantry units, it was also a requirement for victory, and in addition, the appearance of our tanks would shatter the myth that this was a "Sacred and Inviolable Land" and cause Vang Pao's bandit army to collapse and disintegrate.

From 1 to 4 March 1972 Comrade Han, the Chief of Staff of the 312th Division, and Comrade Thap, the Chief of Staff of our army's Engineer Command, accompanied armor officers out to the foot of the ridge to inspect the work of the 17th Engineer Battalion as it prepared the way for the tanks to climb the steep slope. Comrades Khung (the engineer battalion commander), Tuyen (the engineer battalion political officer), and Thuy (the deputy engineer battalion commander) reported that, "All the work of reducing the gradient of the slope, planting route markers, and preparing by-pass sections has been completed. Since the Campaign engineers and the 312th Division have now built a road section almost ten kilometers long and since the most difficult section, that crossing of the 1,800-meter high ridgeline, has been completed, we can now arrange for tanks to test the route so we can see what happens and learn from the results."

3 March 1972. The tank trying to climb Hill 1800 turned over because the slope of the road was too steep. We had to drive in wooden stakes to form a road on which the tank's tracks could get a grip to climb the slope. We had to try again to "level the mountain,"

328

or at least to reduce the gradient of the road. The tanks unloaded all of their ammunition and spare parts and other equipment to lighten them for the climb up the slope. We were very happy that three armored vehicles were able to reach the top and move on into Sam Thong.

On 5 March the 195th Tank Battalion sent two T-34s to make a test run to attempt to cross the 1,800 meter mountain peak, but they were unable to climb the mountain because the slopes of Hill 1800 were too steep (between approximately 250 and 310). That night, the tank and engineer offices held a meeting to review the effort and agreed to continue to try to build a route with a gradient that was not as steep. The 312th Division Headquarters mobilized a force of infantrymen to prepare wooden stakes to be driven into the ground to give the tanks more traction. The personnel of the 312th Division headquarters staff were all sent out to help our tanks make it up the slope. Each man cut two wooden stakes five to ten centimeters in diameter and took them out to the foot of the slope so that the engineers could pound them into the ground. The engineers pounded ten thousand stakes into the ground in the steep sections where the tracks of the tanks were most likely to lose traction and begin spinning. Meanwhile the armored officers and enlisted men prepared large pieces of soft lumber, cutting them into the shape of a triangle. Two men were assigned to carry these pieces of wood along behind the tank so that when the tank stopped temporarily or when it began to lose power, they could immediately jam these pieces of lumber in behind the tracks to prevent the tank from slipping back down the slope while we made temporary repairs.

On the night of 5 March 1972, two T-34 tanks, Tanks 451 and 456, from the 9th Tank Company made the first try to climb the slope. At 2030 hours Tank 451 began its effort to climb the slope. Everyone watched closely. After making it one-third of the way up to the top, the tank hit a piece of lumber. The tank shuddered and stopped, and they began sliding backward down the slope. Everyone had to run to either side of the road to get out of the way. Tank 451 slid almost all the way down to the bottom of the slope, where it reached a curve in the road. The tank then slid down very fast but did not turn over. The tank commander, the gunner, and the driver were all injured, but Driver Do Van Chinh suffered serious injuries and had to be bandaged up and rushed back for medical treatment.

At 2400 hours, after studying what had happened and learning lessons from Tank 451's experience, Tank 456 rumbled forward to try to climb the slope. We removed all of the 85mm shells from the tank to reduce weight, and the tank commander and the gunner would not ride in the vehicle. Only the driver would ride in the tank to control it. The driver would wear a thick quilted cotton jacket and wear a helmet, around which would be wrapped more cloth as a precaution, so that if the tank did slide back down the slope he would not suffer a serious concussion.

Because the gradient was so steep and because there was such a long stretch of steep gradient, during the effort to climb the slope the tank had to constantly stop to rest, and many times it slid as its tracks failed to gain traction. After climbing three-quarters of the way up the slope, the tank again lost traction and its tracks began spinning in place. And so at 0430 on the morning of 6 March the first effort to scale this slope ended unsuccessfully.

At 2000 hours on the night of 6 March, the second night of the effort to cross the ridge, we had our K-63 APCs make the climb first to learn more lessons. By 2400 hours all three K-63 had crossed the ridge safely, one at a time, and were temporarily hidden in Ban Dao at the foot of the opposite side of Ridge 1800.

At 0100 hours on the morning of 7 March T-34 Tank Number 456 again tried to climb the slope. After the tank had made it three-quarters of the way up the ridge, when it reached the fifth difficult curve in the road the tank suddenly slid very quickly all the way down to the bottom of the slope.

We made our third try to cross the high ridge at 2000 hours on the night of 7 March. This time we first sent the tank retriever vehicle up to the top. When the vehicle reached the top of the ridge, it would serve as a fixed anchor point from which it would extend a long cable down for a certain distance as a precaution to be able to pull the tank up if it experienced a problem.

By 2100 hours the tank retriever vehicle had made it safely to the top. At 2200 hours Tank 424 began to climb the slope, but when the tank was just half-way up the side of the ridge, enemy aircraft began bombing the entire area. A bomb hit the section of the road that the tank was on, and the tank slid very fast down to the bottom of the slope. The driver, Comrade Vu Trong Phai, was seriously injured, but the tank did not overturn.

Seeing that the situation was so tense and that it would be difficult for us to continue to try to get our tanks over the ridge, Comrade Han, the Chief of Staff of the 312th Division, agreed with us that we would temporarily suspend the effort to cross Ridge 1800 and request instructions from the Front Headquarters so that we could develop a follow-up plan. [The plan developed was to go around the south end of Romeo Ridge, as Vang Pao had said they would.]

Because of our feverish activities, the enemy was able to detect signs of our reconnaissance activities and to discover our tank road, so the enemy alerted his units to be on their guard, and at the same time the enemy initiated a heave wave of air strikes and artillery bombardment. During just the period from 5 to 9 March, on average there were 120 to 130 attack sorties by tactical jet fighters and four to six B-52 strikes. The high-point was on 7 and 8 March where on each of these days there were as many as 171 tactical jet fighter attack sorties and eight B-52 strikes. As for artillery, they fired up to 1,100 shells per day. The targets of their air and artillery strikes were primarily our artillery positions, the assembly area of our tanks, the areas at the end of our roads for motorized vehicles, and locations of suspected troop concentrations and supply warehouses/stations/caches.

On 8 and 9 March 16 separate waves of B-52s bombed the Hin Tang Valley. Throughout the valley felled trees lay strewn in all directions, and many sections of the forest were set on fire.

On 9 March the tank officers asked the commander of the 312th Infantry Division and the Campaign Headquarters to prepare a section of road northeast of the enemy's Complex 1 in order to be able to move tanks into position to be able to fire directly into the enemy position to support the infantry assault. This request was approved and the 312th Division Headquarters dispatched an engineer battalion to quickly build the road and to dig revetments for the tanks to use to fire at the enemy. This construction was to be completed that very night. [This apparently refers to effort to move the tanks south around Romeo ridge.]

On 10 March, using the newly-built road, 1st Platoon/9th Tank Company, with three T-34s, left Sao Phan and moved up into its firing position at Sa Noc. That night the infantrymen of the 141st and 165th Regiment cautiously crawled up to the enemy's perimeter wire and prepared fighting positions from which to besiege and attack the enemy position.

On 11 March the three T-54 tanks fired 55 cannon rounds that destroyed or collapsed many enemy bunkers. Meanwhile the three APCs and the tank retriever vehicle would accompany the 141st Infantry Regiment in attacking enemy forces on Scarf Hill. On 18 March the armored vehicles surged out ahead of the infantry and roared right through the main gate. When the enemy saw that there were no infantrymen accompanying the APCs, the enemy soldiers ran out, planning to jump up on top of the APCs to destroy them. Our mechanized infantrymen opened the vehicle hatches and used hand grenades and assault rifles to kill the enemy. At that moment, our infantrymen arrived and our forces overran the entire enemy position.

The thing that made us tankers especially happy was that the tank retriever vehicle also participated in the attack and killed the enemy. The tank retriever is a vehicle the bottom part of which is like a tank – it has steel tracks and thick armor. However, it does not have a turret or a turret gun. The primary responsibility of this vehicle is to accompany a formation of tanks to pull out and retrieve any tank that gets stuck. But here, when attacking Hillcrest 3, the tank retriever roared forward, crushed the barbed wire perimeter fence, used its steel tracks to smash and rip to shreds enemy pockets of resistance, and fired its 12.7mm machinegun to support the infantrymen attacking Crests 3 and 4.

15 March 1972. Aircraft attack the road all day and all night. We engineers continue to cling to the road to allow our tanks and supply trucks carrying rice and ammunition to reach the interior. During the months it has spent building the road, the battalion has accomplished its mission of building a road from Ban Phon all the way to Sam Thong. The officers and men of the battalion have experienced and endured combat in keeping with the engineer tradition of "successfully clearing the road," in spite untold hardships and sacrifices.

In early March the five Hmong and Lao Thueng GMs Vang Pao had committed to his deception ops returned to LS-05, LS-20A and LS-32. The eleven PAVN battalions sent to intercept them returned to Skyline.

11 March. Three new Thai irregular BCs - 613, 614 and 620 - arrived in the valley... making sixteen Thai irregulars battalions (8,000 soldiers) total protecting Sam Thong and Long Tieng. PAVN forces were not reinforced.

14 March. Hmong BG 224 on CA pad atop Skyline was overrun by PAVN. The same day PAVN tanks lead attacks around Romeo ridge to hit the Thai irregulars BCs 606A, 607A, 608A and 610A defending eastern Sam Thong and the only way to the base of Skyline. Positions of 606A, 607A and 608A were overrun. However, this assault force was unable to oust BC 610A from its fortifications south of the runway. FAG Spotlight was with those ousted from their positions by the PAVN tanks and spent several days in the middle of the battlefield eluding PAVN infantry, making the final dash across an open area and up a bank to a friendly position somehow without getting shot by pursuing PAVN soldiers firing their AK-47 assault

Positions on top of Skyline Ridge

The "Ramp." Top are eight
supply warehouses. Then Shep's
rigging shed, the two-city block size
ramp, and to the left of the ramp
are the air ops buildings. At the
bottom is the CIA compound.

Kayak and Hog

Kayak, Digger and Ringo   NoMan   Hardnose w/ Whiskey 02

Lumberjack   Air America Chief Pilot Jim Rhyne   Zack

Mule   Ops Ass't Va Xiong   Ops Ass't Judy

Bamboo and Hog among Hmong

Colonel Chanh Nosavanh,
GM 30 commander

Parachutes used to dropped truck
to LS 32 malfunctioned and the truck
fell dead center into Red Coat's hutch.

Redcoat

During a break in the war a football
game broke out

Baby bear

Night life in Vientiane was notorious. "Gabby" pictured above had a speech impediment and could not talk – though many remember having long conversation with her. She may have been a Charlie Bar regular. Another bar – the Purple Porpoise – did not knowing serve journalist out of deference to regular Air America customers. There was also the Green Latrine, Monica's, the Lido and the internationally famous Le Rendezous des Amis where local Asian ladies were known for unique bordello skills taught by the French Madam LuLu. And the most famous of all, the White Rose, pictured above right, where anything boy-girl went. Many of the bachelors from Long Tieng closed the Vientiane bars during their time off. There were also excellent restaurants and less rowdy venues in Vientiane-after-dark, but beautiful, exotic girls lurked everywhere.

The ubiquitous NVA killed during the battle for Skyline

130mm incoming. Shock waves from the impact would hurt your teeth.

Ly Leu, first Hmong T-28 pilots who famously said he would fly until he died. KIA July 1969.

Super Mex case officer for GM 30

Porter landing at LS 32

Kids one year after adoption

Moose and Kayak   Tony Poe and Jim Glerum

Greek and Ringo on the south ridgeline during Skyline attacks

Father Bouchard and Mule

Small O-1 Birddog spotter aircraft flown by the mighty Ravens, who would intentionally draw fire to identify enemy position for Hmong T-28 and USAF jet fighters.

800 lb bomb dropped on the road NVA built down to skyline

Bell helicopter used to support CIA Asian army

Unarmed Air America chopper picking up a Hmong patrol

Frenchy Smith, Air America pilot extraordinaire

Front pages of two Hanoi Newspapers on 14 January 1972 saying
Long Tieng had been captured

Newly built Thai positions near CA   Brad Handley and Will Green

T-28 T-boned into a C-123

Shep Johnson and his famous rigging shed

GM 30 which retook CW pad on Skyline 14 January 1972

Hmong Villagers

Two NVA tanks knocked out by Hardnose's mines

Thai volunteers arriving in Long Tieng

Lao Theung coming in from patrol on the PDJ   GM 22 soldier

On the edge of the fighting

rifles at full automatic.

Mid-March. Final assault plans on Skyline were developed by PAVN Colonel Nguyen Chuong, commander of the 165th Regiment. He was down to fifteen to twenty men per company. He believed the 150 men total he has left in the regiment could breach the Skyline defense (now held by six Thai irregular battalions: 601A, 602A, 604A, 605A, 617 and 618) if (1) rear PAVN headquarters would authorize four tanks to lead the charge and (2) the tanks were able to make their way through Sam Thong to Skyline, then up the road that ran by the CE pad and down into the Long Tieng valley beyond. He promised victory.

****

15 March. Savannakhet GMs 31 and 33 were scheduled to deploy from positions east of Long Tieng to LS 32 where they were to move south in an effort to interdict the Ban Ban Routes 6 and 7 road junction. However, the Lao commander told CIA case officer Montana that the men – now long past their promised sixty-day deployment to Long Tieng – might revolt if sent north.

COS Hugh Tovar and the Lao commander in chief flew out to GM 31 and 33 positions to assess the situation... to see if a revolt of CIA irregular forces was imminent.

Riotous when Tovar arrived, the men were placated to some extent by the Lao commander's comments. Some boarded the waiting helicopters for the flight north. Once this flight of CH-53s was in the air, however, the remaining men and women soldiers in the ranks became restless.

Tovar heard the distinctive sounds of the angry Lao irregulars chambering rounds in their weapons. Someone spoke up in the rear and said the rest of the men/women weren't going. COS swallowed hard. Everyone in front – now all armed with loaded weapons – were looking angrily at him. He looked around; everyone else had melted away. He stood alone... and not knowing what else to do, just stood there. The lonely "Matador."

The Lao commander reappeared and in time negotiated with the men to lay down their weapons and line up for transport back to Savannakhet. For a time Tovar got bragging rights for staring down a thousand angry and armed Asian guerrillas.

During the night of 16 March, BC 610A men at the end of the Sam Thong runway could hear PAVN tanks and armored cars maneuvering to their front (the north) and to their rear.

Early the following morning, PAVN soldiers from the 141st PAVN Regiment began attacking BC 610A. Four armored personnel carriers and five T-34 tanks appeared on the Sam Thong runway. An orbiting Raven adjusted artillery fire from FSB Venus. As tanks attacked the 610A position the defenders fired their LAWS, which seem to bounce off the enemy tanks. Hmong T-28s arrived on the scene and disabled at least one tank, possibly in concert with the LAW fire. By this time two tanks had rolled on top of the 610A command post, leaving crushed bunkers in their wake, and fired down into the trenches.

FAG Wild Bill was in the command bunker but escaped out the back before it was crushed and destroyed. Thai irregulars throwing grenades managed to set one tank on fire before following Wild Bill west to the Nam Ngum River and eventually a pick up by Air America.

By the evening of 17 March evening, the PAVN had cleared all the Thai irregulars from Sam Thong... but again at a considerable cost. They suffered enormous casualties in their assaults and had lost at least two tanks.

In taking Sam Thong the PAVN infantry captured two Thai irregulars155mm artillery pieces and started to direct howitzer fire from the guns on the western end of Skyline.

18 March. PAVN troops overran BC 616 and took positions around the CC pad on the western end of Skyline. With other positions gained on Skyline since renewed attacks began on 15 March, PAVN once again dominated most of the ridgeline.

Midday on 18 March. Wayne Knight, an Air America pilot just back from school in the United States, was out working resupply to the few pockets of Thai irregulars still left on Skyline. He picked up a load for what he thought was going to the CB pad. Bob Noble was the flight mechanic. Noble had been working Skyline most every day for a month and knew at that time that CB was not held by the Thais. It was unoccupied by friendlies as far as he knew.

Anyway, Knight picked up a sling load from Shep Johnson's rigging shed and started up toward CB. Noble, in the back of the helicopter, saw where they were heading and said, "Hell no, don't go in there."

Knight saw another sling load off to the side of CB. Without arguing with Noble in the rear, Knight didn't alter his course and continued to fly in to drop the load... when suddenly - as he got close - a PAVN soldier jumped out of a spider hole near the pad and fired point-blank as the helicopter descended down on him.

Knight was wounded, so was the co-pilot and Noble in the back – the helicopter was pretty shot up, but flyable - and was able to make its way back to the ramp in the valley bottom and land.

Hardnose was near the old CW pad and saw the situation play out... saw the PAVN soldier stand up and empty his AK-47 magazine into Knight's helicopter... and also saw other PAVN firing from shallow holes. Some Thai soldiers were dispatched down to the CB pad to oust the other PAVN soldiers hiding nearby and found the whole area around the CB pad filthy with PAVN from Chuong's 165th Regiment (probably the fifty men remaining in the 6th Battalion)... hunkering in little holes, most half-covered in dirt. The Thai irregulars killed nineteen, captured one, and the rest escaped. (These 165th Regiment soldiers were prepositioned to protect the tanks movement over Skyline and to follow them down into the valley.)

23 March. Thai BCs 601A and 602A were selected (again) to reinforce positions on Skyline. Storming up both ends of the summit, the Thai troops gained toeholds on opposite peripheries. 604A scaled the western slope in two days. Taking a lesson from the PAVN, they climbed halfway up the first night, dug rat holes and spent the daylight hours there, moving up the rest of the way the next night. They attacked and took back CB. These three BCs were joined by BCs 609A and 617 and together began a slow advance toward the center, clearing Skyline of North Vietnamese.

24 March. The prisoner taken when the Thai flushed the PAVN 165th regiment's men from around the CB pad admitted, after a short interrogation by Vang Pao officer, that T-34 tanks were planning to assault down the road from Sam Thong, over Skyline, into the Long Tieng valley within the week. Hardnose knew that was coming, some of the enemy tanks had gotten through the Thai irregulars position, he didn't know when. But with the prisoner's information he put in an emergency order for M-19 anti-tank mines from Udorn and they arrived the next day by a C-123. They were taken off the fixed-wing plane and Greek had them helicoptered up to Hardnose at the CE pad. One of the Thai irregulars at this position had laid mines before, so using his Thai ops assistant, Smallman, Hardnose and the Thai irregular tried to figure out the instructions on laying the mines from instructions printed on the packing boxes.

But with only some general idea what they were doing – and most critical, only a guess on how to arm the mines once they were put in the ground - some of the Thai irregulars took picks and shovels and went down the road on the north side to lay the mines. Despite the serious and dangerous nature of what they were doing – even though they didn't know for sure what they doing – there was a confident, positive air. All afternoon the volunteers laid mines in the road.

During the night of 28 March, PAVN tanks could be heard starting to make their way up the road to Skyline. Tank engine noise stopped when they ran into the newly laid M19 anti-tank mine field. By the time sappers took out the mines it was too late for their attack.

There was little action on 29 March.

Early the next morning Hardnose, listening on his radio in his bunker, heard Thai operators on Skyline scream that four tanks were coming up the north side of Skyline on the Sam Thong road. He called in USAF gunships to take them out.

A Spectre gunship with a 105mm cannon arrived overhead and could clearly see the PAVN tank engine heat signatures on its infrared, but partial cloud cover obscured the mountains. Without visual identification, the men in the gunship were not allowed to fire.

Hardnose yells at them to fire, but they do not.

The tanks continue to make their way up the hill. They are taken under fire by BC 604A at the CE pad with a 75mm field recoilless rifle. The PAVN tanks returned fire, blowing the 75mm out of the bunker and killing the Thai gunner. Panicking, the Thai soldiers desert CE, leaving an open, unguarded path into the Long Tieng valley. Thai Colonel Saen, in the newly reoccupied CC pad west of the road, marshaled the Thai irregulars in the area to move back to CE, when the lead PAVN tank hit one of the last anti-tank mines. It blew the left tread off, blocking the road. As the second tank tried to maneuvered around, it also hit a mine and came to a stop off the side of the road.

The immobile lead tank got into a firefight with Thai irregulars firing small arms. The next morning the two disabled tanks were still there, blocking the way.

****

We learned later that on 1 April one of the PAVN commanders asked General Nguyen Huu An what they should do next. He told them that they have been beat, retreat.

And like that, it was over. Without shouts or surrender or newsmen or pomp or circumstances.

The Vietnam War Its Ownself

****

4 April. The PAVN ceased Campaign Z, leaving behind a rear guard of sappers on some Skyline positions. What remained of the two PAVN divisions headed back to Vietnam. They were clearly defeated and in their reports, said as much.

Their 27,000 main line force lost to a rag tag army of Lao, Thai and Hmong irregulars in the CIA employ.

They suffered more than 10,000 soldiers killed and wounded. Vang Pao forces suffered 2,000 killed and wounded.

Of this number, Colonel Saen reported Thai irregulars casualties during the PDJ/Skyline battle as: 862 KIA, 1,306 WIA, 565 MIA (POWs), and 1,453 AWOL (deserters).

Air America also suffered losses during the battle. In December alone, twenty-four aircraft were hit by ground fire and three were shot down. Between December 1971 and April 1972 in Laos, six Air America crew members were killed.

More Raven and Mao T-28 aircraft suffered battle damage. One Raven was killed. Two T-28s and four USAF F-4 planes were lost in this battle.

****

In their write-ups PAVN commanders gave the following reasons for losing Campaign Z.

(1)   Skyline was a ridge too far. These PAVN solders, mostly new to combat arms, previously worked in North Vietnam rice paddies or in fishing boats, or in Hanoi schools/factories. They were not mountain trained. The soldiers were expected to do too much by commanders who were also not mountain storm troops. Commanders didn't know the difficulties in crossing mountain terrain where there are no trails. They expected their men to carry as much in the mountains as they had in the lowlands. They didn't know the value of water up on those mountaintops. They were beat by Hill 1800 and had to fight on a battlefield Vang Pao constructed. Plus it took more supplies forward than the PAVN imagined. They didn't expect to fight a 100-day battle.

(2)   USAF TacAir performed superbly. Every PAVN report says their regiments had their shirts ripped by the unrelenting USAF. Their

victories on the PDJ came fast and relatively easy... because the USAF didn't show up - they were off SARing. This was not the case later on. The B-52 raid that Hog and Shoua Yang called in early January knocked the socks off two PAVN regiments at a critical time when they were massed for attacks up Skyline. The 165th Regiment commander Chuong, the 165th Regiment commander, said that his unit in particular suffered great damage by the USAF. He also said at the very end, the 165th, which started with upwards of 1,500 men, had less than 150 for the final push and one battalion of those survivors was pretty much taken out when the Thai irregulars found them hiding in rat holes around the old CE pad. The following, from PAVN Colonel Chuong's report on the final push on Skyline, illustrate US targeting efforts and subsequent TacAir and artillery effectiveness:

However, we regimental-level officers were still very concerned, because for the past several days the enemy had been bombing and shelling us constantly. The next morning, as we began to deploy our forces, the enemy's bombing and shelling grew even more intense. The constant sounds of explosions sounded like rolling thunder. The earth shook, our heads and ears hurt, and massive clouds of dust and smoke billowed up and spread out in a blinding cloud that covered one entire area around Long Tieng. Our field telephone lines were cut and we were not able to reconnect them before they were cut again and again. For several hours that morning I did not receive any information from any of my units. Everyone in the command post was on pins and needles because we did not know the status of the preparations of our different units for the battle planned for that day and did not know if anyone had been killed or wounded. At 4:00 in the afternoon the enemy's bombardment intensified even further.

(3)   They underestimated Vang Pao. They give him complete credit for the end- around in February that pulled their fighters from Skyline and gave time for the Thai BCs to reload.

(4)   They underestimated the "hang" of VP irregulars defending Long Tieng.

****

That's what the PAVN, who were there, said. They did not know that other contributing factors included Moose, who developed an effective intercept program that focused U.S. TacAir and local artillery.

Plus they did not calculate the value of Air America pilots who went out every day in aircraft that had, in contrast to U.S. military aircraft, little armor and no guns to resupply all VP's forces. Even at the height of the battle, they got the wounded and the dead out and brought in the new U.S. Special Forces trained troops sent up from the south. Every day Air America made extraordinarily cool contributions, although in fact as author Christopher Robbins said, with Air America extraordinary was average.

Along the same line, the whole logistics chain worked. From Bill Lair sitting on the desk at CIA Headquarters in Virginia, through Jim Glerum in Udorn, through Brad Handley, chief of support at Long Tieng, out to Shep Johnson at the rigging shed, to Air America/Continental Air Services (CASI). VP forces were never at a loss for bullets, water or bread. The PAVN were.

The decision to allow Hog and Hardnose to stay in the valley at night, when the enemy was at victory's gate, was significant. It was noticed by every soldier in VP's force and led to their resolve to stay and fight.

Ambassador Godley and COS Hugh Tovar deserve credit for their ability generally to keep the Washington hand wringers at bay and for getting necessary TacAir support after the fall of the PDJ. And of particular note, Tovar's support to Vang Pao's deception ops – in the face of strong Washington objection – was a deciding factor in the outcome of the battle. In the end it proved Vang Pao was the best general on the battlefield. Plus Soua Yang's knowledge of the only place attacking North Vietnamese could hide was in Vang Pao's farm just north of the CA pad... was absolutely dead on. And Vang Pao's knowledge of steep Hill 1800 and the fact that they wouldn't be able to get their tanks up the grade – was significant in placement of Thai irregulars defensive position south of Romeo ridge.

Hugh Tovar's management style allowed the Stick, C/Udorn, and Dick Johnson, C/Long Tieng, to fight the battle – empowering them with the authority to handle Thai 333 and VP and vigorously supporting their decisions with Washington - was pivotal. In Vietnam, by contrast, all important U.S. military decisions at the time were made in Washington and Saigon, where politics and disengagement were more a consideration than battlefield objectives.

Hugh Tovar, referred to by the international press as the

James E. Parker, Jr.

"Matador" and Ambassador Mac Godley, known as the "Field Marshal," were unusually grounded and competent – greatly respected by the entire U.S. workforce, who they met nightly at the Vientiane airfield. They did what was necessary to be successful on Skyline, rather than what might have been in their best career interest. They stood up to congressional politicians, Washington-based bureaucrats and U.S. military bullies. Together they ran a successful program in a U.S. foreign war where there were not many successful senior-level managers.

U.S. Air Force's B-52s, attack planes, Spookys, Spectres and the enormously brave Raven killed the communist invaders by the thousands.

The CIA forces under General Vang Pao's command held Skyline against all odds, because combat operations were conceived and run from the field. And as Director of Central Intelligence Richard Helms said, the battle was won because of the "special men" in that rag tag multi-national army.

****

I commuted from Udorn during the final days of the Skyline battle... there were no places to stay in Long Tieng or Vientiane. While I was away during the day Brenda was enjoying her role as mother. She would wait for me each night to tell me incredible stories about Mim and Joe, how they were relating and learning English and laughing and crying. She usually had supper fixed and would be talking a mile a minute as I slumped over my plate and ate... and then she would follow me into the bedroom, carrying on more of her stories... even talking to me as I showered and fell in bed. She was so happy.

She was worried that Mim's mother might suddenly appear and take Mim away, claiming a mother's natural right. Brenda said she would die if anything happened to her new daughter. Because of her concerns and because the sixteen- and eighteen-hour work days were wearing me down, I asked Dick about moving my family to Vientiane. He agreed and received approvals from Udorn. Brenda was left to her own devices, however, to travel to Vientiane, find a house, negotiate a lease, and move the car, the dog, the kids and our household effects across the Mekong River into Laos.

No problem, she said. She flew up on 50-Kip and taxied around Vientiane looking for houses for rent. In short order she found quarters within our budget and arranged with the Udorn office to have the family moved north. Labor was cheap in Thailand. It was cheaper in Laos. She hired two maids and a gardener for under $50 a month for the group and they moved into the servant quarters in the back. With the guards who were provided, it was like coming home to a department store at night; there were so many people, so much going on. Maids, guards, gardeners, the dog, wife, children. It was a happy place.

Brenda was brought into the tight sorority of wives in Vientiane whose husbands worked upcountry. Her days were spent mothering the kids, shopping, running the house, playing bridge and socializing with the gals. It was an unusually robust, intriguing life for her and she always seemed so happy, standing on the porch of the house with the kids when I would come in at night.

****

The U.S. Air Force came to bear on the Vietnamese force as they pulled back from Skyline to lick their wounds and head for home. Moose as much as anyone told us that when they eventually began retreating back up the river valley to the PDJ it proved their offensive for this season was over. Their Campaign Z lost.

We were not disappointed with the way the battle had gone. The Vietnamese had taken the PDJ but they had not taken Skyline or killed the CIA army. But no more than a handful of people in Washington knew about our war, about our unlikely success.

The focus of the American involvement in Indochina continued to be South Vietnam. Ours was a generally ignored sideshow. The men who worked upcountry Laos did not consider their contributions in terms of the developing overall U.S. strategy in the region. Most had served in Vietnam with the U.S. military where their work was roundly criticized at home, always looked at in the context of a slowly losing effort. It was more rewarding for us in Laos. There was almost glamor to what we did. Like Helms said, it was the men in the CIA army that made a difference: The Ravens, Sky and Air America... the Thai mercenaries, the Lao Theung, Hmong, troops from Savannakhet, Cher Pao Moua at Bouam Long, Vang Pao and Dhep and Saen and Tovar and Hog and Hardnose and Moose. What a grand experience. Individual, personal. Manly. Adventurous.

--TWENTY-SEVEN--
Va's Porter Crash

About this time young men from the village Va and I had first visited made contact with the settlement at the base of the Red Mountain. They gave the Ni Ban there one of our new radios. When we next flew up Va and I had extended radio conversations with him about his area. Matt Daddio, an Air America Porter pilot, flew for us almost every day then. He was a jovial, even tempered individual who seemed to have a special rapport with his flying machine. Occasionally he would feather the prop as we were flying along and we would glide, soaring with the wind drafts. When we talked with people on the ground, Daddio would slowly bank the plane in an easy circle. He would appear not to be moving at all, holding the stick in one position against his leg. He made flying seem like a natural act.

The Ni Ban of the second settlement said there was no place near his lowland village to build an airstrip but he suggested we think about landing in the valley on top of Red Mountain at an old abandoned landing strip, LS 90. He would send men to the top to secure the high ground, but he only had a collection of old rifles and he needed more weapons, mortars and grenades.

Va knew that the home area of this Ni Ban was on the other side of Red Mountain, in a valley now controlled by a joint Pathet Lao and Vietnamese unit. It was a reasonable proposition to supply him with the weapons he requested so that he could secure the mountaintop in a gradual move back to the eastern valley. We told him as much, and he said, give us weapons and we'll go back home.

Daddio flew us back to LS 272 where I collected carbines and assault rifles, plus some claymore mines, radios and batteries. I asked Shep to rig them for drop from a Porter.

Later in the day we returned in Daddio's Porter over the settlement. We had two loads to drop. The first was in the drop bay in the back of the Porter, with the parachute on top and a static line running to the side of the plane. The other load was behind it, at the rear of the bay area. We made a run over the small field near the settlement where the Ni Ban wanted us to drop the supplies and Daddio noticed that there were unusual wind currents coming up from the different draws. He said he would have to make a steep dip near the field to drop the supplies so they would land on target and not be carried by the currents into the nearby mountainside or down in deep ravines.

Coming around after making the trial run he reached behind his seat and grabbed the handle that would release the bomb doors beneath the drop bay. Like a bombardier he got the field lined up, figured for the wind, dipped the plane's nose and dove toward the field. He pulled the handle as he bottomed out of his dive and brought the plane back up. The load dropped out the bomb bay, the static line caught, pulling open the parachute. As Daddio began to come around for his second drop, we watched as the load drifted down almost into the hands of the Hmong below.

Because the second load was mostly heavy ammunition I had volunteered to manhandle it into the drop bay and was in the back. Va was sitting in the seat reversed beside Daddio.

I pulled the static line in from the first bundle. As Daddio closed the bay doors I began to quickly maneuver the next bundle into position. Daddio continued to come around.

The bundle was heavier than I thought and I had problems moving it in the cramped compartment. I got it to the edge of the bay and it got stuck. Daddio was saying that he was going to be on target within a few minutes. I pushed and shoved and kicked and groaned and cussed but the bundle would not move into the bay. Daddio said he was going to be on target in one minute. I stood over the bundle, grabbed the sides and lifted up and moved it forward, edging it into the bay. I stepped down into the bay and lifted up and felt something give a little bit under my feet. I reached for the load and with two hands pulled it forward as I stepped out. The edge of the bundle tipped forward and then down, striking the bottom of the bay. Suddenly the doors fell open, the bundle was gone, free falling to the side of the mountain below, the static line acting as a streamer.

My knees suddenly were weak as I straddled the open bay, looking down through the bottom of the plane at the ground rushing by below. Va reached and grabbed my pistol belt as Daddio closed the bay doors.

I had had near encounters with death before. I had been only inches away on a number of occasions in Vietnam - I was often unscathed when men were shot all around me, the benefactor of good luck or a Mother's prayer. Why this wasn't my time to go I didn't know. The opportunity was there. I had been standing in the bay pushing up on the bundle, down on the doors. They should have burst through.

There was a well-known story out of Pakse, Laos, in MR IV of a road-watch team that had moved in too close to the Ho Chi Minh Trail and was discovered by North Vietnamese trail guards. Their

Sky officer was in a fixed-wing plane getting a situation report not long after the patrol was spotted by the North Vietnamese and had started maneuvering to get away. The patrol leader said that it appeared to him that they were cut off to the west and he was forced to head back east and find some place to hide and wait out his pursuers. He said he was going off the air to save his batteries. And he disappeared. The Sky officer flew the area every day for the next two weeks looking for the patrol - calling for them on the radio - without luck. Weeks later he was back on other business and got a very faint signal from the old road-watch team and he followed the signal. It led him to the Ho Chi Minh Trail and then east of the trail, into Vietnam. There on the side of a bomb crater he saw a panel the team leader had laid out. Over the faint radio signal the leader said most of his men had been killed but he and a couple more were still alive. They needed food and medicine and batteries and ammo. The Sky officer quickly returned to Pakse. As he was having the necessary supplies rigged, the village chief from the area where the road-watch team had been recruited happened by. On hearing that the team had been found, the chief was ecstatic and asked to go along in hopes that he could say a few words to the remaining men in the patrol. When the plane arrived the second time it flew very high over the bomb crater. The pilot said that they would make a low run south to north. If they did it once maybe they could get away without being hit, twice over the same area so near the trail and they would certainly be shot and they would give away the position of the team. Two bundles had to be kicked out in the one pass. So they made their run. The village chief was in the back with the Air America kicker to help to get the two bundles out the door. As they neared the bomb crater, they kicked out the first bundle. Unfortunately as they were rushing to get the second bundle out the door the village chief got caught in some of the straps, he was jerked out the door and he fell to his death, beating the parachute bundle to the ground.

There was nothing they could do in the plane. It gained altitude and moved off to the west, where, after a short pause, the patrol leader came on the air, booming loud with his new batteries. He said he was thankful for the food and the medicine and the ammo, but, he asked, "why did you send the village chief?"

When I sat down in the back of the Porter, after Daddio closed the bay doors, I was thankful that I had not put these people in the same quandary. "Why did you send the Sky man?" they might have asked.

We resupplied the Ni Ban later in the day with a new load of ammunition and figured that it would take a full week for his people to secure the top of the mountain. While we were waiting, Va suggested that we drive a Jeep he had found near LS 353 to LS 272. Va lived with his wife of less than a year, Bea, a couple of miles from LS 272 and every night and every morning he had to walk the several miles to meet me at the airfield. Though we had almost all the supplies that we needed to do our job and always received requests for additional items, I had been reluctant to ask Dick about a Jeep for Va because of our imminent plans to move back into the Long Tieng valley.

So I told Va to take a couple of days off and go get the Jeep, I'd send him over on a Porter to LS 353. He thought things would go better if I came along. He was unfamiliar with the territory between 353 and 272, though he knew it to be secure. He said he worried that he might run into someone along the way who might want that Jeep. But if a Sky man was along, there'd be no problem. It'd only take one day.

"One day? We can get a Jeep from 353 to 272 in one day I asked? Over that big mountain in between? And it's secure? Yep, he said, and he continued to look at me without blinking, though I sensed he wasn't being completely honest about something.

Two days later when I flew in from Vientiane, Va was waiting with a mechanic plus three other large Hmong, some rope and gas. We took a porter into LS 353 and walked out to a hut on the edge of the village where a stripped down Jeep sat. The mechanic got it running and we headed out of town.

And the road stopped. "No road, Va?" I asked.
"No road," he responded.
"We have to climb over a very large mountain in one day. And there is no road? You said we could do this in one day. And there's no road? We can't do this."
"Can do." Va said looking straight ahead as the Jeep began to negotiate down the footpath into the valley beyond 353. It was a wide trail, though it was crowded with people, and we went slowly, sometimes straddling the trail, sometimes on one side or the other. I noticed there were no other vehicle tracks. I asked Va if anyone else ever drove Jeeps down this trail. He said no, still looking straight ahead. I asked if he had ever heard of a horse-drawn wagon ever going down this trail and he said no.

We finally reached a village in a high valley. As we drove through, toward a river on the other side, people stared. Children, running around a thatched hut chasing one another, saw the six of us moving through the center of their village in that slow moving Jeep and they stopped, dead in their tracks, and stared. It was like the Jeep was a UFO. They simply could not believe what they were seeing. It wasn't me as much as it was that Jeep. The Hmong were descendants of Chinese who had drifted south over the mountains. They had no experience with Western technology and would stare with awe at planes as they flew overhead. Some who lived near villages south of the PDJ that had airstrips had flown in the planes, though first-time flyers always were deathly afraid and always became airsick, causing a smell in those small Air America planes portering Hmong civilians that would almost fog the windows. The majority of the Hmong, however, knew nothing about electricity or world events or medicine or the internal combustion engine. The Jeep was as strange to them, rolling through their village, as it might have been to villagers in ancient China in 500 B.C.

When we got to the river we found people were using a swinging bridge and a log foot walk to cross. Neither, I suggested to Va, appropriate for a Jeep. A mountain loomed large and forbidding on the other side.

I was to the point of saying this is far enough when the driver swung the wheel of the Jeep to one side, taking us on a four-wheel slide to the bottom of the creek bank. We forged the river and headed up the foot path on the other side.

Soon the trail became so narrow and the fall-off to the side so severe that I said I was walking and the Jeep could follow along behind. And I took off walking ahead, but the grade was so steep I tired after only a few minutes. We were going too slow anyway, so I got back in the vehicle and the driver gunned the engine when he put it in gear - so as not to roll back down the trail - almost sending us over the side.

I got out again and took one of the ropes and tied it to the back so the Jeep could pull me along.

And we climbed the mountain and we climbed the mountain and we climbed and climbed and my hands were sore from holding onto the rope but the top was just in sight and we finally reached it and found it was just a ridge we had crested and the mountain went on up in front of us. And the air got thin and it was becoming harder for me to breath and my hands were becoming even more sore, so I got back in the Jeep.

And we got to the high ground in front of us and found the mountain still went up, higher in front of us. And I was fooled another four times, before, finally, we did, in fact, reach the top.

And looking down the other side, I gasped. It went straight down. My fear was the Jeep would start tumbling end over end after it started down. The brakes couldn't possibly hold it. As I stood beside the Jeep, absolutely convinced that we could not travel down the trail before us, the Hmong got out and took the rope that I had used earlier and tied it to a nearby tree. I stood there the driver inched slowly over the edge and the Hmong began letting out on the rope. Which is the way we made most of the trip to the bottom of the mountain. In increments the length of the rope. They would tie it to something and gradually let it out as the driver guided the Jeep down the steep incline. He was the only one in the vehicle and he sat there like the roadrunner cartoon character, waiting for the rope to snap and send him hurdling down the trail like a rocket heading to the center of the earth.

We were near the bottom when we saw up ahead a trail-side stand in which some enterprising young Hmong girl was selling sundries. Like others we had seen along the trail, this young girl was shocked speechless, watching us come slowly down that foot trail. She just could not believe what she saw. Possibly for a dozen generations Hmong and Lao had used that same trail to climb that mountain. Sometime they used small horses as pack animals. But there had never, ever been a Jeep on the trail. Maybe when Father Bouchard walked this way for the first time people might have gawked at him like they looked at us, I don't know, but that girl had never seen a vehicle before.

We pulled up beside her stand, a small rough-hewn wooden table in front of a thatched shelter. Va asked her how much the Pepsis were behind her. There were six on a bamboo shelf. Probably her prize merchandize. Pepsis were in fact used in the mountains of Laos like Americans use champagne at special occasions. She didn't answer but continued to look at each one of us and then back to the Jeep. Va suggested that 200 kip would probably be a good price and she looked at him without comment. As he was counting out 1,200 kip for the purchase, one of the other Hmong got out and got all six Pepsis. Va handed the girl the money but she kept looking at the Jeep from the front to the back, so Va laid the money on the wooden counter and we drove on down the trail drinking the hot sodas, the girl looking at us as we left.

We were in the river valley on the other side of the mountain by late afternoon and it was apparent that we would not get back to LS 272 by night fall if we continued down the footpath that lead through the small settlements. I noticed on the map that a creek meandered in the direction we were heading and emptied into the Nam Nung River, the last obstacle we had to face. I suggested we go down to the creek.

The Hmong phrase for "follow the river" sounds like "today" in English.

While the mechanic charged along as near the side of the creek as he could, spraying water all over us, we kept up the chant, "Today, Today, Today."

Amid the chants I said to myself, let me get back to LS 272 Today, Today, so Dick or Hog won't kill me Tomorrow, Tomorrow.

We got to the Nam Nung River, loaded the Jeep on a raft ferry because the river was too deep to forge, gained the road on the other side and sped down to LS 272, getting there at dusk as the last of the Twin Otters was getting ready to take off for Vientiane.

Va picked me up the next morning in our Jeep, which we named "Today."

****

Within a few days the Red Mountain Ni Ban had secured the high ground around site 90, pushing a small group of Pathet Lao off to the east.

I located a mobile Thai training team in Long Tieng to teach the Red Mountain Hmong how to use rocket launchers and mortars and they accompanied us the first time we landed at the airstrip on top of the mountain.

Our reception by the Ni Ban was warm and though he didn't have the food to offer much of a welcoming party, or "baci" as they were called by the Hmong, we did have a meal of rice and canned meat. Later over hot beer we tied strings on each other's wrist in the Hmong tradition to bring luck. Va and I left the Thai team and returned to LS 272.

Two weeks later, on 5 April, we flew back in. In the way of a graduation exercise the Thai training team had the Hmong demonstrate their new mortar rocket launcher skills by hitting a rock formation I picked at random on the east side of the mountain. Later in a hut by the side of the airstrip we worked out a plan to send some of the men at the position on a reconnaissance down into the valley to the east.

Daddio was flying the Porter later that afternoon that was sent in to pick us up. He had told me before that he didn't like the site, pointing out that it was not the highest point of the mountain, that there were rock formations on either side that looked down on the dirt airfield and made it vulnerable. The PDJ was not too far in the distance and there were no friendly forces between it and us.

To allay Daddio's concerns the Ni Ban had put men on top of the tall rock formation that Daddio saw as he circled before landing. Even at that, he motioned for Va and me, plus the training team, to get on quickly as he landed and turned back around into the wind. The plane was rolling forward for the takeoff as the last man was crawling aboard.

Landing at LS 272 I went to the supply area and began collecting ammunition and web gear I promised to bring back to the site to outfit the men for their reconnaissance. The material we collected filled Daddio's Porter, leaving room for either Va or I to go.

I nodded to Va because no one at the mountaintop spoke English.

On the flight up to the mountain Daddio asked Va to open the door to the plane as soon as they landed and to start kicking off the supplies when they came to a stop. Daddio said he didn't want to be on the ground for more than a minute. Though Va and I had just been there for several hours and felt it was completely safe, Va agreed without arguing.

As the Porter touched down, Va opened the sliding door on the side. When Daddio came to the end of the runway and spun the plane around, Va began to heave the supplies off. Within the minute - some of the Hmong on the position were still running down to the strip to help - Va had the plane empty and Daddio gunned the engine to take off. Va moved back to the seat in the front sitting in reverse to Daddio.

As the plane was gathering speed down the runway the left wheel struck a mine.

The explosion blew the tire and one of the wing struts off and the plane careened off to the left. Straight toward a ravine.

Inside Va opened the forward door. He didn't know what had caused the problem but he knew instantly he would die if he stayed on that plane. Now reeling madly to the left, the left wing almost to the ground.

Forcing the door open against the wind he got a foot out and dove out.

Daddio got his door open under the dipping wing and he tumbled out his side, missing the rear stabilizer of the plane by inches as he bounced and rolled along the ground. Within seconds the plane hit the ravine, crashed and exploded behind him.

349

Not knowing that they had hit a mine, thinking that they were under ground attack, Daddio got to his feet and saw Va lying very still next to the runway.

The pilot yelled and Va rolled over and sat up. He had broken ribs and shrapnel in his back and was in a daze. Daddio, unhurt but excited, yelled again. He ran to the small ops assistant, picked him up and ran off into the bush where he was joined by some of the Hmong from the position and they climbed to the top of a small rise where Daddio slumped down, exhausted. The plane was burning below. Behind it Daddio could see that the mine crater had cut the airstrip from side to side.

Va gradually gathered his senses and sent the Hmong down to get their radio and Daddio called a "Mayday."

Air America, hearing the distress signal - knowing that one of their planes was down - scrambled everyone for the rescue mission that brought Va and Daddio back to LS 272. Daddio was taken directly to Vientiane. Va, though more seriously hurt, was a Hmong and had to be admitted to a local hospital.

Daddio would not be back for a year. He had to undergo a series of operations to repair broken bones and other damage to his body. He was smiling when he came back though, calling the incident an occupational hazard.

Va lay in the open air ward of the local hospital for days because the shrapnel in his back was so near his spinal cord that the doctors were reluctant to operate for fear of causing permanent paralysis. His wife came and camped in a chair beside his bed. His father moved into a nearby village to be with his son.

I drove Today over every morning. When it became apparent that Va needed an operation that called for better facilities and possibly a more experienced team, I took a morning off in Vientiane and found a hospital there where he could be treated. That evening I returned to the LS 272 hospital to pick him up.

His wife said she was going with him.

We loaded Va in a Jeep ambulance for the ride to the airstrip. With his wife in the passenger side of "Today" and his father sitting in the back with a bag of his clothing, we followed. Va was lying on a stretcher in the back, propped up so that he looked out at us. It was the dry season and the ambulance kicked up a rooster tail of dust. I could either lay way back out of the dust or stay in close. I chose the latter, it wasn't a long drive over a ridgeline to the airfield, and I squinted into the dust, looking at the ambulance and Va who was looking back at us. We were going around a curve when Va suddenly became excited. His eyes got big and he began waving frantically at me.

For what, I thought? What could he possibly be that excited about? And he was really excited, trying to sit up on the stretcher, waving. This is crazy, I was thinking, squinting ahead. What's going on?

His father, sitting in the back seat, put his hand on my shoulder and pointed behind us.

Looking around I noticed that Va's wife wasn't sitting in the seat. She had fallen out of the Jeep and was tumbling over the side of the bank behind us, going out of sight.

She had rolled halfway down the slope and was climbing back up, dusting herself off when we returned.

Va didn't know his wife wasn't hurt because the ambulance drove on. People at the airfield were unsure why their reunion was so tearful when we drove up.

Va said his wife didn't have much experience riding in Jeeps.

--TWENTY-EIGHT--
CIA Paramilitaring

I continued to work the ADO and the villagers north of Long Tieng with Khu Sao, another ops assistant, but in May Ringo left for the states and I was assigned his Hmong unit, GM 22.

Nhia was my new ops assistant. A bright, personable young Hmong - he had a swagger to his walk - Nhia was one of the most popular men working for Sky. He claimed he learned everything he knew from Ringo.

The GM was camped south of the PDJ when I took them over, dug in across a no-man's valley from a ridgeline controlled by the Pathet Lao. The North Vietnamese were not in sight and there was some exchange of greetings often between the Pathet Lao and the Hmong GM from across the way.

One morning in late July a flood destroyed the LS 272 rear base. Most of the buildings washed away. Vehicles, heavy equipment and pallets of heavy ammo were strewn down the valley, some hundreds of meters from the now quiet, peaceful creek.

Someday people are going to come across howitzer ammo deep in some clumps of trees and try to figure out how they got there.

The LS 272 flood hastened our move back into Long Tieng. Skyline was completely secure. The main Vietnamese and Pathet Lao units had been pushed back to the PDJ and Hmong patrolled the river valley. Hog and Bamboo came down off the south ridge and we reoccupied the Sky compound. It ended my nightly returns home to Vientiane and I went on a schedule of ten days upcountry and four days with the family. Kayak and I roomed together.

It was summer of 1972, and there were several more personnel changes in the Sky ranks. In addition to Ringo, Bag and Dick, the chief of unit, left. Shep, the rigger, was scheduled to leave in the fall.

It was Shep's second tour in MR II. He was our special person. We loved Shep. He worked hard. Every day. Out on the ramp before the sun came up. Rarely talking, always working, rigging. Getting things exactly right and then checking, rechecking. Absolutely refusing to have anything go out from his rigging shed that wasn't perfect. The right supplies, rigged with the right parachutes, on the right planes in the right order. It was an uplifting experience to work with Shep because he was so conscientious. The salt of the earth. Like Hog and Bag, he had come from the hills of Montana and was for the most part a silent frontiersman.

But he could get drunk on three beers. We marveled at this. We would watch him and listen as he came in the mess hall at night and silently sip his first beer, making no comments. He would get a second beer, drinking a little faster now and he might quietly agree with something someone said and then maybe he'd disagree with something someone said and then goddamnit to hell someone was just full of goddamned shit he'd say and he'd crumple up the beer can and open another and drink almost half the can in one gulp. If I smiled at my friend and he'd say, "What da' fuck is funny Mule? I don't see nothing funny except maybe this whole friggin' group is funny. Full of "girl singers."

"Girl singers" was a Hog phrase. It took me time to get its exact meaning. It meant a man who did a lot of posturing and acted romantic, with half closed eyes, like a male crooner singing love songs. Girl singers. You had to use it a lot for it to make sense. Most politicians were "girl singers."

Once when we still lived in Udorn, Shep and I went out for a beer on a night Brenda went to play bridge with Shep's wife, Jan.

Jan had a glass eye. She was big and blocky and intimidating when you first met her, though once you got to know her, she was a kind and gentle soul. A good wife to Shep and one of

Brenda's best friends.

That night the air conditioner in Shep and Jan's living room wasn't working and the only cool place to play cards was on the landing to the stairs going to the second floor. So Jan set up the card table on the landing. She thought this was OK and no one really argued with Jan, though as I said she was a kind and gentle soul.

Shep had more than three beers out with me, got drunk and wanted to go home. I reminded him that the girls were there playing cards at his house. I suggested that he could just sit with me and maybe drink coffee. I didn't think Jan wanted him to come home right yet.

Nope, he said, he wanted to go home and go to sleep, goddamnit. So I took him home. He got out of the car and went inside. I didn't follow. I think I didn't go in because of Jan, that she might have been angry with me for taking her husband out and getting him drunk, or worse for bringing him home.

Shep went in the house. As he began climbing the stairs, he looked up at the girls playing cards on the landing and he just couldn't figure it out. He weaved back and forth looking up with a confused, curious expression on his face. Jan said sternly, "Shep don't you come up the stairs you drunk son-of-a-bitch, there's no room for you to get by. Go sleep in one of the empty servants rooms or on the couch. You hear me Shep? Don't you come up these stairs."

But Shep wasn't listening because he was looking up trying to figure out why the girls were sitting around a table on the stairs landing. He shook his head in confusion. All he wanted to do was to go to sleep, in his bed, upstairs. So he continued to walk up the stairs and Jan stood up and said, "Shep if you come up here I will hit you." Shep was halfway up the bottom flight of stairs by that time. He jumped up and grabbed the banisters to the next flight and he climbed over, missing the girls. He crawled up the remaining stairs, got to his feet and went into the bedroom and closed the door.

Jan said, "Don't you come out of the bedroom, you son-of-a-bitch. You go to bed and sleep or die, but don't you come back out of that bedroom. We're playing bridge."

Shep came back out in ten minutes.

He had taken off all his clothes and had wrapped a cloth sarong around his waist. He wanted to go downstairs for some reason, but he must have considered the problems this was going to be for him, because he didn't look at Jan as she stood up from the bridge table on the landing.

He jumped over the top of the banister on the top flight of

stairs, with the idea in mind of dropping down to the lower flight of stairs, only he didn't figure for the sarong and he didn't clear the banister. It caught him in mid-jump. He straddled it to keep from falling and started sliding down, which hiked his sarong up.

Just at the time Jan yelled, "Shep, you son-of-a-bitch," Brenda jerked around to see that Shep had slid all the way down the banister to the landing where she was sitting. The sarong, all that he was wearing, was up to his armpits.

"What an asshole." Jan said.

Brenda turned around and found she was sitting 6 inches from Shep's back side. She said, "Yep!"

****

Like the rest of us, VP liked Shep, and admired his work ethic. He planned a large party, or "basi," as a farewell. All Sky was invited. Plus all of VP's officers. The war stopped for Shep's basi.

Hugh Tovar, the CIA station chief in Vientiane, and his French-born wife attended.

Shep did not like crowds. He did not like to be called on in front of crowds. He did not like being the guest of honor, center of attention. And he certainly did not want to go to his basi. Jan told him, "Don't you drink too many beers and embarrass me you son-of-a-bitch. It'll just be a couple or three hours. Just go, drink coke, smile. You don't have to say anything. Just don't drink any beer and get drunk and embarrass me."

But Shed almost died dealing with all of those people in VP's house. Not long after he arrived he went upstairs and had several beers.

After most of the guest arrived, VP called everyone to the table. He sat at the head, Hugh Tovar sat on his left. Hugh's wife, a polished lady comfortable in diplomatic parlor rooms, sat on VP's right and there was an empty seat for Shep and then Jan. Other guest were mixed, boy girl, boy girl.

When everyone sat down, Shep was conspicuous by his absence. VP looked around. "Where's Shep?" he asked. Jan knew; she was very happy that he was upstairs out of sight and she did not answer. A Hmong serving water told VP that Shep was upstairs. VP told him to go get him. This basi was for Shep. He didn't want to miss his own basi.

They got Shep, a couple of Hmong under each arm, and were dragging him down the stairs to the table. Shep's head was on his chest as they dragged him along, his feet bouncing on the stairs behind. Someone at the table called out, "Shep, Shep is that you?" Shep quickly lifted up his head and stared at the dinner table in front. Jan turned around and glared with her good eye. Shep was drunk, embarrassing her, and she was angry. You son-of-a-bitch she was thinking. Shep looked at the people sitting around the table and at his chair like a condemned man must look at the electric chair as he is being lead into the chamber. His eyes got bigger but he got his feet under him - he was at the bottom of the stairs by this time - and he walked stiffly to the table.

One of the Hmong pulled the chair out and Shep sat down.

Two feet from the table. He didn't move closer.

VP looked one way and then another around Hugh's wife trying to say something to the guest of honor. He motioned to some of the Hmong to move his chair in closer and they did.

Shep, now sitting between his angry wife and Hugh's very proper wife, was very uncomfortable.

And drunk.

And he listened to VP for a few minutes but then his eyes began to droop and he began weaving from side to side. He would touch Jan and she would elbow him away and he would lean in the opposite direction and would touch Mrs. Hugh Tovar, who would quickly take in a breath and he would recoil. Back and forth.

And he finally lost his balance and fell off his chair.

Underneath the table.

And he immediately tried to stand up.

Spilling everyone's water.

He knelt back down and then began climbing back up the leg of his wife, though it was in fact the leg of Hugh Tovar's wife. Halfway up, using her leg for a banister, an errant hand hit her right side near her breast and she gasped because this didn't happen often at other dinner parties she attended. Alerted by her gasp, Shep looked up and realized he had his hands on Mrs. Hugh Tovar, who was looking at him strangely. He stood straight up at attention.

Pushing the dinner table back a couple of feet.

And he stood there looking down at Mrs. Hugh Tovar

Jan pulled him down into his chair again as everyone rearranged themselves at the table and the waiters helped clear the spilled water.

All the Sky people, including Hugh, and VP thought it was a hoot. Jan did not. And Mrs. Hugh Tovar did not.

And Shep did not. He sat now frozen in his chair.

355

Then the first dish was served.

Barbecued pigeon.

One report is that the pigeons had been prepared with their tail feathers still intact, sticking up, poised. The pigeons were covered with barbecue sauce. Everyone up and down the table picked up their utensils to clear away the barbecue sauce to get at the meat.

Except Shep, who sat motionless looking at the pigeon on the plate in front of him.

Apparently feeling that he could not handle his knife and fork, Shep reached out with one hand and grabbed the whole pigeon.

And put it in his mouth.

And the barbecue sauce dripped down his chin and into his lap. And he sat there chewing, his eyes half closed, with the feathers sticking out of his mouth, bouncing up and down.

People up and down the table snickered. Jan elbowed him and he looked at her and stopped chewing.

Mrs. Hugh Tovar, on his other side, noticing that Shep was the center of attention, said in her French accent, "Shep, Shep what are you doing?

And he turned in her direction and paused before saying slowly, "Eating PI..geon."

And when he said "PI..geon," he spit all over her.

****

A.H. (alias) arrived for an extended overlap with Shep; "Mr. Clean," with a shaven head, replaced Bag. No one was scheduled to replace Digger who was leaving in the fall. It was 1972 and the war in Indochina was looking for a place to end.

"Zack" temporarily replaced Dick Johnson as the chief of unit. The tour had been difficult for the Dick, because he was placed in an awkward position in his dealings with General Vang Pao... he was between Hog at Long Tieng, who was revered by VP, and the Stick at Udorn, who had seniority and influence. Not everything Dick tried to accomplish got off the ground. But he was very popular in his own right with the entire Sky group. He was cost effective and he demanded accountability from the people who worked for him. He was an intelligent Agency professional. On the other hand Zack, an ex-Marine who had fought in the Second World War, Korea and had served with the Agency in Vietnam and previously in south Laos, did not compete with Hog and the Stick or become contentious with

VP. He was unassuming in manner and had a personality that clicked with Sky, Air America, CASI and the Hmong from the first day. In the valley he was an excellent complement to Hog. Nothing really mattered to Hog other than doing the job. He was there for no man. Zack was different. He was considerate and accommodating in a way we rarely saw upcountry.

****

In mid-August 1972 shortly after we reoccupied the Sky compound the Hmong T-28s began to return to the valley. It was a cause for celebration… the story of the Long Tieng T-28 squadron was always a cause of great pride to the Hmong.

> [[*Bill Lair, a CIA case officer, had initially come to southeast Asia in 1951. His first job was to create what was euphemistically called PARU, a special unit of Thai police responsible for Thai border security. Not long after his work with Lao General Phoumi Nosovanh to retake the Lao administrative capital of Vientiane from Lao (communist-leaning) Neutralist Captain Kong, Lair met and started work with Vang Pao to set up a Hmong army to fight off invading North Vietnamese communist.*
> *Sometime later USAF set up a T-28 training program for Thai and Lao pilots in Udorn. Some of these Asian pilots were eventually posted to Long Tieng under Vang Pao's command, to provide close air support to his guerilla army.*
> *All efforts to convince the USAF to take on Hmong pilots for training was met with long, blank stares, and invariably comments along the lines of: "Those are hills tribesmen. They don't know anything about electricity or indoor plumbing, or gas engines… hell, none of them can drive… they ain't no roads up in their part of the country. They are not part of the mechanical age. They are stone age."*
> *Lair, still commander of the PARU sent one of his cadre to a private flying school south of Bangkok and in due time, this officer received his wings as a fully qualified fixed-wing pilot. About the time of his graduation, Lair located two old Piper Cubs sitting in crates in the back of a supply warehouse in Okinawa; no one knew where they came from. Bill asked for them and since no one claimed ownership, they sent them to him in Udorn still in their crates.*

James E. Parker, Jr.

Bill got local talent to put them together. He and the Stick went upcountry Thailand, just across the river from Vientiane, and leased an old dirt runway the Japanese had built during World War II and a nearby farmhouse.

He asked Vang Pao to send him a dozen smart Hmong to learn English at the old farmhouse, and then to learn how to fly the two gift Piper Cubs by his own PARU pilot.

Bill Lair went back to the USAF T-28 training program in the fall of 1967 and asked them again to consider training Hmong men already knowledgeable of general aeronautics and plane-flying. The USAF trainers said, reluctantly, that they would take a look... so Bill asked that two of the best Hmong pilots undergoing special training at the "Bill Lair airfield" to report to the T-28 school.

Ly Leu (aka Lee Lue) was one of the two selected. A nephew of Vang Pao, Ly Leu was smart, handsome and very brave. He was astonishingly good in the training course once he arrived in the Udorn certification course, in many instances outshining South Vietnamese.

In January 1968 he reported to duty with his assigned T-28 in Long Tieng... and flew almost every day thereafter, often three and four missions a day. He would leave the Long Tieng runway shortly after dawn and would be back from more bombs and fuel my midmorning... back at noon for lunch, more bombs and fuel... and then back midafternoon. At night some of the Raven pilots would notice him sitting in his T-28s after landing, slouched forward with fatigue, gathering his strength so that he could de-plane for supper at Vang Pao's house.

He quickly became a hero in the Hmong nation. Flying out into enemy gun fire day after day after day. Mission after mission. U.S. airmen went home after flying 100 mission in the combat zone. Ly Leu flew 1,000, then 2,000, then 3,000.

He was pointed out to someone from Washington eating supper at Vang Pao's house one night. The official went up to the Hmong pilot, and asked him how long he would fly. Ly Leu looked at him, smiled and said, "I will fly until I die."

That happened 12 July 1969 ... with more than 5,000 mission to his credit, Ly Leu was shot down northwest of the PDJ leading eight T-28s flown by Hmong pilots against an enemy concentration.

358

The Vietnam War Its Ownself

Altogether there were more than thirty Hmong trained as T-28 pilots after Ly Leu. Most died ... every one a hero in the Hmong nation.]]

****

In addition to the veteran Hmong pilots who brought the majority of the T-28 squadron in early that morning from Vientiane, a flight of four newly commissioned Hmong pilots brought up recently overhauled planes in midafternoon. For these pilots, it would be the first time they landed at Long Tieng.

Nhia and I were on the way down to Air Ops from the office in the Sky compound when the flight of four planes flown by the new pilots came over the south ridge. They flew along Skyline and then one after the other they made a slow pass over the valley, back over Skyline. They began banking slowly around to the south to land, one at a time.

The Hmong from the valley came out to welcome their new heroes to the valley.

Nhia and I were standing at the very end of the runway, in front of a huge karst as the young pilots made their flybys.

The first plane touched down and pulled off to the ramp near where we were standing. The pilot had landed short, near the far end of the runway and he had thrown back the canopy to his plane to wave at the Hmong who had run down to the airstrip.

The next plane landed a little further down the runway, because they were coming in quickly now, and he also threw back his canopy and was waving to the crowd as he turned off on to the ramp.

The next plane landed about the same place as the second plane. He was shaking his fist in the air, triumphantly, as he pulled off on to the ramp.

The last plane had trouble getting down and he finally touched down near the end, not far from Nhia and I. And he was going fast. There was some question in my mind right away about whether he had time to slow before he had to turn off on the ramp. I turned to Nhia to say that I thought he was maybe going too fast to make the turn. Nhia was running in the opposite direction. Because if he didn't make the ramp, he ran into the karst ... and we were in front of the karst.

Alone, I got to the balls of my feet. The T-28 was coming straight for me. I didn't know which way to run.

Looking straight at the plane I saw the wheels squall as the plane tried to make the turn onto the ramp, but the pilot was going too fast his turn was too wide. I though he was not going to hit me or the karst behind me he was headed dead-on toward the concrete Air Ops buildings.

His canopy was thrown back. Standing no more than twenty feet from the plane as it rushed by, I could see that the pilot had his hands down and he was struggling, as if he were caught. For an instant we made eye contact. He was alert, confused but not overwhelmed. And then he was quickly past me, his scarf fluttering madly in the wind.

The plane slammed into the bomb-proof side of the building next to Air Ops. From more than forty miles an hour to a dead stop in zero seconds. From a festive atmosphere to a tragedy.

A rocket went spiraling up from the wreckage and a parachute was blown up, weakly, and landed over the fuselage. Dust and smoke drifted up.

And then there was quiet.

I ran toward the plane, which was half buried in the rubble of the side of the building. Within moments Digger joined me. Gasoline drained from the back. There were sounds of clicks and whines.

If the gasoline ignited, the plane would explode and the pilot would be cremated.

Digger and I climbed up, thinking we only had a few seconds to get the pilot out. I shoved the canopy back, which had been slammed shut with the force of impact. Straddling the cockpit, I grabbed the shoulders of the pilot and tried to pull him out. He wouldn't budge. The crackling and popping in the engine in front continued and I could smell the gasoline. Time was important and I couldn't lift this guy out of his seat. "Calm down," I said to myself and I leaned forward to see what was holding him down and there was nothing caught. He was a mess, blood was coming from a dozen cuts.

I was pulling up on his shoulders again, intent on what I was doing, when Digger -- standing on the wing -- tapped me on the knee and said, calmly, clearly, "His seat belt. He's still strapped in."

Digger released the seat belt and I pulled him out, handing him down to some Hmong who had run up to help.

Almost every bone in his body was broken. He died on the medevac down to Udorn.

Brave soldier. Hmong hero. As he passed me he apparently was trying to eject, a simple mechanism activated by pulling up on a handle between his feet. It didn't fire because he had the canopy back. When the canopy slammed forward, the rocket that should have blown him out away from the plane went off.

****

The ramp area in fact was never a safe place. Previously another T-28 with a young pilot landed long, had trouble making the turn on to the ramp and slammed into the side of a C-123 that was boarding Thai mercenaries at the time. The pilot of the T-28 was not killed but the prop of his fighter impaled one of the soldiers inside.

Once I had gone into Air Ops to ask the Greek about using a Porter that had just arrived on the ramp and was unloading civilian passengers; one of the Hmong women coming off ran straight into the Porter prop, which chewed her into small pieces.

Another time H. Ownby, a U.S. Air Force Raven pilot who arrived in the valley during the summer of 1972, was bouncing along the taxiway in his O-1 Birddog spotter plane from the T-28 area when six or seven of his eight rockets accidentally fired. One of the rockets hit a T-28 parked in front of Air Ops, two hit the Air Ops building - near where the Greek was sitting - and several rockets slammed into the karst at the end of the runway, near the top where the Hmong manned a .50 caliber machine gun position. The Hmong, thinking they were under attack, started shooting their machine gun in a wide sweeping arc across the valley, which prompted other sympathetic firing.

H. Ownby sat in his plane wondering what was going on.

Inside Air Ops, Greek was going crazy. Stumbling out a side entrance, seeing Ownby sitting in the O-1 facing Air Ops, Greek yelled, "WHY IS EVERYONE TRYING TO KILL ME? WHY ME GOD? WHY ME?"

****

Va returned to the valley after his hospital stay in Vientiane but soon went to the States to live with my parents, to finish high school and then on to college. I promised to look after his wife and their as yet unborn child.

At Long Tieng, plans that early fall were to train up the GMs, get them re-outfitted and ready for a push to recapture the PDJ.

Digger and I took our GMs to a training facility out of MR II run by Harry M. and Tony Poe. Poe was short for some unpronounceable Polish name. Like Hog, we had heard about Tony Poe throughout our training in the States. A big brawling ex-Marine paratrooper, he graduated from Santa Clara with a BA in English Lit and had been a scratch golfer with the country club set of northern California before joining the Agency. He had worked for the Stick in the mountains of Laos for most of his Agency career. And he had become an alcoholic.

Tony would arrive at the training facility in the morning sober, but by noon he would be tapping into Mekong, the local liquor. He'd drink a bottle by midafternoon and would be loudly drunk.

The locals loved him. He was married to a Hmong princess. Although he didn't speak the language very well, he was an adopted member of the Hmong tribe. A Sky man, a Hmong.

He was missing the middle two fingers on his left hand, blown off in a booby trapped grenade accident. He'd wave that hand around, yelling at the instructors, and everybody would smile and go on with their job.

Tony had given his life to the Lao program and it had consumed him. The Stick had him in a job where he could not hurt anyone, where the love the Hmong felt for him was a contributing, positive factor. VP had no problems about sending his people out of the mountains to Tony's place for training. If it were anyone else, the mountain leader would have been concerned that his soldiers might have been subverted and used against him. But Tony was Sky and part Hmong.

Tony had several children by his Hmong wife. His youngest daughter, possibly eleven, would come by and take him home late in the afternoon. Yelling and screaming at people by this time, he'd calm down when his daughter arrived and would go quietly when she said it was time to go home. The big, hulking, bald headed, drunk brawler following meekly behind the small girl out to a Jeep where she would sit in the front beside the driver and Tony would slump down asleep in the rear.

While the GMs were in training, Brenda, I and the kids took leave and went to Sydney, Australia. We visited the Opera House and the zoo and went shopping and found to our amazement that in July it is not hot in Australia. It was the dead of their winter. In July. How crazy is that we said. No wonder they talk funny. It was a grand experience, seeing Australia through the eyes of our kids, who months before had not known there was a world beyond Udorn.

Tony was sober and entertaining at the graduation of the GMs. VP attended and he and Tony laughed and drank from a bottle of Mekong.

In leaving I told the old war horse good-bye and he yelled at me, saying if we didn't recapture the PDJ, it was my fault, my GM had been trained to a razor's edge and were ready to go.

--TWENTY-NINE--
Return to the PDJ

Digger and I brought our GMs back to Long Tieng in early September 1972 and joined "Than," returning with his forces from MR I and the "Bear," coming in with his GM from MR III to help in the offensive drive. Kayak and Clean with two GMs apiece and Bamboo with the commandos were already on the scene in defensive positions around the valley.

In the early fall of 1972 the buildup of irregular forces to drive the North Vietnamese from the PDJ began. Tahn, a CIA paramilitary case officer, brought his Groupe Mobile (GM) battalion of approximately 800 Lao irregulars from western Laos and set up a temporary camp near the old hospital at the east end of the Long Tieng valley. The Bear came in with his unit from south Laos. Digger and I returned from a training camp run by the legendary Tony Poe, with our two Hmong GMs. Kayak and Clean each with two Hmong GMs, Bamboo with the Hmong commandos, plus all the Thai mercenaries were already in position around the valley. The muddy Long Tieng marketplace suddenly was crowded with hundreds of armed Thai, Lao and Hmong irregulars who drifted from the different camps to drink warm beer in thatched shanty bars operated by enterprising Hmong women in their traditional tribal dress. The Thai mercenaries, taller than the other nationalities, were heavily tattooed and wore distinctive unit scarves, the Lao forces looked like the French Foreign auxiliary with their berets and camouflage tunics, and the Hmong, the smallest and the youngest, looked like dirty mountaineers. There was no friction or fighting between the different groups; they were soldiers marshalling for battle and were restrained, unsure about what lay ahead. The fighting around the PDJ had always been fierce.

Three days before the launch of the offensive, Kayak's forces were assembled, issued extra ammunition and moved out of the valley to the east. The next day my GM was moved by Air

America helicopters and C-123s from the valley north to an abandoned airstrip.

The following day Bamboo's commandos were moved southeast of Long Tieng to a staging area.

The lead element in the offensive, a small path-finding unit of the commandos, remained behind at the Long Tieng air field ramp near two Air America choppers that were scheduled to insert them on a narrow, deserted mountaintop in the northwestern corner of the PDJ. As night fell it began to rain, keeping most of the Hmong villagers who usually congregated around the ramp under cover, out of sight. Near midnight the pathfinders climbed aboard the helicopters. As the pilots warmed their engines and went over their final checklist, only two CIA officers stood by under the protecting eaves of the concrete Air Ops building. Finally one gave a thumbs up to the lead pilot and, without further ceremony, the pilot's heavily loaded helicopter lifted off, skimmed along the ramp and began gaining altitude as it flew down the air field. The second helicopter followed and soon both were lost from sight in the night. Their engines noise faded and they were gone.

Flying by instruments the pilots circled to the west, high and lonely over the rugged mountains - there was no protecting air support - and eventually came down through the weather to where they expected to find the target mountaintop. There was little margin for error.

They broke through the clouds, the PDJ was to their right front, and ahead, clearly defined by recently made B-52 bomb craters, was their mountain. As they descended the pilots switched off all their lights, the flight mechanics, or "kickers," in the back opened the doors, leaned out into the driving rain and helped guide the helicopters to the ground. The pathfinders quickly jumped out and the helicopters lifted off.

Within minutes they transmitted a coded radio message to the commandos, waiting at the staging area, that a landing zone (LZ) had been marked with lights and the commandos could jump in.

Shep had helped give the seventy commandos parachute training. He was standing in front of them at the end of a dirt airfield near the back of an idling Air America C-130 when someone yelled from a nearby shelter that it was time to go. They were a dark, swarthy group, hunched forward in their parachute riggings, their helmets tied down with strips of old sheets Shep had found in the back of a warehouse earlier in the day. They were wet to the bone, some less than fifteen years old and none much taller than their M-16 rifles. Shep walked up to the first man in line and peered in at him under his helmet. The Hmong looked up and smiled. Shep checked his equipment and continued down the line checking parachutes and counting the men off.

There were seventy-seven.

"Hold it, Goddamit to hell. Just wait a damn minute here," he yelled, arresting the movement of the first man who was edging toward the dry interior of the plane.

Shep knew that there were only seventy commandos with parachute training scheduled to make the jump. He went back up the line counting again.

Seventy-seven again.

Seven Hmong, most of whom had probably been assigned support functions at the airfield, had picked up extra parachutes and had intermingled with the others. The Hmong commander came up and Shep yelled, "Buddy, we got seven people here who don't know how to jump, and they ain't supposed to go. I don't know what they're trying to prove, but it didn't get by me." The commander shrugged, unsure of the problem. The Air America C-130 had fired its engines and the wind from the props was blowing the rain back hard at the group. There was no way to determine who the seven interlopers were, the commander didn't seemed concerned, so Shep stepped aside with an angry look and watched as all seventy-seven of the Hmong soldiers boarded.

"They don't know how to jump. Ain't never had any training," Shep said to no one in particular as he pulled his old cowboy duster together against the weather and watched as the back of the plane closed. Within minutes it took off, barreling down the dirt mountain strip lit on both sides by fire from oily rags in # 10 cans.

Twenty minutes later all seventy-seven men ran out the back of the C-130 in their parachutes and landed without injury on top of the lights provided by the pathfinders on the edge of the PDJ.

The next day Digger's GM was lifted by helicopters into the LZ, now firmly secured by the commandos.

There was no North Vietnamese reaction.

Late that same morning my GM began moving toward the PDJ. The men launched with no precision whatsoever, at odd intervals, in small groups, in fits and starts. I would be standing near a forward outpost with one of the commanders. Nhia, my Hmong interpreter, would be lounging nearby with the radios. Groups of Hmong would be milling around and then one or two of the younger boys would move off down a mountain trail, one would have his M-16 over a shoulder, the other would be carrying a box of grenades, cooking pots strapped to the outside of his pack, and then a few more of the older boys would follow and then several more.

Kayak's GM from the south also began heading north toward the PDJ. Tahn's and Bear's GMs from the other regions were held in reserve in the valley. Clean's forces and all the Thai mercenaries were to remain behind in Long Tieng defensive positions.

There was no contact for the first few days. I spent most of the time at the launch site sitting by the radios. Occasionally I would call in an Air America helicopter and recon high over my advancing GM out to the edge of the PDJ.

On the third day, as Kayak's forces came close to a river valley that led down to Skyline, there was a violent clash with North Vietnamese regulars and Kayak's forces pulled back. Tahn's GM was heli-lifted in near the original contact. Because of some confusions in the last couple of shuttles, Tahn was left on the position. He was moving an element of his people to some high ground as the sun went down and was not near a radio to tell any of the last helicopter pilots that he was still out.

It was only when the case officers gathered that evening in the CIA headquarters bunker in Long Tieng, that anyone realized Tahn had not returned. He was contacted through a radio relay on Skyline and gave assurances that he was fine. He said his men were still digging in and they didn't expect any action tonight. It would take the Vietnamese a couple of days to react.

That was not the case.

During the night his position was overrun and Tahn was killed, his face blown away by a grenade blast. Vang Pao and Hog, the chief CIA case officer, went out at first light with a company of VP's personal guards and retook the position and brought Tahn's body back.

I was in Air Ops with the "Greek" watching as other case officers took the limp body from the helicopter, place it tenderly in a body bag and put it on a plane for the rear CIA base at Udorn.

Tahn was a friend, we had trained together in the States. He had graduated from the University of Washington and had served as a Marine combat engineer in South Vietnam. Very adept at leading the Lao irregulars, he was an intelligent, unassuming man, liked and respected by all the Agency officers who worked upcountry. He never said much, but he had strong opinions and people listened when he talked.

The Vietnam War Its Ownself

Dead.

The last in a steady procession of men in body bags moved through the Long Tieng valley; Hmong, Thai, Lao, Air America, U.S. Air Force.

It was part of the job, handling our dead. Early in the year, when the North Vietnamese were attacking Skyline, I would take a fixed-wing Air America plane down to Udorn, Thailand, every night. The bodies of recently killed Thai mercenaries were always the last to be loaded. It was a gruesome sight as the body bags were being tossed on board, often a dozen or more. And I would sit through the flights south looking at the bags, wondering about the men inside, about their families and their past and what they had planned for the future. But it had not taken me long to accept the body bags, in the same way an undertaker becomes accustomed to his work, and after a while I would be happy to see them loaded, because it meant we would be heading south soon.

War forces that on a person. Makes them insensitive to the suffering and dying of others. Searching for moral justification each time a man dies in war is futile and hurts the soul. You dwell on it and the hurt makes you crazy or turns you into a drunk. The sane alternative is to put it out of your mind, resisting introspection and grief. It was understandable how people, like the Air America pilots, who worked for years in the Indochina war, developed detached, unemotional attitudes.

But you can't ignore the loss of a friend.

Sitting with Greek in Air Ops I hurt and cried, silently. Tears ran down my cheek without sound. There are sometime heartaches in our glamorous Lao war fighting... that no amount of experience and strength of character can appease. Losing a friend always hurts.

****

Bamboo's forces secured a narrow hilltop in the northwest section of the PDJ for Digger's people, Kayak's two GMs were moved from the south and my GM was moved to the north. Once Digger's GM was in position on the hilltop, Kayak's forces and mine began moving out to retake the PDJ. Kayak's forces had the first contact and Tahn's GM was moved in, near the clash site as reinforcement. Because Tahn remained in the position the first night , he was killed when it was overrun by North Vietnamese.

The area along the edge of the plateau and in the river valley near where Tahn was killed was bombed constantly over the next week by all the tactical air the U.S. Air Force, U.S. Marines, and U.S. Navy – flying from carriers at sea east of Vietnam – could provide. The Raven FACs in their small, unarmed O-1 observation planes were personally in charge of the air war in Laos. They visually identified ground targets, requested fighters from Cricket, the airborne command post, rendezvoused with and briefed their fighters on details of each air strike. The Raven FAC marked each ground target using a white phosphorus smoke rocket, defined the compass direction heading the fighters could use on their run-in to the target, and defined the specific order in which they wanted ordnance to be dropped on each pass. (1) A single bomb at a time. (2) Multiple bombs dropped on a pass. (3) Or 20mm guns to be used.

The Raven would clear the flight lead aircraft "in-hot" (meaning cleared to drop live, armed ordnance). Lead would call "FAC in sight" to preclude air-to-air contact with the FAC, would drop his bomb then pull up into a low orbit. The Raven would tell Two (the next plane) where he wanted the next bomb to impact relative to where Lead's bomb had detonated – then he cleared Two in hot. This sequence of adjusting the target on each run and clearing the fighter in hot continued until all ordnance available had been expended and the fighters were "Winchester," finished and waiting release to go home. The FAC would provide the fighters with his bomb damage assessment (BDA) then release the fighters to return to base.

The Ravens were a breed apart in MR II. They had all worked as FACs in Vietnam, then volunteered for a secret Project 404 without even knowing to which country they'd be assigned. After arrival in Vientiane their Air Force and Geneva Convention ID cards were taken away by the embassy; their only personal identification became a Lao driver's license. Their active duty uniforms were stored at Udorn. They flew combat in civilian clothing, had no rank in-country, no squadron or commander, and had one extraordinary advantage: no one ever told a Raven where to go or what to do. Highly motivated, each Raven simply saw what needed to be done at the moment and went out and did it on his own initiative. There were no formal flying rules in Laos. Rules of engagement? There was only one: "The ambassador wants every Raven to be on the ground, somewhere, by sunset."

The O-1G aircraft they flew every day was not instrumented for flight at night or in weather. Needle, ball, airspeed and a small whiskey compass were the only reliable instruments they had in the cockpit. Flying a single engine unarmed aircraft that could do a top speed around sixty knots, they flew in a high risk triple-A environment while encountering 12.7mm, 14.5mm, 23mm and 37mm ground fire several times a day. They were neither suicidal nor insane pilots. They were supporting the Hmong, Thai forces, CIA case officers and defending the civilian population of an entire nation being invaded by North Vietnam. Those who survived this intensely Darwinian experience tend to regard their Raven assignment as the best duty they ever had. Twenty of the Ravens who worked out of Long Tieng were killed in action.

To the people who worked upcountry Laos, the Ravens were always respectfully described the same way...."They got balls." Out there day after day in those tiny little unprotected planes. Leading the T-28s in to dead-end valleys. Spotting for sleek, fast U.S. Air force attack planes. The Ravens were like those flag bearers in the Civil War who ran out on the field of battle with their flag streaming, running headlong into the fire of the enemy. They were utterly fearless. They were assigned to MR II for short periods of time, six months or so at a time and we rarely got to know all of them very well. But they were all the same breed: confident and courageous. Nerves of steel.

There was something about their eyes that stopped you when you first saw them on the ramp, told you to be careful, that they were different from anyone else. They looked preppy, but they didn't bluff. They weren't angry, but they were here to hunt and kill the North Vietnamese. It was their job. They killed people. Their eyes said that. Unblinking. The whites were whiter than anyone else's. Fit, alert, ready, lethal. Sky officers often found it confusing why these promising young men were so willing to get in harm's way, so willing to die, but we all considered them one of the most dependable, and most courageous elements in the Lao program. The American equal to the Hmong T-28 pilots.

****

My GM eventually gained the west edge of the PDJ with only light resistance and some patrols ventured out onto the plain itself. They ran afoul of mines, probably left behind by the Thais the previous year, and pulled back.

We established positions on the high ground, along the end of a ridgeline that overlooked the western area of the plateau. Vang Pao did not like the Hmong taking hard positions and there was continuing discussion about the exact employment of our forces. We got to the edge of the PDJ, what next? Were we actually going to occupy the PDJ? Were we going to try and hold ground, and if we didn't seek a hard defense position, where were we going to draw the line this year?

The answer came down finally to Skyline, again. We could not prepare better positions. There was nothing tactical to be gained by re-establishing ourselves on the PDJ. We could in fact deny the PDJ to the North Vietnam if we maintained our soft positions in a crescent around the south and western side of the plateau. And by sitting on our positions overlooking the PDJ, we would probably draw the North Vietnamese out, and we would have the high ground.

So we waited next to the PDJ for the Vietnamese to react. We planned for the Hmong to make tactical retreats, and we would hit the North Vietnamese with our artillery and the U.S. Air Force and Hmong T-28s.

The Vietnamese probably knew we were not back at the PDJ to stay. We didn't have the Thais, the "hill sitters," and we were not hardening our positions.

But you could sense the Vietnamese wanted to attack. It was their nature and if you believed that one of their principal missions was to destroy the Hmong then the target was there for them. We were dangling the bait.

I postponed trips south to Vientiane as we waited for the Vietnamese to attack. I would meet Nhia at the ramp at first light most mornings and take an Air America helicopter out to the GM. Though we were usually aware of activity the previous night, Nhia would always get a situation report from each site as we approached. We didn't land at positions that had recently been probed unless there were critically wounded soldiers. There were some small forward positions we rarely visited because of exposed landing pads. I did get to all the sites over the days we waited, trying where I could to improve their defensibility. The Hmong were headstrong people; when they thought they were prepared, I had problems getting them to make improvements. One of my concerns, a carryover of my American sensitivities, was that in most of the exposed positions, the commanders would have small little spider holes dug in the forward slope and they would send the smallest soldiers there at night with boxes of grenades. When they were probed the youngster would pull the pin on grenade after grenade and toss them out to roll down the hill toward the attackers and it was these smallest soldiers that tended to be the first and the most badly wounded. It was always disconcerting to put young boys in body bags in the early mornings when I would arrive or to see them so terribly hurt being put aboard Air America helicopters, though they never cried.

I spent most of my time at the position of the GM commander. I strongly believed in putting patrols out in front and spent hours getting the Hmong out on patrol and coordinating with the maneuvering soldiers trying to determine were the North Vietnamese were, or where they had been. Ravens were usually overhead and we worked together in targeting U.S. warplanes on suspected enemy locations. Locations we couldn't hit during the day I passed to Dutch at night for B-52 strikes. Hmong T-28s were also on station throughout the days, diving low at suspected enemy positions all across the western edge of the PDJ.

We were never attacked by ground forces during the day while I was out with the GM, though we were occasionally mortared, events that were startling when the rounds would burst nearby, but in fact were welcomed as we called in whatever attack aircraft were in the area. It was not relaxing though, being bait. It was comforting, however, to know I was being served by Air America. The pilots worked the area with daring and cool precision. Despite occasional testy confrontations around the ramp between individual pilots and Sky officers, in the field with my GM they never refused tasking. I was going out to the western PDJ early one morning when Nhia got a radio call from a patrol saying that one of their members, who had been wounded in a confrontation with a North Vietnamese patrol the previous night, was dying. The patrol leader said there was not enough time to get him back to one of the positions. Flying high and to the east we asked them to mark their position with a smoke grenade. Soon off to our front on the sheer side of a ridgeline next to the PDJ, a smoke column began to rise in the early morning haze. B.J. Johnson, one of the more flamboyant pilots, was flying a Twin Pack and he had come up behind us to work resupply that day. As we were talking with nearby units of the GM determining that no North Vietnamese controlled any of the commanding hilltops, B.J. volunteered to go in for the wounded man. He flew below us, descended into the ravine, hovered to get around several tall trees that obstructed his descent, picked up the soldier, made his way back up around the trees and pulled off at an angle for Long Tieng. He and his crew would only get a hundred or so dollars for the hazardous mission, the young Hmong soldier probably did not live and nobody would have ever questioned a decision not to attempt the rescue. It was an unheralded event that work day in MR II but it clearly demonstrates the true day-in-day-out character of the Air America pilots. Because I knew Air America would come get me - no matter what the situation - I never hesitated going out to work the edge of the PDJ.

The North Vietnamese did finally attack in force. They hit both GMs in the north, Digger's and mine, as dawn was breaking one morning when the whole area was socked in with unseasonable foggy weather. They came from the area north of the PDJ, where they had bivouac areas built into the side of mountains. Hundreds of North Vietnamese sappers and ground soldiers moved from their hiding places, across the PDJ and up the hills toward the Hmong.

My GM held through the first assault and then pulled back one ridgeline. Artillery fired at the Vietnamese until the guns were too hot to fire more. The Ravens brought as much air to the fight as they could get. B-52s bombed the Vietnamese concentrations and suspected supply routes. The Vietnamese tried to stay as close to the Hmong as they could to avoid the bombardment and the Hmong pulled back further, finally coming back to LS 15. Digger's forces pulled back and were eventually brought back to Long Tieng.

Within a few days the two Hmong GMs on the south were also hit and they scattered to rally points before pulling back.

A month after retreating to LS 15 my GM began moving back to the PDJ. The main Vietnamese attack force had withdrawn back across the plain, though the GM encountered mines and pockets of small stay-behind ambush groups.

****

I was sitting on the ramp one afternoon waiting for a Porter to come in so that I could fly over the lead elements of my GM when H. Ownby, the Raven, landed for refueling. He had just come in from Vientiane and he came up to me saying he was heading out for an aerial reconnaissance of the PDJ and asked if I would like to go along.

I told him thanks but no thanks. Ravens worked a little closer to the edge than I normally did. "OK," he said.

But I was thinking, I had never been in an O-1 before. I hadn't flown over the PDJ in almost a year.

"It's just a milk run," Ownby continued as he turned to head for his plane.

"I've changed my mind. I'll go," I said and picked up my survival gear and AK-47 as I followed the young pilot to his plane.

And we went up.

And I almost died of fright.

Soaring over the PDJ, north where we knew - Ownby and I knew - there were surface-to-air missiles, over North Vietnamese troop concentration areas, near peaks where the Pathet Lao could have had anti-aircraft weapons. In that tiny, tiny little plane. Without parachutes.

I knew like few other people in the world the nature of the many Vietnamese there below us. And what chance would anyone have if the engine on this little plane quit? If one stray bullet came up and knocked H. Ownby out in front of me, how the hell would I get back? I couldn't fly a plane. And if we did get hit, landed and were captured, what chance in hell would a CIA guy have with the North Vietnamese.

Maybe it was that fear of the North Vietnamese getting their hands on me or my feet-on-the-ground infantry orientation that made me feel so vulnerable and exposed. We were high, but the enemy on the ground could still see us, they could still hear us. I knew thousands of Vietnamese were watching us from below, following us with their guns.

And H. Ownby chatted merrily away as we continued to soar above the PDJ. I was so frightened that I felt pressure on my chest and I had trouble talking.

Finally, gratefully, we got back to Long Tieng. I could hardly resist opening the door before we came to a stop so that I could get out. I had to tell myself to move slowly, carefully, don't shake.

Hog was coming out of Air Ops as I climbed out. He cocked his head to one side as if to ask what I was doing? Sky people in MR II were not hot dogs.

I told him later that he did not have to worry about me flying with the Ravens ever again. Maybe there was nothing wrong with it, maybe he didn't care, but he should know that I would never ever fly in one of those planes over all of those enemy again. H. Ownby and all the other Ravens were crazy.

In all of my experiences I had never been as scared. Before on the ground under fire in Vietnam and out with my GM my fear acted to make me more alert, quicker. I used it. It had been just plain fear up in that little plane with H. Ownby, with no place to go. All of my developed senses to avoid unnecessary exposure to the enemy had screamed at me, "WHAT ARE YOU DOING?"

****

My GM eventually reached the ridgeline overlooking the western PDJ and reoccupied previous positions. Our plans again were to use them to entice the Vietnamese out in the open so that we could pound them with our artillery and aircraft.

At one site the body of a young Hmong killed the previous month was recovered and, rather than bury him there, the GM commander wanted the body sent back to his relatives for the traditional Hmong wake, a ceremony that releases the man's spirit and allows for a dignified death and eternal peace. On the way out to the position that day the commander and I talked about the difficulties in getting a helicopter in to that particular position. We decided that the soldiers had to bring the body down to a landing site on the edge of the PDJ. The commander called ahead and gave the instructions. We landed on the edge of the PDJ near the helipad where the body was to be taken and the commander, Nhia and I, with a couple of Hmong soldiers, walked up the trail toward the position. On the way we met the detail bringing the body down.

The body had been rotting for a month.

And it smelled vicious, was incredibly noxious. Even breathing in through my mouth, my eyes teared and the rancid odor seeped up my nose and exploded. It was battlefield refuge I had never known in Vietnam.

A small banana republic in Latin America was known to use an interrogation/torture technique in which the interrogators would tie the prisoner to a table with his head hanging over the edge. His mouth would be covered with tape and coke pored up his nostrils. Possibly it was the carbonation. Whatever caused it, the prisoner when he finally opens his nose to breath, had to let the coke drain down into the sinus passage and it was like a bullet shot right between the eyes. It was pain worse than hitting a nerve with a dentist's drill. It was the most pain a man could endure without passing out. It was like the pain from eating ice cream too fast multiplied to the tenth power. It was a bomb going off in the skull, behind and between the eyes. Once during a prison riot in this Latin America country, the prison officials were seen bringing in a single case of coke and the prisoners stopped rioting.

The smell from that body was a comparable assault on the senses. It was the worst smell in the whole world that day.

The detail was bringing the body down in short increments, moving off to the side occasionally to catch their breaths.

374

Nhia, who was in front of our group, threw up breakfast when they got close.

It was apparent to me that this body was going to have to be slung under a helicopter to get it out of the area. So I took a radio and told Nhia to go on with the commander up to the position, that I was going down to the edge of the PDJ to coordinate with Air America on evacuating the body.

I walked ahead of the detail which continued with its cockeyed cadence of - take a few breaths off the trail...in...pick up the litter...move down the trail...lower the litter...off the trail for more breaths.

Arriving back at the PDJ, I looked around in the sky for an Air America chopper.

Frenchy Smith was flying in supplies.

Ol' Frenchy.

Ol' Frenchy, give-Sky-a-ration-of-shit, Smith.

I called him on my radio and told him that I had a KIA and asked if he'd drop by my position after he delivered his supplies and take it back.

Frenchy asked if I was sure the person was dead and not just trying to get out and go to the mall downtown Saturday night to rock and roll.

"No," I said, "this one's dead."

The detail arrived behind me and I almost choked. But then I had a thought.

I knew that with the swirling winds of the helicopter that, even though the smell was god awful, Frenchy wouldn't be able to smell this fellow if we put him on board, inside the helicopter. He would be up in the air probably before realizing how special this particular body was.

Frenchy asked me to throw smoke as he came back from dropping off his supplies so that he could see exactly where I was. He didn't want to land in the wrong spot on the PDJ.

Over the radio, Frenchy bayed like a mule as he came in for a landing.

The Hmong with me picked up that body - the nearby grass had begun to wilt - and we ran out to the chopper. Frenchy was keeping up full power, he didn't settle completely to the ground, and the wind turbulence was strong. The kicker threw open the sliding door on his side and we threw that body in and Frenchy lifted off, as the kicker closed the door.

And we fell back, to get our breath, and I started laughing

because I knew in that closed helicopter about right now, Frenchy was smelling that body.

And the helicopter stopped in mid-air. Stopped. It had its nose down and it was gaining altitude and it stopped.

Over the radio I heard, "HOLY GOD ALMIGHTY GOD....GOD....GOD DAMNED."

Other Air America pilots in the area heard the same thing and pilots tied to break in on Frenchy, to find out if he was in trouble, if a MAYDAY was imminent.

"WHAT IS THAT SMELL? WHAT ... GOD ... GOD ...GOD..."

The co-pilot took the controls apparently, because Frenchy continued to yell on the radio and the helicopter turned around and came back over the helipad.

Everyone on board had their heads sticking out the side. The kicker disappeared inside briefly and the body came flying out to land with thud on the ground near me.

But I was doubled over I was laughing so hard. I had never seen a helicopter flown by men with their heads sticking out the windows.

Finally Frenchy came on the air and told everyone to leave Mule on the PDJ.

Mule was not a nice person, he said.

****

I was on a schedule of ten days upcountry and four days down in Vientiane with the family. It was, in real terms, ten days/nine nights up, four days/five nights down, a good distribution of time.

Homecomings were joyous. I would come in on a resupply fixed-wing aircraft or sometimes on a helicopter heading down for maintenance and take a taxi near Poppa Chu's to the front gate of the house. It would usually be early evening and music from Walt Disney movies and other musicals would be on the tape recorder, which on the nights I would be coming home, was always turned up loud. The house would be lit, Brenda and the kids would often turn on every light. I tried to bring things down for the kids, I brought them a little pig once but he ran away the second day. That's what the guard said, though he looked unusually well fed at the time. I brought down rabbits, a dog and an ocelot. Brenda asked me not to bring down any more live things though and I stuck with Hmong toys and web gear, lens from old binoculars, an interesting old pump that looked like a goose.

The kids usually got me off to the side the night I came in and each, individually, would tell me their version of things that had happened while I was away. I could tell their English improved each time I came home. They seemed to pick up a new slang term every week.

Brenda made Mim's and Joseph's costumes for the Embassy Halloween party. Joe was a jack-in-the-box. He was dressed as a clown. We cut a round hole in the bottom of a cardboard box and cut the top on three sides so that it opened like a door, and Joe got inside from the bottom and he'd sing out in his tiny little voice, "Jack in the box, still as a fox......." and he'd jump up, throwing open the top. He'd squat back down and, lifting up the box from the bottom, walk around, before squatting down again. "Jack in the box, still as a fox......"

Mim was dressed as a sunflower. A circle of cardboard petals, each covered with a gauzy yellow fabric, framed her gorgeous little face with a big, toothless smile. Her body was draped in a tube of green fabric. She was the most beautiful flower. How I loved that child.

Joe was my buddy. A clown who loved to laugh. But Mim was my sweetheart, like daughters can be to their fathers. I hurt when she hurt herself. Felt sad when she was tired and crying. She always knew that she would have a sympathetic listener when she talked with me. She always got her way with me.

A part of my homecoming from Long Tieng was to sit down in one of the couches in the living room for Mim to take off my boots. I would usually come directly from the field and my pants, often blood smeared and torn, would be rolled up at the bottom. Mim never asked why I was so dirty or what I did that produced such evidence of pain and suffering. She would get to her knees and push my pants up and unlace my boots from top to bottom. She struggled the first few times, pulling and tugging to get the old army boots over my ankles after the laces were undone, but she got the hang of it soon, knew where to grab them at the heel to get the best leverage. She would lift one of my feet off the floor and straddling my leg, with her back to me, she'd reach down and grab the heel and pull up, grunting, straining, until the boots eased off. When she had both off, she would run and put them in the closet in our bedroom and run back to where I would be sitting to snuggle up beside me and she would bask in the glow of what she had done, sitting there with her Dad,

James E. Parker, Jr.

home for a weekend from the fighting.

The kids knew how to operate the tape deck and loved to play the movie sound tracks. Mim's favorite was the *Sound of Music*. A ritual developed with the song "Do, Ra, Me." After the shoes were off, often when the excitement was waning from the actual coming-in-the-door-homecoming, she'd put on the tape and cue it to "Do, Ra, Me," and race back to my side and look up, right at my lips and I'd sing with the tape, "Do, a deer, a teenage deer, Ra, a ray of......." "NOOOOO," Mim would say as she would reach up to put her hand over my mouth, "It's, Do, a deer, a FEMALE deer, not a TEENAGE deer, Daddy." It was so small a thing, but we both looked forward to it and as time went on we would both start smiling as Mim initiated that part of the evening. She'd put on the tape and I'd start singing, "Do, a deer, a teenage deer...." "NOOOOOOOO."

I was so proud of our family. The three of them were my greatest joy.

The situation upcountry was demanding and dangerous. There was so much giving, warmth and happiness at home. The best of two worlds, so unusually balanced. What other combatant in the 20th century had had it so good? There would always be at least one instance during my home visits when I would say to myself, I am so lucky.

The bachelors, most of the Sky men I worked with, had very different experiences from mine when they came down to Vientiane. They lived in what was called the "R&R" house and spent their nights carousing the local bars; Lulu's, the White Rose, the Lucky Bar and the Tropicana. Lewd, lusty, fleshy, drinking places, holdovers from the anything-goes days of the French Foreign Legions. Set in the tranquil, tropical setting of Vientiane, hard along the Mekong river, it was a bawdy Shangri-La. There were no rules or restrictions to what went on and the Sky bachelors had some very different stories to tell from mine when we returned upcountry.

--THIRTY--
When a Raven Falls

Early one morning in early November 1972 after a four-day home visit, Brenda and the kids drove me to Poppa Chu's restaurant, near the airport ops center. I waited there, drinking coffee and

378

reading until mid-day before a helicopter coming up from Udorn picked me up. Izzy Freedman, our former neighbor, was co-pilot. The area to the north had been covered for days by haze but the skies had finally opened up and Izzy's was among a flock of helicopters heading up to work out of the valley.

Sitting in the middle of the row of seats in the rear of the helicopter, wearing the extra headphone - the "customer" set - I chatted on the intercom with the crew. I could hear the other pilots on the command air frequency (freq) talking amongst themselves, and would occasionally catch glimpses of some of the other helicopters flying ahead of us.

"OK so I'm telling my broker, I know you can buy titanium mine stock," Pilot B.K. Johnson was talking. The airways on the common freq were always busy with small talk. The pilots never stayed on the air long, however, saying a phrase or two and then pausing, to see if anyone else was trying to break in. There would be a quiet, but distinctive break in the squelch as someone came on and went off the air. Conversations were casual, about everyday things, although there was generally no profanity.

"Some of my friends have bought it," pause.

"My broker said, titanium is manufactured," pause.

"It's man made, how can it be mined?" he asked. pause.

"I said I have dumb friends," pause.

"And poor," someone added.

"Titanium is not manufactured," someone else injected, "it's a natural element."

"Oh yea," B.J. said, "Wanta buy some stock?"

"OOOOOOHHHHHH," came over the air from one of the pilots, who was in obvious pain.

"My boss, has a problem," someone said.

"OOOOOOOHHHHHH I gotta go to the john." It was Bill Hutchinson, one of the most senior helicopter pilots flying for Air America. He was leading the pack up north in a Twin Pack.

"Well with one of those super-duper recharged machines you fly," Izzy said before pausing. "You oughta just wander on back through the lounge to the rest area."

"OOOOOOOOOOOOHHHHHHHHHHH, I'm in pain. I almost wish we'd crash so I'd get some relief," from the senior pilot. "How do you make this thing go faster? Oh God, it's a 105."

Because profanity wasn't generally allowed over the open freqs some of the Air America pilots developed the Falcon Codes - common earthy, profane expressions designated by numbers - and a laminated list was often taped to the instrument panel near the radios.

104, "What the fuck, over?"
105, "It's so fucking bad I can't believe it!"
108, "Fuck you very much."
109, "Beautiful, just fucking beautiful."
112, "Let me talk to that sumbitch."
118, "What are you trying to do, kill some fucking body?"
169, "Fuck it, just Fuck it."
272, "One good deal after another."
274, "I'd rather have a sister in a whorehouse than a brother in a Twin Pack."

"OOOOOOOOOOOHHHHHHH, 105, 105, 105," Hutchinson cried.

"There are some people you just can't carry on a trip, you know what I mean," from some unidentified pilot. "Gotta go potty all the time. Reminds me of my first wife." Pause. "No maybe it was wife number two. Wasn't married to wife one long enough to take a good trip."

"OOOOOOOOOOOHHHHHHH," pause.

"MAYDAY, MAYDAY, MAYDAY, I'M HIT." It was a faint but clear signal.

****

"Give us your location," said the senior pilot, Hutchinson, suddenly serious, speaking in with a calm, even voice.

"I'M OVER THE PDJ." It was John Carroll, a Raven who had recently arrived in MR II. A 1962 graduate of the Air Force Academy he had been a test pilot at Edwards Air Force Base, had qualified for the astronaut program, and according to the other Ravens, was certainly scheduled for space flight after he had his "ticket punched" with a tour in Southeast Asia. He had been socked in at LS 20A over the past few days of bad weather and was up on the afternoon schedule to scout the PDJ.

"How high are you, how bad you hit?" the senior pilot asked. Standard Operating Procedures (SOP) among the pilots was that in an emergency the senior man was in charge and everyone else stayed off the working frequency. Air America handled emergencies weekly - mechanical failures, shot up planes, downed pilots - and the response among this group of veterans was practiced and sure. In front of me the pilot reached over and got a map and told Izzy over the intercom to turn to a new heading. Izzy was giving the helicopter maximum power, almost redlining the engine.

"I'M AT FIVE THOUSAND FEET AND DROPPING. I GOT A ROUND IN THE ENGINE AND ITS LOSING COMPRESSION. STILL GOING BUT LOSING COMPRESSION. IT'S THROWING OUT OIL." The pilot's voice was loud, stressed.

The PDJ was 3,500 feet elevation. At five thousand feet the plane had either dropped dramatically since it was hit or had been flying very low. Carroll had in fact been reconning the southern PDJ and had taken a hit from a 12.7 millimeter anti-aircraft round.

"You're going to be OK, don't worry, if your engine is still going you're OK." the senior pilot's voice was reassuring.

"IT'S SPUTTERING. SHIT. THROWING OUT A LOT OF OIL. I CAN BARELY SEE IN FRONT."

"You're flying and we're going balls out to get to you, don't worry, you're going to be OK."

"THE ENGINE QUIT. FROZE. PROP IS NOT MOVING."

"What's your altitude?"

"FOUR THOUSAND FIVE."

"What's your location?"

"SOUTHERN PDJ."

"We've got two choices, you can try and glide into Sam Thong or circle around and land on the PDJ. We'll be in and pick you up. You're OK. What do you think? What's best?"

"THOSE RIDGELINES BETWEEN ME AND SAM THONG ARE TOO HIGH. I'M GOING BACK AND LANDING ON THE PDJ."

A new voice came into play, that of Raven 24, Steve Neal, who began talking to the Raven in the damaged plane. Their conversation was technical, but it appeared to sooth Carroll somewhat and he sounded less frantic when Mike Jarina, flying an America Air helicopter out of LS 05, came on to tell the senior pilot that he was close by and would go in for the rescue.

"OK there Mr. Raven, we're not far from you." Jarina said, "How long can you glide and circle?"

"NOT LONG. SHIT IT'S QUIET UP HERE. ALL I HEAR IS MY HEART."

"You're OK., OK. There are several runways on the southern plains. You know 'um?"

"YEA."

James E. Parker, Jr.

"You want to make for one in particular or land on a road or what? You tell us."

"I WANT TO COME IN ON THE FIRST PIECE OF FLAT GROUND I SEE."

"OK listen to me." It was the other Raven. "Your rescue radio isn't damaged is it?"

"NO, IT'S OK."

"You land, you get out of the plane and you get away from it. Unless you land right on top of some bad boys, we've got time. We're closing in on your position. We'll be there. Throw smoke when you see us coming in."

Before the bad weather we had been carrying only advance elements of Vietnamese along the southern PDJ; most of their forces were north of the plain. If there hadn't been any significant movement the Raven could land safely. Four Hmong GMs were still loosely positioned on the south and the west of the PDJ. They had not reported any significant contact recently. There was all reason to believe the Raven could get down and could be picked up.

The U.S. Air Force radio platform came on to report that fast movers were being diverted from southern Laos, but were several minutes out. The Udorn air rescue squadron had been scrambled and was en route.

Air America had responsibility for the pickup however. Jarina and his co-pilot, George Taylor, were the closer to the southern PDJ by several minutes over the helicopters I was with coming from the south. They were going in first. Jarina and Taylor knew they would not have any fighter support, but they reasoned that time was essential, to wait for U.S. Air Force fighter aircraft or a backup chopper - although both would be on the scene in minutes - was time that might prove the difference in getting the Raven out.

"OK there Raven, my friend, how's it going?" Janira, taking over control of the rescue from the senior pilot, also had a reassuring voice in talking with Carroll, who had heard about the preparations to make the pickup.

"OK. I'M AT FOUR THOUSAND FEET. ON THE WEST SIDE. I THINK I CAN PICK UP ONE OF YOUR CHOPPERS COMING UP FROM THE SOUTH. I'M GOING IN."

"I see him, eleven o'clock, low," someone said.

"OK Big fellow, we've got you. We'll be right down. Get out and away from your plane. Get on your radio. Get smoke. Good luck."

"ROGER. I'M GOING IN, GOING IN SOME BUSHES.

382

GOING IN NOW."

Then there was quiet. All the choppers were at full power. Izzy's helicopter was vibrating terribly. The southern PDJ was in the distance in front. I saw what might have been Jarina's helicopter ahead, close to the first ridgeline and dropping.

"I'M ON THE GROUND. I'M OK. I'M GETTING OUT AND GOING ON MY HANDHELD."

"GODDAMNIT, WE'RE FIVE MINUTES OUT. FIVE MINUTES. GET AWAY FROM THE PLANE. GET AWAY FROM YOUR PLANE. HIDE. GET AWAY."

"I'M OUT, UNDER THE WING. HOW DO YOU READ ME, HOW DO YOU READ?"

"WE'VE GOT YOU TEN BYE. YOU'RE SOUNDING GOOD. GET AWAY FROM THE PLANE."

"...THERE MUST BE FIFTY OF 'UM COMING THIS WAY. THEY SEE ME." The Raven was talking frantically when Jarina's transmission ended.

"DON'T FIRE YOUR GUN. RUN. RUN. ANYONE SEE HIM?"

"...THEY'RE SHOOTING AT......." The Raven screamed.

"WHERE IS HE?"

"I'VE GOT THE PLANE. I SEE IT. OH SHIT. FUCK. THERE ARE GOOKS ALL OVER THE PLACE." Jarina and Taylor were still coming in. Taylor saw six or eight people running around near the downed O-1. Fifty feet away from the plane Jarina began to descend to a hover, hoping the pilot would break from some of the nearby bushes and run to the chopper.

"COME ON, COME ON, COME ON, COME ON." Taylor was yelling over the open mike.

Suddenly he felt the helicopter shudder under the impact of intense ground fire. He could heard the impact of some of the rounds off the engine.

"WE'RE TAKING A LOT OF SMALL-ARMS FIRE, I'M BREAKING AWAY TO THE EAST." Jarina said.

Izzy yelled to Taylor, "SHOOT YOUR GUN."

"SHIT I'LL NEED MY BULLETS IF I'M SHOT DOWN," he answered.

Inside the Jarina/Taylor helicopter, the console dials were going crazy. Some of the rounds had hit the fuel line and gas began pouring from the fuel tank. Immediately the low fuel warning light came on and Jarina struggled to bring the crippled helicopter up and he began heading south. The flight mechanic, Yourglich, began

James E. Parker, Jr.

firing his M-16 at the different people he saw running toward the helicopter as it lifted away.

Three of the helicopters, including Frenchy Smith's, coming on the scene dropped off of their rush to the downed Raven and escorted Jarina and Taylor back to LS 05, where they abandoned the badly shot up helicopter.

Ted Cash and his co-pilot, Roy Heibel, continued on toward the downed O-1. Neal, the other Raven, was directing the first flight of fast movers into the area around the crash site. The senior pilot and Cash talked briefly about making the next charge in to get the pilot. After the fast movers made their second pass, Cash led several helicopters as they swooped down toward the ground.

Cash and Heibel, the first in, hovered near the O-1's wing. The ping of small arms-fire into and around the helicopter made every fraction of a second perilous.

"THERE HE IS. UNDER THE WING," Cash yelled.

"SHIT. HE'S BLOWN AWAY. AH SHIT, SHIT, SHIT. WE'RE TAKING ROUNDS BROAD SIDE," Heibel announced. Most of the other helicopters trying to land were being shot up and they began to pull back.

"I SEE HIM. THEY'VE GOTTEN HIM. HE'S DEAD. WE GOT TO PULL OUT," Cash responded.

There was quiet. Izzy pulled off the power and the helicopter vibration slowed.

A pilot of one of the other helicopters asked if there was any chance the Raven was still alive. Cash said, "No." Everyone on his helicopter saw the pilot under the wing with parts of his body shot away.

Alive and talking one minute, trying to make the best of the situation, trying to stay alive. Dead the next.

Everyone in the air felt tired as the adrenaline began to fade. All the choppers gained altitude. There was concern about Cash because of the rounds he had taken but apparently nothing significant had been hit and he was airworthy.

Because we were at the rear of the group, we were the first to come around and land at Long Tieng. I got off the helicopter as Zack came riding up in a Jeep. I was explaining what had happened when Cash and Hutchinson landed in their helicopters. Soon Frenchy flew in with Jarina and Taylor aboard. Cash bounced out and began examining the different bullet holes in the side of his chopper. Hutchinson who had a harder time getting out of his Twin Pack - burdened by his painful, long overdue call of nature, I suddenly

384

remembered - finally, slowly, got to the ground. And then, walking bent over mainly from the knees down, taking very short little steps, he began to cross the ramp. He got halfway and stopped and stood there for a long time looking straight ahead before walking on, more upright, soiled and sad.

--THIRTY-ONE--

Changes in the Valley

The North Vietnamese forces had indeed taken advantage of the haze to begin moving en masse south across the PDJ and the Raven had landed in their midst.

The U.S. Air Force fast movers, coming from the south to support the rescue, worked the area. B-52 strikes were called in. Aircraft returning from North Vietnam were asked to drop leftover ordnance in the southern PDJ. The area was bombed for days and Vietnamese casualties were high. They paid dearly for the death of John Carroll. Special intelligence indicated that he had shot at the Vietnamese soldiers as they approached and they returned the fire. If he had not fired, the Vietnamese could have waited and may have eventually gotten all the Air America choppers, who would have continued to come in one after the other to try and make the pickup.

In giving his life he probably saved ours.

Though the Vietnamese had suffered hundreds killed and wounded from the bombing they continued their move south. By the first of November were attacking Skyline again.

****

Red Coat left in October and Digger went to Bouam Long to replace him. The deuce and a half truck had been moved out of the Sky bunker by then.

Earlier, Red Coat had requested a large truck to move ammunition and other material around the compound. There were no roads of course in/around the high mountain compound of Bouam Long, but there were various chores near the airstrip that could be made much easier if Cher Pao Moua had a truck. Shep's replacement, A.H., said, "OK, a plane large enough to carry a deuce and a half truck can't land at Bouam Long, but we can drop one in.

385

The Army does it all the time; 82nd Airborne paratroopers jump in an area and right behind them come the trucks. All we need here is just a big parachute."

So they rigged a truck for drop, loaded it on a C-130 and took it up to Bouam Long. Unfortunately the lines got tangled when they pushed it out the back door of the plane and it did a nose dive into the Sky bunker. Fortunately Red Coat was not inside....the engine and cab ended up inside the radio/cook area. It was like Air America bombed the bunker with the truck.

For months thereafter when Air America went up to Bouam Long they said among themselves: Don't land near the bunker, that's where Red Coat parks his truck.

****

Zack continued to be acting base chief until Dick Johnson's replacement arrived. A tall, lanky bureaucrat with no conspicuous talent for the job, the new chief's days were numbered in the valley from the start. He had no rapport with the gruff Air America contingent or the lethal, risk-taking Ravens. He did not seek VP confidence nor did he inspire respect with his Sky officers. He appeared to us to play to Washington, where he had contacts and experience. He would study cables coming in and would often unilaterally compose responses - he saw no need to get others involve. He never participated in the give and take around the map board or in the bar. Zack was never openly critical of the man, in fact he was protective, and forced compliance with an increasing list of administrative chores the new chief levied on the field officers. One of the most restrictive new items was a 6 p.m. organized staff meeting. This meant we had to start coming in from the field around midafternoon. Air America did not run fixed schedules, and when there was contact with the enemy or troop movements or problems with resupply, logical priorities committed Air America to other duties above ferrying case officers back to the staff meeting. The new man understood this to a certain extent, but he was always visibly upset when we came in late. The fixed, formal staff meetings were not popular.

Then there was the chair, and it signaled the beginning of the end. It was a large living room variety of an easy chair and it appeared one day in the briefing room, off the ops assistant's quarters. The new man had it sent up from his household goods or found it somewhere and had the support staff move it in, front and center of the map board. The first night Hardnose came in, saw the new chair, like everyone else, and sat down in it. A "chief's chair" was so pretentious, so unlike anything else ever done in the valley, it was hard to believe that the new man would actually be that out of touch and would have had the chair put there solely for his use. Hardnose honestly believed that it was just another chair, albeit a very nice chair, and he was the first one there, so he sat down. The chief came in, looked down at Hardnose without smiling and cleared his throat. Hardnose said, "Oh," realizing the new man really was out of touch, and he got up. And the next night another case officer was in the chair and the chief came in, glared and cleared his throat and took the seat without comment when the case officer got up.

The new chief did not operate in a vacuum, as insulated as Long Tieng was. The Stick, Hugh Tovar and people in the other MRs soon learned of the chair and how it implicated the man as an officious misfit. His days in the valley were brought to a conclusion by the unlikeliest of characters, the ARMA rep. ARMA, or the U.S. Army Munitions Agency (check to be sure this is the official name), had hired a young teenage dependent out of Vientiane to run the ammo dump off the ramp. He didn't look threatening. He had these enormous feet, would walk around like he was wearing frog feet or clown shoes, and he had long hair that he kept pushing off his face. He was the youngest, least imposing member of the round-eye force at Long Tieng. But he was quiet and competent, worked hard at the ammo dump, near Shep, and things were always in order. A problem came up within weeks after the chair appear that centered around fuses for T-28 bombs. The dump had the right ordnance but were short on the right types of fuses. At a staff meeting this became a long involved subject of discussion. In conclusion the new chief issued complex, confusing instructions on how fuses were to be ordered and stored. The next night Dutch, who was the master of ceremonies at these briefings, went around the room asking the different people if they had anything to contribute. When he came to the ARMA fellow, the guy said, "No, I don't have anything to add." The new chief spun around in his chair and said, "Well just how many fuses do you have?" And the ARMA guy told him.

The next night as Dutch went around the room, the ARMA guy said he didn't have anything. The Chief got up from his chair and said, "Well, now wait a minute, you just want to tell me how many fuses you got?" And the ARMA guy told him. The new chief said, without listening to the response - the number of fuses wasn't important here – "Every night when it comes to you, you give a report on your fuses."

The next night when Dutch began going around the room asking if there was anything more to add to the business of the day, the chief sat rigid in his chair, looking straight ahead, waiting for the ARMA guy. Dutch came to him and the ARMA guy said, "No I don't have anything to add."

The new chief jumped straight up out of his chair, spun around and said, "You're out of here, you're out of the valley. I guarantee it. You're gone."

But he wasn't. ARMA brass in Vientiane made the point to Hugh Tovar, and to the Stick and eventually to the new man, that ARMA was not answerable to the CIA base chief at Long Tieng, and their guy would stay. And Hugh Tovar said OK.

It was not long thereafter that the new man left, short of tour. As he was leaving the Sky compound in the short Jeep ride to the ramp he passed the young ARMA guy walking up the compound street, those big feet plopping along.

And as we quickly got back to a more natural routine with Zack as the base chief, the chair disappeared.

****

One afternoon we received a message that a group of U.S. Air Force officers from the 7th/13th AF out of Udorn would arrive in Long Tieng to brief on the employment of F-111s in our area.

General John W Vogt, the 7th AF Commander, had earlier visited with Vang Pao and had spent most of the day with the Hmong T-28 pilots. Vogt had presence and he conveyed to us who saw him a sense of command, certainly a reflection of his senior military rank and position. He was not a man easily impressed. But after a day out in the Long Tieng elements, talking with the tough hills tribesmen who flew the T-28 day after day into withering North Vietnamese fire - Vang Sue, the senior pilot at the time had more than 5,000 combat missions - Vogt was, according to people who knew him, indeed awed with what he saw. The unpretentiousness of the Hmong pilots and how they mixed with the villagers and guerrillas from the GMs as they walked around the valley made an impression. There was no politics involved or a sterile high tech environment where the old World War II converted T-28 trainers were parked. It was honest warring, primitive, a throwback to the way it might have been in the First World War. The Hmong flyers strapped as many bombs and as many bullets as they could get on their plane and went out and found

North Vietnamese to attack. Flight after flight, hour after hour, day after day. At that time the U.S. Air Force was sending from thirty to fifty sorties of fighter aircraft a day to MR II. Most were fast movers, F-4s, A-6s and A-7s, which were not often used in close support of ground troops who were maneuvering. This major part of our close fire support was left to the T-28s. On leaving the valley that day Vought said the 7th AF could help more and offered the possibility that F-111s from the 474th Tactical Fighter Wing may be assigned exclusively to MR II, probably for close support.

The team coming up from Udorn indicated that Vought was true to his word and that F-111s were in our future.

When the team arrived on an Air America cargo plane they were easily identifiable because we didn't have that many strangers in the valley. They walked more upright than others, their haircuts were shorter and they wore odd-looking-low-cut shoes, like those used for indoor work.

Curious about this new, high tech addition to our fighting force, Kayak and I followed the team up to the Sky compound. As we walked in the Air Force people were finding places to sit among the boxes and weapons and typewriters that littered the main room in the headquarters bunker. Hog was standing off to the side. Bamboo, tall and scruffy, and Clean, shaven headed and bulky, were sitting around Zack at his desk.

The Air Force officers tried to act relaxed but they were uncomfortable and rigid.

Dutch and Hardnose walked in and Zack told the officers that they had the floor.

One of the older men in the group, wearing prescription aviation glasses, began by saying the F-111s (he called them "F One Elevens") had been deployed to South Vietnam for some time, though the media rap on them - what we might have heard - was they ran into mountains. This was overstated. They were in fact very effective, precision bombers, able to deliver bombs in close support to friendly ground troops. Equipped with an on-board computer-aided gyrocompass and capable of off-set guidance from ground beacons, they knew where they were every instance. They could deliver their twenty-four 500 pound bombs on target in all weather. If we knew where the enemy was, marshalling for an attack say, the F-111 could get to them and kill them. They are all-weather aircraft and greatly enhanced the Air Force's ability to provide close support to ground units. In a fire fight, in the rainy season, when heretofore the Air Force was out of action, the F-111 could deliver.

389

James E. Parker, Jr.

"So we're getting F-111s?" Hog asked.

"Roger that," said the Air Force officer.

"Now you know we didn't ask for F-111s," Clean said.

"Roger that," the Air Force spokesman said. "It's been coordinated at very senior levels. The U.S. Air Force presence in South Vietnam is being reduced and the Joint Chief of Staff wants to continue the employment of these state-of-the-art aircraft. With the Vietnamese just starting their offensive here, your T-28s need them. The 474th Tactical Fighter Wing out of Takhli in Thailand is being dedicated for your use in MR II."

I appreciated what the Air Force people were saying and was impressed with the F-111's capabilities, though I sensed something about the presentation that meant more work for Sky. The F-111s were going to take care and feeding and our war was not going to be as private as it had been. The Joint Chief of Staff was not an individual often mentioned in our ops work.

"The 7th AF targeting facility in Saigon has large holdings of potential targets in your area for the planes. But we would like your contribution to this data base," the Air Force officer went on to say. "As you know because of the rules of engagement we are not allowed to have forward observers on the ground in Laos. So we cannot assign U.S. Air Force personnel here - on the ground - to coordinate on the targeting. Raven support is not appropriate. Your Hmong have to be used and we suggest a two-phase program to get this started. First, we get a number of coordinates from you of possible enemy positions, staging areas, road junctions, enemy gun emplacements, etc., to augment our target data base."

Dutch said, "We can provide those. It's something we have plenty of here, targets."

"Second, we train your Hmong radio operators here in the valley and when our F-111 come into the area going to one of the preset targets from the data base and you have new targets, say a position is under attack and you need supporting fire, then your Hmong talker calls up a divert and we scrub the first run and hit the new target. That's the way it will work."

After they finished talking, Zack, looking at Hog said, "I see no problems in getting you coordinates and training the Hmong if the Stick has agreed. Do you Hog?"

"The Hmong will run the radios?" Hog asked.

"Roger."

Hog looked at Zack and shrugged an OK. Later, Hog said the Air Force wasn't seeking our permission, they were giving us a done deal, telling us what they were going to do.

Over the next few days Dutch worked on little else besides collecting targets for the F-111s.

In the valley, Glassman, the senior Sky ops assistant, had been placed in charge of what would be the F-111 radio station, which was named Red Dog Control. He and the other "talkers" were trained by the Air Force team on authenticating targeting information and on communication procedures.

Sky never developed rapport with the targeting officers; they talked a different talk, walked a different walk.

At night in the inner sanction of the headquarters bunker, Clean was the most against their unsolicited help. He said he believed the F-111s flew into the sides of mountains. They had ground-hugging radar but he understood that it didn't work altogether that well. The planes flew most often, according to Clean, on automatic pilot with its altitude set by computer and radar but they flew too fast, too low and when they approached mountains the plane couldn't pull up in time. Even if this wasn't the case often, it meant these bombers made mistakes sometimes, weren't always as on target as they'd like.

"Say we've got some action going near Skyline and the Vietnamese are marshalling for an attack, can we afford to give the F-111s targets 50 meters, 400 meters or what, from our troops? Is their accuracy range within a thousand meters? Maybe they bomb our own people some of the time." Clean pursed his lips. He had in fact been bombed once, in the valley, by U.S. Air Force planes.

The thing that Kayak was concerned about was the imprecise geological mapping of the area and the haphazard way the field commanders often gave coordinates of enemy locations. Plus the F-111s flew on a flat plain. Our ground here was very up and down. A few lateral feet in the air could mean hundreds of feet up and down the sides of mountains. Not to discount the wind drafts that could bounce planes around. "Wouldn't the wind drafts affect the fall of a bomb?" Kayak asked.

I said that in Vietnam while I was there the Air Force used FACs when they supported ground troops. Too much chance of error otherwise. Man was being replaced here by technology. I liked a man sighting for those bombers. Did they use the F-111s in Vietnam in support of ground operations involving American troops, I wondered?

"And the F-111s carried a lot of stuff. Twenty four 500 pound bombs. Not a single bomb had any eyes or conscious after it was released," I went on. "Plus like Kayak said, this is rugged territory here, sheer drops of five hundred, a thousand meters, over-hangings and there were many mistakes in the mapping. Lot of loose variables. Plus we're doing OK without them. We got the Ravens eyeballing in other fast movers. Seems to me we got enough."

Zack called us little old ladies. He said we were afraid of new technology. We couldn't identify with anything that didn't have bodily functions. This F-111 can kill 130mm guns. And if it has had problems in the past, well so what, the F-4 has had its problems - wasn't always on target - and with the crazy unpredictable commitments we got sometimes from the ABCCC - the Air Force radio and command aircraft that overflew our area twenty-four hours a day - we sometime don't get all the F-4 support we want. These F-111s will work for us. Directly. We don't have to clear through ABCCC. Give them a chance, Zack said. You don't have any choice anyway, because the deal has already been made; they are coming.

****

The attacks on Skyline continued to be low intensity probes. There was no indication that the battle for Skyline would be raged with the same ferocity as the previous year. One reason might have been the peace talks that had been initiated in Vientiane. Possibly the Pathet Lao and the Vietnamese were coordinating their field activity with an overall eye toward the negotiations. Possibly they were not as able to launch strong attacks because of the casualties they had taken after the Raven went in or, another possibility, Vietnamese forces could have been pulled out of Laos for deployment in South Vietnam. Ours was still a sideshow.

While the occasional skirmishes continued along Skyline, our main concern was that the 130mms would begin bombing the valley any time. We knew some still operated in the area.

In early December the first enemy round of the season landed in the valley.

However it was not a 130mm round.

It came from an assault rifle. We were expecting a big crashing boom from a 130mm and got a zing. A Vietnamese or a Pathet Lao soldier had made his way through the Thai positions on top of the ridgeline and, hiding in the rocky south side, he began firing at random targets.

"Damned nuisance," Bamboo said.

The following day another sniper opened up from another

position.

Our routine in the valley wasn't affected much by these enemy sharpshooters although we didn't tend to lounge on the ramp the same way we had done in the past. At times I had the feeling that someone was up there on the ridgeline looking at me as I walked along near the Sky compound.

The snipers quickly became just a part of our life. After the first day or so, when we would hear the zing of a round going by and ping off of a rock, we'd dive for cover where we'd wait, smoking a cigarette or reading a book until someone fired either from the valley floor or the ridgeline into the general direction of the sniper. After another pause, we'd put out our cigarette and put away our book, get up and continue on our way again. There was no rush of adrenaline. No fear. Zing and we'd duck. Ten minutes later we'd be on our way again.

But Bamboo was right, they were a damned nuisance.

****

My GM had pulled back from the PDJ and the men were dug in around LS 15. They patrolled east and southeast, occasionally engaging Pathet Lao and Vietnamese. We were unsure how many Vietnamese were in the river valley north of Skyline or exactly what their plans were for the coming offensive. Our plans generally were to hold Skyline, using the Hmong on the flanks as ground maneuver elements and as reserves. My unit at Ban Na, like before, was to draw off some of the North Vietnamese units from the Skyline attack force.

A 105mm howitzer was moved out to LS 15 and the Hmong in my GM began to fire their own close support...mostly by dead reckoning. Thai mercenaries came out and helped set up a fire direction center and patiently taught the Hmong the concept of indirect fire. When they left the Hmong took their own bearings and used sticks and knotted string to align the gun when they fired. They were more or less accurate, although they continued to adjust their sticks for months. And they had a very random way to select fuses. But we were self-contained. We had maneuver elements and artillery and Ravens were usually around. From LS 15 down to the river valley was a little theater of war in the little Lao theater of war. The U.S. Army may be pulling out of South Vietnam but we were still fighting, holding on.

Chuck Hines, Raven 20, filed a report of an activity in

James E. Parker, Jr.

support of my GM at Ban Na:

*"17 DEC 72. Early afternoon. Weather clear. Third "go"
of the day. Was airborne solo in my O-1G out doing routine
visual reconnaissance along north edge of the PDJ. No
backseater. Mule called me on FM frequency 57.65 MHz
and requested tactical air.*

"You are almost overhead my position," Mule said.

*I rolled, looked down and saw a hilltop below me with a
visible Mung defensive perimeter around the top. Mule's
place today. "We're taking a hell of a lot of 12.7 H&I fire
from a small hill nearby, day and night. An irritant. Can
you take it out?"*

*"You have target's coordinates? – or can you mark it with
an M79 willie pete* round?"*

*"No, don't have one of those with me. That 12.7 gun is on a
small hill nearby." A somewhat undefined target. There
were several small hills nearby Mule's place. I picked the
nearest small hill.*

*Called Cricket for air. Only a short wait time before I heard
"BLADE CHECK. TWO." over my assigned UHF
frequency. "Raven two-zero, Blade flight of two F-4s have
you in sight." Fighters rendezvoused and orbited while
receiving their standard, required target briefing sequence.
I put in one willie pete rocket to mark the target, then
cleared lead in hot. Almost immediately I received a
compelling sense that something wasn't right. It was my
usual physical feeling which always accompanies my
intuitive alerts -- a significant tightening across the
abdominal muscles just below my stomach.*

*Mule called and said, "There are friendlies near where your
willie pete just impacted."*

*"Go through dry, Lead. We're moving to another target."
No ordnance was dropped. Blade flight immediately
returned to their low altitude overhead orbit.*

*Looked around. Finally saw where the target, a Soviet
version of the U.S .50 caliber machine gun, had to be in a
round, doughnut shaped trench dug in the earth below the
south side of that hill Mule was on. Wasn't up on a hill.
Constructed on relatively flat ground. Briefed my fighters
on our new target, read the map contours on my 1:50 chart,
mentally converted meters to feet, then gave them the*

target's altitude. Briefed the restriction on their run in's, west to east with their orbit to the south. Friendlies on top of the hill immediately to the north of the white smoke. Nearest safe bailout will be over twenty-alternate runway. Then we went to work.

Fighter pilots rarely saw any visual evidence of enemy activity while putting their ordnance in on ground targets in Vietnam or Laos. Collectively fighter pilots regarded what they were doing to apparently opaque green jungle terrain every day as an organized effort at converting forests to toothpicks. This air strike turned out to be a little different for them.

Marked that doughnut hole in the ground with a willie pete rocket, then cleared lead in hot. "IN HOT. FAC IS IN SIGHT." He added power with throttles to bring his airspeed up to a bit over 400 knots and began descending down on his bomb run. Then over UHF he said, "I can't believe it! I can see that little bastard standing right there inside his doughnut shooting directly at my aircraft with his 12.7." Lead's bomb impacted about 200 meters long and to the left.

"Two, you are cleared in hot." "ROG, FAC IN SIGHT." Two's bomb impacted about 80 meters short. Doughnut gun pit uninjured. Machine gun still firing during each fighter attack pass. Lead was cleared in hot again. His bomb hit the center of the doughnut directly and blew it away. Gave the fighters their on and off times, target coordinates, and BDA: one enemy KIA, one gun and one bunker destroyed. Passed BDA to Cricket. Cricket copied. Fighters departed the area to RTB at their home plate. I continued my afternoon mission – looking for enemy command & control nodes defined by large leaf Bright tobacco randomly planted in vicinity of cave entrances.

****

In late November we received the Air Force radios for our Hmong in the valley to communicate with the F-111s when they arrived.

****

395

I roomed with Kayak in the barracks building. With Shep gone, Kayak was usually the last one off the ramp at night. He would come in the mess hall, putting his toothbrush in his shirt pocket and eat, often sitting by himself reading a book though he would sit and talk with Father Bouchard when the good Father visited. Air America pilots and flight mechanics around them would be involved in animated conversations amongst themselves and with other Sky officers. If they were flying the next day the pilots weren't allowed to drink so they would usually spend an hour or so in the mess hall after their meal, drinking coffee and talking, sometimes reading a magazine or newspaper. Sometimes they'd take food out to the bear, but generally after leaving the mess hall they would go to the temporary trailers, relocated from LS 272, where they'd read before going to sleep. They'd be up in the morning before dawn.

The pilots who had finished their upcountry flying and were catching rides back to Udorn the following morning - four or five a night - could drink and they usually were the only customers in the bar area in the early evening.

Sky officers ate at irregular times. Some - Hog, Bamboo and Zack primarily - ate at Vang Pao's residence. The officers working with the Thais ate in a mess hall at their end of the valley. The Sky officers working with the Hmong would come in and just take some food out of the cooking pots on the stove and put it on bread and walk over to the headquarters bunker. Some Air America pilots also went into the Hqs building at night. It was the quiet inner sanction of the valley, though around dusk it was busy and active. Dutch collected information, aided by Wimpy, Scott and the Big "O," for nightly situation reports, for B-52 targeting and more and more, for the F-111s when they eventually arrived. We usually stood around a map board talking about developments during the day; sniper locations, intelligence reports that had come in on enemy troop movements, patrol reports. Everyone made contributions; Sky people especially among themselves, were not shy. Conversations shifted quickly from subject to subject. Topics would range from a serious discussion on something like the downing of a T-28, to someone suggesting that Digger had been left so long at Bouam Long that he had molded in his hole. We missed the rational contributions Digger made to our evening meetings. He would be leaving in December, to be replaced at Bouam Long by Kayak.

When business was finished the conversation would degenerate into locker room banter with Clean usually acting as the master of ceremony. Hog enjoyed this give and take with the Sky contingent in the headquarters bunker and often later in the bar. He did not participate, however, when any outsiders were around. Prompted, he would be brutal in his comments to Bamboo and Clean. For a period he called Bamboo "the flying zero," because Bamboo appeared to have grounded himself in the valley, rarely ever going anywhere. Hog also would come up with phrases that became part of our language. He'd say things like the "dreaded" Lumberjack had "darkened his door" the other day "for a pair of seconds" to "hunker down" and talk about the Thais. "Not a pretty sight."

His comments stood out because of his usual laconic nature. I'd find myself saying to Zack sometimes during the day when I needed to see Hog about something, "Oh, I've got to go darken the dreaded Hog's door." Or out at LS 15, I'd call in and say, "I'm going to hunker down here for the rest of the day and keep my distance from all you girl singers back there doing indoor work."

"Indoor work" was anything a bureaucrat did and not necessarily to be taken seriously.

Although he had been fighting this nonconventional war for years – initially posted to the forward most bases as a singleton – he had no formal U.S. military training and didn't know how to give orders. He was sort of our trail boss, and his guidance came in the way of conversation, though he always got his meanings across, and to my knowledge there was never any confusion with the more military oriented Ravens or the Air America corps, or with the few of us who worked for him. And he was a like mind with the Hmong and didn't try to impose his will with them as much as they came to agreement about what was to be done.

At night Kayak, the loner, would slip away from the headquarters bunker when business was over and go to our room. He had no interest in small talk. He would take a bath before going to bed, naked, and read until midnight or later.

After our map sessions in the bunker I usually wandered back to the bar. It was not an ornate place. Twenty foot square, there was a door in the back to the dining area, the front door was screen with a spring that slammed it shut when people passed. The room was lit by a bare 100 watt light bulb in the ceiling. There was a plywood bar against a side-wall, liquor bottles lined a warehouse shelf behind it. Beer was in a refrigerator nearby. A dartboard collected dust on the back-wall, a poker table with kitchen chairs was off to the side. There were no pictures on the wall. No bartender. You put money in a cash box when you got a drink, although Clean was usually positioned behind the bar and he would fix you a drink or not depending on his mood.

The place always seemed crowded, maybe because everyone tended to talk loud. War stories predominated...there were many old warriors around. Clean, as an eighteen year old paratrooper, had jumped into Normandy with the 101st Airborne division. He had been around every conflict the country and the Agency had been involved with since. The Air America pilots were equally seasoned and had their share of distinctive personalities. John Greenway, a Bell pilot, had been a B-52 pilot in the Air Force. He said once that his squadron was visited by a shrink and each pilot was given a psychological readiness test. One of the questions was if they were flying for the Strategic Air Command and received orders to fly over the United States and drop their bombs on their home towns, would they have complied. Everyone in the squadron said they would not. Except Greenway. He said he would. You either obeyed orders or you didn't.

Air America folklore was a popular topic and the same stories would change with each telling. There was an incident some years before when an Air America test pilot, ferrying a plane from Udorn to Savannakhet, fell asleep and he overflew Savannakhet, overflew North Vietnam above the DMZ, and woke up over the South China Sea. Depending on who told the story, he had North Vietnamese rockets fired at him as he flew along, asleep; had U.S. fighters chasing him; flew back into Hue and filled up before trying to land at Savannakhet as if nothing had happened; flew back into Udorn via South Vietnam, landed, went home, packed his bags and left. It was always funny. It was like a recurring situation comedy when someone started the H-34 with the sleeping pilot story.

If there was a quorum for a poker game, I played. Zack was the only other Sky officer who participated although Air America pilots made up most of the players around the table. I was a constant winner. Brenda and I went three months in the fall without cashing a check, living off the money I won from Air America playing poker in the valley.

The Air America pilots played poker like there was no tomorrow. They were well paid - although they didn't receive enormous salaries. Helicopter pilots maybe averaged $4,000 a month, which included overtime and hazardous duty pay. But they wore a lot of gold and usually carried large amounts of money wherever they went because they believed they might need gold and money to ransom themselves to safety if they were shot down. In poker they went against long odds, won some big pots but lost many more. "Part of their nature," Hog said. "They like long odds. More action, more adventure in it. No excitement in betting on a sure hand."

I would get to our room before midnight. Kayak was usually awake, reading. He'd stay in one position on his bed for only five minutes at a time and he'd flip into a new position, hitting the pillow with his fist to get it readjusted.

He'd also eat crackers. Constantly. Like a rat. Gnawing away, taking small bites, hours on end.

The incredibly dull books he read tended to be heavy and he'd manhandle them from his chest to his pillow, where they'd make a whoosh sound as they hit the bed clothing. The area around his bed was littered with the big, old books.

Where did he get them?

I often thought the Sky case officers at Long Tieng were uniquely suited to the job: by experience, temperament and personality. All were men of accomplishment, were self-starters. All had years of combat experience. Some were suspicious about stateside society, uncomfortable with the social revolution of the 1960s and some of the Sky behavior could have been looked on as anti-social. Were we this way before we arrived or did we develop suspicious attitudes because it was part of the culture? Why did we love this God-forsaken place, the stone age Hmong or the rowdy Thai mercenaries? We were a closed society of little more than a dozen men by the end of 1972 and there were no other officers in the pipeline to replace us. We were a dying breed and clannish. We were all so different, yet had become so similar.

Why, though, didn't Kayak wear any clothes to bed? I asked around one time. Everybody but Kayak slept in their shorts.

Over there across the room, reading those dull books, eating crackers like a rat, hitting that pillow every five minutes, naked.....he was on the other end of the spectrum from the girl singers of the world.

I just wish he'd wear shorts. And why did he walk around with a toothbrush in his mouth during the day? Why was he so restless, always anxious to get out there in the thick of the action?

Air America, who did not understand this man, said he had a death wish. I lived with him. I didn't understand him.

And who gave him all those crackers?

James E. Parker, Jr.

--THIRTY-TWO--
The Christmas Season in Laos

Shortly before Christmas the Vietnamese brought to bear a new weapon. Before, their sniper fire had not been particularly accurate. They did not have long barrel sniper rifles and used their AK-47s and SKS at maximum range.

But early one morning near the Thai positions at the east end of the runway, there was a zing and a ping from a sniper bullet. Everyone casually ducked and then another ping and people continued to hunker down, scratching and yawning and then zoooooom KABOOOOOOOOOM. As a DK-82 round came screaming in and exploded.

The pinging was from the spotter rifle mounted on a DK-82 that fired a round like the U.S. 4.62-inch rocket launcher. The Soviet gun had two triggers, one to the small caliber rifle mounted on the tube of the DK-82. The gunner would identify his target and fire a round or two with his rifle until he had his target "spotted" and then he would pull the trigger of the larger gun, firing the rocket.

Thereafter the zinging from Skyline got more respect. We'd hear a zing and we'd say, holy shit, and we'd run like sumbitches.

****

With Christmas approaching, the gifts we had ordered from the States for the kids had begun to arrive - dozens of them. It would be their first Christmas with us. Mim and Joseph had some problems understanding the concept of Santa Claus and gift giving, but other kids did not question it. The bottom line for our two was that this Santa Claus thing was very good to children. Christmas was about as much excitement as they could stand. Mim, I know for a fact, almost burst she was so excited.

For herself Brenda asked for a sewing machine.

I had to go to Udorn mid-December to pick up some radios for my GM and photo interpretation (PI) work from overhead photography for Zack. While I was in Udorn I bought a Singer sewing machine for my wife at the base exchange. It had all the whistles and buttons, could do anything. Could maybe be used as a copier or help in micro surgery said the clerk. Came in a nice wooden cabinet. Brenda was going to like it; it was state-of-the-art, top of the line.

The Vietnam War Its Ownself

I took it directly back to Long Tieng. The timing was going to work out well because within the week I was heading down to Vientiane for the holidays.

The day after I arrived back in the valley from Udorn two new DK-82s arrived on the south slope, plus several new snipers. Getting these pests became job one. Possibly some slipped away over the ridgeline at night, but most stayed in place, hiding among the rocks when combined Thai and Hmong forces swept the area. Watching our men scour the south slope of Skyline for the snipers through binoculars from the valley floor reminded me of bird hunting as a kid. Only the game here was deadly and shot back.

I was supposed to leave on December 22nd. All that day I was busy working with Nhia to ensure that our GM were supplied and would not go wanting while I was away. There were a variety of distractions and it had not been a particularly successful day. In late afternoon two DK-82s, which had gone undetected during that day's sweep of the ridge, began firing at the ramp. Most of the Air America fixed-wing planes took off. Which meant that I was going to have to get down to Vientiane on a helicopter.

And I had this large sewing machine in a box.

By late in the afternoon I had done all I could so I left the headquarters bunker. Nhia helped me carry the sewing machine down to the ramp. One of the DK-82s was still working the area, aiming at the ammo dump in an effort to ignite some of the rounds. Several DK-82 rounds landed as we came around the last karst and trotted behind the bomb-proof Air Ops building. I was the only Sky man trying to get out at that time and I joined a group of Thai, Lao and Hmong.

I told Nhia to go on home, that I could man handle the box by myself.

He wished me a Merry Christmas and left. There weren't so many helicopters still in the area and those that were still around didn't want to come in on the ramp, which was hot from the DK-82 fire.

One helicopter finally came in, saying that he was leaving after the first eight paxs got on board or three seconds, whichever came first.

As I trotted out in front of Air Ops, a dozen or more people joined me and it suddenly did not seem appropriate that I would displace some of these people with my box, so I went to the pilot's side of the helicopter when it landed to ask him if he could take this box in addition to eight paxs. He didn't understand me and finally he

401

lifted his hands, palms up and the helicopter left.

Leaving me on the edge of the ramp with this large box. Most of the other people who did not get on were hurrying back to the side of Air Ops. I reached down and picked up the box and heard a ...

Zing.

The bullet hit behind me, near where the helicopter had landed.

"Holy shit," I said running as fast as I could with the box.

Another helicopter came in very soon, landing in another part of the ramp, partially hidden by a karst.

I ran out and asked the co-pilot if he could take my box and me in addition to the paxs and he said sure, but by that time the helicopter had been filled with passengers and there was no place even for me, much less the box.

And the helicopter took off.

And I was the only one left in that particular part of the ramp. I reach down and picked up the box and heard a....

Zing.

Between me and Air Ops.

So I ran the other way, to hide behind the karst.

When the next helicopter came in, I ran out, threw the box on and jumped in behind it. Screw being polite.

****

That night when I got home for Christmas we went to the small Embassy commissary and bought a large tree brought in from New Zealand, tied it to the top of the car for the drive home and later decorated it. The kids were very excited. Christmas Eve we attended church programs and read the "Night Before Christmas" when Brenda and I put the kids to bed. They listened to every word.

Christmas morning we were up before the kids. We laid out all the Santa Claus gifts and set up lights and a movie camera around the tree. Then we sat down and waited for them to wake up.

And they kept sleeping. Why weren't they so excited that they woke up at the crack of dawn?

And we waited and waited. Finally Brenda went in and called them. They woke up gradually and then suddenly they were wide awake. Joe started running down the hall and Mim was right behind him and they turned the corner to the living room and I turned on the lights.

And they froze, blinded. They couldn't see.

I had a LOT of lights.

Both kids squinted their eyes, because the lights hurt. They tried to make out their toys but my million megawatts had a blinding effect. It was hard to be casual and spontaneous at your first Christmas when you can't see what's going on.

The kids didn't know, they thought everybody's Christmas was the same. Toys hidden behind blinding lights.

--THIRTY-THREE--

F-111s and Red Dog Control

Returning to Long Tieng before New Year's Day I was greeted by most of the bachelors who were leaving for their holiday break.

In Air Ops I heard that another one of the Ravens, Skip Jackson, had been killed over Christmas. He was spotting an enemy position in the southern PDJ when one of the planes he was directing came out of the sun and they clipped wings, Skip's little plane immediately spiraling to the ground. He was a very bright person, like a lawyer kind of bookish bright, although he didn't look like a lawyer because he had the physique of an athlete, tiny waist and broad shoulders. He had been the Wing boxing champion at the Air Force Academy, lettered in football, had gotten his masters after serving for a year as an assistant football coach with the Academy football team. A "fast burner" in the Air Force. What a life he was going to have. But now dead. All the joy of Christmas was erased.

In the way of the Ravens, because they couldn't get Skip's body out, they directed a fast mover in several days later to destroy his O-1 on the ground, to consume their comrade inside. Like sailors burying their dead at sea, the Ravens looked after their own.

****

Beginning the new year, the snipers still fired at us from the south slope of Skyline but the Thais had some success in ferreting out the DK-82s so they weren't the bother that they had been.

A group of technicians arrived after the first of the year to solve the problems we were having with our generators. Since we had moved back into the valley the generators had been burning up after only a few days of operation. We'd get in a new generator - heavy, expensive equipment - it'd be installed by techs from Udorn and they'd hang around for a day or two. It'd be working fine and they'd leave. A couple days later the new generator would burn up.

Couldn't figure it out. We had gone through several generators.

The first night the techs went out on the porch of the mess hall and saw the problem.

Half the houses in the valley were lit.

The generators were only large enough to power the Sky compound, Vang Pao's compound, the Thai area and a few other select sites. Not every household in the Hmong nation.

The next day they found one outlet in a rear supply area of Vang Pao's compound that was the switching station for the "Long Tieng Outlaw Municipal Utilities Service." There were about twenty five multiple plugs stuck together coming out of that one outlet, with maybe fifty extension cords attached, running out a window to a lean-to, the switching station for the Long Tieng Outlaw Municipal Utilities Service. In the shed, at the end of each extension cord, were more multiple plugs and more extension cords.

And nobody knew who was responsible.

****

In Vientiane about this time the wife of an Air America official was terrorizing the commissary. An ethnic Lao, she had married an American several years previously who then died mysteriously. She was married next to Pat Thurston, an Air America pilot, but there was something Thurston found unsettling about her and they divorced. She looked around and finally married her third American husband, who worked in Air America flight operations. She was known as a hard, opportunistic lady, unpopular with the other wives who looked on her as a predator and local home wrecker. Possibly because she was not well received by the Air America ladies, the Lao woman did not give a tinker's damn about protocol or accepted norms of behavior in the American community. Cosmetics at the commissary was a case in point. They were purchased in bulk at the base exchange in Udorn and sold at a small glass counter in a corner of the commissary in Vientiane. The woman who ran this concession - who looked on her job as community service - knew basically what products different women liked and she placed her bulk orders in Udorn accordingly. When the Lao woman appeared on the scene, she went up to that counter and bought everything. Every tube of lipstick, every compact, rouge, everything. These items soon appeared on the black market downtown. When the cosmetic section restocked, the Lao woman reappeared and again bought everything. So a limit was put on the amount of cosmetics that a woman could buy at any one time. The Lao woman came in every day thereafter and bought her limit until she had bought out the counter again. She was, in the eyes of the America women, a Lao she-devil.

Then her American husband was found strangled to death.

In the subsequent investigation by the usually inept Lao police, it was discovered that the woman had a Lao boyfriend who had a shaky story about where he was the night of the murder. He later confessed that the woman had put him up to the killing, had in fact grabbed the American's gonads in both her hands while he was being strangled, crushing them.

The American women, as a group, boiled in indignation over the evils of that woman. They could hardly talk about anything else.

The lady was tried by the Lao courts, convicted of murder in the second degree and sentenced to life in a Lao prison.

****

There was continuing interest in the number of Vietnamese coming down to the PDJ to join in the attack on Skyline. There was also interest in the number of Vietnamese who might be leaving because of the peace talks.

In an effort to monitor this suspected ebb and flow of Vietnamese soldiers, Zack increased efforts to send out road watch patrols. Some teams were sent south from Bouam Long. He told me to send some around the northern edge of the PDJ to the area near the abandoned village of Ban Ban, where the road from North Vietnam entered the PDJ.

I inherited Digger's old GM when he went to Bouam Long, so I now had GMs 21 and 22. I told the commanders that we had to get together four 10-man road watch teams and dispatch them to the northeast. I would provide per diem, or bonus pay, plus new equipment, radios with signal scramblers, weapons, binoculars and training. The commanders had to provide the men.

The commanders produced forty more or less healthy men for the job, though none showed any enthusiasm for the task at hand. Road watch work was not part of their culture. Hmong were pretty

405

much here and now type people, very basic in their approach to life. Analyzing movement of the enemy was a difficult concept for them. I was not sure that even if they were ordered to make the maximum effort to get through the North Vietnamese bivouac area north of the PDJ and to move on to Ban Ban, that any of these men would. There was the chance, as the Sky units in the southern MRs had sometimes found, that these teams might just move a few ridgelines over and make up road watch reports and send them back.

Running road watch teams successfully had always been a challenge to Sky. Clean, years before, had the responsibility to send out teams to monitor the traffic on Route six. To enhance security he sent the teams out with homing pigeons. This way there would be no radios for the enemy to vector, no batteries, no need for a rear radio headquarters. The idea was that when the team had a report to send in, they'd put it in the tiny pouch on the leg of one of the pigeons and release it, and the pigeon would fly back to its roost on the karst behind Air Ops in Long Tieng. It was a way to signal in harmony with the environment, Clean said. He had small portable cages built to carry the birds out with the patrols, had made them out of bamboo slivers and nylon thread which were attached to a pack harness. Clean also tested the birds. He carried them several miles south of Long Tieng and released them, watching them fly in circles above him before setting out for Long Tieng, always arriving back to their cages behind Air Ops before he did. He started out with a large group of birds but soon developed what he called the first team, his favorites. These were the birds he selected for the first patrol. He was justly proud of his silent and sure, age-old messengers and helped the bird-carrying Hmong patrol member on with his special pack shortly before the patrol pushed off for their road watch work.

The patrol ate those pigeons.

Ate every one.

****

To check the location of my teams once they were dispatched, I ordered some beacons so that I could fly over the general area where the patrol might be in a Porter and by triangulating, get a true fix on their position.

Nhia and I trained the men near the old hospital in Long Tieng. Some were good, some were not. Three of the patrol leaders knew what they were supposed to do. One was in a daze.

I did the training when it came to the beacons. To mask

their real purpose and to simplify the training I told the patrol leaders that these beacons were the most sophisticated thing of this type available. Made by the same U.S. company that built the spaceship that went to the moon. This was their most important piece of equipment, because with it they stayed plugged into all of the U.S. Air Force. Its interworkings were so complicated that I did not understand it. All they had to know was that they turned it on at midday and let it run for one hour, it would be picked up by satellites and they would be in contact with the overall allied fighting machine. They would not be alone out there. Turn on this beacon and the force was with them.

My plan was to stagger the patrols going out so that I would have one on the way out, one in position, one returning and one in reserve.

I sent out the first patrol, the best one I thought, the end of January and midday a few days later I went up in a Porter with Nhia near where the patrol should have been. I had a very simple handheld antenna that I could turn in the direction of the beacon signal.

There was no beacon signal.

Nhia got on the radio to the patrol and said the U.S. Air Force was very mad at them. They had to turn on their beacon.

The signal came up and I took a reading. We flew to another location and I took another reading. Another location, another reading. Where the three readings intersected was the patrol's location.

They were on a hilltop near the jump off-point. They were not making their way north around the PDJ.

The next day we brought the commander up and he yelled at them and they started moving. From future beacon readings we tracked their progress north.

****

The next day I was lounging on the ramp, laying on top of some canvas, taking the early morning sun, waiting for Greek to get me a helicopter.

Nhia came up and asked to review our schedule for the following day. "We get a helicopter and go up north of the PDJ and spot our patrol," I said, "and then we go on up to Bouam Long so we don't give away the patrol's location and come back and we drop your scuzzy little butt off here and I'm going down to Vientiane and spend some much deserved time with my family."

James E. Parker, Jr.

And I closed my eyes again and got some more sun.

"Why?" I asked with my eyes closed.

"No reason," said Nhia.

After a pause Nhia asked, "Do you know who is flying for us tomorrow?"

I turned to look at my ops assistant, who was as clever and as deliberate as any man I had ever known. He did not ask senseless questions.

"Why?" I asked.

"No reason," he said.

"This is a very good conversation we have going here," I said with one eye open. "Izzy is flying I think, what's up?"

"Nothing."

I closed my eyes again and Nhia continued, "Only you know we fly over my home village. Well not right over but it's off to the west some and you said once that my brother could live with you down in Vientiane and possibly go to school there, that you have plenty of room in the servants quarters behind your house. If we can pick him up tomorrow and if you still think he can stay at your house in Vientiane then he can fly right on down with you. Izzy wouldn't mind stopping for you in my village."

Nhia stood there unashamed, looking me in the eye. I had in fact mentioned one time that we had room behind our house if his brother wanted to live there while going to school. I had assumed his brother lived around Long Tieng, however, or would meet me in the valley.

"Where's your village Nhia?" I asked and he produced a map and pointed to an area west of Bouam Long.

I said, "We don't know anything about this area and Air America doesn't like to fly below high points and ridgelines they don't know for sure are controlled by friendlies. Your village here looks like its halfway down the mountain in a part of Laos I've never been in before. Maybe Father Bouchard is the only round eye to have ever seen this area."

"It's safe," Nhia said. "And Izzy will fly in for you."

"How old is your brother?"

"Twelve."

"OK if we have time and if the pilot will fly in then we'll pick up your brother."

The next day coming back from Bouam Long, Izzy and I were chatting on the intercom when Nhia punched me on the leg. He had his map stretched out on his lap. He pointed to Bouam Long and

408

to Long Tieng and to where he thought we were and then to his home village and he smiled.

I told Izzy that Nhia had a pax he wanted us to pick up.

"Who? Where?" Izzy asked.

"His brother at about..." and I gave him four digit coordinates.

"You are full of crap. No way are we going in there. No way. Tell Nhia no way. No, put the headset on him. I'll tell him."

So I passed the customer headset to Nhia and I looked out the side of the helicopter.

Nhia listen for a few minutes and then he talked a little and listened and talked a little and then he handed the headset back to me. Izzy said we were going in to pick up Nhia's brother and I asked what Nhia had said to change his mind. Izzy said, "I don't know, maybe it was Hmong hocus pocus. Nhia said it was safe and this was about the only chance in the boy's life to get out and its only ten minutes out of our way. I don't know. Nhia's never ever lied to anyone I've ever known. Have you heard of him lying?"

"No." Nhia was a man of his word. He was calculating but absolutely truthful. If he said it was safe, one hundred percent safe, even though this was not that far from China, then I'd believe him. So apparently did my friend Izzy.

We diverted our course and flew more to the west and then north and soon Nhia began pointing out mountains and rivers he knew. He directed us up a long valley and then as he started to give me instructions to pass on to Izzy I took off my headset and gave them to Nhia. He directed the helicopter around a peak and then over a ridgeline and we saw ahead a large mountain village. Down the mountain slightly was an area that had been cleared and some letters staked to the ground. A helipad. The villagers were standing on the mountain between the village and the pad. One individual was standing below the rest near the panel markings. From a distance it looked like he was lecturing the crowd, spread out above him. As we came in closer however I could see that the person was a young boy, looking in our direction holding a cloth bag by the straps in front of him. The bag hung to his knees.

Izzy landed. Nhia jumped out and the young boy came running up through the turbulence of the helicopter and climbed on. Nhia waved to the villagers, got back on the helicopter, tapped Izzy on the shoulder and helped the boy buckle his safety belt.

Sitting beside me I could feel the energy and excitement in the cleanly scrubbed, neatly dressed youngster. Ignoring me his eyes roamed over the cockpit dash, up to the top of the helicopter, out the sides, at the headsets, the automatic rifles, my boots. I put the head set on him and he listened looking straight ahead.

We landed in Long Tieng about nightfall. While Izzy refueled, Nhia and I walked off to the side of the ramp, the boy trailed behind. Nhia said his brother's name was Pao Vang. He had never flown in a helicopter before, never seen television, never ridden in a car or Jeep, never talked on a telephone, slept on a mattress, used an indoor toilet or eaten with a knife or fork. But he is a smart kid, Nhia, said and he will learn fast and he will help around the house. "OK Pao Vang," I said turning to the boy, "you are our boarder. I'll get you back up here educated and toilet trained. But by the by, Nhia, how did your brother know exactly when we were coming?" Nhia said, "He's been waiting for days."

Behind us Izzy cranked and Pao Vang and I got back on the helicopter and we took off, Nhia watching us leave, holding my AK-47.

I liked flying at night. Izzy and I continued talking. We passed high over the mountains, then the dam - the Vientiane reservoir - and finally over the rice fields of the Mekong River valley. In the distance I could see the dim lights of the city.

Beside me Pao Vang was looking around. He did not miss any movement, any flash of light, any sound. His head was in constant motion.

Landing at Poppa Chu's, Pao Vang and I went out back and got a taxi. There in the back seat beside me, Pao Vang continue to swivel his head toward anything that moved. He was suddenly afraid when he saw traffic coming in our direction. And when we stopped at one of the few stop signs in town, he couldn't understand and he knitted his brow. He looked in the different shops as we passed, sometimes turning to look out the rear window.

We got out of the taxi near the front gate at the house and I rung the bell as the guard let us in, Brenda and the kids came running out. They stopped when they saw Pao Vang.

Brenda said she told me not to bring back any live thing. I said this boy was Nhia's brother and he was going to live with us while he learned English.

Walking in the house he almost tiptoed, not wanting to scratch the floor. He looked at the lights, at the windows, at the couches and chairs. Mim talked to him in Thai and he didn't understand. The maid came in and spoke to him in Lao and he didn't answer right away; we didn't think he understood. He kept looking around and then very quietly he said something. The maid smiled and said he was thirsty. She lead him out but in a few minutes he was back looking around. Joe walked up and hit him in the knee with his fist and he smiled and they began to wrestle.

We had been amazed at our kids' discovery of household things that we had taken for granted. We were equally amazed at Pao Vang as he came across the everyday things around us, one by one. The air conditioner. The refrigerator. The telephone. How can sound go so far in "No Time?" he asked the maid.

Pao Vang had an incredible curiosity. Within the four days I had for my home visit he knew where everything was.

I could come in and say, "Pao Vang where are the scissors," making a scissors gesture with two fingers. And Pao Vang would lead me to our bedroom, over to the dresser, down two drawers, under Brenda's underwear, in the back, in a small bag. If that wasn't the pair I was looking for he would take me outside and show me hedge clippers or pliers or back inside he'd hand me staplers or Mim's hair clasp. If I did not stop him he would show me everything in our house that might have resembled something like two fingers scissoring together.

Brenda had given me a Leica camera for my thirtieth birthday and I took photos around town, throwing the exposed film cartridges in a bowl in my study. When a dozen or so cartridges collected I would take them to a local developer.

After Pao Vang had been at our house for three or four months I told him I would take him back to Long Tieng for a visit the next time I came home. Soon thereafter I noticed that the number of cartridges in the bowl increased. There were four or five cartridges one time when I looked and then the next day there were eight or nine.

I found when I had the film developed that the extra cartridges belonged to Pao Vang, who had learned how to use the camera from watching me - although I could not fathom how he figured out the F stops, shutter speed and focus. He had taken photos for his return upcountry. He held the camera out at arm's length and took several pictures of himself. And he used mirrors in most of the rooms to show himself lounging around. He had photos of the telephone lines coming into the house and the toilets and the kitchen and the opened refrigerator, the television set from all angles.

****

411

James E. Parker, Jr.

Back upcountry my first road watch patrol ran into North Vietnamese north of the PDJ and turned back. The second patrol also encountered North Vietnamese and they scattered, individually returning to LS 15. The third patrol was led by the Hmong who was painfully slow in understanding what I wanted. His mission was certainly not going to be successful. His men sorta gazed around most of the time. Nobody talked much in his group. You'd tell them to go over there and wait and they'd go over there and fall asleep.

When they were dispatched they moved north, through the North Vietnamese controlled area and eventually to a hill overlooking Ban Ban where they set up an observation post. They reported clearly on activities on the road below them ... exactly like I had asked them. Their beacon was on at precisely twelve o'clock and went off precisely at one o'clock.

Their information was invaluable.

They eventually ran out of supplies and had to return overland to LS 15.

On the way they were caught in a B-52 strike.

It was difficult to fix blame. They were my patrol. I coordinated on their route. I was around when Dutch made up the Arclight strikes. I had to take responsibility. Hog and Zack made no comments to me about the incident, though Hog's hard look when I told him clearly indicated his reproach. It was the most severe reprimand I was ever to receive from Hog.

I knew the B-52 bombardment hit exactly on top of the patrol. I had taken a reading of their position not long before the afternoon bombing.

I told Zack that maybe all the patrol members were not killed, that some could have made it through the bombing. I asked Air Ops for a twin engine Cessna so that I could go up and post over the area as I tried to make contact with the remnants of my patrol. I sat beside the pilot and Nhia was in the back with the radios, but we were silent as we flew north, fearing the worst...that we would get no response.

When we got over the area north of the PDJ we were very high and we began flying in a wide circle. Nhia called for the patrol.

They came on immediately. All was well. They had no casualties.

What about the bombing the previous day? Weren't there a lot of bombs going off?

Yes, thank you.

Thank you?

Yes, there were enemy all around and the bombs made them go away and hide. The Air Force did a very good job. Bombs landed very close but we weren't hurt. We all gathered close together and we turned on the beacon and put it over our heads. Good beacon. It worked perfectly. We are OK. Thank you.

Thank you Lord.

--THIRTY-FOUR--
Lao Golf

The day the first F-111 came over the Mekong River from Thailand and entered MR II, Glassman was manning the radio.

"Red Dog Control, this is Show Boat 42," the pilot said.

"Roger, Show Boat 42, this is Red Dog Control," Glassman said as he turned and smiled at most of the Sky officers who had gathered to watch this inaugural contact.

"Do you have a divert?" asked the pilot in accordance with the communication SOP. He was in fact asking if Glassman had a new target for him to go to or was he free to hit the target provided to him before the mission by the 7th AF targeting staff in Saigon.

"No divert," Glassman said and the F-111 pilot said "Roger," indicating he was continuing to his primary target.

Within fifteen minutes we heard, "Red Dog this is Show Boat 42, I am RTB [Return to Base]. Good afternoon."

There was a lull in action for the first few days the F-111 were on the scene and there were no diverts. The conversations remained cryptic and correct between the different F-111 pilots and the Hmong radio operators although a noticeable warmness seeped into the communications. It was the first opportunity the pilots had to deal with the Hmong and it must have personalized their work, put them in contact with the ground fighting force working with the CIA. With mountain men. Guerrillas.

For the Hmong in Red Dog Control it was a recurring highlight of their life to actually communicate, in English, with Americans flying up in the heavens. America space explorations had captured the imagination of the Hmong at Long Tieng. For the talkers assigned to communicate with the F-111 in Red Dog Control, it was as if they, in their small way, played a part in the space game, talking to almost astronauts. They looked forward to their short conversations with the pilots almost every waking minute before they came to work. It was amazing to me how proud these Hmong could be over so simple an act. And they communicated that enthusiasm in their transmissions - the pilots knew that on the ground end was someone who really appreciated him and his mission.

****

The protracted, celebrated "peace" talks in Paris produced a cease-fire in Vietnam on January 28, 1973. Shortly thereafter, February 21, peace agreements were signed in Laos. This peace lasted two days. On February 23 USAF bombing was renewed because the Vietnamese showed no intentions of quitting the fighting in Laos. For us the two day peace was something that went bump in the night. We saw the Lao peace accords as an incidental consequence of the talks on ending the war in South Vietnam, not relevant, or enforceable, upcountry. Plus, in the absence of media coverage, no one in particular cared in the United States.

****

The GMs from Savannakhet remained in the valley as reserves, although the Vietnamese did not mount sustained attacks on Skyline. Our GMs were going further and further out on the PDJ and down the river valley without contact.

Shortly before the cease-fire the Bear, from Savannakhet, and I were in Air Ops one afternoon, talking with Greek. It was the rainy season. The weather was bad and Air America was having trouble getting around. The skies over the valley had just opened up and Bear was going up with me to recon the area to the north.

From the Air Force guard frequency on one of Greek's radios, we heard a "MAYDAY, MAYDAY." A very frightened pilot gave four digit coordinates for his location and said he was bailing out.

A Twin Pack had just shut down on the ramp and the pilots were walking across to Air Ops.

Bear and I were out the door running in their direction by the time the U.S. Air Force pilot had finished his MAYDAY signal.

I caught the Air America pilot by his arm and said MAYDAY. He and his co-pilot turned and caught up with Bear and I as we reached his helicopter.

He was cranked and rolling within seconds. We got up in

the air and the pilot called around to get fixes on other helicopters working the area. There were none anywhere close to the downed Air Force pilot who was somewhere east of us.

We were monitoring the guard frequency. The Air Force pilot came on and said he was on the ground, using his handheld survival radio. He had heard people in the distance and he was running up to the top of a nearby peak to hide.

Once activated the survival radio emitted a beacon signal. The Air America pilot slowly turned the helicopter from northeast to east to southeast. He had a directional antenna in the nose and we headed where the beacon signal was the strongest. The closer we got the stronger the signal and the easier to home.

The Air Force radio platform was alive on other freqs getting all planes in the theater heading toward the downed pilot who had been on a rescue mission over North Vietnam and was heading back to Thailand. The planes he was with were low on fuel and had to continue going south. Other planes were in the air, however, and were going all-out to assist in the rescue.

We were the closest and the platform told us to go in. The Bear and I chambered rounds in our rifles. The memory of the unsuccessful attempted rescue of the Raven on the PDJ and Skip's death were still very clear in my mind.

The downed pilot came back up on guard in a low whisper saying people were on the trail below him. Dozens of men. He had a pistol and said he was going to try to hold them off until we got to him.

The Air America pilot told him we were probably close. He asked if the pilot could hear the helicopter.

"YES, YES," he said, no longer whispering, "I HEAR YOU."

Unknown to the pilot he had landed near a friendly settlement, one I had visited often. The people he heard were friendly Hmong villagers who were probably excited about some man dropping out of the clouds in a parachute.

"I SEE YOU, I SEE YOU, COME ON THIS WAY AT YOUR TWO O'CLOCK. I'M AT THE TOP OF THE HILL. I'LL STAND BESIDE THE BIG ROCK, DO YOU SEE THE BIG ROCK. BE CAREFUL THE PEOPLE ARE ON THE OTHER SIDE OF THE HILL."

The Air America pilot said, "Roger, You're going to be OK. I see the rock. Wave your panel. OK good work my friend. I see you."

415

As we approached, Bear and I unloaded our rifles. I could see the villagers crowded near the base of the hill. Some were pointing up to the top where the pilot was hiding behind a large boulder. They had stretched out his parachute and were examining it. Some men had righted the ejection seat, which I suspected would be in the headman's hut that evening.

When we got overhead the rock, the flight mechanic dropped a line from the helicopter that had a large metal ball on the bottom which acted like a sinker.

The line dropped to the pilot, he got on the ball and was hauled back up to the helicopter which had turned and was heading back to Long Tieng.

Bear and I helped get the pilot inside.

He was a very grateful, very happy individual. He said he became disoriented after going through a rain cloud, developed vertigo and had possibly turned upside down. He had ejected because he was afraid he was going to run into a mountain.

He did not listen when we said that the village was friendly. To him, he had punched out over Laos, not far from China and North Vietnam and had been rescued. He probably didn't think there were any friendlies at all in the country.

This was reinforced when the Air Force rescue team arrived in the valley later in the day to pick him up. Jets made passes over the valley as if to tell everyone to keep their heads down. Two Jolly Green Giant rescue helicopters landed in the middle of the runway, with gunners standing by their positions, fingers on their triggers.

Hmong hid along the runway. They were scared, concerned that if anyone looked threatening at the U.S. Air Force helicopters they would have been shot. Hell this was our home, our work place. They acted like they had landed in the middle of the valley of the shadow of death, for Christ sake. We were going to invite them in for a cup of coffee but they weren't smiling and they didn't leave their guns. Not very friendly guests. One of the officers from the Sky admin staff took the pilot down to the back of one of the Jolly Green Giants by himself. No case officer wanted to go out in front of those guns. Those people were dangerous.

When the Jolly Greens took off, the jets made one last pass before disappearing.

Boy oh boy, we said that night at the bar, that U.S. Air Force is tough. Comes from being so far up in the air away from the things on the ground. Don't know the good guys from the bad. We told the Ravens that we wondered what they had been telling their Air Force brothers to make them so hostile acting.

****

Jerry Conners, the Air America base manager at LS 20A, was married to one of the most beautiful women in the world, a Thai lady named Prow. She and Brenda struck up a friendship in Vientiane and Jerry and I got along famously upcountry. Jerry played poker, and I liked my poker playing friends. He and I eventually arranged our Vientiane time together so that he and Prow and Brenda and I could spend time together. On one trip down to Vientiane Jerry said that although he had lived in Laos for several years that he had just heard about a golf course some five miles out of town toward Nong Khai. It was a local operation but a golf course was a golf course. He asked if I wanted to join him in a round of golf. Sure I said, I had a set of clubs at the house so we made arrangements for him to pick me up the following morning. This is just like they do it back home, we agreed. Get some time off. Go play golf.

The next morning Brenda left early with the kids to attend a function at the American school. I waited for Jerry to drive up.

He arrived late. In the back of a samlor, a three-wheel bicycle with a hooded rear seat, the local taxi. He had forgotten to tell his beautiful wife that he needed the car and she had taken off somewhere, so it was samlors or nothing. His clubs were on the seat beside him and he had another samlor waiting to take me and my clubs.

"Five miles in a samlor?" I asked.

"Sure," he said," it's level and we ain't peddling."

And that's the way we went to the golf course. Not necessarily the way it might have been done back home, but close.

The golf course was not like anything back home though. Not close.

It was an open rice field. The only way we knew it was the golf course was because the samlor drivers said it was. There were in fact sticks in the ground scattered randomly around with rags tied to the tops. There was a thatched roof hut off to the side near a shade tree, the pro shop we assumed, but no one was around. We walked out to the closest stick and found that, sure enough, it was sitting in a hole the size of a beer can. We were on the golf course.

We walked back near the pro shop, hired our samlor drivers to be our caddies, helped them on with the golf bags, selected a tee area for the first hole, selected a hole to shoot to, and teed off.

417

James E. Parker, Jr.

There were thirteen sticks in holes in that field, so we had to plot our own course, using some of the holes several times, though all the approaches were different. Since it was a make-your-own course, we made our own rules. If a drive landed nearer a different flag from the one we were playing to, you could play to the nearer flag with a one stroke penalty. Also if you caught the caddy of the other player moving the other player's ball you got a one stroke bonus and the right to hit the other player's ball away from the flag. The other player would have to play it from there. For the first violation you got to hit his ball with a nine iron. For the fifth violation you got to hit it with a driver.

Also we made up our own pars. One hole was a par eight and we had several par sevens. One was a hundred yard par seven.

And we both bogeyed it. Jerry, because I caught his caddy walking toward the flag with Jerry's ball between his toes and I got to give it a penalty hit across the field with my four iron. And I bogeyed it because when I got to the flag we found it was just a stick stuck in a grassy part of the field. There was no beer can size hole. So Jerry pulled the stick out - which left a small hole in the ground - and I had to putt until I got my ball to rest on top of that tiny hole.

We finally finished our round of golf and returned home in the samlors, peddled by our caddies.

It was almost like playing golf back home. Only different. I played par golf that day, the only time in my life.

****

In the days to come upcountry the Hmong talkers began giving diverts to the F-111s when they arrived in our MR. Working up the divert information for passage was complicated but the talkers did their job well, checking and rechecking their calculations. Passing on the divert information also gave them more opportunity to talk with the pilots, which further enhanced their bond.

We received mixed reporting from the field on the accuracy of the F-111 bombing. Then one day one of our photo interpreters (PIs) in Udorn noticed from some overhead photography that an area supposedly hit the previous day by an F-111 showed no signs of any bombing. We requested that all F-111 missions be held up until we could determine what the problem was, whether this was a one-time miss or if it was happening more often. We heard from one of the Ravens that the F-111 targeting people went crazy that we should challenge them on the accuracy of their planes. They sent up a high level delegation to check our computations, test our talkers and generally get us back in line as happy customers.

These people, uncomfortable in dealing with non-USAF people it seemed to us, especially non-USAF people who did not look particularly military, did not have a friendly attitude. Greek for one, thought they were brassy and he stayed close, smiling when they made eye contact, intent on challenging any unsubstantiated knock on the way we did things in MR II.

At the request of the Air Force delegation Greek ordered two Air America helicopters for an aerial reconnaissance that was to end with the two helicopters hovering two kilometers off to the side of Sam Thong within sight of a suspected 130mm position up the river valley north of Skyline, the coordinates for which were going to be passed as a divert to the next F-111. Greek and Hardnose accompanied the targeting officers. Hog and Clean went up on Skyline in a Jeep to watch the bombing run from ground level.

Everyone was in place before the next F-111 arrived. Everyone heard Glassman divert him to the suspected 130mm position. Per the communication SOP there would be no radio contact with the plane from the time it received the divert information until it had released its ordnance and had turned for home. So the team in the helicopters, including Greek and Hardnose, and Hog and Clean on Skyline, kept their eyes on the target. And waited and waited and waited. Finally Red Dog Control reported that the pilot had signed off and had gone south. He had dropped his bombs.

"Not on any target we can see," Clean said.

Greek could hardly contain himself in the helicopter as the Air Force people squirmed and talked among themselves. They left the valley without comment, intent on getting back to Udorn and Takhli so they could staff out the problem.

****

The F-111s continued to fly in our area, however, but we ensured that their targets were further and further from friendly positions. Then one day when Lumberjack was on duty in the Thai headquarters area on the east end of the valley, a 130mm round landed nearby. Lumberjack thought it was one of the more common DK-82 rounds and began calling around to people on Skyline and up in the air, trying to get counter-battery fire. And another 130mm round came roaring over Skyline and hit near the first.

"Holy shit," Lumberjack yelled. "Somebody get that

419

sumbitch."

An F-111 happened to be en route at the time and he was diverted to the nearest suspected 130mm position and asked to dropped all his bombs: twenty-four five-hundred pounders. And he did.

And another 130mm round landed close to Lumberjack. He was now becoming convinced that the fire was not coming from a DK-82 because the ground shook when the round landed, leaving huge craters in the ground.

More rounds landed as another F-111 reported in. Red Dog Control told him to drop twelve of his 500-pounders at another suspected 130mm site and then come around and drop the remaining twelve bombs on the same site.

The F-111 pilot said, "Roger, Red Dog Control." And then there was silence on the air, until Lumberjack began yelling that another big round had just landed.

Then there was quiet again.

"Tonto," a Thai radio operator in a forward position on Skyline, who had been in the middle of the efforts to fix the muzzle blast of the 130mm gun, suddenly came on the air and began yelling, "YOU GOT IT, YOU GOT IT, YOU GOT IT, I CAN SEE IT, YOU BLEW IT OUT OF ITS HOLE."

The F-111 had hit the 130mm gun dead on, confirmed later by aerial reconnaissance. The gun was laying on its side, reduced to rubble.

Lumberjack joined Zack in praise of the plane thereafter; Hog, Clean, Kayak, Greek and I had less to say.

Chera Pao Moua, the commander of Bouam Long north of the PDJ, the recipient of many of the F-111 sorties while we sorted out their dependability, reported that the F-111s had changed things up where he lived. They delivered. Vang Pao, he said, could keep all his GMs, his 105mm and 155mm howitzers, all his mines and rockets - just give Bouam Long the F-111s.

--THIRTY-FIVE--
Hmong New Year

The Hmong New Year, like Tet in Vietnam and the Chinese New Year, came in February 1973. Because of the peace talks or the

F-111s or whatever reason this February, our forces were not under attack like they had been in years past. Vang Pao wanted the troops in the field to celebrate the New Year in traditional fashion.

The tradition involved killing a water buffalo and dressing it for a New Year's day feast. It was important for the buffalo to be sacrificed where the Hmong lived. It was an integral part of the Hmong belief in the trees and the mountains around them. Where the water buffalo was killed was important in bridging the distance between the Hmong people and their environment.

Hog was the first to learn VP wanted live water buffaloes sent out to all forward Hmong positions. It was one of those cross-cultural propositions that sounds simple in each language but had different meanings. Sky and Air America had plenty of planes and helicopters and VP was sure there was some way to get the live animals out to the different sites. It was important to him, important to the Hmong. It did not appear important to us and we saw no value in heli-lifting live buffaloes. Nice buffaloes steaks in cardboard boxes we could do.

I went with Hog to argue with VP on the matter. Maybe, I suggested, we could rotate some of the men from the different sites back to a special area in the valley where they could kill the buffalos and we'd send the meat out to the sites.

VP said no, the water buffalo had to be butchered out where the men lived and worked. He cocked his head and knitted his brow as if confused about why I didn't understand this.

So we went to Greek and said VP needs these water buffalos move to the field.

"You don't mean live, do you," asked Greek?

"Yea, we sorta do," Hog said.

"A water buffalo is bigger than a Volkswagen, weighs a ton. How are we going to get them to LS 15?" Greek asked.

"That's what Air Operations is supposed to know how to do. That's your job."

"You tell Vang Pao to go stick a water buffalo up his ass. We don't have any livestock facilities on our aircraft."

"Greek." Hog said with a meaningful look.

"Oh shit, Hog, how do we move live water buffalo?" Greek asked rhetorically. "I reckon we have to sling them out."

It didn't work initially. The first water buffalo selected to go out to the site was fitted with a belly harness; a helicopter came in and began dropping the weighted line for someone to attach to the harness. The water buffalo heard the helicopter and took off,

421

dragging three or four Hmong behind him.

Tranquilizers were ordered from Udorn. The next buffalo was doped up for his sling ride. This time the buffalo stood with his head down and allowed the helicopter to pick him up and in time he was delivered to one of my positions near LS 15.

Thereafter for several days, Air America slung out water buffalo to the different forward positions. It was a strange sight standing on the positions watching Air America helicopters coming in with those doped up buffalo. They looked like the Brooks Brothers logo.

I had long since found out the Hmong had better eyes than I did. They had better eyes than I did with binoculars. I would be waiting on a site for a helicopter and the skies would be empty and a Hmong would look in the distance - without squinting - and say "Chopper." And I'd look and not see a thing. And Nhia would say, "Yep, sure is." And I'd take my binoculars and scan the sky and maybe find a speck way in the distance with the binoculars, that maybe was a helicopter, or it could be dirt on the lens.

Once they spotted a helicopter and I got the binoculars and could just make it out, and they said nope it wasn't ours, it wasn't coming our way. And they were right, but it took me another two or three minutes watching the speck to see it moving laterally.

One helicopter arrived on a site I was visiting without its water buffalo, which must have fallen off en route. The kicker got on his stomach and was going to guide the helicopter down so that the animal would have a soft landing and there was no animal at the end of the sling.

The pilot said, "Shit, we had him just a moment ago."

Nope, one of the Hmong said, there wasn't a water buffalo there at least since Sam Thong. Which meant that Hmong had not only seen that helicopter from ten miles out but he had seen he wasn't slinging anything either.

And I believed him.

We often wondered if there were any Hmong along the way who saw that water buffalo fall from the chopper. Why'd Sky send the buffalo that way, they might have asked. Or if they didn't see the helicopter and suddenly a water buffalo dropped out of the sky at their feet they would have said, Damned thing was flying.

Greek's real problem came in getting water buffalo to Bouam Long. It was just too far to sling buffaloes up one at a time. Plus we were deep into the smoky season and it was a constant struggle getting Air America to fly helicopters up over all that haze.

Greek ordered up an Air America Chinook, a large transport helicopter that had a sizeable lift capacity.

A.H. and a case officer from Savannakhet pitched in and worked on getting the buffaloes ready for the flight. A.H. said, "The plan here is to dope these animals until they drop and then lift'um onto pallets with a fork lift, strap'um down and put'um on the Chinook two by two. We can get eight on."

The water buffaloes were led behind air ops where the tranquilizing and palleting was done. By the time the Chinook arrived from Udorn the eight water buffaloes were on the ramp, in neat rows lashed down to their pallets. They looked like they were ready for mailing. Their legs were hog tied, like a rodeo animal, and they were laying on their sides, strapped to the individual pallets with heavy webbing.

A.H. was justly proud of his cargo.

The Air America pilot said he wasn't carrying them to Bouam Long.

The Greek exploded. "You, worthless, scum sucking, over-paid bus driver, what do you mean you ain't carrying these pallets up to Bouam Long?" He took some anti-acid pills as he said this. Air America, Greek thought, often did things to drive him crazy.

"I don't do animal acts," said the pilot. "How long are they tranquilized for? How long they going to lay there peacefully and sleep?"

Greek said, "Hell I don't know, we'll ask A.H. Hey, A.H. how long have you got these cows tranquilizer for? Long enough to get to Bouam Long, right?"

"Yep," said A.H.

"How do you know, A.H.?" asked the pilot.

"Well I've just been doing this air freight of water buffaloes for a week and I know, or I knew before you two started arguing, that there was plenty of time to get to Bouam Long."

"OK," said the pilot, after consultation with his crew, "We will take your cows up to Bouam Long on two conditions. One, I use temporary, emergency chocks at the rear of the rollers (two tracks of rollers ran the length of the inside of the helicopter.) If one of those animals so much as bats his eyebrows, shows any signs that he's coming off Dr. A.H.'s drugs, they're out the back door, all of them. I do not want a half crazy water buffalo loose inside my helicopter flying over clouds near the PDJ. You can understand that can't you, Greek?"

"What's number two?" Greek asked.

James E. Parker, Jr.

"A.H. goes with us."
"Are you crazy," A.H. exclaimed.
"Or you Greek," the pilot said.
"Are you crazy!" the Greek said.
So they sent the guy from Savannakhet.

And halfway to Bouam Long one of the water buffalo blinked, and no one saw it.

And then he blinked again, and no one saw it.

And then the water buffalo must have realized that he was lying down in an unfamiliar place and he wanted to get up and look around. And he tried to get up.

And the crew said, Holy Shit. They removed the chocks from the rear of the roller tracks and the water buffalo continued to struggle on the pallet, kicking more and more violently. The pilot put the nose of the helicopter up in the air, dropping the rear. And the water buffaloes began to go out the back, two at a time. The one buffalo who had begun to struggle was just getting one of his feet out of the pallet webbing when he disappeared.

The North Vietnamese on the ground probably reported, "We were bombed by eight buffaloes today."

****

For himself VP decided to have a large baci at his compound in Long Tieng during the Hmong New Year. He invited the Stick, Hugh Tovar, the Ravens, all Air America and Thai mercenary commanders.

There was a large turnout. Zack brought his wife and son up from Bangkok. They were the last to arrive, coming in over the valley about dusk on a Beach Baron aircraft. The valley was socked in. The pilot circle for several minutes but reached a point quickly because of his low fuel where he either had to punch through and land or head back to Vientiane. On one of his last circles Greek, who was working in Air Ops, noticed a small opening near the east end of the runway and told the pilot he could try and land but it would require some quick turns around a karst to get in and down on the runway. The pilot said he was coming in. The hole in the clouds was closing fast as the pilot guided the small plane down and in around a karst to land first on one wheel and then down on two, hard, and rolled to a stop on the ramp. Hog was there in a Jeep. As Zack's wife got out and got into Hog's Jeep to go to VP's compound she said it was nice of Hog to come down and pick them up. He said slowly, "Hell

424

ma'am, I just came down to watch the crash."

Outside the assembly hall where the baci was held, Hmong girls in their colorful skirts tossed balls back and forth, a traditional courting gesture. If a Hmong boy broke in and starting tossing a ball with one of the girls, it was taken as a very serious public show of affection and marriage often ensued. Inside, Hmong bands with their flutes and drums alternated playing. There were tables of sticky rice and pork and peppers and greens and chicken and water buffalo. On other tables were assorted bottles of liquor and tubs of beer.

And there were good, stout-hearted men around. Thai, Hmong, American.

At one point, Hog, Zack, the Stick and Hugh Tovar were standing in a group. From across the room I thought that I had never worked for better men. They had extraordinary character, unknown to the outside world and to the American public which they served so well.

The group broke up and Zack came over to where I was standing with some Air America people. One of the pilots, who had flown up just for the baci, was well ahead of everyone else in drinks.

I said that Hugh Tovar was a fine man, a man of culture and education. "Look at his hair," I said, motioning over to Hugh. "I have seen that man get off a helicopter going full torq and it didn't mess up his hair. Didn't put a hair out of place. That's class."

The Air America pilot said, "It'svsa a hairpiece, that's why it looks soo neat." He slurred his words.

"No it isn't," said Zack. "I don't know a lot, but I know for sure that Hugh Tovar doesn't wear a hair piece."

The Air America pilot took a few steps back and looked wide-eyed at Zack. "You don't believe me, you don't believe me, you don't believe me, you don't believe me."

"No," Zack said, smiling.

"I'll prove it tooo you," the pilot said, still slurring his words. He bent over and put his Mekong drink on the floor and dusted off his hands. Walking in a staggered line across the floor, he went up to the circle of men that Hugh had just joined - we thought to look very closely at the station chief's hair from the rear.

But he moved beside the man standing to Hugh's left and turned back to us to give us a big, exaggerated wink before turning back to the circle of men as if he was interested in what was being said. Slowly he began to snake his right hand up behind the man standing next to Hugh.

When his hand got about shoulder high he leaned back so

that he could see Hugh from the rear and then he quickly reached up and grabbed his hair.

The pilot may have honestly expected to come away with a hairpiece, but Hugh had a full head of hair and the pilot almost yanked him backwards to the floor. As Hugh tried to get his balance, the pilot continued to shake him by his hair. Hugh said, "Ouch, God Damnit," and he slapped the pilot's hand away.

THIRTY-SIX
Shadow War Politics

Soon after the baci we got the first message about BDA.

BDA, bomb damage assessment. An Air Force term. They wanted to know how effective their F-111s had been. They needed BDA. The cable demanded BDA.

Previously when we received bureaucratic tasking upcountry, someone got the word to the Stick in Udorn and the base stepped in and either did it themselves or told the requester to go away.

This time the Stick said he couldn't help.

We were caught in the middle of an Air Force situation - we had been penetrated by the USAF and were part of their equation now. The Air Force office in Vientiane maybe resented our direct targeting of their planes. The F-111s program did in fact obfuscate the need for so many Air Force bureaucrats in Vientiane so proprietary interests were involved. For a bureaucrat, that is a life-and-death proposition. These detractors in Vientiane said the F-111 commitment to MR II was a misuse of Air Force resources. Our BDA was necessary to determine their cost effectiveness.

But we didn't have BDA on all the strikes. We had sent the 474th Tactical Fighter Wing some damaged small-arms weapons from an air attack and Zack had helped Vang Pao write a letter of appreciation that included the phrase "Whispering Death," a transliteration of the North Vietnamese term for the F-111s. We also knew the North Vietnamese were extremely hesitant about any massing of their forces and we were not being pressed on Skyline, or on any of our other positions like we had in years past. That was prima facie BDA evidence to us.

But the Air Force brass in Washington, possibly prompted

by the Air Force bureaucrats in Vientiane, continued to hound us for more detailed reporting.

We had necessarily diverted the planes to targets at times out of eye sight of the line troops out of reach of guerrilla patrols. We had no way to assess the bomb damage other than to make aerial reconnaissance, which we did, but we were flying over old targets, over enemy territory and it was dangerous and began to take up all our time. Especially mine. I was doing most of the field BDA work.

And the cables kept coming asking for more BDA. We responded to most, but they kept coming. It was like an insatiable animal. BDA for the F-111s was taking over our lives.

Finally we received a cable saying the Air Force had to go before a hostile U.S. Senate in a few days to justify spending a significant part of their budget on the F-111s, presently in use in our region. We were on the point. Give them BDA.

We had been captured and mastered by our tools.

We renewed our field work and finally collected in the main room of the headquarters bunker of Long Tieng to write the definitive BDA cable.

Two weeks later our words were delivered by U.S. Air Force brass before the Armed Forces Committee of the Senate. We read them word for word in the "Stars and Stripes," the military newspaper we received several days late.

Times were changing. First the Joint Chief of Staff and now the U.S. Senate was getting involved in our work. It was being reported in international newspapers. MR II had become a topic in the Washington political scene and we knew in Long Tieng that the end of our secret war was near.

Resigned to our fate, we still marveled at the magical relationship between the Hmong talkers at Red Dog Control and the F-111 pilots. They never met. They only used 150 odd words in English total, but they communicated volumes. The mountain men and the astronauts. And as Cher Pao Moua said, the F-111s were worth everything else we had, put together. Some felt if the war had gone on the 474th Tactical Fighter Wing fighter wing would have destroyed every sizable NVA unit in MR II. However Sky would certainly have lost its autonomy to run the war and we would have had to engage in bureaucratic battles, which we were not experienced in. The F-111s came with a lot of baggage.

It was better with just the troops. Our guys against their guys. Commandos lining up on some dirt strip in the rain in the middle of the night with their helmets tied down with old sheets, going off to jump in to a little opening next to the PDJ, if they could find it. Getting live buffaloes out to forward positions and brow beating commanders to get their men out, patrolling, engaging the enemy. Firing our 105mm howitzers using strings and sticks for sighting. Moving our GMs out to high ground, enticing the enemy to attack. It was what Hog, Clean, Kayak, Greek and I knew about. Zack was the only visionary in the group.

****

One night about this time we received word that a Thai had been severely wounded in an accident and would certainly die if he were not evacuated before morning. Al Cates, the senior pilot in the valley that night, volunteered his Twin Pack crew to go out on the evacuation. Charlie Basham was his first officer. It was a foggy night; as the helicopter was trying to make its way into the site, it crashed. The helicopter came to rest between the Thai and North Vietnamese positions.

Cates came on his radio immediately and relayed back that no one was hurt, though the chopper was disabled, and that they would stay near the helicopter until morning.

Lumberjack contacted the Thais at one of the nearest friendly positions and told them to go down to the crash site - they could see the helicopter on the ground even in the fog - but not to try to make contact with the Air America crew until daylight. They were to surround the site to ensure that the North Vietnamese did not sneak in and take the crew prisoners.

Cates' radio stopped working and they were cut off, under the fog. He did not know that friendly Thais were coming down to cordon off the area. But they heard the sounds of people surrounding them and they expect to be attacked at any minute.

The co-pilot, Charlie Basham, was a large man - 285, 290 pounds. He liked to say he was so fat that in a small helicopter with another large man as pilot they'd be so heavy that the only thing they'd be able to carry would be "verbal messages." He sat beside Cates, leaning against their crashed helicopter, listening to the noises around them, holding his handgun, shivering, scared. In getting out of the plane he had lost his watch and at one point he asked Cates, "What time is it?"

Cates said, "One a.m."

After what seemed like four hours he asked Cates again, "What time is it?"

The Vietnam War Its Ownself

Cates said, "Five after."

****

In Vientiane Brenda normally had the kids up eating breakfast in the morning before seven. One morning Joseph heard a plane overhead as he was finishing. He yelled and ran outside through a door that lead off the dining room. Brenda sent Mim back to her bedroom to change clothes and followed Joseph outside.

Mim was in her second year of kindergarten by this time. The wives in the area alternated in taking the neighborhood kids across town to the American school in the Embassy housing compound. The lady driving this day lived a couple of blocks away.

In the back Brenda and Joseph sat on the stairs and watched three bombers making practice runs near the Chainimo Army Garrison across a field behind the house. They had a front row seat and could see the planes dive down, come up, circle around and dive again. Finally the planes dropped some bombs and Joseph clapped his hands as the planes came around and headed back to the airport. Joseph jumped up and down waving as the planes passed low over the house.

Mim came out with the maid who had helped her dress. Brenda took her by the hand to the car and with Joseph standing on the floor in the back, looking out between the front two seats - his favorite riding position - they drove to the neighbor's house.

Brenda blew her horn when she got to the front gate, but the guard was not around. Strange.

She got out and opened the gate herself and drove in.

The lady came running out, screaming, "BRENDA, BRENDA, BRENDA, GET INSIDE THE HOUSE, GET YOUR CHILDREN, GET INSIDE THE HOUSE, HURRY, HURRY. THERE'S A COUP."

Brenda, appropriately concerned, scurried Mim and Joseph inside, joining the woman and others under the dining room table. Kids, maids, guards, everyone. The lady tried to squeeze Brenda, Mim and Joseph under - though in truth there were parts of people sticking out.

In a pile, under the table, the woman explained that they were bombing the army camp behind our house. She said she was worried that our house was in the line of fire. She was so thankful Brenda and the kids were safe.

A coup, asked Brenda? Real bombs? Behind our house?

429

James E. Parker, Jr.

****

Upcountry we began to plan our next dry season offensive but were not surprised to receive messages from Washington to stand down, to hold our own, and put aside plans to go on the attack. Visitors from Washington speculated that our war was over. Vietnam had been conceded, they said. There was no longer a will to fight or to win there. A popular phrase was, "Let the Vietnamese fight their own war." "Vietnamization" was in fact the U.S. government's fig-leaf means of extricating itself from South Vietnam. And if the United States pulled out of the fight to protect South Vietnam, there was no chance we would be allowed to continue fighting in Laos. Our mission was in support of overall U.S. objectives in Vietnam. The U.S. government did not come to this part of the world to protect Laos.

The morning of 22 February 1973 the last F-111 "crossed the river" into Laos, delivered its ordinance and was gone.

All was quiet in MR II. The war had been going on for a long time. And now it was quiet.

****

About this time in Vientiane, my wife faced the certain prospects that a family member would die, for her a far more serious matter than a cease-fire and peace negotiations.

Most American families in Vientiane had pets. We had Harry, our lucky mongrel dog from Chapel Hill, who was an adjunct to Brenda's everyday life. He slept on the foot of the bed or on the floor at Brenda's side. During the day he followed her around from room to room, sitting alertly at her feet when people came to visit, turning occasionally to look in her eyes when she laughed or called out to one of the children.

All the pets in Laos lived under the threat of heartworms, a disease prevalent in the tropics. Transmitted by mosquitos, heart worms entered the blood system and traveled to the heart where they set up housekeeping, eating at the muscles until there was nothing left, and the heart burst and the animal died. Heartworms were a terminal condition.

A veterinarian came up to Vientiane every two months, took blood samples of pets had them tested in Udorn. On return trips he always seemed to report on one, sometimes two, heartworms cases.

Sometimes the vet returned to find out that the animals had died in the interim. There was nothing that could be done for those that were still alive. He often euthanized the animal rather than to leave it to die gradually, painfully with the owner.

The gym of the American school was used for the vet's clinics. Some of the wives who arrived early would find out which of the pets had tested positive for heartworms. If they knew the person some would, out of a macabre sense of theater, wait until the owner came in to receive the bad news.

Brenda came in the gym during the April visit with Harry and accompanied by Mim, who she had just picked up at kindergarten. She noticed a group of women standing off to the side. She waved as she went up to the young doctor, greeting him warmly, saying that Harry was in for his blood test results.

The Vet looked her in the eye and said Harry had tested positive for heart worms the last time he had come up. Positive sounded good to Brenda and she said as much, asking the Vet where he wanted to take Harry's blood this time.

"You don't understand," he said, "Harry has heartworms. I'm sorry."

Brenda stood very still for a moment, turned and looked at the women standing nearby, suddenly aware of what was going on. Then she turned back to the doctor and she was angry.

And she started crying, demanding that the doctor do something. He said there was nothing he could do. She said, "Please do something. SOMETHING. SOMETHING."

And her balled-up fist were pumping and she said, "YOU WILL DO SOMETHING. SORRY IS NOT ENOUGH."

My wife had come a long way from North Carolina. She had not liked the Orient when she first arrived, but it had been very good to her, and she was comfortable, happy. She had two children she loved very much. A good home, friends, a husband who enjoyed his work.

She had learned to do for herself when I was away, which was most of the time. She thrived in the Lao culture. She was not easily intimidated or put off. She was not afraid of noises in the night. She could look after herself and her loved ones like a pioneer woman.

This dog, who was looking up at her as she raged, was very precious to her and she was not going gently into that quiet night suggested by the vet. She did not consider accepting this young doctor's decision that her dog was going to die. He did not

431

understand that he had to do something, so she continued to say loudly, "DO SOMETHING. DO NOT TOUCH ME. DO SOMETHING." She was crying but her voice was strong. Her eyes, through her tears, were intense and angry. She was breathing hard; she looked like she was going to hit the man.

And she did not look like she was going away.

The vet said, "The only thing that can be done is to give the animal strychnine. But it has almost no chance of success. You try to kill the worms in the heart without killing the animal. It's a fine line. Hair thin. I don't know when it has ever been successful."

"GIVE ME THE MEDICINE," Brenda said quickly, loudly.

The doctor gave her seven pills, taken from a valise he carried. He said, "Give the dog one pill a day and then pray. If he begins to vomit, you have to stop, because he will discharge enough poison to kill other animals. You have to promise me if he upchucks that you will stop, accept his fate."

"And," he said, "you have to realize that there is almost no chance that it will be successful, that you might be giving him enough poison to kill him. Or that he will go through all this, and the heartworms won't die."

Brenda had not stopped crying. She had understood everything that had been said.

She drove home with her dog, her daughter and those seven pills. That night she gave Harry pill number one.

The next day she gave him pill number two and day three Harry was sick. He was in pain. His eyes were not clear and he wobbled when he tried to walk. Brenda helped him get about and she cried.

I had just left for upcountry and I did not know what she was going through.

The next day Harry was so sick he could hardly get up and he fouled the rug by Brenda's bed. The next day, day five, he vomited. Brenda held him and told him not to do that, please don't do that.

She had promised to stop the medication if he couldn't take it anymore, but she didn't. She gave him his sixth and his seventh pill. Harry laid quietly, breathing irregularly.

There was no change on the eighth day when I returned from up country. The next day he was up and moving around.

When the vet came back in two months Harry was his old self and he tested negative for heartworms.

Brenda said she knew it would turn out that way. Harry's

magic. He's a good dog and he's lucky.

You're a pioneer woman, I said, feeling very proud of my wife.

"Feel happy about Harry," she said, "don't think about me."

****

The Laos cease-fire settlement finally took effect and eventually allowed for Pathet Lao administrators to come to Vientiane and assist in running the country. Pathet Lao military forces - host to our North Vietnamese enemy for so many years - would also be garrisoned in the capital.

It was a strange sight to see those former enemy soldiers standing on the street corners of Vientiane when I came in from the valley.

We had been so intent on keeping them out, to protect the local government. That was our mission. I remembered Ambassador Godley standing in front of us saying it was important to hold Skyline, to stop the Pathet Lao and the North Vietnamese from threatening Vientiane. He invoked the name of the president, spoke about the good our efforts could mean to the overall U.S. position in this part of the world. Stop the Communist from moving south, he said. And here they were. It was hard to understand, how we could have worked so hard, have been so successful and yet loose the country to the politicians. It was like the referees had decided the game.

It was approaching June, and the summer rotation was upon us again. Kayak, Bamboo and Dutch left as did many of the support people. They were not replaced. Zack, Hog, Clean and I, plus administrative officers, were left to work with the Hmong. Most of the Thai mercenaries and their Sky advisers were sent south. We went from thirty eight CIA officers of all stripes in MR II to eight.

The war was over and the tough, resilient, Hmong fighters who had supported American objectives for so many years - had been in our employ for so long - were unsure about their future. They needed schools now and hospitals and more chicken farms. Industry to generate cash. They needed alternatives to opium farming. We could make a difference, Zack, Hog, Clean and myself. We began looking at sites for the different projects. Our daily routine changed from war mongering to social work.

Hugh Tovar departed Vientiane, replaced by Dan A., a well-known manager in the CIA East Asia Division. He had a reputation for being an effective station chief at his other postings, but he was ruthless in his dealings with subordinates. There were stories about agent operatives brought to tears by the man. He loved to intimidate according to the rumors that preceded him, and he had no compassion for the feelings of those around him.

That did not bother us. What concerned us upcountry was that Hugh Tovar, who knew the sacrifices the Hmong had made, was leaving and a man who had no sweat equity with the program was going to be in charge. At the eleventh hour a new boss.

It didn't seem fair, but there wasn't anything that we could do about it.

In late July we received a message from Vientiane, which was replacing Udorn as our principal correspondent. The message said that we were to facilitate the intent of the cease-fire by disarming the Hmong.

This was ludicrous. The Hmong were not going to give up their weapons; they would have been slaughtered. But there again there was no need to consider what would happen to them if someone took their guns, because they would not consider giving them up. They would have disappeared into the hills first. They were a primitive society. The Hmong were not going to give anyone their weapons, not to Sky, not to anyone.

Zack wrote a message back saying as much.

Soon another message came up from Vientiane asking us to provide a timetable of departure for everyone in the valley, except for Hog and a support officer, who would be staying. Everyone else would leave. Vientiane station wanted to know when.

We got together and wrote a cable about chicken farms and schools and hospitals and why we were needed to assist the Hmong during this transition period.

The next cable did not mention our response. It asked for a timetable by the end of the week.

Cold hearted, insensitive bureaucrat, we thought. Vintage Dan A.

We didn't respond.

On Monday we received a blistering message saying that we were to provide to the chief of station personally a list of our duties and the earliest dates we could leave.

We sent a message back respectively talking about chicken farms and hospitals and schools.

Dan A. flew up the next day.

This business about our departure and our moral

responsibilities to the Hmong were not the only items in which we were in dialogue with Vientiane, Udorn and our headquarters. We were involved in a variety of other activities: dismantling equipment, drawing boundaries on areas of Hmong control, wrapping up papers on subjects of intelligence interest. The Chief of Station Dan A. ostensibly was coming up to discuss a host of issues. But we knew the main reason for his visit was to discuss our departure and our concerns about the chicken farms.

This was good the small group of us said that night in the almost deserted bar. We were sure Dan A. was the problem. Hugh Tovar would have understood. We have the chance to win over the new man when he got to the valley, educate him on the long history of the Hmong's close work with the Agency, sensitize him to our residual obligations.

He was coming to us, which was a manly way to handle this. But we had home field advantage and we had him outnumbered.

Hog, Clean and I, with the Sky officers working with the Thais, were in the main room of the headquarters bunker when Dan A. came walking in the next morning. Zack, who had met him on the ramp, made the introductions.

He did not make much of an initial impact. He was slight, pale and mousey looking, someone who wouldn't get a second glance on the street. The altitude was having its effect and he was breathing hard. He was dressed like a city dweller, like he belonged behind a desk somewhere. Who did indoor work. Not the type individual to take on the Long Tieng garrison.

He began by saying that we had done a good job. Few people knew how well. However he said it was expected. If we had not done a good job, we would have been replaced with people who could.

His mousey looks belied his tough language, the firmness in his voice.

The war is over up here, he went on to say. Your job is done. Time to get on with other things. It's like digging a ditch, he said. When you're finished, you put down your shovels and you go home or to another job.

Put down your Hmong. Go home.

They have been well cared for these many years they worked for us. They can look after themselves now. Our job is finished here.

You are public servants, employed by the CIA - but you work for the American people - and you have a position of trust. You

435

cannot afford to have divided loyalties. When there is some question about your loyalties, it's time to stop, step back and have someone remind you of your obligations.

You've gone native, some of you. You smell bad. You think your opinions are the ones appropriate here. You're a little lost in the forest, boys. No one forced the Hmong to fight for us. This is their homeland. We've helped them defend it all these many years. Our job's over and we have to go. They got along without us for eons, they'll survive. There are professionals in other organizations who know more about chicken farms and schools and hospitals than you ever will, who are itching to get up here. Leave your schools and chicken farms and hospital building to them. The Hmong will be OK. Go on to your next job.

Anyone got any doubts on this, any questions?

No one did. Clean left and I left in the fall. Zack left the next summer. Only Hog remained.

****

Some of what's been written about the "Secret War" emphasizes hellish U.S. bombing in the countryside, often comparing it to tonnage dropped in Europe during World War II. USAF General Curtis LeMay famously said that in Southeast Asia, "We ought to bomb 'um back to the stone age." Sounds right, but doesn't fit. USAF bombing of the PDJ region during the heavy fighting period from the summer of 1970 to the summer of 1972 was only a small fraction of the upwards to 8 million tons dropped in all Southeast Asia. And as for the bombing during the Battle for Skyline, it was very focused.

USAF, Navy and Marine TacAir actions shouldn't be taken out of context, anyway. North Vietnamese invaded Laos and the bombing was in reaction to that.

There should be no mention of U.S. bombing in northeast Laos without first some acknowledgment of the North Vietnamese military incursion into the Hmong heartland.

Thousands of people were killed in the Lao war. Yet it was a time and a place where millions were killed in China, Korea, Vietnam and Cambodia.

Cost? Senator Stuart Symington, chairman of the Senate Armed Services and Foreign Relations Committee, observed that the CIA's annual budget in Laos was approximately what the U.S. military spent per day in Vietnam.

For the Hmong, winning the battle for Skyline – ultimately winning the military fight for Laos - was a testimony to their strength of character. It provided, after all's said and done, an honorable departure for those who came to the States – and most who fought in Vang Pao's army came to the States.... They were not beat. That is part of their heritage. They were not forsaken.

For the officials in Thailand who facilitated the recruitment of the tough and effective Thai irregulars and their deployment to MR II to fight in the secret war, they lived up to their side of the bargain, we lived up to ours, and the Thais were able to protect their border when communism was spreading throughout Southeast Asia.

And for the Thai irregulars, they got a chance to do something with their lives. They were common people, everyone, who did very uncommon things up there on that ridgeline.

Air America/Ravens, they had the time of their lives. They did things few can even imagine.

Another interesting characteristic of the CIA's Lao program was that although a large number of case officers and Air America pilots had a combat Special Forces or Marine background, many had no prior military experience at all. This includes Hog and Bag who were former Montana smoke jumpers. Plus Vint Lawrence and Moose who were hired right out of college; Vint out of Princeton and Moose out of Columbia. They made significant contributions not based on military doctrine or experience. Credit goes to the Agency's human resources staff who ladled these men into the paramilitary workforce. Also Pop Buell, a middle-aged retired farmer from Indiana who worked for the International Voluntary Service (the Peace Corps predecessor), once trekked entirely around the communist-infested PDJ doing a census of Hmong villages. He brought a sense of humanity and love of the mountain people of Laos to the program. Plus there was Father Luke Bouchard, a Catholic missionary who walked the Lao back country tending his Hmong flock.

He kept the case officer corps humble. As they went about their work out in the PDJ to Long Tieng battlefield, a case officer might take an Air America helicopter or CASI Porter into some isolated dead-end mountain valley where they were sure to be the first Americans to ever visit, to find Father B there washing his only set of clothes, dirty from tending sick in the area or from setting a farmer's broken leg.

He was one of the most loved members of the American team, although he saw himself representing a higher authority.

James E. Parker, Jr.

It is also interesting to note the small number of Americans assigned Long Tieng. Many Americans supported the PDJ/Skyline/ Long Tieng fighting from a distance - out of other CIA installations in Laos (where they had their own regional wars to handle). Plus there were Air America/Raven/CIA rear echelon people in Udorn and Vientiane; support crews from AF bases throughout the Southeast Asia theater; as well as Department of State, Department of Defense, CIA and National Security officials in Washington. But at the point of attack, there were no more than 100 Americans out on the battlefield during the day – and most were in the air; Air America fixed-wing and helicopter pilots with their flight mechanics and kickers; Ravens, USAF, Navy and Marine TacAir pilots; and aerial flight controllers (Cricket, Alley Cat and others). On the ground during the day there were about ten Americans around the ramp and the CIA base – communicators, Intel analyst, air ops, support, and Raven mechanics. But on Skyline and to the north, actually on the ground in the battlefield, there were only ten to fifteen CIA case officers working thousands of Hmong guerrillas, village militia, Thai irregulars and Lao SGU.

With local ops assistants, field commanders and FAGs, that was enough. At night when the North Vietnamese were attacking the ridgeline, and our Asian proxies were digging in for fierce fighting – when the battle was decided - then just three or four CIA case officers remained. Everyone involved in this lean workforce had good judgment, self-confidence and unique qualifications for the stress and danger of working out of the Long Tieng valley. They were not everyday people... and they didn't come together by happenstance.

Again, the CIA human resources people deserve credit for finding these good men who successfully made their way through comprehensive CIA evaluation and training for selection to the Lao program. It is also interesting to note that in this very small and select case officers work force was a Chinese-American, Mexican-American, African-American and two Native-Americans. The Lao program proved that good horses don't come in a particular color.

****

In late November 1973 Hog drove me down to the ramp where I was to catch a plane south. I was going to pack the family out of Vientiane, go back to the States for some home leave, and return to Indochina.

I had requested and received orders to Vietnam.

438

The Vietnam War Its Ownself

Hog parked his Jeep in the shade of the Air Ops building and squinted into the sun. In his slow Montana drawl, he reminded me what our chief had said, that the fighting was all over. He thought a tour in Vietnam was after the fact. He said I ought to return to North Carolina and maybe open up a Mule's Feed and Seed store. South Vietnam didn't have much a future.

"Nope," I said, "it's my war now. It seems to me the Americans on the scene there now don't understand what we've gone through fighting this war -- the human price we've paid. To them, it's just some other man's war. Someone who was around early on ought to be there now to speak for the Americans who died. Don't you think?"

Hog, who was tough and unsentimental, shrugged.

We sat side by side in silence. I had requested an assignment to Vietnam because I was frustrated with the way things had turned out in Laos and, as naive as it might sound, felt I could make a difference in Vietnam. There was no question that I enjoyed paramilitary work but I was also motivated by a sense of unfulfilled duty. Perhaps these feelings had been fostered by General Heintges at my OCS graduation when he said that I was among a group chosen to uphold the dignity of our country. Perhaps it was because I had gotten out of the military when our country was still at war. Maybe because I had come to realize I had a lot invested in this war. Memories of my friends and compatriots who had died -- Patrick, McCoy, Goss, Ayers, Castro, Slippery Clunker Six, the Hmong, the Thai mercenaries, the Ravens, the Air America pilots -- stayed fresh in those baskets at the back of my soul, where I had put them so that I could get on with my life. Sometime when I was alone, I would take down one of the baskets and look at the contents, and then put it back. I felt a soulful obligation to ensure the sacrifices of my friends in this war were not overlooked.

"Just something I got to do, I reckon," I told Hog. "Just got to do it."

Hog looked away, but smiled. "The dreaded Mule," he said.

****

When I processed through Udorn after leaving Long Tieng and Vientiane, the base was almost deserted. In two years it had gone from the nerve center of the private CIA war in Laos to a building of caretakers.

Air America drew down. All the Thai mercenaries who

439

were returned to Thailand were discharged. The Hmong GMs were disbanded, and the irregulars for the most part returned to their villages, but they did not give up their weapons. Someone shot the Sky bear and he was butchered for his meat, which was reportedly very tender after so many years of drinking beer.

The Stick retired, so did Tony Poe. Hog and VP eventually left the valley as did all the remaining Hmong ops assistants, T-28 pilots and VP's officers. Sometime soon thereafter a Communist Pathet Lao unit moved into Long Tieng and set up an office.

One of their first orders of business was to arrange the transfer of all the T-28s to the Pathet Lao headquarters at Phong Savan. Former pilots in the pro-U.S. Lao National Air Force were located to move the planes.

To ensure that these non-communist pilots flew the planes to the Pathet Lao base and not into Thailand or to some Lao or Hmong hideout, a Pathet Lao guard was put in the back seat of each of the old fighters with a brace of pistols. The Lao pilots were told if they tried to land at any base other than the one known to the guards they would be shot.

One of the older pilots was the last to leave Long Tieng. With his Pathet Lao guard sitting behind him in the T-28 with drawn pistols, he took off, made a low pass over the valley and then flying slowly, he turned and headed north.

As he gained altitude, with the PDJ in front of him, he came to the edge of the territory controlled by the Hmong.

And he punched out.

Leaving the young Pathet Lao guard in the rear seat of the open cockpit.

With no way to fly the plane.

As the pilot drifted down in his parachute near a friendly Hmong village the T-28 went out of sight, heading north, certain to eventually run out of gas and crash.

With that final bit of derring-do the pilot salvaged a piece of dignity for us all, and got bragging rights for the Hmong and the United States.

In the hearts and minds of Sky, we never lost.

--THIRTY-SEVEN--
Vietnam Transfer

On the way back to the States, Brenda, Mim, Joe, and I stopped in Hawaii and stayed in a beach bungalow at the Kahala Hilton. Bob and Linda Dunn were living on Oahu at the time, and they showed us the island as if they owned it. We went on to Los Angeles, California, where we made an obligatory two-day Disneyland visit. Then, we drove a car across the southern United States for a company that transported cars from coast to coast. It was an almost new Mercury that was being repossessed from a sailor in San Diego. We returned it to a car dealer in Charleston, South Carolina, and then went on to North Carolina in time for Christmas. The kids assumed that everyone traveled around the world like this.

After the holidays, I went to CIA headquarters in Langley, Virginia. I spent a month on the Vietnam desk and read up on the deteriorating situation in South Vietnam.

On 3 March, we departed for Taipei, Taiwan, where Brenda and the kids would stay while I served in Vietnam. The wife of a man whom I had known in Laos and an Agency support officer met us at the airport and delivered us to our quarters in a comfortable housing enclave in downtown Taipei. A neighbor said the name of the development was "Mortuary Manor," after a funeral home at the head of our street.

The kids were not sure that this was the best place in the world. When I left for South Vietnam, Brenda was in the process of moving to another development of forty or fifty houses on Yangmingshan Mountain, which overlooked Taipei.

At Tan Son Nhut Airport in Saigon, a CIA station driver met me. He drove to the U.S. Embassy through streets clogged with traffic -- motorbikes darting in and out among the larger vehicles, bikes, and pedicabs, with the passengers sitting in front, competing for road space.

Standing in front of the main gate of the Embassy, I remembered that Duckett and I had stood in the same place seven years before. We had been intimidated by the Embassy then and reluctantly gone inside, only to jump out of the way when Embassy staffers came by. It seemed less forbidding now.

I met with the CIA's deputy chief of station, who told me that I was assigned as a case officer to the Mekong Delta, which included all of the area below Saigon. He said, in the way of an

Jr.

overview, that what was happening in the Delta countryside was of extreme interest to policy makers in the States. I was to work hard at developing new sources of information on enemy political and military activities, get as many reports I could from the existing agents whom I would be handling, and work closely with the Special Branch of the South Vietnamese police, but I was not to let them lead me around or recruit me to report the war the way they see it. My job was to work on building up unilateral -- not liaison -- operations. He said that I was needed and there was much work to be done. "Plus," he said, "your presence out there reassures the South Vietnamese that the United States is still at their side."

Later, I took a pedicab to the Duc Hotel, a resident hostel used exclusively by the Agency. Sitting in the front of the three-wheeler, with the wind in my face, I could smell the city, the exhausts and the cooking odors and the ripe human smells brought out by the tropical sun. Horns blew. Bikes whizzed by. The street noises produced a sense of excitement and vitality. Most of the people did not look at me or show any expression -- hundreds of thousands of Americans had come this way before.

In mid-March 1974, almost four months after I had said good-bye to Hog in Laos, I jumped off a helicopter in Chau Doc, South Vietnam, a Delta province capital bordering Cambodia. My new boss, Don K., was waiting on the tarmac. A tall, lean, goateed intellect in his early thirties, Don K. was a career intelligence officer who had been busy in another part of the world when he was drafted into the CIA's clandestine corps to serve in Vietnam. He had little in the way of a military background, but he knew people and he was adaptive.

Don drove me to our downtown office/living quarters compound on the Bassac River. By the standards of the Lao program, we had palatial accommodations, as well as a large service staff, mostly Chinese, of cooks, maids, mechanics, and drivers. Our guard force was all Nhung, descendants of Chinese mountain tribes, who had served with the CIA for years. Several interpreters and translators worked in the office. The office staff was multilingual, and English, Vietnamese, Cambodian and Chinese were spoken.

Among my assigned contacts was a squat and unusually quiet Cambodian, Ros [alias]. He had been a CIA agent for years and had done everything that had been asked of him. If he understood what his Agency case officer wanted him to do, he did it. He traveled on intelligence missions into Cambodia under a number of guises, often as a hawker selling sundries that he had purchased in the local

442

market. Ros lived by his wits. He carried a knife among other weapons and had killed before when cornered and questioned about his activities.

His reports of missions into Cambodia were detailed and informative. Initially it took me hours to debrief him because I had no background on the interplay among various groups in Cambodia, which included the Khmer Rouge, Khmer Krom, North Vietnamese, Vietcong, and Cambodian government forces. But Ros was patient, and I soon became conversant with the border situation and the stark, brutal realities of life in Cambodia.

On the South Vietnamese side of the border, the Chau Doc office collected both military and political information from a variety of agents. The military information was straightforward. North Vietnamese forces dominated the countryside. They moved with impunity from their sanctuaries in Cambodia through Chau Doc Province and throughout the rich farming region of the Delta. The Government of South Vietnam (GVN) forces held all of the cities south of Saigon, as well as the lines of communications, roads, major waterways, and other major components of the infrastructure, but the GVN's influence in the countryside was limited. In some areas, it was restricted to the ground under the feet of its army.

The farmers around Chau Doc, for the most part, didn't care about the war or for that matter, the government in either Saigon or Hanoi. If they took sides, they were at risk of being killed. The farmers wanted to farm, and they had no interest in politics. Their traditions were nondemocratic. They didn't understand the reasons for the U.S. involvement, and they didn't make eye contact with soldiers moving through their areas. The country people did what they were told by whatever force was around at the time.

I liaised with the military and, because I knew most of the Air America pilots, became the outrider for the office. Often I went to Ha Tien on the coast. Once, while waiting to talk with the district chief there, I walked out to a cemetery on a windswept knoll overlooking the ocean. On some of the tombstones were names of Frenchmen, most with military rank. French Foreign Legion perhaps. "Mort pour La France" was inscribed on the tombstones. A beautiful place this country, this hill overlooking the ocean. Vietnam was a country worth fighting for. But what was that Kipling poem the Cavalry sergeant quoted about Westerners making war in Indochina?

> At the end of the fight is a tombstone white
> with the name of the late deceased.

James E. Parker, Jr.

And the epitaph drear:
"A fool lies here
who tried to hustle the East."

I thought the epitaphs were correct, and the poet wrong. These Western men who died in Vietnam were not fools, they were patriots, who died in the service of their country. The fools were Western politicians and bureaucrats who did not know the beauty and vitality of this land, who thought it was a little, insignificant "pissant" country where it would be easy to impose the Western will.

****

When I went back to Taipei for my first family visit, Brenda had moved the family to the development on Yangmingshan Mountain. Our house, tucked in behind the Chinese Cultural College, was only a five-minute walk to a spectacular overview of the city. At night, the lights from Taipei went as far as we could see.

The kids had started kindergarten and Brenda was working part time. Her life was more hectic than it had been in Vientiane; there was more to do and more wives around as friends and neighbors. The development swarmed with children, and our kids had no lack of playmates. Brenda played bridge and handball and had evenings out with the other wives. My family was very much at home in Taipei.

After I returned to Chau Doc, I spent my days in developing information on Cambodian and Vietnamese political and military activities. Part of the conventional wisdom in 1974 was that the North Vietnamese military was stronger than the South Vietnamese, but the long-term consequences were not widely discussed. This was because the CIA station in Saigon, an insulated, bureaucratic, personality-driven institution, held the notion that the future of South Vietnam was assured because of secret, off-the-battlefield developments that they were following, but of which the field officers were unaware.

As a direct consequence of this perspective, CIA officials in Saigon did not encourage military reporting, particularly reporting from GVN military sources, "liaison sources" as they were called in the trade. Station personnel in Saigon considered GVN information to be biased and unreliable. I found it strange that people in my organization in Vietnam did not have the same trust in our South Vietnamese allies as we had in our Lao compatriots. Maybe because in Laos we ran the war and had a vested interest in winning. Here, now, we only monitored the situation. And those who managed the intelligence collection effort for the most part had political backgrounds and did not care about the opinions of military commanders. This message was conveyed to us in the field by the use of the CIA intel grading system.

Each intelligence report submitted from the field to Saigon and to Washington was eventually given a grade, from ND to 20. If a field report was not disseminated to customers in the intel community, it received an ND (non-disseminated). A report that was disseminated but judged by the analysts to be of marginal interest received a grade of 1, a disseminated report considered to be of some value received a 5, and a report of significant value received a 10. If a report attracted significant notice and had some hard, critical information that would have an impact on policy it received a 20.

Most liaison reports were graded ND, 1, or, at most, a 5. On the other hand, political reporting from unilateral agents received 5s and 10s.

The troubling aspect of this political reporting from the South Vietnamese countryside was that unilateral Vietnamese agents run exclusively by the CIA were found, time and again, to be fabricators.

There were a number of reasons for this. Most of the CIA case officers who served only one tour in Vietnam did not speak the language, were poorly trained in the esoteric of Vietnamese operations, did not fully understand the complicated interactions within the Vietnamese political arena, were manipulated by their translators and interrogators, and, despite all this, were pressured to produce intelligence reports. The CIA officers who put out the most reports were the ones promoted. Numbers -- reports and grades -- spoke more clearly than the reports themselves.

Over time, a subculture of professional Vietnamese fabricators, "intel producers," had developed. Operating in the alleyways of Saigon and on the fringes of the American community in the provinces, they satisfied the CIA's need for political information -- any information. As they moved from province to province, they created agent nets, cultivated relationships with translators, found out what was needed, developed their contacts with CIA officers, and convinced the latter that they had privileged access to Vietcong or North Vietnamese political plans. When they were placed on a salary, they began selling fabricated reports. They based the information on local newspaper articles or marketplace rumors, or, more often than not, it was just pure invention.

James E. Parker, Jr.

It was hard to believe that CIA analysts in Saigon, inundated with all that manufactured mush, could have had any idea of what was happening. Or perhaps the invented political "intelligence" from these phony field sources was so broad that the analysts could choose their own conclusions.

****

In June, after I had been in-country for four months, the CIA base chief called me to his office in Can Tho and asked if I would like to take over a province by myself.

"Yes, sir," I said. "What province?

"Chuong Thien."

"Chuong Thien?" I asked incredulously.

Zee, an old friend, had just been assigned to Chuong Thien. Some people had given him the nickname "Deadman," because Chuong Thien province, on most people's maps, was VC-controlled. Only the capital of Vi Thanh, the location of the ARVN's 21st Division headquarters, was under South Vietnamese control.

"Zee is being transferred out of Chuong Thien," the base chief said without elaboration. "It is yours if you want it. Go down and show the flag. The 21st ARVN Division has the security responsible for most of the Delta. Even if Saigon Station doesn't want to know what the ARVN are doing, and what they think about the enemy, I do."

So I took the job and flew down in an Air America Porter airplane that afternoon for a short overlap with Zee. As we approached the town of Vi Thanh, I told the pilot that we were awfully high if that little airport way down there was indeed where we were going. He showed me his map. It was all red around the town, which indicated enemy control. There was no approach area. The only way to get in was to get directly over the town and spiral down. This we did and delivered me dizzy to Zee below.

Terry Barker, the local State Department/USAID (United States Agency for International Development) representative, was also on the ramp when I jumped off the Porter. He and Zee were the only Americans in the province, a point they emphasized on our way into town -- that the whole American community showed up to welcome me. They said there was a siege mentality about the place. ARVN forces did not leave town unless they were in battle formation. The badlands began right outside the city gates.

As close as we were to enemy forces and as dangerous as

this place was supposed to be, the compound was surprisingly open. A barbed-wire fence ran around the football field-sized area where I was to live and work. A single Nhung guard stood by the main gate. I was to inherit a staff of ten local workers, two of whom were translators and ops assistants.

After dropping off Terry at the compound, Zee took me to meet General Le Van Hung, commanding officer of the ARVN 21st Division, who welcomed us warmly. Speaking English slowly but clearly, he said that his division was responsible for the whole lower Delta. They were outnumbered, but he did what he could, picking and choosing his confrontations. He could not go charging every enemy bunker because he would lose his men quickly. Because he was in this war for the duration, he had to husband his forces and his resources. He said, matter of factly, that he could not turn the tide here. If he began to get the upper hand, he reasoned, the North Vietnamese would bring in more forces.

"Why fight a losing battle?" I asked.

"What are my choices?" he asked, smiling. Slowly, he added, "This is my country."

On the way back to the compound, Zee began talking about the realities of this war in the same way that we had talked about it in Laos. He said Vi Thanh was the worst place in South Vietnam. There was no reason for hope in Vi Thanh. The enemy was all around. He said he had argued with the base chief in Can Tho that we should pull out. Why risk the capture of Americans here during the eleventh hour? It is all over, he said. The country is lost.

As he continued to talk, I thought, well, this is the reason this guy's leaving. His doomsday reporting was too sharply contrasted to the enormous number of other -- primarily political -- field and Saigon-based reports, that said everything will work out. Zee was calling the cards as he saw them at a time when Saigon Station said the real game was being played under the table, out of sight.

After Zee left, I moved into his room in the two-bedroom main house on the compound. Terry had the other bedroom. That night after supper, Terry suggested that we sit on the front porch. Slumped in a rattan chair, I balanced a glass of tea on my stomach. I couldn't see Terry sitting half hidden in a chair to my right.

"We're surrounded by VC and North Vietnamese regulars. Just you and me, you know," he said. "There are no other Americans around to bail us out if the bad guys come after us."

"Yep, I'm getting that message. Just you and me down here in God-forsaken Vi Thanh."

James E. Parker, Jr.

"Yep, and I'm a draft dodger," Terry said quietly.

Because my companion was out of sight, I just stared straight up at the ceiling of the porch. Draft dodger, what's he doing in Vi Thanh with me, surrounded by VC?

"How'd you get here?" I said aloud.

"Damndest thing. I was in college in Texas in 1969, and I didn't have a clue what I wanted to do with my life, though I was aware of what Uncle Sam was doing with uncommitted youngsters over the age of eighteen. I was thinking, I want no part of going to war in Vietnam. I wasn't an antiwar activist -- I'm just not demonstrative that way -- but there was so much ambivalence about what we were doing fighting a war halfway around the world from where we lived. For what? Killing and napalming and bombing? What could possibly justify what we were doing? Hell, I'm from Texas, Alamo country, but try as I might I couldn't justify our military involvement here and I was certainly not going to participate as a U.S. soldier. So out of college, to avoid the draft, I joined the Peace Corps. It's that simple. For the same reason some people went to Canada, I went into the Peace Corps.

"Got sent to a small island on a Micronesian atoll -- one hundred by five thousand meters. That's all. Just me and 350 natives. A resupply ship came by once every two to three months with mail, though sometimes it forgot to stop. But on the positive side, I wasn't in the Army, wasn't in Vietnam. Then one time when the resupply ship stopped -- I had been on the island for a year and half then, I think -- it stopped and there was a letter from my draft board back in Texas, saying, come on home son, your number's coming up and you got to go do your duty. Whatever you might think, here in Texas we don't consider Peace Corps work a deferment." He paused a moment, "Want some more tea or something?"

"No, I'm OK," I said. The sun was almost completely down and it was pleasant on the porch. Cool. Terry's slight Texas drawl wore well, and he told an interesting story. Although he was describing himself as someone very unlike myself, he was a kindred, rational spirit.

"So I went home," he continued, "took a physical for the Army on a Friday -- passed it, unfortunately -- and was prepared to go in the Army on a Monday. But Saturday, now I know this is hard to believe but it's the truth, on Saturday, I got a call from a U.S. Agency for International Development fellow who offered me a job. I called the U.S. Army on Monday and told them to stick it. This was late 1971. Took training for about ten months and USAID sent me to

448

Vietnam. Trying as hard as I could to stay away, it's where I ended up. I've been here in Chuong Thien Province ever since." He paused.

"And you know what, I've become very proud to be part of the U.S. effort to keep this country free. I believe our intentions are noble, and I have humble respect for the soldiers fighting for freedom here."

"What changed your mind?"

"Being here, knowing the people -- they're good people you know, hardworking, family oriented, proud. You met General Hung. Colonel Canh is the province chief. I'll introduce you. These two are dedicated South Vietnamese patriots. And the others here in Chuong Thien, the farmers out there, they have it so tough, but you know, every encounter I have with them, they smile. Every time I fly out to the districts, they seem glad to see me, they smile and ask me to eat with them. They are so humble, so easy to like. And they just want to farm and family. That's pretty much what they do -- farm and family - - and I'm a big fan. I think they should be able to do that without the Communists telling them what to do, who to share what with. I can understand why I was unconvinced about our warring effort when I was in college, but I know for sure now that we were right in coming here to help these people stay free. What we're doing here is worth dying for."

Texas Terry Barker, I thought, did not betray his Alamo roots. This was a tough guy, and I was lucky to have him with me in Vi Thanh. He had been here for three years, wonder if he thought I was Alamo/Vi Thanh material?

I asked if the local security situation was as bad as everyone said.

"Yep," he said, "maybe worse. The enemy owns the countryside. But I don't think they are going to come across the field in the back and attack this compound because," he paused, "they never have. They don't want to. The Communists want Americans out of South Vietnam and capturing or killing civilians like ourselves might change Washington's resolve to get out. Attacking us here would make the papers back home, and the North Vietnamese don't want negative press. They're not stupid. They read the papers too. Even the VC out there in the Chuong Thien boonies know what's going on in the *Washington Post*. And you know what, we're low priority to them. What damage do we do? I don't harm them myself, my USAID programs probably indirectly help the local Communists. And nothing that you do is apparently disruptive.

"So we get along, out here as far from Washington as you

can get, we and the bad guys get along. There's something like a truce between us. Zee didn't believe it. He thought the end was near, that he was at risk of being attacked on the whim of some local VC commander."

Sitting in the half-light on the front porch that night, I thought a case could be made on both sides. I agreed with Zee that there was a short future to South Vietnam, but my sense was that we would not be attacked here, that I was safe as long as I didn't threaten the local VC. However, it wouldn't hurt to double the size of the night guard and to keep a loaded gun at my bedside.

That night, we decided that if the bad guys did sneak into the compound and come into the house, they would probably be gunning for me, Parker, the CIA guy. I figured that I had to convince them that they didn't want me, Parker, but Barker in the next room. Barker, not Parker. Maybe it was a typo, maybe they had just misunderstood their orders, which I would try to say was easy to do, confusing the names of Americans.

Right, said Terry.

Over the months that followed, I worked to develop information on the situation in the lower Delta. I spent hours at 21st Division headquarters and finally obtained a permanent pass to visit the G-2 and G-3 sections. General Hung spent most of his days in the field. His command helicopter left early most mornings to make his rounds of the isolated positions and talk with his field commanders. I met him most often at night, sometime over supper, sometime for drinks. Occasionally we met during the day in his office. Our contacts became relaxed and comfortable over time. We enjoyed one another's company.

Terry introduced me to the province chief, Colonel Canh. He was the ARVN soldier of the year prior to coming to Chuong Thien, an honor he received in part because of his heroics in a battle with North Vietnamese main-line forces near An Loc. He had been terribly wounded and lost part of his face. When I met him, his disfigurement had been corrected to some extent by plastic surgery, although the first thing my eye went to was the long scar running along his jaw. Canh had a positive attitude about the war, as dismal as it was in Vi Thanh. He was a soldier's soldier, brave and incorruptible. He traveled alone by sampan at night to remote outposts to deliver salary and supplies and to lift the morale of his soldiers. He said that he had good men and they would fight the Communists until they died or until his country was free.

At night, Terry and I had to work hard to entertain ourselves.

Our favorite past-times were playing rummy and watching 16-mm movies. During our rummy games Terry got up to owing me $18 zillion. Then we played one hand double or nothing and he came back even. We received only five or six movies every other week. The first time that we showed each movie we invited our Vietnamese counterparts. Although Terry and I watched the same movies again and again, we never tired of the musicals.

My parents wrote that everyone in the States was talking about Watergate and the prospects of Nixon's impeachment. Everything was a downer. Fortunately, some distance on the other side of the world from those sordid going-ons, we blissfully played cards and watched musicals and did not feel deprived.

We also played tennis at the old MACV compound across the street and read several books a week. And we played chess -- conventionally at first, and then battle chess. We placed a thin piece of board across the middle of the chessboard so that we couldn't see the placement of the other person's pieces. After arranging our pieces anyway we wanted, we lifted the board and flipped a coin to see who went first. These were bloody skirmishes. Each lasted fifteen minutes or less.

General Hung's outlook did not change while I was in Chuong Thien. He was convinced that the real struggle for the Delta was under way in other places, possibly in Saigon parlors. A Buddhist, Hung believed in fate; whatever happened with whatever consequences, was the natural order of things.

Hung thought his role as 21st Division commander was to keep his division together, to maintain communications and keep everyone alert, to fight for survival, and to take the net advantage from any engagement. He did not believe in trying to win the war or in squandering supplies. Survive and things will take care of themselves, he said.

I usually called for an Air America plane and flew into Can Tho once every two weeks. During alternate weeks, I tried to find time to visit a neighboring province, either Rach Gia or Bac Lieu. A person could get cabin fever by staying in Vi Thanh too long at a time, plus it was safer to meet the few unilateral agents whom I handled away from Vi Thanh. I maintained a schedule of twenty-eight days in-country and six days with the family in Taipei.

There were no direct flights from Saigon to Taipei so I always transited Hong Kong. Sometimes I laid over in Hong Kong for a few hours on a shopping errand for Brenda. On these excursions, as I had done on my R&R from infantry days in Vietnam,

I took the Star Ferry back and forth to Kowloon. The cruise was soothing and I always compared those times with my life in Vi Thanh. There was so much industry and energy here, so much to see, so much going on. I felt so safe on the edge of the crowded Star Ferry. In Vi Thanh, life was very quiet. Its days were measured, and gloom and doom permeated the place. And danger always lurked nearby. Hong Kong was a reaffirmation of life. One round trip on the Star Ferry convinced me that a world, prosperous and alive, lay beyond Vi Thanh.

Homecomings were also uplifting. I could see how much the kids had grown between my visits. Their lives were full and challenging. Undeniably American kids now, they had their slang and their favorite junk food and their Hollywood heroes.

Mim and I still had our special times together. She appeared honestly disappointed that I wasn't wearing boots for her to take off when I came home, but she took off my shoes anyway. Once when I came in, she took off my shoes and socks and because she was in a playful, happy mood, she ran into her room and came back with fingernail polish and painted my toenails red. I never removed the polish but just let it wear off in time. It was Mim's special mark on me.

Brenda's sister, Betty Jo, came to Taipei for a visit during the fall of 1974. After dinner one evening, she and Brenda went to the Grand Palace Hotel to buy postcards. When they had finished shopping, Brenda pulled away from the curb near the entrance, as she chatted away with her sister, and made the first turn leading out to the street, she found herself going down the stairs from the hotel to the street below -- in our 1971 Oldsmobile.

The doorman came running up to driver's side of the car and with his hands over his eyes shouted, "No, No, No, No."

The car wouldn't back up. The rear tires were lodged against the top step.

So the doorman called everyone in the area, workers, guests, everyone -- the car was surrounded by Chinese. Brenda put the car in reverse and gave it the gas as they pushed it up the stairs. When she drove off, they all applauded.

Back in Vi Thanh, I continued to send out my dispatches on the situation in Chuong Thien and the lower Delta to what I perceived to be an uninterested readership in Saigon and Washington. My grades were mostly 1s and 5s. I tried for balanced reporting, without sensational language, but the message was clear that the Communists dominated the countryside and the long-term prospects for GVN forces were bleak.

One day, field officers were called to Can Tho for a briefing by the CIA's chief analyst in Saigon. I had heard that he was from North Carolina, so I was looking for an educated redneck in the hope that we could have a substantive give-and-take on the situation in the Delta. I was excited about the visit. It would be my first opportunity to give my views of the situation directly to someone in a position to make a difference.

As it turned out, I was very disappointed. Frank Snepp was a condescending, pedantic elitist who ventured south to give us a "big picture" lecture, resplendent with insignificant order of battle information and minutiae on North Vietnamese personalities, trivia gleaned during his years in the air-conditioned confines of Saigon.

Snepp's talk did not reflect the realities of the countryside. It had no sense of sweat and no military or historical perspective on what was going on where we worked, where the war was being fought. Plus, he didn't ask us any questions.

Despite the recent setbacks to the South Vietnamese troops in the central and northern parts of the country, the southern area, especially the Delta, was secure, he said. Generations of case officers would follow in our footsteps in the Delta. Eventually there would be tacit understandings to the negotiated cease-fire, signed in 1973, with which both the North Vietnamese and the South Vietnamese could live. There were factors at work, not apparent to us in the field, that ensured this to be the case. There is no question, he said, that South Vietnam will survive.

It occurred to me much later that no reasonable person could have believed that the North Vietnamese, who had suffered a million casualties in this war, were going to stop short of complete victory. Maybe, I thought later, Snepp was part of a U.S. government conspiracy to keep us at our posts in the field while we waited out that decent interval until North Vietnam took over the south.

Then, I thought, no. Our government isn't that smart when it comes to Vietnam. This prediction of a North Vietnamese-South Vietnamese co-existence is just foolish enough for our policy makers to believe.

At the bar, later that night, I told Snepp that despite what he might think, the North Vietnamese were not going to stop this side of a complete victory in the south. The South Vietnamese military could not stop them. Hung's 21st Division was among the best that the ARVN had, but it was overwhelmed and was only waiting for the end. There was no democratic future for South Vietnam. Snepp, accustomed to briefing world leaders, looked at me strangely and turned his back without comment.

On my return to Chuong Thien, I was in a gloomy mood so I decided to visit the local orphanage, one of my all-time favorite places. The small Catholic chapel and orphanage complex was on the edge of Vi Thanh, across a small river. I drove a motor scooter to the river and yelled to a boy who poled a boat across to pick me up.

Most children orphaned in Vietnam were taken in by members of their immediate families because it was part of their culture and it was common for extended family groups to raise their orphaned relatives as adopted siblings. The children taken to an orphanage were often deformed, sickly, or disturbed and beyond the ability of their families to care for them. Many of the children in the Vi Thanh orphanage were horribly disfigured. The nuns gave them loving care, which was reflected in the faces of the kids. The children were always either happily at play outside or sitting dutifully on little pots -- all in a row -- doing their daily business.

When I visited the orphanage and sat under the trees to watch those scrawny, deformed kids laugh and play, I always felt better. It was often the high point of my day, to go over to the orphanage after work, and I frequently carried the kids around the play area on my shoulders.

For Christmas, Terry and I enlisted the help of our parents in the States and Brenda in Taipei to get enough gifts for all the kids. We bought cases of ice cream and candy in Can Tho and invited everyone in the orphanage to the compound. Remembering how excited the children were in Udorn, Terry and I sought to make the Vi Thanh Christmas party just as joyous. The party turned out grand. We had a wonderful holiday.

THIRTY-EIGHT
My Bodyguard

The North Vietnamese launched a coordinated offensive in the northern areas of South Vietnam in December 1974. There was no subtlety. They got their conventional forces on line and charged straight at South Vietnamese positions. After each attack it appeared to us that they waited for a response from the United States. When there was no response, they attacked again. On 6 January 1975 the

The Vietnam War Its Ownself

North Vietnamese captured Phuoc Long Province, north of Saigon.

Finally, the U.S. government did something. It reduced the size of the official American community in Vietnam, which clearly indicated that our government had no confidence in the ability of the South Vietnamese to survive.

In late January, as a consequence of the reduction, Terry was transferred out of Vi Thanh. I would be the only American left in the province.

Jim D., the new CIA base chief in Can Tho, asked if it was tenable, and I told him that it was and the only thing I feared was fear itself. If the local Communists had not attacked when only the two of us were there, I figured they would not attack now just because I was alone.

After I put Terry on the plane, I called aside the chief guard, Loi, and told him that his job was being changed from his previous duties of ensuring that his men changed shifts on time, stayed awake at night, and received correct pay. From now on, his main job was to be my bodyguard -- that is, BODYguard. He was to think about the safety of my body at all times. He was to move his bed to the room of the guardhouse near the corner of the main house where I slept, and he was to be within several steps of me all day. If I was in the office, he was to be in the office. If I ate at noon in the house, he ate at noon in the house.

Loi stood almost at attention. Wide-eyed, he took in everything I said.

If I went to division headquarters, I wanted Loi to go to division headquarters. If I rode the motor scooter at night he rode his motor scooter with me. If there was any danger, anything out of the ordinary, he was to get between me and it. I wanted him to take spears in the chest. I wanted him to die before I died. I wanted him to be a living, walking, talking shield. That was his job. If he didn't want it, I would get someone else, either here or in Can Tho.

Loi, after waiting a second to be sure I was finished, said he understood. He said he would take spears in the chest if he had to.

"What are spears, anyway?" he asked.

The first night after our talk, I was riding my motor scooter, with Loi right behind me on his. The route, which I had taken before, ran past the market and out to the northern edge of town, then on a built-up road to a bridge and back by the orphanage and home.

At the edge of town, Loi came up beside me and sputtered, "Where are you going?"

"Down to the bridge."

455

James E. Parker, Jr.

"No, No, No."

"Why Not?"

"Bossman, the bridge belongs to the local VC," he said.

When I told him that I had been going there for weeks, he slapped his forehead with the palm of his hand and said, "Are you crazy?"

So I didn't go down there anymore, but I checked Loi's information and found that it wasn't entirely true. The VC tax people were there only some of the time.

Also, when Terry left, I asked one of the interpreters to help me have a talk with the cook. The kitchen had been Terry's responsibility. He paid the cook and bought the things she needed in Can Tho. Her name was Ba Muoi. In English that's number ten. She was the tenth child born in her family. Naming children by number was an ancient Vietnamese custom that promoted family unity by giving each child a place. Ba Muoi knew how to prepare about nine dishes, which she served on a rotating schedule. We almost knew what day it was by the meals she prepared. I asked her to vary the menu. It would make my stay much more pleasant. I liked Vietnamese food. Don't always cook Western, I told her, give me some down-home, Vietnamese food. For example, I said, I pass the market often and see these giant frogs. I used to hunt frogs as a kid, and I want some frog legs. Try fixing me Vietnamese frog-leg food.

There was some distance between what I intended and what I had for my next meal. I think maybe the phrase "down-home" got garbled in translation.

Ba Muoi went down to the market and bought some frogs. She put them on her cutting board, chopped them up from the heads to the ends of the legs, and served them in a soup.

I had frog soup. Not fried frog legs, but frog soup, with frog lips, frog eyes, and other green stuff swimming around in it. I had lived with the mountain people of Laos for a couple of years and ate some odd things, but I never saw anything as unusual as that woman's frog soup.

I told her to go back to her nine meals.

She was walleyed. When I told Brenda, she said that was what she expected me to say -- my maid was a walleyed older woman -- but I said it was true and she was a grandmother too. Because both of Ba Muoi's eyes looked out opposite sides of her head, she had a blind spot in front and had to walk with her head cocked to one side.

Ba Muoi had been working at the U.S. compound in Vi Thanh since it was built years before. Someone, sometime, had told

456

Sundowner on the roof of
CIA compound with Caesar

Brenda, Mim and Joe on an overlook
near our house in Taipei, Taiwan
where they lived while I was in Vietnam

Christmas party Vi Thant, South Vietnam 1974. Terry is holding one
of the youngster on the left near the pile of gifts. Each child got a
present for their very own.

The Vi Thant compound. On the left is the house Terry and I lived in, though for the most part it is where I lived alone. Notice the screen door Loi tore down in getting in the house to protect me from incoming rockets. The guard quarters are in the center rear of the compoundand my office is to the right. The town was surrounded by VC and they would have had no problem to get in and destroy us, if that what they wanted.

On the right is my Vietnam interpreter in Vi Thant. In the rear is my Chinese interpreter. Loi is in the center and on the left is a Nung guard.

Loi, my personal body guard, who I was not able to get out.

With the 6 January 1975 NVA capture of Phouc Long
Province, the end of South Vietnam was at hand

The indomitable George Taylor, who flew me out to the US Navy with
the first load of KIP, took me back to the USS Vancouver that night
and the next day came back to pick up the rest of the CIA base in Can
Tho. This Bell was one of two used to evacuate the KIP and the CIA
base.

The USS Vancouver which answered George's call as we helicoptered out to the US Navy fleet. We landed on the rear and I was escorted up to the bridge to meet the Captain and explain myself.

Ed Flink, captain of the Pioneer Contender

Pioneer Contender

LSD type I piloted from the mouth of the Bassic up to Vung Tau

Tug boat barge used to take refugees from the Vung Tau pier out to
the Pioneer Contender

Pioneer Contender crowded with refugees. I said good-bye to Vietnam from the upper most deck.

her to make up the beds at eight o'clock in the morning, and she would come into my bedroom to make up that bed at eight o'clock, whether I was in it or not. And I swear she went into Terry's room to make up his bed for months after he left. She'd go into his room and say, "Oh," and then go into the kitchen.

One weekend morning, I heard her come into the house while I was still in bed. I got up and walked over to the closet to get dressed. She walked into the bedroom, intent on making up my bed. It was eight o'clock although because the curtain was still pulled, it was dark in the bedroom and she apparently did not see me. She headed for the light on the bedside table where I kept a 9-mm pistol, loaded and cocked, when I slept. I had been reading late the previous night and had dropped my glasses on the floor beside the bed. They were in Ba Muoi's blind spot, and she stepped on them, mashed them flat. She stepped back, cocked her head to one side to see what she had crushed. When she saw they were my glasses, she backed out of the bedroom, leaving them flat on the floor.

I went outside a few minutes later with my flat glasses and I said, "Hey, what happened to my glasses?"

She said she didn't know.

****

One night some VC came into the cluster of houses across the field from the compound. They carefully put together some wooden troughs aimed across the field, placed rockets in them, and fired them in our direction.

What we pieced together later was that some of the merchants had slipped through the VC checkpoints without paying taxes on the goods that they brought into town.

The VC tax collector was letting the merchants know that he wasn't happy with this.

The first rocket whizzed over the compound to explode in the market beyond. Loi came tearing out of his room and came to my bedroom window.

He started yelling, "Hey, Boss, Boss, Boss, Boss!"

Another rocket came zinging overhead and Loi dropped to the ground, but then he was back on his feet by the window, yelling, "Hey Boss, Hey Boss, Boss."

Another rocket zinged overhead and Loi kept yelling but I didn't hear anything. The air conditioner was going, and I was in a deep sleep.

One of the guards at the rear of the compound had a night-vision scope. He yelled to Loi that he could see them across the field. It looked like they were getting ready to fire again. Loi ran around to the front of the house and hit the screen door to the porch with his shoulder. It flew open, but the front door of the house was secured by a small bolt lock. Loi slammed against it as another rocket zinged overhead.

I began to come awake as Loi burst through the front door, and I was wide awake when the rocket exploded in the market behind him. When Loi charged across the living room into my bedroom, I was certain that he was an attacking VC or North Vietnamese. I reached for my 9-mm and Loi saw me going for my gun. He screamed and jumped to stop me from shooting him.

I had adrenaline surging through my body. I had the strength of a thousand men, and Loi and I wrestled mightily -- until I recognized him and calmed down.

Another rocket went off in the market. Trying to protect my body, as I had ordered him, Loi was lying on top of me.

"Get off me, you fool," I said.

****

My routine during the day remained unchanged. I would wake up around 0730, breakfast at 0800 while I listened to the news on the radio, and then a Jeep ride over to the Operations Section of the 21st Division headquarters to get a report on military activities in the lower Mekong Delta over the previous night. If there was a serious incident, my subsequent visit to the Intelligence Section would usually focus on the implication of the incident to the overall security of the region. I often visited the Special Police offices on the way back to the compound. If they had a VC suspect in the interrogation center or if they had special intelligence on VC/North Vietnamese intentions, I would go over their reports. We also ran several joint operations and I would meet with the individual South Vietnamese case officers to discuss developments. Some of the bilateral operations were substantive, but most were obviously fabricated to get money from me, or to give the Special Police an excuse to travel out of Vi Thanh. As I reported to Can Tho once, "Some of their stuff is chicken salad, but most is chicken shit." They produced little intelligence.

In the afternoons I usually went back to division, but most of the time I wrote reports and managed the few unilateral CIA operations run in the province. The Air America courier flew in from

Can Tho twice a week. I would go days without seeing an American.

At night I refused to be idle. If I grew tired of reading, I invited the guards and translators to play chess. As a group, collectively, they knew how the pieces moved. I faced Loi across the board and the guards and translators stood behind him. Talking fast in Vietnamese among themselves, they discussed every move, sometimes arguing, sometimes poking at different pieces on the board. When they finally came to a consensus on a move, Loi slowly and cautiously advanced a piece. As I reached toward the board to make my next move, often without much of a wait, they looked at me and back to the board, paused and started talking again. They never won a game.

On the other hand, I never beat Loi at tennis. Once or twice, deep into the game, I managed to even the score. Then it was as if Loi said, "Oh, what, even?" and he'd slam a serve back at me so fast that I couldn't react, as if to say he was still in control.

I asked the compound manager to build a Ping-Pong table so that we could play at night on the porch. All my people were very good at Ping-Pong; unfortunately I was not. One night I said to Loi, who was toying with me as we played, "Loi, I can't see. The light is reflecting off my glasses. We're going to have to move the table so the light is over my side." Loi said OK, so we moved the table down the porch. Not only did Loi's side have much less light, but we had moved the table so far that he had little room to maneuver. The end of the table was less than four feet from the end of the porch.

"Hey Boss, this not fair," Loi said. "I can't see. I can't move."

"I can't hear you. Who's serve?" I asked.

I began to win a fair share of the time, but I constantly had to put up with, "Hey Boss, this not fair."

My evenings with General Hung were more serious. He would ask about my family, about the United States, and about current events. He had an interest in American literature and I would often talk about American authors and their works. Although I read two or three books at week in Vi Thanh, I had not read many of the books Hung asked about. For his part, Hung would talk about Vietnamese history and stories of Indochina wars. He always spoke deliberately, slowly. He smiled often, even when discussing serious issues. He was uniquely self-confident and had a calming aura about him. He was very easy to like and we developed a deep friendship.

In February, at the insistence of his superiors in Can Tho and Saigon, Hung's forces attacked a large North Vietnamese unit on the eastern fringe of Chuong Thien, in the infamous U Minh Forest, long a Communist stronghold. The attack was Hung's largest operation since I had been in the province and he agonized over the operations plan. He used what South Vietnamese Air Force he could get. Although he had an abundance of artillery pieces left by the U.S. Army, he had difficulty moving the equipment into place because of the paucity of flyable helicopters, and he lacked the right supplies to adequately outfit his attacking force. For example, he had plenty of claymores but no activators and plenty of artillery ammunition but rusty fuses.

As it turned out, he suffered extensive casualties.

His men fought bravely. Reports coming from the field reminded me of skirmishes in Laos. I could understand his anguish, and I knew how proud he was of his men, who were taking casualties but continuing to press the attack.

When the battle was over and the North Vietnamese had been pushed back into the U Minh Forest, General Hung was not sure if he had, in fact, secured the net advantage. He had used much of his limited resources. For what?

A few days later, the most god-awful odor drifted through my compound. I had smelled it before -- rotting flesh, dead people. An interpreter said that the division morgue was located between our compound and the orphanage.

The bodies of many of the soldiers killed during the operation were waiting to be shipped out. In addition to limited transportation, there was no refrigeration and some of the dead were from areas now completely controlled by the North Vietnamese.

Mercifully, Hung managed to move the bodies within the week. We were almost to the point of abandoning the compound.

In late February, a team from the International Commission of Control and Supervision (ICCS) arrived at Vi Thanh. The team consisted of four nationalities: Hungarians, Poles, Indonesians and Iranians -- Westerners, most of them, with round eyes. I was excited, and I went to see them the same day that they came in. They were civil but obviously uncomfortable with me because I was CIA.

I was not to be put off, however, and went back the next day. They were correct but unfriendly.

So, Loi and I went out and hit tennis balls. I felt like Robinson Crusoe with his man Friday.

****

The following month, Ban Ma Thuot fell, and ARVN Supreme Headquarters in Saigon had to realign the standing forces vnorthern edge of Can Tho and the general was asked to accompany the detachment. He was assigned as the deputy ARVN commander for the area south of Saigon.

On 20 March, Hue fell.

On 30 March, Danang fell.

In Can Tho, General Hung was courteous to Jim D. and the officers working in military liaison out of the American consulate, but his remarks made obvious that he was more likely to be candid with me than with officers whom he was meeting for the first time.

With the collapse of the ARVN forces in the north, military reporting suddenly became job one in the Delta. Jim called me to Can Tho on two occasions to meet with Hung for a briefing. The second time, he told me to move up permanently so that I could meet Hung on a regular basis. Another reason was that consulate staffers often found Air America pilots uncooperative and many of the pilots were my friends. Jim thought that I could improve the overall relationship.

I planned to visit Vi Thanh weekly or biweekly thereafter to check on the compound and to get a briefing from Colonel Truong, commander of the 21st Division element left behind. My departure was an ominous sign to my interpreters and the staff, especially Loi.. As long as an American was on the scene, they weren't going to be forgotten. They had a fatalistic view about the future and they wanted to be at a launch point when the light went out. They were aware that the North Vietnamese were pushing down the coast above Saigon and that most of the South Vietnamese forces were falling back.

Promising them that I would not forsake them, I said that I would be back as often as I could. They were to continue doing the job here and let me know what was going on. I left that day with most of my personal items. I had been in Vi Thanh for nine months, most of the time as the only American. As the Air America Porter was making its tight spiral to gain altitude over the city, I saw the staff standing silently in the compound as they watched the plane leave.

My work routine in Can Tho differed greatly from that in Vi Thanh. The nights, however, were about the same. Wasn't much to do in Vi Thanh at night, and, in Can Tho, everyone went to ground early because of the 2000 curfew. Each morning, I walked to the consulate from my apartment down the block, and it was crowded with people trying to get in to get a visa for the States. I had to fight my way through the crowd, past the local guards and the U.S. Marines, into the secure base area. The first person I always saw there was Jim D.'s secretary, Phyllis F.

The general drawdown of official Americans continued.

Every morning as I passed Phyllis's desk, I saw piles of automobile, office and apartment keys from people who had left the previous afternoon or evening.

After the fall of Ban Me Thuot, the North Vietnamese were moving south without much resistance. The North Vietnamese occupied more and more territory every day. Sometimes, no one was sure exactly who controlled what area. Some South Vietnamese military forces in the Delta deserted their positions. Some South Vietnamese military and provincial officials just walked out of their offices and headed to Saigon to catch planes out of the country. Air America pilots did not want to take just anyone's word on the security of an area where they were asked to fly or where they were asked to land. Relying on the trust that we had established in Laos, most of the pilots worked with me, as well as Mac [alias] and Sarge [alias], two other CIA officers at the Can Tho base. Mac, another North Carolinian, had previously worked with Air America in southern Laos and knew most of the pilots. Sarge spoke fluent Vietnamese and was a long-time adviser to the Can Tho interrogation center. He had been in South Vietnam for years and knew the lay of the land and in the Delta better than any other American in country.

The principal officer at the consulate, Consul Gen. Francis T. ("Terry") McNamara, had the unenviable job of trying to identify all U.S. citizens in the Delta to ensure they had the means to leave if they wanted to. He was assisted occasionally by Lacy Wright in Saigon, previously a State Department officer at the consulate in the Delta. It was difficult to determine sometimes who was entitled to U.S. citizen status. Some Vietnamese women had returned from short marriages with GIs in the States. Even if their status was clear, the eligibility of their extended family was always fuzzy.

In one case, McNamara was required to fly to a province close to the Cambodian border for a personal interview. He tried to arrange this directly with several Air America crews, but they either told him to get someone else or said that their helicopters were down for repairs. McNamara, in fact, had a history of altercations with Air America pilots. Once, he had asked a pilot to shut down out in a field in an area that the pilot thought was not secured. After a loud shouting match, the pilot said that he was leaving. McNamara could come with him or walk back. McNamara, of course, left with him but was fuming.

McNamara asked Jim D. to intervene on his behalf with Air America so he could get out to the province close to Cambodia. The next morning, I went with McNamara to the airfield at Can Tho and waited for the Air America helicopters to come down from Saigon.

Cliff Hendryx, an old poker-playing friend, was captain of the first chopper to land.

I asked McNamara, who had a scrubbed, neat, office look about him, to wait in Air Ops until I had talked with the pilot, and I walked up to the helicopter as it was shutting down. Cliff opened the door. His helmet was lying on the console beside him.

His eyes were bloodshot, and he had not had a shave in several days. He had a thin, gaunt face, and his stubble made him look like a mountaineer. He also reeked of garlic. The kicker in the back was handing him a slice of watermelon.

"Muley, how you doing, fuckhead?" Cliff said. Most Air America pilots did not know my real name.

As he ate the watermelon, with some of the juice dripping down his chin and onto his shirt, I explained what McNamara wanted and what I knew about the area where he wanted to go, which appeared safe. Cliff picked up a *Playboy* magazine and put it in his lap to catch the juice. I said that I would go along because I knew some of the ARVN in the area. Cliff didn't voice any objection to the mission. He finished his watermelon and lit a cigarette. He was smoking and spitting out watermelon seeds when McNamara walked up. The Congen looked at Cliff -- the smelly mountaineer -- for a long moment. He finally said that he had changed his mind, turned on his heels, and left.

"Well, fuck him," Cliff said.

--THIRTY-NINE--
The Light at the End of the Tunnel

An area of increasing concern was Route 4, which ran west and southwest out of Saigon, north of the Bassac River, and down into the Delta. Elements of the ARVN 7th Division protected the road, and General Hung arranged for me to be briefed by General Tran Van Hai, the 7th Division commander. Hung said that he had served in the 7th Division himself when he was younger. The American adviser at that time was the legendary Lt. Col. John Paul Vann, a man who would become an authority on the ARVN and would eventually die in South Vietnam. I flew out by helicopter to 7th Division headquarters and met with Hai in his office. An Oriental copy of a U.S. Army officer, Hai was a chain smoker and neatly dressed, with his sleeves folded up above his elbows. He spoke excellent English.

The eyes in his pudgy face were hard, and he was not friendly. I asked him about the situation.

"You want information, U.S. government man. I want helicopter parts. I want ammunition."

"You're talking with the wrong man, that is not my job."

"You are U.S. government. The U.S. government promised to keep us supplied so that we can fight. We can do it, we can continue to fight, if we have bullets and planes. Tell your government that and I will tell you what is happening here."

"I will. I will report that you are short of supplies."

Hai looked at me for a long moment. Finally he said, "You Americans don't always keep your word to us Vietnamese 'slope heads.'" And he continued to look at me through his cigarette smoke as he waited for my reaction.

When I did not respond, he shrugged and started his briefing. He said his men had interlocking positions down Route 4 and out to the Cambodian border to protect the underbelly of Saigon. The area was mostly open rice fields. Morale was good, and he could hold out against a division-sized North Vietnamese force for a short period of time. Morale would collapse, however, if his division was set upon by a larger force and if its ammunition began to run low, and he expected that a large North Vietnamese unit would attack soon and that he would have no source of resupply. He faced the NVA 9th Division commanded by Maj. Gen. Di Thien Tich, who had been fighting in this area since before 1965.

"Tich is maybe the best field general the NVA has," he said. "You know what the slogan of his division is? 'Obliterate the enemy.' That's me. You know what the slogan of the army helping me is? 'Fuck your friends.'"

There was venom in his voice. The ARVN was collapsing in the North, and he was sullen, bitter about his fate. Unlike Hung, Hai was not philosophical about the future. He was angry.

I suggested that there might be a negotiated cease-fire that would protect the sovereignty of the Government of South Vietnam. The general looked at me without speaking. I had no idea what he was thinking.

Later, back in Can Tho, I reported on my meeting with the 7th Division commander to Jim D. and told him, in conclusion, that the general wanted more bullets and spare parts. Jim D. knitted his brow and looked at me. "Put it in your report to Washington, then, don't tell me like I got what he needs in the closet."

I went downstairs to the base map room, where I had set up my work space, and wrote a cable for dissemination to Saigon and Washington. I thought about Snepp's briefing and wondered who was right. Snepp should have met with good General Hung, although I remembered that Snepp had said in his briefing that information from ARVN sources was biased. Realistic was a better word.

Every morning, the crowd in front of the consulate seemed to get larger. Every morning, there were new keys on Phyllis's desk. Every morning, there was bad news about the North Vietnamese pushing down from the North.   Sarge, Mac, and I continued to travel throughout the Delta as we gathered information and looked after the local staffs in compounds that had been abandoned by departing CIA and USAID officers. Wherever we went, we promoted the line from our Saigon station that the Delta of South Vietnam had nothing to worry about -- there would be a negotiated peace. I repeated this message time and again without blinking my eyes. It was a better out than saying what I believed -- the clock was ticking and the end was near.

After consultation with CIA management in Saigon, the base chief decided to close some of the compounds in which there were no Americans. Rather than return the equipment in the compounds to Can Tho, Jim decided to turn everything over to the South Vietnamese government officials in the provinces. He told those of us going to the field to terminate all local support staffs, and he instructed the base finance officer to draw a large amount of U.S. and Vietnamese currency from the Saigon Finance Section to cover their termination and separation pay.

The Agency, however, had long-term responsibilities to some of the special agents who worked out of the compounds to be closed. Jim told the deputy base chief, Tom F., to draw up a list of these key indigenous personnel (KIP) who had tenured employment with the CIA and to work on ways to protect them.

Tom was uniquely suited to the task. He was one of the most experienced Agency paramilitary hands in Indochina. In his first CIA assignment in Thailand during the 1950s, he handled a one-man office in a small town on the Thai-Cambodian border and met other Americans only on quarterly trips into Bangkok. His total immersion in the Oriental culture served him well. He knew the soul of the Indochinese farmer.

Although Tom had tough standards, he was compassionate and fair when it came to dealing with the Vietnamese and deciding who deserved our special consideration and protection. Because the

465

number of people had to be realistic -- we couldn't take everyone who wanted to leave the country -- Tom included on the KIP list only those staffers and agents who had done sensitive work. Maintenance staff, guards, and cooks were not included. In Vi Thanh, the only two people who qualified were my two interpreters. Loi, the senior guard, did not.

I drew a cardboard box full of Vietnamese piasters and a box half full of American currency as an advance from the finance officer before leaving Can Tho to close my old compound in Vi Thanh. Loi met me at the airfield and peppered me with questions about the situation in the north. As we drove into the compound, I told him that we were closing down and I wanted him to prepare a list of all the equipment -- every typewriter, every rifle, every knife and fork, every towel, every pencil. The interpreters were sitting on the porch of the main house when we pulled in. I told them to work on the employment histories of all the employees. I wanted to know when each man started to work and his terms of employment. I told the two interpreters that they were being transferred to Can Tho. Loi was carrying my bag into my old bedroom and overheard me. He stopped and looked at me in the hope that I would say, "Loi, too, you're going to Can Tho," but I did not. I turned and walked toward the office. Tom had said, "No guards."

I was going to have to pay off Loi and let him fend for himself. If there was a negotiated halt to the North Vietnamese advances, he would face the prospect of finding a new job. If the GVN was near collapse, as I believed, Loi would almost certainly have a bleak future. Either way, he was on his own. He was despondent and dejected, and he thought that I, personally, did not want him. Loi had worked for the Americans for most of the previous ten years, but he wasn't on the first team with the interpreters. I avoided Loi, although there were times that afternoon and evening when he tried to talk with me alone.

The next day, we resumed our inventory, and I started individual meetings with the staff members so that I could pay them off. I sat behind a desk in the open bay area of the office, with the boxes of money on the floor beside me. As each of the workers came up, usually with one of the interpreters standing by to ensure that there were no missed communications, we discussed each one's employment history to arrive at the exact length of service with the U.S. government. Most had termination bonuses of one month's salary for each year of employment, plus there were other considerations, such as leave earned and not taken, outstanding loans, breaks in service. Another factor that confused the exact termination figure was a period during which contracts had been written in U.S. money amounts, which implied that U.S. rather than Vietnamese money was owed. When we arrived at a final amount, usually in two currencies, I counted out the money from my boxes. Then, the workers counted it out and signed for it.

Finally, everyone was paid except Loi. I called him into the office, and the interpreters left. With his hat in hand, he stood in front of my desk and cried. He said that he didn't want his money, he didn't want to be laid off, he wanted to continue working for the U.S. government.

I told him that it wasn't in the cards. My chest hurt and my eyes watered, but there was nothing more to say. Loi wiped his eyes and looked at the floor.

My voice breaking, I told him to sit down and let's figure out what he was owed. I gave him every consideration and added six months' salary as a bonus for being my bodyguard over the last few months. I laid an impressive amount of money on the desk. He signed for the money and stuffed it into his pack.

That night, I went by the orphanage for the last time. I said good-bye to the sisters, and they told the kids that I was leaving. One boy with crossed eyes, and possibly retarded, shook his head no. A sister was holding him. I tickled him under his arms, and he laughed.

The province chief arrived the next morning, and I asked that his staff check the serial numbers on all of the items before he signed for them. By midday, everything had been accounted for, and the province chief signed for the compound.

As a final piece of business, I asked Loi to drive the two interpreters and their families to Can Tho. I was thinking that maybe I could find something for him to do later, but I did not tell him that. He looked closely at me to see if there was hidden meaning in my request, sensed there was, and enthusiastically said he'd get the men there safely. I could trust him.

They arrived in two days, having fallen in with a military convoy. I sent the two interpreters to General Hung's headquarters, where I had located office space for them, but I had found nothing for Loi. Mac and Sarge, also closing compounds, were having similar problems in dealing with long-time staffers who had done non-sensitive work. Large numbers of Vietnamese, who had been good loyal employees of the U.S. government, were looking for seats out if the Americans were evacuated. I told Loi to go home in the truck that he had brought from Vi Thanh and see his wife, do something with his money, and come back in one week to my apartment. Good plan, he said, relieved to have continuing contact with me.

By the first of April, all CIA compounds in the Delta had been closed except for My Tho, Chau Doc, Rach Gia, and the base offices at Can Tho. Including immediate families, we had a list of fewer than 150-Kip.

Bill A., another base officer working out of Can Tho, located an American with a Vietnamese girlfriend who claimed to know of an island out from Rach Gia that was loosely controlled by the GVN and did not have a Communist presence. The island might be useful as a temporary safe haven for our KIP if we needed a staging area away from Can Tho. Conceivably, if South Vietnam fell, we could move the people to this island for later pickup by the U.S. Air Force or Navy.

In early April, My Tho was hit with rumors that the VC were ready to launch human-wave attacks on the city. The men in the Agency compound finished shredding classified documents and left for Saigon in the fastest vehicles available. The compound was ransacked that night before the Nhung guards could get control and roust the intruders. I went up the next day to close it permanently.

The staff was assembled in the courtyard when I arrived, apparently ready for what they anticipated would be an inquisition into how the compound walls had been breached and some of the compound property stolen. I listened patiently to their stories and sent the senior Vietnamese staffer at the compound to get the province chief's aide-de-camp. When he left, I told the remaining staffers to line up outside the office and come in to see me one by one. With four exceptions I was going to pay off all of them and dismiss them from U.S. government employment.

I had finished paying off the staff, who were quickly leaving to put away their money, when the aide-de-camp arrived. I told him that I was turning the compound over to the province chief in forty-five minutes, and I wanted someone there to take responsibility, plus a guard force. The aide-de-camp left, and I dispatched the four men who had been designated KIP to get their families and start making their way to Can Tho. I had closed the compound in a little over two hours, compared with the two days to close Vi Thanh.

As I waited for the province chief, I walked around the compound. My Tho, the first province south of Saigon, had been used as a support base for some Saigon operations. The compound was an old French villa, comfortably outfitted with nice furniture. A dozen vehicles were parked in the motor pool/garage, the offices had typewriters, copying machines, photo equipment, the game room was filled with movies and recreational equipment, and the kitchen had a vast inventory of stainless-steel cookery. The province chief arrived, out of breath; I told him that I was turning over the compound to him. He signed a receipt hand-written on a piece of notebook paper and I left with the remaining money and the staff receipts in a box.

As I was being driven out the gate I observed the province chief, anxious to see exactly what he had been given, hiking up his pants and walking into his new facility.

****

A few days later I left the consulate with Sarge at the end of a long workday and we went to the Delta Club for dinner. Glenn R., one of the senior officers at the base, was the club manager. For weeks, he had almost given away all the perishable items. A T-bone steak dinner with a bottle of wine cost less than a dollar. Mac joined us and the three of us had a feast. In pain from overeating, I returned to my apartment before curfew and went to bed early.

The first explosion jarred the apartment building, and I was awake immediately. Several more explosions followed. I decided that the explosions were on the other side of the consulate, and my apartment wasn't in danger. Jim D. came on the handheld radio and called Don K., who was on duty in the base area of the consulate. Don said that the explosions were artillery rounds landing in the shanty area down the road. He couldn't imagine why the VC were firing there.

Jim asked for a head count. As we were calling in, Don broke in to say that a fire had started near the impact area. It was growing fast and coming toward the consulate.

With almost everyone accounted for, Jim received a preliminary report from a base asset at General Hung's headquarters. The South Vietnamese military's best guess was that the VC were firing rockets randomly into town as harassment.

Don came back on the radio and said the fire was building in intensity. He could feel the heat when he opened one of the rear windows by Phyllis's desk. We heard several more explosions.

I got up, dressed, and went to the roof of the apartment building. The flames raging beyond the consulate were higher than any building in the area. The street below was becoming clogged with people trying to get away. Sirens went off on the other side of my building as fire trucks tried to make their way through the mob.

The wind was swirling and tossing around ashes and bits of charred wood. The fire was so intense that it was pulling air into it but a natural breeze was blowing our way, and the wall of flames was leaning in our direction. There was no doubt that the fire was heading toward the consulate.

Several helicopters with searchlights passed over. The noise from the street below competed with the loud popping from the fire.

Glenn lived in an apartment immediately across from the consulate. He confirmed to Jim over the radio that the fire appeared to be heading in their direction.

Don, knowing Glenn lived close by, said, "Ah, good to know I'm not alone in this part of town."

I said that I was also nearby.

Glenn volunteered to go across the street to help Don. Jim told the radio communicator and me to join them so that, if the consulate had to be abandoned, we could shred the files in the vault and remove or destroy the communications equipment.

The fire was getting closer, Don said, and the building was getting hotter.

I went down to the street level, and the guard in front of the building helped me open the door against the screaming people outside. Suddenly, I was out in the middle of the masses. I was initially carried away up the street before I got my feet under me and began pushing my way against the crowd. It was like swimming up a raging river. If I stopped pushing forward, I was swept back. People were carrying personal items on bikes and carts, on top of their heads, in baskets. Children were screaming. Several pedicabs, filled with household items, were mixed in with the crowd. An armored personnel carrier, leading fire trucks, came down the street. Sirens were wailing. People were screaming.

The guard at the front gate of the consulate helped me get inside and pushed away people who were trying to get in through my legs. Glenn had already arrived, after a struggle just to get across the street. In time, the communicator also arrived.

It was hot in the base offices and even hotter near the rear windows. The fire covered the whole skyline to the west. Ash swirled around the building. We heard loud popping and burning noises. Sirens were still going off pell-mell in the street over the roar and screams of the crowd.

The communicator went into the commo room and Don, Glenn, and I went into the vault and began shredding the personnel files on the most sensitive of the active operations in the Delta. We had a sense of urgency and moved quickly and quietly. Periodically, we ventured out of the vault to look at the fire. It was still intense, but, as we finished the shredding, it did not appear to be gaining on the consulate.

Don went down to the commo room to help the communicator prepare items to be destroyed or removed.

After he left, Jim called and told us to destroy the money in the safe. The finance officer gave us the combination over the radio. Soaked in sweat, we went into the finance office where, against the near wall, sat an old black Wells Fargo-type safe, with a safe dial on one of the double doors and a heavy brass handle on the other. We tried the combination and pushed the handle down after spinning the dial for the final turn. Slowly, we opened the doors and there -- from the bottom to the top of the safe -- were stacks of money.

Glenn whistled and we both stared inside the safe. I had never before seen that much money in one place -- U.S. tens, twenties, and hundreds, plus Vietnamese piasters. A person could work hard all his life and never make the amount of money that was on even one shelf in that safe. It was a sight right out of Hollywood, a CIA safe filled with money.

We could hear the popping from the fire. I wiped sweat from my forehead. Glenn picked up the radio and asked Jim D. if he was sure that he wanted us to destroy all this money.

"Yep," he said.

Picking up a box of piasters, we went to work at the shredder, but it was quickly obvious that it would take us hours. We had to take apart each bundle and separate the money into piles small enough to get through the shredder. So, we rolled a couple of fifty-five gallon drums, equipped with thermal chemicals for emergency destruction of paper, into the finance office and filled them with the remaining Vietnamese money.

We put the American money into cardboard boxes. There seemed to be something patently wrong about destroying hundreds of thousands of dollars of U.S. currency. We told Jim, if we had to abandon the consulate, that we would destroy the Vietnamese money in the drums and take the U.S. money, with the communications stuff, to Glenn's apartment across the street.

Don came back upstairs and said we were crazy if we thought we could get across that street, still clogged with people, with boxes of money in our arms.

"It's only paper, burn it, shred it," he said, looking at Glenn and then me.

Standing in front of the safe, I said, "We can't do that."

"Why not?" asked Don.

"Just can't. It's not right. I come from the South and we just

471

don't do things like that down there. Just look at all that money. We'll put it in the trunk of one of the cars down by the motor pool and we'll drive across the street. It's taxpayers' money."

"It's paper," Don yelled.

"It's money," I said.

So we carried the U.S. taxpayers' money down into the commo room and stacked the boxes alongside the equipment Don and the communicator had prepared for removal.

We went back upstairs. The fire had not come closer and appeared to be diminishing, although a wall of fire still covered the entire area behind the consulate. We had done all we could. I got a cup of coffee and slumped in a desk chair.

Glenn went on the roof where the Congen had set up a crisis center to watch the fire. McNamara was wearing a flak jacket and a helmet with a large white star painted on the front. He told a consular officer later that he considered himself equivalent to a brigadier general in the U.S. Army.

With the fire in the near distance, the star on that man's helmet looked to Glenn like a reflective bull's-eye. Apparently McNamara was seeking some visual inference of rank at this significant point in his life, but "foolish" was the only word that came to Glenn's mind. Glenn told McNamara that he was leaving the consulate to see that his Filipino engineer contractors were safe. Seeming to take that as a request, McNamara was debating the safety factors of someone leaving the consulate as Glenn turned and left.

The fire eventually subsided and the crowd in the street in front thinned out. As we found out later, the fire came to the edge of a small river and burned itself out. Shortly before dawn, I returned to my apartment for a few hours' sleep.

When I returned to the consulate at midmorning, the finance officer told me that he thought my concerns about destroying taxpayers' money was silly. He said it was newly printed currency that could be just written off the books. Since the U.S. government still controlled it, the money was just paper.

"Easy for you to say," I replied. "You have never been told to shred a million dollars before, or however much was there. To you it might be just paper. Not to me. You don't burn money."   "You serious?" asked the finance officer.

"Yep," I said. "'Cause you know what, one of these days I'm going to be low on funds, maybe broke, and I don't want to feel any worse, knowing I once just burned money. Besides, look at me, listen, you don't burn money."

Later that morning, an officer in from Chau Doc who had

been unaccounted for the previous night -- he had slept through everything -- came into the consulate. Still unaware of what had gone on, he told me I looked like hell; life in Can Tho was obviously too hectic for me, and I ought to go back to Vi Thanh.

****

I continued regular visits to General Hai, commander of the ARVN 7th Division. He rarely smiled. Usually, he was sitting in a wooden lawn chair beside his desk, half-hidden in cigarette smoke, when I visited his field headquarters near the Cambodian border. Our times together often involved his recollection of what he described as the "U.S.A.'s haphazard" military involvement in his country.

His words usually ran something like this: "There is enormous difference between our cultures, yet you Americans expect us to think and to act like you. In fact, we do not like you or your policies... you hear me. We don't like you telling us what to do. But we need your help in order to survive and we know that it is to your advantage to see us survive. That shouldn't give you a right to meddle in our affairs, our culture. You are here like a visiting three-ring circus. Who asked for the news people? And USAID. We were doing OK before. Where did all these 'civic action' things come from? What were they? Nation building? The Vietnamese culture goes back to the beginning of time, and you are telling us how to live and work and govern? Does this make sense?

"And why wasn't your military in Cambodia? The North Vietnamese were, why weren't you? If you came all this way to stop the spread of Communism, why didn't you go on into Cambodia, where you got Communist camps, and knock them out? Why aren't you in Laos? Why don't you use some of your big equipment to plug up the Ho Chi Minh Trail through Laos? It's a simple military situation here. Simple. Why are you acting like such fools?

"We Vietnamese think you are fools. What do you say to that, CIA man? You are a fool, working for a country of fools."

I sat quietly although I thought, where did this word, "fools," come from? The poet Tennyson and now from this South Vietnamese general. Tens of thousands of U.S. servicemen had died trying to keep his corrupt government afloat. They were not fools.

In time, after the general had called me names, after he had ranted about the way the war had been fought, often repeating himself, had blown himself out, we talked about the here and now -- the situation in his area of operation.

473

In those meetings at his headquarters, the general and I had become comfortable with one another. Not friendly, but comfortable, we knew our place. Possibly this was the result of my two years in Laos where I had made many Oriental friends, or maybe it was that the general sensed my sympathy and my respect for his sense of duty, honor, and country at a time when others were thinking only about themselves. Perhaps we were comfortable with each other because I was his most frequent visitor.

Throughout early April, the North Vietnamese Army met only occasional resistance and continued to close on Saigon from the west, north, and east. Although some ARVN forces, especially the Hoi Chanh special units and elite regulars, went down fighting, the South Vietnamese could not stop the NVA's progress.

Senator Frank Church, speaking for the U.S. Senate on 10 April, said that enough was enough, the South Vietnamese military was on its own. Congress rejected President Gerald R. Ford's request for $720 million in military support and $250 million in economic support to South Vietnam. It allocated money only to evacuate Americans from South Vietnam.

The next day, I flew by Air America helicopter to meet with Hai. He did not rise from his lawn chair to greet me when I walked into his office. Almost out of sight in a smoke cloud, he said slowly that my government stinks like leper shit. Senator Church is worse than Hitler. Americans have no honor. Our military violated the universal soldier's Code of Conduct by turning our backs on a comrade in arms, abandoning him on the battlefield.

He stood up and came up close to me. I noticed that his eyes were red. His hand rested on the grip of his pistol and he stared at me, loath and anger in his eyes. He tensed, reached a point of action and his fingers tightened around the gun handle. Then the moment passed and he sighed. "I should kill you," he said, "in the name of all the good men who died in this war. I should kill you because your government did not try to win this war."

I stood my ground, but I was shaken. Quietly I said, "The war is almost over. The fighting has been done. You must accept the way things turned out. You have to accept fate."

"I heard your Kissinger said the other day that Vietnam was finished. Does he know we're still here? Does he know we listen to what he has to say? And " Hai asked.

I did not respond. The general finally shrugged and speaking in a voice that displayed no energy, he gave me an update on enemy deployments that he had obtained from an observation aircraft under his command that had recently flown along the Cambodian/South

Vietnam border.

Finally when there was nothing more to say, I took my leave.

--FORTY--
Promises and Confrontations

Every morning, more and more South Vietnamese gathered at the front gate of the consulate in hopes of arranging travel to the United States. As news spread about the NVA's advances, the crowd became more desperate. Reaching out to show me letters and pictures, many people pleaded, "Look, help me." Anxious to avoid involvement, I never paused or made eye contact. I worked my way to the front gate, and a local guard opened it slightly to let me through.

Glenn R. approached me in the consulate one day and asked if I would consider adopting two kids. He knew that my wife and I had adopted two Thai children. Sarcastically I thanked him for thinking of me, but I had too much work to do to get involved in something that personal and I told him no. He insisted and said that the mother of the children was in a small interview room off the lobby of the consulate. It wouldn't take long to hear her story.

Glenn led me to the room, where I met a beautiful Vietnamese woman, in her late twenties, wearing a demure "ao dias," the traditional local dress. Speaking softly in broken English, she said she had two American-Asian children, a daughter age four and a son, two. She loved them very much and was concerned that the North Vietnamese would treat them badly when they took over the country.

"The Communists slaughtered all half-French children when they won in North Vietnam," she said. "They will do the same in the South with children who are half-American. I do not want my children to die." She started to speak again, opened her mouth, closed it, and then, still looking at me, started to cry, wide-eyed and sorrowful.

After all my years in this war, I knew the only way to keep my sanity was to avoid agonizing over the suffering of others. So, I remained detached and told the woman that we did not know for sure that the North Vietnamese were going to occupy the Delta. People in Saigon who knew more than either of us had said that we were OK down here.

James E. Parker, Jr.

"You do not know," she said. "I know that in a matter of weeks a North Vietnamese man will be sitting in this room, talking with me, deciding the fate of my children -- like you are now. Please take them. Please. Let them live. Send them to your wife."

I finally said that I would come by to meet them, but I could not promise anything. My main interest was in getting out of that room and back to my work.

I'm not sure why, but I did stop by her row house that night. She had drawn a map. The house was on the way to the airport and easy to find. The two children were outside. The little girl, with her intelligent, sincere eyes, reminded me of my daughter, Mim. The boy, a toddler, was active, loud, inquisitive, and unafraid. They were grand-looking, healthy, everyday children. The girl escorted me inside, but the mother was sullen and did not move to greet me. Without smiling, she flicked her hand toward the couch, motioning for me to sit there. She sat in a chair across the room. She introduced the children. The boy finally broke the awkward silence by climbing up the back of his mother's chair and falling, with a thud, into her lap.

The woman ruffled the boy's hair and renewed her efforts to get me to take her children. I told her that I could not do that now -- the North Vietnamese were not at our doorsteps; they were to the north. She would not want to send the children away unless she knew the Americans were leaving. Because I was still here, I reasoned, no decision had to be made now. We could wait.

"OK," she said, "but, if before you come back, the Delta is attacked by the North Vietnamese, I will take my children to you at the U.S. consulate."

At the consulate that night, I got a telephone call through to Brenda in Taipei. Excited to hear about the kids, she started asking questions and making plans at the same time. Then, she paused and said that the woman must understand that, if we adopt her children, she cannot come back later and say, "I got out and I want them back."

"I will not be used," Brenda said. "Look after yourself, and tell that woman I understand her terrible anguish and we will give those children a good home."

I relayed this to the woman the following night when I went back to visit. She whispered, "Thank you."

****

The next day, 15 April, I flew back to the 7th Division at first light. As usual, the general harangued me for the conduct of the United States. "Where are South Vietnam's friends now when she

476

needs them? Who can I call on? The enemy is at our door, my country is on the verge of being occupied by a hostile neighbor. Who will come to our aid?"

His observation plane had noticed a concentration of North Vietnamese on the other side of the Cambodian border that was beginning to swell in number. He said new heavy equipment was arriving twenty-four hours a day.

"Where are your bombers? We have them in the open. Now is the time to get them. They are marshaling in front of my men. I need help. Help me, CIA man."

As usual, I left him sitting in one of the wooden lawn chairs in his office, looking at me through his cigarette smoke.

Returning to the base I was late for a general meeting with the chief of station, Tom Polgar. We were to learn later that Polgar had come to Can Tho specifically to investigate the reason why General Timmies, his principal liaison officer with the ARVN, had changed his assessment of the defensibility of the Delta after a recent visit to the base. I had spoken with Timmies and had gone with him when he met with General Nam, ARVN commander for the Delta, for a briefing on the military situation. Timmies, a venerable old soldier who had been around the South Vietnamese Army for decades and had known most of its commanders since they were junior officers, had developed a Saigon attitude -- elitist, urban, theoretical -- about life in the countryside. He did not want me in the room when he met with Nam, but I knew that Nam was giving Timmies a picture of the situation that tracked with what his commanders at Supreme Command in Saigon wanted the U.S. government to hear.

Later, on my own, I arranged for Timmies to meet with Hung, whose briefing differed from the normal ARVN party line. Hung said that the South Vietnamese could not defend the Delta, and the North Vietnamese knew this. If all the South Vietnamese marines and rangers and other regulars and irregulars, who had lost their positions in the north and were streaming into Saigon, were brought to the Delta, organized, and put in fighting position, they could not hold. They did not have the right supplies and they had the feeling that they had been abandoned.

Polgar wanted to neutralize this opinion at the source. His position was that the North Vietnamese would not occupy Saigon and could not take the Delta.

As I walked into the meeting, I had to take a seat close to the front. Like Snepp before him, Polgar said that there would be generations of other case officers after us assigned to the Delta, this thing about future generations of case officers apparently being a catch phrase in Saigon. He said, unequivocally, "South Vietnam will survive."

From the back of the room, Tom F. opined that the resolve of the ARVN to hold out was in question. I agreed, adding that I thought the North Vietnamese were certainly intent on taking Saigon and the Delta by force. North Vietnam was run by military people who had been fighting this war for decades. They were unlikely to sue for peace when they could win.

Polgar was unmoved and ended the meeting with a positive statement about the rocky but generally bright future of South Vietnam.

Later, after Polgar left, Tom F. sulked at the Coconut Palms bar, "Either that guy is crazy or we are."

I said, "He's the chief of station, Tom."

"Well," he conceded, "then we're crazy. But crazy or not, I know this, the North Vietnamese are going to win this war, flat out, whether that desk warrior likes it or not."

We eventually heard an interesting story. Polgar spoke fluent Hungarian and was meeting privately with Hungarian members of the ICCS, the peacekeeping force in Vietnam. They told him that the North Vietnamese had no plans to occupy Saigon or the Delta. This same information was being passed by Anatoly Dobrynin, the Soviet ambassador in Washington, D.C., directly to U.S. Secretary of State Henry Kissinger. This apparently orchestrated misinformation from two separate sources made a convincing case to American policy makers on the viability of the South Vietnamese government.

The information was not totally incorrect. The North Vietnamese did not hope to take Saigon within the year and had no occupation plans for the Delta. However they never wavered from their intent to occupy all of South Vietnam in time. And the Government of South Vietnam was not viable. It was corrupt and totally out of touch with its farmer citizenry. There was no hope that it would survive.

Polgar, however, and possibly Kissinger believed the Hungarians and the Soviets against all reason.

****

On 17 April 1975, Phnom Penh fell to the Khmer Rouge -- Cambodia was now in the hands of the Communists.

I began visiting General Hai every day. He reported that the North Vietnamese forces continued to assemble just over the

Cambodian border. They were bringing in armor, portable bridges, and artillery. He also said that fresh troops had arrived, probably, he thought, to lead the attack forces against Saigon. It was the only realistic target for them, the general said. They were assembling more of a force than they needed just to attack the 7th Division or to secure Route 4. Once they launched, there was nothing but open marshy country -- the Plain of Reeds -- between the border and the southern city gates of Saigon.

Jim D. put his hands over his ears when I briefed him on Hai's prediction about a pending attack on Saigon. He didn't want to hear it. Saigon Station continued to put out intelligence reports supporting a negotiated cease-fire, and there were enough other pessimistic reports out of the ARVN. Possibly, he suggested, the North Vietnamese planned to use this force as a cocked gun at the head of the South Vietnamese government to force negotiations. I said, nope, these NVA troops out there in front of General Hai were going to occupy Saigon. I suggested to him that U.S. politicians in Washington and the U.S. government people in Saigon, who are calling the shots, thought in terms of indoor work, such as negotiations and compromises. "I know this war out here in the countryside," I told him, "and it's about over."

A U.S. Navy armada was assembling off the coast of South Vietnam. Possibly it could be considered a deterrent to major North Vietnam attacks in the Saigon environs, but we understood that its primary function was to ensure the safe evacuation of Americans from the country. Mac, flying along the coast one day in an Air America chopper, said that he could see Navy ships to the edge of the horizon.

Under pressure from Washington, U.S. Ambassador Graham Martin ordered all but essential personnel to leave country. We were reduced to twelve officers at the CIA base in the consulate -- the only U.S. government facility still open outside Saigon.

I visited General Hung occasionally in Can Tho. He was aware of the military situation throughout the country, but he remained calm and resigned as he waited for the outcome. Not one of the Delta's sixteen provincial capitals was under North Vietnamese control. Possibly half of the population of South Vietnam was here and out of harm's way. He would sit and wait.

During our 19 April meeting, General Hai told me that there Cambodia was now in the hands of the Communists.

I began visiting General Hai every day. He reported that the North Vietnamese forces continued to assemble just over the

479

James E. Parker, Jr.

Cambodian border. They were bringing in armor, portable bridges, and artillery. He also said that fresh troops had arrived, probably, he thought, to lead the attack forces against Saigon. It was the only realistic target for them, the general said. They were assembling more of a force than they needed just to attack the 7th Division or to secure Route 4. Once they launched, there was nothing but open marshy country -- the Plain of Reeds -- between the border and the southern city gates of Saigon.

Jim D. put his hands over his ears when I briefed him on Hai's prediction about a pending attack on Saigon. He didn't want to hear it. Saigon Station continued to put out intelligence reports supporting a negotiated cease-fire, and there were enough other pessimistic reports out of the ARVN. Possibly, he suggested, the North Vietnamese planned to use this force as a cocked gun at the head of the South Vietnamese government to force negotiations. I said, nope, these NVA troops out there in front of General Hai were going to occupy Saigon. I suggested to him that U.S. politicians in Washington and the U.S. government people in Saigon, who are calling the shots, thought in terms of indoor work, such as negotiations and compromises. "I know this war out here in the countryside," I told him, "and it's about over."

A U.S. Navy armada was assembling off the coast of South Vietnam. Possibly it could be considered a deterrent to major North Vietnam attacks in the Saigon environs, but we understood that its primary function was to ensure the safe evacuation of Americans from the country. Mac, flying along the coast one day in an Air America chopper, said that he could see Navy ships to the edge of the horizon.

Under pressure from Washington, U.S. Ambassador Graham Martin ordered all but essential personnel to leave country. We were reduced to twelve officers at the CIA base in the consulate -- the only U.S. government facility still open outside Saigon.

I visited General Hung occasionally in Can Tho. He was aware of the military situation throughout the country, but he remained calm and resigned as he waited for the outcome. Not one of the Delta's sixteen provincial capitals was under North Vietnamese control. Possibly half of the population of South Vietnam was here and out of harm's way. He would sit and wait.

During our 19 April meeting, General Hai told me that there did not appear to be as many new additions to the North Vietnamese forces collecting across the Cambodian border. They were repositioning in their assembly area. He thought that when they began to line up with the new troops close to the border behind the bridge

480

units and heavy attack tanks, their push to Saigon would be imminent. It would take them seven days to get from their sanctuaries in Cambodia across the Plain of Reeds to the underside of Saigon. The general's 7th Division forces could only slow their progress.

"We cannot stop them," Hai said. "There are too many, we are too few."

On the morning of 21 April, Xiam Luc, one of the last ARVN strongholds north of Saigon, fell after a heroic stand against a vastly superior North Vietnamese force. The president of South Vietnam, Nguyen Van Thieu, resigned later that day.

I flew out to 7th Division headquarters on 22 April. It was dark inside Hai's office. He was sitting in his regular lawn furniture-type chair near a small table and couch, and smoking.

"The NVA's heavy tanks are lining up. The new, young troops are falling in formation behind them. They were getting ready to launch. Saigon will fall to the North Vietnamese in seven days," he predicted. "29 April 1975."

Rising his cup of lukewarm coffee, he proposed a toast to all the soldiers who had died and to our future, but he did not smile.

The remaining base officers were in the consulate when I returned that afternoon. They gathered in Jim's office and listened quietly when I reported on my visit with General Hai.

"A week," Jim D. said when I finished. "He's saying attacks on Saigon will start next Tuesday, 29 April." He had developed an appreciation for the 7th Division commander's reporting over the past month. Although Hai had a morose attitude, the information obtained by his observation planes and his analysis of that information had proved to be accurate, corroborated by overhead and other special intelligence.

"That's a shame," the base chief continued to muse as he looked off into space. Finally, he said, "Saigon doesn't want to hear this. They've sent out more developments on the negotiated peace theme today. Do we try to get anyone's attention back in Washington?" He paused. "As if they care. They've already given up on South Vietnam."

"First," Mac asked, "do we believe it?"

"I do," I said without hesitation, "Saigon will fall in seven days." No mysterious force, no promise by the Hungarians, nothing the CIA leadership in Saigon could imagine would prevent it. The North Vietnamese had more than 100,000 soldiers in an ever-tightening circle around Saigon. North Vietnamese would occupy the city in seven days. Standing in the base chief's office, I was sure of it.

481

Jim polled the others in the office. No one doubted Hai's information.

We had seven days.

In the map room, I sat down at my desk and began to draft the report of my meeting with Hai. Jim asked that I keep it lean, leading with the general's statement that he believed Saigon would fall in seven days, followed by the general's reasoning that the North Vietnamese were preparing to launch from their sanctuaries in Cambodia west/southwest of the city and they would be moving through an area where they could not hide. Their intentions were clear to Hai. They'd get to Saigon in seven days because ARVN 7th Division forces would not be able to stop them.

At dusk, after some small changes to my draft we sent the report to Saigon and Washington.

We gathered in Jim D.'s office the next morning to receive our work assignments for what we considered to be our last week in Vietnam. Jim told me to continue visiting General Hai until he evacuated his headquarters, which was on the edge of the North Vietnamese advance and to work out arrangements with Air America to have enough helicopters on hand for evacuation in the event of an attack against Can Tho. The South Vietnamese military ability to provide for our safety could suddenly deteriorate. Mac and the Sarge would continue to collect most of the KIP in safe houses around town and in outlying areas.

Tom was to continue working on the means of getting the KIP out of the country. He told Bill A. to pursue the possibility of the ex-GI and his Vietnamese girlfriend providing a back-door escape route through the island off Rach Gia. In developing this option, Bill was to truck the base's speed boat from Can Tho to Rach Gia and to position barrels of fuel on the island for possible use by Air America and boat crews.

Jim would work with McNamara to come up with a practical evacuation plan for the remaining Americans at the consulate. We were to stay in contact with Phyllis. It was no time for performing missions of mercy or focusing on anything but the job at hand. Jim wanted us to coordinate with him on everything we did. We were to carry our passports wherever we went. We were to leave no loose ends. If we had to go right now, we would just get up and go.

"There is to be no 'Oh, wait, there's something I've got to do across town,'" he said. I thought about the two children.

Our primary rally point for the evacuation was the CIA housing compound and club, the Coconut Palms. Tom sent a work crew there later in the day to cut down all the trees around the tennis court in order to facilitate helicopter landings.

After the meeting I helped arrange with "O.B.," the CIA air operations officer in Saigon, for three Air America helicopters to remain in the Delta twenty-four hours a day with at least two parked on the Coconut Palms tennis court at night. Pilots would rotate back to Saigon every other day.

I visited General Hung in Can Tho later that day. He reported that North Vietnamese forces had launched across the border near General Hai's forces early in the morning and were heading toward Saigon. Hung had begun to direct the limited South Vietnamese Air Force and artillery resources available to him in the Delta against the advancing enemy, but, as yet, the North Vietnamese advance had not been impeded. He remained calm but he kept his family close by.

Jim D. and McNamara were not able to agree on a joint evacuation plan for the consulate. Sitting around Phyllis's desk, we sometimes heard them yelling in McNamara's office below us. One confrontation went something like this:

Jim: "The safest, surest means of evacuation is by helicopter."

McNamara (louder): "There are not enough helicopters to go around, there are too many Vietnamese that we must get out."

Jim (louder): "What Vietnamese do you have to get out?"

McNamara (still louder): "I do not answer to YOU. Listen to what I'm saying. If we have to evacuate, this consulate goes out by boat down the Bassac River. Period. End of discussion."

Jim (softer): "That is ridiculous. We might have to fight our way out, and we are not combatants. We get up in the air, and we go out by helicopters."

McNamara (softer): "We cannot control the helicopters. I have had my experiences with your Air America helicopter pilots. They have the last say. They could leave us all here. They are wild, uncontrollable animals, the Air America people. We control our own destiny if we go out by boat. I have many, many Vietnamese -- and Cambodians -- I am obligated to get out, and going by boat is the only way we're going to do it. I am the senior man on the scene here, do not forget."

Jim (even voice, determined): "I have my people to protect, and I have helicopters. My people go out by helicopter."

McNamara (screaming): "You will do what I say or, God as my witness, I'll have you out of here. You -- Hear -- Me?" We heard a crash, like an ashtray hitting the floor. "Get out of my office."

In normal times this shouting and bitter wrangling would not have happened. But this was a situation of unusual proportions and in view of the personalities of the participants, it was not unexpected. Jim D. was a large, forceful, competitive Irishman, a Georgetown law school graduate, and a world class tennis player; two of his sons were All-American tennis players at Stanford University. Terry McNamara, a career diplomat, had firm ideas of his responsibilities and powers as the senior American official on the scene. He was intelligent and tenacious, and he did not back down. Both men sincerely believed in their separate positions.

McNamara's plan, however, was dangerous. It was sixty miles from Can Tho down the Bassac River to the South China Sea, and a boat filled with Americans certainly would draw attention. It could be overtaken by South Vietnamese forces or worst, attacked by VC or North Vietnamese who occupied positions along the river. Only recently, a base officer had been shot in the head while he was riding on a boat near Can Tho.

Second, McNamara was not an experienced boatman. He had no idea how to negotiate the navigable channels or their locations, especially where the river lets out into the ocean. And he didn't have access to the radio frequencies of Air America, the U.S. Navy, and ARVN units. He would have been completely out of communication during his sixty-mile run down the river. Obviously his plan had not been developed by anyone with a military background.

Third, McNamara's plan did not provide for the safety of the CIA officers. We had no cover. If we were captured by the North Vietnamese, as was entirely possible, McNamara suggested we tell them that we were USAID engineers, which would not have held up during any type of serious interrogation.

Although Jim explained all these points, McNamara was not to be dissuaded. He approached some of the base officers in an effort to obtain their support for his plan.

****

Our original support officer had recently left to take his family out of the country and was replaced by an officer from one of the abandoned CIA bases to the north. When the old support officer departed, he left all the keys to the supply warehouses with Phyllis. She tried to get the new man to take them but he told her to get rid of them herself.

"Get rid of them?" said asked, not knowing exactly what that meant.

"We're only twelve here now. We aren't running any operations. We don't need supplies. I'm busy. Help me here." And he walked into Jim's office.

She was standing by her desk, looking down at the pile when the Sarge and I told her we'd take care of them for her. We raked the well-marked rings of keys, plus a book listing safe combinations, off her desk and into a shoe box.

"Whoever owns these keys," I said, "Owns what's inside those warehouses."

Phyllis said, "I don't bloody care. I just want to clear my desk. Thank you."

There were a lot of keys, maybe a hundred. Glenn, as head of the Delta club, was aware of an impressive amount of supplies on hand in the warehouses. He was the custodian of a few of the storage bins that held equipment that had been passed down from club to club. During the height of the war, when hundreds of thousands of American troops, officials, and contract workers had been in Vietnam, there were clubs in every province -- there were USAID clubs, officers' clubs, enlisted clubs, Special Forces clubs, MACV clubs, private engineering company clubs, hospital clubs, and so on. As the Americans began to pull out, various clubs were consolidated, and the best items, including jukeboxes, slot machines, bar accessories, restaurant equipment, lights, signs, and stereo components were turned over to the consulate clubs that remained. As the last club in the Delta, Glenn's was the proprietor of the primo of primo equipment left behind. Other merely very good bar equipment was stored in the warehouses.

So, if there was so much interesting stuff just from the clubs, who knew exactly what else was out there in the warehouses. We could only image all of the sexy CIA stuff that we would find.

When we arrived at the compound, the guard at the gate wanted to see some identification. We showed him our embassy badges, but he said it was a restricted area and we needed special permission to get inside. We fished around in the box of keys until we found the badge of the departed logistic chief, which satisfied the guard. He waved us through.

We drove up and down past the warehouses as we tried to reconcile the building numbers with the tags on the keys. Finally, we stopped and opened one warehouse with a key that was clearly marked. It was filled with weapons -- crates of carbines, M-16s, Swedish Ks, AK-47s. In a fenced off area were special sniper rifles.

There were pistols with silencers, pistols with scopes, and pistols that converted into rifles and concealed weapons. In another warehouse, we found knives, machetes, night vision equipment, more scopes, binoculars, and web gear.

There were refrigerated warehouses and air-conditioned warehouses. We discovered electronics equipment -- what looked like hundreds of different types of radios -- projectors, furniture, typewriters, pool tables, linoleum tile, baby cribs, kitchen stoves, furniture, generators, crystal, silverware, maps, uniforms, claymore mines, books, Bibles, and hundreds of unmarked boxes. The motor pool had new Jeeps and cars, some with armor, some with oversized engines, and some with oversized tires.

"It's all ours, Sarge, all ours," I said. "I think that when I was a Boy Scout, if I had known there would be a chance to go through something like this and pick out anything I wanted, I couldn't have waited. You know what I mean? I would have been anxious all my life to get here. Is this a boy's dream or what?"

Eventually, we left the complex and tipped our hats to the guard. We had not taken a single thing; there was nothing there we needed.

Amazing, I thought as we drove back to the consulate. All that money we were told to destroy, all the goods in those warehouses -- amazing. The sheer volume was staggering. And all of it would be left behind in seven days.

--FORTY-ONE--

KIP Collection

I visited the mother and her kids almost every night. At first the children were suspicious of me because their mother was so distraught when I was around, but the boy's natural curiosity brought him closer and closer to me until he came naturally into my lap when I arrived. Before long, he was taking off my glasses and investigating what I had in my pockets. The girl often sat beside me and held my hand. She examined my fingers and occasionally looked up at me. She spoke some English and usually looked at my lips as I talked.

The mother always sat in her chair across the room. She had taken the kids out of school and kept small plastic suitcases packed with their clothes by the front door. On advice of the Consular

Section, I had her sign a note giving up her rights to the children. The note and the children's birth certificates were in one of the bags.

It was clear after a few visits that the mother hated me. My countrymen had gotten her pregnant, twice, and left, twice. Both men had said that they would marry her, but they had dropped out of touch. And now my country had abandoned her country, had dropped out of touch and broken its promises.

Her comments were in this vain, "Is this American way to be a friend? You don't care about us. You used us. You. Yes, you. You and your countrymen. I cry inside all the time. I will die soon because of you. You have destroyed my life. My country. We trusted you. You used us and now you leave. Good-bye, Vietnam. Sorry."

I told her I could not explain how the war had turned out the way it had, but I promised her that, if I had to be evacuated, I would come by for the children. She would probably know if an evacuation was under way. I told her to stay in the house. She was not to try to bring them to the consulate because I could miss them on the way. If we left, I told her, I would have little time. The kids had to be at home.

Sometimes, the girl went over to her mother as we talked and wiped her eyes or held her hand or leaned against her. She looked back at me, confused, unable to understand what made her mother cry. Why exactly her and her brother might be leaving with me some day.

The boy could not remain serious for long, and he squirmed. When he slowed down, his body tiring from a full afternoon of rowdiness, I knew it was time to go home.

After a while, the woman stopped seeing me off when I left. Usually the girl was the last one I saw as I got in my Jeep and left. She stood with her arms wedged in the door frame, her colorful suitcase near her feet. She waved as I turned the corner and looked back.

****

We had four days to go. All of our Delta KIP were identified and in separate areas. Bill A., assisted by Larry D., an officer from a closed base to the north, had visited the island off Rach Gia several times and made a convincing case to Jim D. that it was ready to receive our KIP if evacuation through Saigon or to boat out at sea was not possible.

Jim sent Glenn to Saigon that day with what turned out to be three missions. One was to arrange for evacuation of fifty Delta KIP who had homes or families in or near Saigon. He was to try to put them and their families on aircraft leaving Tan Son Nhut Airport in Saigon. His second mission was to arrange for a U.S. Navy ship, with a landing platform, to position itself off the coast somewhere near the mouth of the Mekong as a receiving station for Air America helicopters shuttling people out of the Delta. The third mission was to talk with CIA management in Saigon and, if possible, Ambassador Martin, in an effort to get permission for us to evacuate our KIP to the Navy platform, to the island or through Tan Son Nhut.

The same day, I went out to the 7th Division area on an Air America helicopter. General Hai's headquarters had been evacuated. The tents and building of the command complex had been torn down. All I could see on the ground were scars from the old structures. Deserted bunkers ringed the area. Off in the distance, near the North Vietnamese line of advance, we saw large dust columns like those made by armored vehicles crossing open fields.

Returning to General Hung's headquarters at Can Tho, I found the general serene, as usual. He said that the 7th Division was mobile and that the North Vietnamese forces were large and not temporizing. They were moving aggressively toward Saigon.

Glenn telephoned Jim from Saigon. He said there was bedlam at the Embassy. Everybody was talking; no one was listening. No one, other than a few close associates, was able to see Ambassador Martin. Word was that he was not acting rationally; he was walking around in a daze and unresponsive. His secretary had been asking people for amphetamines. No one wanted to make decisions, so the ambassador's existing orders not to facilitate evacuation of Vietnamese civilians by any element of the Embassy had not changed. People were getting out, however, through Tan Son Nhut, Glenn said, and he had been successful in getting the fifty Delta KIP on a nonscheduled flight out of the country within the next couple of days.

Jim told Glenn to continue working on getting a Navy platform and permission to evacuate our KIP. He added, "Oh, and Glenn, don't let them forget about us down here."

Early the following morning, Sunday, 27 April, the few of us who were left gathered in Jim's office.

He began by saying, "Things are deteriorating as fast as we predicted. Cable traffic this morning indicates to me no one knows what's happening. Everyone in Saigon is breathless, confused. As far as I can tell, here, we're ready to go. We'll have two Air America helicopters working for us today and Parker says we have good pilots.

If we get the word to evacuate right now -- Parker, Mac, Sarge, will work on sending the KIP out of the country by helicopter. Everyone else goes to Coconut Palms." He paused and looked around the room. "We assemble there and we go out with McNamara by boat. That's the plan for now. We send the KIP out by helicopter and we go out with the Congen by boat. He has a couple of landing craft tied up at the State Department compound that are ready to make the trip down the Bassac. He's got the Marines and boat pilots and God knows he needs our help. That's what happens if that telephone rings right now with orders to get out of Dodge." He looked down at a pad on his desk and made a check mark.

"Number two. But we can't wait for that telephone to ring to do something. We got to decide what to do with our KIP, and we gotta do it. Our options are: One, we can move them to the island off Rach Gia. Two, we can send them out to the U.S. Navy. Or three, we can send them to Saigon in hopes of getting them out through Tan Son Nhut. We can just start doing one of these three things or we can try again to get Saigon's permission. What do you think?" he asked the group.

Tom suggested that sending the KIP to the Navy ships now was the best, going to the island was number two, and sending them through Saigon was a distant, improbable third. He agreed that doing nothing -- waiting for the evacuation order -- was waiting for events to overtake us. Mac suggested that we get Glenn in Saigon to try one more time to get permission to move the Vietnamese out to the Navy and, if he can't, that we move them to the island.

Jim said Mac's plan works. Glenn would be contacted that morning with instructions to get permission from someone in the Embassy, or at Tan Son Nhut airfield, for us to move the KIP to U.S. Navy ships offshore.

As a back-up, Bill A. would take a helicopter to Rach Gia and continue work to prepare the island as a safe haven. In either event, we were moving our KIP tomorrow, 28 April. We had them at launch sites, we had two helicopters at our disposal and the clock was ticking.

In the morning I would load up one helicopter with the group from Chau Doc and either head east to the armada of U.S. Navy ships at sea or go south with the group to meet up with Bill A. on the island. So as not to cause panic, all the KIP would be told that they were being moved to an evacuation point near Tan Son Nhut airport in Saigon.

Jim said, "There it is. Go out and make it work."

Several days before I had moved from the apartment near the consulate to the Coconut Palms, the Agency compound in Can Tho, which was on the way to the airport and convenient to the house of the kids. I had left instructions with the guards at my former apartment house to send Loi to the compound when he returned from visiting his family.

Loi was waiting beside his truck in front of my apartment when I pulled into the compound later that morning. He had a pensive look and tried to make eye contact as I got out of my Jeep and walked over to him. I told him that the situation was deteriorating. He was to get his family and return to my apartment here the following evening. He hugged me and left. We were together only a few minutes.

For the rest of the day, I collected KIP from separate safe houses and moved them into groups. I told them that they would be moved to Saigon the following day for eventual movement out of Vietnam by airplane from Tan Son Nhut.

Jim telephoned Glenn at the Embassy in Saigon and passed on our plans. When he finished, Glenn hung up the telephone, took a deep breath, and went outside to the parking lot. He found a Jeep with keys in it and drove out to the MACV compound at Tan Son Nhut, where he met with Rear Adm. Hugh Benton and asked him how long it would take to have a U.S. Navy ship within reach of evacuation choppers from the Delta.

Benton, claiming surprise that someone was taking action on a sealift, said, "You are the first Embassy person to come to me with a request for U.S. Navy support. The first. I've had ships steaming around in circles for five days waiting for instructions. Let's get on with it."

Glenn asked for a time and place where the Air America helicopters could find the U.S. Navy platform. Benton said he'd have something ready in a few hours and promised to advise the coordinates when he got them. With that information, Glenn tried to telephone Jim in Can Tho but was told by the operator that the lines to the Delta were down.

When Glenn returned to the Embassy in the commandeered Jeep, a red-faced, angry George Jacobson, the ambassador's special assistant, confronted him. "What in the hell is going on? What is this request in to Admiral Benton to evacuate people out of the Delta? On whose authorization? And why didn't this request go through this office or through McNamara? You people know anything about proper channels? You taken leave of your senses?"

"They're Vietnamese," Glenn said. "Long-time CIA agents. That's who we're evacuating. We don't have access to the Tan Son

Nhut gateway for these folks like you do. Or are there other plans to move our key local people from the Delta that we don't know about? And McNamara knows about this. He has been moving his people out of country for days through the airport here. Well ours are old CIA agents. They don't have a clue, we don't have a clue how to move them through Saigon and get 'um booked on flights out. Our people have no passports, no destinations, no nothing. No one's helping us. We're just doing what we can. That's all."

"I beg your pardon, McNamara didn't know about this," Jacobson countered. "He blew his top when I called him a few minutes ago and asked what was going on. Blew up. He said you have been trying all along to make your own evacuations plans, to take over, and he was going to put a stop to it."

"Look," Glenn told Jacobson, "Saigon's gonna fall in two days. Two days. Forty-eight hours. Poooof. Gone. No chance to get our people out then. It's now or never. McNamara's can rant all he wants but this thing is bigger than he is, there's more at stake. We're just trying to do in the Delta what you're doing up here... getting people out, while we can."

Jacobson seemed understanding, although he was oddly unaffected by Glenn's report that the NVA would be in Saigon soon.

In parting to answer an anxious call from a colleague down the hall, he said, "Well, good luck. I'll try to help with McNamara."

Glenn took the ambassador's special assistant's manner to indicate that he supported our effort to move the KIP to the U.S. Navy.

While this conversation was taking place in Saigon, McNamara was calling Jim into his office. He yelled that he had just heard from Saigon that Jim was acting as if he were the law unto himself in the Delta. Jim called McNamara hypocritical -- everyone in the consulate knew that McNamara had facilitated the evacuation of his Cambodian in-laws, plus cooks and drivers and others of questionable eligibility through Tan Son Nhut while refusing to allow the base to evacuate its more vulnerable KIP.

McNamara yelled that he was in charge and that Jim was "fired."

Jim returned to the base offices and cabled the Saigon CIA station.

Unaware of the problems that Glenn and Jim had encountered that day, I returned to the consulate in the early evening before curfew and called Brenda. I told her that I thought I would be home soon, that I would be flying the Delta the next day but that

James E. Parker, Jr.

things were under control. She wasn't to worry. On the way back to the compound I drove by the kids' house but the lights were out. I hesitated before going in, then decided that I would see them the next evening and give the mother a radio.

Returning to the Coconut Palms, I learned about the latest developments in Jim's ongoing problems with McNamara. As we were discussing the ramifications, Jim walked in and said McNamara had just been told in State Department communication channels to continue working with him -- he wasn't "fired" -- and to stand down on objections to evacuate CIA KIP. Tan Son Nhut was mentioned in the text. Although there was no reference to taking the KIP directly out to the U.S. Navy, Jim said that's what we're going to do, first thing in the morning.

At first light the next morning, Monday, 28 April, I went by the State Department club complex. One of the Air America helicopters was going to land that night on top of the compound, and several trees had to be cut down. The tree-cutting crews was at work as I left.

Air America pilot and my close friend George Taylor was flying for me that day. He had just landing from Saigon when I arrived at the airport and I briefed him on our plans. The Sarge, who would be getting the people ready to go at the different launch sites, had already left on a chopper to meet the group driving in from Chau Doc.

The airport was quiet. There was nothing to do but wait for the Sarge to call in that the Chau Doc group was ready. Standing on the tarmac, near the radio room, I had the sense of pending conflict, not unlike the feeling that had I here in Vietnam ten years before as we staged for heli-borne assaults. There was so many unknowns about the day ahead. We had to be ready to pluck people from rooftops and empty fields, and then just head out to sea. Was the Navy going to receive us? Had they gotten the word? And it was hard to tell what was happening around Can Tho. Would we be overrun by fleeing South Vietnamese soldiers or attacked by North Vietnamese? Where exactly was that large force of North Vietnamese moving on Saigon? At last report, they were only a few miles to our northwest. Had an element been sent to occupy Can Tho?

I had worked with copilot Taylor, an implacably cool individual, going on four years. He said, "Mule, I've never seen you so tense." Trying to reassure me, he said that we could stay in contact with everyone from the helicopter, so we decided to take off and see how the tree-cutting work was going. Taylor said it would stop my pacing. As we were gaining altitude, the Sarge called in to say that he

492

had the Chau Doc group in a field west of Can Tho and was waiting for us to come in for a pick up.

We headed due west and soon landed in a field where the Sarge was waiting for us. The Vietnamese agents and their families -- wives, children and some unexpected parents -- scrambled on board with their luggage. We lifted off with twelve people, including Ros, my former Cambodian agent. Flying high, we headed due east down the Bassac River to the South China Sea. As we neared the coast we could see U.S. Navy ships.

I had on the customer headset. Taylor contacted a Navy air controller and told him that we had Vietnamese on board and that U.S. Embassy officials had directed that they be taken to the U.S. Navy evacuation force.

--FORTY-TWO--
Broken Promises

As we left the coast and flew toward the Navy ships the Vietnamese were becoming agitated. I told Ros to let them know that we had to change our plans. We were not going to Tan Son Nhut. It was for their good. They had to trust me. I did not want any problems from them.

One of the KIP moved beside me and yelled in my ear that he had to get to Tan Son Nhut, that a relative was bringing all his money from Chau Doc. He would go back with me on the helicopter. He insisted that he could not leave Vietnam without his money.

I looked at him for a long moment and told him to shut up. I saw no need to be diplomatic.

The Navy air controller asked Taylor again who had authorized the evacuation. Taylor said the U.S. Embassy, and he added that an embassy officer was on board and could explain. The air controller told us to circle between the Navy fleet and shore.

As we circled, we saw one of the ships, with two distinctive helipads marked on the rear deck, move out from the armada. A radio operator from that ship, the USS *Vancouver*, came on the guard frequency. He told us to come in and for the U.S. Embassy officer to meet with the captain before anyone else got off.

Armed U.S. Marines surrounded the helicopter as it touched down. A couple of Marines quickly approached one side, and I got off to meet them. They escorted me off the helipad and up a flight of stairs. A Navy officer, with an unfriendly expression, then took me to a stateroom and asked for identification.

Producing my passport and U.S. Embassy pass, I explained that the people on this helicopter and other groups of people on their way were Delta KIP.

"Delta KIP?" he asked in a flat voice.

I told him that I was with the CIA and these people were agents who had worked for our organization for years. Their evacuation had been coordinated with MACV and the Embassy in Saigon. I said that he could get confirmation by contacting the Embassy but he could rest assured that this was authorized and necessary. If these people did not get out, they would be killed when the North Vietnamese took control of the country.

The officer looked at me without expression. Obviously the Navy at sea had not gotten the word because our KIP were unexpected.

This guy decided their fate and it was up to me to win him over.

I said I had to return to coordinate the evacuation of the rest. We had about 150 total. Time was critical. I encouraged him to check with his superiors. I did not blink.

He reluctantly agreed to take the Vietnamese, although he never smiled.

I thanked him and went back to the helicopter. Ros was the first one off, then he helped a woman, who had been sitting, wide-eyed near the door of the helicopter, to the deck. The remaining Vietnamese seemed reluctant and hesitant but they followed. As the helicopter revved up and lifted off, we saw the Marines lining up the people beside their luggage.

In the air, Taylor said that he had no doubts Muley could talk the Navy into taking on some passengers without tickets.

We flew back to the airstrip in Can Tho. Mac came running out to the tarmac and gave Taylor instructions on where the next KIP group was to be picked up. The other helicopter was already en route to the Navy ship.

Throughout the day, we moved KIP offshore. I was at the airstrip as the people in the last group were being assembled for what they, too, thought was a flight to Tan Son Nhut. The pilot, Bob Hitchman, was to return to Can Tho after this last flight to the Navy boat and land on top of the club, where the trees had been cut down that morning. It was going to be dark when he returned, and he was unsure if he could find the exact building. I told him that I'd go along,

I could find it in the dark. Mac was on the tarmac, and I asked him to tell Jim that I'd be in later.

Like the group from Chau Doc, the people in the last group were also upset to see us flying toward the South China Sea instead of Saigon. I had fallen asleep on the flight and was awakened by one of the Vietnamese at my side who wanted to know what was happening. I told him curtly to calm down, everything was going to be OK, and he'd thank me for it later. He started to object and I leaned in close to him and said slowly, "Did you hear me? Calm down. Shut....... up."

As we made our approach to the ship the sun was going down and the ship's lights were on. In the area under the landing deck, I saw an assortment of lights and shapes. The ship's air controller broke in on his landing instructions to say that the captain wanted to talk with someone in authority on the helicopter, either one of the pilots or somebody else. Hitchman said they had just the man. Mule.

"Mule?"

"A U.S. Embassy man is aboard," Hitchman said.

"He's just the man the captain wants to talk to," the radio operator said.

When we touched down several Marines with guns came to the helicopter door. One Marine pointed to me and motioned me off. They escorted me, as though I was under arrest, up the same flight of stairs that I had climbed that morning, and the same Navy officer was standing on the bridge.

We went into his cabin and he asked me again, harshly, who had authorized this evacuation.

I said a rear admiral at MACV, I couldn't remember his name.

The captain said nobody in Saigon knew anything about this. No one. I asked if anyone in his chain of command had talked to the ambassador's special assistant, Jacobson.

He didn't answer. He seemed tired of talking with me.

He said that his ship was to be in position in a matter of hours possibly to lead the Navy up the Saigon River to evacuate the Embassy. He was not in the CIA-support business or the refugee business. He was going to put us off at another ship. Now. And he was going to go on with his mission.

"Us?" I asked.

"You and all those ratty looking people of yours below deck who themselves know nothing about this. They are below deck demonstrating, trying to attack my Marines. You, my friend, are going to lead those people off my ship. Now, go say good-bye to your helicopter. You belong to me. And to those people of yours down there."

This man, I surmised, was not to be argued with. But I heard myself telling him that I had to get back to the consulate. I was thinking about the two children and Loi.

Ignoring my statement, he said, "You take your people to this merchant marine ship beside us and tomorrow -- if we don't go up the Saigon River tonight -- I will send someone over to pick you up, and your helicopter can come get you and take you to your consulate. It is the best deal I'm offering, and I have been very good to you. Plus, you don't have any choice."

He had indeed been very good to me today and he had a point -- there were a lot of Marines outside. I went back out on the bridge and down to the helicopter. I told Hitchman to come back and pick me up in the morning, that I had to move the KIP.

The people on the flight were already off the helicopter. As it lifted off, the Marines lined them up and searched their luggage. One of the Marine officers asked if I had any weapons. I showed him my 9-mm, which he said he'd take and hold for me.

"Thanks," I said sarcastically and, though I was on a U.S. Navy ship, gave it up reluctantly.

I followed the last helicopter load of KIP as the Marines escorted them off the helipad and down into the ship. We came out below the deck and there we saw, under bright floodlights, landing craft tied up near walkways along the side. All of the KIP, sixty-seven people, had been herded into a corner of the docking area. Marines were standing around them with drawn weapons. Some of the more aggressive of the Vietnamese were staring angrily at the heavily armed U.S. soldiers.

One saw me and yelled. The rest looked up, and some called out my name.

"These are not VC," I said to a Marine standing to the rear. "They are pretty good people."

"Couldn't prove it by me," he said. "They are awfully pissed. And they were all armed."

I broke through the ranks of the Marines and went into the circle of Vietnamese.

One of them said, "Do not tell us everything is OK again. It is not OK."

Many of the women and children were crying. Some of the older people were almost frozen with fear. They had expected to be in Tan Son Nhut this night, not under arrest in the bowels of a monster

496

foreign ship at sea.

One of the Navy men called out that the boats were ready. I turned to see two of the landing craft being prepared to launch from the side docks on the inside of the ship.

I led 117 tired, confused, angry, disheveled Vietnamese and one Cambodian through the ranks of the Marines and divided them into separate groups for the two landing craft. When we were on board and outfitted with life preservers the landing craft moved away from the dock and out the back of the ship.

Surprisingly close by was another large ship at anchor. The ocean was calm as we made our way toward her. One of the sailors in the landing craft used a loudspeaker to attract the attention of someone on the ship's deck. A rope ladder came over the side and the end of it dropped into the sea. The landing craft pulled in against the ship and aimed their floodlights up the side. The KIP began to climb up the ladder. A crane extended over the side of the ship and dropped a net on a line. Navy seamen filled the net with the KIP's luggage and hauled it aboard. Ros and I were the last ones out of the boats. I was tired and had to labor to climb the ladder.

On deck I was introduced to a Marine Captain Garcia who was in charge of a detachment of US Marines pre-deployed on this merchant marine ship to ensure the safety of the crew if it was used again to transport refugees. He said the ship's master wanted to see me. This is becoming a common request, I said. I followed him up a couple of flights of stairs. Lights from Navy ships winked and flashed all around us. It was hard to tell how many vessels there were; there appeared to be hundreds. Below me were the open, empty holds of the cargo ship. In the distance, I could see the landing craft returning to the rear of the Navy ship.

A middle-aged, beefy individual welcomed me aboard the USNS *Pioneer Contender*. He said he was Merchant Marine Capt. Ed Flink and asked who the hell I was and who were these people.

"They are Vietnamese staffers of the U.S. Consulate in the Delta," I said.

The captain said, "That little four-year-old child down there works for the consulate?"

"Staffers and their families," I replied.

I was very tired and did not want to go through another confrontation. All I wanted was a full night's sleep and to be up early in the morning so that I could get back to the U.S. Navy ship and return to Can Tho. I did not want to make conversation or problems.

"Listen, my friend," Captain Flink said, "I was recently told

James E. Parker, Jr.

to go up to Danang -- you know Danang -- to pick up some Vietnamese staffers of the U.S. Consulate there. Didn't get what I expected. Got Vietnamese Rangers who terrorized my ship. Thousands of them. So I don't believe you. I believe I'm getting set up again." He paused. "What am I supposed to do with these people? I don't have enough food. I don't have facilities. Just me, my crew and these dozen US Marines out here on this boat. I'm being told all the time what to do. So you tell me what do I do? You tell me. What do I do?"

"I don't know," I said. "My people probably have some food with them. They can sleep on the deck. They will be no problem. I will be no problem, especially if you have a spare bunk, or, if you don't I can go down there with my people and sleep."

The captain continued to look at me. "Where's your grip? I've got a room for you, but I'm telling you, I don't want any trouble with those people down there and I don't have anything for them to eat. Maybe some food for tonight. That's it. They can stay in this first hold here. It'll get them out of the weather. And I'll have the galley make them some food for tonight. But that is all. Period."

"OK," I said. The situation was settling itself.

"Where's your grip?" the captain asked again.

"I don't have one. It was not my plan to be here tonight. I'm here courtesy of the U.S. Navy."

I went down to the deck and followed a Marine into one of the forward holds. The Vietnamese followed me. Some were still grumbling. Others were tired, like myself, and just wanted to find some place to lie down. This ship, for all her rust and cavernous space, was more friendly than the Navy ship had been, and her crew was accommodating.

Ros and a few of the other men, on instructions from the crew, went to the galley and came back with pots of hot food. I said good night to the group and went up to the mess hall. After a hot meal, I sought out Captain Flink.

He was standing on the bridge with a cigarette and a cup of coffee. The Navy ships were in the background. I explained to him about the deteriorating situation in the Delta and the danger these people would face when the North Vietnamese took control of the country. I expected the Government of South Vietnam to fall within the next couple of days. There was much work that I needed to do, and I had promises to keep. I was anxious to get back to Can Tho.

He listened sympathetically and then said, "Sure. But like I said earlier, you aren't the first person from the U.S. government to come to this ship from Vietnam and talk about evacuating people.

498

You all act like you're on a deadly serious mission. And you are. You all are. I know. But I think it's beyond you a little bit. Ain't no one in control."

Then he paused and looked toward the ships on the horizon. "I was on my way from Hong Kong to Singapore and was told to lay in near Hue to evacuate some Americans from Hue, only we were too late. So at the end of March, they told us to go on to Danang and evacuate some Americans there. Some of your people came on board and said something much like you just did, that they had some people to evacuate because if the Commies caught them they'd be killed. Well, what ended up on my ship were those South Vietnamese Rangers I was telling you about. Wild, crazy people. I took two loads out of Danang -- thousands of 'em, there were so many they couldn't all find room to lay down -- and the Vietnamese Rangers that second time took over my ship. Took over my ship. Killed, raped, robbed. You could hear gunshots all the time. Soldiers were walking around with bloody knives. We had to lock ourselves in the pilothouse. I only had a crew of forty, plus some security, but there were thousands of those wild, crazy Vietnamese people.

"They finally shot some of the worst once we docked at that island, what, Phu Quoc, and the people got off, but I'll tell you, son, it was hell. We found bodies all over the ship after everyone got off. Babies, old women, young boys. Cut, shot, and trampled to death. And it all started when some of your friends came aboard talking about taking on some good Vietnamese refugees who'd be badly treated if the Commies got 'em. Well, if they were talking about those Rangers, I know why they would have been treated badly. They were crazy."

"It'll be different this time. They're only sixty-seven civilians with me," I said, aware that I wasn't the only one trying to find my way safely through this morass. "I'm sorry about your problems before. We won't be a problem." Flink rolled his eyes and in short order showed me to my quarters, a stateroom with bunk beds and a shower. He said that he had taken the liberty of providing some toilet articles out of the ship's store for me.

I thanked him, shut the door, and fell across the bottom bunk. I was asleep before my head hit the pillow.

****

The following morning, Tuesday, 29 April, I was up before 0500 and on the bridge.

James E. Parker, Jr.

The *Pioneer Contender* was alone.

There were no U.S. Navy ships around -- nothing but flat sea for as far as I could make out in the half-light.

"Where's the Navy?" I asked the two men on duty in the control room.

"Left in the middle of the night, I think. Pulled out to the north."

"Oh, give me a break," I said. "Where's your radio? How do I call the U.S. Navy?"

"Sparky's still asleep," one of the seamen said. "He don't have no communication with the Navy though. We do have this," he said and offered a small portable radio, not unlike a Radio Shack Christmas toy.

"Who do you talk to on this?" I asked, in an incredible tone.

"Ship Control, I think, is the call sign. It's part of the Sealift Command," he said.

The seaman was not used to a lot of questions from strangers in his control room at this hour of the morning.

"Yeah, OK, that's what I want, Ship Control, I want a pickup," I said.

I walked out of the room onto the bridge and turned on the radio. The frequency was crowded with transmissions. Some weak, some strong.

There was no Ship Control, although a common call sign was Tugboat Control. I made several efforts to call but got no response. Finally, a ship relayed to Tugboat Control that the *Pioneer Contender* was trying to reach him.

"Yea, what does she want?" Tugboat Control asked in a decidedly unmilitary tone.

"What do you want, *Pioneer Contender*?" asked the intermediary.

"I'm an embassy officer on board, and I want a pickup for delivery back to the USS *Vancouver* so that I can get to Can Tho. Where's *Vancouver*?" I asked.

"We don't know. Tugboat Control doesn't know. That's naval operations."

"What does the *Pioneer Contender* want?" asked Tugboat Control.

"It's some guy trying to get on shore. Everyone's trying to get out. He's trying to get in."

It was hard to tell exactly what was going on with Tugboat Control. Apparently, it was involved in a massive way with what we had been doing on a small scale the previous day, getting Vietnamese civilians out to ships, and probably operating some distance from the lonely, empty sea around us. Evacuating people from Saigon, I guessed.

There was nothing I could do. I was stuck on this merchant ship sitting at anchor.

I returned the radio to the seamen in the pilothouse and asked them to get me if the U.S. Navy reappeared. I went back to my stateroom, took a bath, and went back to bed. At midmorning, I awoke, dressed, and went out on deck.

Ros was standing close by and listening to a commercial radio station on a portable AM radio. He said the station was reporting that North Vietnamese troops were entering Saigon. The U.S. Embassy was being evacuated. The radio broadcast was crowded with the voices of excited people.

We swayed at anchor. Seagulls squawked overhead, but there were no ships anywhere in sight.

Saigon evacuated. North Vietnamese troops entering Saigon. The best and brightest Americans in Saigon said it wouldn't happen. In the Delta we had believed Hai, and he was right, to the day.

The consulate in the Delta was also certain to be evacuated. I thought about Loi and visualized him waiting at my apartment with his family. Loi would be quiet, trying to calm his family, and unsure if he should stay at the apartment any longer. He must be wanting desperately for me to show up.

Nearby in another part of Can Tho, the mother would be huddled with her two children as they waited for me. She would not go out; I had made that clear. Don't leave. Don't go to the consulate. Wait for me. She would be crying. I could almost hear her across the ocean. And cussing me. Right now, I thought, she is inside her house looking at the door and pleading, "Where is he? I have been abandoned again by American men, this one leaving my children behind to die."

All these people waiting for me, and I was trapped at sea, sitting at anchor, cut off from the world.

I sought out Sparky, who said that he had only shortwave to the Philippines in addition to the tiny portable used to net with Tugboat Control.

"This big boat and that's all you've got? Two dinky radios?"

I ate with Captain Flink at lunch. The evacuation from Saigon was continuing. I suggested that it was an exciting break in his normal routine.

"I ain't set up for all this. I can't take people," he said. "I've got no food, no sanitation equipment. The people making all these decisions don't know this. I'm supposed to carry cargo. That's C-A-R-G-O. Your sixty-seven people are more than I can handle. I don't like people. Especially people who don't speak English. I don't want this ship ever again considered as a people carrier. You appear to be a nice guy, all of you people are nice guys, but I don't want you on this ship of mine. Or those Vietnamese marines. I want boxes of things that don't talk some foreign language, carry guns, eat, and shit."

Throughout the afternoon, we listened to the AM radio station and Tugboat Control. The Americans were on their way out of the country, and evidently thousands of Vietnamese, as well.

I felt my anxieties begin to drain out of me. There was nothing I could do. The war was over for me. Thinking back over the past few days, I knew that I had done all I could do. I wished that Loi and the woman and her children had not been traumatized and hoped that they would be treated fairly by the North Vietnamese. I'm sorry, I said to myself a dozen times. I couldn't help it that I wasn't there.

There was a certain peace on the *Pioneer Contender*. I had been the subject of so much scorn recently -- from the woman and from the 7th Division commander. Now it was all over.

As dusk began to fall that evening, the newsman on the AM radio station said that all of the Americans had left the country. For the first time in hundreds of years, it was under the complete control of the Vietnamese. The Western devils were gone.

FORTY-THREE
Air America to the Rescue

After supper, I looked over the paperback books in the ship's library, and wandered down to talk with the KIP. Most of them by now were appreciative of our efforts to get them out of the country, although a few of the older women continued to cry. Some of the men said they would remember this day for the rest of their lives. Ros, as usual, was quiet. He was the only ethnic Cambodian in the group, but that made little difference. He had always been a loner.

I wondered how the evacuation had gone in Can Tho. We had been ready. Jim D. and Tom F. had proved themselves to be very capable. In the face of uncertainty, when the safest course would have been to do nothing -- no one would have blamed them if the KIP didn't get out -- they had done what they thought was right. Everyone except the base officers and Air America yelled at them. Tough guys, they had probably gotten out without any problems, I thought.

In fact, I found out later that there had been some problems in Can Tho. Early on the morning of 29 April, both helicopters, which had remained in Can Tho overnight, were dispatched to pickup points to get the last of the remaining KIP and take them out to the Navy. Later, in the consulate, Tom was talking with one of the Marine guards downstairs when someone told him that McNamara had just received a telephone call from the Embassy ordering the evacuation of all Americans in the Delta. When he got up to the base offices, Jim was reading a flash cable from Saigon with a parallel message ordering the evacuation of base personnel.

Tom said, "We were right. To the day."

Jim didn't comment. He told the support officer to bring his money to the logistics compound to pay off the last of the base guards. Turning to Phyllis, he asked her to gather the few sensitive records that were left so that he could destroy them and he also told her to advise everyone to move to Coconut Palms to stage for the evacuation. Tom was dispatched to the radio room, where he told the communications operator to shut down and either destroy the coding equipment or take it with him.

Within minutes the support officer was ready with a large pouch of money, Jim had destroyed the last of the sensitive records and everyone hurried out the door. Phyllis was the last to leave. She calmly counted people off as they left, reached in and turned out the lights, shut the door, and walked out.

Jim, Tom, and the support officer went to the logistics compound and met up with the chief guard, who had his supervisors standing by. They all went upstairs in one of the buildings to make the final termination payment. This had been a major concern of Tom -- that we maintain a cohesive guard force no matter what happened in the Delta. He had had long talks with the chief guard, not unlike my conversations with Loi in Vi Thanh, to get assurance that the Americans would be protected to the end. Tom had told the Nhung that neither he nor his men were going to be evacuated. He had to understand that Tom would not make any provision to get them out, but he would provide adequately in the way of a termination bonus. The guard, who with an Agency staffer, had received the CIA's highest award for bravery for their activities during the Tet offensive of 1968, agreed. This would probably mean that he and his family, in addition to his guards and their families, would have to go into hiding after the Americans withdrew because they were incorruptible anti-Communists, supportive of the Americans to the end. But the guard didn't question his role. Like so many other Agency jobs, he accepted his last assignment by saying he would do good.

At the Coconut Palms, the guards let the base people inside and locked the gates. Phyllis accounted for everyone except the communications operator and radioed Tom.

While Jim and the support officer were paying off the senior guard people, Tom went down to the dock where several Boston whalers (stout, flat-bottomed fishing boats) were tied up. The Air America choppers had not been seen since they had departed early that morning with the last load of KIP going out to the U.S. Navy ships. Tom had heard that American officials in Saigon were being evacuated by helicopter. He felt sure that their Air America helicopters had been diverted to the capital. The CIA people in Can Tho would have to leave with McNamara in his landing boats, which were tied up downriver from the logistics compound at the State Department club.

After inspecting the Boston whalers, Tom called McNamara to tell him that the base people would be coming down the river in their small boats to join his group. McNamara said he had already pushed off and would wait for them in the middle of the Bassac River. He said the CIA communicator was with him.

The group at the Coconut Palms overheard the radio conversation, and everyone moaned. Now their evacuation would involve moving by Jeeps from the Coconut Palms to the logistics compound and then down the small river in the Boston whalers to the Bassac River for the beginning of what certainly would be a hazardous trip to the South China Sea.

Tom was squeezing his eyes shut in anticipation of what lay ahead. Around him in the logistics compound, workers were busy with the end-of-the-month inventory, mechanics were doing maintenance work on various vehicles, and other workers unloaded a truck that had recently arrived from Saigon with supplies. A voice broke in on Tom's radio. George Taylor, copilot on one of the two Air America helicopters, (Weiss was the pilot) was saying that both choppers were returning to Can Tho. Tom looked up and, way off to the east, could just barely see them.

He was almost giddy when he said, "Oh, you are so beautiful."

"Yeah," Taylor said, "we almost ain't here. On the way back, Air Ops in Saigon ordered us north to help in the evacuation, but we said we had some good customers in Can Tho and had to return there for one last trip before we headed up. You did want us to come back, didn't you?"

"I wish I had as much money as I'm glad to see you," Tom said.

The pilots of the other helicopter, Hitchman and Goering said that they were low on fuel and needed to gas up before they did any more flying. Mac got on the radio at Coconut Palms and suggested that one helicopter land where they were and the other in the logistics compound. He would help direct the choppers to a fuel dump somewhere in town.

Tom ran upstairs to get Jim and the support man. When they left, the chief guard suddenly found himself in possession of the Vietnamese money left on the desk. Downstairs, the CIA men moved to a cleared area in the compound near the front gate, and Hitchman landed -- blowing off the roofs of dozens of sheds in the community of lean-tos right outside the fence.

Weiss sat down his helicopter at Coconut Palms and picked up the base people there. Mac had on the customer headset. He had been working the helicopters over the past few days and suggested that they try first to get fuel at the airport. This idea was discounted out of hand by the pilots because no one answered the radio in the control tower there. There was no telling who was in control of the airport by now. The next suggestion was the Shell compound on the road to the airport. Although neither pilot had landed there recently, they knew it had a pump and a landing zone inside the compound large enough for two helicopters to be refueled at one time.

Weiss's helicopter, with the people from the Coconut Palms, reached the Shell compound first and made a pass overhead. No one on the chopper saw any unusual activity below, so Weiss brought it around and landed near several rubber bladders of fuel. Within minutes, Hitchman's helicopter containing Tom, Jim, and the support officer landed behind them.

Once both helicopters were on the ground, a group of armed Vietnamese soldiers came out from behind a building and lined up by the pumps.

"Goddamnit," Mac said, "we were so close to getting out of here."

"Oh, shut up," said Weiss, "they probably just want a ride out of the country."

"They ain't got no luggage," Taylor said. "Plus, my bet is people who want out come running up to the helicopter. They don't stand in front with guns in their hands."

James E. Parker, Jr.

Both helicopters settled down, although the pilots kept up full power and the battey-de-battey of the blades continued loudly.

Weiss said, "OK, here's what we're going to do. Two people go over there beside those Vietnamese and pick up the gas nozzles and bring them back to the helicopters and give us a squirt. We don't need to top off. Just enough to get us out of here."

"I'll go," said the flight mechanic in the rear helicopter. "Who's going up there?"

"Mac," Weiss said.

"Mac?" Mac asked.

"Look, we have submachine guns. You go over there and get the gas nozzle and come back to the helicopter. If they try to grab you, drop down and we blast them with automatic fire."

"There is no chance in hell we can get away if we start shooting. There must be a dozen of them. You going to kill them all or what? And how we going to get fuel if everyone starts shooting? This ain't the movies, you know."

"You got a better plan?" Weiss asked. "We have to have petrol. It's right over there."

"OK," Mac said, "if they try to get me -- shit, look at them, some have AK-47s -- if they try to get me, I fall down and you guys blast 'em and then I get up and try to make it back to the helicopter."

"Right."

"OK."

Mac slowly, awkwardly, got out of the lead helicopter and walked stiffly toward the rack holding the gas nozzles. The flight mechanic from the other helicopter was somewhere behind him. The Vietnamese did not show any expression. Hopefully, they were going to ask for a ride out of the country, Mac thought. Please don't want to capture me. Please don't want to kill me.

Picking up a nozzle, Mac walked back to the helicopter. He looked one of the kickers in the eye the whole way, as he watched for any sudden movement by the kicker. Anything sudden and Mac was dropping to the ground. But then, he thought, I've got to be sure because if I drop, the pilot and Taylor and the kicker are going to start shooting.

The kicker had removed the gas tank cap on the side of the helicopter, and, as Mac walked up, he went back to lean against the helicopter near his gun.

The flight mechanic in the rear helicopter passed him with another hose and nozzle.

Mac starting pumping the gas, and he pumped and pumped. Finally, he realized that no one in the helicopter was going to tell him

506

when to stop. They were all intent on staring down the Vietnamese in front of them.

The flight mechanic from the rear helicopter had finished pumping gas and was screwing on the cap to the helicopter gas tank.

"Hey," Mac yelled over the noise of the helicopter to the kicker, "is this enough?" The kicker didn't hear. Mac stopped pumping and went over and grabbed his arm. The kicker jumped straight up.

"Is this enough?" Mac asked again. When the kicker said that it was, he went back to the nozzle, extracted it from the fuel line, and began to walk back to the nozzle rack. Halfway there, Mac thought to himself, I don't need to take this all the way over to where those men are standing with their guns. I'll just drop it here.

And he did.

When he turned to go back to the helicopter, one of the Vietnamese shouted, "Hey, you."

Mac was facing the helicopter and watching Taylor, who was vibrating because of the high torque of the engine. Mac knew that Weiss had an automatic rifle in his lap. The flight mechanic, the gas hose in his hand, stopped, frozen, and looked wide-eyed at Mac.

Should he drop to the ground? Was this it? Mac was rigid, tense. His face was suddenly wet with sweat.

"You. You," the Vietnamese said loudly behind him.

Mac turned around, ready to drop.

"You have to sign for the gas." The Vietnamese offered a clipboard, Mac signed it, and got back on the helicopter.

The last American on the ground in Can Tho, and one of the most thankful to be leaving.

****

I went up to my stateroom early that night. Captain Flink woke me up around midnight.

"There are planes buzzing my ship," he said. "Why are there planes buzzing my ship? Do they have bombs? You caused all this. They are North Vietnamese jets and they want to kill you, and your people and they are buzzing my ship."

Behind him, outside, I could hear a jet scream by, low.

"Jets?" was all I could think to ask. A lot had happened during the past few days. I was on a merchant marine ship. A strange beefy man beside me was accusing me of something that had to do with jets. I didn't have a lot of experience with merchant marine ships

507

or jets, and I had trouble putting things into perspective.

Someone came running up to the cabin and told the captain that boats were coming at us from shore.

Still confused, I thought, boats?

"Goddamnit, man," the captain yelled at me. He wheeled around and left.

I dressed and ran outside to the bridge. Standing by the captain, I watched two boats slowly make their way toward us. The captain ordered the anchor hauled. Jets continued to buzz the ship and the two approaching boats. It was a friendly sort of nuzzling by the aircraft, I thought, and I suddenly realized that the two boats were the landing craft with McNamara and his staff. I told Captain Flink that everything was going to be all right.

That was clear when I looked at the boats through the ship's binoculars. They were flying American flags.

"The consulate is coming," I said. "You've got more guests."

"Jesus H. Christ," the captain exclaimed. "I think I would rather be attacked by jets." After a pause he said, "I'll tell you this, my friend, I don't know how you'all did this, but I know if you hadn't been on this ship, I would have been out of here. Those two boats would not have caught me until I reached Singapore. I don't like jets and unidentified boats that come out of a country the Communists have just taken over. You people don't understand. This is a C-A-R-G-O ship."

Talking through a relay, I tried to get someone at Tugboat Control to pass the word to the Navy that the U.S. Consulate group was arriving at the *Pioneer Contender*. Finally, someone netting with Tugboat Control said that they would pass the message.

Sparky tried to get Sealift Command on the shortwave to get instructions on what to do. In his messages, he said the captain urgently requested permission to get under way.

As the boats approached, the captain threw the rope ladder over the side and ordered his crane in position to take on the luggage.

I contacted Tugboat Control again and asked if they were interested in two landing craft to assist in the evacuation. Otherwise, we were going to cast off them off. Tugboat Control, usually slow to answer any of my calls, immediately came back and said through the intermediary that landing craft were exactly what they needed. They asked if there was any way we could bring them up to Vung Tau, a coastal town near the mouth of the Saigon River.

I remembered that McNamara had hired some river pilots to drive the boats down the river, so I figured they could drive the boats to Vung Tau. The captain was busy with instructions to get the two landing boats tied up beside the ship near the rope ladder, so I asked someone in the control room, "How far is Vung Tau? How long to drive one of those landing craft there?"

"Eight, ten hours," the man at the wheel suggested.

I went back on the bridge and stood beside the captain. Borrowing his loudspeaker, I called down to McNamara and asked if his river pilots were up to taking the landing craft to Vung Tau. He answered through his loudspeaker that he didn't think so.

Two of the first people up the ladder were Filipino engineers who had maintained the generators at the consulate. I asked them what was wrong with the pilots, and they said the Vietnamese crew had disappeared before the boats left Can Tho. There were no river pilots on board; they had learned how to drive the boats themselves.

"Good," I said, "We're going to take those boats to Vung Tau. You guys and me."

Most of Vietnamese who arrived with me were on the upper deck as they watched the on-loading of the consulate crowd. I yelled for Ros, and he walked quietly out of the crowd. When I told him to get his stuff together because we were going for a ride, he turned without a question and went down a staircase to get his gear from the hold.

I went back to the portable radio, called Tugboat Control, and asked them to confirm that they seriously wanted these landing craft. Was this important or just something that would be sort of nice. Tugboat Control responded immediately and said the boats would make a difference in whether some people got out or not. It was important to those people.

I had left Loi and the kids, but perhaps I could help others. Maybe it was a trade-off. Putting the radio down, I told the captain that a Cambodian, a couple of Filipinos, and I were going to drive the landing boats to Vung Tau.

Flink said Sparky had just gotten word that the *Pioneer Contender* was also to relocate to Vung Tau to help in the evacuation. He suggested that I go in front of him with the two boats. He would hold a straight reading north and pull back to match my speed. All I had to do was keep looking over my shoulder and guide on him.

Ros and the Filipino engineers were on the deck. When everyone had cleared the landing craft except for a couple of men, we went over the side of the ship and down the ladders.

The Filipinos got into the rear boat. McNamara was still in the other boat when Ros and I climbed into it. He put the last items into the net and then motioned the crane operator to lift it. He had the

509

consulate's American flag with him and he was wearing his helmet with the word Congen and a big white star on the front. I welcomed him to the *Pioneer Contender* and told him of the arrangements to get the landing craft to Vung Tau, but he was exhausted and couldn't have cared less about what happened to the boats. He was glad to get to the ship. They had been fired on coming down the Bassac River, he said, but everyone was safely out.

"Good," I said, "go up, take my stateroom, take a shower, go to sleep. See you in the morning."

Ros and I were then alone in the boat, and we didn't have the faintest idea how to drive it.

The captain yelled through the loudspeaker to untie the lines holding us in. While Ros did this, I went into the small pilot area and tried to figure out the controls. Gauges on the console indicated that we had plenty of fuel. The throttles and the gear shifts for the two engines were prominent in the light from the gauges. With the steering wheel in front of me, that was all I needed, I thought.

The Filipinos threw off the ropes holding the two boats together at about the same time that Ros untied the ropes holding us to the *Pioneer Contender* and we were free.

I moved the throttles and rammed back into the other landing craft. After I changed gears and gave the boat more gas, I looked up to see that we were heading straight toward the ship's anchor chain. It was a long way up to the deck. The captain came on the loudspeaker and told us to stand clear of the anchor, which was coming out of the water.

Easy for him to say, I thought. I finally got control of the boat by putting it into reverse again and backing out some distance away from both the ship and the other landing craft. Ros came around behind me and watched as I played with the controls.

I finally stopped backing up, but I couldn't see directly in front of the boat when we were going forward. The controls were in the stern, where all the weight was, and the bow stuck out of the water like a shield. To see straight ahead, I had to walk over to the side of the boat while Ros held the wheel or turn the boat to one side or another. Also, because it was empty and the bow was high, the boat was difficult to drive. Wind and waves turned it from one side to the other. One second I was going due north, then a wave hit the front and I was going due west. I finally moved the boat off the port bow to the front of the *Pioneer Contender*, which had just gotten under way. The other landing craft fell in behind us.

--FORTY-FOUR--
Farewell Vietnam

We were a small parade heading north that early morning -- my landing craft in front, bouncing from one side to the other, then the less erratic landing craft and finally the monstrously large cargo ship. I tried to find a good medium speed. The faster we went, the more our bow stuck out of the water and the more affected we were by the wind and waves. The slower we went, the more we fell under the bow of the large ship behind us. I had to turn every minute to make sure we were staying on line.

When I got tired, Ros took the wheel. He struggled with it, and veered off to one side, followed by the landing craft behind us. As we got on line again, I thought that the crew of the *Pioneer Contender* surely must be cussing us as unfit sailors.

The wind picked up around 0400, and we were violently tossed around from side to side. Every time I turned around, my neck hurt. I tried to motion to the Filipinos to take the lead, but either they did not understand or did not want the point. Doggedly they stayed behind me.

When the sun came up, I had a chance to look around the pilot station after being in the dark all night. I found some lights. Why weren't they on when I got in?

And then I looked at the gears. I had only one engaged. Putting both engines in gear, the boat settled down to the more steady motion that I had admired in the Filipinos' boat.

Around 0800, the *Pioneer Contender* suddenly accelerated. Despite our best efforts to stay in front, she passed us to the east and was gone. Nice guys, I thought.

I had motioned the other boat to come up beside us and we were traveling along more or less even when Ros tapped me on the arm and motioned to the west. My first thought was that we had come in close to shore. Then, I thought we were drifting toward an island, because we were going forward, but it seemed the island was closing.

I tried to increase our speed, but the more I throttled forward, the more erratic the boat became. And the island was getting closer.

The Filipino's boat moved ahead, leaving me to fight the back and forth motion of the landing boat.

The island kept getting closer and I was unable to stop the

drift. Then I noticed boats between us and the island. Ros took the wheel while I reached for binoculars and fixed them on the approaching boats. They were filled with people. And that wasn't an island behind them, but many more boats, also filled with people.

The boats were overtaking us. What are those Filipinos doing that I'm not doing, I thought desperately, because their boat was moving ahead. They must have a better boat. That was no consolation because behind me, maybe a hundred boats were bearing down, straight at us. For what? Who told them I was here? I was taking this very personally. Perhaps they weren't coming at me. Perhaps they were heading to Vung Tau, and we were just in the way.

I could barely see the *Pioneer Contender* on the horizon. She wasn't extending the distance between us, and I wondered if I should be so lucky that she was, in fact, at Vung Tau. I had no way of knowing exactly where we were. All I knew for sure was that this haggard Cambodian and I were somewhere off the coast of Vietnam the day after the Americans had been evacuated and a hundred boats were rushing up to us. Could they be North Vietnamese attack boats? No, they must surely be South Vietnamese boat people heading to Vung Tau, I decided, so I turned the boat southeast to get out of their way. And they turned in my direction. The whole fleet. Why me? The Filipinos' boat continued to move toward the *Pioneer Contender*.

The first boat, lightly loaded with civilians, reached us from the rear. We had no weapons, thanks to the U.S. Navy, but Ros had found a knife somewhere. He looked to me for instructions, but I decided that we could not fend off one boat, much less the many others behind it.

I told Ros to yell at them to go on to Vung Tau, that they would be taken care of at Vung Tau. Ros went to the side of the boat and yelled. I had never heard him raise his voice before and was surprised at how squeaky it was.

The people on the boat ignored him, and someone threw a rope over a cleat on the side of the landing craft. Another boat came up on the other side and lashed on. People from both boats began piling into the landing craft. As other boats arrived, they tied onto the first boats, and their passengers scrambled into our craft. Soon the only place where we did not have boats around us was to our bow. The tongue of the landing craft prevented them from making purchase there.

Quickly our landing craft filled with people, settling the bow into the water, and I could see the ocean in front from the driving console.

More boats were coming up behind, but it was becoming

increasingly difficult to see them because so many boats had tied up to one another. I told Ros to get four or five men and bring them to me. Within minutes, he was back with a dark, swarthy crew. I told him to say that their being on board was no problem and I would look after them once we arrived at Vung Tau, but we could not take on any more passengers. I wanted them to go around and cut the lines holding the boats to our craft.

As Ros translated I looked up and saw dozens of people, some carrying guns, scramble over the boats toward us. I grabbed two men in the group and pointed to one side. I pushed one of the remaining men to the other side and told them to hurry and cut the ropes. Ros repeated my instructions, and the men leaped away, calling on some of their friends to help.

Within minutes we were free of the boats and we pulled forward. It was a wonderful relief to find that the landing craft maneuvered nimbly and could make speed with a full cargo. I located the tall silhouette of the *Pioneer Contender* in the distance and gave the boat full power. It surged ahead, and we began to leave the fishing boats behind.

I passed the Filipinos' boat, which had stayed well ahead of the boats that overtook me. By midday on 30 April 1975 we were near the *Pioneer Contender*, which sat amid an assortment of oceangoing vessels, barges, fishing boats and U.S. Navy ships. The port city of Vung Tau was off to the northwest.

Tugboat Control had mentioned meeting me south of Vung Tau, but no boat came out as I headed north. When I came alongside the *Pioneer Contender* the captain welcomed me over his loudspeaker. I yelled up that I had some more guests for him. Very special people, every one. He shook his head, but soon the rope ladder dropped over the side.

The first officers yelled down that a U.S. Navy tender was coming soon to pick me up. He told me to hurry with whatever I was doing and get ready to go to the ship, but I said that I had to deliver the landing craft to Tugboat Control before I did anything else.

"Your friends have already left," the first officer yelled. "Come on."

I pretended that I couldn't hear him. After everyone was off-loaded, Ros pushed us off from the side of the ship.

With the Filipinos following, we went out into the swirling mass of boats and debris. The harbor was ravaged by the war's end. Refugees were clinging to anything that would float, paddling with their hands and pieces of boards, standing in boats, holding children, arms outstretched to us and oceangoing vessels. Oil spills and litter swirled with the tide.

I saw what looked like hundreds of Vietnamese standing on a pier as they waited to be loaded onto a barge that was being moved into place nearby. A U.S. Navy ship, maneuvering in the northern part of the harbor, fired into a hill overlooking the evacuation area. I moved toward shore, past the barge near the pier and tried to find someone in charge. Four or five large oceangoing tugboats were in the area. As we came alongside one, I yelled out and asked for directions to Tugboat Control.

"Tugboat Control? Are you tetched? Bloody Tugboat Control was in Saigon. The docks at Newport. They pulled out last night." The sailor had a distinctive Australian accent. For a moment I thought I was hallucinating, that overnight I had traveled into the twilight zone. The voices at Tugboat Control had been American and I assumed the tugboats and other evacuation craft would have been crewed by Americans. I had also expected an organized evacuation of people, where there would be a clear need for the landing boats. But before me was a crowded, chaotic harbor clogged with thousands of hysterical refugees. And a sarcastic Aussie appeared to be in charge.

"Pulled out, are you crazy? Where'd they go?" I asked.

"Out to sea. They're on the *Chitosa Maru*. They brought this barge down the Saigon River. We needed your boats before we got the barge, but that's it. You supposed to meet them, mate?"

"Yeah."

"We're almost finished here. We've only the *Pioneer Contender* left to load."

"You don't need these landing craft?" I asked, suddenly very tired.

"Nope. We did, now we don't."

"You want these boats?"

"No."

"Well, I've broken my ass and was almost sunk trying to get them up here. You hear what I'm saying?"

"We're finished."

"I brought these boats up from the mouth of the Bassac River for you to use in evacuating some of those people over there!" I was getting angrier by the second.

"OK," said the Aussie. "OK, tie up to me. We'll use them."

We tied both landing boats up to the tug and were taken back to the *Pioneer Contender*. As I walked toward the rope ladder, the Aussie said, "Hey, you're the last American. Aren't you supposed to turn out the lights?" I shrugged and turned to the ladder.

514

When I climbed up and got on deck, I learned that I had just missed the Navy tender. Captain Flink said she probably would be back to pick me up but not to worry if she didn't. I could have my old stateroom back. He said he'd like that anyway, so that he'd have someone around to help him deal with all these people.

"Thank you for the stateroom, my friend," I said. "I am going to bed. If anyone calls for me, if the Navy boats comes back, tell them to go away."

As I turned to leave the bridge I looked around. With the advantage of the *Pioneer Contender*'s height, I could see U.S. Navy ships out to sea, the chaotic harbor, and the beaches, crowded with people and personal belongings.

A tugboat, under power, now held the barge against the pier. The press of people reached from the beach to the end of the pier. As the crowd surged forward, some people near the end were pushed off into the mass of humanity fighting for space on the barge below. The tugboat crew was unfazed and kept the barge steadily braced. The crowd suddenly surged forward again, and more people were pushed off, some falling, screaming, into the water. Two gangplanks were crowded with refugees slowly making their way into the barge. Everyone was carrying something -- women had children in their arms, men had suitcases, boys bags, soldiers guns. Everyone was pushing frantically, desperately.

Suddenly, an artillery round whistled overhead and landed in the middle of the harbor. Then another, as if the enemy gunner was registering his rounds. The people on the gangplanks continued to press forward. I saw their mouths open wide in horror when the tugboat reversed its engines and began to pull the barge slowly away from the pier. Men, women, and children, tried to jump on board, but many were not successful. As the tugboat and barge moved farther away from shore, I could see people in the water behind them. Slowly, the boat and barge turned and started in our direction through the maze of smaller vessels -- makeshift rafts, fishing vessels, South Vietnamese Navy lighters. More shells began to land randomly in the harbor. A U.S. Navy ship moved by us briefly and fired her huge deck guns in the direction of the North Vietnamese gun position, but the ship soon fell back and the incoming rounds continued. Smoke from fires near a warehouse on shore drifted by us out to sea. A low wail from thousands of desperate people drifted across the harbor.

From Vietnam, ARVN helicopters, singly and in groups of two and three, made their way out to sea in search of a receptive U.S. Navy ship. One helicopter, awkwardly flying alone, suddenly

515

James E. Parker, Jr.

exploded, like faulty fireworks, and debris rained down on the sea south of the barge making its slow way toward us.

Looking over the harbor, back to Vietnam, I thought about my ten years' involvement with this war. I had landed here in Vung Tau during the buildup of American forces in 1965. Now, as a CIA case officer, I was the last American out.

I had been so young when I arrived. I thought about leading men into combat, and I remembered battlefield events, both frightful and funny. Clear images swirled before my eyes -- lost friends, arrogant American bureaucrats, angry South Vietnamese generals berating me for abandoning them on the battlefield. I had put so many people into body bags. I was leaving friends behind.

And I saw antiwar slogans, talking heads on TV, student demonstrations. I remembered coming home as a soldier, proudly wearing my uniform, and how Dad shook my hand and how Mom, crying, ran her trembling fingers across my lips. I remembered coming down from the fighting in the hills of Laos -- the kids squealing when I came in the front gate, all the lights on in the house, Brenda standing on the porch smiling, Disney musicals blaring in the background.

But, mostly, I remembered the fighting. I shut my eyes and heard the familiar sounds of battle -- bombs going off, bullets whizzing overhead, helicopter blades whirring noisily above me, men screaming. I remembered the surges of adrenaline as my body tensed when I heard noises in the jungle night. I remembered holding Goss when he died and saw the young North Vietnamese soldier struggling gallantly to live. I smelled the dead from the ARVN 21st Division morgue. I felt the tight confines of the tunnel at Cu Chi when I knew a wounded VC was nearby, underground, in the dark. I saw the VC coming up out of the hole and I saw the muzzle blast as he fired at me. I heard Slippery Clunker Six reciting poetry, and I remembered standing by his body bag at Minh Thanh. And always the civilians -- the children huddling next to their mother in Can Tho, the farmers refusing to make eye contact, the orphans playing at Vi Thanh, and Loi protecting my body. I saw the Oriental moon through layers of jungles and the sun rising in the mountains and setting over rice fields. I could taste the lukewarm, iodized water from my canteen and Castro's C-rations stew, and I could smell putrid sweat and feel the rain and the heat and the pain and the anguish and I heard myself yell at Patrick not to die.

My mind was briefly out of control. Everything I had seen or heard or thought or done in this war merged together and then into the chaotic scene before me and I stopped and looked at the Vung Tau

516

harbor and the thousands of South Vietnamese refugees who were trying to follow us home.

What was the value to all this?

Standing on the bridge of the *Pioneer Contender* and looking back at Vietnam, I suddenly sensed -- in a startling moment of clarity -- that even though we had lost, we had done right by coming here to fight this war. History will look kindly on our good intentions to save a country from being overrun by an aggressive neighbor.

We did not win because the government that we came to save, the Government of South Vietnam was incompetent and corrupt and did not represent the people. And we did not win because American politicians and policy makers were guilty of incredibly bad decisions, from start to finish.

It seemed to me the lasting legacy of this war was the men who answered their country's call and gave their lives in Vietnam. In a time of shifting values, they reaffirmed the ageless principles of duty and country. They acquitted themselves in the finest traditions of American fighting men. They died young, in battle, with honor. Heroes, every one.

Facing the shore, I saluted them, slowly, with military precision.

I stood silent for a moment, turned and went below.

The war was over.

****

Loaded with thousands of Vietnamese refugees, the *Pioneer Contender* heaved anchor early the next morning – 2 May 1975 - and pointed her bow to the east. Vietnam faded behind us.

EPILOGUE

General Le Van Hung

At 7 p.m.PM on 30 April, 1975, General Hung, the former ARVN 21st Division commander and my friend, called his wife into his office in Can Tho. He told her that ten townspeople had come to him and asked him not to fight the advancing VC in their city's streets. The communists would shell the city and leave it waste, they said, and many civilians would die. Hung told his wife he understood and had agreed not to turn Can Tho into a hopeless battlefield. He also said a contingency plan to retreat with some of his soldiers to an isolated area of the Delta had been compromised and was no longer viable. Surrendering was not an option. He could not even bear to meet with Major Hoang Van Thach, the ranking VC in the area. He would not flee his country. He had an obligation to the men who had given their lives in its defense.

He was left with one honorable alternative, he said. He must take his own life.

His wife cried and pleaded with him to reconsider. "Why can't we leave for a foreign country like the others?" she asked.

He reminded her again of his obligations to his country and to his soldiers. And he continued, softly, slowly, "Don't let me lose my determination. Continuing to fight now will only bring trouble and loss not only to our family but to soldiers and civilians also. And I don't want to see the sight of any communists."

He stood, embraced his wife and wept. Finally he said,

"Hurry up and ask your mother and the children to come in to see me."

When his mother-in-law and the children came into his office, he said goodbye to them, kissing each child.

All the soldiers in his outer office came in next, lined up, expecting orders.

Hung told them the fighting was finished. He said the country was lost because of poor leadership in Saigon and asked their forgiveness if he, personally, had made mistakes. The atmosphere was solemn. "I accept death," he said. "Good-bye, my brothers."

He saluted them and then shook each man's hand. He asked everyone to leave. Some of his men did not move, so he pushed them out the door, shook off his wife's final pleas, and finally was alone in his office.

Within moments there was a loud shot. General Hung was dead.

****

General Tran Van Hai

On the morning of May 1, 1975, at the mobile headquarters of the ARVN 7th Division, General Hai's first lieutenant military aide came into his office.

General Hai lay face down at his desk. Alone during the night, without saying good-bye to anyone, he had committed suicide. A half-empty glass of brandy, laced with poison, was near an outstretched hand.

"Duty, Honor, Country"

GLOSSARY

ABCCC - U.S. Air Force Airborne Control and Command Center This 24-hour-a-day overhead air force platform coordinated air force support and provided radio relay services to Sky officers on the ground

abort – To suddenly cancel a mission.

ADO - Operation de L'Armee de Defense, the Hmong village militia originally organized by the French. General Vang Pao was chief of the ADO when he was initially contact ed by the CIA.

AIRA - Air Attache's office at the US Embassy.

Air America – the name of the CIA's proprietary airline operating throughout Indochina, but primarily in Laos.

air ops - This term was commonly used to indicate (1) the building by the Long Tieng ramp where landings and takeoffs were coordinated and (2) the overall business of Air America and Continental Air Service support to the field in Laos.

AK-47 - Soviet. Avtomat Kalashnikova automatic assault rifle used by the North Vietnamese. Fired a 7.62 mm bullet, was easy to maintain and use. Hmong forces used a number of captured AK-47s .

Alternate - aka LS 20A aka Twenty Alternate aka Long Tieng. CIA and Vang Pao headquarters in NE Laos.

Alley Cat – The orbiting USAF command center that took over from Cricket at night up in the Lao NE.

ao dias - A traditional Vietnamese woman's dress, which is always worn with pants because the long skirt is slit all the way to the hip on either side.

APC – Armored Personnel Carrier

Arc Light - Code word for the US Air Force's B-52 Arclight Strike Zones were rectangular map grids passed to the Air Force (by the coordinates of the corners) for bombing

ARMA - Army Attache's Office in the US Embassy - Provided ordnance, including T-28 bombs and fuses, to CIA forces.

ARVN – Army Republic of (South) Vietnam.

AWOL – Absent without leave.

B-40 – PAVN designation for the Soviet RPG-2 rocket propelled grenade.

B-52 - The Boeing B-52 Stratofortress came under the Strategic Air Command. First flown in 1952, it was designed to deliver nuclear bombs. The aircraft had a range of 7,500 miles unrefueled. After the Big Belly modification its bomb load was approximately 60,000 pounds.

baci - Hmong term for a party (welcoming baci, Hmong New Year baci, wedding baci, farewell baci). If the host could afford it, liquor was provided. Mekong, the local liquor, was usually the drink of choice, although Vang Pao served White Horse scotch. At some time during a baci, the host knelt in front of the guest of honor and tied a cotton string around the guest's wrist for luck and prosperity. Once the string was tied in a tight knot, the host usually downed a shot of liquor with the guest. The host then moved off, and other Hmong knelt to tie strings around the guest's wrist, followed by an exchange of drinks. If there was work to be done after the baci or the next day, Sky men usually insisted on a toast only with the host. Twenty, thirty, or forty Hmong could be waiting in line. Visitors from Washington, unsure of the custom and not wanting to offend anyone, would go shot for shot with the Hmong, until they toppled over. Though Sky officers often passed on the liquor, they appreciated the strings. They might have said, among themselves, that the strings were just Hmong hocus-pocus - had no actual bearing on a man's fate-but they never took them off. The strings were part of the required uniforms worn upcountry Laos by CIA officers.

backseater - The Meo officer-also known as a Robin-who sat in the backset of the 0-1 and, as a Lao national, was able to validate targets for a Raven and authorize strikes. They constituted a small, trained corps in Gen. Vang Pao's forces.

Ban Na – LS 15. Due west of the PDJ. Site of fierce fighting between the RTA and PAVN 165th Regiment in late 1970 to early 1971.

BC – Battalion Commando (Thai irregular units of 550 men)

BDA - Battle damage assessment, US Air Force term for after-action reporting on the effectiveness of its bombing missions. This was an integral part of CIA duties associated with the employment of F-IIIs in MR-II, Laos

BG - Bataillon Guerrier, or Warrior Battalion

Big Red One - The U.S. 1st Infantry Division

BLU – 82 – A massive bomb filled with a slurry explosive known for its tremendous concussion effect. Delivered out the back of a C-130

Bouam Loung - Lima Site 32: Mountaintop base for Hmong warrior Moua Cher Pao. After the fall of Phou Pha Thi, Lima Site 85, it became a critical U.S. intelligence gathering post.

BPP – Thai Border Patrol Police.

c

C-4 - A plastique explosive carried by military personnel in Vietnam, which would burn like Sterno when lit.

C-46 - A large aircraft made by Curtiss, called the Commando. It had two Pratt and Whitney R-2800 engines. The first of these airplanes was built in the 1930s.

C-47 - The most extensively-used transport during the 1930s and 1940s. This two engine aircraft was made by Douglas and designated the DC-3; also known as the Gooney Bird.

C-123 - A large aircraft made by Fairchild . Powered by two P & W R-2800 engines, it was the largest STOL (short field take off and landing) aircraft in the Air America inventory. A USAF workhorse.

C-130 - The Lockheed C-130 Hercules is a four-engine turboprop military transport aircraft designed and built originally by Lockheed. Capable of using unprepared runways for takeoffs and landings, the C-130 was originally designed as a troop, medical evacuation, and cargo transport aircraft. The versatile airframe has found uses in a variety of other roles, including as a gunship (AC-130) and aerial command and control platform.

C-Rations - Combat rations

Campaign" Z" - PAVN campaign in MR 2 (dry season, 1971-1972) to kill all the irregulars under command of Vang Pao and occupy Long Tieng. 27,000 PAVN soldiers were committed to the fight again approximately 4,000 irregulars. They lost.

Caribou C-7 - DeHavilland DHC-4 twin-engined STOL tactical transport aircraft, capable of carrying up to 32 troops or 8,740 pounds of cargo.

CAS - Controlled American Source, the term used for the CIA in Laos.

CASI - Continental Air Services International - a private airline that augmented Air America work in up- country Laos. It provided Twin Otter and Porter planes for field support work. The pilots were generally considered easy to work with. Although not a wholly owned CIA proprietary- created to serve the needs of the Agency.

CBU – Cluster Bomb Unit

Chapakao - Call sign used by the Hmong T-28 fighter pilots.

Charlie - Short for "Victor Charlie," meaning VC or Viet Cong

Chinook CH-47 - twin-engined, transport helicopter with rotor blades fore and aft.

chieu hoa - Amnesty program enabling VC to defect with safety to the South Vietnamese government side

claymore mines – Anti-personnel mines containing thousands of little steel balls that blow outward, covering an arch of about 120 degrees.

CORPS – In South Vietnam, there were four military corps: I Corps was the northern most region of the country. On the north was North Vietnam. Hqs city of I Corps was Hue. II Crops was the next region going south and covered most of the South Vietnamese Central Highlands. Cam Ranh was a large US naval base in this region. III Corps was right above Saigon. IV Corps was the Delta. Can Tho was the central city of the region.

COSVN - Central Office for South Vietnam: Field headquarters for the Viet Cong's political wing, the National Liberation Front (NLF), located inside Cambodia, northwest of Saigon. Often sought, but never found by the American and South Vietnamese forces.

Cricket - The radio call sign for the orbiting command center that controlled U.S. air in northern Laos during the day (redesignated as Alley Cat at night).

customer - Air America phrase for CIA case officers.

d

defensive perimeter – In Vietnam when infantry settled in for the night they made a circle in the jungle or where ever they were with the Hqs unit in the center and the men facing out in a protective circle.

DEROS – Date of Estimated Return from Overseas. Your ticket home.

dreaded   - Hog term used in much the same way the British use "bloody." "The dreaded ramp," Hog might say, "is this war's bulls-eye."

dust off – Medical evacuation mission by helicopter. The term maybe comes from the great amount of dust thrown up by the rotors as the med evacs come in to land.

e

E&E - Escape and evasion. A tactical process by which one tries to escape from an enemy-controlled area; also, the signature CIA paramilitary training course In addition to a hand gun or assault rifle, each CIA case officer and Air America pilot carried a military E&E kit when he was working in the field.

ETA   - Estimated time of arrival.

exfil - Short for an exfiltration or egress.

f

FAC - Forward air controller. Usually a USAF jet pilot flying a slow unprotected O-1 Bird Dog spotter plane.

FAG - Forward air guide, usually an Asian, who help direct fighters onto targets from the ground.

FSB - Fire Support Base. An artillery battery set up to give fire support to surrounding units.

fast mover - Any military jet that delivers ordnance.

559th Transportation Group - Secret North Vietnamese unit that operated the Ho Chi Minh Trail. Based in Vinh, North Vietnam,

flack vest - An armored vest issued to American soldiers. They were hot, heavy, and often not worn despite the protection they offered.

FNG - Fucking new guy– Used throughout Indochina by American forces to refer to new replacements.

g

girl singer - Hog term used to describe a man who puts on airs and acts in a pretentious manner. It was taken from the visual image of on overdressed male lounge singer, strutting around on stage with half-closed eyes, who tried to appear romantic while warbling a love song to no one in particu- lar. Hog said most politicians were girl singers.

GM - Groupe Mobile. A French military term for a regiment-size unit of approximately eight hundred Hmong. There were six Hmong GMs in MR-II in 1971. Groupement Mobile, or mobile group. Under the French system , a multi-battalion force brought together on a temporary basis for a specific operation. Although initially faithful to the French concept, beginning in March 1961, the FAL formed permanent Groupements Mobiles averaging three battalions apiece, comparable to regiments. Beginning in 1967, the CIA also formed permanent GMs averaging three to four irregular battalions each.

gunships - A tactical innovation of the Vietnam War, the first gunship was a modified World War II C-47 Gooney Bird cargo plane, redesignated as AC-47 and known as Dragonship, Puff, or Spooky. Also in Vietnam a combat helicopter, commonly a UH-I "Huey" armed with multiple machine guns, rockets, and automatic grenade launchers. Primarily used in close support of infantry operations. Also used to support Gen. Vang Pao's troops in Laos, under the auspices of the Lao Air Force, and the 14th Special Operations Wing of the Air Commandos. AC-119 Flying Boxcars were also modified, using aerial parachute flares to operate at night. C-130 cargo planes were later converted to AC-130 gunships and were used extensively over the Ho Chi Minh Trail and became the best truck- killer of the war.

grunt – Originally slang for a Marine fighting in Vietnam, but over time applied to any soldier involved in ground combat.

h

H-34 - Sikorsky H-34 Choctaw helicopters was the dated (deliveries to the U.S. Army began in early 1955) work horse of Air America used all over Laos. However in the high mountains of NE Laos they did not have the lift capacity to carry much cargo or troops.

H&I - harassment and interdiction, commonly called H&I fire. Artillery bombardments used to deny the enemy terrain which they might find beneficial to their campaigns. The targets for H&I were general rather than specific, confirmed military targets.

HE - High explosive, as in HE rocket.

hang - A term, as defined by CIA people in Washington, DC, in the early 1970s, to describe people who could "hang in there" when the going got rough. "The man's got Hang, " was the most popular phrasing and, in SOG/Washington circles, was usually used in reference to Hog, who by reputation, stayed in the thick of the fighting in Loos and never come out. According to old-timers at Long Tieng, however, the phrase came into the up-country language from the Lao word, "hang" (phonetic), which means a man with a strong heart; a man who stays and fights. The Lao phrase "Loo me hong lie" (phonetic) means that he is a man with resolve and principle. The phrase Hog used most up-country was, "The man has no hang," a rough translation of the popular Lao phrase "bo me hong" (phonetic), which means he is not strong and cannot be depended on - he will not stay and fight.

Headquarters 333 - Thai headquarters for paramilitary operations in Laos, located at Udorn RTAFB .

highly dangeral - Hog term used to indicate anything risky. It originates in a radio message from one of Hog's ops assistants who was describing a very dangerous field situation.

Hmong - One of several tribes who, over the course of several thousand years, drifted south out of China into the mountains of Laos. Other tribes include the Yao and the Koo. Because the rugged terrain of the mountains separated the Hmong, three dominant groups evolved in Laos. The Flower Hmong and Stripe Hmong, known as peaceful, agrarian hill people, lived in the western section of Laos. The White Hmong, who lived around the PDJ, were considered the least civilized and the most tenacious warriors. Vang Pao was military leader of the White Hmong from the late 1940s to the mid-1970s. Touby LyFong also had considerable influence in this clan, although he tended to focus his work on political and social programs. (Note: The name Hmong is used as both singular and plural. Aka also known in the pejorative as "Meo.")

Hmong hocus-pocus - Anything in the Hmong culture that Sky people did not understand.

Ho Chi Minh Trail - A camouflaged highway network, in the jungled southeastern Laos corridor occupied by the NVA after 1959, across which flowed supplies and soldiers for the war in South Vietnam.

Huey - The Bell UH-1 Iroquois (unofficially Huey) is a military helicopter powered by a single turboshaft engine, with two-bladed main and tail rotors. The first combat operation of the UH-1 was in the service of the U.S. Army during the Vietnam War. The original designation of HU-1 led to the helicopter's nickname of Huey.[2] In September 1962, the designation was changed to UH-1, but "Huey" remained in common use. Approximately 7,000 UH-1 aircraft saw service in Vietnam.

i

ICC - International Control Commission

Indoor work - Bureaucratic nonsense.

Infantry platoon - In 1965 the US 1st Division was organized into 3 Brigades, each with 3 Battalion, each with 3 infantry companies, each with 3 infantry platoons. In the platoon were 3 rifle squads that included 2 fire teams of 5 men each and a squad leader. Plus a heavy weapons squad which included 2 M-60 machine guns. The hqs unit of each platoon included a radio operator, a platoon sergeant and a platoon leader.

Irregulars – generic terms applied to all soldiers under command of Hmong war lord Vang Pao in the CIA Army of Laos.

j

JLD – Joint Liaison Detachment. Cover name for the CIA base in the Udorn AFB.

Jungle's Mouth - Nickname for the western edge of the Plaine des Jarres.

k

Karst - Rugged rock column that juts straight up in the air. It is found most often on valley floors.

KIA – Killed in action.

Kicker - Term used for flight mechanic on Air America rotary wing and for cargo master on fixed-wing planes. The word's origin is associated with the job on transport planes of pushing or "kicking" rice and other supplies out the side of air delivery planes.

Khumu - Also known as Lao Teung. A tribal group in Laos who believe that their ancestors were responsible for the ancient stone jars on the Plaine des Jarres.

Knuckle draggers - Phrase used to describe CIA's SOGers, alluding to their possible close kinship with the gorilla family.

I

LAW - Hand carried, shoulder fired Light Anti-tank Weapon

Lima 22 – Air America designation for the main airfield on the central Plaine des Jarres.

Lima Site 5 – Pa Dong. South of the PDJ. First headquarters for the CIA army under Vang Pao.

Lima Site 15 - Ban Na. West of the PDJ. Site of fierce fighting between the Royal Thai Army and the North Vietnamese 165th Regiment.

Lima Site 20 – Sam Thong. Former USAID center in NE Laos, just over the ridgeline from Long Tieng.

Lima Site 20A – Long Tieng. Headquarters for the CIA and for Hmong War Lord Vang Pao.

Lima Site 32 – Bouam Long. North of the PDJ. Mountain foutress commanded by Cher Pao Moua. Always surrounded by North Vietnamese and attack often. It was new overrun or occupied by communist forces during the Vietnam War.

LOH - (pronounced "loach") Light observation helicopter.

Long Tieng – valley 20 miles southwest of the Plaines des Jarres in which the CIA and Vang Pao had their headquarters. See Lima Site 20A

LS - Abbreviation for Lima Sites, landing airstrips in Laos Sometimes, the designation did not include the S; the airfield at Vientiane was designated L 08. The airfield in the Long Tieng valley was LS 20A. Although pilots and customers often said the whole phrase, Lima Site Twenty Alternate, it was most commonly referred to as Twenty Alternate or, more simply, the Alternate. When the Hmong civilians moved into a new area, they often built a Lima Site, and an Air America engineer had to fly up by helicopter and inspect it before a fixed-wing plane could land. These Lima Sites were often dug out of the sides of mountains ; severe wind sheers and drafts affected take-offs and landings. There was little margin for error in landing.

LSD – Landing boats used by the Can Tho consulate to evac down the Bassic river and then driven up the coast of Vietnam to Vung Tau to aid in the evacuation of refugees.

LZ - Landing zones. The LZs by Hmong villages were cleared areas where fixed-wing pilots aimed air delivery of supplies, such as rice. By Hmong and Thai defensive positions, LZs were primarily landing areas for helicopters. They were usu- ally designated by two-letter combinations of white cloth staked to the ground. The LZs on Skyline were in the C series: CA, CB, CC, and so forth.

m

M-16 - American 5.56 mm infantry rifle

M-60 – American 7.62 mm machine gun.

M-79 - A grenade launcher. The shoulder-fired weapon resembled a sawed-off, hugely bored shotgun, and could lob its projectiles more than a hundred meters.

MACV – Military Assistance and Advisory group.

Mekong - The river that feeds the Mekong Delta of South Vietnam. Also separates Laos and Thailand. Also, a very inexpensive Thai liquor, not much different in taste from Southern mash bourbon. A few drinks can cause a normal-size Occidental man to fall over backward.

'Merican - American. This southern-accented word was initiated by Hog to describe any person or ideal that represents American common values. "Hard work 's the 'Merican way So is good pie."

Mercenaries – aka Thai irregulars

Military regions - There were four MRs in Laos: MR I in the northwest, MR II in the northeast, MR III halfway down the eastern border, and MR IV in the south.

n

NCO - Noncommissioned officer. A person bearing one of the sergeant ranks in the armed services.

Ni Ban - Hmong village chief. Elected by the people, the Ni Ban decided when the village moved, ruled on domestic disputes, settled property rights, and selected the men to join the GMs.

Ni Khong - An official appointed by Vang Pao and Touby Ly - Fong to coordinate activities of the various Ni Bans. Ni Khongs usually were former Ni Bans. They ruled on territorial matters and differences between Ni Bans. Disputes that they could not settle were passed on to Vang Pao or Touby LyFong.

Nipple - Nickname for the marshy lowlands jutting off the southern Plaine des Jarres.

NVA – see PAVN. People's Army of Vietnam.

o

105 mm artillery – US. 102 model was first introduced in Vietnam 1966. Has an effective range up to 7 miles.

155 mm artillery – US. This towed heavy artillery piece was used in Vietnam and Laos and has an effective range up to 9 miles.

130mm field gun – Soviet. The M-46 was developed in the 1950s from the M-36 130 mm naval gun used on ships and for coast defense. It is has a maximum range of 23 miles.

14.7 AAA gun – Soviet. Has a range of 3,000 meters horizontally and 2,000 meters vertically against low flying planes. Has a 600 rpm rate of fire.

37 mm AAA gun – Sovet. Used effectively in WW II to kill more than14,000 Axis planes. Often mounted in a 4 gun carrier. Maximum range - 5 miles. Also known as the "Jane Fonda gun;" she was famously photographed sitting in one of the firing seats in a quad rack during her visit to Hanoi during the Vietnam War.

81 mm mortar - A medium-weight, smooth-bore, muzzle-loading, high-angle-of-fire mortar used for long-range indirect fire support to light infantry, air assault, and airborne units across the entire front of a battalion zone of influence. 3 mile range

60 mm mortar - The M224 model is a smooth bore, muzzle-loading, high-angle-of-fire weapon used for close-in support of ground troops. 2 mile range.

4.2 inch mortar – Rifled tube that can fire a M3 high explosive (HE) shell packed 3.64 kilograms of explosive charge, placing it between the 105-mm HE shell (2.18 kilograms of charge) and 155-mm HE shell (6.88 kilograms of charge) in terms of blast effect. Range: 2 miles

OCS - Officer Candidate School. Schools run within each service to train men and women from the enlisted ranks to become officers.

Ops assistants - Hmong or Thai men who assisted Sky case offi- cers in the field. They were used as interpreters, translators, area experts, radio operators, and bodyguards A close bond always developed between a case officer and his ops assistant.

p

Padong - Lima Site 5: Mountain encampment where CIA and U.S. Special Forces teams trained Hmong in 1961. Vang Pao's first headquarters. See LS 05.

Pair of second - Hog phrase that meant a short period of time.

Parrot's Beak - A Cambodian salient just northwest of Saigon, across which the NVA sometimes infiltrated units, especially during the 1968 Tet Offen- sive.

PARU – (Thai) Police Aerial Reinforcement Unit. Unit first used to train Vang Pao's hills tribe guerrillas in Laos. Created by CIA case officer Bill Lair.

Pathet Lao -   Lao hill   people   who supported   the Communists and were hosts to the North Vietnamese in Laos. Predominantly from the Hmong and Kao tribes, they rarely became involved in confrontations with the Hmong GMs. Lao Communist movements included: the People's Party of Laos (Phak Pasason Lao--PPL); the Lao Patriotic Front (Neo Lao Hak Sat-NLHS), the central committee of which commanded the armed forces known as the Lao People's Liberation Army; and the Patriotic Neutralists. But by any name, these groups were little more than front organizations manipulated by Hanoi.

PAVN - People's Army of Vietnam. Before 1975 called North Vietnamese Army (NVA).

PDJ - Abbreviation for Plaine des Jarres, or Plain of Jars, a two hundred and fifty- square-mile plateau in the mountains of Laos near the North Vietnamese border. It is named for the stone jars that litter the landscape; origin of the jars is unknown. As critical terrain in central Indochina, the PDJ is a trading center and often a battlefield. It is the homeland of the White Hmong. Fertile plateau with moderate climate, named by the French for the ancient stone jars found there. Colonial French built homes here.

phi - The spirits that the Meo believed inhabited everything, from rocks to humans, from trees to airplanes.

Phou Pha Thi - Lima Site 85: Ultra-secret U.S. navigational site guarded by Hmong. Overrun in March 1968 by North Vietnamese Army.

Porter - A Swiss-built short-takeoff-and-landing (STOL) air- plane used by both Air America and Continental Air Services. A single engine plane usually flown by a single pilot. Abbreviated name for the Pilatus Porter, a light STOL aircraft used by Bird & Son/CASI.

PRC - 25 - Portable Radio Communications, Model 25. A back-packed FM receiver-transmitter used for short-distance communications. The range of the radio was 5-10 kilometers, depending on the weather.

PRC - People's Republic of China

r

Ramp - The city block-size asphalt tarmac at the west end of the Long Tieng runway that was the hub of CIA activity in MR II.

REMF - Rear-echelon motherfucker-the name given to all people stationed away from the combat areas.

Red Dog Control - Hmong radio hookup with the US Air Force's F-111 bombers. Hmong talkers sat for hours in front of the dials on their radios-silently waiting for transmissions from the F-111pilots and working on their messages to their heroes, to the "almost astronauts."

RLAF – Royal Lao Air Force

RLG -   Royal Lao Government

ROE -   Rules of Engagement , by which the U.S. military sought to control and limit the war.

RON -   Remain overnight.

RPD – A 7.62 mm communist machine gun with a 100-round, belt operated drum that fires the same round as the AK-47.

RPG – A communist self-propelled rocket.

RTA – Royal Thai Army

RTG – Royal Thai Government

RTB - Returning to base, a phrase used by F-111 pilots to tell the Hmong talkers at Red Dog Control that they had dropped their ordnance and were returning to Thailand. The pilots often used the words, "I am RTB," and sometimes followed this phrase with "Good afternoon to you," or "Nice talking to you," or "Have a good day." The Hmong talkers seized on these farewells-they asked Sky officers hundreds of questions about the exact meaning of each phrase. At first, they usually repeated the farewell in signing off, but they eventually interchanged the phrase. When an F-111 pilot said "Good afternoon to you," for example, the Hmong might sign off by saying "Drive carefully. And thanks." The Hmong talker would then sit back, stare at the radio dials, and beam.

RTO – Radio operator, usually a PRC-25.

s

S-1 – Designation of personnel staff for a field unit

S-2 – Designation of intelligence staff for a field unit.

S-3 – Designation of the operations staff for a field unit.

S-4 - Designation of supply staff for a field unit.

S-5 – Designation of civic affairs staff for a field unit.

SAC - Strategic Air Command, under which the B-52 bombers were flown.

Sappers – North Vietnamese special assault troops. Used for a wide range of missions, sometimes by themselves, or sometimes as spearheads for a main-force echelon. The Viet Cong also deployed sappers particularly after Tet Offensive losses had made large-scale attacks hazardous. Called *dac cong* were an elite, especially adept at infiltrating and attacking airfields, firebases and other fortified positions. About 50,000 men served in PAVN as sappers, organized into groups of 100-150 men, further broken down into companies of roughly 30-36 men, with sub-divisions into platoons, squads and cells. One of the sappers in the spectacular 1968 Tet Offensive attack against the US Embassy for example, was once a driver to the US Ambassador.

SAR - Search and rescue. An elaborate procedure under Air Force rules involving the suppression of ground fire by fighters before Jolly Green helicopters attempt a pickup.

SGU - Special Guerrilla Unit. The most effective of Vang Pao's troops, using helicopters, were organized into these small combat units.

Sky - Term used by the locals for the CIA in up-country Laos.

Skyline - The towering ridgeline that guarded the north side of the Long Tieng valley.

Slick – Helicopter for transporting troops. Often "Hueys."

Spec-4 - Specialist Fourth Class. An enlisted rank immediately above Private First Class. Most enlisted men who had completed their individual training and had been on duty for a few months were Spec-4's, Probably the most common rank in the Vietnam-era army.

Spectre and Spooky – C-130 gunships (AC-130H and AC-130U). Different avionics and subsystems aside the two aircraft have many similarities. All of the weaponry aboard both is mounted to fire from the left (port) side of the non-pressurised aircraft. During an attack the gunships performs a pylon turn, flying in a large circle around the target, allowing it to fire at it far longer than a conventional attack aircraft. The AC-130H Spectre was armed with two 20 mm M61 Vulcan cannons, one Bofors 40mm autocannon, and one 105 mm M102 cannon. The AC-130H Spooky has all that in addition to a 25mm gun.

SOG - Special Operations Group of the CIA Directorate of Operation. It was responsible for staffing the Lao program The CIA Special Operations Group should not be confused with the US Army Special Operations Group, which saw extensive action in Vietnam. Although they had some similar paramilitary missions, they were two separate organizations.

SOGer - Any CIA case officer working in SOG Also, see knuckle draggers.

SOP – Standard operating practice or procedure.

sortie - One attack, or operational flight, by a single military aircraft or single formation of aircraft.

Swedish K - submachine gun. A popular CIA and SOG weapon.

Sweep operations – In Vietnam when an infantry unit lined up and moved through an area in search of the enemy. Initially with the 1st/28th

Infantry battalion, 1st Division, that meant getting everyone on line and advancing into a jungle area. However in time it meant each platoon lining up by squad files to move through thick foliage. Problem always was keeping the different units on line... that one file didn't get so far ahead of another that they would be taken as the enemy.

t

T-54 – Soviet medium tank. First developed and used in WW II, they were the main stay of the North Vietnamese armor corps.

T-28 - A propeller-driven, single engine airplane that was the only figher and bombing plane flown by the Lao Air Force.

Tahan Sua Pran – "Tiger soldiers." Aka Thai irregulars. Thai volunteers. Thai mercenaries.

Tan Son Nhut - The large airbase on the outskirts of Saigon. The airfield was used by civil and military aviation, making it one of the busiest airfields in the world. Hundreds of thousands of American soldiers arrived and departed Vietnam through the Tan Son Nhut terminal.

Tet - Vietnamese lunar new year festival, celebrated as a national holiday

Triage – The sorting out of patients according to the criticalness of their needs, i.e., those who need immediate surgery versus those who need lesser care.

Twin Pack - A Sikorsky S-58T used for heavy sling loads in sup- port of field operations It was usually flown by senior pilot.

Twin Otter – DeHavilland DHC -6 turboprop STOL utility tansport aircraft capable of carrying up to 20 passengers or 4,280 pounds of cargo. Flown by Air America and CASI in Laos.

u

Udorn Air Base - Northern Thai air base. Location of CIA headquarters for its operations in Laos.

UNITY – Program to deploy battalions of Thai volunteers to Laos (1970-1974). Also known as the 333 units. Soldiers sometimes called Irregulars, mercenaries, volunteers and/or Tahan Sua Pran (Tiger Soldiers).

v

VC – Viet Cong. Viet Cong: Military units of indigenous South Vietnamese Communists. Almost ceased to exist after the 1968 Tet offensive.

Viet Minh – Communist guerrilla forces fighting for independence against the French.

VP – Vang Pao, Hmong War Lord and General in the Lao Army. Head of the CIA army in NE Laos.

w

White Mice - The National Police of South Vielnlm. K.IDiil: corruption and their willingness to be used for political called because of the white hats and shirts of their uniform.

Willie Pete - white phosphorus ordinance. Ravens used it to make a smoke plume which functions as a spatial reference on the ground in the vicinity of a target.

Selected Bibliography

Books

Abramson, Rudy *Spanning the Century* Morrow New York 1992

Anderson, Charles *The Grunts* Presidio Press Novato 1976

Andrew, Chris *For the President's Eyes Only* HarperPerennial New York 1996

Baker, Mark *Nam* Random House New York 1981

Broyles, Jr. William *Brothers in Arms* U. of Texas Press Austin 1986

Castle, Tim *At War in the Shadow of Vietnam* Columbia U Press New York 1993

Cates, Allen *Honor Denied* iUniverse Bloomington 2011

Chantrakiri, Rueng *A Man named Dhep* Clet Thai Bangkok 1992

Clark, Eugene *The Secrets of Inchon* Putman New York 2002

Conboy, Kenneth *Shadow War* Paladin Press Boulder 1995

Davis, Charles *Across the Mekong* Hildesigns Press Charlottesville 1996

Devlin, Larry *Chief of Station, Congo* Public Affairs New York 2007

Dodd, Jan *Vietnam: A Rough Guide* Penguin Books New York 1996

Donovan, David *Once a Warrior King* Random House New York 1985

Fall, Bernard *Street Without Joy* Stackpole Mechanicburg 1961

Fall, Bernard *Hell in a Very Small Place* Lippincott Philadelphia 1966

Freedman, Lawrence *Kennedy's Wars* Oxford University Press New York 2000

Gaddis, John Lewis *We Now Know* Oxford University Press New York 1997

Glasser, Ronald *365 Days* George Braziller New York 1969

Goulden, Joseph *Korea, The Untold Story* Times Book New York 1982

Haas, Michael *In the Devil's Shadow* Naval Institute Press Annapolis 2000

Halberstam, David *The Best and The Brightest* Fawcett Crest Bloomington 1993

Halberstam, David *The Coldest Winter* Hyperion New York 2007

Halberstam, David *The Fifties* Fawsett New York 1994

Harriman, Averell *Special Envoy* Random House New York 1975

Hathorn, Reginald *Here There are Tigers* Stackpole Mechanicburg 2008

Helms, Richard *A Look Over My Shoulder* Random House New York 2003

Jennings, Phillip *The Politically Incorrect Guide to the Vietnam War* Regnery
Washington 2010

Karnow, Stanley *Vietnam: A History* Penguin Books New York 1983

Kissinger, Henry *Ending the Vietnam War* Simon&Schuster New York 2003

Kissinger, Henry *White House Years* Simon&Schuster New York 1979

Lanning, Michael *The Only War We Had* Ivy Books New York 1987

Lanning, Michael *Inside the VC and the NVA* Fawcett New York 1992

Leary, William *Perilous Missions* University of Alabama Tuscaloosa 1984

Logevall, Fredrik *Embers of War* Random House New York 2013

MacGregor, Sandy *No Needs for Heroes* Southwood Press Australia 1993

Maclear, Michael *Vietnam: The Ten Thousand Day War* Mandarin House
London 1981

Manchester, William *American Caesar* Little, Brown Boston 1978

Mangold, Tom *The Tunnels of Chu Chi* Random House New York 1985

McMahon, Robert *Major Problems in the History of the Vietnam War* Health
Lexington 1990

McMaster, H.R. *Dereliction of Duty* HarperPerennial New York 1997

Mersky, Peter *Naval Air War in Vietnam* Kensington Publishing New York 1981

Methven, Stuart *Laughter in the Shadows* Naval Institute Press Annapolis 2008

Moore & Galloway *We Were Soldiers Once... and Young* Random New York 1992

Morrison, Gayle *Sky is Falling* McFarland & Company Jefferson 1999

Parker, James *Codename Mule* Naval Institute Press Annapolis 1995

Parker, James *Last Man Out* Random House New York 1996

Parker, James *Battle for Skyline Ridge* Mule Press Las Vegas 2014

Petcharawises *People of the Hills* Duang Kamol Bangkok 1980

Plaster, John L. *SOG* Simon&Schuster New York 1997

Polifka, Karl *Meeting Steve Canyon* Karl L. Polifka Virginia 2013

Prados, John *Lost Crusader* Oxford Univeristy New York 2003

Prados, John *Safe for Democracy* Ivan R. Dee Chicago 2006

Robbins, Christopher *Air America* G.P. Putnam's Sons New York 1979

Robbins, Christopher *The Ravens* Crown Publishing New York 1995

Roddy, Ray Jr. *Circles in the Sky* Infinity West Conshohocken 2009

Schlesinger, Arthur *General MacArthur and President Truman* Transaction Publishers New Brunswick 1992

Shackley, Theodore *The Third Option* McGraw-Hill New York 1981

Shapley, Deborah *Promise and Power* Little, Brown Boston 1992

Sibounheuang *White Dragon Two* Altman Spartanburg 2002

Singlaub, John *Hazardous Duty* Summit Books New York 1991

Snepp, Frank *Decent Interval* Random House New York 1977

Sorley, Lewis *A Better War* Harcourt Brace Orlando 1999

Sibounheuang *White Dragon Two* Altman Printing Spartanburg 2002

Stieglitz, Perry *In a Little Kingdom* M.E. Sharpe, Inc Armonk 1990

Sullivan, William *Obbligato* W.W. Norton New York 1984

Thornton, Richard *Odd Man Out* Brassey's Washington 2000

Toland, John *In Mortal Combat* Morrow New York 1991

Trest, Warren *Air Commando One* Smithsonian Institute Washington 2000

Warner, Roger *Shooting at the Moon* Sreerforth Press S. Royalton 1996

Weiner, Tim *Legacy of Ashes* Anchor Books New York 2008

Willenson, Kim *The Bad War* Newsweek New York 1987

Zumwalt, Jr. Elmo *On Watch* Zumwalt & Consultants Virginia 1976

Declassified Official U.S. Government Documents and Tapes

• Memo on Pres Eisenhower's advice to incoming President Kennedy that it is in the U.S. interest to maintain Lao neutrality. Memorandum of a Conference in the White House on January 19, 1961 attended by President Eisenhower and President-Elect Kennedy.

• State Department review of significant events in Laos during the mid-60s. Foreign Relations of the United States 1964-1968 Volume XXVIII Laos 1 January 1969.

• Godley saying to Kissinger that Lao SGUs for the most part defend Long Tieng. Most Hmong have left the fight. Kissinger says Nixon wants "maximum" effort in Laos. Memorandum of Conversation. Source: National Archives, Nixon Presidential Materials, NSC Files, Box 547, Country Files, Far East, Laos, 1 April 1970– 11 August 1970. Top Secret; Sensitive. The meeting with Godley was held in Kissinger's office. Holdridge forwarded the memorandum to Kissinger under an

August 5 covering memorandum. Kissinger approved it on August 10. Washington, July 23, 1970.

• Discussion on the use of Thai Khmer SGUs in southern Laos. Memo on use of Thai Irregulars in northern Laos

• Memo from DCI Helms to President Nixon on Thai personalities including Dhep.

• Discussion on assignment of Thai Irregular soldiers to Long Tieng. Attacks imminent. 1040 U.S. personnel ceiling discussed. Minutes of a Meeting of the Washington Special Actions Group. Source: Foreign Relations of the United States, 1969–1976 Volume XX, Southeast Asia, 1969–1972, Document 88. September 10, 1970

• Foreign Relations of the United States, 1969–1976 Volume XX, Southeast Asia, 1969–1972, Document 93. Memorandum From the Assistant Secretary of State for East Asian and Pacific Affairs (Green) to the Under Secretary of State for Political Affairs (Johnson). October 9, 1970

• Foreign Relations of the United States, 1969–1976 Volume XX, Southeast Asia, 1969–1972, Document 94. October 23, 1970

• Minutes of a Meeting of the Washington Special Actions Group. Source: National Archives, Nixon Presidential Materials, NSC Files, NSC Institutional Files (H-Files), Box H–115, WSAG Meetings Minutes, Originals, 1971. Top Secret; Nodis. The meeting took place in the Situation Room of the White House. According to Kissinger's Record of Schedule, the meeting ended at 4:37. (Library of Congress, Manuscript Division, Kissinger Papers, Box 438, Miscellany, 1968–76) Washington, February 9, 1971, 3:15 p.m.

• Agreement to use US Army Cobra gunships on med- evacs in Ban Na. VP prospects for next dry seasons using Thai SGU. Number of RTA cadre committed to irregular force. Minutes of a Meeting of the 40 Committee, Sam Clemente, March 31, 1971

• Memo of Souvanna Phouma request for additional Thai military unit to Long Tieng. President Nixon approves. Memorandum From the President's Assistant for National Security Affairs (Kissinger) to President Nixon. Source: National Archives, Nixon Presidential Materials, NSC Files, Box 567, Country Files, Far East, Thailand, Thai Involvement in Laos. Top Secret; Sensitive; Nodis. Sent for action. Holdridge and Kennedy sent this memorandum to Kissinger on April 14 (Maybe 1970, but probably 1971) recommending that he sign it and indicating U. Alexis Johnson had cleared it. Washington, undated.

• Haig says Long Tieng survived last PAVN attacks due Thai irregulars Memorandum From the Deputy Assistant for National Security Affairs (Haig) to President Nixon Washington. Includes the following statement: "The energy and enthusiasm displayed by General Dhep, the Thai Commander, have raised morale considerably among the Thai irregulars. Morale is better today than at the beginning of April. This in turn has had a favorable effect on the morale of General Vang Pao and his Meo troops." And... "Generals Dhep and Vang Pao believe that the Long

Tieng situation has been stabilized for the moment and they are beginning to think in terms of offensive action of their own beginning in June." May 7, 1971.

• Telegram on Thai PM's attitudes about Thai irregular soldiers in Laos Telegram From the Consulate in Hong Kong to the Department of State11. Source: National Archives, RG 59, Conference Files, 1966–1972: Lot 73 D 323, Withdrawn Box 14/15, Folder 943. Secret; Nodis. Drafted by James L. Carson (S/S), cleared by Nicholas A. Veliotes, and approved by Green. Also sent to UNSTO and repeated to Bangkok and Vientiane. Hong Kong, May 29, 1971, 1630Z.

• Minutes of a Meeting of the Senior Review Group Washington, June 8, 1971

• Memo of Military situation on PDJ. VP plans to replace his Hmong SGUs with Thai irregulars   Memorandum From the President's Assistant for National Security Affairs (Kissinger) to President Nixon Washington, July 3, 1971.

• Staff Report to the U.S. Senate Committee on Foreign Relation regarding the war in Laos. For the Subcommittee on U.S. Security Agreements and Commitments Abroad. Lowenstein and Moose report on their April 22 to May 4, 1971 trip to SEA for an update on the war in Laos. Includes details of Thai irregulars under command of Vang Pao at Long Tieng, Laos. 3 August 1971

• WSAG Discuss using VP's recent capture of the PDJ as spring board for peace talks. Sullivan establishes the dialogue. Minutes of a Meeting of the Washington Special Actions Group Washington, August 10, 1971

• USAF "Summary: Air Operations Southeast Asia" Headquarters PACAF, August 1971. 1 September 1971.

• Nixon Tape 82-1.Speaking to the cabinet, Nixon says purpose of our efforts in Laos at this point is to give time to get U.S. out of Vietnam. President says, "Asian boys should fight Asian boys." 4 November 1971.

• USAF   Contemporary Historical Examination of Current Operations (CHECO) Air War in Northern Laos 1 April-30 November 1971, December 1, 1971 112

• Nixon Tape 639-2   Unidentified briefer tells Nixon that the NVA have launched a major offensive in Laos. Lost includes two T-28s and three F-4s - one being shot down by a MIG over Laos. 18 December 1971

• WSAG on loss of PDJ 18-21 Dec '71 Washington Special Actions Group held December 23, 1971, in the White House Situation Room to address the emergency situation created by the North Vietnamese attacks on the Plain of Jars in Laos in the early morning of December 18.

• WSAG on how to hold Long Tieng Washington Special Actions Group held January 3, 1972. Information Memorandum From the Under Secretary of State for Political Affairs (Johnson) to Secretary of State Rogers11. Source: National Archives, RG 59, Central Files 1970–73, DEF 1–1 US. Top Secret; Nodis. Drafted by Sullivan.

• Nixon Tape 646-2   Nixon says, "Laos just maybe can't be saved." 12 January 1972

• Nixon Tape 648-4   Kissinger tells Nixon that the NVA still haven't taken Long Tieng. "The main thing in the north is that we gain time." 17 January 1972

• Discussion of Kissinger secret peace negotiations with the North Vietnamese Minutes of a Senior Review Group Meeting, Washington, January 24, 1972

• Nixon Tape 665-3   Kissinger to Nixon: "We have given Long Tieng 4 weeks of B-52 bombing support. NVA face almost nothing there. Every week there (for the NVA) puts us ahead." 3 February 1972

• Godley argues against "thinning" Thai troops at Long Tieng Message From the Embassy in Laos to the Department of State. Vientiane, February 11, 1972, 1115Z. No distribution outside Department. For the Secretary from Ambassador. Bangkok eyes only for the Ambassador.

• Response to Godley explaining background to "thinning" Thai troops message. DoD official comments on "stupid" tactics at 20A.   Joint Message From the White House, Department of State, Department of Defense, and Central Intelligence Agency to the Embassies in Thailand and Laos. Washington, undated, but shortly after February 11, 1972

• Memo explaining how U.S. military could frustrate Long Tieng defense Memorandum From John D. Negroponte of the National Security Council Staff to the President's Deputy Assistant for National Security Affairs (Haig). Washington, February 14, 1972.

• Message from Abrams on situation at Long Tieng On 5 March, 141st and 165th are 6K from Sam Thong. 148th 16K NE of 20A. 335th at Skyline. Road finished from PDJ. 174th returning to Skyline. 8 March 1972

• Memo from Negroponte to Kissinger on CIA request for Strength II   General doubt in Washington that forces presently protecting Long Tieng can hold out against concerted PAVN attack. VP has suggested another deception op back to PDJ. Most in command structure approved. 10 March 1972

• Memo from Carver to Helms on DoD air support to VP Carver report on meeting with Sec Laird on DoD problem with allocation of air resources. "Vang Pao gets what Abrams doesn't need." 13 March 1972

• Nixon Tape 665-3   Kissinger to Nixon: ... (because the USAF didn't deliver bombs on schedule because of the weather)..."We must have the world's worst Air Force. (The NVA) Still haven't taken Long Tieng. They must be weaker." 30 March 1972

• Message from JCS in WDC to the field   From Moorer to McCain (CiC, Pacific) and Abrams (C, Military Assistance Command, Vietnam) that reports: Thais say that the U.S. providing TacAir is the quid pro quo for them providing irregular soldiers. They want more TacAir. If not, they will pull out of Long Tieng. 8 April 1972

• WSAG discussion of "maximum efforts" by PAVN to take Long Tieng. Minutes of a Washington Special Actions Group Meeting. Source: National Archives, Nixon Presidential Materials, NSC Files, NSC Institutional Files (H-Files), Box H–116, Washington Special Actions Group, WSAG Minutes (Originals) 1–3–72 to 7–24–72.

Top Secret; Sensitive. The meeting took place in the White House Situation Room. . Portions of the minutes are printed in Foreign Relations, 1969–1976, volume XIV, Soviet Union, October 1971–May 1972, Document 118. Washington, April 17, 1972.

• Godley says the PAVN pulled back. In Washington: "The one bright spot in SEA... (is) Long Tieng." Message From the Embassy in Laos to the Commander, Military Assistance Command (Abrams). Vientiane, April 19, 1972

• WSAG "Thais have done very good so far at Long Tieng" Minutes of a Washington Special Actions Group Meeting. Source: National Archives, Nixon Presidential Materials, NSC Files, NSC Institutional Files (H-Files), Box H–116, Washington Special Actions Group, WSAG Minutes (Originals) 1–3–72 to 7–24–72. Top Secret; Sensitive. The meeting took place in the White House Situation Room. Washington, May 4, 1972

• Telegram from U.S. Embassy in Bangkok to U.S. Vice President, advising that Thai irregulars in Long Tieng kept Long Tieng from being overrun by the PAVN earlier in year. FOREIGN RELATIONS OF THE UNITED STATES, 1969–1976 VOLUME XX, SOUTHEAST ASIA, 1969–1972, DOCUMENT 164 164. Telegram From the Embassy in Thailand to the Embassies in Japan and Bangkok, May 13, 1972, 1005Z. 6634. VP Only. For The Vice President From Unger. Subject: Thai-U.S. Relations and Your Visit to Bangkok. This message provides background on current Thai-U.S. relations and, where needed, talking points for use in your discussions with the Thai leadership.

• USAF "End of Tour Report" ('71to '72) Colonel Stanley M. Umstead, Wing Commander, 7th Air Force, Korat RTAFB 7 May 1973.

• Department of Defense "Report on Selected Air and Ground Operations in Laos and Cambodia" 10 September 1973

Articles and Documents

Ahern, Thomas A. "Undercover Armies," Center for the Study of Intelligence, Central Intelligence Agency, Washington, DC 20505

Air Facility Data Pamphlet for Laos Listing of all Lima Sites and Lima positions in Laos. Revision No. 6, June 1, 1972

Air and Space Magazine "The Ravens of Long Tieng" by Ralph Wetterhahn, November 1998

Boyne, Walter J. "The Plain of Jars," Air Force Magazine.com

Doolittle, Jerome "My Genital Strategy" Penthouse Magazine July 1973

"AIR AMERICA AND THE WAR IN LAOS, 1959-1974," Thesis, presented to the faculty of the University of Texas at Dallas in partial fulfillment of the requirements for the degree of Master of Arts in History, The University of Texas at Dallas, May 2010

Genovese, Lia "The Plain of Jars: Mysterious and Imperiled" PhD dissertation, School of Oriental and African Studies, University of London. February 2012

Greenstein and Immerman "What Did Eisenhower Tell Kennedy about Indochina?" The Journal of American History September 1992

Leary, William M. Interview with Richard Helms, 16 September 1981, Oral History Program, Lyndon Baines Johnson Presidential Library, Austin, TX

Leary, William M. "The CIA and the 'Secret War' in Laos: The Battle for Skyline Ridge, 1971, 1972," 34 p.

Leary, William M. "CIA Air Operations in Laos, 1955-1974: Supporting the Secret War" 21p.

Leary, William M. Typed notes from interviews, newspaper articles on Secret War activities 200 p. approx.

Leary, William M. "Air America: Myth and Reality"

Leeker, Joe F   "Air America in Laos III – in combat, 23 August 2010"

Marek, Edward   "LS-36 , 'The Alamo' in Laos"
http://www.talkingproud.us/Military/Military/LS36Alamo.html 18 November 2012

Matthews, Thomas   Diary that Matthew (also known by his callsign "Ringo") kept from 10 February 1971 to 10 June 1972 on his day to day activities as a Case Officer with a Hmong GM at Long Tieng.

Newspaper Bangkok Post   "Long Cheng attack by N-VN troops." December 22, 1971

Newspaper Bangkok Post   "Fate of Key Lao Base Uncertain" January 14, 1972

Newspaper UPI   "Laos Retakes Ridge Near Beefed Up Long Cheng" January 17, 1972

Newspaper The Nation (Bangkok)   "New Strategy will Secure Long Cheng" January 17, 1972

Newspaper Dispatch News Service International   "U.S. Bombing in Laos: An Inside Story" Michael Morrow, January 1972

Newspaper AP   "Intense Fighting on Ridge" January 22, 1972

Newspaper Washington Post   "The Question is How to Get Off the Tiger" by Stacy Lloyd, February 6, 1972

Newspaper Washington Star   "Mountain War in Laos Grim" Tammy Arbuckle, February 27, 1972

Newspaper Washington Post   "CIA-Backed Laotians Face Hanoi's Best at Long Chieng," Laurence Stern, March 1, 1972

Newspaper Bangkok Business Leader "Some Meo Tribesmen would rather resettle than fight," April 30, 1972

"Cover Story on Lt General Withun Yasawat," pp 11-86. February 1988

O'Dell, George   O'Dell's (also known by his call sign "Digger") lesson plan: "The CIA and the War in Laos" that includes an overview of CIA involvement in Laos, duties of a paramilitary Case Officer and overall retrospection.

Polifka, Karl   "An Account of my time in South East Asia, First Tour Forward Air Controller, Walt 21 in Vietnam, Raven 45 in Laos"

Rand Corporation for Advanced Research Projects Agency of the Department of Defense   "Organizing and Managing Unconventional War in Laos, 1962-1970" Douglas Blaufarb. January 1972.

Rand Corporation for Advanced Research Projects Agency of the Department of Defense   "Revolution in Laos: The North Vietnamese and the Pathet Lao." Memorandum RM-5935-ARPA, September 1969

RTA record of Thai irregulars at Long Tieng 1971-1974   Chronology of Thai irregular BCs, 601, 602, 603, 604, 605, 606, 607, 608, 609, 610, 613, 614, 616,617, 618, 620 plus the "A" reorganized units of some of these groups reconstituted from the PDJ force.

The Vietnam Archive, Oral History Project, Texas Tech U. Interview with Bill Lair conducted by Steve Maxner, December 11, 2001

Tovar, Hugh B   International Journal of Intelligence and CounterIntelligence, "Chronicle of a Secret War" review of Jane Hamilton-Merritt: Tragic Mountains: The Hmong, the Americans, and the Secret War for Laos, 1942-1992, Summer 1995

Tovar, Hugh B.   International Journal of Intelligence and CounterIntelligence, "Managing the Secret War in Laos," review of Timothy N. Castle: At War in the Shadow of Vietnam, U.S. Military Aid to the Royal Lao Government, 1955-1975, Fall 1995

Tovar, Hugh B.   International Journal of Intelligence and CounterIntelligence, "Chronicle of a Secret War (III) Laos: The CIA's Biggest Venture," review of Kenneth Conboy, with James Morrison: Shadow War: The CIA's Secret War in Laos, Winter 1995

University of Texas at Dallas Air America collection   Daily Air America air ops log, drafted by air ops officers Tom Sullivan and Jerry Connors. 141 days, from 9 December 1971 to 29 April 1972. (approximately 250 pages)

PAVN Reporting Translated by Merle Pribbenow

Bio: General An   "New Battlefield" [Chien Truong Moi] Colonel General Nguyen Huu An (as told to Nguyen Tu Duong), People's Army Publishing House, Hanoi, 2002 (Second Printing) pages 1-274

Bio: General An   "My Days on the Plain of Jars" [Nhung Ngay O Canh Dong Chum]
By Major General Nguyen Binh Son People's Army Publishing House, Hanoi, 2003
(Second printing) page 12

Bio: General Chuong   General Nguyen Chuong [Nguyễn Chuông] People's
Public Security [Cong An Nhan Dan] newspaper, http://www.cand.com.vn/vi-
VN/phongsu/2009/1/106215.cand 21 Dec 2009

Short Campaign Z overview "Military Encyclopedia of Vietnam" [Tu Dien Bach Khoa
Quan Su Viet Nam] Compiled by the Military Encyclopedia Center of the Ministry of
Defense Chief Editor: Senior Colonel Tran Do People's Army Publishing House, Hanoi,
1996 page 105

Bios: Vu Lap and Hung   "Military Encyclopedia of Vietnam" [Tu Dien Bach Khoa
Quan Su Viet Nam] Compiled by the Military Encyclopedia Center of the Ministry of
Defense Chief Editor: Senior Colonel Bui Vinh Phuong [Bùi Vinh Phương] People's
Army Publishing House, Hanoi, 2004 page 513

Bio: Gen Vu, One-eyed Armor commander   "Following the Tracks of our Tanks,
Volume 1" [Theo Vet Xich Xe Tang, Tap 1]; Tank-Armor Technical Service Chronology
of Events [Bien Nien Su Kien Nganh Ky Thuat Tang Thiet Giap]; and "The Dao Family
Name in Vietnam" [Ho Dao Viet Nam].

1953 Invasion of Laos   "The Road to Dien Bien Phu" (Duong Toi Dien Bien Phu),
by Senior General Vo Nguyen Giap, with Huu Mai, People's Army Publishing House,
Hanoi, 2001 (Third Printing, with Additions and Corrections)

1953 Invasion of Laos   "Military Encyclopedia of Vietnam" [Tu Dien Bach Khoa
Quan Su Viet Nam] Compiled by the Military Encyclopedia Center of the Ministry of
Defense Chief Editor: Senior Colonel Bui Vinh Phuong [Bùi Vinh Phương] People's
Army Publishing House, Hanoi, 2004

1953 Invasion of Laos   "Military Encyclopedia of Vietnam" [Tu Dien Bach Khoa
Quan Su Viet Nam] Compiled by the Military Encyclopedia Center of the Ministry of
Defense Chief Editor: Senior Colonel Tran Do People's Army Publishing House, Hanoi,
1996

Vietnamese Campaigns in Northern Laos   "Military Encyclopedia of Vietnam"
[Tu Dien Bach Khoa Quan Su Viet Nam] Compiled by the Military Encyclopedia
Center of the Ministry of Defense. Chief Editor: Senior Colonel Tran Do People's
Army Publishing House, Hanoi, 1996 pages 97-149

Campaign 74A   "Military Encyclopedia of Vietnam" [Tu Dien Bach Khoa Quan Su
Viet Nam] Compiled by the Military Encyclopedia Center of the Ministry of Defense
Chief Editor: Senior Colonel Tran Do People's Army Publishing House, Hanoi, 1996

Index

467